THE SACRED WITHIN MOUNTAINS:

Singing with the Sidhe

THE SACRED WITHIN MOUNTAINS:

Singing with the Sidhe

Anne Gambling

Lorian Press LLC
Lorianpress.com

THE SACRED WITHIN MOUNTAINS:
Singing with the Sidhe

© Copyright Anne Gambling 2024

All rights reserved, including the right to reproduce this book, or portions thereof, in any form. Anne Gambling has asserted her right to be identified as the author of this work and photographer of her interior images.

Cover art (from *The Card Deck of the Sidhe*)
and Book Design by Jeremy Berg
Photographs by Anne Gambling

ISBN: 978-1-939790-68-2

Gambling, Anne
The Sacred Within Mountains/Anne Gambling

First Print Edition: December 2024

Printed in the United States of America,
the United Kingdom and Australia

DEDICATION

I swear I begin to see little or nothing in audible words,
All merges toward the presentation
of the unspoken meanings of the earth,
Toward him who sings the songs of the body
and of the truths of the earth,
Toward him who makes the dictionaries of words
that print cannot touch.
Say on, sayers! Sing on, singers!
Delve! Mould! Pile the words of the earth!
Work on, age after age, nothing is to be lost,
It may have to wait long, but it will certainly come in use,
When the materials are all prepared and ready,
the architects shall appear ...

(Walt Whitman: "A Song of the Rolling Earth" 1856)

• • • • • • •

In honour of the Ancestors, in honour of Hope
In honour of the Alliance between Humanity and Faerie,
We companions of the Way of Love dedicate this text,
as with all our work, to our dearest Sister:

<Gaia>

ACKNOWLEDGEMENTS

I apologise for being a broken record, but as with my two prior volumes in this trilogy of Sidhe-partnered and co-produced works, I say:

As <u>ever</u>, none of our work (<u>or</u> its setting down in text) would have been possible without the foundational efforts of David Spangler, Jeremy Berg and Mariel of the Sidhe. 'Chapeau' all round. We are <u>truly</u> indebted!

Ditto goes to my dear Family – immediate in Human'd skin, Amici'd in blue, OneEarth'd in any/all myriad forms of Being, physical and non- (big shout-out to Tree and Mountain here!), as well as to TeamSky and all cosmic kin. All gods, all goddesses, all sages and saints:

"Thank you, thank you, and again – thank you!"

But to add to that now in relation to the particularity of <u>this</u> text and its 'prescient' (Amici words, not mine!) work-program:

None of it could have been achieved without my dear, dear Body staying the distance in partner'd space/time to work with all ye All (physical, subtle and gift'd more) in resonant loving (visceral!) intersect. Thank you, Body – for your courage, compassion, patience, perseverance, grace, gratitude, <u>and</u> trust! You have taught me so much! I am truly in awe of you, and the miracle <u>you</u> made (as a 'lab-rat' of one).

Ex-Volume

https://www.nestedfishes.org hosts my evolving library of writerly works offered freely to the conversation on Peace. In its various 'reading rooms' you will find the texts cited in this book – whether in atrium (essays), on fiction shelf (prose), in poetry corner (bardic works) or by entering the krypta's performance space for all resonant voice. Please feel free to explore!

CONTENTS

Prologue	i
Stretch 1: The Wisdom Of Ages And Sages	1
Der Ruf Der Berge	7
Mountains/Dragons Without End	20
To The Power Of Five	39
Stretch 2: In Company Of Stone Giants	69
Joining Mountains	76
Intermezzo (1)	113
Walking The Garden; Weaving The World	122
Joining Mountains (Continued)	145
Intermezzo (2)	170
Stretch 3: Exploring Song	176
Whole Earth Partnership	182
Sasso And His (Stellar) Waale	199
Of Bens, Bogs And (Scotty) Dogs	238
Return To Source (Code/x)	265
Song To The Power Of Seven	293
A Temenos To Song – Anwa In Form	317
Epilogue	352
Appendix 1: The Song/S Of/For/Through/By/As Gaia	354
The Skychild's Song	355
SimpleSong	356
Song Of Gaia	357
Appendix 2: The (Original) Card Deck Of The Sidhe In Amici Hands – A Primer	359
Appendix 3: The Snowball Of Becoming	364
About The Author	368

PROLOGUE

    This volume has its roots in the same stone-sentient co-working space as my first Sidhe-partnered text, "Awakening to Home" (Lorian Press LLC, 2016); likewise, its underlying spirit of intent is to support the continued evolution of Gaia's crystalline consciousness.
    I say Sidhe-partnered with good reason – without their prodding, support and subtle co-authorship that first documentation of our together-work would never have seen the light of Human or Sidhe day, nor our second co-production: "From the Common Grail Within" (Lorian Press LLC, 2020). Over time it has emerged with stunning clarity that our shared field research (in company of the original Card Deck brought into being by Lorian's David Spangler and Jeremy Berg with Mariel of the Sidhe) has been as necessary an engagement tool for potential Sidhe-Human collaboration in their world as in ours. Indeed, right from the start, a subtle 'book launch' where "Awakening" was promoted to curious and sceptical Sidhe alike was a revelation to little me – all this on the back of 'workshops' we co-hosted with a similar focus.
    Like any artefact birthed and gifted to the world of Time, a text commands a presence and life of its own. I have to admit to my delight that after our co-produced texts' first toddler steps down the years, they continue to walk Gaia's

spheric plane, as handy a reference and companion volume published by a Sidhe version of 'Lorian Press' as the one paper-bound on this side of veil by Jeremy and his pit crew. And now to have a third (Sister) text to join the party, trip through meadows flower-bright and fragrant? How happy can a fey book-child be!

While this volume in one respect chronicles the work program which constellated over the past several years with Sidhe colleagues I most affectionately call 'Amici' (friends), it is unnecessary to peruse our earlier work to make sense of what is written herein. Prepared as a stand-alone narrative, any cross-referencing to earlier work will be presented in context. Nevertheless, as all royalties from its sale, just as for the others, are gifted back to Lorian to further their own work, the reader may enjoy having all three tomes on his/her actual/virtual bookshelf to bolster Lorian's coffers a smidgin more. Thank you, in advance, on their behalf.

This text has been written to cycle through three stretches of Songline. Commencing with the overarching sacred wisdom that Mountain sequesters, stewards and guards on behalf of Gaia's evolutionary consciousness, the narrative shifts to the specific nature of our work with stone giants in the second stretch, before delving into the role Song plays in our collaboration to sing up a whole Earth partnership with every footsoldier'd step in our own or each other's "shoes" (to quote an analogy from David's first "Conversations" with Mariel). Each section is prefaced by an introduction to frame the discussion to follow; select appendices stand ready to round out the volume; other references are housed on my nestedfishes web presence.

Now, just a caveat about my style (for want of a better word) of textual expression which subscribes to the adage that the Story's need to tell itself shall take my pen where it wants to go, with you dear Reader (hopefully) content to bounce along on our inky ride. While EM Forster's dictum calls for sitting down alone to "struggle with the writer", I trust it shall not be too arduous an undertaking herein. Suffice it to say that while a (loose) structure exists for the text, content is apt to shuttle back and forth like a warp in Einstein's space-time with various rhizomatic tendrils (or threads in the telling) exuberantly marching off like Deleuzo-Guattarian ant armies to show up (in another guise) via a parallel dimension (or chapter as the case may be). In point of fact, such 'structure' (or lack thereof) mirrors my engagement and experience of the Sidheverse (and other subtle realms). Outwith the usual linearity of a (Human) Time'd well, it is one I attempt to honour by writing from its everywhere-everywhen plane, not least because the audiences for these texts exist across multiple dimensions.

To visualise how form follows function in this regard, imagine the book's content as a 4D spheric plane (2D rendered for simplicity's sake). Lain out on its smooth-as-glass surface, like a holocratic map of 'horizon' landscape, the plane hosts many in-time content 'events' in space represented as discrete points of light.

By taking a full (Stanley-knife'd) cross-section of plane, making sure to intersect the rim's holistic knowing of everything inwith sphere, a seemingly random capture of individual elements can itself become a view of the whole. No longer a sampled 'moment', its potentiality fans out to become its own 3D sphere teeming with content 'life', like a Chinese globe lantern full-bound and lit from within. Now, introduce Time to the particularities of this latter spatial equation and see its perspective suddenly expand from an individual phenomenal 'flashing' to an own 4D'd 'universe'.

Another (and perhaps more prescient) way to look at the book's content (as a mirror to my subtle engagement) would be from an 'ice core drill' perspective, one which includes Time in the scientific equation as matter-of-course. Still, the 'sample' needs to engage rim-to-bookend'd-rim for the holistic principle to work. In fact, the reader will find as pages turn that our Amici'd partnership delivers us out to the thin Blue line of Earth's atmospheric extent on the ride. By visualising the 'core drill' doing its bit (pun intended) to cross-sect the entirety of Gaia's spheric frame – thin Blue to thin Blue – you approach some sense of the extent of our work, inwith and of an ensouled full reach.

Like a pond's biodiversity expanding under microscope, with the viewer's awareness including a before-and-after, a this-and-more, there is one last aspect to writerly process I would like you to consider. Imagine that our moment of content extracted in the above sample (3D captured to 4D fanned) is so excited by its own witnessed becoming that it wants to return to spheric plane, dive straight back in between those bookend'd pages to intersect a veritable infinitude of other fanned-out moments expressed in text, and for the potentiality of its Joy of cross-fertilisation to bring a next best ever-new to blessed re-creation. Freaky? No – for this is how it works when your own thoughts and considerations, Reader, enter the equation, when the content this volume houses has the opportunity to offer its (excitable) dynamic knowing back into the collective pool of our OneEarth Commons – a 'hadron collider' par excellence accelerating each and every particle whizzing round its mercurial track.

Yes. A book is a receptacle of shared experience, in its writing, in its reading – the relation of its content to its very self demonstrates the spheric nature of Time as a Space whose shape is round, and in whose 4D frame we are all co-participant, and all co-creative. Perhaps you will find letters, words, sentences (metaphorically) all a-jumble, punctuation (symbolically) all askew. But: Voila! Our hope is that sense-making comes into being when you 'drop' out of head into heart to simply bathe in the text, rest subtly awash in its fundaments of Presence.

Indeed, Kisha, a protagonist in my work of major prose fiction "The Taste of Translation" (2011), had an analogous experience which may help explain our Amici'd proposition:

"Once she had a dream ... a typewriter began to tell the story, typing by itself. All she had to do was watch as each sheet was lifted through space to a workshop bench where the text was laid out, stacked and bound. A frenzy of words tumbled out of the typewriter in their desire to tell the story of what happened. And she watched everything become ordered, everything in its place, linear, rational, believable. All she need do was watch.

"But suddenly it went awry. The words, the very letters began to float off, detach themselves from the completed pages of the story while the typewriter still pounded, producing more, yet more words. No! she cried aloud in the dream. Stop! And reached up, tried to catch the letters and words, return them to earth and finite logic. Ream upon ream of gobbledy-gook swirled about her head, bobbing in a chaos of thought, merging, separating, scattering, like fireflies tugged by a turbulent breeze. No sense to the text, no meaning to the story, no language in which it could ever be understood. Who could possibly translate such a mess?

"But the letters seemed happy, the words satisfied to float in an airborne harbour, and no amount of poking, prodding, imploring or urging could put the story back the way it was. We have leavened your dust into seeded loaves, they explained. Our rhizome clusters host real meaning. Here, you will find your truth. Nothing for it. She surrendered to their supremacy, their insight into best-fit, and when handed a needle and cotton, she understood her task was to stitch a fine cloak from their scattered snatches. As translucent as muslin, she tried it on for size, looked in the mirror, the sheer wrap following the contours of her form ..."

Form following function. Thank you for sharing your story, Kisha. Of what is housed 'in-frame'.

I readily concede that the raft of symbolic imagery, mixed metaphors and language used to describe our work can be difficult to navigate (the above Stanley-knife'd example inclusive), as well as the revolving door'd cast of characters populating this volume being an odd lot (myself most of all!). The symbology, of course, makes sense to me because it is the language of our subtle communication, honed to the shared <u>wiring</u> of consciousness evolved over time to enable said communication. My job? To tease out the various relations as best I can to facilitate my own understanding before sharing it with a third party (as appropriate) in text. Nothing if not unwieldy, akin to pulling teeth, and at times requiring <u>hours</u> of re-writing for the most innocuous of paragraphs (I kid you not), it is the task of a translator. While I am no Walter Benjamin, his subtle philosophic sponsorship underpins my efforts, and I offer his words (1923) into your potential pool of Forster'd 'struggle' likewise:

"The language of a translation can – in fact, must – let itself go, so that it gives voice to the intentio of the original not as reproduction but as harmony ... (and) allows the pure language, as though reinforced by its own medium, to shine upon the original all the more fully ... When translating from a language very remote from his own (the *translator) must go back to the primal elements of language itself and penetrate to the point where work, image and tone converge."*

The words guiding me here ('intentio'; 'harmony'; 'pure'; 'primal') describe our Amici'd "work, image and tone" well, acting as the convergent <u>root-stock</u> on which my translation, via this text, is <u>grafted</u>. The use of specific vocabulary to describe certain aspects of process and/or certain <u>modes</u> of Presence is implied here. While others have honed taxonomies of the subtle worlds according to their language preferences, so have we. A preferred expression for the subtle realms is 'Malakut', for example, the Arabic word for the intermediate world of the soul in Islamic (Sufi) mysticism, the place "where the body is spiritualised and the spiritual is embodied" according to renowned scholar Henri Corbin. The reason? Simply because my first major journeys <u>in</u> (many years past) walked in Ibn Arabi's footsteps, "alone with the Alone".

Likewise, whenever we speak of 'source' – Love, cosmic ancestry, sacred well/s of sagic knowledge etc – it is generally ever-coupled with 'code/x', thus speaking to a twin proposition that whatever is <u>encoded</u> in the various wisdom treasuries into which we have the supreme good fortune to tap has its roots in our OnePeople'd 'source' in the Generative Mystery. A codex is a most ancient and hallowed of manuscripts. Here, on our wee micro-plate, we offer you Memory's codes (recovered), and fresh-envisioned, of what it means to be Us.

With that, I wish you much Joy exploring the multidimensional world of this text, and offer many blessings on your longer-than journey of Life – with Gaia, with Sidhe, and with Song!

STRETCH 1:
THE WISDOM OF AGES AND SAGES

Mentors to process; conversation partners to coalesce latent knowing into manifest being; companions constellating selves and/or tools in support of our Amici'd task in a right-time-right-place sort of way ... Before arriving at the 'music' of our collaboration it is important to paint the 'maths' – to share my understanding of the geometry to this sacred geology, divining (with a rod as a-glow as any Shiva'd lingam) the root-knowing of aeons on which our latter-day blessing praxis has been built.

The Sacred <u>within</u> Mountain/s – in and of itself, in and on behalf of Gaia. All stone is sentient, all stone a fractal of primal ground, an ongoing record of Gaia's geologic origins, a creation story 4.5 billion years young, and still in the co-making. "Awakening" documented our Amici'd acts to 'sing up' the connection between home nodes across the world <u>through</u> stone and <u>with</u> stone – mirroring the work of ancestral energies 'awakening' this most physical of wisdom containers. Stone as partner, Star as partner, Sidhe as partner. This Gaian Commons we share is a diagram of equals, a holocracy of co-determinant interbeing where each has a role serving the whole; where each is sacred in the eyes of the whole. A knowing which found expression in symphonic voice at a particular point in our co-productions thus:

Whether Star or Stone,
Human, Faerie, Garden Gnome,
whether Brother of Flame
or Sister of Light,
itinerant monk a-wander,
or ashen hermit staying put,
animal vegetable
mineral manufactural,
we all share the Fate of our planetary Blue.
We all bear witness to the Truth of sacred Yule ...

This planal non-hierarchical connection I feel to the all of the All – as Family sharing a single planetary Home, a tiny Blue marble in the inkiness of Void (as the Apollo 8 lads described) – informs my wholehearted loving <u>embrace</u> of Mountain as an expression of the Sacred in a whole Earth landscape where <u>All</u> is sacred.

To the core of FeltWorld have I plumbed, at the farthest extent of (thin Blue line'd) atmosphere have I sung. But the in-world locale of <u>intersect</u>, where Heaven <u>meets</u> Earth, where respective energies comingle <u>and</u> commune, where Light streams between stellar realms and earthen kin via leylines of subtle watersheds a-flow, is (in <u>my</u> understanding) the preserve of Mountain. Mountain as Presence. Mountain as Conductor. Mountain as Lightning-Rod. Here, Life <u>stretches</u> itself to 'touch' Source, to drink of the Joy of Being – to share, via <u>root</u>-known networks (Land-Sea-Sky'd), the Love of All <u>with</u> the all.

My Love is part of this 'all' as it is for each of us; and my task, with Sidhe Amici, is to partner the <u>enspirited</u> geology of Mountain <u>kin</u> via the circular economy of Gaia's 'Ecology of Light' – in Song. Tree, I know, shares this horizont/vertic'd role – touching Source, flowing Love's Light in-out, offering its Presence as container, conduit and magisterial companion of Gaia's way. No coincidence that in many traditions a World Tree hosts Creation-energy, as does a World Mountain. Yes, I have travelled Tree; I have 'met' their lineage holders, and with Sidhe Amici partnered these kin to common purpose. An example is housed in "Grail Within"; by the end of this volume we will see how Mountain/Tree twin. But for the meantime let me focus on Mountain ...

•••••

Different world faith traditions and mythologies assign specific mountains to be containers of the sacred – this not only represents an holistic understanding of Mountain's role but fulfils a need for majestic sites of sequestration and veneration. These peaks take their job seriously and I honour them. But I honour all others 'unchosen' as highly. On a diagram of equals none stands above the other (no matter what the altitude); our 'sight' is only limited by imagination (or lack thereof), or by the mediating role played by various sacred texts (their human 'gatekeepers' and/or via oral tradition) rather than trusting to or having the opportunity for direct unmediated experience of Mountain sentience oneself. All this I interrogate in later chapters but let us set the imaginal scene with a few 'stone giants' that oft go unseen or unremarked.

What of, for example, the peaks that, over aeon'd Time, have been sand-papered and eroded to undulating bedrock, to murmur their knowing across a horizon scape rather than by (relatively geologic-recent) vertic'd up-jump? What of the cliffs and headlands which fringe wide oceans – high and wild in their own wave-and-wind-swept way as any alpine setting? What of deep-sea mountains far below the surface of our everyday cognition? What of all those poking noses up out of the Blue which are called 'islands'? What of volcanos that lose their topknot to a vent of laval exuberance, crater'd cauldrons now hosting Macbethian witches of alchemical bent instead? What of all Mountain knowing 'locked' in ice, now melting to flood the world with its particular brand of Joy?

In short, Mountain is a state of mind – in space, in time. A marriage of spirit-geology, ensoul'd of Body – as are we all in incarnate form. Take this to its logical conclusion and no part of our 'Third-Rock' out from Sun is <u>not</u> Mountain, has not played an active part in stewarding wisdom, oozing it forth from core at some point in DeepTime-Tectonia'd history. This is the knowing of ages, and sages, I shall delight to tell – one to be found everywhere, everywhen, everyhow-which-and-why.

That said, it was with especial joy to read in David's "Conversations" with Mariel, when the volume first entered my orbit a decade past, as I (coincidentally) sat with a dear longer-than (mountain) friend to begin a (shared) reading adventure, I was not alone in understanding the <u>reach</u> and <u>depth</u> of Mountain; Sidhe too fundamentally recognise their integral 'mattered' nature to furthering Gaian consciousness:

"(A mountain) is a major conduit through which the energies of stars and earth meet ... (it) is for us not a geographical feature as much as a presence and an energy field. ... Some are more accessible than others ... (some) prefer to be left alone as they are doing their work in deep solitude ... Most, though, are happy to engage ... When I go into the mountain, then, I am entering into the energy and life of one of the great servants of Gaia, one who itself can perceive the cosmic energies and draw them into our world ... Mountain spirits are among humanity's greatest allies in the changes that you face, though you don't realise it."

Ah, but Mariel, I certainly did realise, though at the time of reading "Conversations" I had no idea of the (vast, daunting) undertaking to which our Amici troupe would be asked to (future) contribute. At that stage, I had done little more than connect home-mountains across the world – carrying a simple 'message stick' of blessing to the summit of each so they could chat to each other as well as offer me an opportunity to join their infinitely wise and minerally conversation. Looking out my 'window on world' in a 'forgotten (alpine) valley on the border of Time', I was able to collapse time and space, 'hang' with my Cloud-Catcher, watcher watching East over a wide southern Pacific sheet of shared Home. Later, more stone giants would actively join our little mountain collective, in meditation, with the thought:

"Wherever you are, I'm there too."

The familial alliance I experience with stellar kin is equally ripe for active engagement in stone – over-ever-over. As documented in "Awakening", for example, our TeamBerg/TeamSky ('Berg' = 'Mountain' in German) troupe sang up the Stars within Earth for a specificity of home-places, one which Mariel's counsel to David generously underpinned from the start:

"In you, stars and earth meet. … In partnership with us, our desire is for you to become like the Old Ones, who stood and formed the first circles. … You are less child-like than you were then. In some ways you have become darker, but in other ways you shine more brightly and carry a hard-won wisdom and connection to the world … you are in touch with the life within matter in ways we are not. If you will listen, it speaks to you with voices we do not hear. We know the voices of starlight but you hear the voices of the fire within earth and matter."

The Life within Matter, said Mariel. The Spirit within Geology. Within the (Third-Rock) fact of our planetary home, Star/Stone comingle, merge, twin. Dance! Sing! This I feel in-Body, in the very blood/bone of matter'd existence. The Amici call the consciousness of physical matter with which we 'surface-dwellers' are blessed and into which we can connect the 'Magic of the Mantle'. Long have I experienced it – the burble of Joy beneath feet, 'Star' radiating out from 'Stone', Lorca's duende at work dervishly whip-whirling a real-time connection to me, and to incoming stellar. We are a bridge species, like Mountain, like Tree, for good reason. When we three together join to sing the connections alive in the blood/bones of Gaia's physically magical home? Cool!

Specific geologic types 'sing' Gaia's knowing differently. Sidhe, for example, are most aligned to limestone – portals in and through to catacomb'd treasuries. But attuning to granite/gneiss I have found the most enduring to 'anchor' purpose, as well as protect chthonic vaults of wisdom. Like Gaia herself, we all have the capacity to reveal the magic of our mantle in-world, to wear (as she does) a stellar 'Soul-at-Skin', secrete a stellar 'Sink-at-Surface', connect the sheer wonder of our own personal self-sovereign enspirited 'geology' with that of cosmic kin. (Malakut) mountains may constellate as me-sized brothers or sisters, while their material twins have me puffing up steep paths, but it would never have occurred to me to include a section in this book relating the philosophic, mythologic, cosmologic background to this in-grained felt-sense – mine or via sacred text – until a chance encounter which, as a rhizome of 'becoming', generated much fuel for our work in its snowball'd wake.

See, I have a dear friend of longer-than standing. A gnomic figure of contrary worldview, I delight in tickling his fancy with whimsical 'what ifs'. A classic meeting-of-opposites, one day – many years ago – he told me of his brother, as different from him as chalk to cheese, a tall streak of a thing with long wild hair, a follower of an Indian guru. He and I were in email touch off and on over the years, but I mostly found out about his adventures via my gnomic friend.

When I first began research on this project with the Amici (from an intriguing vision in 2015, they 'upped the ante' to a point where, by early 2017, there was nothing for it but to get busy), I stumbled across an archived newspaper cutting which cited my friend's brother. A surprise in itself (my googling had gone from 'Messner' to 'Kailash'), here I was reading his thoughts about a mountain, holy to four faith traditions, and considered the incarnate spiritual axis between Heaven and Earth. I laughed out loud and sent the link to my gnomic friend. As one would expect, this elicited a direct response from his brother, who relayed the backstory to his interest – a story which involved meeting a member of the party responsible for transporting Gandhi's ashes to the mountain in 1948. As 'Gandhi' is a placeholder in my memory drawers for a significant Malakut meeting, this left me suitably gobsmacked at the rhizomatic synchronicity facilitated by my gnomic friend.

About six months later, down under for our usual hemispheric pilgrimage, we were invited to weekend with the (garden) gnomes (my friend's wife is as tiny a treasure) at their mountain retreat which rests in my overall Stretch of (homecome) Song. As his brother had recently moved to a town which lies in the shadow (and divine shed) of (my) Cloud-Catcher (brother) an hour or so further South, it seemed a good opportunity to invite him up for brunch. We would be meeting face-to-face for the first time.

Prior to this, however, I had been Malakut-ing. In a subterranean temple space (nary a gnome in sight), my task was to lead the 'pink' chant: "Life-Love-World-Breath, Love-is-Celebration!" This went on/on as different Presence/s arrived, as a congregation of joyous younglings lined the stage. It seems Christ would also visit – understandably they wanted their Song perfect. 'Flying' home afterwards I traced the coastline, taking 'memory-pix' for our Amici'd map. And now, exhausted by our pre-dawn work, I was still thinking through its next steps when my friend's brother arrived – suddenly, and with a big plastic bag of tomes. No small talk, no formal introductions, he announced: "I hear you're writing a book on Sacred Mountains."

An open mouth my sole (soul?) response. This Amici'd workstream so huge an undertaking, I had not even contemplated a book as part of the mix, let alone

one which addressed the sacred nature of our mountains' work. How on earth had he come to this idea? An idea which implanted itself in the soil of my more-than fertile mind? Ah, but this is how it (the big IT) works when the Amici start 'playing' around. To add to this (seemingly) foregone conclusion, it seems the bag contained his favourite books on his favourite mountains to help me, viz:

Kailash – the object of my (at that stage of mountain game) research

Arunachala – of which I had never heard, but when he told that it was home to Sri Ramana, I nodded slowly (he of the Sruti note in my essay, "Universal Resonance", and this the place of his in-cave hum'd knowing)

Khangchendzonga – third tallest worldwide (and I with a penchant for the sacred no. 3?); I was to discover her later, mediated by Sikkim Temi tea. Yum!

The thing I needed to work through, however, was that if a book on our project was to be mooted by Sidhe and me alike, why the need to document the human wisdom intersect when we were all on the same page, actively engaging the sacred within mountains – any and all? Ah, I (finally) realised – because of Mariel's commentary above:

"Mountain spirits are among humanity's greatest allies in the changes that you face, though you don't realise it."

Much wisdom has been lost, fragmented down the ages, amongst which Mountain's knowing stands forlorn and forgotten or appropriated by specific traditions to the seeming exclusion of others who do not share their particular expression of 'faith'. Time to re-state it plain and in fresh dress, not for me or my Amici who <u>live</u> this connection as daily matter-of-course, but to remind all, on either side of our cousinly Common'd veil/vale, of the Sacred <u>vested</u> in Stone and to which we <u>add</u> – with each blessing, each 'Hello the House', each pilgrim'd mantra and up-sung kora radiating out through watersheds high and wide, sequestering Love's Light in PeaceSinks vast and deep, for offering to any/all of Gaia's glorious world, when (their) seeds sown deemed ripe for reap.

With that 'why' to this text's 'what', dear Reader, I welcome you to the various chapters which follow, documenting the wisdom of ages, and sages – of Mountain as container of the Sacred.

DER RUF DER BERGE

Growing up at sea-level, on the shores of a southern ocean, I could never quite understand the fascination mountain-climbing had for so many. I knew it had something to do with an attraction to wild places, commensurate with an ability to wander far from the madding crowds our species had spawned. But from where I sat, there were plenty of places to engage the wild without getting high. This perspective was, however, most likely a function of living in a landscape devoid of high wild; in my part of the world, we could enter the rainforest'd belly of Rainbow Serpent, traverse the sparse spinifex of her outer skin, or drench ourselves in the limitless ocean from which she emerged. Perhaps climbing mountains had something to do with a deep-seated <u>desire</u> to explore the beyond – further than the farthest horizon, higher than the faintest cloud. Yet I could accomplish same by simply communing from a rocky headland with a white-capped sea, barely moving a muscle save the one of my imagination.

Of course, these musings occurred long before I found myself on migration to Heidi's own Land, small, 'eng' (a perfectly narrow word to mean just that), landlocked to boot. Not a stretch of salty H2O within cooee. Here it was difficult to see far, beyond the boundaries set by geologic time unless you climbed out of the valleys (preserve of human endeavour) into the high wild where Nature remained (mostly) untamed. At its most rational, this was fair explanation. Yet, as Pascal held, the heart has its reasons of which reason knows nought. And it was into this space I found myself, trying to understand how and why my outer senses could seemingly take light-years to acclimatise to a completely foreign environment while in the inner-most sanctum of Soul, a <u>felt-sense</u> continuously prevailed that I had come <u>home</u>, as Peter Matthiessen wrote:

"In another life – this isn't what I know, but how I feel – these (Himalayan) mountains were my home; there is a rising of forgotten knowledge, like a spring from hidden aquifers under the earth."

Likewise, I engaged a soul-restlessness placated only by walking, and living, the high wild of this new/old landscape of the heart. I had been 'called', as so many before; I had heard 'der Ruf der Berge' (the call of the mountains). While the rhizomatic path this pilgrim pen traverses will result in many instances of 'der Ruf' of the Sacred within (and through) Mountain, we will begin at the (in medias res'd) 'plot-point' that kick-started our project's 'Snowball of Becoming'.

"Appendix 3" houses the 'snowball' model, and the Sidhe-partnered story of its development for the interested reader. A tool to focus action at any given moment, the 'snowball' cycles from the initial stage of building desire, through mapping a project's landscape or terrain (with the additional descriptor 'terroir' to denote and capture the <u>flavour</u> we bring to task), to growing consciousness of task, self <u>and</u> other, in order to 'call in' further allies on both sides of veil/vale. Here, Mariel's comment is relevant:

"Once you set forth your intent, we can blend with the field you create and enhance its capacities to connect and to manifest."

A tidal flow exists between this 'step' and its prior (landscape) in the spirit of becoming as it is 'walked', at ebb with Moon's wax and wane. From here we begin to develop 'product' – i.e. the action (or artefact) – which is our Amici'd 'micro' act (wrapt in the purity of our intent, hence always lily white). This we offer into the 'macro' or collective pool of same as a 'becoming myth' to share beyond our small troupe in support of Gaia's own dynamic and continued mythic 'becoming'. A lot of words, I know, but we have a simple mantra to call this process forth:

A Snowball of Light
That becomes and becomes –
So it is, when all is Love …

Here is a simple example – stone/mountain/Gaia-relevant:

In praise of the 'forgotten valley on the border of Time' which called me home to this Land and where I first met the Amici, I composed "Onsernone Long Poem" (OLP) a verse narrative of epic length woven in and around the seasons, directions and elements. Intimately 'micro' on one hand, I soon realised it was a Love Song to Gaia – the valley a microcosm of her entire planetary Beauty, hence the work a celebration of same. I performed several cantos in the high wild of its composition before deciding the best thing I could do was gift the entire work back to the Earth from which it was born. Christmas Day 2016, with several family members in attendance, I 'planted' OLP in the slope above our village in a wee calico bag (lily white!) from a Himalayan foundation called 'Shed the Light'. It seemed sweetly symbolic, as was the planting locale – in sight of two mountain 'besties' who overlit its writing. The 'snowball' had cycled through my desire to write the homage, to sketching out its landscape'd framework, to becoming conscious it was not just the valley I wanted to honour but Gaia herself, to 'making' a product which twinned this micro/macro proposition, before gifting a personal creation 'myth' back to the whole. So it is, when all is Love.

While the above example seems 'contained' in and of itself, I am always amazed how each lily-white 'act' feeds into a more expansive snowball'd becoming outwith Time. Here again the reader is invited to think of a 3D core sample fanning out its 4D exuberance before diving back into the dynamic whole of expression, cross-fertilising with other samples and landing even bigger 'fish' on my (spheric planal) plate. My task? To keep diligent notes of the different puzzle pieces as and when they arise in the event that, like a juggler with too many balls in the air, the 'snow' either melts before it can be actioned (leaving me, at least, wet, bedraggled and cold) or that it compounds with such energetic speed that the weight of the thing buries us all in a 'drift' of avalanched proportions. Such notes, reflecting a thinking/writing-through process on the way to actually 'becoming conscious' of task, therefore serve to moderate 'desire' to align an eventual action with its in-Time potentiality to 'stick'.

With that as preface, herewith the 'plot-point' which (unknown at the time) kick-started my 'becoming desire' for the eventual manifestation of project this book's task is to tell …

'Twas a visioning experience that presented while I was deep in the process of documenting "Awakening" – dateline September 2015. An experience which stayed on a pending pile for 18 months or so, added to (but never amplified) by other encounters, it intrigued and concerned me in like measure. But its central tenet never faded. The fact that the vision presented in the same intersect as my entry into the inner sanctity of the Alps, Sasso san Gottardo, said something was afoot beyond my (conscious) intent to visit any Sasso.

Literally translating as the 'rock' of St Gotthard, this catacomb'd redoubt burrows into solid granite and marks the true 'heart' of Switzerland, the centre of the Alpine chain that exploded in a battle of plate tectonics some 20 million years past. In a section of "Awakening" titled "Meeting Mountains Redux", I described my intent to meet Helvetia, the genius loci (or angel, dependent on one's vernacular) of this peace-sunk Land at the heart of Europe, within her heart.

I wanted to ask permission, seek her blessing before stepping out to walk her Songline all the way cross-country, to sing up, on her behalf, Peace-Love-Light for the all of Gaia's world with each breath, with each press of (my) sole to (her) soul. I knew I had to do this physically for the psychoid unity of the undertaking to begin on the right foot (so to speak); it meant meeting her inside Mountain before I could walk the full stretch of her outer Mantle as a 3D/4D (up-hill/down-dale) cross-section, rim to (border'd) rim, space-time'd, proposition.

Intersecting the Sasso visit was, by coincidence, the red ('blood') Full Moon, September's total lunar eclipse. We set the alarm for 4am, but I was lucid a few minutes prior, returned from an Amici party where a large group had gathered to witness the 'Red Lady' (as they call her). Here, Moon was huge, much 'closer', almost physically present on a sunny hillside, green-grassed, daylit. Yet still so visible, so red? Later, after our family's 'physical-peek' and 'wow', we went back to bed where I had a chance to return to the Malakut; now the after-party was in full swing, and I had delight meeting 'cousins on my mother's side'. These 'usual suspects' I could make sense of, but the visioning experience?

OK. Here goes …

I am on 'the edge of the world', learning about nodes connecting different (major) regions of the world. I see one, for example, on the southwest coast of Latin America with a diagonal line through to northwest United States. Effecting a triangulation with an in-between node, the central 'crux' of line shoots up into space. I see another which is vaguely Middle East/North African-commensurate but the 'map' in which I stand (and over which I fly) is different to the physical world, so I am unsure of exact locale.

At this point an energy signature which, at some level, is aligned with David's arrives in a Lorian class-type context to talk about energy lines, power, and how the 'forces' can get it wrong when engaging humanity, either distorting or killing if the differential is not properly managed. Very unwieldy to work with this solo is his counsel. I observe as he busily writes to various buddies to warn of the unpredictability of the energetic forces within Earth at this time, how they are manifesting to engage the crises of our time but (perhaps) our intentions are misleading or ill-conceived (as usual) or just plain deceptive (ego-driven); this is how/why things go wrong. He seems very concerned.

Another Lorian-aligned energy signature arrives; we begin to talk 'Sidhe'. My partner F also arrives to demonstrate how I should 'anchor' myself (via a resonant-vibrational hum) in the veracity of Mountain via a specific cliff I 'know' well. I then travel with the former into Sidhe zones where we work with a flaming branch, phoenix-lit, from a tree in a family's garden. Time is running 'down'; periodically she blows a horn to 'inform' someone of our actions – it seems we need to light a bunch of 'stations' with the burning branch before Time is 'extinguished'. Yet it should be done slowly, moderately, methodically; when 'contaminated' with the energy of urgency it is not done well.

To say this vision was confusing does not describe half of it. A subtle communique covering seemingly unrelated territory (to my mind, at that time), as well as vastly different work practices or streams with which (I assumed) I had no experience? I scribbled it out, popped it on a pending pile, and tried to see it simply as a 'cautionary note' in the spirit of Mariel's:

"The aetheric planes of the earth are cloudy and polluted; the lens has imperfections in it that can distort the forces that are released. There is much to be done before either of us can safely recapture what once was."

As we were working with known PeaceSinks (albeit in home territories stretched across the world) at that time, I trusted our Amici troupe were on 'safe ground' with our underlying fidelity of intent. I continued to script "Awakening" and plan the PeaceWalk across Helvetia. But what I had been shown of the geometric geography of energy 'nodes' in different regions of the world <u>unassociated</u> with any known 'home-map' was nothing if not intriguing. The desire to 'become' had been seeded.

It would take another year and a half (and more – ad infinitum!) till a moment arrived when I 'suddenly' began to understand the scope of what we were actually being asked to do. Thereafter slumping in a puddle of daunted self-doubt at this undertaking (an UrWerk* to all intents in time <u>and</u> space), no amount of snowball could shift me to consider the magnitude of its 'becoming product' without seeking (physical) David's real in-Time counsel to amplify what the Malakut revealed of the unwieldiness of in-Earth energies, counsel which will be shared later, at the appropriate juncture in this narrative.

(*UrWerk. Noun. Collective. German – hybridised. Ur = Ancient. Werk = Work.)

For now, however, I want to return to my central proposition that on a spheric planal diagram of equals ('Universe high and just as wide') no mountain is any more or less sacred than another. This embodies my understanding that the macro is mirrored in the micro in each context. Just as a water droplet contains the entire ocean in its very self, each fractal of the whole hosts the whole at core – the spark of Love that animates is no more or less in each than in all. The Buddha's teaching speaks to this:

"There is Love at the centre of all things and all things are the same thing."

As does Rumi's beautiful:

"Lovers don't finally meet somewhere. They're in each other all along."

Odd 'maths', you may think, before we attend the 'music', but there are two quick 'routes' I want to follow here for the reader who has not encountered my work before. In partnering our Cousins of the Commons, I am constantly exploring what I, as Human, can do to sing up the Stars within the Earth across a border Faerie/Sidhe* cannot cross.

(*Apropos labels: My Amici call themselves 'Elven'; others I have met introduce themselves as 'Pixie'; down under are my 'Shining Ones'; in another region of world the 'Sunny-Side-Up peoples'; Swiss talk of Wild-Folk/Wildmännli; and I'm sure the provenance of the 'Harlem Globetrotters', self-described, is clear. Point being that as far as I can tell these are like any human descriptors which connect us to place, culture, tradition, history-of-contact et al).

The important thing is, as Mariel says:

"We are <u>star</u> people because we bring the Stars to Earth. But we can only bring them so far; there is a <u>threshold</u> we cannot cross, but you can, if you will dance the stars inward and outward with us."

In such spirit, let me first look at the plan to 'walk out' from Helvetia's heart as a <u>physical</u> and <u>subtle</u> proposition, to 'dance' the stars inward and outward with each 'singing' step.

On a micro level I envisioned this as an opportunity to enliven long <u>dormant</u> lines by actively 'singing up country' with my Peace-Love-Light mantra to support Gaia's (macro) crystalline consciousness in, as Mariel says, an ongoing "<u>choir</u> of unfoldment and evolution". But another 'micro' was implicated in this walk: Helvetia, the genius loci herself. Albeit on a grander (physical and subtle) scale than little I, by <u>blending</u> my Light with hers in Song across an entire stretch of terroir (after inviting her blessing via Sasso-sanctum'd petition), I envisaged the unfoldment of a fresh (Land-Sea-Sky'd) <u>self</u>-leyline in my, thereby her, thereby Gaia's, subtle and physical <u>structure</u> – simply by twinning <u>my</u> Self with <u>her</u> Land, simply by <u>sharing</u> the same stretch of Song, merging our respective 'mantles' to gift blessing out/on to Gaia's whole.

This practice speaks to Australian Aboriginal tradition, of course – nomadic ritual which enacts (and sings) pilgrimage as a way-of-being, as daily matter-of-course. In Bruce Chatwin's landmark and lyrical text for a Western audience ("The Songlines", 1987), he writes that pilgrimage re-establishes the original harmony which once existed between humanity and universe, citing the Buddhist principle that in travelling the path, one becomes the path:

"Arkady, to whom I mentioned this, said it was quite similar to an Aboriginal concept. 'Many men afterwards <u>become</u> country, in that place, Ancestors.' By spending his whole life walking and singing his Ancestor's Songline, a man eventually became the track, the Ancestor and the song."

My practice until that point had been to charge and energise connections between specific hemispheric nodes (Swiss-Aussie) within a stretch of steward'd HomeSong in the lattice of Gaia's planetary crystal. The PeaceWalk I envisioned now extended such Self-stretches across a vaster 'becoming landscape', one emerging as walked, navigated as sung. At some point, 'words formed':

"*I am an itinerant monk, ever unterwegs (i.e. 'underway'); Pilgrim for Love. Amen.*"

It seemed to capture what I was proposing. I assume this was Soul talking, sharing what I had 'signed up for' upon incarnation this time round in the spirit of Emerson's observation that the Soul contains in itself the event that befalls it, 'for the event is only the actualizing of its thoughts'. Well, here was a 'long' event, both spatially and temporally if ever there was one.

Peace-Love-Light – shared ground, shared way, shared goal. Our (shared) essence involved pilgrim staff (happily self-dubbed PeacePole), legs, voice, backpack, hat, sunnies and all in between eagerly making holistic connection to the All of the One on behalf of One and the Same. I visualised a living thread of Light walked through Helvetia's PeaceSink, the potentiality to blend her Gaian Songlines of geology and spirit, and through my (micro) human act to rebind (macro) humanity to Land via the paths Ancestors had inscribed in/on her skin – akin to Aboriginal Dreaming, which teaches to walk and re-walk the Ancestors' becoming, to sing and re-sing over and over the Songlines they steward. Why? Because they believe:

"*An unsung Land is a dead Land.*"

With this 'walk', therefore, I committed to extend (micro'd) stewardship of (macro'd) Earth in the spirit of Mariel's commentary:

"*The Earth is still a planetary crystal with energies vibrating and coursing along a vast latticework of connections. The phenomena you call the 'leylines' are only an outer representation of this, the manifestation upon the physical of these deeper lines of living energy and consciousness*".

Now, intersecting this is the second route on what I feel I can offer to a partnership with Sidhe across a threshold they cannot cross.

I know we all work on different aspects of restoring and evolving Gaian holism and I hope and pray all our shared work will bear fruit, for Gaia, for All, in the fullness of Time's watch. What I have learnt thus far from my attunement to stone sentience, to Mountain's sanctity (and beyond), is that the more we (humanity) know ourselves and our connection to Land (by embracing and embodying the 'consciousness of matter' – as self, as other), the more Gaia comes to know herself and her connection (to 'Third-Rock' physicality).

It is as if by extending our consciousness, in holistic inclusivity, to engage the sacredness at the core of each expression of Life, we help to evolve and 'open' Gaia's beautiful limitless heart further, and further to shared relationship, inwith and of the Body of her full reach. Not simply engaging Gaia as an overlighting or underlying World Soul that 'sponsors' our work, or for whom we work, but actively inviting her participation as fully-fledged co-performer in our enduring loving service as she actively invites our co-performance in consciousness-building.

This I 'learnt' before my active working engagement with Sidhe, when a planetary Being, a 'keeper-presence' (or guardian) of Gaia's DeepTime-Tectonia'd memory, whom I know as Gondwana, arrived to share her wisdom. It was in the context, as Bruce Chatwin writes, that:

"*In Aboriginal belief ... if the songs are forgotten, the land itself will die.*"

I had 'seen' this – Gaia torn, wrenched from her planetary home by humanity's forgetfulness, by our continued desecration of her 'magic mantle', our unabated disrespect for <u>elemental</u> cohesion and <u>harmonic</u> energetic balance in our approach, as we (in Gregory Bateson's prescient rhetoric) "arrogate all mind" to ourselves ... seeing "the world around as mindless and therefore not entitled to moral or ethical consideration". In such a space of grief and 'mourning', of literal com-passion (to suffer with) Gondwana spoke. She said Gaia's evolutionary consciousness would only be <u>ripe</u> for full (lotus-blossom'd) manifestation:

"*When the Spirit is once again at One with the Third ...*"

I understood my work involved <u>re-singing</u> a connection into being between Gaia's bruised and battered Spirit and her (equally) exploited Earth. To heal, the World Soul desired nothing more than to re-unite in <u>divine</u> marriage with the sanctity of her 'Third-Rock', the <u>physical</u> fact of our beautiful, beautiful world. In 'singing up country', I saw my task as weaving threads of Love's Light between spirit and geology (vertically to intersect incoming stellar) and between physical sentience and itself (horizontally via leylines of 'root-knowing' through Land, Sea <u>and</u> Sky). Further, I understood that the <u>depth</u> of my engagement would only truly support Gaian holism if 'spiritual' practice were enacted physically and 'physical' spiritually; I needed to <u>walk</u> in the footsteps of the Ancestors, to 'know' Land as it was originally sung into being – I needed to re-trace the paths of great planetary beings, and leave my trail of loving Song, like theirs, as a gift <u>imprinted</u> in Gaia's skin, infusing her subtle-physical bones in one.

Again microcosm-macrocosm – the onus on <u>us</u> to 'know' Land, <u>and</u> its Spirit, so it may know itself. Reciprocal recognition by another name or the 'Way of Love' which embraces both path <u>and</u> voice (Luce Irigaray's *la voie de l'amour* and *la voix de l'amour*). Amongst other examples of same, it reflects the underlying intent of the well-annotated hadith:

"*I was a Hidden Treasure and wanted to be known so created the world that I might be known.*"

While a roe deer buck in the forest one day rendered the message to me thus:

"*Through your eyes, I see myself.*"

In Gaia's <u>incarnate</u> form, as a <u>function</u> of the Generative Mystery, it is as if she (as Treasure) stays hidden from herself commensurate with the extent of how 'veiled' <u>we</u> are from our true nature to engage and attune to the consciousness of <u>her</u> matter, that of our planetary home. The more we 'see' and the more we 'know' – thereto so does Gaia. My practice of 'mirroring Joy' speaks to this, but walking <u>and</u> singing has the added benefit of sharing it out across Land as a living leyline of resonance in perpetual dynamic motion.

Recently, Gondwana's words amplified to include:

"When we the Crone become, when we the Land become ..."

The statement speaks to Gondwana's own DeepTime-Tectonia'd cronedom-crown worn on behalf of her 'younger sister', Gaia, the one who agreed to <u>be</u> this world, yet (understandably) needs in-time and in-space <u>rooted</u> elder presence support of this longer-than undertaking – both here in dense elemental physicality <u>as well as</u> beyond the thin Blue line of planetary atmospheric extent. I have seen the 'Hand' which delivered Gaia to Earth, but it stands just as ready to pluck her Soul out of this grand experiment and take her home to the Stars …

Yes, what I have seen may speak to Gondwana's role as 'Hand', but it also speaks to our ability to be the 'Hand' of partnership likewise. Indeed Gondwana's 'crone' comment was captured in a quote of Mariel's earlier, repeated here because of its relevance:

'In you, stars and earth meet. … In partnership with us, our desire is for you to become like the <u>Old Ones</u>, who stood and formed the first circles. … You are less child-like than you were then. In some ways you have become darker, but in other ways you shine more brightly and carry a <u>hard-won wisdom</u> and connection to the world … you are in touch with the <u>life within matter</u> in ways we are not. If you will listen, it speaks to you with voices we do not hear. We know the voices of starlight but you hear the voices of the fire within earth and matter.'

Reader, you may think I am getting into some freaky (or at least odd-ball) cosmology here, but "Awakening" amply began the disclosure of the creation myths and familial relations which have been shared with me according to my mode of symbolic understanding. Obviously these are the subject of different interpretations by a variety of world faiths, indigenous or latter-day religious. But no matter how expressed, the root stock is Love. Couple that with the Common Ancestor of 'Sidhe-and-We' in the lineage of cosmic humanity and there is <u>nothing</u> of the Universal Commons that does not share the same primal (in-time) vine.

To conclude this chapter, therefore, two last observations about my experience of the consciousness of matter, the notion of twinning ourselves with Land to 'hear' and honour its voice – to call up and verily embrace a self-Earth consciousness, to live as micro 'Gaias', our own incarnate <u>matter'd</u> consciousness in intersect with that shared by each other form of sentience, including our darling World Soul herself.

Firstly …

In a Malakut setting, I once sat at a kitchen table with a Sidhe companion – I know her as MakerMan because she helps choreograph our Amici performances in subtle and physic'd space. ("Appendix 2" houses a 'who's who' of my Card Deck Amici.) We were discussing interconnectivity over a cup of tea (a common practice – I am never without a cuppa whether in material or Malakut dimensions!) when, suddenly, a richly textured carpet unfurled on the floor beside us. It depicted the inky night sky, a female shape clearly discernible therein. Like a constellation, yet with stars so tightly packed her form could clearly be seen without any need of imaginative projection. The figure was depicted standing, one arm raised, as if in the midst of a dance. Words formed as, together, we beheld this image:

"*We come from the stars and we return to the stars.*"

While this was something previously shared by other sources, I had never encountered it in such ornate visual expression before. I was then handed a small ball and understood it to be like a starseed (a set of which I once received for 'planting' our Amici'd intent in fecund soil). This ball though was warm, glowing, 'alive'. Compared to an actual starseed (an orb of pure light), it was solid, dense - really like a ball.

I intuited it was our stellar ancestry within; it was called our 'Earth-consciousness'. For the stellar realms to connect with us as intended, our task was to return this ball to the stars – not as individuals but as the human collective. There it would be absorbed by the energies, their reciprocity of same enabling the continued 'evolution' of Earth-consciousness here in physical space-time. How this ball could 'return' to the stars I learnt in two demonstrations – one where I myself rolled the ball directly into the female form in carpet (who, by this stage, was called 'Mother'); the other where the ball traversed a difficult maze-like concourse on the table before dropping down onto the carpet, there to be re-absorbed. Enduringly, throughout, was the refrain:

"*We come from the stars and we return to the stars.*"

I returned from the space energised; such a compact demonstration of process and purpose! Now I found myself within earshot of a joyous chorale; unlike angelic choirs encountered, these voices presented like a scout troupe or 'hi-ho' worker detail – youthful, marching down a path below my window. I longed to join their expression of praise and immediately I could – not as vocalisation, but as waves of energy surging through me and spontaneously radiating out. This would be my Song, my expression commensurate with theirs; 'praise' accompanying each inflowing, inpouring, outpouring, outflowing wave. A felt-mantra, a Body-constituted-mantra shared on/on as self-Light, participant in being and flowing the world with blessing.

'Twas an in-house demonstration of what my own ball of Earth-consciousness could do, how it could connect and 'return' to stellar realms as a recurrent cycle of energetic praise fuelled by Joy to contribute, fuelled by Love to serve. How precious an instruction in the purpose of humanity's in-world presence! Writ large are we simultaneously of the Stars and embedded in Earth. Here, in the heart of FeltWorld, is our work, a difficult maze-like concourse to be negotiated, granted, but ever with the possibility to stream our Joy from the glowing ball of warm dense living Light we carry within. Our inheritance, our gift, to gift on.

Secondly …

As a ten-year-old my youngest, D, went through a stage of reading a raft of mountaineering books to supplement his desire to climb all the mountains of all the world. I said: Let's just start (Heidiland) local; as a family, we summited about two dozen that year (the irony of piggy-backing him up mountains as a whingey pre-schooler is not lost on me, but I digress). One evening he sat on the couch in shock – this particular Swiss alpinist (since passed at the tender age of 40) had described in graphic detail his unsuccessful rescue of a fellow climber on Annapurna, including the hallucinations he experienced of his friend seemingly calling to him as he shovelled ice and snow atop the corpse during a blizzard. I read the harrowing chapter myself, similarly dumbstruck by the situations these fellows encounter, and the risks they knowingly undertake in the well-documented 'death zone'.

Why?

The perennial question remained on my lips as I headed to bed but in my wandering of the Malakut that night it was more than successfully answered by my encounter with a Presence who intended, it seemed, to complete my induction into 'Mountains 101' in equally graphic detail. This teacher was female energy-pure and she said, quite matter-of-factly:

"*You are all called; everyone hears der Ruf der Berge.*"

As soon as these words formed, the rhizome of my brain flooded with Light. Connections synapsed all over its known world in randomly-enacted quantum leaps. Tangential lines-of-flight, they nevertheless brought me to the same core of cognition, including (but not exhausted by) the following:

An experience of 'self-naughting' years before which saw me embrace a 'me-sized' Malakut mountain as a natural expression of my Love for its sheer beingness;

A later instruction to consciously greet the spirit of mountains we physically climb in order to heighten the resonance of connectivity between our 'mattered' selves;

The realisation of the sheer power of creation and destruction at work in Nature on a scale and at an intensity that cannot possibly be expected to spare any Life in the wrong place at the wrong time; and

That a vast majority of mountaineers have no conscious awareness lain over an unconscious primal urge to heed the call of high wild.

The Presence brought this latter line-of-flight into sharp relief via a complementary teaching she called 'Sherpa-knowing', which compared the ego- and/or technically-driven goals of those they serve (as guides and/or packhorses) to their <u>lived</u> experience of the high wild. 'Sherpa-knowing' was therefore equal parts intuitive, genetic, religious, cultural – an understanding of <u>ever</u> being at the mercy of Nature's sublime force, to the <u>elemental</u> energies of Land and Sky. Hence the intoning of "Om mani padme hum" as a constant mantra tuned to their footfalls on the path – to act (equally) as protective shield or, if protection impossible, to afford comfort by still (ostensibly) gracing lips at the moment of passing.

Throughout the teaching, I felt the Presence of this overlighting <u>collective</u> Himalayan entity as female, something which came as a complete surprise to me given the energetic power I experienced. My cultural background would suggest such strength should be male, but the spirit revealed herself as all-woman – fierce, strong, protective, nurturing. It literally felt like the 'mother' of all energies. She then spoke her name: Kali. Another synapse pulsed with life. Kali – the Hindu goddess of time and change, the consort of Shiva and keeper of 'shakti', the sacred force. The primordial cosmic energy of creation and destruction was hers to wield, she a true UrWerk-er in the canon.

Kali showed me her power. I <u>lived</u> her stone mountains quaking and cracking, crumbling to form the soil in which Life took hold. I 'saw' the whole chain of Life on Earth emanate from this force in an incredibly vivid flash, rich in colour, texture, sound, and one in which I experienced my own calling, my own 'Ruf der Berge'. Kali said: "Surrender" and without thought I did, throwing myself face-down on the ground, <u>loving</u> her, binding myself to her, becoming <u>one</u> with her. Rock, stone, earth, grit, dust – I merged with the heart of FeltWorld and in so doing, absorbed its energy as her gift of Grace. Universal resonance sang in my veins and a blinding white Light filled my inner vision, an explosion of clarity as to the purpose of this ritual – to <u>honour</u> the matter of which we are made, wherefrom our Body has come, and to whence it shall return.

Kali. Kali. Kali. Instantly I realised what lacks in many mountaineers' understanding. Likewise are they called, her all-woman call stirring their loins no less; they long to 'mate' with this energy. But surrender their very selves into her care as Sherpas do? In typical Western patriarchal fashion, instead they try to dominate, "knock the old bastard off," as Hillary so ineloquently put it, failing to recognise, to <u>revere</u>, her majesty and pre-eminence in this, <u>her</u> domain. So many leave debris and waste to foul her sacred places, letting their competitive spirit or a commercial imperative 'guide' their actions in the high wild. So many are corrupted – by ignorance, lust, arrogance, greed. But still she calls. So she may teach, so we may learn her laws – of how the world works, of why we must let be, let be, so it <u>can</u> work as a whole living <u>breathing</u> system, and why <u>all</u> destruction, including our own, however violently it may seem to take place, is a necessary part of that selfsame law. As eternal as the cycle of creation and destruction is her call, so we may understand our place in the world, that the threads of our existence are as intimately woven into the web of Life as any and all.

Regardless of how confronting it was in the moment, my conscious re-acquaintance with the law of the Ancients was appropriate – direct, unmediated experience is how I learn best. A shamanic initiation in its own right, my physical and subtle connection to stone sentience suddenly morphed, via this dramatic encounter with Kali's energy, into a binding and holistic psychoid unity of shared geology, shared spirit. Mountains 101 indeed. Let us move on …

MOUNTAINS/DRAGONS WITHOUT END

I have several intimate conversation partners when it comes to 'talking' Mountains. With each I sit long, and return to their sacred wisdom again and again, ever walking further along the mystic trails their texts set before these more than willing feet. To a person, they document my own experience – of mergence with Mountain, physical and subtle. How the sanctity, the stillness of stone invites them into the sanctity, the stillness of spirit, the 'caves' where their own teachers dwell, Body-Mind at one with the space of their communion.

While I know of the Abrahamic traditions' connection to the Sacred within Mountain/s, the various passages in their holy texts which reference same, and the desert fathers/mothers as well as other anchorites (including Eastern Orthodox, Sufi) whose hermitage and connection to Source intertwine spirit/text, for reasons of which I (like Pascal's reason) am unaware, despite my genetic and cultural background, this Annie-heart in this lifetime's skin attunes more readily, seamlessly even, to the writings of Eastern mystics, principally Taoist and Buddhist. Both Chan/Zen, with its blending of Taoist principles, and Tibetan, which found its way to Japan as esoteric Shingon, figure in this (latter) mix. Hindu traditions never made headway, regardless of my gnomic friend's brother or my years-past meeting with Kali. Indeed, hearing her speak her name meant that once

I returned from the Malakut, I went on an immediate search for information to explain why she had actually shown up in this context, so unaware was I of her 'stature' in the canon.

The intent, therefore, of this chapter is to share with the reader insights from my favoured traditions via outtakes from my most treasured volumes, and how they support my longer-than connection to Mountain as well as underpin an understanding of what our Amici project could offer to Gaia's evolutionary consciousness. To call us to scene, however, I need to skip this rhizomatic tendril ahead of itself a wee while to the third section of book – "Exploring Song" – to quote a specific verse from one of my compositions. "Thine Eyes" was written in the spirit of my last chapter's (roe deer buck-mediated) observation:

"Through your eyes I see myself."

It forms part of an "In-Frame" Cycle of Song, whose (2019) performance, while solitary of voice, was symphonic in length. The relevant verse goes:

Mountains Dragons without end
Generating resonance
Echo to divine Presence
Look close with these, thine eyes.
Each reflecting its own kin
Each is wearing Soul at Skin
Sink at Surface blending in
To see with these, thine eyes.

The reference to Mountain is clear. The reference to Dragon, if the reader is unfamiliar with Eastern mythology, less so. In this respect, Dragon is River – all waters a-flow, the full shed between (Mountain) Source and (primordial) Sea implicated in Dragon's 'river-flight'. The fact of elemental Water as the of/in-Earth partner to elemental Wind (aka above-Earth Air), with Fire as their in-between elemental connector thread, helps explain why Dragon is the mythic beast of choice, quite happily cross-dressing and dissolving boundaries no matter how its fragrant fiery Breath-of-Life manifests. Sailing Sky-waves to generate lightning strikes as readily as snaking through (and/or 'becoming') Rivers, Lakes, Seas, as well as slicing clean through Earth as 'liquid lit' energetic meridians of rhizomatic proclivity, Dragon (as serpent or Nessie or any other basilisk'd creature), is a charming companion of Love's Way or, as Gimli says in his broad Scottish brogue to Aragorn at one point in LOTR3:

"Very handy in a tight spot."

If one considers that Mountain, vertically connecting Heaven-Earth, has 'responsibility' for elemental Aether (or Space as the Tibetans call it) as well as anchoring the elemental (Earth-dense) 'base', while Dragon busily whip-whirls the horizontal (relatively speaking) tribe of three 'middle-schoolers' into shape, shunting exuberant electrically-charged ions this way and that, there really is nothing more needed to engage the primal <u>root-knowing</u> of Earth-consciousness than by partnering these two 'guardians' or 'stewards' of the (elemental) way – at least in our (simple-mind'd) Amici work of "harmonising the resonance of elemental sentience in skin – micro/macro'd and all in-between – amen" (as our invocatory mantra invites them to table). But once again I am getting ahead of myself. This particular line of (harmonic) flight will be fully enfleshed by the close of chapter. In short, however:

"Very handy in a tight spot."

Now to begin with Dogen, the 13th century Japanese Zen master, whose "Mountains and Waters (i.e. Dragons) Sutra" is lyricism itself:

"The appearance of the mountains is completely different when we are in the world gazing at the distant mountains and when we are in the mountains meeting the mountains … From time immemorial the mountains have been the dwelling place of the great sages; wise men and sages have all made the mountains their own chambers, their own body and mind. And through these wise men and sages the mountains have been actualised. However many great sages and wise men we suppose have assembled in the mountains, ever since they entered the mountains no one has met a single one of them. There is only the actualisation of the <u>life</u> of the mountains; not a single trace of their having entered remains."

In his commentary on Dogen's text, John Daido Loori says:

"To realise the mountains as one's own body and mind is transformative … <u>Intimacy</u> is the dwelling place of the great sages … To realise all form as one's own body and mind is to dwell in a universe that is unborn and inextinguishable, a universe that has no beginning or end."

Intimacy – yes; my embrace of a me-sized Mountain, Kali's induction via sweaty gritty earth, the way my body sings with the 'chi of shared circuitry' when it comes into resonance with Mountain's <u>in-stellar</u> Life. A purely physical manifestation – of 'sizzling' fingertips, 'seared' palms or soles of feet, solar plexus 'stretching' beyond skin, leaping to engage like a sprinter out of the blocks. My energy responds to its <u>loving</u> welcome of mine, as 'Presence' on a diagram of equals which 'dances' our shared Way of Love on. A connection akin to vertigo at times as I am pulled into Mountain's embrace – chthonic, heated, shunted direct to Acqua Termale'd (thermal waters) font …

"The Amici Files", appended to "Awakening" (and available on nestedfishes. org) amply wax lyrical on my self-apprenticeship in the ways of Mountain, Dragon. A felt-sense of mergence pervades, yet one which is coupled with a clarity that, in the space we share, we nevertheless remain our own 'selves'. A sense of togetherness, therefore, infuses the scape, as if moving past the ritual of reciprocal recognition to a state of <u>centred</u> co-belonging, of twinned 'being-with', as if via its energetic <u>outreach</u> Mountain affirms my prior 'bow' of greeting as much as honouring my entry to its 'domain'. 'Tis a cone of Light we share and which flows, via Dragon's enspirited veins, as liquid silver'd gold through all worlds and times of Gaia's all. Held in their generous embrace no matter <u>what</u> happens, one could say it is my 'Sherpa-knowing' by another name.

I 'hear' the resonant hum tuned to a lower vibratory pitch than my 'chi', granted, but as we both 'sing' in the same Gaian choir, the full membrane of World Soul holds <u>both</u> our notes in a harmonium of communion. A key task in connecting home nodes across the world (see "Awakening") was to discover the extant 'note' of my glacier-erratic'd anchor-stone in garden grail (affectionately dubbed MossMan-Findling because of his relation to the bardic Heart Stone in our Amici Stone Circle – see "Appendix 2"). Sitting long in meditation to hear his burble within, like the quiet settled breath of a child's deep sleep, I could attune to and write out from this shared space a specific 'awakening' melody, to draw him 'out' with my Love, alert him to the task ascribed to his portal'd presence.

The principle, and lived fact, of 'universal resonance' underpins the interconnectivity of each our discrete piles of matter'd consciousness. An eternal base note underlies the 'musica universalis', or Harmony of the Spheres; first proposed by Pythagoras (in our Western tradition), it holds that each member of the solar system produces a unique hum, or orbital resonance, as it spins through time and space. Bring this discussion down to micro fractal'd level here on Earth, and you reach the extant note of a stone's unique vibration, 'split' from Mountain which carried its 'mother-lode' knowing. The following quote by the late writer (and Buddhist practitioner) Peter Matthiessen, on his Himalayan encounter, is relevant here, as well as gorgeously poetic:

"The secret of the mountains is that the mountains simply exist, as I do myself: the mountains exist simply, which I do not. The mountains have no 'meaning', they are meaning; the mountains are. The sun is round. I ring with life, and the mountains ring, and when I can hear it, there is a ringing that we share. I understand all this, not in my mind but in my heart, knowing how meaningless it is to try to capture what cannot be expressed, knowing that mere words will remain when I read it all again, another day."

In "Nine-Headed Dragon River", where this text appears, Matthiessen continues to write of his induction into the mysteries of Mountain thus:

"The ground whirls with its own energy ... in a slow spiral, and ... in this vast space and silence, that energy pours through me, joining my body with the sun until small silver breaths of cold, clear air, no longer mine, are lost in the mineral breathing of the mountain ... I grow into these mountains like a moss. I am bewitched."

Matthiessen's 'whirling' is the vertigo-like connection I experience, but it also describes the way I 'see' the elementals come into harmonious resonance. Seriously, though, his writerly genius is on full view in the above quote. 'Mineral breathing': What a divine expression to describe this felt-sense, brimful of luminosity!

Matthiessen goes on to describe how the stillness of stone invites one <u>in</u> to the sanctity of spirit:

"This stillness to which all returns is profound reality, and concepts such as soul and sanity have no more meaning here than gusts of snow; my transience, my insignificance are exalting, terrifying. Snow mountains … serve as a mirror to one's own true being, utterly still, utterly clear, a void, an emptiness without life or sound that carries in itself <u>all</u> life, <u>all</u> sound."

It is a stillness I inhabit daily when in <u>conscious</u> seamless boundless connection to Mountain. It means I do not need to enter meditation as much as it enters and surround-sounds me – a cave or con' of silence ever-extant, its note ever-present, a perpetual under-breath (or current) to inter-being'd relation. The place where this is revealed and 'actualised' (to draw on Dogen's language) most particularly is the tiny stone cottage we steward 'in a forgotten valley on the border of Time'. Built more than 400 years ago from fragments self-split from the rambunctious ridge overlighting village ("a breadknife in need of smoothing to a more functionally acceptable blade," as I wrote in the epic OLP in whose shadow this poem was 'planted'), our home is a patchwork'd <u>fractal</u> of Mountain, a literal 'chip off the old block', as are all hereabouts. As Kisha remarks in "The Taste of Translation":

"Nothing looked the same in the Swiss south. All was stone. The houses and barns – roofs of stone, walls of stone, floors of stone. Stone. All stone. But they couldn't eat stone. So terraces were laid, crops sown, all edged with sturdy stone walls."

So here I am, encased in stone that fulfils the function of an anchorite's cave as well as any chiselled by hand or 'badger-mole' burrowed amongst the roots of peak itself. Yet such a 'by-product' (or indeed, foundation stone) of in-home connectivity was the farthest thing from my mind when 'becoming desire' to put down roots in this Land, commit to 'staying put' within its landlocked lines, began its snowball'd 'house-hunt' rumble. Yes, I knew Home had found me when the cottage spoke its 'stillness' thus:

"People have slept well here; at Peace."

Decades ago, however, I did not realise the profundity of this statement for my (future) work, that the Amici were already hovering, that "der Ruf der Berge" had decided to literally anchor itself in this tiny treasure. Emerson's Soul … It takes a long time for my (simple) mind to catch up with what it ever-knows. But as this is a perennial Annie-time-lag, I won't labour the point.

• • • • •

Shifting the perspect a mite, let's move to symbology – to the runic script which houses, within itself, both the form and function of Mountain. There are two strings to interrogate here, both Taoist of (primal) origin.

'Tao', of course, is most usually translated as 'Way' or 'Path' and references the underlying order of the Universe as much as <u>our</u> 'way' to align with <u>its</u> Harmony on the 'path' through Life. There's a delightful comment Lao Tzu makes in his "Tao Teh Ching". I can almost see this little old Chinese sage sitting at his dais, trying to figure how best to express the inexpressible, bring language to the numinous, finally shrugging and simply penning:

"I do not know its name; so I call it Tao."

A key principle of Taoist philosophy is that of 'wu wei' – literally non-ado. 'Wei wu wei' is thus doing through non-doing, action through no action. Anything we actively do (the word 'striving' figures highly here) is against the natural harmony of the Universe. The metaphor of water and its yielding nature is oft-cited – water is without will, yet creates great landscapes (says Dragon, with a glint to eye). With its Source inwith Mountain's cave-of-heart, water exits, spills forth, its Dragon-breath carving, as <u>natural</u> matter-of-course, vast valley'd sheds on its homecome way to Sea. Respect for the pre-eminence of the elementals, for coming into harmony with the <u>truth</u> of their <u>nature</u> by following our own, is implicit in this view, viz:

"Tao never makes any ado,
And yet it does everything ...
All things will grow of themselves ...
When the desires of men are curbed, there will be peace,
And the world will settle down of its own accord ..."

True. Nature. Nothing. Special.

In the Taoist (and by extension Chan/Zen Buddhist) lexicon, for something to be 'true', it acts in natural harmony with the Universe. 'Nature' lives this (naturally!), by existing in concert with Time, yielding like seaweed to an ocean current wherever whenever however it is 'tugged'. The eminent Zen monk Shunryu Suzuki explains it this way:

"Something which comes out of nothingness is naturalness, like a seed or plant coming out of the ground. The seed has no idea of being some particular plant, but it has its own form and is in perfect <u>harmony</u> with the ground, with its surroundings. As it grows, in the course of time it expresses its nature ... For a plant or stone to be natural is no problem. But for us there is some problem ... To be natural ... we must work ..."

'Work' – to cinder the veils of conditioning, to reclaim our true nature, reveal our Light to the world, partner Gaia, our World Soul to fully evolve her own. Something I call wearing 'Soul at Skin', bringing 'Sink to Surface'.

Helping me with my own 'work' down the years was a delightful Malakut wander I once took while ruminating upon being 'at one' with the natural world. Quite unexpectedly I stumbled into a Sun-soaked grassy meadow brimful of snails living Life far beyond the limitations of my miniscule worldview. Bending low to observe their activity, I watched a snail climb a blade of grass. Over and over, up and down, up and down. Each time, I thought: "But that's just not possible; it'd be too heavy!" My mind would try to 'see' a human-logical 'reality' – blade of grass bent-double, snail less than vertical in progress, but over and over, the expression of its 'true reality' was repeated. This snail, like all others in the meadow, was making its way slowly, steadily, effortlessly up a single wispy blade of grass, a solitary stem which remained tall straight true, unbowed by its companion's actions. As I watched, slowly dissolving that intransigent knuckle of (my) human purview, words formed:

"*True nature.*"

Yes. The blade of grass was following its true nature – to stand tall – just as the snail was following its – to climb. A lesson about perception – not just mine (trying to make the image 'fit' what I thought I should see) but the snail's. It didn't think of itself as 'snail', or as something separate from 'grass'. This was not a case of one separate entity encountering another but both being one-and-the-same in shared space. The boundaries between 'self' and 'other' were blurred, in fact non-existent. The snail and blade of grass were so seamless in their 'reciprocal recognition' that neither remarked where one ended and the other began.

True nature guided each's individual behaviour as well as their collective undertaking, their energies merging to achieve a single common purpose, an activity facilitated by 'wei wu wei'. Simply by being themselves, and following their own natures (a snail to climb, a blade of grass to stand tall), they could share a moment of complete oneness and (supposed!) gravitational impossibility. Thomas Berry's "communion of subjects" in living Malakut colour.

Suddenly I understood how this 'micro' example extended to the snail's interrelation with any and all expressions of sentience in this landscape – its true nature expressed in, of and with everything else. I literally saw the snail merge with the blade of grass as well as with sunlight, breeze, dewdrop, on and on throughout the entire meadow. Everywhere I looked, true nature was being enacted; each remained itself yet seamlessly, simultaneously, was co-existent, at one with all. Of course, expand this teaching, in a Taoist sense, to full 'macro'd' extent – to come into harmonious co-resonance with the underlying order of the Universe – and we can see the extraordinary potentiality of living true nature. "Nothing special" (Suzuki would say with a sagic shrug). But: Oh, so special for those of us reclaiming what once forgot!

More on that later. Let us return to huggable Mountain and our Taoist adepts.

A key 'tool' of Taoist practice is the "I Ching" (Chinese Book of Change), which rests its oracular skill on the combination of trigrams to form a hexa- (here we go with 'maths' again) which are a mix of yin (Earth) 'broken' lines and yang (Heaven) 'solid' lines. With eight different trigrams in the model, 64 hexagrams are the result. Each hexagram expresses a particular aspect of the underlying 'Tao' (or Way) – i.e. the natural order of Universe. Containing several layers of text and subject to numerous levels of interpretation, the "I Ching" is considered the oldest of Chinese classics, having captured continuous attention for well over two thousand years. The specific commentary I consult was written in 1796 by Liu I-ming, who was also well-versed in Buddhism and Confucianism, in a translation by the inimitable Thomas Cleary.

With my website logo featuring the yin-yang symbol of opposites uniting as nestedfishes in solitary fusion, the holism which results when self and other meet as partners on a plane of consistence (i.e. diagram of equals), it should not be too far a stretch for the reader to see why this volume of Taoist wisdom speaks my 'language', especially given the mystical and profoundly lyrical way in which it is written. Stemming from ancient tradition, the trigram for Mountain comprises two yin topped by a yang. Simple – Heaven above, Earth below. The yin in the middle, to my mind, represents the 'flow' of Light between the two – a channel which facilitates their communion as well as comingling elemental energies (here, think Dragon and his tribe of 'middle-schoolers'). In Taoism, the Mountain trigram represents inner essence, that which is enduring, immutable, beyond change. A particular hexagram (whose name escapes me, as well as its contrary tri-) demonstrates the firmness Mountain displays when meeting the mutable energies of the phenomenal world; its signature text:

"Let Wind enter; keep Mountain still."

Another way of saying the Buddhist: "This too shall pass", and thus encouraging patient detachment to any 'dragon-ey' high-jinks which delight to surprise, it has become family shorthand for any clan member feeling overwhelmed by a situation. The visual quality attached to the expression is perfectly illustrative of the life skill, or quality (like Courage), to stand self-sovereign. No matter what outer forces 'buffer' our borders, our core (Mountain) remains intact. Always. And that core is expressed (in-world) by Mountain's mineral essence – a 'mirror' (as Matthiessen holds) to our own or, as 9th century Sufi master Sahl Tostari says:

"The secret of divinity is yourself."

To which (as a perpetual Aussie tea-apprentice) I delight in appending Thich Nhat Hanh's:

"Drinking a cup of tea, the seeming distinction between the one who drinks and the tea being drunk evaporates. Drinking a cup of tea becomes a direct and wondrous experience in which the distinction between subject and object no longer exists."

Shakespeare could quite happily tag along on this mystic meander – a rose by any other name would smell as sweet (and one which I lovingly attributed to a Sidhe Card Deck Dancer).

But just as drinking a cup of tea, sharing breath with a smelly rose or simultaneously 'being snail' while 'being grass' cannot be discounted as anything less than sacred communion, felt-sense engaged, the psychoid unity inherent in conjoining Human Time with Mountain Time – inner world of (its/our) self with (its/our) outer same – equally delivers a cathartic 'a-ha' to the chamber of my heart. Indeed, when – in the same intersect as Card Deck's arrival in my Heidiland letterbox – the "I Ching" toppled (of its own accord) out of the bookshelf and opened at a hexagram I had not yet encountered (Mountain, so-called because upper and lower trigrams are – you guessed it – Mountain), the synchronicity was too neat <u>not</u> to honour its counsel in my 'naming' ceremony for the Deck's Howe into whose 'hollow hill' we go:

Mountain above as Mountain below
one does not have a body;
walking in the Garden
one does not see a person.

The text's 'signature' is translated thus:

"Joining mountains; thus do superior people think without leaving their place."

Hmmm. OK. Something to remember – and something I was reminded (again) to remember in the context of sketching out our daunting Amici UrWerk!

Nevertheless, returning to our geometric line (of ant-army'd Taoist flight), at an exhibition of the 18th century Zen abbot Sengai's art and calligraphy some time ago, I came face-to-face with a thick-brushstroked parchment which spoke in ways (I assume) were unintended by dear Sengai (the catalogue giving no clue beyond a cryptic non-title). I literally said:

"Oh my gosh! He's scripted the word, TAO, uppercase, and in English!"

To my sight, in this 'mergent' moment, the prevailing trigram of runes matched perfectly the <u>sense</u> of Tao as well as the context in which Tao acts to <u>link</u> interdimensional realities (as well as underlie same). I saw the 'square' (or T) of 'Earth' at start of line, the 'circle' (or O) of 'Heaven' at end, joined by the 'triangle' (or A) of Mountain at centre. I saw the whole 'Way' unfold in simple runic representation as I read left to right but could easily have (Japanese-) read right to left (but that wouldn't have spelt Tao to my brain – an associative resonance for which I am grateful, being the simple-mind'd lass I am!). What immediately jumped out at me was Mountain's position in line-up, <u>between</u> Heaven-Earth; as well, its simple portrayal as a triangle perfectly 'fit' an (outer Toblerone-worthy) pyramidal (Matterhorn) shape. In the same a-linear flash, I saw the triangle's 'A-frame' represent both the 'Aum' of Sri Ramana's resonant hum (Sruti note) of primal creation (in-world expressed by Mountain's beingness) as well as 'Acqua' (water) sourced from Mountain's minerally 'Termale'd' (thermal, fiery) bones, thus connecting Dragon to the equation.

Now, the intriguing thing was he had not composed this as a vertical calligraphic work (as is the Japanese norm), but horizontal. I thus viewed it in the same 'planal' spirit – its 'landscape' rather than 'portrait' format convincing me it was a 2-D 'diagram-of-equals' representing 4-D knowing. Such that I immediately saw the word 'TAO', immediately saw Mountain's position reinforce its "I Ching"d trigrammic role, immediately saw the work present – in fresh 'dress' – a sacred <u>and</u> harmonic geometric equation. As a 'diagram-of-equals' horizontally expressed, thus non-hierarchical, it meant – to my simple mind – that Heaven Mountain Earth (if read right-to-left) or Earth Mountain Heaven (vice-versa) formed a balanced holistic framework of Being lain on primal Ground via the harmonic resonance of elemental sentience in parchment'd 'skin'.

Thank you, Sengai! I now had our UrWerk's requisite cosmology and Mountain math'd 'Music' in one. Suffice it to say, the image joined our Amici runic library post-haste for which a mantra, to invoke 'housed' energy during its inscription, is:

"*Tao of Way walked by all filial kin …*"

(NB. If you would like to view the image, it is on Sengai's wiki page under the title: 'Universe' which is someone else's interesting 'take' on an untitled work!)

A wee rhizomatic aside before moving on. The geometric form of circle is oft-found in Zen art. Known as the 'Enso', it represents the Void and, in a play on its shape, is usually described as a cake. In another Sengai work, simply of the Enso, the accompanying calligraphy says:

"*Eat this and have a cup of tea!*"

What a <u>delightful</u> exhortation for a little Aussie tea-apprentice – cheers to the 'Tao of Tea'!

•••••

Let us now look at the architecture of Mountain vis-à-vis its standing presence in Gaia's living room. Big. Pyramidal (even if most pass on taking up Matterhorn's particularity of dress). A-'framed'. Robust. Each fractal'd chip off the old block too. But <u>Wind</u> can enter. <u>Water</u> can flow in/through/out. <u>Fire</u> (lightning) can strike, and its audible companion-'breath' (thunder) rumble. Mountain's <u>Earth</u> takes all that Dragon dishes out (or in) with equanimous poise. Porous, its skin. Like ours. The density of matter'd selves may be different, but not the Light of consciousness which fills our well, nor the potential to radiate same, engage in loving co-being with the all of the All. Our porosity enables us to know boundaries yet at the same time embrace interconnection. Just as I feel myself melt/merge with Gaia's surrounding Commons, so does Mountain. Meditating in my cave of heart twins <u>my</u> practice with Mountain's <u>beingness</u> in an inner sanctum'd kiln room, a "ten-foot-square hut within" made manifest by the card in Amici Stone Circle (see "Appendix 2"). A temenos, to all intents, it blends "energy and substance", as Mariel attests. Once entered of the Howe's "mountain above as mountain below", the kiln room is where our Amici collective meets, where we welcome partners and companions of the way to shared table.

While the hum of universal resonance, connecting us to the very Ground of Being, underpins all – within Mountain's cave or out in the phenomenal world of Dragon's flow – it has no desire to shut out Life as lived in Gaia's Commons, nor do I. Mindful awareness, heightened, begets an <u>expansionary</u> sense of interbeing with all whom I come into 'touch'. Bird calls, traffic noise, spilt milk, silent snow; none are privileged (or labelled as distracting annoyances to praxis). All is at it is on Tao's (trigram'd) way. Mountain has this state of porous 'horizontal' mind down pat. For me it takes work – to be aware, sensitive to needs (inner/outer), yet remain focused on intent (ditto), whether in caves (of heart), out-in-world or anywhere in between. Boundaries ebb, flow, and I try to 'dance' the tidal rhythms intuited. Gregory Bateson calls this "transforms of difference" which I feel as a translational interplay between 'being' Mountain and 'flowing' Dragon or as Mariel describes: "Grounded fluidity."

In "Exploring Song", I will discuss this further, but for now – following the architectural spatial line – the dance tends to manifest as a spontaneous desire to hug (for want of better word) aspects of my immediate and, at times, not so immediate environment. In sustainability-speak (an old stamping ground), one could describe this as an extreme form of stakeholder outreach. No longer an observer, distant or separate from the 'object' of my contemplation, I actively participate in Thomas Berry's "communion of subjects" as simply another horizontal expression of All That Is, one where the 'I' of 'me' becomes a redundant (and constricting) construct. Instead I stay open to learning – to understanding and negotiating said "transforms of difference" from a self-sovereign 'zone' of Soul-informed reference.

In this respect, Sun is my brother as surely as Worm my sister, or fledgling Oak on the back verandah my child; all of us sharing a single familial Self greater than the sum of our parts – that of precious interbeing'd Life in and with our wonderful Gaia. Bateson's "ecology of mind" morphs from abstraction to experiential reality; no 'thought' enters equation with a felt-sense akin to suddenly shedding a spatial 'shell', self-Light bursting beyond the arbitrary boundaries set by skin to touch and be touched, hug and be hugged, kiss and be kissed by the Beauty of world, Love the source code/x to begin this snowballing wave of joyous expression. An ancient primal urge, discovered 'anew', I <u>live</u> the SkyChild's wonder to see the world for the very first time (each time!). And with a Crone's emerging perspective cleaved thereto, it manifests as Song (to be explored further in our third section of volume).

In living the Dance of Mountain/Dragon "being/flowing the world with blessing" (as described in our work), I know that every 'event' I am presented with (in inner cave or outer world) has meaning (Emerson's Soul refers) and if I have not intuited its meaning, I have not looked deep enough into the message, or let it ripen long enough in Psyche. My subtle colleagues connect in a variety of ways – non-physically or by prompting physical 'interventions'. I know energies shape-shift and I need to be ready to engage them in attuned form. The Amici (and, by extension, other dear subtle kin) know which 'buttons' to press so I take notice – that there is a message, for example, in the Patrouille Suisse acrobatic team doing a fly-over at a particular moment during our 'work'; or that when a beetley bug comes to visit, to not shoo its (local version of) 'sacred scarab' away. Nothing can be 'perceived' as annoyance or distraction. I listen and try my best to tease out the meaning from each encounter.

Horizontal mind. Lateral connectivity. Rupert Sheldrake's principle of morphic resonance by another name, or Carl Jung's a-causal synchronicity which begets psychoid unity by another. As simple as taking Gondwana's counsel as gospel: Listening, with the _ear_ of the heart; seeing, with the _eyes_ thereof etc/etc/etc till each sense enjoins the dance to infill the Annie-Commons (sense'd) with mindful awareness. One day, I hope, my architecture – as presence and temporal-spatial inter-cognition – will be as big and pyramidal and A-framed and robust as Mountain. But in the meantime, I will give myself up to continuing apprenticeship, this time at the feet of another sage, a particularly cool old dude, Han Shan, whose life of interbeing with a cool old 'berg' provides inspiration and celebration in one …

Reading Gary Snyder brought me to Han Shan whose name literally means 'Cold Mountain'. A 9th century recluse, his Taoist/Chan poems were written on rocks and, according to the preface to a collection at the time, transcribed by a local Tang Dynasty official. Whether this (and/or he) is myth is not the point. The poetry speaks the wisdom of a life lived in the embrace of Mountain's inwith/outwith architecture or, as Goethe holds, "crystallised music".

In each poem an osmotic existence is described in full expressive flow, which leads Snyder to rhetorically wonder: Is it he or his dwelling which is the subject here?

Men ask the way to Cold Mountain
Cold Mountain: there's no through trail.
In summer, ice doesn't melt
The rising sun blurs in swirling fog.
How did I make it?
My heart's not the same as yours.
If your _heart_ was like mine
You'd get it and be right here.

One-and-the-same, of course. His ears, eyes (and so on) of heart are fully-attuned. Yet Han Shan's (or Mountain's) teasing prod for readers, too, to cleanse Blake's "doors of perception" is apt – a beyond beyond the furthest horizon is waiting <u>inwith</u>. Together with Dogen's wise men and sages, Han Shan invites us to foment an energetic current of Love (at heart) coupling spirit and geology, twinning our own Body-Mind with Mountain, and thereby manifesting a <u>harmonium</u> of crystalline musical interbeing.

Radical philosophy? Hardly, from his perspect (or Goethe's, probably – he loved to hang out in the Alps). "If your heart was like mine, you'd get it," he writes. Taut-strung like a Pythagorean monochord, their shared resonant hum of Life, <u>living</u> the singularity of Being's breath, flows in and through an architectural <u>frame</u> which has no name:

> Cold Mountain is a house
> Without beams or walls.
> The six doors left and right are open
> The hall a blue sky.
> The rooms all vacant and vague
> The east wall bears on the west wall
> At the centre <u>nothing</u>.

Emptiness pure, openness to the divine assured, Sengai's 'Enso' rendered as quadrilateral (Earth) rather than cirque (Heaven). Han Shan's embodied knowing may be an architectural "frame of no name", but one which sings/sings/sings in its cosmic choir'd 'absence'. For his part, Peter Matthiessen finds that:

"The emptiness and silence of snow mountains quickly bring about those states of consciousness that occur in the mind-emptying of meditation ... the earth twitches and the mountains shimmer, as if all molecules had been set free: the blue sky rings. Perhaps what I hear is the 'music of the spheres', what Hindus call the breathing of the Creator and astrophysicists the 'sighing' of the sun".

These lines are taken from his Zen journal, "Nine-Headed Dragon River". There's that Dragon again. Mountain can't go anywhere without him! Returning to Matthiessen:

"Soon all sounds, and all one sees and feels, take on imminence, an immanence, as if the universe were coming to attention, a universe of which one is the centre, a universe that is not the same and yet not different from oneself, even from a scientific point of view: within man as within mountains there are many parts of hydrogen and oxygen, of calcium, phosphorous, potassium, and other elements ... (and) an instinct comes to open outward by letting all life in, just as a flower fills with sun."

Matthiessen quotes Dogen's description of his own experience of 'universal resonance':

"When I am enlightened, at that moment the mountains and rivers are enlightened, and vice versa ... as I practice, everything is practicing. To realise this invests each moment

of our life with great significance. This moment is not just for us, just right now, but for all space and time. When we really perceive that, we can feel the trees and rocks doing their enlightened practice."

Trees and rocks at enlightened practice? Definitely! This is my experience of the everyday. I look out my 'window on world' here in our 'forgotten valley' direct onto the face of an Annie-sized 'Cold Mountain'. I feel our shared existence-in-space despite and perhaps even because of the deep chasm vale'd 'void' in-between. A relational dance which backbones the next section of this text, ours is a perpetual psychoid unity-in-the-making as complete and seamless as Han Shan discovered in his high wild home:

Spring water in the green creek is clear
Moonlight on Cold Mountain is white
Silent knowledge – the spirit is enlightened of itself
Contemplate the void: this world exceeds stillne

Dogen gave a complementary dharma talk the same year he delivered his "Mountains and Rivers Sutra". Appropriately enough, he titled it "Valley Sounds, Mountain Colours":

"In Song China there was a man who called himself Layman Dongpo … A literary genius, he studied the way of dragons and elephants in the ocean of awakening. He descended deep chasms and soared freely through clouds. One night when Dongpo visited Mount Lu he was enlightened upon hearing the sound of the valley stream. He composed the following verse for his master:

Valley sounds are the long broad tongue.
Mountain colours are no other than the unconditioned body.
Eighty-four thousand verses are heard throughout the night.
What can I say about this at a future time?"

In giving this talk, Dogen told his monks:

"You may regret that mountains and waters <u>conceal</u> sounds and colours, but you may rejoice as well that the moment of enlightenment emerges <u>through</u> mountains and waters."

In asking his students to open their minds to the possibility, he asked:

"Who can fathom this water? Is it a bucketful or does it fill whole oceans? In the end was it Dongpo who was awakened or the mountains and waters that were awakened? … Once a monk asked: How do you turn mountains, rivers, and the great earth into the self? The master said: How do you turn the self into mountains, rivers, and the great earth?"

Indeed.

"It was the silence she loved most. The sounds of the silence not man-made. The sounds instead of bird calls and the wind rustling leaves in trees, the sound so quiet that it drummed and buzzed in her ears and behind it, another sound, a low hum, the hum she heard above and behind the noise her feet made tramping through the forest, or the noise her hands made pushing away branches which marred her passage through. Another

sound, this hum, deep and resonant within her, audible only if she made no interruption herself with words, with laughter, with song. The hum still there, the hum that came best and fastest and loudest when her mouth was closed. The hum a sound from deep inside. Ah, she thought, now I understand. This is the sound of silence. This is the sound of my soul breathing."

I scribbled the above text many years ago, sitting on the verandah of a simple 'ten-foot-square hut' in the middle of a cicada-chirred forest, half a world and lifetime away from the 'snow mountains' of my now. My thought at the time, that the low sound I perceived – a deep and resonant hum <u>beyond</u>, yet <u>within</u> self, a seeming 'foundation-breath' <u>beneath</u> all other sound – was actually Soul presence, I can only describe as unconscious heart-knowing. That this breath twinned with World Soul's and each expression of sentience in creation likewise was unconscious yet <u>known</u>. As with Matthiessen, stone provided the pervasive connector thread; <u>its</u> matter'd consciousness, within and <u>of</u> the most basic and humble building block in Gaia's architectural arsenal, outreached to dance with my own, bring me 'home' to the self of Dogen's "mountains rivers and the great earth".

Earth, literally, was my way in to the felt-experience of universal resonance in skin, and for which Kali delighted in completing my induction. William Blake's take?

"Great things are done when men and mountains meet."

Agreed! And I hope the reader is ready for what our "I Ching"d journey of 'joining mountains' reveals. For the moment let me just say that if one considers that Life itself is bricolage in skin, that we ourselves are a palimpsest with the capacity to cinder the veils of our own <u>unknowing</u>, to let our self-Light shine through, out, flow into the world with the intensity and bright beingness of a crystal cluster'd heart forged in the fiery furnace at the core of Mountain, then there is nowhere our Dragon <u>cannot</u> fly …

• • • • •

Now to round out this chapter and in-herald the next.

What I have attempted to do herein is bring the human wisdom tradition of recognising the sanctity of Mountain into focus, concentrating on Eastern philosophy with which I more readily attune. Yet in working with the energies of stone sentience and indeed partnering their very essence – great beings in and of themselves whom I love dearly as co-equal family – I know that whatever has been said or written in the human sphere is limited <u>and</u> limiting regardless of how ancient the texts. The boundlessness of knowing Mountain as Mountain knows <u>itself</u>, as DeepTime-Tectonia's <u>root</u> of Earth-consciousness, as anchor to and bridge-'species' for the inflow of stellar stream, cannot be 'framed' by our small minds. We see only our partial intersect with same and even then – as with all numinous encounter – cannot express it as adequately as we would like so others may 'see'.

Of course, it is not only in respect of Mountain but all universal wisdom with which we, as a species, come into touch. Engaging with the Sidhe broadens our perspective or, rather, re-awakens us to <u>shared</u> primal memory if we are open to their way of framing the respective mythologies. Life-long I have found myself trying to plumb to the source code/x of Being beneath <u>all</u> language – the pure space of Benjamin's 'intentio'. Ever do I fail (like the unnamed narrator of Beckett's "Worstward Ho") but my hope is that over time I fail better with each switch-back of path up/down this particular (hollow hill'd) Howe – inner or outer skin traversed. For example, before hearing the 'call' to serve Gaia in the deep recesses of Earth memory, Tectonia'd spaces far removed from human dimensions, I had researched, extensively, world faith traditions for a major piece of prose fiction, "The Taste of Translation", to work through the premise that the 'root-stock' of all creation is Love. Of course, I am not the first nor the last to have investigated nor come to such a place of (self-) understanding. But I wanted to share that information as a preliminary comment to what follows – the opinion of Mountain itself ...

I have communed, in this forgotten valley on the border of Time, with my glacially-smoothed, lily-white quartz-spined Cold-Mountain brother/lover/friend across the way for decades. He knows, <u>intimately</u>, my (amicable) battle with the architect charged to renovate our cottage, such that a 'portal' could be opened direct between me and Mountain, me and Sky, to enable our interbeing 24/7 via an arched non-Juliet-balcony'd 'window on world'. We speak, heart to heart; one word, shared: "Love." It was, and remains, as simple as that.

Deep in the thought-space of our Amici'd Urwerk some years ago, one weekend we happened to host, for a too brief time of togetherness, dear friends not seen in ages. Being Spring, my Cold Mountain (Pizzo Ruscada) was a <u>dazzling</u> snow crystal in a sea of translucent blue. It made me so happy he could wear his best dress to bring our friends' city-selves Joy in connecting to the high wild.

We had walked, talked, eaten and drunk ourselves cheerfully silly, including a sunny midday wander to the next village where an organic vintner introduced them to a tasty valley drop over a platter of cheese, whose rinds could casually be offered (over the edge of stone table) to Moose, a more than ample hound in residence. Before leaving, the vintner showed us a next lot of vines ready for planting out. His description, as well as the sight of these <u>grafted</u> younglings, stirred a strange sense in my heart but I could not put a finger on it at that precise moment. I felt an energetic tug from Ruscada and looked across at his broad inscrutable face. Physically, as well as subtly, overlighting the whole of valley reach, I knew he had an opinion on this.

Later that afternoon, before our friends' long drive South, we sat in the garden (or 'Green Room' as it is dubbed) over a cup of tea – chatting, admiring the view a last time, reliving aspects of the vintner visit. Suddenly Ruscada entered the conversation – taking <u>precise</u> aim at the grafts we had witnessed. The context for his speech (as it swirled to life in my mind) was my sharing, on previous evening by the fire, pictures of a family trip to Japan. Our friends had found the vermillion-painted Shinto 'Torii Gates' beautiful. Portals between dimensions, gateways to temple'd precincts (on either side of veil), I described how Buddhism had co-opted the Shinto architectural form for their own temple entrances, like vines 'grafted' onto older 'root-stock'. At this Ruscada took over in a rush of (mineral) verbiage.

I pointed to him across the way, and explained (his/our) thesis that world religions may have assigned holiness to <u>certain</u> mountains but that <u>all</u> mountains deserve reverence. I told how my 'window on world' similarly enacted a Torii-like relation, as an arched portal to sacred communal space with one who may go unnamed, unremarked in this or that 'official' canon, but is no less <u>integral</u> to a world ensoul'd equation in the 'eyes' of Earth-consciousness.

His/our thesis, therefore, was that any/all are sacred, and can be 'sung' awake to their inherent birthright by our participant-witnessing, reciprocal recognition and (down and dirty Kali'd) Love. In saying as much, I told how, after <u>years</u> of conversing across this split gorge'd valley, we made pilgrimage to his summit with a token gift of community to lay at his altar'd (stone cairn) topknot, to look back and wave (together) to the window'd hologram of 'me' across on this side of valley and thus 'formalise' our connection. And that afterwards – to bind this brother to another on the other side of my hemispheric stretch of HomeSong'd world – we had taken a small fractal'd token of Ruscada's spine down under for a walk up my 'Cloud-Catcher', Wollumbin, in similarly anonymous ritual offering.

No external (historico-cultural-canonical) authority mediated the act nor sanctioned either peak a 'worthy' pilgrimage destination during incarnate life. I said I was sure this was not how it was intended at human'd start either; when Moses toddled up a hill or Muhammad retreated to his cave, or Milarepa flew on a sunbeam to the top of Kailash, they were each just doing their mythologic bit for universal law with a <u>local</u> in-skin 'friend', <u>embracing</u> direct mystic knowing in the spirit of Dogen's sutra'd sages, as were we. But over time, with the embedding of each numinous experience and learning in sacred text, a hierarchy had established itself where, in the canon of true nature, there really only ever-exists a diagram of equals:

True. Nature. Nothing. Special.
(So Suzuki would say.)
And this makes her smile.

The above lines are from the poem: "Muted Earth" (see "Grail Within");

they speak to Gaia's desire for us "to return to the true and the real at the core of FeltWorld home." And, in Ruscada's (grubby) allegorical hands – that day, post-vintner-visit – humankind's shift away from core was put into stark relief by the lived experience of grafted vines. The further they grew (vertically) away from the 'root-stock' implanted in earth, while (horizontally) being 'trained' along lines of wire'd 'flight' (where fruits-of-the-vine could form 'discrete' partial-perceptive receptacle bunches of the whole), the less in touch they were with source code/x, with their original primal root-knowing stretching through vast reaches of Earth.

Indeed, being a different varietal altogether, disassociated from the stock onto which they were grafted, hence no ancestral root-connection of their own, only 'mediated experience', I wondered aloud (on Ruscada's behalf as much as mine) if a discrete 'hand' of grapes could be analogous to the tragic tribal behaviour vis-à-vis the foreign 'other' which continues to co-opt religion for geo-political ends, tragically observable and documented loud/long on the Angel of History's (horrified) watch.

I said if we consider what the root of all faiths' direct connection to the divine has taught – no more no less than Love, pure – it is the same for/in/of Earth consciousness. Yet while each particular vine was grafted onto stock which, of itself, connected in, to the sanctity of the (mineral and subtle) bones of (Earth's) Love, the actual grape variety was too 'delicate' itself to take root in the soil. But (Ruscada/I said): We are not 'varietals'. Humans are of the original stock. When we commit to connect, to reawaken and enliven, again, our connection to source code/x? Plunge our hands into the soil and celebrate the sheer fact of our true nature – Love-in-form where none is 'foreign'? The roots of the Sacred are in Earth herself, here-now, I said (Ruscada cheering me on), and drew upon Mariel's wisdom of the in-Earth lines of living energy and consciousness of which leylines are their outer physical representation.

Mountain's DeepTime-Tectonia'd root-knowing carries all this in its mineral bones and breath (generously shared!), plumbing to Gaia's very core, coursing information along and through a vast latticework of Dragon-excitable 'currents'. But when the diagram-of-equals is forgotten? And the sanctity of Land as a whole, of Mountain (plural – any/all) as connector thread through to Source and beyond, lies unremembered while a few 'robust' (trusted, holy) vines become the (sacred) root-stock for a vast range of fragile varietals who only know Life 'above' ground? No direct connection in, hence mediated and closeted off in a membrane of self-other wariness? That only 'this' mountain is holy and only according to 'my' religion, hence?

Ruscada's manifesto was a plea from the heart, on behalf of all who share common Gaian ground – Mountain'd and more. Observing this or that variety (of faith tradition) grafted onto the root-stock of ages (and sages hanging out with their 'local' buddies), he lamented (as did I) humanity's sharing of only the slimmest of primal connection, already so far removed, and self-removed at that, from ancestral genetic memory.

And to compound the separation (continuing with the metaphoric learnings of a grapevine- 'enlightened' afternoon), 'tis wax which binds the fragile varietal tip to root-stock, to protect it from outer world. Requiring a constancy of temperature to 'take', it hardens the youngling to no-return, 'veils' its sight of the whole as it grows up and out exuberantly, in fruitful transcendence, without ever looking back and down to the immanent ground of origin'd birth. Like the hardening of ego in a child as it grows, like the forgetfulness of whence primal come. Resilience ensures survival in one respect, yes, but closes borders to an 'all-Earth-commons' as a result.

What 'melts' wax? Fire. The Dragon fire of Love at Mountain heart, the liquid Light we share out from Source, all the way to (homecome) Sea. How to suck all these grafted 'tribes' back down to Source (like sap in reverse) where they may meet and merge with the sacred code/x which brought the all of the All into being in the first place, to understand all is divine? So their sense of community can expand exponentially? So all may see there is no 'foreigner', only multiplicities of unique and wondrous expressions of the 'All-That-Is' in Gaian ground?

As Ruscada (via Annie) wound up this little speech (to blank stares around the table – it was a pretty full-on download from my perspective too!), one of our friends lifted her phone to take a pic of the view, as a memory-marker in time. There's a better spot, I said. Come upstairs to our attic room, to the Torii gate herself. Here is where Mountain is framed by and frames a most relevant 'view' – onto a whole world of luminous 'rising suns' present to the Presence of divine (self-) Presence …

TO THE POWER OF FIVE

I am nothing if not an optimist. Where others may see an ominous cloud, I as natural matter-of-course remark Hope seaming a silver lining at its wing or note a patch of blue fast-following in its wake. Over a lifetime of having my 'naivety' scoffed at, and my 'gullibility' at the inherent goodness of the world derided, I am quite used to it by now. Instead I am thankful that, no matter what 'events' Wind whips up to rock (my) Mountain, at times shaking it to its very foundation, nothing can part me from this (inner) SkyChild innocence and wonder, of what is possible if we simply trust to Love and live, daily, a practice of celebrating and honouring the sheer blessing of our incarnation on Gaian ground so we may serve Love's purpose here.

And, no doubt, each and every 'event' (Soul-thought to actualisation) has been intended to make (my) Mountain more robust (A-framed to boot) despite (indeed, because of?) all trauma lived. At end, however, the wise words from the Gospel of John: "Perfect Love casts out fear", as well as Christ's counsel to Julian of Norwich: "All is well and <u>shall</u> be well", serves to underpin a life-long connection to the <u>constancy</u> of Paul's Letter to the Corinthians (1:13) as it continues to unfold in my miniscule experience, bolstering my 'rock' of self to weather any/all passing storm/s:

"Love bears all things, believes all things, hopes all things, endures all things. Love <u>never</u> fails."

In the silent calming inner space of Peace, which (true-naturedly) arises from such a fundamental trust in Love – no matter what happens – Mr1300BC (a longer-than subtle companion to whom I 'apprenticed' myself for many years) arrived one day in meditation with some reminders of his own. Central to his wisdom was the need to always keep the door of my heart fully open so I always had access to Love's Light. There was strength in 'owning' my vulnerability; what had previously been tagged 'naïve' or 'gullible' by others was, in point of fact, Courage – to not be swayed from the path (Self-) assigned, come-what-may, to not 'shut down' my connection to the Sacred in the face thereof. He spoke kindly, but firmly; said:

"Noli timere. Don't be afraid. Don't <u>ever</u> be afraid."

• • • • •

This chapter will lead us through a preparatory discussion on engaging elemental energies before arriving at its application in our Amici Urwerk in the next section. Again, my learning and understanding arose via the mechanism of Eastern philosophy, beginning with the perennial Taoist symbol of the yin and yang fishes, <u>nested</u> together to unite the opposites – of heaven and earth, spirit and matter, male and female, and so on.

This symbol was one of the earliest in my runic 'library'; indeed my website is named as such. The nesting of the fishes represents my belief that Love is the foundation for Peace. By hosting a 'spot' of the other's colour within each 'fish', their respective energies may connect and commune, speak to each other, and transform duality into solitary fusion. In the same way we interconnect with all creation, whether we are aware of it or not, via the 'spark' of Love – the creative energy animating all Life – at the core of self. As unique manifestations sprung from the same primal Ground – Love's energy alchemised and transformed into whatever 'shape' the particularities of our function demand – this spark (or spot) (of self-Light) stays as our enduring signature-code in the overall cosmic fabric.

When we recognise, respect and consciously work toward understanding Love's 'spot' in its myriad of rainbow-lit colours expressed by other manifestations of Life in the universal Commons, regardless of how different we may appear in outer form, Love has the capacity to propel us toward real and lasting Peace – in relation to ourselves, each other, and universal purpose. We incarnate into an astonishing and intricate web of interrelation whose holism is succinctly captured in this Taoist symbol, and whose potential for harmonious co-existence (if the precepts are <u>honoured</u>) I find best expressed by the master, Lao Tzu:

All beings support yin and embrace yang
And the interplay of these two forces

Fills the universe.
Yet only at the still-point,
Between the breathing in and breathing out,
Can one capture these two in perfect harmony.

By transposing the word 'dance' for Lao Tzu's 'interplay', the following poetic lines of TS Eliot's "Burnt Norton" speaks the 'language' of our Amici praxis – the firmness of Mountain (yang) engaging the flexibility of Dragon (yin) to conjure the all of the All into being:

At the still point of the turning world. Neither flesh nor fleshless;
Neither from nor towards; at the still point, there the dance is,
But neither arrest nor movement. And do not call it fixity,
Where past and future are gathered. Neither movement from nor towards,
Neither ascent nor decline. Except for the point, the still point,
There would be no dance, and there is only the dance.

Such that the equation, to my (simple) mind, follows the logic (self-formulated):
To <u>be</u> Peace, <u>think</u> Peace, <u>live</u> Peace, we simply need to <u>be</u> Love, <u>think</u> Love, <u>live</u> Love.

When we open our hearts to what we share, not what separates self from other, Peace is as easy as Breathing. And Breath (as we know) fuels Song. In this respect, the logic follows that our (micro) Amici (lily-white, pure-of-intent) acts (of Love, in Song) contribute to the peace-sunk wells of Gaia's evolving (macro) consciousness; our acts containing the whole within the modesty of minute 'firefly' (singing) sparks of Love …

• • • • •

While at its most basic we have the two forces of yin and yang united in harmony or, in other words, amply enacting the underlying cohesion and order of chaos-in-action, Kali's creation and/or destruction as lived (breathed) phenomenon, my understanding of the <u>alchemical</u> proposition that Love, as source code/x, 'ignites' the cauldron, for creation to 'become' in the first place (most amazing snowball <u>ever</u>!), was delivered as a Malakut Tibetan-style teaching long years past. Presented as a vertical continuum, it centred on the five elementals – from a base of Earth through Water, Fire and Air (Wind) up to Aether (Space), the last being the link to cosmic consciousness (Universal Mind or Ground of Being).

Think of a chorten, here, with its five levels representing the Buddha, or a Japanese gorinto (stupa) whose geometric building blocks house such elemental symbology, and for which a sweet yukimi (stupa'd stone lantern) is simply perfect for an Amici-partner'd garden grail, viz:

Earth (cube) – Water (sphere) – Fire (pyramid) – Air (crescent) – Aether (lotus or organic spire)

The point of the teaching I received, however, was that the 'order' I had in mind was back-to-front. For my work practice, I should not be thinking from an

Earth-conscious (or ying) perspective but from a Heaven-commensurate (yang) one in order to support the 'drawing' of the energies in and down – i.e. I should focus on how Malakut <u>matter</u> 'becomes' then shifts through to the physical plane. With images concentrated on how dust forms and coagulates, it spoke to a notion I had once entertained about 'enlightened' specks of dust (aka the spark of Love at the core of each Life).

As I had gifted this notion to my Bosnian War refugee, Kisha, in "The Taste of Translation", so that she could host a conversation with her Mountain 'partner' on the prospect, it may be worthwhile for the reader to have this context before I proceed with the teaching I received:

She made a last round of the garden, watered the small punnets of hope instructed to guard against rhizome incursions, cleaned the house and climbed the stairs to the attic to farewell her view. Afternoon sun bathed the bed and spotlit a column of dust in suspended nonchalance. Dust. After all her cleaning, dust!

Plain to the eye in the shaft of light but no doubt, at sun-shift, new dust would be revealed, and she sat on the bed, wrapped in sunlight and dust, tiny specks bobbing about her with the random delight of a bottle floating at sea, adrift, with no thought of destination. Yet arriving somewhere, eventually, to tell stories of the journey, of life itself as a speck of dust.

She sat and wondered: What's the difference between me and a speck of dust?

Is that a trick question? asked Samir.

She ignored him, thought: Does dust have memory of where it's been or plans of future bright? Does dust know anger, frustration, fear, pain? Disappointment? Love? Does dust know Love? Her brow furrowed at that one.

I'm serious, said Samir. Are you doing this on purpose?

Perhaps we should drift, she wondered. No plans, no future, no memory, no past. Just a string of todays where everything is revealed in its true light and true measure, the siege simply a breeze which skittered us about, our whims unheeded as much as these innocent specks.

Ah, said Samir. But here's a thought – is it better to be aware of this or not? Is it better to be an enlightened speck of dust or are we just as blissful (or not) by the turns of fate as an ignorant speck? None of us knows our destiny, where our message-in-a-bottle bobbing on a vast and trackless sea will beach us, what hazards we'll face in the stream, which rocks will bruise and scrape or slice us to shreds as we're carried past. It all just happens. So what sort of speck would you rather be?

He spread his arms wide atop Pizzo Ruscada and parted the clouds of unknowing which clung to the peak, wind-shifting them with an invisible breath. Now she could see him full in the kiss of the sun.

I'll take enlightened, she grinned.

He laughed, whooped his joy. This is how it ends, Ki-. And how it begins. At the end of a journey of no end from a big bang before beginningless time. Never without the hope that a spark will pierce us, illuminate us, enlighten us, we humble specks of dust.

Love! he cried aloud. Love! That's the spark!

And she couldn't help but agree as he conjured an image of billions upon billions of radiant dust stars, a universe of twinkling dust fireflies, all filled with the light of Love.

With that as preface, the teaching asked that I flip the elemental continuum on its head in order to engage the simple salient fact that all 'arises' from Aether. I myself was in the 'Unmanifest' – from this space I had the possibility to 'manifest' whatever it was that required manifestation if I followed the correct alchemical 'line'. The (dusty) roots associated with the lesson made abundantly clear to me how the process worked as a continuous 'swirl' of energy gradually densifying and coagulating through this (inverse) elemental chain.

The densest dust being Earth-<u>conscious</u> 'matter' (as a final in-world <u>subtle</u> outcome), it was thus a fusion of all (its) prior stages in continuum as well as an exact <u>corollary</u> of Aether as a <u>pre-existent</u> fusion of all (its) following stages. In other words, how it was taught, so I could apply it in our work, was that the five elements exist as a consequent 'whole' or 'mass' of consciousness in the Unmanifest, where Love's alchemic 'ignite' was required to release their 'stream' of <u>becoming</u> consciousness according to respective degrees of (snowballing) manifestation.

To bring symbology to the science, one could speak of the process as Dragon's 'flow' – from an <u>aetheric</u> (Mountain) beginning in Love's primal ground, Dragon acts to manifest, at the Earth-matter'd 'end', a like (Mountain) <u>becoming</u>. The marriage of spirit and geology as yin-yang'd nestedfishes thus already exists in the Unmanifest, <u>inwith</u> the Ocean of Being which is, at the same time, Source. Whether in-world <u>or</u> beyond, for the specificity of <u>our</u> Amici work, I saw Dragon's task as continuously flowing the 'swirl' of consciousness back and forth as (Water Fire Air) Breath while Mountain maintained its solid functional presence (in whichever form – Earth'd or Aether'd). Now, if one overlays this geometry onto Sengai's Taoist rune from the previous chapter? We have Mountain as Earth (square), Mountain as Heaven (circle) with Mountain as Dragon (triangle) connecting the (wayward?) middle-schoolers in between.

I know it seems complicated and, at surface, a confusingly contradictory melange of concepts when first apprehended. But I hope that the following sections of our text provide enough evidence to demonstrate that, for our Amici troupe's UrWerk purposes, this really was a fundamental lesson, even if delivered (seemingly) ages ahead of our actual application of the principle! Later, skipping forward some years, and post-dating the work documented in "Awakening", I found myself increasingly engaging something I called the 'Blue' via gaps in 'Time's script'. At the time I had no requisite language to describe the felt-sense of an intense working (colour-coded) elemental mergence, finding I could only express the various dimensions of the 'Blue' I encountered in poetic tongue – such that I penned one!

"Song of the Blue" (2016) is annexed to "Grail Within" (2020) (and available in the nestedfishes.org poetry corner). But looking back at its composition now, I see it represented a first seriously-conscious expression of my understanding of the cosmology of our praxis, given it had arisen from a space of interbeing akin, in the above teaching, to the first Malakut fragments of aetheric 'dust' swirled to creative 'becoming'. Yet at the time it seemed like a stand-alone text written to capture insights from an experiential zone of perennial inquiry until, in the wake of ritually agreeing to undertake this UrWerk at 2017's Spring Equinox in company of the Amici, I was formally inducted into a specific Sidhe methodology for working the 'Blue'. "Whole Earth Partnership", a chapter in the third section of volume, puts the outcomes of this process into context. But relevant to our discussion herein is the specificity of Blue's role in the elemental equation as revealed by my induction.

It focused, once again, on an energetic continuum but this time presented horizontally rather than vertically. A process I seemed to already be comfortable using, my (self-) consciousness affirmed I could actively 'teach it on' with the Amici crew in (subtle) workshop settings. Again, a densification process featured whereby the key concept, and its alchemic formulation, was:

"*Everything arises from Aether.*"

In this space of lateral engagement, however, our partnering task would concentrate only on the first stage of continuum, the process of drawing out the elementals from their 'mass' of consciousness in the Unmanifest and working Aether's energy of 'becoming' to kick-start (as it were) the rest 'waking up' to task. Surprisingly (or not) this stage was completely Blue.

The Blue was its beginning and the Blue was its outcome, the manifestation (by close) of the full (first) stage. Our 'line' (or length of 'Elven-rope', so-called) to draw the Blue 'mass' out, to kick-start an elemental 'power of five', was lain flat (on a diagram-of-equals) and likewise blue (in hue). During the induction I was reminded that the previous day in meditation I had seen myself with blue legs (strange but true). As if, by walking the Blue out across Land, I became the Blue, actively inhabiting the (blue) alchemical 'line' (or 'stretch of Song') to draw out the elementals in this first (blue) stage.

Once I acknowledged and reflected on what had already been shared, it was time to go back in for a next download. When I observed the following, I realised the intimate connection of the Blue to the Tibetan-style teaching from years before.

I watched a bird 'crunch' a seed; a small bird, nevertheless it had an extraordinarily strong beak. The seed looked like a golden ball in its mouth;

proportionately it would be as if we had a gobstopper in our 'beak'. A very powerful visual image of <u>potentiality</u>, once crunched, the seed released golden wisps, like flowing dense threads, which completely dissolved the seed into space. That is, the seed was fully transmuted (post-crunch) into the golden threads – no residue or debris of its 'seed-self' remained. This had returned whence come – back into the Blue.

I understood the crunch of seed released the first <u>material</u> densification of consciousness into the world, that which had been formed by our elemental work (in the Blue). I saw that this put the solid dense warm glowing 'alive' ball of 'Earth-consciousness' (that I needed to roll back into the stellar carpet, my discussion with MakerMan refers) into the <u>fullness</u> of its in-Time potential. With the Amici, we were operating at the stage of stellar 'reciprocity' to enable continued evolution here in physic'd space. Our task, along the lateral continuum I had earlier seen a-flow, further increasing its conscious matter'd <u>density</u> as it engaged (material) world, was to nevertheless concentrate on the Blue, at the Unmanifest 'end'.

In relation to the stage demonstrated by the bird's seed crunch, the Blue thus operated as the <u>pre-conceptual phase</u> of material manifestation which I enacted in meditation to affirm accord – curling into a ball to 'release' the golden threads of consciousness, and fulfil our 'human' role in equation – across the threshold which Mariel confirmed to David that Sidhe cannot cross. Here was union, a 'divine' marriage clearly aligning Malakut and material, Sidhe and we; the Blue its commencement, the Golden where the shift 'happens' – threshold to physical world.

Putting pieces of our UrWerk puzzle together later, I realised that several months <u>before</u> this Sidhe induction, I was directly contacted by Dragon whom I already 'knew', of course, but in the context of UrWerk, arrived with a specific task for me. As an over-Presence to all Flow in and through world, his message was contained in an empty cirque. The Enso of Sengai (or any other master), this appeared in vision as a thick swish of black executed as a single fluid brush stroke. A 'whole of story' did Dragon tell me from within this Enso; I kept going over it again and again, in image and text, writing while kneeling, bowed, in a temple quadrangle rimmed by long scrolls, banners, fluttering pennants. A direct mystic encounter of the <u>fact</u> of the Void, Dragon's message was painted in Breath and framed by the cirque. Here, in this space, was the place of our (Blue) praxis, my task not only the work itself but to be its scribe.

In personalised form (at the time) I had only one Dragon friend (but really, does anyone ever need more than one?): Seiryu, Jade Guardian of the Eastern Torii, 'born' of the Land of Rising Sun, intimately acquainted with MakerMan, my choreographing Amici 'heart stone'. But in (personalised) Mountain form, the reader will find quite a cast of characters assembling as we proceed; a cast in which Ruscada's root-knowing is seamlessly intertwined – attuned, intimately, to a whole world of luminous 'rising suns' just waiting to be up-sung and brought into being from the Blue ...

•••••

At this juncture I would like to shift the narrative to Aboriginal cosmology and its intersect with the elemental teachings shared above. A key actor here is Winpa, the Lightning (or Thunder) Boss, who conjures storms to sing up the waterholes of Western Desert Dreaming (yes, a Sky 'Dragon' by another name, as is the Rainbow Serpent who sang Land into being).

Firstly, however, to revisit "Awakening" where I described my deep abiding 'white-fella-black-heart' connection to birth-country, a "Great Southern Land", as Icehouse's song lyrics attest:

Standing at the limit of an endless ocean.
Hidden in the summer for a million years.
You walk alone with the ghost of Time ...

My country is ancient, skeletal, weathered, stoic in deep silence like a desert ascetic; eroded to bedrock, proudly ochre'd is her (burnt) skin. She wears a cronedom mantle on behalf of an even more ancient mother, Gondwana, who (at time of writing) remains locked in Antarctic ice. Sixty-five million years has Australis stood her ground since separating from home; in point of fact, the last to shyly leave the folds of Mother's skirt. This we share. This I know.

Aboriginal Dreaming holds the stories of Land – the stories Land passed to her first inhabitants for safe-keeping, markers of DeepTime-Tectonia memory. Seamless mergence of spirit and geology is described in the myths of legendary totemic beings singing up country, <u>and</u> all inhabitants, to existence; wherever the Ancestors walked their footprints left a trail of Song, of Life. The result is a labyrinth of invisible pathways crisscrossing my island home. Bruce Chatwin writes that by singing the world into existence the Ancestors had been poets in the original sense of the word 'poesis', meaning 'creation':

"In theory, at least, the whole of Australia could be read as a musical score. There was hardly a rock or creek in the country that could not or had not been sung. One should perhaps visualise the Songlines as a spaghetti of Iliads and Odysseys, writhing this way and that, in which every 'episode' was readable in terms of geology."

Other world traditions talk of similar markers of evidence, remainder'd reminders in stone of 'contact' with the great prophets of history, 'gods' to all intents. Physical imprints left in the skin of Land – a foot or hand marking a 'stopping place' on their pilgrim's way through world. I, for my part, have encountered same – unexpectedly, confrontingly – here in Helvetia's domain. Not written into any sacred text or passed down by oral tradition; no. But seen with 'thine eyes' in the deep recesses of our own catchment. An UrAlt (ancient) scape, older than Memory, older than Animal was my sense of this place, a steep thick-forested slope of stone silence. Nought more. A place where DeepTime-Tectonia had dramatically upjumped its 'Sink at Surface', then left untouched, uninhabited all the long millennia since.

Yes, there were wisps of energetic signatures (Animal, Faerie) having lightly passing this way, but none had put down 'roots'. The roots were its own, unadorned, and the air <u>thick</u> with primal Presence. The resonant hum of Soul-breath (micro-macro'd) infused the entire scape. This was my sense – a sense matched (paradoxically) by my direct encounter of the deep wide <u>Earth-brown</u> Aboriginal-brown presence of Gondwana in Australis' sand-paper'd-by-aeons stone-silent 'Soul at Skin'. Vertical, this Helvetian home-place, to the other's horizon, but somehow Gondwana had found me here and, to honour her perennial counsel to "Listen", I moved slowly down this unknown slope of Ruscada's flank following our climb of his heights on a different path in order to weave a fresh 'loop' to our shared Mountain-Dragon Songline.

A huge dead Larch, Winpa-bolt'd, in-herald'd the commencement of shift in the energetic mix; a 'Faerie-Ring' of (live) Larch chatting on a small knoll followed. A little further along, a bright <u>blue</u> splotch of paint on a tree trunk. Meaning? Hiking paths are marked with red/white stripes. In such spirit ("Song of the Blue" having recently been penned), I took it as MagicMan whimsy to alert me to an 'outwith Time' encounter. For, over a next ridgeline, down into a gully came an explosive shift of energy. Dense with an age ne'er-fore encountered here, in Helvetia. Shift immediate, dramatic. The vertigo of a 'threshold-experience' almost took me over the edge, into <u>its</u> Void; I needed to stop, steady myself into its loving (yes) embrace – its silence, coned, cradled my non-fall – while two boys (six legs) trotted on, happily oblivious.

Seemingly predating anything 'Animal' (physical or non-), the space suffused a symbiosis of shared or collective knowing. Acting like a sacred wellspring of the most ancient root-knowing of Mountain-Tree, stone/wood kin. It felt as if the alchemy of the elementals themselves were bubbling away in a cauldron at surface, in which I was participant-witness to the 'golden-wisps' shift. The physical link between stone/root-knowing was extraordinary – older and more <u>loving</u> their symbiotic embrace than anything witnessed at surface. Entwined. Familial. Huge boulders, tumbled down from Ruscada's craggy cliffs, deep/dark with mystery, the secrets of original world, now wrapped (and let be, let be) in their forest 'cloak'. I heard:

"Ancestors."

Far deeper than any Human, Faerie, or Animal ancestral energy which, by comparison, feels youthful (skipping, singing), here were Gaia's 'Earth-Ancestors', revealing themselves <u>on</u>, and <u>as</u> her mantle. Here DeepTime-Tectonia said: "See me. Witness our primordial work."

((Apropos 'mantle': While in geologic science, 'mantle' officially describes the layer beneath Earth's 'crust', the outer surface we most readily intersect, I use the word 'mantle' to describe a full zone of DeepTime-Tectonia'd <u>interbeing</u> in the spirit of my Amici's 'Magic of the Mantle' observation, as well as to capture the sense of affirmation I made when agreeing to actively partner Sidhe in shared worldwork for Gaia, as described in "Awakening":

I wear a mantle of starlight here in the world to
bring the energy of the Stars streaming to Earth

This spoke to Mariel's call for us to formally step into the Stone Circle with an intention – mine in this case literally 'mantled' – micro-macro'd, in service to Gaia.))

A chthonic zone, a layer so <u>recessed</u> in Earth's psyche, housing the consciousness of <u>her</u> matter, had found me here in Ruscada's kilt; I knew it housed Gondwanan root-knowing as surely as my connection down under. So too in the 'Ent-like' quality of forest clearly on view. I have felt 'tugs' from discrete ancient Tree-Keepers at other places in this valley, and know that alp-herds in centuries past consciously left particular exemplars on meadow verges as guardians of place. But this forest was complete, <u>sufficient</u> unto itself – for example, a Beech <u>actively</u> mothering half a dozen babes of another species amongst her roots, or two different species sharing trunk, stone, breath – <u>becoming</u> the other, <u>sharing</u> a single self. In another case, one species' branches reached to purposely hug the trunk of another species. No whimsical imagining on my part needed; the space communicated its intent loud-and-clear in subtle-speak. So much UrAlt Love in form! So fortunate my witness in order to mirror this Love with 'thine eyes', in a space <u>saturate</u> with Cernunnos'd presence! I will gush liberally about my connection to this ancient being at a later stage in narrative, Reader, but in the moment, the harmonic resonance this forest <u>embodied</u> was summed up in his wise observation (once shared):

"We all work within our sphere of influence."

In DeepTime-Tectonia, this applies to root-knowing that stretches as far as far can go …

The forest opened onto a clearing, its energy subtly dissolving into the next stage of path; a liminal zone, it demonstrated in physical fact Gregory Bateson's 'interface' where difference "makes a difference". Here, a Larch family had been Winpa'd out of existence, and I could see straight through to the pyramidal peak that overlights our valley headwaters. In this moment, Presence 'rose' from its apex. A dark majestic shape, of outstretched wings, infilled with elemental power, it spoke to the (vertical) connection of Earth and Heaven via Mountain, as contained in Sengai's Taoist rune. A multi-layered message, I simply honoured its force and turned to find myself staring directly at a ginormous split boulder on the opposite side of path. I 'saw' immediately the impression in rock for what it was. 'Twas the paw print of WolfMother, genius loci of our high wild (raw and free) river shed, etched huge as a wall in a split cliff'd boulder three times the size, sliced in two by the sword-wielding hand of Zeus. Literally struck by awe, I nevertheless realised it mirrored the peak's arisen Presence; here, elemental forces had rent the fabric of space-time as surely as anywhere to leave their ancient calling cards as birthmark'd scars, as tattoo'd brands in tough geologic skin, to say:

"I was here. And this is what I made. On behalf of Gaia; on behalf of the All."

Yes, before the era of Peace sunk deep in Helvetia's subtle bones, the elements did battle till they their harmonic balance, their pitch-perfect resonance, their collective <u>sentient</u> oneness found. Here in this place of Mountains Dragons without end was the echo of divine presence.

Having made pilgrimage into the high wild headwaters of WolfMother's domain some years earlier I knew her signature, even if this a first time in the particularity of this place, nowhere 'near' the locale of prior meeting. My task at that time? To bless the Source of our personal (Dragon) waters, offer a small token of hemispheric community to its pristine sacred pool spilling from the heart of stone, 'becoming' the mighty river which would find its homecome way to Sea via the Venetian Lagoon. A ritual I had already message-stick'd on behalf of Mountain 'bros' stretched across the world, now it was Dragon's (Dogen'd) turn. A story told in full in "The Amici Files" (annexed to "Awakening"), salient aspects thereof will appear in the chapter "Joining Mountains" to come. But relevant to <u>this</u> discussion is that prefacing <u>that</u> pilgrimage, the great ancestral being of place, WolfMother, had herself welcomed us to country. Now to find her calling card in stone skin here? That, from our forgotten valley on the border of Time, she was 'channelling' Gondwanan root-knowing all along into my (unconscious) orbit? Oh, my goodness!

In the wake of this 'doubling', a psychoid unity'd event seaming Malakut to material in any/all dimensions, to (additionally) find WolfMother patiently present at the Gaian Throne in Card Deck of the Sidhe? Enacting its own (Chatwin-like) Songline which affirms every ancestral 'episode' is readable in terms of geology?

The creation myths of many indigenous cultures mirror and/or share the fundaments of Aboriginal legend-making in their own tongue, but as Australia is the Land of my birth, and Gondwana her (thus my) 'Mother', it is the one I know and most readily tap (i.e. 'recognising' the geologic signature of this mother even when she shows up in Helvetia). Cosmic humanity's "creation story", as told by Mariel to David, emanates similarly from such a timeless well, where signature-recognition is attuned to Song because, simply, it arose through Song:

"The simplest metaphor is that our ancestors worked with sound and spoke or sung into being whatever they were seeking to manifest. ... (Like) a living tuning fork, able to *produce variable frequencies within itself and in collaboration with others, ... the world itself was like a giant vibrating crystal singing in the vastness of the cosmos, and our ancestors came to sing with it in a choir of unfoldment and evolution."*

Over long millennia Aboriginal culture learnt to know their Mother, read her ways, sing in concert with her Land as they walked. But what binds me, a latter-day 'whitey' to Aboriginal ancestral stories; how does their knowing intersect my cognition of elemental sentience?

With a connection forged, principally, on the notion of pilgrimage as permanent state, Aboriginal nomadic practices are ingrained with spiritual significance. Duty of care for Land, for a 'stretch of Song' which selflessly shares its bounty with human stewards, is an act of community, of participatory co-creation with elementary forces. Vested with responsibility to continue singing as part of a (micro) universal choir of 'unfoldment and evolution', whether as rain-maker, bush-tucker-maker or any-which-way-maker, ritual ceremonies of invocation and gratitude underpinned daily life for each skin-group.

To keep the singing alive down generations was to keep the consciousness of Land alive to its co-creationary role – a functionary 'symbiosis of sharing' for which Song is the relevant form. Singing means walking, tracing ancestral paths ever-over to infuse Love into physically manifest leylines while deeper-intersecting the living rivers of (Blue) consciousness streaming through Earth (yes, this I have seen), to ensure they ever-flow fresh, and like a well-tuned carburettor, continue purring like a contented SkyChild kitten of Native Cat Dreaming.

My sense, therefore, is that when we touch, physically, psychically, into one 'bit' of Land, having passed over many bits as part of a stretch of up-sung journey, we touch into all bits, sending Love vibrating through the all of All. This I call 'root-knowing', and to which a micro-Cernunnos'd 'sphere of influence' can exponentially be macro-applied. My sense is that when we feel our way into the wonder and joy of rhizome, of unending interconnections, the effect (in like measure) opens us to the experience of kinship with the all of Gaia's world, the in-Earth matter'd consciousness inherent and alive in the lattice of our "giant vibrating crystal".

This is my lesson from Aboriginal Dreaming. While each clanship group may have stewardship (responsibility or guardianship) for a particular stretch of ancestral Song, their several verses are part of an unending melody in which all Ancestors participate, in which all sentience perennially sings, like Proclus' 'heliotrope' to Sun's daily glory. And, when/if we understand that our participation in a single Earth community likewise has no definable boundary save (perhaps) the porous atmospheric thin Blue line beyond which Life-breath is extinguished, that our participation stretches across and through vast tracts of sentient space (leyline'd Land-Sea-Sky), that a 'symbiosis of sharing' inwith and of the Body of Gaia's <u>full</u> reach is our birthright <u>and</u> inheritance, participant in and co-creator of the glorious web that binds each to the other to the other without end (and all back to the One of Love), then and <u>only</u> then, will we hear Gaia's voice sing loud and strong <u>her</u> Song in universal choir – <u>her</u> birthright and inheritance, full-bound as <u>spirit</u> to her Third-Rock'd <u>geology</u> in like measure to <u>our</u> full-bound and mirrored connection to this, our shared sanctuary'd Home.

Muted is Gaia's voice, muted is the harmonic resonance of her elemental sentience, <u>in</u>-skin. I must listen close to engage her Soul-breath, her Sruti note. In some places her kitten 'purrs' but in others it is almost completely masked, rendered full-'mute' by the 'unsung'. Our task, everywhere everywhen everyhow, is to partner Earth's Song, to sing <u>her</u> Land, Home.

• • • • •

"Awakening" houses the story of my 'call' to return down under as <u>partner</u> to a specific stretch of HomeSong. While mine is an 'eastern-sea-wild' Dreaming, I had (albeit unconsciously) connected into another – beyond Great Divide, a mountain range extending along the Pacific seaboard – during several years living 'out West' as a 20-something. What I experienced, and the Song to which I attuned, extended far across continent, it seemed, but did not start to actively burble from the fecund swamp of Soul till I began stewardship of a peace-sunk pure patch of forest by the name of 'Maleny' about 10 years later (and to which the text in previous chapter: *"It was the silence she loved most ..."* refers). Hence, when specific visioning involving Aboriginal energies began in its wake, my intuition was the opportunity arose not through an alignment with cultural perspectives per se, but from deeper engagement with the sentience of Land herself. My respect for this wisdom tradition is undeniable, yet I am more than cognisant of the genetic and socio-cultural 'otherness' I bring to said awareness. It was as if I came into resonance with ancestral Dreaming from 'bottom-up' rather than 'top-down'.

By way of analogy, drilling through the differing 'levels' of Earth-consciousness, as if on subtle archaeological dig, I 'see' how humanity's contribution (or impact) touches, most keenly, the uppermost layer of 'mantle' – metaphoric 'topsoil' so easily prone to erosion if not managed correctly, if its 'geology' severed from the 'spirit' of overarching genius loci. This I sense as a 'deep-natured' ancestral Presence percolating with the <u>power</u> of 'full fathom five' deep.

Plunging further, to the very bedrock at 'heart' of FeltWorld, I engage the strength and simple beingness of temenos, a temple'd space which mirrors our 'sunk deep in settled stone' kiln room (of Card Deck self-naming – see "Appendix 2"). It was in this place I realised embedding our <u>human</u> Love deep in the Earth via the conscious recognition of the very <u>miracle</u> of our material incarnation (rather than floating in existential ambivalence around on the surface of her face) would deliver more <u>sustainable</u> Joy and Peace into our own self-reservoirs while at the same time contributing to Gaia's PeaceSink at the particular location of our 'rootedness'. This was the beginning of my understanding of task, if you like, on which – latterly – connecting home nodes across the world and singing stretches of Song with Sidhe partners ("Awakening"s preserve) ramped up to snowball-become the UrWerk described in this text.

Once, however, many years ago, Mr1300BC demonstrated a correlation between these initial insights and a musical score, such that <u>each</u> place was linked to <u>all</u> places in a web of Song and attunement. 'I saw' the five lines of a stave, and how each line of music harmonised with its sister-brothers. Across the five lines, each represented a different dimension, medium <u>and</u> technique; for example, some lines represented instrument, others voice, emanating from material or Malakut, Earth-energies or stellar-; this vision was summarily amplified when I actively began to partner Sidhe. Each line of 'music' presented horizontally – as its own Song- line – yet was completely attuned to counterparts above, below in a full 'Choir of Commons'.

Now, if we consider applying this matrix'd 'stave' of Song to the 'power of five' elementals on Amici continuum – horizont <u>and</u> vertical? The infinite potentiality of 'harmonium' comes into (interdimensional) focus. However, as I have no idea how to present such an interwoven geometric fabric for readerly understanding (given that I am no maths whizz to begin with), you will just have to take me (and Sidhe) at our Cousins-of-the-Commons'd word.

We do have an expression for this, though. Harmony 5.0 or (in shorthand): H5.0. And this is where the 'maths' <u>fully</u> meets the 'music' …

My propensity for attuning to Aboriginal ways of seeing (and being) arose as a function of plumbing the elemental dimensions of Earth-consciousness – from FeltWorld heart, on the way back out I connected into Aboriginal resonance singing its 'line' of 'stave'. It meant that, <u>before</u> "Awakening", I occasionally met presences in these (tonal) zones. Once I observed a Women's Song to heal Land at Uluru; this was after I helped move 'food' supplies to 'higher' ground <u>within</u> the Rock (the lower levels increasingly 'tainted' by impure energies). Another significant encounter involved the ancestral 'couple' of the 'W-clan', emanating from their (Western Desert) beyond. In charting a way to future, they affirmed their active embrace of learnings from <u>other</u> traditions toward a holistic, inclusive 'world' spirituality. We had sat at round table – drawing on the energy of other traditions was a path to furthering one's own learning, they felt. Pilgrimage (or 'walkabout') meant leaving the fold, the known, to go out in the world, experience the new, return with fresh perspective – thus better serve Gaia. In a later encounter, I met clan members following this guidance:

"We are from the (new) W, but the (original) W lives on …"

I understood that the power of change and transformation lies at the heart of their wisdom tradition, as it does with all in a dynamic living Universe, 'open and connectable across all dimensions'. This, of course, is analogous to learning the history and wisdoms of the Sidhe (and vice versa) so as to walk in the footsteps of <u>our</u> Common Ancestor, thereby embracing the full 'harmonium' of shared Song Mr1300BC demonstrated and singing it on.

To this end, and crosshatching prior lines of flight, was a Malakut journey I made in company of a girl. It seems I was her 'singing teacher' and this would be her first public performance. We needed to reach an auditorium far to the West of our usual 'stamping ground', <u>walking</u> the full way, following the (Song) line of a 'highway'. <u>Five</u> 'kilometres', it nevertheless crossed half the continent. We lived the red dust, intense heat, full desert-critter'd deal, but finally arrived. During performance I stood at the back of the hall while she took the stage. I strongly remember the melody needed to end on a high clear note. And to make sure she was 'in key' (still a 'learner'), we asked an elder presence observing from the back row if she could tune to his 'tuning fork'. I have no idea if he played it or not. I could hear no sound accompany the conclusion to performance. Still, to my ear, she accomplished the high note pitch-perfect (and held it long, unwaveringly) as if her <u>inner resonance</u> was completely 'sound'. So proud of her! I stood, and clapped and clapped and clapped.

Of course, I offer the reader these pearls in order to string a semi-logic to our Amici narrative. At the time of my 'singing teacher' duties, any inkling it could be applied to our Urwerk described in this volume was still (happily and sleepily) resident at (tempestuous) full fathom five Shakespearian depths.

Again, years prior, and 'outwith' a Time-commensurate intersect <u>except</u> for Kali's Mountains 101 induction, I journeyed a full Malakut day (night) in company of Song – invited to visit a community across the other side of 'home-ocean' (i.e. diagonally hemispheric from my sandy stretch of salty H_2O – 'eastern-sea-wild' to its 'pacific-north-west'). For a 'conference', in which I did not participate, at a 'teaching centre' I had never seen in either dimension, I was asked to sing the 'high harmony' to an male elder's main (Song) line – for this task, we needed to be 'horizont' as if lain side-by-side on Mr1300BC's 'stave'. This was my sole/soul contribution to the gathering, but apparently it would support participants to meditate. I had been welcomed earlier to the centre by a different elder – female – whose energy signature was absolutely ginormous. When she came to embrace and thank me for my attendance, I found her so wide and tall I could only manage to get my arms to reach the breadth of hips in reciprocal hug. This reminded me strongly of my embrace of the 'self-naughted' Mountain (described in previous chapter). If it had been 'me-sized', how much larger was <u>this</u> Presence?

My singing, and its harmonising function as a gift to the group, was the most potent memory, however – a riff on endless repeat. Intriguingly, it was the '<u>chorus</u>'

to John Denver's "Country Roads". Was the female elder '<u>Mountain</u> Mama'? Were '<u>Blue</u> Ridge' mountains an outwith-Time message? To: "Take (all) home to the place (we) belong" in meditative micro-macro?

At this point we need to return to Australia's Western Desert and the intersect of an in-Time event with the above choral work, following in the wake of W-clan ancestral encounters some months earlier and my witness of the "Crone" (aka Gondwana) at her worldwork, a poem penned in honour. Our annual pilgrimage down under that year included a trip 'down to Sydney' and a multi-day hike of World Heritage Gondwana Rainforest 'on the border'. Coexistent with a stretch of HomeSong, it hosts stands of Antarctic Beech, memory-markers to "a time before time, a place before now". While I have no desire to bore you with a month-long travelogue, some germane anecdotes from each will be useful to the next section.

In Sydney, I took the boys (partner F, younger son D) to an Aboriginal Arts Co-operative after introducing them to stunning Museum-housed exemplars of same, the idea to acquire several quality-crafted 'souvenirs' for nearest and dearest back in Heidiland – the boys with a 'show and tell' opportunity, having now learnt some relevant history at the Museum. Coincidentally this particular co-op only stocked Central Australian work. As well as the usual artefacts and designs on anything from scarves to cushions, there were stacks of canvases piled on a long low bench. An older woman behind the counter took no notice of us while a mid-aged man, whose look belied both Aboriginal and Afghan (trader) heritage, regularly did the rounds.

The beauty and relevance of Aboriginal art (and I have to admit here I am most familiar with Central Australian, i.e. Western Desert, work) is its rendering of a 2-D planal 'view' of a skin-group's stretch of Song while housing 4-D ceremonial knowing to mediate ritual re-enactment of the Ancestors' own Song. In so doing, they literally call in the 'power of five' (elemental dimensions) as the work facilitates the Ancestors' 'arrival' into ceremonial space itself – spiralling up from chthonic depths or down from stellar heights as the case may be.

In its own tradition it is akin to a Tibetan mandala – kalachakra'd (in-Time) of place (five-level chorten'd). But rather than build a human temple as representative of the various aspects of Buddhahood, Land itself enacts the architecture, the crystallisation of <u>its</u> music; verily it <u>is</u> the 'chorten' in its own 'power of five' skin. Sung into Being by the Ancestors at Big-Bang'd beginning and re-sung at each in-Time ceremonial marker thereafter, no more nor less is needed than the extant <u>note</u> of respective geology vested with relevant genius loci'd spirit. Couple this with the five-power'd elemental continuum – horizon as stretch of Song outlaid, <u>simultaneously</u> vertical as dot-painted 'stopping place' portal through which an Ancestor spirals – and we have an Earth-<u>conscious</u> cosmology staring us in the face.

To tease out the 'power of five' nuances of this latter statement a wee more, the artwork of region was only latter-day 'painted' as enduring artefact – and, following its commencement in the early 1970s as therapy for those dispossessed of ancestral Land, increasingly as a form of commodified outreach for a Western market. Yet if we return to its source-code as <u>lived</u> experience, the <u>physicality</u> of scripting to sand while singing or story-telling, or marking to flesh (self or other) for ceremonial Dance in company of Song, or simply as 'map' held in mind as home-stretch walked and sung, we find all five senses actively engaged to form a '<u>common</u>-sensed' whole. As a fully sensorial embodied <u>activation</u> of humanity's <u>incarnate</u> role as <u>bridge</u> species between Earth-consciousness and (common) ancestral cosmology, this mandala-of-self – unfixed and mutable, seamlessly mergent with the dynamic space of act – becomes a more-than-worthy reference point to the chapters which follow.

OK, back to the shop in Sydney …

At one point, we each wandered different areas. Suddenly I heard the man yell: "Don't touch that!" The object of his fury was D who had picked up a didgeridoo. Hmmm. D high-tailed it back to me, F also joined; we decided it was better to roam as a pack. We settled on flicking through a <u>random</u> stack of canvases (with the proviso none may be affordable). Flick, flick, flick. None spoke – all too 'bright' and 'pretty'; Women's Dreamings, they would be perfect for family/friends but did little to remind me of Malakut spaces I had wandered.

By now nearly at the bottom of the pile, a work veritably jumped out to tug at my heart, like a pup's doe-eyed beseech at a rescue centre: "Me! Me! Choose me!" Completely contrary to each canvas prior, the work was intensely plain – deepest brown on a thick black ground, its inner 'dot-work' white, flush with a geometry of scape more square than cirque'd. At odds with all before, as well as Men's Dreamings I had seen in ochre'd tones at Museum, this work said: DeepTime. This work said: Chthonic Earth. The depth and colour of Gondwana dirt – it was this which attracted me to wrench it out of stack, its perfect colour match to the hoodie I had worn for years from a local clothing 'brand', named? You guessed it: Gondwana.

The man approached with piercing eyes and an inscrutable expression. D shrunk. I thought: Oops. Maybe this too is a 'don't touch' moment? We held our breath. He stared at me, and said (with emphasis, marked):

"Either you have a <u>very</u> good eye for art; or you are very <u>very</u> lucky."

Que?

It turns out the work was by the younger brother of two incredibly 'famous' artists, their fame founded on two aspects – the work, of course, but also the fact this family (of nine) walked out of the (western) desert in 1984. The last to do so – 'first contact' nomads. Having seen nothing of white life <u>or</u> black community life, they were encouraged to 'come in' by extended family members, whom they had met unexpectedly at a water bore only a fortnight earlier, to look for marriage partners (i.e. to not narrow the gene pool any further) and re-forge community. Yet, having made the choice, they began to paint their Dreaming several years after relinquishing the nomadic life to stay connected to country, to express their loss. In current generational 'degrees' of Aboriginal art, therefore, it meant this work was absolutely raw, unmediated, direct, a scratched-in-the-sand experience of Land's Dreaming, wedded to a minimalist colour spectrum, offering (warily) only the bare bones of this sacred Story.

Now to a World Heritage rainforest.

Antarctic Beech – *nothofagus moorei* – is a relict of the supercontinent from which we were the last to break off in that far-distant past. Sailing North at the stunning rate of 5-7cms/year was not leisurely enough a traverse, however, for *nothofagus* to adapt to new parameters like heat and the sparse rainfall that came with it, as a result remaining only in small pockets of cool temperate fire-free rainforest at high altitude along eastern seaboard, of which our stretch of Song is its northernmost 'stand'. That said, it certainly adapted sufficiently to ensure we can witness its lived beauty at all rather than relying on rare fossil pollen records to tell an extraordinary story. For *nothofagus* learnt to reproduce asexually – stubbornly coppicing new trees from the roots of old when no longer able to produce viable seed in increasingly difficult conditions. An evolutionary marvel, these gentle giants are generally in family groups, so-called 'Faerie-Rings' from a single clonal individual; some specimens date to 12,000 years.

According to Yugambeh Dreaming, the region was sung into existence by "Woonoongoora", Queen of the Mountains; the plateau of our traverse the rim of a caldera formed from a vast shield volcano whose remnant plug, my 'Cloud-Catcher' of brother'd twin (Ruscada) across the world, was to the South, demarcating an end to my stretch of HomeSong. We detoured off the main track to "Tullawallal", 'place of many trees', its own mini-summit, to commune with these 'senior citizens'. The side-track spiralled slowly, up and around the hill, and while I did not consciously realise it at the time (having no image in mind of what I would find there), I was drawn to move slowly, mindfully, participant-witness to a Songline unspooling before my feet. Sharing space and breath, it was as if the path and I journeyed back in Time.

As I approached the top, 'I saw' them – the elders, dear Ancestors of Yugambeh Men's Dreaming. Rising out of non-existent mist, in the midst of a grove of ancient trees above me, each with a twinkle in his eye and a smile on his lips in welcome. There they sat, a crosslegged collective, faerie-ring, within a faerie-ring. 'Twas a strange feeling, I so small – below, beneath. For a few seconds I wondered how to approach the space; I had literally lost the path in my surprise! Eventually I found an appropriate spot for a last brief ascent and arriving, discovered my elders had turned to stone. Vast slabs of moss- and lichen-bespeckled igneous rock now formed the ring of shared presence with *nothofagus* kin.

Serenity filled the cocoon brought into being by elders and trees as one, a place of shared beingness we were invited to share, a place of (I felt) <u>continuing</u> worldwork – the Sacred sung into existence aeons past still sustained its extant voice, a <u>true</u> note in the musical score of Gaian resonance. As a mark of thanksgiving, as a 'bridge' in the absence of bridge, I placed a hand against an elder tree's clonal trunk while my other rested on a stone elder, offering a prayer for their continued presence, for <u>holding</u> this place open and present to all. I softly felt the thread of connection pass through me and down, to return 'heartbeat' whence chthonic-come, to effect on their behalf the mirroring of a joyous yet peace-sunk settled space of communion and facilitate its sharing through the root-knowing grid of Gaia.

• • • • •

Reader, you may wonder if we are ever going to close-out this discussion on the 'power of five'. To be honest, I have been wondering the same myself (hence the caveat at start about a story going where <u>it</u> wants to go!). It's been a rollercoaster ride, granted, but I promise this is a last parse before we move on, in next section, to effecting 'praxis' from 'research' – even if both exist happily, yet most frustratingly, outwith any Time-logic'd sequence to enable such efficacy. With that, thank you, Reader, for supporting me in the 'struggle'!

Here, the intent is to in-weave some other (at the time, unremarked) cogent threads to the telling centred on what was 'sown' in the wake of publishing "Awakening" in 2016. A 'gap in the script' in its own right (which began the Blue's ample inflow), it begged the question: "What next?" for our Amici crew. This line of flight followed the (geographic) argument that having connected homenodes, and strung our length of 'Elven-rope' across the world as a fresh leyline in Gaia's grid, what could we achieve <u>if</u>, as 'Companions of the Way of Love', we consciously took said Love "on the road" (to darling Jack's dharma bum'd 'beat') in outreach to the genii locorum of other Lands? To a stone (in circle) the response was: "Emissary."

An 'ambassador of goodwill' despatched from Helvetia's settled peace-sunk purity with subtle gifts of communal spirit to share and an open heart and mind to learn, plus PeacePole ever at her itinerant monk'd side? Sure! Two family journeys were (coincidentally) planned for this 2016 year – to Spain, a 'known' space in its role of opening me to purpose (home to a subtle sister who once said: "There is not enough Love in the World"), and to Japan, a complete (geographic) 'blank' even if I was already devoted to Basho, Sengai, Dogen and Tea!

The first, as 'pilot', revealed much; this offered the opportunity, in advance of latter, to begin non-local outreach and thus facilitate deeper contact once in Land. While we had no active plan to hike or climb during either visit, contact in each case remained anchored in my practice of listening for the 'extant' note of <u>enspirited</u> geology, as revealed by Mountain (mantle'd) specificity, in order to effect communion. "Awakening" describes my practice of "Hello the House" as such a form of outreach, but over time this greeting stripped itself out to a bare minimum, the simple intoning of:

"I am the Love sunk deep in settled stone."

Thereafter would I wait, and listen (as Gondwana had counselled), for a like-echo rippling out from the heart of (this particularity of) stone. I formalised non-local outreach to the spirit of Nippon at a Summer Solstice ceremony in our Amici garden grail which had taken a central role throughout "Awakening". Now, with a Zen-inspired garden extending TreeMother-MossMan-Findling's original cone-of-connectivity further on to a <u>very</u> mature Japanese maple, a venerable squat-meditating master alongside garden wall (whom I call BuddhaAncestor), I was able to meditate under his umbrella-like dome at Solstice – on a flat stone 'cushion' I lovingly named Gondwana. The fence which backs this section of garden, installed when a four-legged lad joined the family line-up some years prior, has sturdy wooden uprights to anchor its simple unpainted pickets. By happy chance, the Zen garden 'extended' our grail exactly five uprights in length. Immediately I saw the opportunity to empower these as PeacePoles (in honour of Masahisa Goi's life and work) by asking my artistic daughter to script the kanji for Peace ('Heiwa') onto each. To confirm and <u>seal</u> the 'harmonic resonance of elemental sentience' enduringly <u>resident</u> in our grail space via ongoing rituals of alignment, I also asked her to sub-script each pole with the kanji of its respective element in vertical-horizont continuum thus:

'Sora' (Aether) 'Kaze' (Air/Wind) 'Hi' (Fire) 'Mizu' (Water) or 'Tsuchi' (Earth)

With the Zen garden designed to flow down the side as a (gravel'd) 'River of Enlightenment' toward TreeMother's 'Ocean of Being', it should come as no surprise that Tsuchi's PeacePole 'just happened' to back MossMan's stone, his 'extant note' being the first in our quiver. Hi's PeacePole, meanwhile, 'just happened' to rest behind BuddhaAncestor's meditative cone of silence, blithely representative of the 'earth-fire' at Mountain heart; at BuddhaAncestor's maple'd foot, a stone lantern (yukimi) completed the elemental (chorten'd) equation.

A main focus of meditation aims to 'twin' the harmonic resonance of <u>my</u> elemental sentience with the grail's and, by extension, the macro proposition it calls into being. This harmonising function centres on the relational interbeing of my five physical senses with the five elements as they are brought to incarnate Life in my Body (as for all of us). As (self-) embodied knowing, 'universal' (macro) H5.0 in intersect with little micro-Annie completes a 'power of (my) five' awareness <u>inwith</u> physical skin. From here, as Love's Light, it radiates out again as conscious blessing. The grail thus acts as a cauldron for <u>working</u> the alchemical contract (of self with universal) as well as <u>delivering</u> it back (via grail) into Gaia's crystalline grid.

The holism of my '<u>common</u> sense' (as physic'd five), expressed in/through Gaia's 'Commons', comes into play when interweaving our harmonised resonance into the fullness of elemental sentience across the five lines of Mr1300BC's stave. As an attuned harmonium 'singing' <u>along</u> the full vertical-horizont continuum as well as <u>with</u> the full continuum – where none receives preference over another, each an agent of change in our diagram-of-equals – the opportunity to energise, enflavour and quicken the <u>holistic</u> elemental force as a coalescent dense 'ball' of Earth-consciousness evolving within us <u>and</u> within Gaia cannot be overstated. In essence, it's about <u>living</u> our true nature; we are an (incarnate) alchemical mix of elemental energy for which our physical senses provide an active gateway <u>in</u> to engaging their harmonising function <u>inwith</u> skin if we 'twig' to co-creative commonality (of all senses, all elements) as holistic fact. The harmony of the wave is the <u>fact</u> of the wave; the harmony of the heliotrope is the <u>fact</u> of the heliotrope; the harmony of little micro-Annie is ... Point being: The <u>fact</u> of incarnate existence evolves our Earth-consciousness in like measure to Gaia's. Discussed earlier from a different perspect, in this context it looks at the inherent 'power' of <u>living</u> the 'five' as Love, as Light, as Song. The form of practice may vary, but its underlying function is the same – serving Gaia by <u>truly</u> being us.

For now, back to a garden grail's 'becoming' ...

In short, it all seemed fit to purpose; to be honest I could not believe my luck. Our 'brief' to landscape gardener had none of these aspects in mind. Perhaps his Soul was in on Emerson's gag? Or Amici had done some 'mind-mining' on my unconscious behalf? Who knows! But the result was, in hindsight, completely in line with our (ongoing) micro-macro intent.

So: All good at Solstice. 'Emissarial' mission to the Land of Nippon described – not only on our Amici PeaceWalk-ing behalf but in reverent memory of my (personal) Sky-Father, a WW2 veteran whose own 'ghosts of Christmas past' had sent him to an early grave when I but an 18-year-old 'child'. He knew, of course, that he had left too soon, so had flown – at the moment of his passing a hundred miles away in physical space – along my stretch of 'eastern-sea-wild' to tell me he must leave; tell me in that long and (at that stage in life experience) frighteningly black tunnel linking the worlds, that I needed to walk on alone through this plane of existence. Alone, with the Alone. Hence <u>never</u> alone ...

In the near wake of Solstice, a night arrived when the Malakut was charged with thought, an energetic buzz that refused to let me settle. I found myself in non-descript spaces; my task to light candles. At one point I held two used matches in my hand; these had lit their respective candles earlier it seems. Later I held two fresh matches but was unsure for what or where these needed to be applied. At end, I stood on/at/with Moon to watch Earth 'unfold' (as I described the process to myself). I saw points of 'a-proximate' Light illumine across the globe; the message was that these would 'ignite' lines of connectivity in-between. I 'saw' leylines at work but how would/could my two fresh matches be used in this context?

At breakfast, F checked the news websites (as an ex-journo this is a difficult habit to break).

Woah, he said. They voted for Brexit.

OK, I thought, that explains the energetic buzz in global 'field'. I had sensed the <u>intentionality</u> of this outcome about a week earlier but, as I never actively follow the news, had no idea when the actual vote was. My point to F had been, however, that dominoes had fallen in other regions of the world but now it would be the turn of the West – Brexit would be followed by a Trump presidency, I said. The desire for chaos to erupt could not continue to be plastered over by an 'orderly' West. The cracks (of own making) too big, I said. The old must crumble for the new to be revealed; all needs be stripped away to return to the essence.

But why had I been hanging out with Moon overnight? And what were my matches for?

In the moment of F's 'woah', I had had a sudden 'flash' of old alliances centred on regional geography splitting asunder for new to emerge along 'a-proximate' lines of flight. Granted, this could account for what I had seen, but my work was not in 'human dimensions' – so?

I decided to go for a walk along our local creek – an energy continuum with active subtle presence often conducive (together with fresh air) to uplifting insights in the exact moment I need them. During a meandering contemplation, three image-messages stood out:

The need to recognise the <u>energetic</u> value of 'scrub turkeys as disruptive technology' (a species long-misunderstood by Aussie householders who love a 'neat and tidy' garden).

The <u>evolutionary</u> value of carrying 'spores' from the old on a grand adventure to the new; here, Antarctic Beeches, committing to embrace same and adapt their <u>wiring</u>, featured (I saw their overlighting angel sign a contract to 'try' – both intentionality <u>and</u> choice implicated).

Lastly, the lessons of Gondwana-as-primordial-Land herself breaking up – the <u>seismic</u> fault lines leading to continents drifting apart, reforging/reforming …

At this, Gondwana arrived in the midst of what I thought (till then) was a self-conversation; she offered to teach, continue the lesson if I would simply: "Listen." (All while walking along the creek.) I saw a long timeline unravel – back <u>and</u> in. I saw Earth 'unfold' as it had overnight, but now it was FullDark; there were no 'a-proximate' points of light, no interconnecting lines of flight. In the moment, the only thought was:

"<u>Subtle</u> plate tectonics."

At that a <u>thump</u> of energetic resonance exploded deep inside and I experienced an immediate <u>physical</u> connection to Moon. This was the age (and longevity) of wisdom that Gondwana was offering to share. I saw how these two Beings had 'midwifed' Gaia's Earth-conscious <u>geologic</u> birth into existence; I understood they were Sister-energies in task. Together with Kali, they formed a seeming goddess-triumvirate (three faces of a single energy) which spoke to the 'three faerie godmothers' of princess'd lore. Following this download (courtesy of a rickety 'thump'), I was directed back to two strong Malakut encounters of my own aeons past.

First, 'Mother' had been cuddling a beautiful flaxen-haired girl (pre-teen) with <u>emerald</u> backlit eyes and asked me to take over. She had been sitting on Mother's lap but with me she simply stood in her pretty dress and smiled up while being introduced. I immediately recognised her, said: "I have known your older sisters." In the moment, I remembered a much earlier Malakut encounter in the garden of 'Great Mother' where I first met this girl-child but not yet been asked to take over her care. On that occasion I simply observed her SkyChild's joy in the arms of Mother, plunging her face over and over into a switch of jacaranda blossom and laughing with the sheer wonder of the 'physicality of things'.

The second was a Mr1300BC lesson: "This was a thousand-year dream …" (said).

He was talking about the 'Human Time' scale of upheaval in <u>its</u> framework of intersect with Gaia's planetary Being, and the need to work through all <u>transitional</u> forms of consciousness to a potentiality which <u>could</u> reveal itself a (mere) thousand years hence. It was shown to me, yet without any indication I was involved in such 'Human Time' scale work. Indeed, I had been told, even earlier again, that my task was to "play like a rock"; apart from embracing a me-sized Mountain at that stage, I had no idea where such a line of flight could head. Nor how Kali's induction, <u>sealing</u> my Mountains 101 'knowing', would fit into its overall work 'script'. Now, following my self-apprenticeship in Light-work (documented in "The Amici Files") and actively partnering Sidhe to shared outcomes ("Awakening"), it seemed I was being invited to learn from Gondwana (and Moon) about the DeepTime-Tectonia dimension of <u>their</u> Gaian engagement – with the potential to <u>deepen</u> our Amici work into, literally, 'Mountain-Time'.

I remembered the 'map of the world' on whose edge I had stood nine months earlier, post-Autumn Equinox '15 on the eve of journey into Helvetia's heart, when Moon had donned her Red Lady cloak – chthonic, Earth-'fired' was her colour that day-night. I remembered how, as "Awakening" drew to a close earlier in the year, I found myself in a Malakut space writing about our <u>next</u> work. At some level I knew it was important to describe my early working-through of its proposition in an "Epilogue" to book, so shunted a chapter of documentation across the pond to Jeremy post-haste. It centred on:

"*Stretching the Boundary to the Heart of Stone."*

As I wrote in "Awakening", to in-herald this next work, I needed to affirm an understanding to <u>earth</u> myself in Gaian ground simultaneous with connecting to the <u>aether</u> of cosmic energy. I saw this as a function of being 'barefoot' in either context – physically sensate, skin-to-skin. Most delightful was how this alchemical reaction was brought <u>into</u> my Body and optimised – by drinking tea! Lady Grey for earth-conduit, Earl Grey for universal. Ah, my Amici certainly know which symbolic buttons to press! Later, a single word joined this stable: <u>Chthonic.</u> It was used to describe the destination of a group excursion beneath mantle; so intensely FullDark, my only conscious memory was of arriving back to Mountain's 'outer skin'. I said to an Amici colleague that I had not realised how 'messy' a chthonic encounter could be; it manifested as a laval-red fountain out the top of my head! Yet fit to purpose – within Stone Circle I was the 'flame' at centre <u>anchoring</u> their 'Ring of Fire' in-world; at the same time their fiery standing stone action <u>protecting</u> my 'inner' work like a bell-jar prevents Wind wavering or sputtering a candle. All of this spoke to Mr1300BC's observation that:

"*Love in itself is Fire".*

A glowing permanency of shared presence ensued, yet the Amici still thought I needed a specific 'bodyguard'. He stepped forward – fit, healthy, long dark hair pulled back in a ponytail. Sweaty, covered in grit, dirt and soot, his task was to watch out for me in this volatile setting. The Dancer, ShapingMan (see "Appendix 2"), had taken form at last. He reached out, shook my hand – casual, but very professional. With his longer-than experience singing up ancestral country, 'reading' campfire embers for clues, I more than welcomed such skills to 'shape' our chthonic engagement. Again, I remembered my encounter on the edge of 'map of world' – how I was reminded to 'anchor' myself in a cliff of rock to negotiate whatever needed negotiating in this new (unknown) work. Yes, I would trust ShapingMan to constellate this relation.

In hindsight, our Amici troupe was 'prepping the space' even then for heading further into FullDark inner-Earth zones – a bit Jules-Verne-ish in a way. But what suddenly jumped out at me now was a memory of 'Gondwana-brown' – the <u>tug</u> of intensely dark and pungent colour in the artwork of Western Desert Dreaming origin, discovered at random in that Sydney gallery years earlier. Outwith Time (at the time), the artwork was now beginning a slow sashay to front and centre. I looked at it with fresh eyes. It looked at me with ancient ones.

"*Hmmm,"* it said.

"Hmmm," I said. *"Are you channelling Gondwana by any chance?"*
"Who me?"

Feigning shock, it looked back over its shoulder to where, deeper than Gondwana-brown, the artist had applied a thick layer of FullDark black. Painted direct onto a blank canvas Void, the Unmanifest from which all arises ... I reflected on my overnight vision – standing with Moon watching Earth (Gaia) 'unfold' her 'a-proximate' points of light for (fresh) interconnecting lines of flight. A map of potentiality, to all intents, which perhaps we could help bring into being if I would simply: "Listen." Thereby (really) learn. I needed to slow my long-<u>conditioned</u> "Human Time" back down/in to "Mountain Time" – DeepTime, Tectonic Time – and:

"Wait, listen, learn."

Mirroring what seen/experienced in Malakut nine months earlier, whether phoenix-torch'd or Annie-match'd, lighting these 'stations' needed to be done slowly, methodically. In order <u>and</u> in-Time. I needed to <u>partner</u> Time here in a space where it did not/could not run fully down but remain unextinguished – simply slowed while I waited, listened, learned. Again I was reminded of my "Epilogue" to "Awakening" where, in the exuberance of flaming circle's self-incarnation, I announced (to whomever would listen):

"The crystal beacons are lit!"

I had been reminded of the scene in LOTR3 when Pippin does his bit to light the beacon of Minas Tirith, setting up a chain reaction of beacon-lighting along a full stretch of Middle Earth Mountain 'Song'. Aragorn then does his bit to tell the King of Rohan. While the King pondered for an <u>inordinate</u> number of film-seconds, my exuberance could not be stemmed:

"The crystal beacons are lit! Gaia calls for aid and we 'Horse Lords' from the North, through the Gate of the Stars shall answer!"

The relevance of 'crystal' to the equation followed the trajectory of my felt-sense as a self-sovereign crystal pillar a-flame, thus intersecting my desire to walk Love's Light out from Helvetia's crystalline heart, radiating it as Song wherever, whenever through Gaia's glorious world. The image which accompanied the statement was a memory of snow swept up to aetheric heights by high winds over a blessed mount. Caught by Sun's set, the snow crystals veritably <u>burned</u> with glory against a backdrop of Blue. The phenomenon was so exhilarating to watch and its memory so enduringly fresh – a reminder to all we Amici that our constancy of praxis – of praise, of blessing, of joyous participative witness, <u>and</u> loving co-creation would keep the flame of our grail's crystal beacon ever-lit.

Thus did I conclude "Awakening" with the following statement of longer-than commitment which seemed, upon re-reading in the 'light' of overnight vision, as well as preceding phoenix-torched encounter, to be opening the way <u>very very</u>

wide to a next (best) work detail:

"So is it done, our work? No, never done, no matter how many lives we walk the Earth, no matter how many skins or mantles of starlight we wear. Time is ever of the essence. The Stone Circle's incarnation as a cauldron 'charged' with its own (vertical) alchemical remit continues apace, and so do we keep walking the thread out into the (horizontal) world, singing up country, singing a Songline of Love, of crystalline consciousness, into being, over, ever over – in honour of the Ancestors, in honour of Hope, in honour of the Alliance between Humanity and Faerie. And all for our wondrous Gaia."

I looked at the text with fresh eyes. It looked at me with a babe's six-month-old ones.

"Hmmm," it said.

"Hmmm," I said. *"Are you channelling Gondwana, by any chance?"*

"Who me?"

• • • • •

Let me introduce you to 'Dawn-of-Time'. I have a feeling he has hovered in and out of view over the years but in the days leading up to our 2016 Autumn Equinox ceremony following all outlined above, I had a most intriguing encounter with this Presence. To set the scene, and relevance of his arrival in intersect, our general template for rituals of ongoing alignment involves "12-Days-of-Consciousness" in advance of Equinox or Solstice (as the case may be), the last five of which comprise "120-hours of Mindful Harmony". This involves opening the Stone Circle gates in order of their relationship to elemental continuum each sunset to enable the swirl of densifying energy to gradually 'become'; it ensures any/all subtle collaborators entering through the gates slowly attune to the resonance of grail space without energetically overwhelming me with a single 'party-central' nightclub vibe. On the final eve, a full 'current' of energy comes into play to in-herald "36-hours of Ceremony & Celeb" thereafter. Mostly I close up the shop on the morning of 22nd (of whichever month). But if the energy still needs time to 'speak' its counsel and/or I have not yet completed all intuited tasks pertaining, it can take a few more days. Onto the template are grafted specific alignment practices relevant to each in-Time marker of Celtic calendar. Autumn Equinox coincides with UN International Day of Peace, thus speaking to our work in a most particular way – Sidhe as 'People of Peace' so-known and my subtle activism and wordsmithing focused on 'Peace consciousness in the 21st century' in the (last) decades pertaining to same. The fact we Amici found each other in order to continue our respective PeaceWork as collaborators is one of those happy mysteries of Life. As is the fact the UN Day of commemoration was first introduced during the Bosnian War, the setting for "The Taste of Translation", something of which I had no idea when I penned the novel, all on the back of a subtle sister's words:

"There is not enough Love in the world."

One more thing: This Equinox begins birthday month with Sun's shift to Libra, always a time of heightened subtle activity for me. As a result, as an Amici work crew we use this time to review the year that has been and set up the yearly 'program' to come. So, with that as backdrop, let me (finally) introduce you to Dawn-of-Time …

He came knocking on the (Makakut) morning of a (material) 'pre-birthday treat' which would see us in a (replica) 18th century Japanese tearoom at an art museum downtown for a Chado ('Way of Tea') ceremony with suitably certified master. At some point in my encounter with Dawn I was handed a hessian sack of seeds with the instruction:

"With the sack of seeds be wary till March."

I understood this to mean I should not 'plant' or 'distribute' them immediately, but wait, and consider their use carefully. The thing was that my <u>receival</u> of the sack was outwith Time. March was three months ahead of when our meeting ostensibly took place. Hence, Dawn's comment alerted me to the need to take close note of what would future-happen around the Winter Solstice. Potentially, as an in-Time marker, it may 'shed light' on what I should do.

The use of the word 'wary' was potent. Not a word I would normally use, it stopped me in my tracks. I took note of my excitement in the space to receive these seeds, a situation which could easily lead to my natural exuberance to immediately tackle whatever needs tackling to get out-of-hand. I needed to wait till Time was ripe – Spring. Yes, this made sense. I needed to be patient, observant, watchful till then. In other (Gondwanan) words: Listen.

The scape constellated as a community in a dry desert-like region. The community was spread out; small adobe-style dwellings, terracotta in colour, blended well with the surroundings. It reminded me of desert father/mother terrain in Egypt. I met a fellow in one of the dwellings a couple of times, just in passing. He was doing his work; I was doing mine. But when I took my dog for a walk around the village, following a wide path up an incline toward stony fields and bare hills, he suddenly appeared at my side with his. We made small talk. I noticed he had changed 'clothes', shapeshifted form, but knew it was the same energetic signature.

How he 'presented' was quite intriguing. He was fully composed of red carpet; not only in his suit of clothes, but even his skin, face – everything. I noted the red carpet was old and worn in patches; in some areas, tufts of carpet, its very fibre, was completely missing. All that was left was the plain 'woven' mat beneath, exposed in odd places. He was a complete hotchpotch of old and less-old. Nothing was regenerating; it was more as if he were aging at different rates. At some point in the future, though, all would be 'worn through' to bare element. On his feet were rope sandals, like medieval Japanese monks would wear.

We wandered up the hill together till reaching a raised platform. Semi-roofed and 'framed' on three sides, it was like a pavilion or verandah, square in shape. Dark wood was its timber flooring. The whole structure sloped down toward the back; plain, bare – nothing in or on it. Here we decided to rest a while. He lay down; I sat on the edge. He told me about his project (whose content was FullDark to surface me) but as he told, I had a 'flash' of the last time he 'incarnated' with this brief. At the world's 'dawn'. On that occasion he had failed to 'complete the wiring' because of whatever circumstance. I saw that the makings of project were not lost, however. They just needed to be revitalised, further developed. He was keen to continue and (hopefully) get it fully done this time round. Yet he was weary, unsure if it were possible. His 'aging process' had much to do with it – understandable for one working since the 'dawn of time'. Into this quiet conversational space, I reached over, held his arm in support, said:

"Don't worry; this time Mummy's here to help."

Well. 'Mummy' (apparently) meant me!

He asked me to lie down beside him, but because of the sloping floor, I was hesitant. I felt myself tilting, sliding back toward a FullDark chasm at the back of platform, was concerned I would tumble into an unknown 'void' pre-dawn (of time). He purposefully assured me: Don't worry. It'll be OK; we won't. But as I continued to feel unstable in this position, I pulled myself upright and consciously exited the space, lifting myself 'back' to the here and now.

The 'locale' was called: "Bay-Root". While pronounced like the Lebanese capital, its spelling mirrored the German city, Bayreuth, associated with the composer Wagner. This latter line of flight connected the notion of his operatic 'Ring Cycle' with Nietzsche's thought of 'Eternal Return' which seamlessly segued (in my mind) to the concept of 'Amor Fati'. I had been handed a sack of seeds but needed to heed the cautionary note associated with their delivery. This certainly was a cryptic clue with much ancient mythology thrown in for good measure!

Just prior to Equinox, however, we met again. After a long journey by various modes of public transport through Swiss-style lowlands, I found myself walking beside a fast-flowing river. Sitting on a fencepost beside the path, he waited for me to arrive. Now he presented as a very 'lit' suave timeless gent in a completely white suit who easily fell in beside me so we could walk on together. Content now with the energetic 'fit', I found I could see straight through to the <u>constancy</u> of his 'deep nature' while the serenity of his smile settled any previous sense of instability I might have had. I knew F would be equally comfortable with my new travelling companion. This could work; 'Mummy' was here to help.

●●●●●

We have covered a lot of (Gaian) ground in this chapter, Reader, and I appreciate you staying the course. Much more will be covered in the next section to 'enflesh' spare geologic bones and bring the abstract into the realm of lived praxis. For now, though, let me simply set the scene by (subtly) shifting the narrative out another six months to Spring Equinox 2017, specifically the days prior to the "12-of-Consciousness", when I was trying to come to terms with what – by that stage – I finally realised was being asked of our Amici crew, and thus needed to design a relevant ceremony to confirm both understanding and commitment to task.

In this period, I received a final instruction (or reminder) on the 'power of five' and what H5.0 as a <u>twinned</u> alchemical proposition could manifest – the harmonic resonance of elemental sentience in seamless conjunct with our own 'common-sensed' empowerment, the wonder and <u>ability</u> of incarnate presence alive to colour-coded consciousness. I watched the elements 'bend', saw their response to our working with their energy – transmuting, transforming, metamorphosing according to whatever specific purpose we desired to 'magick' into being, as true partners to an aligned outcome. But? The reminder was that the foundation for our/any 'snowball of becoming' must be Love – unconditioned, unconditional <u>loving</u> service offered back to the sacred pool of Being's Ground whence come. We have this ability, this capacity, to shape and mould, envision and manifest, but too often we can be attracted by glamour, power, greed – the all-too-human failings of our species when we slip from heeding the voice of truth at heart: Love.

'Tis the (lily white) purity of <u>our</u> intent which enables the elements to manifest with purity and dance <u>their</u> alchemic Joy toward a co-creative harmonically resonant 'event'. Like attracts like. Corruption arises when we are corruptible; muddied outcomes fomented by muddied intent – ambiguities, negativities, ego-driven hungers. The 'Form of the Good' can only emerge when the Good is its source – within us as much as the forces with which we work. A 'divine' alchemical marriage can only be divine when we ourselves bring divinity to the elemental equation, when we ourselves are the harmonium we wish to sing through all worlds and times, in <u>concert</u> with all worlds and times of Gaia's glorious all.

In the space of reminder, I again see the five lines of Mr1300BC's stave. I see myself writing it out, again – the instruction about <u>how</u> it all works on horizon <u>and</u> vertical continuum; how everything arises from Aether and within Aether is the <u>purity</u> which brings us to incarnation, which brings the All to incarnation. I see Aether, the first 'Blue' – there she is, expressing her Joy at the <u>infinitude</u> of elemental continuum; there she is, commencing the <u>magic</u> to 'chain reaction' our beautiful Blue Planetary Soul, Gaia, to incarnate Form.

All the while, I hold a stone – small and perfectly smooth, pure as white muslin in my hand; obsessively washed, over and over, by the aeon'd waters of Hope, like the ill-treated mothering Perdita continued to do, <u>constant</u> in her care of all foster pups in Dodie Smith's "101 Dalmatians"; like Gaia continues to do,

<u>constant</u> in her care, no matter how we may ill-treat and disrespect her, no matter how forgetful we may be of the counsel of ages and sages.

I finally finish writing, and tell the Child everything I have written – the Child of Divinity, the 'Form' conceived from our marriage of the 'Good', from the purity of our intent fused with the harmonic resonance of elemental sentience, to <u>be</u> the harmonium. He nods and says:

"We begin tomorrow."

'Tomorrow' is a Monday. 'Tomorrow' comes and with it a delivery to my garden gate – of eight mounds of 'dark knowing'. Rounded, moulded – they are stone, and smooth. Their colour Gondwana-brown. The full elemental string has been strung through to the <u>densest</u> of Earth-consciousness. Each the size of a small Findling. Not delivered heaped in a pile. No. Each its own discrete container, a reservoir of wisdom within its own space, yet each equally an integral member of the whole on this diagram-of-equals. They arrive at the border to our garden grail. It is our task to bring them in, and work their elemental energy with the purity of our intent, with the <u>fidelity</u> of our Love, we Amici della Montagna della Luce, we Fedeli d'Amore to each and all …

STRETCH 2:
IN COMPANY OF STONE GIANTS

UrWerk. Noun. German. Ur – Ancient. Werk – Work.

'Ur' is a very useful prefix to refer to anything ancestral, primordial, indigenous, archeologic – animal, vegetable, mineral, manufactural. It is also the name of an extinct species of wild bovine, widely distributed through Europe, Asia and North Africa. The ancestor of domestic cattle, in English it is called: "Aurochs". Something to remember for later, dear Reader.

'Werk', meanwhile, is a handy catch-all for a raft of interconnected English meanings. The <u>act</u> of creation itself, the <u>site</u> of such creation, the <u>craft</u> applied to bring the creation to light, a creation of <u>immense</u> magnitude, as in opus, or the full <u>body</u> of created 'works' – as in oeuvre. Even in pronunciation it bespeaks a toughness or tenacity; the effort required to wrench a creation from reluctant and incubatory cosiness (a process I have likened to pulling teeth). All that energy and dense weight of expression is lost when we say 'work' in English.

Think of the Titan, Atlas, and his holding aloft of the weight of celestial sphere. Now that was (is?) an UrWerk. One could say the 'dimensions' of our micro-Amici task fit this 'snowball' model, at least in terms of endurance, strength and our offering of support to Gaia. In "Exploring Song" we will look at this further.

'Ur' pronounced, of course, sounds the same as 'Uhr' which refers to any sort of 'work' which marks the passage of Time as well as a specific moment of clocked 'Time'; '3 o'clock' is '3 Uhr'. Now, to this Sengai 'cake', let's add a small measure of synchronous synchronicity by going for a rhizomatic meander to the ancient Sumerian city of Ur, where archaeological evidence suggests their giant sundials, of some six millennia past, were one of the oldest forms of clocking Time. On the back of this last tidbit, it should really be no surprise why UrWerk is an appropriate noun to describe our Amici 'work', one of DeepTime-Tectonia service to Gaia's experience with and expression of Earth-consciousness. Nibbling on this (Ur) cake, while enjoying a cup of fragrant tea, with Sidhe-inflected whimsy I invite the reader to venture back (in mind) to the place I first met Dawn of Time; it is eminently possible my 'naming' of him encompassed locale in a more 'literal' sense than I imagined 'at the time'. While an 'outwith' encounter, it would not surprise me if he were the prompt for our project 'title' – a micro-word for a decidedly macro-undertaking.

Along this arc of Ur/Uhr'd illinearity, there is an in-Time meeting of relevance which extends (and sub-texts) the discussion of last chapter where I describe the 'seeds' of emissarial duty sown in the wake of publishing the 'fieldwork' of our Amici partnership ("Awakening").

But to place this meeting in context, I need to backtrack a little further. As a co-created artefact, the text of "Awakening" had come together very fast; in only a couple of months, <u>everything</u> that had 'happened' in the past four years following closure of my last major work, "The Taste of Translation", tumbled out onto the page. In an attempt to re-group and get my head around a zombie'd sense of energetic malaise – on one level cathartic, yes, but on another involving a feeling of complete (cognitive) disfunction – we continued with rituals of ongoing alignment but little (surface) else till the day "Emissary" popped in.

Now, I know well the buzzy energy released by a collective 'snowball of becoming' in its process of deciding to become <u>no matter what</u>. The Stone Circle – as an engine for and container of this energy – can at times reach quite 'noisy' heights with the range of voices eagerly entering discussion. At the 'core' of Circle, I find myself in a dual role – to honour and hold the 'space' as it grows, while ensuring no part of puzzle is left unconsidered: 'No rock left unturned,' as they say – metaphorically or literally in our case! As with an orchestra, its conductor ensuring (via PeacePole'd baton) that the brass does not overshadow the woodwinds, at times I find <u>smoothing</u> the energetic resonance inwith and beyond Circle, like the coverlet on a fractious babe's crib, a real effort – especially when I add my Annie-exuberance to the mix!

I am no adept like Mr1300BC; hence, the entirety of dynamic in its see-sawing attempt to find harmonious balance can manifest within my Body-Mind complex as a 'pushy kid on the block' as easily as if an overwrought child who has had <u>too</u> big a day out. My Amici are a wonderful crew, bringing in Sidhe healers at any stage of a process to soothe frayed nerves or give energy boosting tonics. Some of these are really tasty to boot! However, in prepping for the Summer Solstice, with its focus on non-local outreach to the genius loci of Nippon, I found myself in a right state of energetic disarray – terribly scattered in thought yet completely mired in inactivity. Thus very concerned I would 'let the team down' by being ill-prepared on the day, by not having enough <u>time</u> to do our outreach justice.

I know I have shared this anecdote before, in "Grail Within", but it bears repeating given our need to harness the principle of 'partnering Time' to requisite psychoid-unity'd effect under the 'material light of day' while operating under the 'Malakut' same. My problem (back then) focused on the notion of 'slippage'. Ever since "Awakening" had 'outed' itself, Life had felt 'odd', and I thought my sense of 'time' was somehow implicated. Unlike the regularity of heartbeat that keeps a settled fluidity to its encircled momentum, an energetic 'arrhythmia' had set in. Time seemed to 'skip a beat', stop, hiccup, or go racing off in any direction at the drop of a hat. It felt like being in a washing machine that does a few rounds happily enough and then either stops or does an about-face or shifts 'program notch' to a different stage of cycle. But that would still be rhythmic, and follow a (set) pattern. I could pick no pattern in this new 'script', however.

When there was no shift to this felt-sense after months and it hampered work output to boot, I began to worry. Deciding to take 'time out', and write through my frustration in the hope of directly engaging the 'symptom' to approach a potential underlying 'cause', I began:

"*Time is slipping ...*"

As these words 'formed', I was instantly cognisant of a Presence entering (through the back of my skull in point of fact) who was no Sidhe healer. The energy was so big that I had to speak the words as they were scripted, scribbling as fast as I could in my journal to catch all 'It' had to say. By speaking the words, I hoped to slow the momentum somewhat, thus 'hold' the energy better in a space from which I could write out. Here is its full encapture ...

Time is slipping; Time is slipping through cracks; gaps in the script open and don't seem to want to close again. Time says: *There's not enough Time for all you want to do, to say, to think, to feel, to experience, to remember, to repeat, to deepen, lengthen, widen the trench.* Time says: *There's not enough of <u>me</u> for you to do what you will.* Time says: *That's why you notice the slippage, the staccato, the rhythm arrhythmic, like a heart beat gone awry.* Time says: *Watch me, watch yourself.* Time says: *Watch for when the gaps open, for that is when you are <u>free</u> the script to write.* Time says: *It is Time. Live in the gap. Do not remark me and my passage.* You are beyond that space, where all is me (Time) bound. You are beyond and when beyond you cannot step back,* *you cannot be in the space of me anymore; this is what you have remarked in the wake of closure; this is what you must embrace for it is where you already are. There is no arrow of Time you can march to/join the march for. Anymore ...*

Intense download. Tough counsel. It was only when writing the first sentence from a self-perspective that I realised exactly who had entered, hence shifting to direct reportage from that point on. The felt-sense of shift was dramatic. As the words, 'Time says' exited my mouth, I almost lost it with the combination of vibrational tremor coursing Body as Psyche began battening down the hatches, saying: "Oops. Here comes a scolding from big ol' papa bear ..."

But the scolding never came, and I settled into transcribing the whole of his matter-of-factual 'you're-just-going-to-have-to-live-with-this' speech. That said, the asterisk marks the spot where tears began to drip onto the page (a humbling runic memory-marker of its own in my journal) – tears which reflect a child's sudden fright at a dark unknown 'beyond'. Indeed, the way Time used the word 'closure' to describe "Awakening"'s publication implied that this 'event' had closed-out a phase to in-herald a next. No matter what I had written in conclusion to the book, or the fact Time said I was already <u>in</u> this next space, I needed to <u>accept</u> it in order to 'embrace' it – yet rI emain eternally grateful for his direct intervention rather than leaving me to wallow in a slough (of self-despond, and more).

Over the course of our UrWerk, I have often returned to this text (most recently in recounting the episode here for you, dear Reader!), and will surely continue to do so for I find it rich in wisdom, practically applied. Especially the exhortation to 'live in the gap' touches both symbolic and personally resonant chords. As an affirmation, that I am 'free' the script to write from this space 'outwith' (a wonderful Scottish word!), a space where Time displays none of its usual (human-perceived) control functions (arrow'd, enslave'd, chain'd, bound), segued of its own accord to the realisation we could <u>engage</u> Time as an active <u>partner</u> to our work.

It 'fits' the diagram-of-equals – Time is a Space whose shape is round, a dynamic Presence bringing each cross-section from 3D to 4D. It fits my understanding of the purity needed in-self to 'bend' elements to holistic outcomes. Affirming our pure (of Love) Amici intent in each request of Time to partner and support an in-Time 'act' has proven to be a magical extension to praxis, correspondent to the Taoist principle of wei wu wei, and adding another dimension to our H5.0 quiver. (When seen from the perspect of vertical-horizont stave, we are now at a species of geometric form this simple maths mind cannot get her head around; but I digress.)

In such spirit I return to Dogen's Sutra, its simplicity of Being (Mountain) and Flowing (Dragon) as daily (micro) matter-of-course within an interbeing'd watershed (of inner sage in outer place) connected to all watersheds of our sacred (macro) Gaian world. When Time does not 'bind' activity, but offers itself as an inclusive 'frame', open and connectable across all dimensions; when Space does not 'bind' us to a specificity of locale, but offers itself as a vast potentiality of rhizomatically root-known Song, a landscape that 'becomes' as it is up-sung, our opportunities to co-create Love in the sphere of Earth-consciousness are limitless. Of course, Lee Irwin says it so much better. His wonderful book, "Visionary Worlds", holds that our ability to <u>design</u> reality is limited only by our imagination. He coined the expression 'mergence' into the bargain, one I oft-use to describe my experience of the world as an ever-increasingly expansive interactive sphere of 'becoming' – <u>grounded</u> in Love, <u>fuelled</u> by Love:

"Our ability to discover patterns of emergence, of shared correspondences, of the magical links and leylines threaded through <u>all</u> worlds and conditions, opens the horizons of knowledge to an increasingly greater spectrum of possibility (and …) can lead to increasing insight and empathy with all worlds and beings (where …) each individual contributes to the whole."

In the last chapter, I described my entrée to chthonic depths and the work we trialled to 'hold' a laval flame of incarnation steady in Stone Circle. In the same intersect as Time's arrival in through the back door (so to speak), I sat in meditation, breathing through the connection between stellar and earth energies as usual when it spontaneously transmuted from laval to blue flame. This was definitely a startling shift in dynamic.

I sensed the blue flame as a more potent manifestation, yet the crystal pillar of me within remained pure white – radiant with self-Light, comingling incoming stellar, untouched by the change in energy 'emission'. I felt no different, simply abiding, <u>being</u> Mountain, a cone of controlled energy, <u>holding</u> a form to enable a functional remit. But I could see how it now <u>flowed</u> as blue Dragon breath into the world (through leylines Land-Sea-Sky'd) and found it most intriguing. An image arose of geologic bergkristall's formation under the most intense pressure and heat within stone. As a literal translation in English, 'mountain-crystal' is quartz or rock crystal – whether transparent or translucent, it is stunning to behold. I remembered the words I put into the mouth of Ibn Khaldun, a 14th century polymath in "The Taste of Translation" when marvelling at rock crystal vials:

'Look at them!' he says excitedly. 'The scientist al-Biruni was enthralled by this material – crystal fast-frozen within its clay bed. Imagine – water frozen, never to unfreeze!' And indeed, the perfection lies within this unity – the fineness of air fused with the clarity of water.

The alchemy described in this 'fiction' (reflecting what scientists of the era assumed) struck me afresh in this context. Water – Air conjoined to form an 'Ice' (white) 'Rock'; all brought into being when the extreme intensity of (blue) Fire ignites a 'reaction' within Earth (stone) – an Aether-arisen 'visionary world' that should, to all (pure) intents be White at (Mountain) core, and Blue in (harmonically resonant and roaring Dragon) surround.

The Blue intersects and intrigues from my sensed 'holding pattern' of form and function did not end there, however. Several weeks post-Solstice when (post-partnering Time) I was feeling a wee more settled in (stone) skin, I meditated further on these insights, and found a whole stream of Blue'd 'becoming' unravelling (in reverse) along a curve of pre-Ur/Uhr'd Werk. "Awakening" documents, for example, the need to symbolically anchor the 'soul' of home in a blue-green tone that 'merges' forest and sea on living room wall – <u>subtler</u> than turquoise, <u>deeper</u> than aquamarine (whimsically called 'Wishlist'). This sent the rhizome skating decades back to the 'consequent chunk' of aquamarine daily donned at my neck which then shot off to the top of Sydney Harbour Bridge (after a little city-climbing adventure, in tourism-office issued <u>blue</u> overalls no less) where I described to D a bit of 'Blue Mountains' history (to the West), and how its name came into being – from the heat haze of eucalypt oils sucked into atmosphere. Material elements returning to the aetheric whence first come, a <u>visual</u> ring cycle of Song. This brought me back to meeting Sidhe (when I did not know about Sidhe), lighting Song's return to Howe with blue gentians from previous alpine excursions.

Everywhere I turned my attention a spectrum of Blues appeared – on the cards, within the inner sanctum of meditation room, a 'ten-foot-square hut' without equal – as I continued to hold form in Circle. And suddenly I saw no crystal, no surrounding cone of flame. All was Blue which kept extending out from my form, the Circle a micro-membrane of our planetary Blue in space, infilling the whole of hut as an act of 'holding' for Gaia; as an inner grail of garden grail this seamlessly merged with out-of-house Blue or (as a Card Deck Dancer, whose shorthand name is "Beauty", described):

"Material-aethereal; all one and the same in my reality ..."

Quite. And now in mine too! My attention was drawn to the Tibetan Kalachakra mandala on wall, a beautiful artwork containing each aspect of wisdom – spheroid chorten radiant with Light gradually (aetherically) <u>densifying</u> to deeper Blues the further it retreats into cosmic depths, at the same moment touching into Soul's inner-most blue flame'd surround of pure crystal (self-) Mountain. Love uplifted from Being's Ground returned, by us (as us!), in metamorphosed form, its ordered praxis in each direction, horizont or vertical of 5-D'd stave (Time-partnered, Kalachakra'd), fit to universal purpose.

I returned to the memory of Blue Mountains – simply breathing their way through day/night. True-nature'd is their expression of Blue's alchemy, the harmonic resonance of elemental sentience in primal colour, <u>uplifted</u> from FullDark to commence the unfold in space-time from no-space-no-time. <u>Potently</u>

blue, <u>pervasively</u> blue. Infilling the 'gap in script' where I (Time-partner'd) dwell, where I am free the script to write, with dear Amici, for our darling Gaia – Blue. No wonder Song/s (of the Blue) desired more than anything to be written …

JOINING MOUNTAINS

When the "I Ching" tumbled its "Joining Mountains" wisdom out of the bookshelf on a cold Winter's day in late 2014, I could have seen this as a nod of acknowledgement to the mountains I had already ostensibly 'joined' the previous Summer – the 'message stick' of community from a Cold Mountain here (Pizzo Ruscada) delivered to a Cloud-Catcher down under, southern-most outpost to my stretch of HomeSong 'empire'. There, my watcher (Wollumbin in local Aboriginal tongue) watched East across an unending sheet of Pacific (Blue), but equally monitored marked page of continental geography North-South along an 'eastern-sea-wild' coastline; so too West – further and further into the baked Gondwana-brown interior of this 'sunburnt' Land. Just as diligently Ruscada overlit our full stretch of valley terra here, upstream-down, winking in my window of home as readily as any other along thread of gorge; while from the heights his 'watch' reached far in each compass'd direction across Human Time borders regardless of their insignificance to Mountain Time life.

I cannot remember the exact moment when the idea seeded itself in my mind to link these two home-brothers via a walking thread of me as (little) sister. But I do recall it merged Kali's 101 with lessons learnt from Aboriginal Dreaming to form a homespun mini-spider's web in an Annie-becoming 'myth', this self 'stretched' across hemispheric world between two deep-rooted homeplaces. Previously I would feel torn, rent, homesickness keen while boarding a plane, consciously uprooting this 'tree' each time, from each place. A sense of 'always leaving there', I needed to shift the narrative to 'always being here' – no matter which 'here' it was.

The 'snowball' had ramped up its energy of 'becoming' the previous year but, after a serious cyclonic season took out the path to Cloud-Catcher's summit, our pilgrimage instead centred on a multi-day circumambulation of the caldera's rim – the Gondwana World Heritage trek described in "To the Power of Five". Constantly, however, I was aware of his presence. Ever a companionable view onto his knobbly crown spied on horizon, an opportunity to line-of-sight 'speak' my intent – to try again, 'same time next year'. Our walking communion was fit to purpose, I saw. As well as meeting the (stone) elders of Tullawallal wrapt in embrace with ancient Gondwanan trees, now I was more aware of the depth and extent of Mountain root-knowing – old as Time, deep as Tectonia'd memory was its Sink-at-Surface upjumped, its Soul-at-Skin worn. While an 'extinct' plug of an ancient shield volcano that had its last hurrah some 23-million years ago in one respect, I sensed its extant laval Life still rippling subterranean veins of Earth-consciousness, and stretching far beyond what a winking peak would suggest. This laval flow reached as far North as Mother's-Head in whose lee I would (future-)steward a home, and actively partner Sidhe, as documented in "Awakening".

When we finally did manage to deliver Ruscada's message stick to Wollumbin's summit cairn the following Summer, it was clear he had been awaiting outreach as eagerly as I was ready to effect it. Our energy signatures were coming closer and closer into resonance with each conscious re-commitment to intent, and I heard my wee stone of blessing carried in pocket, having already trekked 10,000-miles, also murmur its own "Hello the House" excitedly. The night before our climb, we slept at the foot of the mountain in a small cabin. A blinding presence woke me before dawn in a 'welcome (<u>back</u>) to country'. See, I had made this trek some 30-years past, at a time of no conscious understanding as to why I had been 'called'. Profound was my humility in the moment of such unexpected re-welcome, of the sheer fact of Mountain memory – its intimate knowing of whose energy signature had tramped this path before. Hours later, arriving at summit, I closed eyes in prayer and found myself immediately (surprisingly) tugged down-down-down, into the very heart of his living Fire. Peace, I felt. Ancient Dreaming Peace, he housed. I could have communed a lifetime in this inner 'cave' we shared, such was the resonance of ringing silence, of my sense of <u>primordial</u> homecoming.

But? Purpose fulfilled, stone squirreled, it was time to retrace steps down through birdsong'd rainforest. Along the way my wise stone giant delightedly shared a philosophic conversation about unconscious <u>and</u> conscious 'singing'.

Yes, Joy lives at the core of 'Song', how we express (aka 'sing') our Light in-world, but in interbeing'd co-relation, expressing the 'true nature' of community (Gaian Commons), Wollumbin described how he consciously <u>absorbs</u> each joy-lit 'speck-of-dust' into subtle bones to radiate out in a continuous loop, or 'water-cycle' of Love's Light. Maybe he was taking his 'cloud-catcher' role literally, but the visual analogy offered in conversation worked for my (simple) mind. Yes, I saw the forest's expression of 'joy-in-song', on its own <u>extant</u> behalf as well as that of all Life it hosts, was rooted <u>in</u> and in harmonious resonance <u>with</u> his 'water-cycling' role – the symbiosis of sharing by another name. But his point was that the joy of a recurrent cycle of happy hikers through his domain also (even if unconscious) was ripe for subtle reap.

While my preferred way to 'sing' is quiet, contemplative, consciously prayerful, for example, a child's bubbling laughter, a jogger's concentrated sweat, or the chatter of dreadlocked hippies salt-caked from an early morning surf could be just as generative to the harmonious resonance of <u>this</u> genius loci's elemental sentience when its underlying spirit, like that of Proclus' heliotrope, emanated from the same 'well' of Love's Light. Each trekking his 'spine', whether that day or any day, he held in a cone of embrace, offering each an opportunity to <u>micro-contribute</u> to his macro-water-cycle in their respective way to express Joy. A 'mirroring' moment in miniature, this was Wollumbin's 'take' on how a PeaceSink aquifer fills.

Now, it is eminently possible that the extraordinary strength of resonance I experienced with the mount that day, as expressed in multiple ways, had another precursor on its snowball'd rumble up/down hill than the one alluded to above. The previous week I had similarly found the 'chi of shared circuitry' (mine with enspirited geology) ramp up in an equally extraordinary manner. We had driven 'out West' for some days in a region of known ceremonial Aboriginal use; many thousands of years old was the rock art in these National Park 'galleries', a place where different skin-groups congregated for sacred ritual in the cool of gorge, cocooned from the surrounding dusty western plains by a labyrinthine water-carved network of sandstone.

Hiking happily along one day, 'singing up' country on the way to a particular sacred site I had also visited some 30-years earlier, I recalled how, at that stage, unconscious 'knowing' had led me to this territory and how 'blown away' I had been by all witnessed. Now I shared my joy of return – consciously, mindfully – in the way I 'sang', and spontaneously outreached in physical space to greet a large boulder 'guarding' the entrance to area. My! I have <u>never</u> felt such a charge of conducted energy shoot up my arm. It literally felt like I had put my finger into a live power socket, such was the electric surge recoiling up into my shoulder. Like the friendly mate-ish punch on arm that leaves the recipient saying: "Ow! What was that for?", it seemed I was being 'blown away' all over again!

Yet in my (overwhelmed) surprise, the exhilaration accompanying act cannot be overstated. Reciprocal recognition pure; the strength of Ancestors' 'welcome to country' may have caught me completely off-guard, but perhaps that was the point? Nothing could 'muddy' these waters of communion; no wee Annie-mind was getting in the way of a heart-to-heart meeting between Land and my inner depths. It meant I was suddenly (dramatically!) in touch with the magic held enduringly within hearty healthy robust and weathered stone. Well and truly alive, 'awake' to sacred purpose, aeons of ceremonial 'singing' had embedded a constancy to co-creative Life retained still in subtle bones. And it had no hesitation in sharing such fragrance with little me. With supreme thanks/good grace!

In light of that experience, perhaps my Cloud-Catcher's <u>blinding</u> presence in his 'welcome to country' could be similarly perceived? That with the 'chi of shared circuitry' so heightened, my shared resonance with Land having 'amped up' far further than a normal base-burble of (carburettor) kitten gently purring, I was energetically wide open to receive a 'lightning-flash' hello? Regardless, the most salient fact was of the connection effected – as <u>loving</u> an energetic mountain embrace as I could <u>ever</u> hope to receive, and one which brought renewed Joy at its memory each step of my (silent) singing way to summit and back, through swirled shape-shifting 'water-cycle' mists and more. Indeed is he a brother in the <u>truest</u> sense of word. And since, blissfully, our line-of-sight communion has been seamlessly effected via the constancy of Ruscada's presence either in scape, or in 'Torii''d outreach – physically, subtly.

With that as a longish preamble, let me return to the opening sentence of this chapter – that while the "I Ching"s "Joining Mountains" prompt could be seen as a (hindsight) commentary on that little stretch of community brought into being earlier in year, I did not see it as such. The esoteric in me looked instead for 'inner' mountain clues to mirror its 'superior people' exhortation on back of previous oracular counsel offered. And, not finding any of the latter in this little former, I said a quiet "Hmmm" and popped its inscrutability back on the shelf …

• • • • •

While "Awakening" as a project had connectivity-through-stone as its underlying theme and the need to re-awaken stone to its ancient use as anchor to and facilitator of same (vertical or horizont), I never actively saw my Mountain/s as part of this 'work'. While my connection to Mountain provided me with a (rock-solid) foundation which our Amici partnership could 'tap', to harness the fractal knowing of each 'chip off the old block', Mountain (as placeholder concept) acted more as overlighting 'godfather' to process rather than full-on participant. Yet this was despite our work being 'backed' by a 'crystal mountain' I had seen in Malakut (at the same time the "I Ching" made its remark) which I understood to be symbolic of Gaia's planetary crystal reaching up to comingle with stellar energies.

In the end, what it demonstrates is that there are multiple levels of interdimensional knowing on our spheric diagram of (Mountain) equals. Each 'view' of the whole is partial, just as each view of Mountain is dependent on one's (lowland) perspective, or according to which degree of (compass) overview taken in from (upland) heights. In the moment of "Awakening"s work our attention clearly needed to focus on one tiny bit of one fractal'd sliver of (Sengai's) cake in order to mindfully 'eat' its 'whole' while having a (perennial) cup of tea! In short, not biting off more than we could chew (in between sips of Earl or Lady Grey) – it was our first together-project after all. In this context, a (tasty) piece of cake by the name of 'crystal' was prepping itself for interrogation (or meditative munching); offering an important intersect in our work with 'raw tools', all understandings and reflections thereto were captured in an essay ("Crystal Knowing") published in "Grail Within". Here, however, in respect of "Joining Mountains", Mariel's description to David is a useful starting point:

"Perhaps the image of the crystal with its latticework of nodes and connections is a way to illustrate our differences. You took from our Common Ancestor the capacity to be a node in the lattice, while we took the capacity to form connections ... Together we are the complements that create a whole, living matrix, one capable of singing the energies of the earth back into the places of physical matter and into our world as well."

With the idea of complementary skills that we Cousins of the Commons bring to partnership, I offer another relevant Mountain 'stopping place' from "Awakening"s pages – a beautiful svelte limestone plateau'd peak called, appropriately, Silberen (Silver). As she would continue to feature in our Amici work this time around, let me apprise you of our shared story.

Located in a remote valley two hours' drive from home, our family's first toddle up this hill was a (self-) birthday treat many years past. While officially occurring 'pre-' my partnership with Sidhe, it did postdate, by a couple of seasons, my meeting of 'wee folk'. "The Amici Files" appended to "Awakening" contain this background, including research into the legends of Wildmännli (as they are called). Both delightful and fascinating, a key actor in these tales is Chamois, a species of alpine goat-antelope (caprine); from their milk, Faerie-cheese is made. Receiving a (Malakut) gift of same is a real (and tasty!) treat, while (physically) meeting Chamois in the wild is always special – their reciprocal recognition (or "through your eyes I see myself") connects me into the Sidheverse web of any region I happen to traverse – either as in-herald of presence or shape-shifting Sidhe him/herself (i.e. "through my eyes you see").

Thus chosen, had I, this 'birthday-mount' because of the legends hereabouts, to see what I could 'see', blessing all the while. During the climb, I had mused on her name, Silberen, which brought a notion of starlight to mind. This, in turn, surfaced a memory of the 'Star-Geist' I had seen in Malakut a fair while earlier – an encounter (recounted in "Awakening") during which my interlocutor (who turned out to be MakerMan a year ahead of her arrival in Card Deck) demonstrated how to 'conjure' the Geist (spirit) of a mountain (Berg) so the two could 'take flight' together as 'Star-Geist-Berg-Geist'. I took the memory no further, however, intrigued instead at all the 'new' I was encountering – such a variety of different karst formations, delightful flora microclimates peeking out as we crossed her high wild plateau! Within her depths, meanwhile, elaborate systems snaked, into which only experienced cavers ventured. I pictured Tolkien's "Mines of Moria" (Khazad-dum et al) minus its squealing goblins, grumpy cave troll, and flaming Balrog.

At the summit, it was clear why Silberen was named thus, the plateau like sheet foil reflecting Sun's glory back to the face of Sky. We picnicked in full sight of a chain of snowy peaks to the South, the most inspiring of whom is Tödi with his broad glacial slash. This was another reason I chose Silberen as my treat – to get 'up close and personal' with his majestic hunk of rock. Some years earlier, full hemispheric family complement, including hound, complete (the year of D's two dozen summits), we climbed a mountain in a neighbouring valley to surprisingly find (for me at least) Tödi leaping out of the ground directly before us. As his visage is the 'big bomber' in alpine line-up spied from our village far to the North (admiring his glacial slash burn bronze at Dawn an especial gift on the walk to train), to be so close was simply riveting. I wanted another bite at the cherry and hoped Silberen could offer it. Yes, indeed! Happy birthday, Annie! Picnicking, I connected into the peace-sunk sentience of place, and saw it expand well beyond her boundaries of silvered skin to comingle with all brother-sister peaks and rise as a unified 'force'. Swept up in her 'boundary extension', the resonant hum veritably oozing from each pore, the only words which surfaced for me in the moment were German:

"Im Einklang mit dem Universum."

While its literal translation, 'in harmony with the universe', does not do justice to describing my felt-sense of seamless harmonic resonance, it was all I had. <u>Intimately</u> experiencing the mirror at <u>its</u> work of Joy, as a radiant and shone-<u>through</u> reflection of pure Light, I instantly felt drawn to contribute in Song. Now, this was definitely something new in my 'being-with mountains' repertoire. While my Joy was comparable to the time a scout troupe singing Gaia's praise had me longing to join in (after learning about the dense ball of Earth-consciousness recounted in the chapter, "Der Ruf der Berge"), on that occasion Song presented as energetic waves of Light surging through and spontaneously radiating out.

Now, however, real Song burst from my lips. I could have done a Julie

Andrews, I suppose, but what exploded un-thought from heart was a particular women's yodelling call. Discovered the previous year (as a documentary's signature theme), I had immediately attuned to its evocation of the strength of female energies high wild-encountered; it instantly reminded me of Kali's presence as 'all-woman'. Encompassing, to my mind, an ancient Alpine vocalisation of same, I had occasionally sung it (in the shower) to see if I could 'hit' the high notes, but never felt drawn to publicly attempt it. But in hearing Silberen's 'siren call' from deep within her core express itself as an outward surge of Joy, I instinctively wanted to accompany her soundwave. I flung my arms wide as a first note rushed out to share this group hug with all creation – the extraordinary simplicity and magical wonder of existence in and contribution to our World Soul's expression of her precious Self.

Of course, this was ripe territory for a teen's embarrassment at a mother's weird ways, but over time, D has learnt to cut me a bit of slack on birthdays … The following Summer we returned as full family complement to share this new discovery on our 'Tödi-viewing' map. A lovely day, with other friends joining, we were a gay party chattily moving up the path. It gave me the chance to actively 'dawdle' at the rear of pack, and outreach to lads and lasses with my ritual 'Hello the House' greeting. Soon enough, I came into resonance and words formed:

"*The Sinkholes of Peace.*"

I feigned to see the entry to Faerie amongst the deeply-scored and water-runnel'd limestone slabs, the hidden passageways that hairy-footed Wildmännli took to scurry out of sight of our heavy boots. The connective thread grew stronger all the way. I touched a boulder and immediately tapped into the chi of shared circuitry. Post-summit, we headed down the 'back' way as we had the first time – the route forms a perfect pilgrim's cirque for connecting into the 'Howe'. On this slope Silberen cradles an Urwald (primeval forest) in her skirts, and I came to a place where the resonant hum was particularly strong. The path veered left across a 'land-bridge' between two grotto'd cave entrances but I felt a tug straight ahead, into the 'hollowed' hill itself. Fresh words formed:

"*The Magic of the Mantle.*"

I stopped for a moment to consider this, 'heard' nothing more, continued walking. A simple verse invocation, as if on behalf of as well as energetically aligned to the spirit of Silberen, then arose to the steady beat of my boots:

"*May the magic of your mantle bring the energy of stars streaming here to Earth.*"

In my mind I had connected my affirmation to "wear a mantle of starlight here in the world to bring the energy of the stars streaming to Earth" to Silberen's like 'duty'. A little further on, a female voice suddenly jumped into the midst of the verse and said:

"*Shall we work together?*"

Understandably this stopped me in my tracks. The voice sounded 'Faerie'-pure – a sing-songy lilt 'bouncing' on air. The memory of the Star-Geist surfaced afresh. I picked up a hunk of limestone threaded with the 'Light' of other sedimentary material. Different minerals, fused in shared <u>compact</u>, this would seal our 'alliance' beyond, it seemed, "Awakening"'s closure.

While I had no idea what lay around the corner, I refer the reader back to the last chapter where the Stone Circle's "What now?" seeded emissarial tasks. Specifically, the 'mission' to the Land of Rising Sun, Summer 2016, is implicated here and all the magic, whimsy and synchronicity that journey encompassed. Returned home, having explored as much of Japan as one can within a fortnight at Shinkansen-speed, I fell, seriously flat, back into 'daily life'. Living a Hayao Miyazaki-inspired "Midsummer Night's Dream" (most brilliant anime director <u>ever</u>) was my idea of an endless Shakespearian "Twelfth Night" of joyous triangulated Love (with sacred geology), each MagicMan-instigated comedy of errors included. I felt my loss keenly, especially for Fuji-san (the ultimate pyramidal dude) who personally greeted us as we flew in at Dawn one hot August morn, directly North from southern hemispheric chill over the serene blue of Pacific, as vast in latitudes crossed as it is in any number of longs …

Probably this sense of loss, indeed of <u>homesickness</u> as I described it, was based on the fact it was altogether too brief a time to drink in the fullness of wonders of this extraordinary archipelagic length of volcanic (Dragon-breathed-into-being) terra, or to investigate potential for 'emissarial outreach' to lead to any <u>lasting</u> relations. In advance I had been alerted to a 'line' in the enspirited 'geography' of Japan, specifically Honshu where we would concentrate, like Basho, our 'narrow road' travels. I saw this from above, as if a relief map yet with wilderness densely covering its topographic surface. My (unseen) interlocutor confirmed the line was not a (seismic) <u>fault</u> (or split) in scape but more a connective or bound energetic 'presence' within Land – like a Songline that would intersect our own. Our journey would take us along and through this 'line'. <u>Out</u> of the experience, apparently, I would understand <u>much</u>.

The information was presented in terms of: This is fortuitous; this is intentional – i.e. although not <u>my</u> intent (Japan a 'blank'; we had sought advice from a travel agent), it had come into being of its own 'im Einkang' accord, <u>its</u> energy working to, it seems, fulfil underlying intent. At the time I saw it as speaking to (self-) doubts about doing a 'standard tourist thing' but in the wake of journey, it most assuredly bore fruit. The 'line' revealed itself; being 'torn' from its emerging understanding too soon is what led to my sense of 'loss'. Subtle contacts made, including Sidhe from 'Sunny Side Up Village' (what an adorable name!), were memorable and intriguing; I connected into several landscape 'scripts' centred on Dogen's wise men and sages inwith the 'line', and its Mountain/s Dragon/s (without end), but for the moment, and in the context of this chapter, let me concentrate on Fuji-san.

It is well known the role Mount Fuji has in the national psyche, and how 'natural' it is for Japanese people, even if (to all intents and purposes) they present as rule-bound secular 'salarymen', to meld spirit and geology in their reverence of the mount. The historic <u>culture</u> associated with Buddhism's arrival in Japan is central to this – coming from China infused with Taoist influences, it merged with the older Shinto whose roots were in shamanic indigenous practice. Ceremony is thus part and parcel of daily life – whether in tea-making, rice-washing or tying ropes around sacred temple cedars. Bowing before this perfectly conical peak with a crater for a top-knot is simply the result of aeon'd mythology still <u>lived</u>; circumambulating the crater's eight shrine'd peak is part of this pilgrimage, as well as paying homage to the fiery heart of mount <u>inwith</u> crater, the ultimate 'shrine of the depths', so-called.

It was not our fate to walk Fuji-san's path this time. Perhaps never. Who knows. But the physically relational encounters I had via line-of-sight 'view', sometimes distant sometimes close, using each opportunity to effect blessing, let him 'see' and thus recognise me, came home (somehow!) as 'live memory'. He would pop up in meditation as 'flash vision' of cheery hello but this, paradoxically, had the effect of compounding my sense of being far away from the physical presence of this great being. It was only when I could properly label this sense for what it was ('homesickness') that a remedy jumped out. I needed to treat Fuji-san as a 'node' in my self-grid of home.

Somehow this Land, which was not 'officially' home-turf, spoke as if home turf. And what is 'home', or 'kin', if not honouring one's relations and relationships, drawing the net wide and round to bring all to a shared hearth, wrapt in a group-hug of loving embrace regardless of how we present in skin? Effecting emissarial outreach may have begun our (familial) connection in temporal-spatial intersect, but taken to its logical conclusion, once recognition is reciprocate, clearly we are 'companions' henceforth on Way-of-Love walked. Our network thus exponentially expands as the stretch of Song extends; all filial kin of Gaia's Commons met along the way are invited to share in singing up shared country – each form of sentience (physical or non-) may contribute their loving song to Gaia's 'Land' in a world-wide-high-deep (Third-Rock) band!

I remembered the spiritual <u>inclusivity</u> the Aboriginal Ancestors of W-clan described to me in the Malakut – that in charting a way to the future, the active <u>embrace</u> of learnings from other traditions toward a holistic vision could not be ignored. For me that active embrace centres on, is verily rooted in the bones of Gaia – spiritual inclusivity as geologic inclusivity; the 'round table' hosting (spheric) discussion no more no less than the <u>all</u> of Gaia's Commons. Diagram-of-equals rendering the 'power of five' in 2D, taking <u>any</u> 3D cross-section through the whole, making sure to intersect the 'rim' (of <u>her</u> inclusive Self) 'fans out' an own holistic panorama, in Time-partnered 4D. Walkabout <u>does</u> mean leaving the fold, the known, to experience the new, return with fresh perspective – all in order to better serve Gaia as the Ancestors attested in our conversation. And yes, this little Annie-emissary with her open heart and mind to learn, with subtle gifts of communal spirit to share, was committed to living it. Indeed, in the Land of Rising Sun, had unexpectedly found a fresh 'home-node' opportunity had come home with her, like a souvenir tucked in a memory-drawer of her Library of the Heart.

But how to enliven, maintain the connection in skin? I wandered the grail where I had begun non-local outreach several months earlier. I weeded the River of Enlightenment, swept the garden (any size) as witnessed in each temple visit. In the Zen aspects integrated in advance of journey, we had created a lasting connection to Land. There was nothing more I felt should be added, but it was too 'stretched' and 'diffuse' an energy 'field' for what I had in mind. I needed to discover a specific way to connect with this new-found and (at some level) re-discovered 'big brother', in the same way as with other brother-sisters in stone down under. No 'message stick' existed; no trek to a summit cairn had taken place. Yet I needed to trust it was possible to effect union in line with what I had seen; a note in my journal the week after our return captured it succinctly:

"*Overnight spaces continued the theme of being 'present' everywhere. A scenario involving depth/width/extent of <u>connecting</u> seemingly alpine locales (cowherds) with similar in Japan. Context: Edo-era farmsteads, <u>sunken</u> hearths …*"

I remembered what my 'forgotten valley' said each time I left for return to city'd North:

"*Wherever you are, I'm there too.*"

My Torii gate onto Ruscada's visage may exist physically but I still 'saw' its arched portal in meditation, could connect to Ruscada and, by extension through to my Cloud-Catcher down under, walk and continue to sing a stretch of Song that had come into being <u>because</u> of a map enscripted on heart, a 'line' in the spiritual 'geography' of me …

It was at this exact intersect in thinking-through that, by <u>absolute</u> coincidence, and with supreme thanks to the trees for giving their life for such psychoid unity to be effected, our neighbour at back decided to thin out a section of thick yew along the boundary which had apparently grown beyond its (tall) 'hedgy' intentions. Overnight, our village view at the end of street – of Alps lined up, Tödi as crowning glory – suddenly became my personal window's outlook. Oh my goodness – what a revelation! I had no idea he was there!

From this perspect, Tödi was centrally 'framed' (within window frame). Believe me, Reader, I was <u>never</u> so keen to clean Blake's 'windows of perception' as I was on that surprising day! I greeted this great (local) master, and wrote exuberantly in my journal:

Tödi-san! So clearly revealed these dawning morns ... an opportunity to connect directly with you on behalf of all mountain spirits ... Finally a 'Cold Mountain' literally in direct line-of-sight from this ten-foot-square hut too? What <u>absolute</u> luck!

In hindsight, it was probably my spontaneous use of the honorific 'san' that set the snowball rumbling, intersecting two lines of flight in the rhizome of this brain. Soon enough I was asking Tödi to send blessings on my behalf to Fuji-san through his <u>root</u>-known 'line-of-sight' network. It seemed like the most natural thing in the world – this was 'my' approach to partnering. With a child's innocence, simply a case of 'asking nicely', I reasoned, then stepping back to let the Universe take over. Purity of intent founded on Love's ground was a given – this child just wanted to be a 'big helper' at Mother-Gaia's side with the rest of family.

It reflects how I connect with our Amici crew – 'family' its key descriptor too. A working family, yes – but family nonetheless. All are "Cousins on my Mother's side", as my extended Elven family were once introduced to me, but the <u>core</u> team – swirling, making contact via my 'self-apprenticeship' over the years, to finally fully <u>activate</u> thanks to the work of David, Jeremy, Mariel in bringing the Card Deck to 'life' – is truly nuclear (in each sense of word). I may look back in surprise that by "Awakening"s close, we had organically reached such a familial point of interbeing'd relation from a seeming 'standing-start' (literal in the case of Stone Circle!), but all I can surmise is it was/is helped along by my natural predisposition to find the 'spot of colour' in the other (nested) fish to enable communion and thereby facilitate holistic fusion of whatever (lily white and pure) snowball'd intent we desire to see 'become'.

I may grump at MagicMan's practical jokes but he is the crazy jester brother each team needs. I may stand in awe of MakerMan's choreographic skill, but as an older sister from whom I learn <u>much</u> there is nothing cold or standoffish in our relation. I may feel most connected with my bardic MossMan twin given the centrality of Song to our work, but I will never forget my depths of longer-than relation to VanDiemen'sMan 'backing me' with his love – he with whom I stood looking North (to the Stars) whence we had originally come ...

Now I have cause to wonder – in the spirit of how the expression of familial love can lead to any number of magical outcomes – whether my Amici crew had any hand in our neighbour's 'slash and burn' approach to hedge-trimming? It seems to fit with Mariel's observation:

"Once you set forth your intent, we can blend with the field you create and enhance its capacities to connect and to manifest."

Nevertheless, once again I thank the trees for giving their lives to effect this opportunity, and turn to my (raw) journal notes to describe how such a snowball can grow from an innocent inner-child uplifting her desire for all manner of 'becomings':

It's as if this all happened outwith Time, in the Blue 'gap in script' the poem wrote into existence pre-; my learning to actively embrace this fact, and trust. It's as if my homecome intent is now so integrated into daily life, so embedded as true-natured connectivity, that it expresses itself 'simply' as a harmonium of interbeing within the entirety of Gaia's rhizome. Outwith Time, outwith any specificity of Place. The 'theme' of being present everywhere ... True-natured, it arises – no 'thought' or active 'will'. Love's wei wu wei at its instinctive best. Like walking the dog along the Findling Forest and asking Larches on the meadow above to send greetings down to our 'forgotten valley' in the South. Never forgotten! Likewise, Tödi connecting with Fuji-san does not only generate an experiential connection for each with me, but each with each other – my conscious loving 'wish' brings their direct unmediated interrelation into being. Or where an interrelation (potentially) exists, my continued blessing heightens the resonance flowing through root-known networks of Earth-consciousness. Being 'present' everywhere – deepening, widening, extending ...

Weaving connections not only between myself and sacred spirits of place but with each other on any/all levels, any/all dimensional planes of 'existence' ... It's as if we're helping re-awaken lifelines, rivers of Light within Gaia's full Earth-conscious watershed simply by maintaining a constancy of matter-of-factual loving attention. Something begun with home-nodes, yes ... but when everywhere is home? And everywhen? And everyone/thing? Oh, the Joy of weaving!! My Peace-Love-Light mantra a constant subtext to thought, walk, act; Love naturally pooling in fingertips for release to the All; the thump at solar plexus when in especial 'touch' with an energetic force. Simply dusting. Simply ironing. Simply 'washing the dishes to wash the dishes.' I don't know ... I could go on and on. But it's a different feel this time to homecome from a journey with an intense need to hook a seeming 'non-home' into a home-grid.

What I was describing above was the pervasive harmonic resonance which seemed to carry me through all space/time to arrive at a sense of rootedness in the All, the All of Home. I wondered whether this was an entrée into thinking like Gaia, like a planet. That in emissarial outreach, being a pilgrim for Love through all space/time as 2016 had shaped itself into being, I was becoming more attuned to Gaia's fullness? No clue. But it felt transitional, and on the back of Time's counsel (see introduction to this section), a mite concerning with its seeming 'preface' to a next stage of rollercoaster'd work. I was grateful, therefore, when a poetic text arose from Soul-depths to hold my hand through this process of (major) becoming:

Trust. In the Pure Land,
the Steady Hand, in the
Small Boat afloat on a
(sometime) tranquil sea.
Outwith Time. Alone with the Alone.

Walking sailing singing. This is me:
A life's true-natured being.
And this life simply Yours …

Each time a 'fear-of-the-unexpected' or 'what-if' moment surfaced over all days months years since, this self-text continues to strengthen (my) Mountain resolve to keep door of heart fully open, to always look straight into the face of come-what-may. Each phrase is underlain by a bunch of (inner) reference points, but as a 'whole' I am sure its meaning is clear to the reader. But, you may wonder, where is the physical connection that seemed so necessary to my sense of interconnectivity, to effecting psychoid unity? The (window) sight-line began the process, yes, but now? My birthday (again) loomed. And the Amici popped in with a suggestion of what 'berg' we could venture up. But before anyone thinks I am a serious alpinist capable of doing a Messner on a mammoth rock-ice giant, it was not Tödi himself.

During Stone Circle ceremony of ongoing alignment at Autumn Equinox which, as previously mentioned in-heralds 'birthday time', I received an unexpected visit from the Wildmännli of Silberen with an invitation to come visit on the weekend. I saw their Sinkholes of Peace, and while scanning terrain also saw – up in the heights, on glacier-smoothed plateau where we had picnicked in full sight of Majesty's bowl – their actual 'village' home. Such a surprise! It constellated as an apartment block several stories high, extending at least 10-15 individual balconies wide along the front. Stepped back into slope, each was painted either snowy white or glacial blue in a pretty chequerboard pattern. Imagine: Each little railed verandah with a most-brilliant view onto Tödi et al. How wonderful a treat this would be with (Enso) birthday cake and thermos'd PeaceTea! Being a (benevolent) H5.0 world, the weather gods decreed stunningly perfect hiking conditions for our Malakut visit to be physically realised. The journey began pre-Sun's peek over horizon – Moon's waning crescent, Sirius' chatty radiance, Orion still high. The whole distance I intoned:

"You magic-mantled mount; know that we come, with love in heart, blessings on tongue to Hello your gracious House. Tödi-san, Fuji-san – all through Silberen-san!"

The valley where we left the car two hours later was still in shadow when we began to climb – Sun hidden behind the ridgeline. I had not realised, on previous excursions, that the path tracked East to crest summit. Literally it would be like walking through the Card Deck's Gate of Rising Sun – to Tödi-san, Fuji-san, all facilitated by darling Silberen-san! My amazement did not end there, however. Arriving up top, I realised this view onto Tödi exactly matched that of my (now-revealed due to tree-lopping) 'window on world' at home. It meant Silberen must also (lowly) be in line-of-sight. No wonder Wildmännli could directly deliver their invitation; no wonder this presented as an opportunity for physical skin-to-skin connectivity!

In remarking this, I also saw a physical 'loch' (hole) in the next ridge over; it intersected the valley below Silberen's heights – something not previously 'seen', as I had always been too intent on revelling in Tödi's forever-snowy crown. Now I saw how this giant 'rose' up behind the ridge – the view, through this massive hole in (lowly) ridge, entered the base of his rock-mantle'd hide. Here was root-knowing's actual sight-line to Tödi drilled (literally) through skin, the loch like a 'gap in script' enabling a direct line from my home, even if 'un-seen', to stream Love's Light on and through. This may not seem interesting to the reader on first observation, but the twig on consciousness arose not only from the geologic 'geometry' of equation but the language which described it, 'loch'. In German it means hole, cavity or void; in Scots-Gaelic a lake – in-Land or Sea-linked. In pronunciation, 'loch' is close enough to 'lock' to evoke the twin sense of a locking mechanism on door/gate, as well as the enclosed 'chamber' in a canal for vessels – an 'air lock' (cavity) being similar for entry/exit between 'differential' zones.

In the context of the word presenting to describe what I saw (i.e. it spoke itself in German), its intent was to bring portal and security considerations to my attention together with 'flow' as evinced by the word's (Scots) use for bodies of water. The most important aspect, however, was it revealed a physical form charged with alchemically-elemental function. Whatever Light 'streamed' via this continuum of home, Silberen, Tödi-san and Fuji-san negotiated this portal as a necessary 'loch/lock' (a 'transformer substation' if you like) in the Earth-conscious script of enspirited geology. Bateson's 'transforms of difference', too, a relevant analogy here.

In any case, I was 'seeing' this (now) for a reason – a portal'd 'gap' was key to how the energy of place worked. With the Card Deck's 'Gate of Rising Sun' as its direction on compass'd grid, MakerMan its steward, it is obvious who choreograph'd 'loch' into my mind. Nevertheless, in the moment I put all this on a pending pile in brain to return to my profound excitement of being-with Tödi-san, on my special day, at the express invitation of local Sidhe! I called out:

"You tell Fuji-san! You tell him I brought Genmaicha in Kirin's Rich Green Tea bottle today for a tea ceremony of especial blessing! You tell him that we honour the thread as sung into being and have strung the thread further now between home and Silberen and you – direct line of sight all the way through to him! You tell him this 'line' is live with our Love, and full-bound to the 'line' I saw in his Land!!"

Sinkholes of Peace greeted us at every turn that day. An emissary was sent to 'guide' our way: Chamois. During picnic, dotterels – four of them, each fleet and light of foot – appeared from amongst the limestone, camouflaged in her silver-grey heights. Like tiny kodama (tree spirits) from Miyazaki's Mononoke, they scurried, stopped, scurried, stopped – were we following? Faeries-in-feathery-form, magicking mantle beneath winged feet, they tugged my attention away from Tödi-communion where I suddenly saw …

… the whole <u>sweep</u> of limestone coming in from North-East. From Silberen herself I saw <u>back</u> to Säntis (he of 'I'll hold your back' fame in "Awakening") and the Churfirsten (Seven-Sisters of ancient lore whose mid-point-mount, Brisi, was the Malakut locale for Star-Geist's arise and which I had climbed the previous year in honour). From this perspective, I saw the entire Alpstein (as the region is known) as a <u>stunning</u> River of Light trailing South-West to where I sat on Silberen's wide stellar-shone-through plateau, acting like a broad-as-breaching-whale 'radio telescope' receiver and transmitter in one. A big 'dish' (in astrophysics vernacular) which, at some level, I intuited the first time atop her heights with her 'mirroring' and 'encapture' function. Again, no wonder this was the place to anchor the 'call'; no wonder it was here that I heard:

"*Shall we work together?*"

Oh, my gosh! You lucky lucky <u>lucky</u> Wildmännli to live here, Disney-whistling while you work together with so many magnificent 'Gipfels' (mountain peaks) in your inter-stellar'd sight! I spread arms wide, hugged the Universe, and in this <u>sheer</u> space of Sidhe-infused whimsical Joy, lifted up the piece of picnic chocolate I had been nibbling before any dotterals got busy with attention-seeking behaviour. A family tradition to carry a bar in backpack for ritual handing round the weary team in celebration of 'summiting', in self-whimsy asking:

"*Can I have a Gipfel Chocie for every Gipfel I see? Or only the ones I climb?*"

We trekked across Siberen's broad back before commencing our descent; my yodel silent this time – I wanted to send it deep into Earth-consciousness not out into cosmos. Along a 'spine' of ridgeline, I stopped to make my offering into a moss (pillow) crevasse below crest. Shells lifted from my 'eastern-sea-wild' shores, blessings of shared community, these message-sticks a gift of Love all the way from 'Source-to-Sea'. I continued, and suddenly spotted at my feet was an own gift in return. A perfect silver-white feather, sublime as snow, no mark of ancillary colour to disturb the purity of moment (or intent). I could not believe it! F must have walked right over the top of it without 'seeing' and/or it only materialised for my 'sight'? And F the 'ornithologue' always on the look-out for his elusive snow grouse? (Ptarmigan, we call them.) I laughed out loud at MagicMan's wit and brought home this best-of-bestest birthday gifts to rest on altar in my ten-foot-square hut, a temple which, like Mariel's, is "one of substance and energy" – a <u>sacred</u> meeting place for a <u>working</u> family that lives, breathes, loves in plain interdimensional sight, now with a memory-marker as fitting as <u>any</u> for a Star-Geist's flight …

• • • • •

As previously described, Gondwana (Dreaming) found me before I was (consciously) aware of having found her – here, in small landlocked Heidiland, with its 'peace sunk deep in settled stone'. Once she said: "Listen," however, things proceeded apace that (2016) year. Yet it was still a shock when we were commissioned with a specific action – to plant a PeacePole in the volatile Body of United States in the lead-up to presidential election. The story is shared in full in "Grail Within" ("Crystal Knowing", a reflective essay on the centrality of raw 'rock-ice' to our praxis) but the model, for an UrWerk requiring global outreach, was (to all intents and purposes) piloted in this (subtle) version of first-responder action.

As I sat in meditation with no 'thought' a few days before the 'big day', I heard the Angel of America cry out. In the moment, the genius loci named herself Liberty; she was hurting, badly, with all the divisiveness in her 'shed'. No sooner had I connoted this than Helvetia entered the meditation, said: "Go. Go now." With no idea what was required, how it would unfold, or how 'I' could help, I 'flew' out from Source – the only way I knew, East, across the Pacific, my homecome Sea. And once the Pacific crossed, the only place to go was Mountain. Rainier, I chose, Pacific North-West, a 'fire-lord' like my brothers on western rim. I offered a <u>crystal</u> totem, aetheric-<u>fractal</u> of Helvetia's peace-sunk heart in garden grail, into his (active) volcano.

I saw it ignite, burn, flare. The pole stood strong; neither wavering nor disintegrating, staying firm, receiving his fire, transmuting it to liquid Light to flood Liberty's shed, bring healing to her wounded Soul. On the homecome way, I flew to Fujisan to 'anchor' this act by planting another pole, then South to Wollumbin. Ditto. Like tent pegs pounded into the ground, on a stormy windy night, with guy ropes strung between, taut-held in check despite the blustery (Stateside) conditions, a triangulated 'Rütlischwur' (sacred oath) between three Brothers of Flame, root-known to each other under deep oceanic crust, stretching across 'pacific' waters.

I reflected on 'why' these nation-rooted Presences shared such deep unthinking enduring 'brotherhood'. Mr1300BC arrived for a chat, pushing my focus from Human Time to Mountain Time, that of tectonic kinship rather than neighbourly (or not) geo-politics. And then pushed me deeper still – to the space where these genii locorum, in <u>pure</u> compassion, Love at heart of <u>their</u> unmediated Earth-consciousness, <u>huge</u> micro Beings in the fullness of Gaia's macro, were outreaching <u>through</u> a shared (ocean) puddle, one they <u>rimmed</u> in fire, and one which did not operate in hierarchies of 'power' but according to <u>interdependencies</u> of spirit and intent, geology and geography, all on a 'pacific' plane of consistence. This was the vast extent of realm, of Dogen's Mountains and Dragons where I had to date (to put it politely) only been "looking through a bamboo tube at a corner of the sky":

"*Eastern mountains master travelling on water. Accordingly, these activities are a mountain's practice ... (this) is the <u>bones</u> and <u>marrow</u> of the Buddha Ancestors. All waters appear at the foot of the eastern mountains ... Walking beyond and walking within are both done on water.*"

Eastern mountains, through the Gate of Rising Sun, offering their loving practice via the water which appears at their foot – this Pacific daughter of primal Mother who first cloaked Gaia's luscious body some four billion years past, whose name bespeaks the harmonic resonance implicit in our precious Blue. I needed to remember the diagram-of-equals (Mr1300BC said) – here in plain sight was the 2D rendering (of planal 'map') through which <u>any</u> cross-section intersecting rim offers the potentiality to fan the whole of its knowing out (3D) where Time can enter the equation, manifest this 4D 'event'. The specificity of this alchemic action, on PeacePole emissarial mission, had (at <u>its</u> genii locorum'd core) the desire to re-harmonise the resonance of elemental sentience being tipped out of balance on Human Time's watch via crystal forged at Mountain heart delivered through Dragon jade waterworld:

"*Water is the true dragon's palace ... Water is water's complete virtue.*"

The waters of limitless Pacific facilitated our action/s as surely as the strength of eastern mountains walking their bones and marrow beyond and within. I meditated in the Circle, found myself on a terraced bank watching a lad below use a machine to smooth an 'earthen' path or channel. It was one of those noisy hand-held pounder thingeys – a mini-steamroller, I suppose. He noticed me, looked up with intense blue eyes and tousled blonde curls around a fresh young 'worker-energy' face. He needed big earmuffs to block the sound, yet smiled. With thanks to his selfless Amici service, this trench would allow our liquid Light to flow – East through the Gate of Rising Sun. Oh, my mountain brothers looked adorable in their protector-energy 'suits', constellating as golden samurai – armour-sheathed, silver-sword'd. It pressed so many Sidhe-whimsy buttons, yet their serious dedication to task clear since the start.

In the midst of all this, I was approached by a group I know as the 'Rugby Sevens', asking me to 'sing' with them <u>again</u>, as if this shared action a specific 'performance' in which they had participated but another loomed, a 'new' song for which I did not (yet) have a song sheet. The approach took place in a huge congress locale – many round tables and participants, people milling as if between sessions, a subtle 'United Nations' to all intents, an assembly of all actors helping in whatever (form-functional) capacity they could to moderate <u>and</u> modulate the situation State-side. The Rugby Sevens, I knew, emanated from the mountains of Hong Kong. Fuji-san must have called them in. I had no idea how they would physically constellate, having never visited the area, but understood they acted as a 'back-up line-out' along full western Pacific rim for any troublesome situation at his 'Gate of Rising Sun' (as a fan of rugby, the symbolic connections fit; again, I appreciated the effort to make translation easier!). In short, they were tasked with ensuring defences went unbreached no matter what.

It was during a break in congress proceedings that the team captain came over from his table to ask me. He was pure rugby physique (solid, boofy, bald head); when I looked to his peers, all were likewise statured. Robust lads. I apologised; I did not know the words to this 'new song' but from his point of view this presented no problem. I would receive a song sheet, and my 'vocal performance' would be clear. He seemed confident I would need no rehearsal and be able to dive straight in. I joined him to greet the team – all were mountain 'bodyguards' in a sense; joining us was a woman from a different table whose 'energy signature' also fresh to me. We made small talk; like me, she did not know the drill, but we agreed we could manage – graciously accepting their invitation to contribute, now awaiting our song sheet of the 'new'.

Another of our Amici actions was to clear muck from 'The Narrows', so-called, to assist flow. Everything I had learnt in self-apprenticed Light-work, flowing liquid Light out from Mountain source through Dragon river of my 'pure' (peace-sunk Helvetian) shed was able to be put into practice as a cleansing operation. Within the slim squeeze of (this) gorge, the muck of thought forms, fears and conspiracy theorists was stuck; parasitic dark energies could easily squirrel themselves into these festering backwater pools to grow, multiply, block an entire system of arteries of Love's Light through world or shunt their hate through living leylines of Earth-consciousness to taint the purity of other locales. We handled this via 'filtration' grasses – bundles of organic matter in different colours and textures assembled in a variety of mixes according to need. Like sea grasses which cleanse and re-oxygenate waterways, to relieve the psychic 'pollution' here we added them to gorge sites to trap dense matter, negativities, from continuing their flow downstream through watershed, in an effort to neutralise and gradually dissipate impacts of and in 'The Narrows'. Only liquid Light could traverse the grasses, filtered and untainted, pure in the healing it brought all the way from Source to Sea.

This was hot and sweaty work! At last I was on a metro 'home'. The train quite full, standing beside me hanging onto a toggle was the big bald leader of the 'Rugby Sevens'. He too was looking forward to going home to sleep. A tough day at work but still happy, serene, upbeat. Our service rewarding in and of itself. We would meet again when the 'new songsheet' was ready, and yes Reader, here we are …

To conclude this 'Pacific' tour, let me say that while I am not one to study earthquake activity around the world there was a moment, with Gondwana's presence ever-hovering, I had a few niggles about my learning of subtle plate tectonics. We had concluded our active support, yes, but a couple of days later I had occasion to wonder if anything would ever be enough to support this transition in the Americas when the literal 'ripple effects' of everything occurring that Stateside November re-crossed the Pacific in sub-terra form – viz. earthquakes striking off the coasts of New Zealand and Japan. The impacts could have been much worse, in sites of greater human habitation during daylight hours, but I will never forget the quote from a NZ local describing the 'witching hour' sensation he experienced during this complex two-minute geologic dance:

"It felt like sleeping on a waking dragon."

Being 'Middle-Earth', no doubt Smaug was on his mind. But in the moment, I understood that the forces of Earth-consciousness were doing their best to absorb these 'shocks' to our entire planet's energetic system, shocks unleashed by an intense fracturing of State-side psyche. Mountain brothers, Rugby Sevens and Gondwanan DeepTime had stayed their watch to smooth the colicky babe's coverlet as best they could. With thanks/good grace, we all work within our sphere of influence. Amen ...

• • • • •

Finally it is time in this chapter to take up the main narrative line in the general territory of "To the Power of Five's" conclusion where, about a fortnight prior to Spring Equinox 2017, in early March, eight mounds of 'dark knowing' were (subtly) delivered to garden gate. Their arrival intrigued me but (fortunately) it did not take too long to connote purpose. In the previous month, much had happened on Malakut front; when seen in context, I realised each mound 'housed', in its own discrete 'earthen' container, a reservoir of wisdom still 'dark' in knowing – of itself as much as a potential role it could play in relation to our work.

So, what had been happening the previous month?

As preface, let me say that I work closely with the energies of Moon. While I have generally kept my monthly practice in sync with hers down the years according to 'snowballs' which desire to 'become', it was only when invited to participate in the Amici's 'Red Lady' eclipse party, end-September 2015, that I began to actively engage her as a partner-presence in our work. That eclipse, of course, coincided with my meeting of Helvetia – within the beating heart of her Mountain – and the subtle communique re 'lighting' stations across the world.

In the wake of eclipse, more of Moon's 'lineage' was shared – including her Sister'd relation to Gondwana (which Gondwana later confirmed). Over the years I have also had the privilege to meet a community of subtle presence residing within her 'catchment' whose chief role is to energetically 'bless' Gaia and with whom the Sidhe work in close collaboration. And, as recounted earlier in the text, I often find myself 'out' with Moon to observe Life on Earth. In short, it is a salient perspective for connecting with the all of the All from a zone of much 'motherly' Love and nurturing patronage for the continued evolution of Gaia's wondrous self.

Indeed, I cannot stress highly enough how important Moon's role is to supporting Earth-consciousness – one which fits a 'model' of faerie-godmothering. While Gondwana the sister 'underlighting' the full evolution of Gaia's crystalline and radiant core from a space of DeepTime-Tectonia'd planetary 'birth', and Kali the sister 'whip-whirling' elemental alchemy in its creative dance of 'change' through spheric space-time, Moon acts as a serene 'overlighting' sister – setting a rhythmic metronome for all inwith Gaia's membrane to find their harmonic resonance, re-settle into new forms and patterns of being, find their 'homecome' place. Her tidal push/pull, wax/wane integral to process – she and Sun an intimate mirroring <u>intentional</u> team in the cyclic dance to nurture Life <u>inwith</u> the Life of Sky Child, Gaia, herself 'homecome' to Earth. Moon's geologic age is crucial here – forged in the same heart-fires as Gondwana, her task of spinning 'overlight' has thus offered a steady percussive pulse to Earth-conscious process over all the aeons since Time (here) began.

Once I decided to fly up to Moon for a 'no-occasion' visit, just to be-with her loving self, 'lifting' myself steadily higher into her fullness. A real delight, for as I drew closer I saw her 'colours' – wondrous! They mirrored those of Winter mountains – black-greys to silver-whites with the palest of pink-blues swirled in and about, like a Swiss pre-dawn when Sun just beyond horizon begins to soft-wash-prepare Sky for the day ahead. Yet here colour was <u>embedded</u> in Moon's form as a <u>constancy</u> of praxis, surprising me, but the message clear – I was seeing <u>into</u> her subtle geologic substance, her stone sentient mirror to Earth in all (their) <u>shared</u> colours. The experience was brief but very lucid. Flying closer, I found myself on 'approach'. Here the colours, shape, <u>form</u> of her mantle exhibited <u>nothing</u> of the craters or mute greys we are so used to seeing. Suddenly the thought arose: Oh, I need to 'land' somewhere. But where? At this I observed, looming, a 'Tree of Life'. A huge Apple Tree, full-leafed, laden with ruby ripe fruit, lay prone on the ground – i.e. <u>flush</u> with Moon's <u>flesh</u>. Here I could land, greet Moon, and engage her 'gardening' community.

Moon acts as 'base camp' for a vast array of subtle and Sidhe activity in which I am blessed to participate with Amici. Gathering the 'threads' of Light (deep wisdom trails offered by Elder-Beings throughout solar system and wider galaxy), moulding and shaping these to 'digestible' form (an alchemical proposition – see my previous discussion in "To the Power of Five") for delivery on and into Gaia's realm; different tasks are performed according to a monthly (and annular) Moon-cycle regimen – seeding, anchoring, ripening, harvesting (thus mirroring the seasons) includes the requisite incubatory or fallow days during her 'Dark' (when we are busy on 'composting duties'). While our Amici work is necessarily in-world, shifting that first incarnation of the Blue, 'planting' its (now-digestible) Light in Gaia's flesh, it is always fun to go visit and help out at 'Moon Mother's community' when the opportunity arises.

The month prior to our eight mounds arriving at garden gate had been Moon's New Year. Lunar celebrations principally celebrated in Asian traditions, this year our Amici Imbolc ritual – honouring the Celtic goddess, Brigid, spirit of hearth and home – came hot on its heels. Both have as intent the in-herald of Spring, 'seeding' the new, hence a focus on clearing out 'stale' energy at home. With the Celtic calendar backboning my (solar-inflected) 'indigene' practice, and my 'nearness' to Eastern philosophical perspectives as well as Sidhe connectivity to Moon directing me lunar, no wonder our Amici crew 'Spring-cleaned' in material and Malakut alike!

Latter tasks expressly focused on our village 'in a forgotten valley' – F happily hacking into our (subtle) 'green room' while I helped prep party locale in a meadow very 'close' to Sun. I should have realised something loomed to centre activities there rather than garden grail here. This is "The Amici Files" territory – my self-apprenticeship with Light-work, Acqua Termale's source, WolfMother's shed, and latterly Gondwana's 'upjump' from Ruscada's tectonic folds. I should also have realised something was afoot when we noted an Amici 'neighbour' pruning a huge apple tree against his wall. Not only were branches toppling onto our shared stone 'path' but I saw the tree had, in its exuberance, sent out roots in amongst the stonework of steps, including a fresh seeder trunk materialising through the wall. The interconnectivity of this space with Moon's 'garden' work was ripe for interrogation. But I wasn't thinking along those lines – yet. It was party time. And I needed to help another dear Amici hoist her 'melon' trees atop a pergola so they would not disturb the guests beneath. Apparently it would take ten years before she would reap her first harvest. Isn't Gaia's subtle ecology fascinating? There is so much we can learn!

Meanwhile, in material space, I busily cleared out the ten-foot-square hut of all 'surplus' accoutrements. Surplus, in they were still treasured memory-markers, but sitting in a drawer of altar cupboard went unengaged. Looking through these I noted all were relatively robust and decided to shift them to garden grail, either e hung from the withered crone-like branches of TreeMother or arranged in the mulch at her base. In the process I noted all emanated from my (or F's) binding to past continental energies – mine the Americas (latterly re-engaged via Helvetia's 'first-responder' action) and F's African (latterly re-engaged via the arrival of a new son to the fold, R – life-partner to daughter, H). In handling and connecting with the memories these tokens housed, I entertained a whimsical thought:

"If the grail connects me, via symbolic interlocutors, through to home places and other lands emissarily engaged, what possible connection via memory trail or meditative

process rather than physical contact?"

The thought stayed where it was; I went back to cleaning. But in the wake of Imbolc celebs, in deep HMed (shorthand for 'horizontal meditation', a Pythagorean 'incubation' technique) one day a very abstract visioning scenario spontaneously presented. Repeated over and over, it involved sheets of white paper, blank, large. As if wrapping paper, but thick and strong. I saw myself busily take each sheet as it 'materialised' from the Void to lay on top of the last. At the same time, I had something (not visible) which I wrapt before a next 'set' of paper (similarly enclosing something) was stacked on top. I called these 'acts' – each its own 'thing', with its own set of wrapping paper, in a pile. I wondered what I was up to. The only word which arose to describe the practice was: 'Accumulating.' At this, I found myself on a ship; it seems I had been working on these acts down in the hold – literally 'below decks'. I returned to my cabin. Following me was a dwarf who flopped down, absolutely tuckered out. Hovering while I was at task, now he could relax too. A dear gnomic friend, I looked closely at how he constellated – this could give me a clue to our 'acts'. It was a real Caribbean look, even down to his reggae-rasta hairstyle. In any case, he must have been super-cold, because he had assembled as much warm gear as he could find here – purple slippers from the cupboard, a funky hoodie dressing gown from across the hall, a thick grey beanie from downstairs. I said: "You warm enough yet?" This fortunately elicited a grin. He looked absolutely adorable, the gown so big it covered his little hairy Wildmännli feet – most practical in the circumstances!

Another symbolic activity spurred on by this Spring-clean energy was my consumption of the last dregs of pure water sourced from Helvetia's heart – a litre bottle filled from the mineral spring that rose within the Sasso san Gottardo fortress had returned home with us from the small visitor centre at its entrance 15-months earlier. The day after Imbolc, a particular grail-like goblet (of blue glass) which hosts 'Faerie-wine' at each Amici ritual suddenly spoke:

"Fill me with the purity of your intent, the purest of pure."

I knew it meant the Sasso water whose desire to intersect these 'acts' wrapt in lily white. But beyond? No clue. Following, I saw myself writing yet had no 'knowledge' of content. However, someone had been in, added to the work, writing a sentence in amongst mine in a different coloured pen. All the time I heard water flowing and twigged: Our task was to attach a tap to the pipe to access this flow. Later I sat with Amici family and looked at my 'hairy' (Amici) feet. I thought: Oh, that's growing well! A 'brother' served porridge, rimmed in <u>blue</u> potato mash – whatever I was up to would need good basic 'food-as-fuel'. Things were bubbling to the surface of consciousness, but when would they 'break ground'?

While hindsight is a wonderful thing to sort through the many clues resting amongst Malakut bedclothes (still) lying in a mussed mess in the wake of our Liberty action, it came together in Mind's (simple) conscious world when I found myself performing a task for Sky-Father. This Presence was introduced to readers of "Awakening"; at chapter close, his godfatherly history will be shared, but for the moment let us stay with the task.

By now we are at Moon's Full a fortnight following her New (Year) when, typically, causes and conditions ripen for some welcome 'illumination' to the puzzle. Initially the space constellated as a 'new' home working environment. It overlooked a huge lake within a cirque of mountains offset by crystalline and glacial blue sky. We could access the lake directly from a wide terrace-cum-pontoon jetty over the water off a full glass-fronted 'inner' living space. I understood this to mean the water 'belonged' as part of our space; no border in-between. Our home was not the only one on lake, though; strung out either side were 'connected' spaces; circa a dozen. A high dam wall (unseen) flanked its far shore. This was a shared facility, and an 'entity' was responsible for keeping the lake brimful, 'in-pumping' from the surrounding shed, because its primary function was as a 'receiving' mirror for incoming stellar energies.

Here, my work of 'mirroring Joy' to infill Helvetia's PeaceSink was implicated; now I saw how this work intersected Moon's at her Full – serene and brimful, receiving all of Sun into herself to mirror Joy on and <u>into</u> Gaia, thus filling a font with 'liquid Light' for sharing out into world. Within the scape, the lake's surface mirrored the <u>stillness</u> of everything 'arising' from its own 'depths' – Land <u>and</u> Sky. A pure H5.0 expression of cosmic connectivity. I 'heard' the rhythmic metronome at work – back and forth, each mirroring 'event' doubling the last, tuned to the constancy of pitch pipe at ear-of-heart. The harmonium's function was fully revealed in this form, sheer equipoise of planal 'sphere'.

A <u>settled</u> proposition, I was later to learn, for once established, energised <u>and</u> inducted to aligned purpose, a whole squad of 'pit crew' would maintain this framework of 'intervention' on our UrWerk's behalf, serving the 'entity' with responsibility for the reservoir. Thus was the micro-macro proposition. It put me in mind of an "I Ching" wisdom gifted many years ago during my (so-called) 'seven years in the wilderness'; as part of my practice, I was handed a wood-planing tool and had set up at a stretch of Wall to gradually thin the veil between the worlds till returned to a shared original pristine and holistic scape – minus Wall. "The Amici Files" contains this self-parable but when the task was first assigned, I asked the "I Ching" for clarification.

Well, either MagicMan was doing a tricksy hover even that far removed in my dim dark past or Mr1300BC has a funny bone after all because my question: "What is my task at the Wall?" returned the wry answer: "Reduction". Well, obviously! The text fortunately expanded on his droll remark with:

"What is the use of two bowls? They can be used to receive. Mountain (still) above lake (joyous). Rejoice then still it!"

"Ah! Alles klar!" (as they say in German). Reminded now, I saw how the Water-Cycle of Love's Light, Ring-Song'd as Joy operates as subtle and physical 'twins'. Mountain receives in its bowl (aka source, spring, well); Lake receives (twice) in its own – from the <u>flow</u> of Mountain's source (out) and from reflecting Mountain's <u>being</u> (still). Two bowls infilling selfsame PeaceSink – the knit of spirit/geology in stillness of Joy <u>mirrored</u>. All the while the metronome tick-tocks back-forth, steadily, and Moon smiles beatifically in her contribution to the circular economy of Gaia's 'Ecology of Light' (in completely fit-to-purpose functional form).

To find myself in this 'new' home working environment was quite a profound affirmation and extension of practice in itself. But then Sky-Father arrived. There were a bunch of tasks where he needed my support but the one I concentrated on in the moment was letter-writing. Now, these were 'business-style' – nothing to do with core family. He had received correspondence from various entities, my task to respond on his behalf. Everything went FullDark; when next 'conscious', I was at a post office counter with several large packets which were sent off after a bit of a kerfuffle, but all good. On leaving the space, I felt the world 'shift'.

This was <u>very</u> pronounced. The only other times I have experienced such sensation is during a couple of (relatively minor) physical earthquakes – a 'whooosh' of <u>movement</u> that has nothing to do with 'air' nor coupled to an ancillary rumble or rattle of physical artefacts to disturb the purity of <u>its</u> expression. In the complete <u>stillness</u> of moment, there is only the 'shift'. In this Malakut post office the 'shift' was greater but still 'sourced' from a like space of Earth-consciousness. I felt myself lean 'into' a non-existent slope to retain balance. No one else in post office had remarked it. Two things came to mind: The letters I had posted had something to do with Gondwana and subtle plate tectonics, plus Dawn of Time's pavilion was somehow involved.

Within a day the rhizome took off in earnest. The whimsical thought out in garden grail about connecting other Lands via <u>memory</u> trails intersected Gondwana's 'underlighting' role on sacred physical plane with Moon's (joyous lake) 'overlighting'. As sister 'memory keepers' of Gaia's DeepTime-Tectonia I could engage both in this 'new' home working environment. This synapsed line-of-flight then flipped to the continents breaking up, a geography assignment (complete with working model) I had helped D with years earlier where I (and he) learnt quite a bit about earthquakes along fault lines and the whole ocean 'subduction' bit. A (self-) quantum leap took me to how this operated as a slip/slide motion. Bingo! There went the lightbulb. Sky-Father's letters were to genius loci 'memory keepers' on <u>each</u> continent to kick-start the creation of a 'nodal' web of entry points (in an "all-of-Gaia-is-home" macro-sense) we could manifest in micro-garden grail. At that point I cried halt: "Slow it down, guys. I am only a small human. And this is for our Equinox ceremony? Hmmm." Word formed:

"*Thinking Time.*"

Exactly. However, this was also a reference to a decades-old favourite in our indie-rock family song sheet, "Closing Time", whose closing line is:

"*Every new beginning comes from some other beginning's end.*"

Exactly. However, now the rhizome kicked me back to the 'close' of Time shared in the subtle communique 15-months earlier (its 'seed' Sasso-water'd by this stage) where the lighting of 'stations', while needing to be done before Time 'extinguished', also needed to be conducted slowly, moderately, methodically. Hence, we were back to?

"*Thinking Time.*"

Exactly. There was no way something of this magnitude and complexity, an UrWerk of loving outreach across the full 'stretch' of Gaia's HomeSong could be achievable in a single Equnioximage ritual earmarked for five (short) weeks hence. This 'snowball of becoming' needed tempering and considered <u>thought</u>. Nevertheless, I felt the <u>thrilling</u> desire of each member of our Amici crew rippling through my starblood veins to honour Sky-Father's patronage <u>and</u> intercession, to attempt this 'new' beginning from our previous beginning's 'end'. I wondered, though, how I was going to 'psychoid unity' this – merge the spirit-geologic equation to facilitate harmonic resonance of elemental sentience across a full plane-of-Gaia 'diagram of equals'. Having seen, in subtle communique, on-Earth 'nodes' effect <u>triangulation</u> with in-between central 'cruxes' to intersect stellar energies, I realised our support of such work could be a more than relevant continuation of "Awakening"s project, partnering "Sidhe, Star and Stone" (with little me). It spoke to the true <u>depths</u> of what we 'Cousins' could effect, as Gaian <u>citizens</u>, in concert with Earth's role in full 'Cosmic Commons', thus answering (once more) Mariel's call:

"*Together we are the complements that create a whole, living matrix, one capable of singing the energies of the earth back into the places of physical matter and into our world as well ... (yet) there is a threshold we cannot cross, but you can, if you will dance the stars inward and outward with us.*"

Still, the serious cautionary note of communique niggled – the unpredictability of energetic forces <u>within</u> Earth, manifesting to <u>engage</u> the crises of our time, but if the differential not properly managed? Hmmm. Not only was I thinking of Mariel's counsel of the aetheric planes being 'cloudy and polluted', but my own experience of how we, as an Amici crew, operate. As preface, here are several of Mariel's comments from "Engaging with the Sidhe":

"*My <u>body</u>, like yours, is made of matter, but the matter of my world is less formed, less conditioned, than yours. It is more primal and fluid. You would probably say it is less like matter and more like energy, but these are two different states of one thing ...*

This means that our world has landscapes much like your own, but these landscapes exist on multiple levels of perception and energy. Some are very close to your world and here and there <u>merge</u> with the physical dimension; in such cases, the land mimics your land closely, and <u>the two may affect each other</u> ..."

This accurately describes my experience of the way <u>shared</u> Malakut workspaces manifest. They mirror certain aspects of our densely physical world (hence my desire to bind actions via physical <u>and</u> subtle methods in the hope of assuring in-Time manifestation) but heighten other aspects to enable energetic 'manipulation' (shaping, moulding or bending) of less-<u>substantial</u> forms (tools, acts <u>and</u> 'engineered' space). Nevertheless, we need to take care how this substance and our work team 'intersects' the dense material world, something which was thrown into glaring relief as the Amici prepped our Liberty (pre-US election) action.

I was with a group of extreme 'researchers' in full alpine climbing gear who had assembled in our 'forgotten valley' to investigate potential impacts (positive, negative) of our involvement. They were working high in the steep moraine'd slope above our 'base camp' and had been called in (apparently) via the Stone Circle Dancer: "Gravity always gets in the way when you don't make a big enough leap." In their case the aphorism seemed to be as literal as it gets for a Sidhe scout troupe. One fellow, who had travelled '2300km by car from Peru' to join, 'died' in a crash en route. All this I heard second-hand, of course, but suffice it to say I was seriously in awe of their ability and dedication to task.

Their research involved a hand-held contraption with a sensor probe. Like a cross between a metal detector and Geiger counter, its purpose was to monitor 'geyser' activity <u>within</u> the mountain, i.e. where the primal 'Acqua Termale' was under pressure or could dangerously and unexpectedly breach the surface in other spaces – blow a liquid Light 'fuse' by another name. This in itself demonstrated the level of caution we needed to integrate into our work practices or sites, a bit like receiving a 'foreign affairs travel advisory' for specific no-go zones.

But what I found most intriguing (at the time) was our heli-ride back to base. A direct vertical plummet <u>at</u> speed, G-force pure had us hanging on for dear (subtle) life. Yet the purpose was to demonstrate how we 'intersected' or 'merged' with the physical world. I saw the regular heli pilots who service our valley doing their courier jobs to and from farmsteads above the despatch point on main valley road, each long line carrying a large heavy palette-load in either direction – real 'grunt work'. Just as these pilots needed to ensure they steered clear of electricity lines or gondola cables strung between different outposts, our Malakut pilot had to avoid the same lines <u>plus</u> every other one – i.e. the physical helis, their loads and lines.

Until this point it had not occurred to me how much 'overlap' there was between dimensions. We would all be in a right mess if any 'immaterial us-thing' touched a 'material them-thing'. If we snagged on a line, it would mean the end of us <u>and</u> them – definitely a sobering thought! To a very real degree, we Cousins of the Commons share space – physical and non-physical need to respect certain norms, rules of engagement; time-space events must be harmonised. Of course, with the principle of interdependent co-arising, everything is and always has been implicated in such a shared living universal system, but the <u>specificity</u> of what I lived in a working context really hit home. The Amici heli was energetically material enough to need to 'work around' and give 'wide berth' to <u>any</u> level of materiality to fulfil its work detail safely.

In same context, I see the aftermath of 2016 US election – the <u>intensity</u> of pressure State-side, a huge psychic 'whoosh' of breath long-held at 'what will be, who will win?' suddenly released, ricocheting across Pacific to, within a few days, manifest a 'super slow roller' deep sea earthquake (as one local described it) off New Zealand's coast. Tectonic fault lines carry much <u>weight</u> in their subtle bones too, but like all elemental forces seek to return to a point of <u>equilibria</u> from the chaosophy of (Kali's) tumult, to re-align sentience with the harmonium of Gaia's UrAlt presence – her 'hush' of resonance at core of FeltWorld heart, her Sruti note of beginningless Being, <u>her</u> Peace sunk deep in settled stone ...

Yes. Many reasons to invest in "Thinking Time" – even to <u>begin</u> a cautious approach to this UrWerk. Thus did sheafs of paper start populating themselves and the dining table morphed (for only the second time in Annie-history – the first being a PhD's rhizomatic web) into a mind-mapped Alice-in-Wonderland-like (black) rabbit hole. Luckily it is a long and wide dining table. I needed all its three-square-metres to get the (literal) grey matter from a (simple) mind <u>plus</u> an entire Amici crew's inputs into some form of coherency!

As I have already built much scaffolding in preceding chapters as well as this one on our work-process, we will 'cut to the chase' as they say with a string of salient points:

- Mountains would anchor our continental nodes through their root-known 'spheres of influence' and facilitate a 'symbiosis of sharing' via their source-sea-source'd sheds to form an interconnected worldwide (water-cycle) web (WWW) network of liquid Light (that 'circular economy' again), thus extending Mariel's original comment: "(A mountain) is a major conduit through which the energies of stars and earth meet ... a presence and energy field" to an all-of-All (in-Time-and-out) proposition.
- Helvetia would act as our central crystal-hearted pivot – from here I would send out emissarial despatches framing our work in the context of Sky-Father's initial outreach.
- The delivery of <u>eight</u> mounds of 'dark knowing' were for a reason; I

needed to focus outreach on eight ex-Helvetia continental Mountain-'keepers'.

- The cautionary note of subtle communique 15-months prior re unwieldy forces meant we would concentrate on associative resonances – outreaching through and via <u>already-established</u> loving relations to 'newbies' on (Gaian) block rather than risk being 'fried' by differential differences (i.e. known Mountain 'quantities' acting as our emissaries out into the field).
- An established process to write 'Open Letters to Sacred Spirits of Place' (genii locorum) in advance of <u>physical</u> emissarial outreach – instituted with Spain (LaCon) and Japan (Rising Sun) – would provide our model for subtle contact henceforth.

I looked out my windows on world – one North, one South of Helvetia's peaceable heart. In a crazy synchronistic quirk of amor fati'd fate, I worked the (cartographic) numbers and realised (now) my two homes were in a direct North-South line, Sasso san Gottardo smack bang between the two. Yes, Switzerland is a small country but this was freaky geography. It meant, on a 2D planal cirque of Helvetia, I could use this <u>perfect</u> 3D cross-section of 'home' to fan out into a 4D … You get the picture. A case of micro-macro staring me in the face for decades, but now? I couldn't <u>not</u> use this knowledge to construct a matrix of associative resonance and extend our lengths of Elven rope from a central node of Mountain connectivity every which way – including to the Stars and back. The other thing I had up my sleeve? Australian heritage; here Gondwana revealed herself to me with greatest clarity, the last to leave 'home', break from motherlode. I understood the import of genetic <u>inheritance</u> we, as Land, carried. We are born of the dust of DeepTime-Tectonia worn at skin – full-exposed to close scrutiny and direct engagement on a 2-D continental cirque of eroded scrubbed-back to its bare essence <u>form</u>. Here Land reveals, sink full at surface, the inner <u>function</u> of Gondwana's sacred work; <u>plus</u> it was still understood and actively engaged by a skin-group who only walked out of the desert three decades prior to my encounter with a work by one of their own in a Sydney gallery? Where I felt myself tugged into depths its colour conjured via an 'already-known' Gondwana-brown arising from the black Ground of limitless Void? Our Amici Urwerk would be called Gondwana Dreaming, in her/their honour.

I remembered how long-long-long years ago Mr1300BC threw a most cryptic clue my way:

"*Mystics know to conjugate the rhythmus of the nine spheres.*"

Accompanied by an image of a spinning sphere, I saw <u>eight</u> hollowed-out dark spheres within an encircling ninth. A bit like a very weird ball-like holey (Swiss) cheese but all dark, dark, dark. 'Conjugate'. Despite a wordsmith, 'tis not a verb I actively use. Meaning: To inflect, combine, unite, bend, modulate one's voice in pitch or tone … Um. Song? My medium for all the above verb 'lines'? In grammar-speak: The process of changing the shape of a base infinitive to account for its application in 'space' and/or 'time' … Um. Peace? Love? Light? These were my words, the base 'note' in each Song at heart wherever its infinitive 'line' led. Over decades I had circled his statement. Now it made sense – the shape of Song, to bend Song to a 'line', to unite all Songlines on a 2D plane which, when 3D cross-sect'd and 4D fan'd out, could take account of any old (dark holey/holy?) Swiss cheese.

Yes! Finally I had an 'in' to Mr1300BC's wordsmith'd cryptogram! And, like his Acqua Termale puzzle (described in "The Amici Files"), whatever its primal (Genesis) source, as a personalised specificity for my 'this-life-in-this-skin' work it meant harnessing the Love, the Song of my 'One Place' out of an infinite number of (base) 'Names', to offer our grassroots 'local' (micro) acts (wrapt in lily white) into a manifest 'global' (macro) pool of singularity-shared 'One Life'. With our UrWerk's 'becoming' snowballing at speed, no more abstract circling of statement required but its active application of 'base infinitive' in space and time envisioned – our contribution to an enspirit'd geologic psychoid unity of Gaia's consciousness of 'One Life'!

Thus would Helvetia act as my personal specificity – central (spinning) pivot of our continental outreach enacting the encircling ninth of eight hollowed-out dark spheres at same time. A microcosm to Gondwana's macro, steward to the tectonic Earth-conscious 'genetic memory' of Gaia's macro, our task to 'enflesh', 'enliven', 'en-star' with Song these eight (continental) hollows of 'dark knowing' within her (spheric) 'motherlode'. It was only at this point (see? simple mind in delayed action!) I realised the eight mounds delivered to garden gate had been 'scooped' from encircling ninth (of cryptogram) (here, visualise a watermelon-baller at work). We could 'conjugate' the rhythmus as discrete propositions, moderately, methodically, as the subtle communique had counselled. Each a 'Howe' in the fullness of its (Sidhe-woven) base infinitive. Hollow-hill 'voids', our task to enter through Mountain, to enact (as "I Ching" advised):

"Joining Mountains. So do superior people think without leaving their place."

I trusted it would be possible to effect an (outer) physical spirit-geologic intervention via (inner) subtle same. Our task to infill each container with Love's Light, and connect one to the other to the other without end for all Mountains house Dragons when all said and done. Well, we were still no closer to Spring Equinox but at least the map on dining room table was having fun populating itself with a rhizomatic dance of (metaphoric) red threads. At this point in the chronology, Mr1300BC arrived. Or, rather, I was out visiting him, for his first comment was:

"You come to me, anchor-free ..."

I found myself in a serious workspace, having a serious conversation with the 'boss'. Pleased with our 'scoping' work so far, he said I was at '70' now; '100' being perfect congruency with task orientation and vibrational integrity. Sensing my disappointment, he was at pains to confirm this was positive; now we could move on to the <u>real</u> work. Indeed, he recognised how exhausting instructional downloads can be for me, and seemed to express relief I had come through this testing time intact! 'Well-rested' was his expression (I guess it's all relative ...).

We then discussed 'The Daphnes' – the image which accompanied this was a renaissance-era rendering of a garden-idyll, dancing nymphs, as if uplifted from Greek myth. When its wisdom needed integrating to process, I would find this at the 'National Gallery'. Hmmm. We parted and I thought I could return to 'well-resting'. Instead, I arrived in a conjoined space where a woman explained my 'contract conditions' and outlined various aspects of detailed work planning I needed to take into account. At one point I commented on how complicated and regulation-heavy this all seemed which drew the dry remark:

"If you think bureaucracy on Earth is bad, try Galaxy-wide."

OK. That put me in my place! At one point, passing a long desk in completely 'empty' space, she tripped over 'nothing' which revealed itself to be a minute character peddling away on a (tiny) standing bike, at work beneath (my) desk. Its name (i.e. function)? 'Filing Tray'! Suffice it to say Filing-Tray (complete with 'e-Bike') has been a stalwart member of our (stellar) crew ever since. How lucky can we be! With Equinox looming, my research focused (exhaustively, I might add) on an appropriate set of eight (continental nodal) mountain 'keepers' as well as access ways 'in' to their resonant hums 'signatures' with my own. Here I wanted to ensure that, even though our outreach would occur through associative Mountain 'allies', we could minimise the potential for any energetic equivalent of 'cold call telemarketing' response – of 'phone' slammed down in small human ear.

Important to consider, too, was my 'small' stature or, put another way, to locate Mountains which constellated as 'me-sized', thus harnessing my self-naughting induction to Mountain wisdom years before as well as reflect how I naturally outreach – in child-like Joy to any/every other on a non-hierarchical diagram-of-equals. I did not want 'layers' of thought-forms intruding (re specific 'famous' or 'sacred' mountains) to muddy or intimidate an unmediated connection – heart to heart, pure of intent. Of course, one could say you cannot get much 'bigger' than Fuji-san in a national psyche but that 'just happened'. Already daunted by task, I did not want to make it any 'bigger' than it needed to be. Additionally, I had no desire to attempt outreach to holy mountains with enough on their plate already holding humanity's prayers and petitions, or famous peaks with tourist hoards plying overstressed backs.

Here, I would remind the reader of Ruscada's speech at the close of "Der Ruf der Berge" – that while countless mountains may go unnamed or unremarked, none is any less integral to a world ensoul'd equation in the 'eyes' of Earth-consciousness. Indeed, when Ruscada/I made our little 'grafting' speech, we did not get to talk about the responsibility of designated holy peaks, the <u>weight</u> they carry when a diagram-of-equals of muskateers around the globe could share the load. We did not get to talk about the geo-politics of Chinese oppression Kailash bears on behalf of all Tibet's peoples. We did not get to talk about 'what if' the atomic bomb had missed Hiroshima and taken out Japan's own Sumeru (Mt Misen on the isle of Miyajima) instead, not only obliterating all life but all faith and hope bound to deep psyche. We did not get to talk about the fate of dear Everest with its 'traffic jams' of climbers on the Hillary Step or how, perhaps, like in Carl Jung's recounting of the ancient legend of sacred spring gone underground (that once 'commercialised', its sanctity vanishes to re-appear elsewhere) this could spur such an outcome for Chomolungma likewise. There were too many blank stares around the table as it was. But these were the thoughts keen to spill from a (shared) heart to describe further our concern and our <u>desire</u> to support all Mountain sentience to awaken to sacred purpose. In the end what motivated me was the opportunity for any and all to have an opportunity to participate in this UrWerk, in the same spirit as I 'hear' a tiny pebble or sea-washed shell cry: "See me, see me! I want to help Gaia too!"

In effect we were designing a 'Mountains Mandala' of eight continental champions radiating out from Helvetia's crystalline core to form, in their own way, a Tolkienese 'Fellowship-of-the-Ring' (Song), in our case: "Nine Companions of the Way of Love" serving Gaia's full-woven Songline, just ripe for the upsinging. A caveat, however. As the subtle communique contained a 'map' of the world different in some aspects to one physically outlaid, I meditated long in the Stone Circle to 'arise' which continental 'aspects' would best reflect the <u>intent</u> of this Dreaming and the 'access nodes' into its wisdom. It revealed the following names of tectonic and <u>rifted</u> memory-keepers down through DeepTime:

- Crone: Australis' World Heritage (Gondwana) Soul worn at Skin
- Gateway: Japan as (volcanic) Rising Sun Torii-gate entry to Asia
- LaCon: Europe's <u>edge</u> where African-European plates collide
- Cradle: Africa's centrality to Humanity's outwalk of Song
- IceWorld: Antarctica – polar pole'd and aurora'd
- Roof: Tibet – Trans-Himalayan plateau-
- Nafta: North American plate – un-of-wall
- Latam: South American plate – tropic-to-tundra

In choosing resonant mountains to catch the sense of each memory-keeper, I felt it important to honour and extend the Ring of Fire alliance commenced with our Liberty action. This would also concentrate associative resonances around the Pacific Rim, which I had already intuited as a daughter-keeper of primal Mother-Ocean knowing in the same way Crone presented as a daughter-keeper of Gondwana Dreaming. Together they enacted a Mountain-Dragon dance on regional stage with the potential to 'flood' the world with Joy. Here, associative resonance extended to my HomeSong connections as well as Amici relationships established through emissarial outreach as well as the Liberty action.

While Wollumbin (Crone), Fuji-san (Gateway) and Rainier (Nafta) are peaks known to the reader based on events recounted in the text to date, and with whom my spontaneous un-thought work for Lady Liberty obviously set the scene for this global undertaking, the journey of discovery to other continental keepers was sometimes direct or, as described, requiring emissarial 'intervention' via known allies. By end, however, we had assembled our 'Fellowship of Gaia' into a nodal matrix of (six) 'Brothers of Flame' encircling, as a protective Ring-of-Fire, (three) 'Sisters of Light' – Roof, LaCon and Helvetia. With the latter supported by Australis' Crone-knowing (the link between Wollumbin and Ruscada sound), I saw the three Sisters as (radiant) Earth-conscious receptacles of the 'faerie-godmother' wisdoms of Kali, Moon and Gondwana respectively. With strong intimate connections to LaCon and Roof, confident their Light-work would 'flow' in situ, I concentrated my outreach (as Helvetia's emissary) to the Brothers, or as I was to self-describe in an affirmation:

"An itinerant monk, ever unterwegs, Pilgrim for Love. Amen ..."

The order of approach (i.e. singing up the connection) to integrate the eight 'mounds' into a full 'rhythmus' of nine spheres I knew would be important. The beacon-lighting would need to 'flick' from one to the other in conscious sonorous fashion. And, as previously mentioned, associative resonances would guide my way – out from Helvetia's heart. Yet in collecting my thoughts regarding what (if any) emissarial outreach to undertake at Spring Equinox (fast-approaching) I was surprised to find my two 'window-brothers' North-South of 'hemispheric divide' (respectively: Tödi-san, Ruscada) knocking on the glass with their proposal to not only 'open' the way through their aligned portals but actually attend to my foot-soldiering self out in the 'field'. In so doing, it confirmed the need for robust 'bodyguards' in like form and function to bolster my encounter with any 'remote' stone giant across our wide Gaian world.

Another example of wonderful storytelling for my (simple but symbolic) mind, herewith the notes of how their proposal was presented:

In a Malakut space, I observed 'Knights of the Good' perform a ritual on a field of conflict, working to render benign a 'Balrock' (note different spelling). I saw it 'tethered', ambling about like a gentle giant. The ritual worked to nullify any volatile outpouring of energy in order to engage its 'neutral' or pure essence. The (two) knights worked as a team; it was a simple ritual to bring the whole into balance if they followed 'due procedure'. The knights' work was effortless; I saw harmonic resonance <u>easily</u> achieved. All flowed as matter-of-course because they did not deviate from practice. An important point: No sense of force or control to the 'tethering'. The Balrock had as much desire to serve within <u>its</u> framework of being as any – unpredictable or unwieldy 'lashing out' was due to imbalance, ill treatment or (as the subtle communique back in 2015 described) misleading or ill-conceived intentions on our part.

In one respect, this was a follow-up to the 'power of five' instruction shared earlier in text – how the elements 'bend' or respond to <u>purity</u> of intent and <u>constancy</u> of practice, aligning in alchemical 'service' on a shared 'Way of Love'. In another respect, a follow-up to Mr1300BC's 'Way of the Knight' parable about the 'volcano mountain' we house within (aka our self-Light), an alternate way to explaining the saying of Christ in the gnostic Gospel of St Thomas:

"If you bring forth what is within you, what you bring forth will save you. If you do not bring forth what is within you, what you do not bring forth will destroy you."

In this context, 'bringing forth' or outreaching with the <u>pure</u> essence of our (volcanic) Light of Love occasions our meeting of an interlocutor on a like plane (diagram-of-equals). As 'Perfect Love casts out Fear' (1 John 4:18), fear was not my problem. But the communique had counselled how <u>unwieldy</u> it could be working 'solo' in these chthonic zones; meanwhile I had described the knights' actions as '<u>effortless</u>'. Would I pass up on their support? Never! I was happy to have Helvetia's 'Knights of the Cloth' out in the field with me singing full-time! We agreed to work through, and sing-up, each connection as its own loving proposition. Only one 'Balrock' at a time, my two robust stone giants either side guarding and girding resolve.

With that the Amici arrived to inject a bit of whimsy to our sobriety. I re-watched a family anime favourite with the details 'Malakut-tweaked'. A specific scene involves the hero playing a flute which leads to several prairie dogs rising up from their holes to 'sing' along. He giggles, says: "I'm putting an orchestra together!" Another character sarcastically responds with La-De-Da which the dogs likewise mimic, while a flying lemur dashes about – trying to pounce before they drop down into holes again. In my (Amici) case, the scene had the eight discrete mounds of 'dark knowing' dotted around as 'hollowed hills' in their own right (reprising their own 'rhythmus' of nine spheres). As I (Helvetia's flying lemur?) pressed down (or touched into) one mound, <u>levelling</u> it to primal 'Ground', others sprang to (up-sung) attention. While the need to commune, sing to <u>and</u> align with each discretely to bring its nodal wisdom to Light was affirmed in the demonstration, my practice would nevertheless 'activate' the whole.

With relief I stepped back from a concern that nothing could (or would) start 'happening' (in support of Gaia) till all continental nodes were up-sung. The

Amici's response? Our UrWerk would reap the most out of its shared harmonic resonance as long as I took time to know each intimately; the specific vibration or tonal quality each held in the "Song of Gaia" required dedication to its discovery. Yet we could still work the energy of the whole while each was being honoured – the root-knowing networks were intact, after all. This was confirmed later in the process from another perspective – how the stone giants actually 'saw' and experienced me as I approached in outreach. Again, delightfully communicated:

On a sloping Malakut pathway, I played ball with a boy who was 'higher' up the path than me. We bounced a baseball of rainbow colours to each other – he had one, so did I. A simple game but it said so much about the 'how' of our 'what'. I realised each ball, as a fractal of Self sent on emissarial mission, contained our respective extant (base) vibrational note which painted a 'rainbow of incarnate resonance' – how delightful! The bounce 'action' released the ball's Song (extant note) into 'the Commons'. A mechanism to 'sound' intent, the other player could either decide to play (i.e. catch the ball post-bounce) or not – reciprocal recognition, 'Way of Love' by another name. The bounce also served to anchor engagement in shared primal Ground. At the same time, an (invisible) energetic current flowed (as Love's liquid Light) along the (ley) line of ball toss which, when 'caught' post-bounce, anchored the energy in the other player's embodied knowing likewise. This 'doubling' served as scaffolding for a robust intimate yet still self-sovereign zone for engagement within the 'frame' of the game by calling into play our common nestedfishes spot of colour by which communion effected.

In the same context, I met Ruscada – he climbed down out of the stands at the baseball game to talk to me on the 'playing field'. We stood together while he showed me blueprints of 'energy patterns' – drafts, prototypes, generations, derivations. In a sequence of A4 flipcharts, these gradually grew more recognisable, infilled with detail. We discussed 'targets', which version was most understandable. Even I was included in the line-up! His point here was that the patterning 'software' enabled mountains to recognise me according to which version they found most understandable. Cool! I understood our work was not 'hit-and-miss' – the more I attuned I became, the more 'accurate' these blueprints would become. Yay!

• • • • •

A point came in this quantum of preparatory work where I returned from HMed in the Stone Circle to find myself (surprisingly) luxuriating in the feeling of being 'settled' into a stream of work with dear kin rather than (the usual) daunted and overwhelmed by a seeming waterfall of informational downloads. I had been visited by a lively youthful regal presence aligned with Moon's 'Stairway to Heaven' Dancer community who said she would be back 'Monday' with more tools. The touch of her energy signature, in silver-white appliqued robes, same (subtle) fabric, texture as my 'rainbow-fluorite' set (purple/green to connect Heaven/Earth), lifted the weight of work from my (small) shoulders, confirmed it as a shared 'burden' across a full team.

So did I luxuriate in the (brief) respite this awareness offered, and contemplated how the path had opened along disparate tracks to now converge on a task of planetary scale. I thought of connecting home nodes across the world; I thought of my original self-work with Light; I thought of my learnings to 'play like a rock', 'embrace a mountain', find the source of our valley headwaters, add my purity of intent to its flowing Love out into world, then continue my waterway'd gifting of Light via stone and shell 'containers' while walking-singing across the length-breadth of Helvetia's hills and dales, heights and vales over years.

I thought of my acceptance into a lineage and workstream which crossed humanity's ancestry in matter'd form to embrace active Sidhe partnership, and return us, together, 'up the line' to our Common Ancestor in support of Gaia's evolution at her deepest layers of planetary consciousness. I thought of the paradox of needing to understand DeepTime origins of Us-as-Kin and Gaia-as-Sister to reforge bonds rent asunder and walk into a future 'down the line' as Family, reunited (TeamSky, TeamBerg) within a Gaian Commons of inclusive loving service – all was fracturing, yes (as Gondwana had stated), but 'twas necessary for all to heal.

To appropriate Leonard Cohen: "The crack in everything is how the Light gets in." No matter what 'happened' I knew we would stay true to longer-than task, trusting to the unfold of Earth-consciousness along an arc of Time not of our making, yet with whom we actively partner in its H5.0 'universe', thereby ours. Partnering Time in the time given us (this time, in this skin); where on Earth is there 'time' for despair? What a waste of energy when our task is Joy! Living and working the Joy of Gaia's Commons, contributing to its deep wells of Peace, Love and Light, mirroring Joy to double the impact. Like Churchill: Courage, first of all qualities; and never giving in to the dark of despair. Love's Light our shield and spear to pierce any jolly old Cloud of Unknowing lurking in sad sorry depths of unhealed trauma. Not easy but doable.

I thought on, luxuriating in the whole interweb I could call on for aid and strength – either known or unknown, ever amazed at who showed up at my door when a snowball such as this began its desire to 'become'. I marvelled that walking 'alone with the Alone', as I do, unaligned to any specific track, cobbling together tools and tricks from a treasury of traditions all lain on Love's Ground, was also a paradox – how being fully open to come what may, accepting my vulnerability, my courage to give something of this scale a 'try', had become a beacon of radiant Light, broadcasting news (via affirmations) but also needs (via discussion in Stone Circle). And, into this space of luxuriating, contemplating, suddenly I was sucked 'home' to Helvetia's crystalline heart with the re-realisation of crystal mountain of which my 'pillar' a fractal. A very firm self-reminder from

Soul depths issued forth:

"*You are Mountain. You are Crystal-at-Core.*"

I was consumed by pulsating Light, out from (self-) core, with a strength which made my limbs rise, push against resistance, confirm a conviction to stand self-sovereign in task "shoulder-to-stone-shoulder, battle-worn and scarred" (as I wrote in a Song dedicated to our work). The strength of Mountain which <u>defies</u> gravity, defies the <u>weight</u> of despair, to become, just like the seed which contains within itself an entire tree – the will to contribute to Life! To thrust through surface of being, to rise up from mantle, stand tall and say: "I am". No matter what:

"*I am*", "*This is*" *and* "*We must!*"

With all humility I could not imagine any of this occurring till it did. With the assembly of as many allies a girl could possibly want in a lifetime, it 'just happened'. And here I stand <u>equal</u>, crystal beacon 'lit', acting as a conduit for a full planetary crew according to Liu I-ming's sagic "I Ching" commentary on the hexagram that (literally) dropped its knowing out of the bookshelf at the same time as a 'crystal mountain' vision appeared prior to "Awakening"'s call:

"*Joining mountains. Thus do superior people think without leaving their place. With mountain above and below, one mountain joins another, and so on, so that a thousand mountains, ten thousand mountains, present a single image of* <u>*stability*</u>. *Being in place means being immutable, stabilised in the right way. Thought that is properly stabilised (i.e. grounded in the Way of Love) encompasses all reason and responds to all things: Indeed, when you know the One, all tasks are done ...*"

Well, at some outwith level, perhaps, 'all tasks are done', but Time-partner'd? Our Amici crew still had an awful lot on our UrWerk task-list – one which has stretched years and along an array of concurrent tracks since the fateful days of which I write. To preface each action in those early days – confirm commitment, request support – the same Song filled our Stone Circle over and over. Tuned to Ed Sheeran's Smaug track, <u>our</u> focus was firmly on calling up fiery Hope in full knowledge of our responsibility to 'try':

Oh misty heights of the mountain below
Keep careful watch over all our souls
And if this UrWerk should come to nought
Please hold a prayer at heart (for all our souls):
Home home home ... Home home home ...
Home home home ... Home home home ...

The final 'ring' of Home, sung as woven thread in the same 'rowing' spirit as our Sailors' psalm (a 'charm' to call up Peace-Love-Light as we sail Gondwana's 'Book of Voyage' through leylines Land-Sea-Sky'd), specifically references my journey Home to 'Sacred Pool' in company of Sky-Father long years past. Described in "Awakening", and for which a Dancer in Deck its memory-keeper, a short review of its salient points to close chapter. The journey, in respect of meeting MakerMan over a cup of tea (when the stellar carpet of our origin story unfurled), shows another side of task while in service to (and with) our sister Gaia – the aim to gift the dense ball of Earth-consciousness home to the stars.

In my encounter, Sky-Father wore his (Cernunnos) half-stag, half-human dress – calm, settled, ancient. Already at this stage of self-apprenticeship I understood the extraordinary extent of our connection; a knowing so deep no communication was required. We made our way through a grove of skeletal trees above a pond, but while the group followed him toward a clearing beyond, I felt an immediate desire to <u>skip</u> down some wide stone steps to the pond which I named 'Sacred Pool'. I literally felt like a young child coming home from kindergarten, only recently independent, out in the world, full of Joy to be <u>home</u>, having made it back on my own after the <u>big</u> adventure of the day. Reaching the water's edge, I knelt down to greet the pool – a presence in its own right as well as all ancestors who lived eternally in its depths. Hands rose to greet me. I felt so blessed, so loved – all acknowledged my homecoming with Joy! When Sky-Father returned with the group, we entered the pool. Instantly I floated while he and 'Elders' walked its surface. As to lineage, words formed:

"The Mother is the Mother of the Father and the Brother and the Child."

Sky-Father's Mother, went the logic, was Sacred Pool <u>it/herself</u>. No wonder I had such desire to greet the pool for its own sake; here was my UrMutter pure! The location morphed into a cavern deep within the cradle of Earth where we sat as our origin story was projected on its ceiling. In Song and Image we basked in the calm of our delight but as the Story proceeded, Time skipped forward to post-date our current 'negligence' in duty-of-care (key words 'emissions' and 'we have to leave') to see the world gradually re-absorbed into the Stars with fiery explosions and much Light; we would be 'repatriated' Home – heads hung in shame. Yet I returned from this space deeply settled; the profound Love experienced in the company of our entire 'Sky' lineage suffused me. Finally uplifted to consciousness from the depths of Soul wisdom was the knowledge of starblood flowing through my subtle veins, as with us all. And, in remembering our shared Story, <u>why</u> we are here, I felt intimately grounded in (and inducted into) the courage needed to challenge the potentiality of such a shameful outcome.

Here was confirmation of why <u>we</u> needed to stand in the sovereignty of our incarnation – here, now – and for which the Song in Stone Circle served to remind all Amici crew of the depths of our responsibility to 'try'. It was time to design an Equinox ritual, step into the grail, and affirm our commitment once more …

INTERMEZZO (1)

It may seem odd, Reader, that I am recounting events from so many years past in such detail. Indeed, without the rigour of my journal notes, I would have little memory of the specificities described. This manuscript intended to see light of day at the close of 2019 when everything was (naturally) fresh in my mind and thus comprising recent history rather than constituting the need for a deep dive. But at the point in narrative where I closed the last chapter, ready to take up my pen again within the next days, I was suddenly blocked from any more activity. Not by the act of writing itself, but by pain – intense – gripping my back.

As anyone who has experienced deep penetrant pain (physical, emotional, psychic) can attest, it puts all other (relatively minor) considerations on a metaphoric backburner while the root-cause is investigated, understood, embraced and (hopefully) healed. So it was for me when Cancer (blood/bone) was diagnosed a month prior Covid's global diagnosis. The world hunkered down; I hunkered down. The Amici arrived, saw into the <u>length</u> this hunkering would require (Annie-personal; human-collective) and agreed to pop the book in a drawer.

Instead, I was spurred with an inordinate energetic desire (for a Mind with a lot of hunkered decisions to make and a dear sweet Body in serious need of 'tea and sympathy') to co-produce "From the Common Grail Within" (2020). The intent? That if things went completely 'belly-up' in the Annie healing stakes, we still would have shared fundamental myths of planetary creation and evolution, including the role of our OnePeople (Sidhe/We) in support thereof. Myths rendered in Story and Song (our micro-experience of the 'great work' spoken in bardic tongue), in our Amici 'skin-language' (to coin an Aboriginal expression), these were prefaced by essays documenting our applied praxis of Anwa and the weaving of Love's Light in Song.

Breathing a collective sigh of relief when the "Grail" volume was complete (without this Annie-'singing-bird' falling off her perch!), it was shunted across the pond into the safe hands of a Jeremy (Berg = Mountain); the wizardry of Lorian Press could now take over. I could retreat to cave-of-heart, and apply everything learnt about Anwa, Love's Light, Song (Mountain, Dragon <u>gleefully</u> tagging along) to my own healing journey. Yes, I understood the purpose of my (Body's expression of) Cancer; it had arisen in subtle realms in the early stages of UrWerk as a potentiality – that in going deep into Gaia's pain, to the very core of <u>her</u> primal (blood/bone) wound, it could trigger something (as deep) in me. But I thought our work negotiated this successfully. By the time I was writing the manuscript our work-process of joining mountains, lighting beacons, and weaving the world had completed itself.

Ah ... but no. The wound desired to be engaged on <u>physical</u> plane; <u>its</u> decision to shift from subtle to physic'd writing itself into existence via two acts which affirmed my ever-service to Gaia – "Muted Earth", a poem penned from the <u>place</u> of Gaia's pain; and the inscription of birth contract in (Annie-) skin (described in "In-Frame").

Both 'myths' – the latter personal, the former planetary – are housed in our 2020 volume. Both were intended to be part of this manuscript's flow but I, like the Amici, thought we may be out of (Time-partner'd) time. I needed to not only understand and bear witness to our depths of discovery in script but, like ekphrasis, inhabit the iconography, embody the physicality of creation as com-passionate participant-witness – as with Gaia's, so too mine.

Com-passion – to suffer with. Yes. It is part of my birth contract; it is part of my commitment to service. This time in this skin and, with any luck, the gift of healing my Body's garden would bring healing gifts to Gaia's (garden) well-being (Being's <u>wellspring</u>) likewise. This is how every invocation was and continues to be written, a case of (as we whimsically express it):

Everyday Delight for Everyday Adepts –
rooted in the Earth, seeded with a smile,
an Acorn becomes Itself – in Time ...

The beauty of a more-than-four-year delay in publication has, however, been an absolute blessing, I must say. More opportunities to share happy tales of co-creation which appear in the third section of volume: "Exploring Song". Thus are 'old memories' (anno '16-17) brought (as much as possible) into a here-and-now of ever-fruitful collaboration.

The purpose of this "Intermezzo"? To reinforce the main points from the "Anwa" and "Song" chapters in our 2020 book – to affirm the 'how' of the 'what' in our work, down all years 'fore and hence, to bring fieldwork praxis <u>and</u> practicalities into Sidhe/We Anwa'd discussions. The following, therefore, represents an outtake from that text to affirm the content to come.

• • • • •

"Anwa: A faculty, a way of life <u>and</u> a state of being. We come <u>at</u> Anwa <u>through</u> Anwa."

So did the Amici show up at 11.30pm one night, just after Annie-lights-out. As the statement was co-spoken (i.e. describing a <u>shared</u> tenet in as <u>precise</u> a formulation as we could muster in a pure 'Us-as-Us' moment), I knew I had to scribble it down immediately. And I am so glad I did – capturing the modality (skill), process (flow) and sovereignty (presence) we bring to the <u>lived</u> praxis of second sentence. Sharp, blunt, to the point. Forget the grammar, Annie, it's about harnessing, blending, moulding, shaping, and <u>partnering</u> Anwa, together with <u>other</u> Beings' expressions of Anwa, to <u>create</u> holistic Anwa-<u>inspired</u> outcomes that serve the <u>totality</u> of Gaian life. <u>In</u>-spired, <u>breathed</u> into existence. Nothing is <u>not</u> infused with Anwa. It's as simple as that – 'micro-macro and all in-between' (as our weaving rituals decree).

As with many languages, the nuances in the Sidhe word 'Anwa' cannot be captured precisely in another tongue. There are Swiss words, for example, hybrids drawn from all-over this tiny Land, to which I cannot succinctly apply a direct one-on-one translation, but I certainly 'know' what my interlocutor is communicating and can eagerly contribute to the discussion out of own experience even if reduced to body language to facilitate understanding. But how to get inside the <u>lived</u> experience of a word from within the particularity of a person's <u>use</u> of word, encompassing a <u>personal</u> worldview as much as the <u>collective</u> historico-cultural-economic-and-so-on coining of word in the first place and/or its 'morph-in-meaning' over time? So much is bound into syllabic form beyond a few letters in a certain order. Thus do I understand well the conversational conundrum David and Mariel experienced in a simple discussion of 'Anwa'. It is why hybrid-words abound in our Amici circle, examples of which include 'Alternavism' (to describe various aspects of praxis) and 'Intelliginstinct' (skills I need to cultivate). In similar spirit, we play with phonetics which cross language boundaries. My point being that we know what we mean and the context of its application but can it be directly apprehended by others?

Here are David's and Mariel's discussion on the conundrum:

"Anwa is a complex concept that does not render itself easily or simply into your

language. It represents a property that all things possess, but it also represents our response towards that property. You might say it is our participation in the universal nature of this property, which put very simply is the intent and desire of life to be itself in harmony with all other life. Using your terms, I could say Anwa is both a noun and a verb. It describes a state of being and a state of doing. It describes how we relate to our world, and it also describes that in the world to which we are relating. It encompasses a dynamic relationship that we have with equally dynamic and unfolding life. Anwa is like breath to us. It is a natural part of who we are. To be Sidhe is to relate to Anwa through Anwa."

The quote appears in "Engaging with the Sidhe" (2017). I, however, only had an opportunity in 2019 (post-UrWerk close-out) to read it. Not only I, but the Amici were fixated on their rendering of the concept – how 'abstract' their discussion had been. It needed 'bringing down to earth', down into the grubby trenches of our work out in the field. In deep Malakut zones of enquiry and discussion, I sat busily writing a lengthy text on our shared behalf about Anwa from an experiential fieldwork perspective during which I thought:

"This is fascinating! It hooks everything we've ever done into the structural framework of David's conceptualisation of the faculty with Mariel, thus bringing it into a dimension of felt-experience, of active working-with, plus demonstrates its application as true-nature'd matter-of-course!"

I saw myself write (and delight in re-quoting this co-produced paragraph!):

"There is nothing that is _not_ infused with this expression of the Divine, and the creative fluidity of partnering Sidhe and their _skilled_ approach to working this interconnective _sense-force_ will better serve Gaia's evolutionary consciousness than if we keep puddling along on our own 'separate' tracks. Instead of muddying the waters with labels, therefore, let's just write about what we do as an Anwa-conscious Amici workcrew in our grassroots everyday. Let's just document how we _live_ our OnePeople'd common ancestry as true nature and apply its wei-wu-wei'd dance in-world!"

An important point we discussed was that in working the inherent _energy_ of co-creation, we (as humans) need to be aware of when to step _out_ of the (Anwa) stream so that cognition can kick in and process what requires _doing_ to ensure our active involvement supports the unfold of an action rather than hamstrings it. The _density_ of our (human) construction is a necessary adjunct for work to 'stick' on this side of veil – the grounded fluidity we bring to the equation supports actions that require _literal_ 'planting' in Gaian soil. We are two sides of a single One-People'd coin, after all, and in other contexts Mariel has spoken long about the respective qualities we bring to shared partnering table. In this respect, Gaia's _physical_ Self vis-à-vis our physicality serves to _anchor_ Anwa's 'dance' of Love's Light in (healing vial'd) containers of physic'd space; the very _fact_ of our incarnation facilitates the psychoid unity of actions 'seeded' in Earth ('rooted in the soil of Gaian existence' is our ritual text here), thus expediting the 'shift' from subtle to physic, and ensuring sticking power. Here. Now. In-world.

This aspect of partnership cannot be stressed highly enough. Stepping <u>out</u> of Anwa's stream is necessary for human partners in Sidhe co-productions in order to enact specificities of in-world action, but with a rider to <u>ever</u> ensure being able to step back <u>in</u> again, re-connect to a <u>same</u> cycle of dynamic unfoldment. Never losing the connection is critical to the <u>continuity</u> of work cycle engaged. Within this context a word arose to describe the sense of 'step-shift':

"*Equipoise.*"

The synonyms of 'Equipoise' include 'harmony', 'balance' and 'equilibrium' which look at the 'equi' part of word. The Amici, however, were at the 'poise' part – a state which encompasses stance (being) and dance (flowing, or 'doing' as Mariel calls it); Anwa as both noun and verb. Yet, while demonstrating a perpetual now of self-presence (being) and dynamic engagement (flowing), there is a third aspect to 'poise' – the <u>unfolding</u> of future potentiality which Anwa embraces in Self-Other'd relation when we are 'poised' (or prepped) for action in response to whatever here-and-now of 'stance' and 'dance' we encounter.

This could be as immediate as a 'first-responder action' or a longer-than coalescence of energetic 'grunt-work'. Step-in. Step-out. Stay poised. No. Matter. What. We call this aspect of faculty: 'Come-what-may' (romance); 'romance' a cue word for the <u>loving</u> engagement we bring to <u>any</u> relational work in/out of Anwa's stream as well as step-shift in-between. For example, stepping 'out' could be seen as a separation or severance of energy, of giddy vertigo, but when handled consciously, sensitively in and with Love, could be likened to the sweet kiss of farewell – damsel on tip-toe, barely reaching the chin of her (Sidhe) beau in <u>unwavering</u> equipoise, stance steady following dance (sweaty!) till next 'come what may' step in.

What facilitates our equipoise in each of the three emanations of its single whole? Love. Of Self. Of Other. <u>Trusting</u> in the truth of what we make, together, with the purity of our intent to serve Gaian purpose. Once, I heard/told myself in meditation: "Only when the Light pure is within me, can the Light pure be shared." If our intent is pure, grounded in Love, then Love's (liquid) Light carries this quality as true-nature'd matter-of-course into and through world.

Phonetically pronounced the same way, though with a slight difference in spelling is the Arabic word for divine Light: 'Anwar'. In mystic Sufism, this 'Light upon Light' describes the entry and circulation <u>in-world</u> of 'Anwar' as an 'unfolding' of the Sacred as Itself (<u>within</u> All) as well as to facilitate relationship of All (<u>with</u> All). This understanding of 'Anwar' backboned my self-apprenticeship in Light-work and its flow for many years before we (Amici) found each other. In one respect, therefore, learning of the Sidhe faculty Anwa was like coming home to a known and remembered quality. Yet to consciously <u>partner</u> Sidhe on

Anwa'd outcomes, I needed to <u>trust</u> in their <u>skilled</u> application of its potentials, to see 'inside' <u>their</u> experience of Anwa, provide insights from my experience of Anwar, and thus speak the same 'language'.

Also joining the Anwa/Anwar party (with its own language and runic symbology) was training in Reiki. Following a random conversation with a random stranger at (yes) a random party, I realised my (random) thought in the early days of UrWerk had been taken up by the Amici in (typically) non-random fashion. See, I was concerned my self-apprenticeship in Light may need 'ramping up' to cope with the quantum of work envisaged and/or my confidence to tackle same. Enter (completely random) Reiki conversation. Here was a technique to hone 'raw-skills' and help keep me focused on task. While principally a healing modality for human clients, why not for Gaia as a planetary being? Why not for better attuning to interstellar energies? Why not as a toolkit integrated into my 'grounded' Anwa praxis? Indeed, as soon as I committed to this course of training, a strong message arrived from 'higher-dimension' subtle allies – they were looking forward to welcoming me to 'Alpha-Cen's Sprachschule'. Cutely expressed, this was code for the constellation of which my homecome Southern Cross is part, at a language school I did not know existed! As I would be meeting with a Reiki-Master on our forthcoming annual pilgrimage down under, to see if we attuned, it was generous information in advance that learning Reiki, in my birth-country, would improve (simple mind'd) Annie's 'translation skills' on multiple fronts!

• • • • •

At this point let me introduce you to 'Golden Duck'. A 'vessel' of Anwa, it simply showed up one day to support our UrWerk. We had assembled in a 'group house' with other teams from different parts of 'Sidheverse'; here, I wrote a letter describing how to work with its energy:

"Golden Duck lives on a waterway steadily flowing through Gaia's world. Always 'on the move' between Source and Sea, Golden Duck isn't a fleshy feather'd 'live' duck but a solid gold sculpture happily bobbing along. Golden Duck looks like a decoy from my place of witness on riverbank, but is definitely no 'sitting duck'. It <u>flows</u> where the river takes it (i.e. wei-wu-wei-ing the Way of Love) while its very <u>being</u> remains immune to any hunter's rifle (i.e. its stance solid). Nothing can harm Golden Duck's presence <u>or</u> its treasury within, which is greater, deeper, wider than the dimensions of a simple duck (golden or otherwise!) would suggest (like Hermione's beaded bag in 'Harry Potter').

"Golden Duck is our partner to purpose – infilled with and 'ausstrahlend' (i.e. radiant) of Peace-Love-Light. It has strength and presence <u>and</u> conviction of intent. Nothing can tamper with this duck or its contents. Brave Duck! And what comprises its treasury? A <u>vast</u> repository of wisdom on Love's Light as well as every conceivable <u>tool</u> for its application! Such that simply by <u>being</u> itself, Golden Duck <u>flows</u> blessings thru all the waters of all the world. Yet each of us is welcome to 'reach out' from riverbank to

access its wisdom equally for it is ever-replenished by Love at core like our never-ending Chamois cheese that regrows each magical night as long as a single thimbleful remains in bowl (a Sidhe legend of our Wildmännli here in the Alps).

"This 'dual function' in 'single form' will be very useful to our work. Simply <u>observing</u> Golden Duck's self-action helps spread Peace-Love-Light through the world (<u>all</u> are connected to water – for Life <u>and</u> for the duration of Life); likewise, we can 'dive in' to Golden Duck's 'resource library' for use in our outreach programs, accessing <u>anything</u> depending on task or orientation, and watch how it instantly replenishes for any other team's use in their workstream. Hence, Golden Duck will always be fully available to us here <u>within</u> the grail but at the same time continue to glide <u>inwith</u> the grail of 'world' – water deep, flow constant – sharing blessings simply by <u>being</u> itself which each act of 'witness' from riverbank serves to <u>flow</u> (magnify <u>and</u> multiply) as a mirroring action on through world. Brave and Loving Duck! How lucky are we!"

Indeed a brave, loving duck – enacting <u>and</u> invoking selfless service to Gaia's 'Ecology of Light'!

In "To the Power of Five", I describe working according to a H5.0 'songsheet'. Anwa is another expression to explain a like engagement with elemental energies as they <u>bend</u> to the purity of loving intent to unfold an arc of 'becoming' and <u>midwife</u> potentiality toward manifestation according to the causes and conditions ripe for same. All the language is there – the energetic swirl of 'Light upon Light' forming around the 'seed proposition' (a resonant presence of Light in <u>itself</u>) which acts to coalesce a <u>network</u> of co-creative partners to share in helping <u>its</u> Joy to become Life. All the language is there, too, in our model of the 'snowball of becoming' (see "Appendix 3"). Our Amici work? Simply: "Anwar'd-Anwa-in-Action" – subtly 'planting' intent before physically enacting whatever ritual action is envisaged to increase the 'sticking' power of said action in-world. There can be many (vertical) layers and (horizont) dimensional planes of 'shift' from subtle to physical before the psychoid unity of an action takes 'root'. Patience is key (we work on DeepTime-Tectonia's watch, after all!), together with the lived experience of ritual in a <u>constancy</u> of praxis. I remind myself daily of the (seven) 'perfections' I need to bring to task: Courage, Compassion, Patience, Perseverance, Grace, Gratitude, <u>and</u> Trust. In this way we Amici can, through and with Anwa, '<u>melt</u> into each other' (as Mariel says), equipoised of stance, dance and (come what may) romance.

Mentioning the 'seed proposition' above in context of a network of co-creative partners (beyond We/Sidhe) who contribute <u>their</u> expression of Anwa to same is amply demonstrated by our work with a micro-version of Gaia's Seed Earth (see David's work for more elucidation on this concept). In our (grubby) trenches it manifests as a spheric shape similar to a geodesic dome (i.e. home infilled of light). 'Flat-packed', the Seed is reduced to a slim 'slice' of Gaia's (Whole) Earth so we can 'travel-lite' (with/as Light – get it? MagicMan's cheery contribution to bolster sweaty spirits!). Once our 'stopping place' in scape is reached, the Seed is tossed, springing open to its full spheric extent which 'ignites' its own physically manifest (Light) becoming in-world once 'contact' is made with the ground (or something solid or dense).

I was offered 'sight' onto multiple versions of these geodesic flat-packed 'blueprints' – they related to or (better said) had been gifted into the care of myriad different species and incarnational beings. Each had its task to 'manifest' a whole (i.e. construct the full shape and spring it open in a 'contact-ignite' relevant to its species or incarnational work). Each of these then 'nested' or coalesced into a single overarching model – hence partner'd action with the Whole of Earth to realise a shared envisioning of our Whole Earth. In a way I was privy to seeing into Gaia's Seed Earth-layer'd 'fore-dimensions'. This confirmed the responsibility and active partnering of all species to task. I saw, for example, 'Tree' action in service to the whole, 'Stone', 'Insect', and more. Each action (inwith its geodesic dome) was, like our Amici work, aimed at strengthening their structures via 'Song' along enlivened lines of energetic or vibrational resonance. And with each I saw how it diffused or seeped through from subtle to physical (a very exciting 'shift' to witness and engage!). Thereafter each Seed Earth worked to support the strengthening of other inter-dimensional elements inwith the Whole of Earth once it was nested into or seamed onto the Whole Earth.

Each interconnecting line or rod (to come back to the geodesic analogy) of Love's living Light operates as a 'stretch of Song' between 'stopping places' (nodes or storage tubers in rhizome-speak) where Peace-Love-Light can be sequestered, and anchored in subtle-physical intersect. Attested by Australian Aboriginal Dreaming practices, the (Song) lines are like roots, but also strong bones. Important, however, is that 'free space' between each triangulation (of geodesic rod-like structure) stays 'free' or 'empty' – like the Enso, offering co-creative zones of potentiality where all species and beings can come together and contribute to Gaia's emerging holism (PeaceTea and RockCake optional). A fresh vision (for my eyes) which took the role of 'active' mothering and nurturing, and placed it in a broader context of 'midwifery'. Just as it takes a village to raise a child, it takes a Commons dedicated to community to bring our full planetary beauty to manifest reality.

• • • • •

Dear Reader, thank you for staying the distance thus far in volume and quietly absorbing the magnitude of (Cancer's) spanner-in-the-works for our micro-dedication to serving Gaia. I have to admit to an underlying 'trauma' when considering my (eventual) return to this text. It was right here, in this tiny 400-year-old cottage, my cave-of-heart in a 'forgotten valley', that Pain asserted itself with its "See me!" cry while I continued to busily sit and write. It could wait, I thought (as so many of us do). But no. It stamped its (big) foot and said: "Now!" The text up until that point, literally the last paragraph of prior chapter, 'houses' the memory of Pain's moment/s on (Annie) stage.

I (latterly) could keep writing 'beyond' this point (slowly, gradually) but could I ever return to edit/review this first section of text? Or would it again arise 'something nasty' in Body? Seems silly, I know, but rational thought has no place in the Body-Mind of lived trauma. So how did I/we return? It had to be here, in this same place, our high wild raw <u>and</u> free valley – alone with the Alone, my 'pretty fire' front-and-centre, and my Amici ever in loving support. With thanks/ good grace let us continue our story.

WALKING THE GARDEN; WEAVING THE WORLD

I have already introduced you to the Zen nook along garden edge, the symbolic importance of its physical presence in heart. Walking Gaia's garden (any size) is a constancy of praxis when I need to think something through, to let knowing percolate up from Land, stream down from Sky – personal, planetary. So did I wander out to Zen nook one day when considering (with the Amici) the content of our intro-ritual (aka stepping-up-to-UrWerk) earmarked for Spring Equinox '17.

There, in contemplative silence, I remarked (as if for a first time) the stones placed in and/or flanking its 'river of enlightenment'. I counted. The stones watched. (The Amici giggled.) And suddenly I saw the eight (subtle) mounds of 'dark knowing' delivered to garden gate in physically stone-sunk animation. Right there in garden grail were eight consequent chunks of Mountain at my feet just ripe for awakening to world-work service. At source, meanwhile, I spotted my 'Knights of the Cloth' – sitting, waiting all along for me to remark their (ever-) presence at back of 'True-Sister's-Island' (so-named) from which we would step out in emissarial outreach. The Amici happily skipped the 'river' down to sea; I, meanwhile, walked slowly, meditatively, asking each stone to name itself. Which mound would it agree to steward, accompany, anchor, mirror in continental collective? Which reservoir of 'dark knowing' would it offer to draw out?

Clear to me now was our process; the Song sung, with Love, to MossMan-Findling years past (documented in "Awakening") would underpin efforts again. Trialled, successfully, to connect nodes of HomeSong across the world, now causes (and conditions!) had <u>literally</u> materialised to awaken and connect nodes worldwide in Gaia's HomeSong. The micro of macro revealed in this tiny patch of terra, this mini-stretch of (Zen-nook'd) Song? The coincidence of landscape architect's (number of) stones and their placement a year earlier was dizzying, but still I walked, and listened, as they spoke not only their sovereignty, but their solidarity with application to sacred task.

Naming, followed by outreach in a particular order, based on associative resonances outlined in our last chapter – downstream from 'source' all the way to 'sea'. And that's when it happened. I looked anew at the Aboriginal artwork, my 'very-lucky' find in a Sydney marketplace (see "To the Power of Five" for backstory), and started counting. How could I have missed this before? Staring back at me from the face of canvas were eight equivalent mounds of 'dark knowing' conjugated within and uplifted from the stellar heights <u>and</u> earthen depths of an Aboriginal (ancestral) Dreaming "Ninth". A Beethoven-worthy choral symphony in paint, with its own "Ode to Joy" at breathing heart? How could I have been so blind! Delivered to garden gate were these eight, delivered to <u>our</u> ninth, Helvetia's starlight suite. Dawn of Time was in on this. 'Something' was swirling to life. And her name was/is/ever will be "T".

• • • • •

I don't know how it works but this is now it works
I don't know how it works but this is how it works
I don't know how it works but this is how it works

This the incantation muttered as I am drawn to this, that or other, trusting Soul to not lead me astray, trusting intuition, trusting heart-knowing (call it what you will) – amply admixtured by the synchronistic prods, pokes and offerings by a plethora of companions of the Way (of Love) in various skin'd or un- guises. In this particular instance, when waking to birdsong and planning a 'big walk' into the heights as a last blessing to valley before the need to return North, instead the words start arising, populating a chapter (this) I had not planned on writing whilst here, but "Sasso" (intended) has kindly stepped back to let T take centre stage. (Sasso really is a charmer, but I digress.)

I do not have much time and she is desperate, at last, to have her story heard, told, witnessed. T, who for <u>so</u> long demurred from being 'exposed' in this volume, who urged me time and again to find a way to share her knowing <u>without</u> sharing her knowing, has finally offered an olive branch. "Tell it this way," she whispers, "and I will respond …"

Dearest T, whose name I <u>cannot</u> speak, for she is a Dreaming from the ancient world, from the primal depths – of FullDark in Time's Tectonia. A record in paint, but first scripted to sand, her Story told, danced, then scrubbed out – the ephemeral of her spirit's arise in-time erased, farewelled with thanks/good grace, enabling her to return to her elemental nature, retreat, withdraw, be sucked back to the depths from which emerged till next called forth to <u>ground</u> a ceremony in the vast desert reaches of inland Australia.

Dearest T, whose name I <u>will not</u> speak out of respect for her maker, respect for her true nature, respect for the Ancestors who first brought her Dreaming up from the depths to engage a <u>concomitant</u> humanity, who worked with and for her to sing the Land awake, to sing the Songline on. T, who came to me – to tell her Story, gift her wisdom direct into our Amici'd hands – to steward on, to <u>enfold</u> a whole world in our weaving work. T, who offered us her very Self to <u>anchor</u> this work of weaving-the-world.

Yes, her work had been centred on, and curated by and for the Land of my birth, that of her maker, but she had been apprised, it seems, of what the whole of Land, of Gaia's <u>full</u> extent, Third-Rock a-spin through the infinity of cosmos needed to <u>sing</u> the Whole-Earth Story on. "Use me," she said, "in your efforts to weave. I gift myself into your care …"

By the end of this volume, Reader, you will meet another of the ancients, from a different tradition, who likewise said: "Use me". But we will stay with T and what she would tell, for it unfolded the all-to-come.

Many threads had (unknown to little me) been stitched into place to preface the moment of T's offer, the magnitude of revelation she desired to share. There was the sourcing of artefact which holds her Presence in the first place more than a decade past, told in "To the Power of Five" but here enriched with her memories <u>sandwiched</u> to mine. She remembers, well, laying prone in a musty pile of canvases countless miles from her birthplace, a place where salty sea formed the pungent scent on air rather than red plains dust. Buried beneath the exuberance of women's work piled atop, Dreamings in bright colours which spoke of Land's abundance, of the gracious gifts of Earth. Desert yam, bush tomato – it mattered not. Each and every painting scripted Joy-of-Life; vibrancy oozed audibly from each painted pore. But while each and every were admirable, none spoke 'my' language. T heard the flip-flip-flipping through the pile, felt my approach, knew when I stopped. 'Twas when she was exposed to Light. Harsh. Fluorescent.

I stared at this sole exemplar – the only one ancillary to verdant theme in entire pile. Rather than wearing its soul at skin, this one's message hidden, sunk into, <u>beneath</u> a single chromatic key. Within black there is white – this I had known since long, a Taoist wisdom speaking to the uncreated Light. But here, seaming one to the other was the deep dirt of Earth sentience. This too I knew – Gondwana brown. When the twig came on consciousness, I knew not to second-guess or question the intuition. The knowing was immediate, as immediate as so many other (more costly) acts in life (see "Awakening" for a mortgage-worthy example).

Had T been yelling from far beneath the surface exuberance of Land's bounty piled atop (an irony not lost on me) to be excavated from her 'burial site'? To breathe the fresh air of day, albeit far from her birthplace in a desert workshop, blank canvas on bare earth, conjured to life by a barefoot master with a simple stick and three paint pots?

When the dealer approached, Time hiccupped as he looked from T to me and back again. He was a trader – Afghan as well as Aboriginal blood flowed in his veins. Once he softened to our ignorance (and innocent interest), he told the 'Tale of the Nine', one of whom was T's maker (also named T), born amongst saltpan and spinifex, the last to walk in from the raw wilds of western desert just a few decades earlier. It made national headlines at the time; they were the subject of much anthropological enquiry as well as caution. Guarding against basic disease for which their immune system had no defence? Minimising contact with white folk till integrated with their own? Softly, softly – at the very least more compassionate practices had developed over the past hundred years.

But how had I missed this in the press? These were the selfsame years I, a child of sun'n'surf coast, made home 'out west', drove corrugated tracks, red dust spiralling in a chariot's wake, walked Dreaming paths not my own but which touched, deeply, my white fella (black) heart. I knew I couldn't stay too long in this country; its harsh climate overwhelmed my need for lush green; its parched earth, while fully 'alive' of bush tucker, too 'foreign' for a mango- and pawpaw-raised lass. Nevertheless, its spirit thrilled me with 'otherness', whispering Land's elemental songs on a crackling fire, billy tea brewing while a bandicoot nosed around camp. No coincidence I yearned to return, bring family here years later. They would understand more about me by trekking this raw wild country as well as Gondwana's coastal fringe.

T's maker, a shy youth whose birthyear was reckoned to be several post-mine, took up the paints of his older brothers. But where they created monumental works which hang in the famous art museums of the world, T's maker stayed quiet, stayed small, stayed in/with the desert (mother) who had gifted his skin <u>this</u> Dreaming. I still see T's maker as he was, even though the 'provenance' pic which accompanies an Aboriginal artwork's certificate of purchase (as proof-of-making) shows a mid-aged man in a dusty tin shed sitting cross-legged with T, a simple canvas fresh-minted held up to camera flash. Stoic are they both of expression, like a Gondwana version of Grant Wood's "American Gothic":

We are the Land and the Land is Us. (said)

The trader proffered a Wiki page and old newspaper articles as evidence.

Perhaps T had been stuck at the bottom of pile because he never thought she would be saleable; she did not even host the ruddy hues of more known ochre-inspired works that 'sing' the desert colours. No, she was darker, deeper and to a 'white' sensibility morose of tone. Perhaps it just needed someone who hangs out in DeepTime-Tectonia to see her Beauty for what it was. Lucky it was me; "very lucky" as the trader wryly remarked.

• • • • •

T sings the original Dreaming. Although I did not (consciously) know it at the time, it was her Gondwana-brown seaming which spoke, connecting me into whatever it was she would tell, in time. In good time – hers, not mine. But gosh I loved her well – fostered, like a wee foundling discovered on Soul's doorstep. Invoice settled, safely swaddled, I clutched her scroll to breast – the most precious cabin baggage imaginable – carrying her thousands of hemispheric kilometres across time, space to the alpine heights of Helvetia. We would cross her primal lands in the plane, 10,000kms up in the sky. Did she feel the tug as we hurtled on/past? Stretching her Songline, an umbilicus strung from the heart of stone, now vertically, horizontally, spherically strained by Gaia's colossal Third-Rock girth?

But earlier than this/that, I wondered:

Did it hurt, T, to be wrenched from your maker's arms? Or was it a pact already sung into being as first paint was applied to bare skin, smearing your lily-white canvas, pure, virginal, with the black of original Mystery, that cosmic dark <u>potency</u> in which uncreated Light resides, the all-of-all of potentiality incubating pre-Big-Bang singing, mirrored in the peatbog-fecund primeval ocean which, once, covered all the world? The black needed to dry, yes, 'ripen' its knowing before brown could be 'applied', before Gondwana could emerge as Land onto which could then be plotted the lily-white stellar coordinates so you could always find your way home. No matter who chose you from a musty pile – already far from home. A home, and Dreaming, you could re-enter from this landlocked otherworld of walls doors roofs as foreign to you as a desert's hot breath to me.

I see your maker sitting on/in the dirt, bent over your emerging form; I see his paint stick at its work; I see him mutter/hum your Song, chin tucked close to his chest:

Dot-dot-dot. Dip the stick in white paint pot.
Dot-dot-dot. Dip again, continue work.
Dot-dot-dot. You-are-Me and We-are-Three.
Dot-dot-dot-dot-dot …

No more meditative percussive praxis can there be for walking and singing the Land into being – each bare footstep to raw skin'd Earth; each repeat performance to canvas, ensoul'd. Yes, I see him still at task; T's maker – this sweet boy who walked in, mute, from the desert, torn too from primal ground. Given clothes, given shoes (they didn't last long), given paint and canvas where before he would sit, script Story/Song in the dirt at his feet. Just another layer, just a palimpsest. Here, lad, said those who had come before, those who had been born into these dusty settlements a generation removed from desert mother origins.

Here, boy, take these paints, let your Song <u>stick</u> in the human realm, assume enduring voice in acrylic dress (and in the process earn your bread). Each/all set sail but T found her longer-than home, her longer-than steward, that day in a Sydney marketplace. Oh, she was coddled! This next best 'rescue child' of mine, unframed. Just a plain wood stretcher at back to offer strength and hung on wall in inner sanctum where each/all on Love's altar said: "Welcome."

In those early years of our together-life, I and sweet silent inscrutable T, my focus was mostly on her brown seam – Gondwana as the <u>glue</u> between primal night and stellar white. In those years, Gondwana simply offered her quiet resonance to a symphonic binding with down under home, one that found expression and longer-than residence with the 'Shining Ones of the Sea' (see "Awakening"); one that set to train the praxis of sacred (and secret) 'tsuringa' message sticks in various skin'd forms (ditto). But a moment came when Gondwana wanted to share, specifically, her Dreaming story and how we could 'work' with this. Now, years later, I realised she arose from/through T to gift me insights in 'language' that would make sense to a simple mind, in language that would suggest what we could make together <u>beyond</u> a simple binding of home with home. I realised that all 'apprenticeship' tasks undertaken, tests 'passed', and the growing fluidity of our Amici work had widened, deepened, extended the trench of what we could offer to world, to Gaia's evolution of consciousness – as a holistic proposition – just as my own evolved in (embodied) tandem …

I had no way of knowing at the time but in the moment Gondwana said: "Listen", revealed her direct presence, intercession, support for our UrWerk (not even knowing it was our task to perform or support such an UrWerk!), it was abundantly clear T had facilitated this and (as will soon be shared) sanctioned it, seeing a future potentiality which, once little me was 'apprised' of same, became a domino tumbling par excellence, a rollercoaster ride that only now I am able to tell – for this, after all that, T has now (at last) sanctioned. With thanks/good grace.

Yes, I know my praxis of walking, singing, sole-pressed-to-soul infuses Love to Land in the spirit of Aboriginal Dreaming Songlines. Yes, I know we are all part of Gaia's OneEarth, bound by DeepTime-Tectonia'd root-knowing far beneath surface considerations which stretch the Songlines as far-as-far-can-go through world. Yes, I know to honour, and bless as I enter 'new' territory, on metaphoric bended knee give homage to Mountains, Waters, Ancestors, Flora and Fauna (my "Hello the House" praxis). Yes, I know, at some deep resonant burbling level, that Gondwana stands at back, she whose earth has <u>made</u> me, she who carries in her dense and dusty bones the primal code/x of DeepTime-Tectonia'd origins.

Yes, all this I know but so much I do not, nor will ever. In any case, it is time to turn the stage over to T, for her to tell as much as she wants about her facilitating backboning patronage of our work. Please be patient, Reader, with this stream-of-consciousness transcription of her voice. We shall see how we go, shall we? Over to you, T …

I remember the day I chose to come, tell her (Annie) of my joy that she would take up this mantle and complete the puzzle, the jigsaw of pieces placed by DeepTime indigene'd wisdom and her own white world's in shared framework. That's what I saw, this potentiality, and that's what I placed before her eyes. And a moment came, in my telling (I am a part-time teacher, at best, after all, and it is difficult for me to 'step down' into this role from the stellar depths-heights and 'hold it together' so a professional voice can emerge rather than the passion I feel thru all times and worlds, my home, heart worn on a sleeve I do not have), …

((Yes, Annie, I know your heart is warmed and pounding and stretched beyond measure by writing this down/out for me; I know you must speak aloud the words as you write for your small shell/container cannot hold within the energy I bring but stay with it, sweetness – all is well, and ever, as you are so fond of self-quoting Julian of Norwich's encounter with divinity.))

Yes, a moment came in my telling when I lost it and shining tears flowed forth in my <u>potent</u> joy that I could share inwith <u>this</u> group, with this one who said she would take up the mantle, bring my knowing to world and, with Love, weave it on. To enable my arise, my emergence (full and frank) from canvas, several precursors, waymarkers were needed. With support of her Amici (here I must thank MakerMan for her wise-woman-Sidhe'd intercession – they make good working partners, but I digress), Annie saw the need to formally ask permission of the Aboriginal elders whose tradition I serve, whose Dreaming I host – permission that they would <u>release</u> my knowing into her care and let me come into the full blossoming and flowering that the jigsaw's potential bespeaks. (She has an expression for this – 'recovered memory, fresh envisioned' but again I digress.)

Oh! I saw the letter she wrote to formally ask permission of the elders in subtle realms! So full of Love and so pure of intent in her desire to serve Gaia, a whole-of-world consciousness support in its unfolding. She lay down her and her Amici troupe's provenance, a CV in a way, and said look to the record of what we have made, ask for references if you like – Gondwana at least will tell you are hearts are true! The 'dark' (mounds) had been delivered to her garden gate; she had intuited their purpose as continental anchors for a global alliance of mountain champions to join together, support the increasing flow of stellar 'Blue' into the Body of Gaia's 'Green'. Robust consequent stones, of physical mass <u>and</u> presence, existed in her Zen Garden, edging its River'd journey from (mountain) source to (ocean of being'd) sea. Delivering the 'dark' to <u>infiltrate</u> the consciousness of their matter was a precious timely Amici task in overall process.

She had already assigned 'brothers-of-flame-sisters-of-light' monikers; now was time to formally free my knowing from the corset binding me to the specificity of ancestral Land and demonstrate, in vision, what we could 'make' for Gaia as an holistic proposition.

And oh, she knew how this could be misinterpreted, misunderstood, the whole language of cultural appropriation and colonial usurp descrying the purity of her intent. Knew, so wrote her letter to the source – to the maker's <u>spirit</u> from her very own spirit; drawing words up/out of soul-depths to speak true her troth, waters from Love's well fuelling each word penned, a cosmic language with no need of translation. "Dear T of the P, dear T of the Nine," she wrote (in fact) (for my maker's name and mine share the same first letter) and offered it to our gods, posted it 'home' to our Ancestors, and then waited – to see what they willed to be done …

Ha! Who would have thought she could uplift the innocent child of my maker's mid-aged hand from spirit depths with her heartfelt plea? But here he was, arrived in thru Window-on-World as if re-delivering me to her ten-foot-square hut, hanging me up on wall (approving placement to all intents), before re-donning flying goggles and setting sail in a 'Tiger Moth' biplane with a broad cheeky grin as if a 'Koala Brother' from her own child's TV screen come to life! That was the first step in (my) process of shedding corset. Following, He released me – the Great Ancestor who walked/sang our Land into being from/out of (my) primal mud. I saw how she watched, absolutely stunned (I can understand why – 'twas a confronting, challenging sight for a small human not even of our skin to witness) as He rose out of canvas, great thick trunks of legs lifting up/out of peat-black mud, giant arms swinging as off/back to our home constellation amongst the stars He strode. Once, He looked back, nodded to her, affirmed his accession to her request. Sky-Father, she called him in deep-heart-understanding, and stayed with the experience all the way thru to its close.

It needed this (latter) act, see; not just what she assumed needed (letter to maker) to release me fully into a potentiality to partner. For when my maker, T, created me, T, as sacred container of his Land's Dreaming, he sang 'awake' my stellar origins in painterly incantation, sang awake my Great Ancestor's 'presence' as a loving overlighting force to the enduring anchored spirit of Land I house. With her letter, soul-to-soul and 'posted' home to the Ancestors in Love, she (in a way) reprised the role of a suitor seeking permission of a father for a daughter's hand, which, when he rose and strode back to the stars, affirmed his agreement of this divine marriage, Annie-&-T, inwith a constellation of OnePeople'd communion.

Frame. Named. Here/now. Free. Homecome-welcomed. Released to shared soul-purpose to serve all of Gaia, not just my (as hers) <u>birth</u> Land. And in a monumental download (for her small human mind to hold), accompanied by many shining tears (mine), I took this opportunity to teach the wisdom on, offer it into the shared hands serving world. Here is what she saw:

((I will now pass back to sweet Annie to describe in her own raw voice the vision of *what could be made, for Gaia … Thank you for listening to my story …))*

Dear Reader, you cannot imagine my relief when T arrived this morning and said: Now! (or never). I had reached a point, after so much fruitless coaxing to please let me tell of what we have made, what she inspired and inspirited (literally) us to make, after so many avenues explored, so many: "How about this?" (conversations). What would work without revealing too much of the treasury of secret (men's/women's) business (an Aboriginal expression for the depths of Dreaming that can only be shared within a miniscule circle of initiates) emanating from her catacomb'd troves? So many attempts led to dead ends, her (mother-of-pearl'd) lips clamm'd tight shut, stubbornly un-budged by my implores, that it would help others make sense of our work, place it within the framework of WorldSong, of what Mariel had to David described, we Amici simply a set of tools (wrapt in tulle) for each performative outing on Gaia's high wild raw and free (concerto) stage.

Indeed, I thought the chapter would (post-title) be a series of blank pages (Jeremy would have loved that bit of unsustainable publishing – not!). The chapter still needed to be present even if its slate wiped clean post- (inner) performance or outed on what I call (after Zourabichvili, after Deleuze & Guattari) a 'plane of intimate exteriority'. Wiped clean, each time, like Suzuki's beginner's mind or when the makers of each Dreaming cycle scripted, sung the stories in sand, then scrubbed them out post-ceremony. Sand mandalas to all intents (like Tibetans craft for their gods) for the Ancestors' arrival-departure – up from Earth spiral'd, down from Heaven ditto'd, in a quintessential vortex of Breath-<u>reciprocate</u> flow, each time a first time, round the ring we go.

Yes, like beginner's mind, but our cupboard (unlike old Mother Hubbard's) was far from bare. I had tussled, veritably wrestled with this notion of shifting inner wisdoms to a public plane decades past in my PhD research in an attempt to find a way <u>through</u> to telling, to sharing what had been shared in the canonical halls of sages (down the ages). At the time of PhD, I quoted Virgil's dilemma, nay verily invoked Virgil's <u>desire</u> to tell as my own (which confounded the academy no end; thank heavens for Jungian psychology to provide the 'jargon' for keeping my work, marginally, within the bounds decreed by 'scientific rigour'!).

For T, it seemed like the only way to tell <u>without</u> telling – a chapter of X number of blank pages, like a sacred performance stick-drawn by my Shaping Man in original Card Deck, danced in the round (of seasonal indenture), by bodies smeared and daubed in sacred symbology, then wiped away from the sands of time, scrubbed clean at the waterholes of wisdom, so the next new could ever rise (afresh). And yet, and yet … T was committed to canvas, as portable as a tsuringa stick, or travelling icon. A mere fifty short years since such permanent Dreaming 'markers' of ancestral Presence were able to 'fly-out' from HomeSong, see beyond with physic'd eyes, tell their Story to a physic'd humanity beyond primal shores. And here was T, post-letter, post-my-beseech, freed to tell in her own voice (a first time in intimate company) and freed now (again, by her own hand) to commit a version of same to print in this chapter. Phew!

Life is liminal (this we know); the ephemeral ever-dwells beneath soil, its rhizomatic (rainbow) serpent shifting, moving, writhing below turf till a moment comes when it springs forth, cries: "Catch me if you can in my brief moment above Land!" Which is what happened this morning, in this place, when T, far from the wall on which her 'likeness' dwells, (prodded by Gondwana in Ruscada's skirts no doubt: "Come on, girl, give her a way in to pen your ken") arrived pre-dawn and said: "OK, here we go ..."

Well, Reader, what a ride and it ain't over (as we all know) till the Fat Lady sings. We have enjoyed the overture (thank you, T!); now 'tis time (for me) to put flesh on these gnawed gnarly crone bones, tell our Amici'd part of tale and how it serves the Gaian good in weaving-the-world.

•••••

After I penned the letter, asking (please!) to harness T's work as a Mountains-Mandala melding energy and substance, I entered one of the deepest meditations I can recall in which I saw an 'Anne-cosmology' (relevant to task) interweaving the stellar realms with the stars-in-the-earth through the nodal 'reservoirs' (receptacles) assigned – in-Zen-skin, in-T-canvas, and via in-world peaks. It was in the ritual of their 'naming' that their one-and-the-same <u>interchange</u> as 'grail-beings' was forged.

Apropos 'naming': In Ursula Le Guin's "EarthSea" realm, Ged's apprenticeship as mage involves needing to learn a thing in all its seasons, weathers, humours before he can truly know it and thus speak its name with any power, use it as a tool, or partner it to shared purpose. He needs to get <u>beneath</u> its skin, to where its essence dwells, to honour its 'being' as itself. A process of initiation, of relational interbeing, was implied and so it was, equally, with my conscious act of naming.

Words (strongly, unequivocally) now formed: "Circumambulate." I 'saw' myself as a pilgrim, walking each node's Songline from outer to inner, to call up its energetic thread between upper-lower, singing the "Awakening Song" all the while. Retracing the path out again, in <u>exactitude</u>, was essential. The power lay in <u>explicitly</u> engaging T for T to engage <u>her</u> work (to support <u>our</u> work). The layers of 'activation' were thus multi-fold – first honouring the work's creation by maker's hand, then, via 'tracing' the path in/out, walking in the footsteps <u>of</u> the footsteps of the Ancestors, thus replicating T's maker's process as well as binding me/us to T's spirit-geologic 'holism'. Once I understood (and therefore completed) this entire process in self, 'formal transference' could occur. The Ancestor rose out of canvas, strode off/back to its cosmic origins while T's maker skipped off through the wall of hut with a grin, tools of trade in hand, antique flying cap on his head.

'Twas a powerful affirmation when I saw the Ancestor leave, head 'North', speak <u>its</u> Dreaming name aloud to me in mind, affirm its origin in a specific stellar constellation known well. A dark spirit energy matter returning whence come, it walked <u>huge</u> over Land before rising to Sky while I stayed put. Well-rested, cosy, sunk, <u>held</u> in/by Land, the pure Mother-Love of embodied immersion via a precious-precious Dreaming courtesy of a random find in a random marketplace of a far-from-random artwork.

While the Ancestor was still present, here I was, just 'humming away', thinking: "We're all vibrating together; I'm at and/or we're all at/in time/concert with the same vibrational frequency of Land as it/herself – spirit and geology <u>are</u> one, and I 'one' with it! So cool!"

The Ancestor chose this moment to 'exit-stage-left' (perhaps bored with my 'la-la-land' effusing?). A deep message was imparted by its farewell – an acknowledgement its work here was done. 'I' had been apprised of task, and actively sanctioned to harness its <u>applied</u> wisdom to a Whole-of-Earth ontology. At this I had a 'flash' of desert nights around a campfire, watching this Ancestor's constellation shift across Sky. I felt into the aeons <u>consolidated</u> in a single moment ingrained in T's canvas iconographic 'likeness' – the <u>echo</u> of original in generational time ever-present. The Mother-Ocean 'mother lode', a repository of DeepTime wisdom from Memory's treasury seeping up from homeland and into me. Yes, I understood 'in-Self'. Transference had been effected. To premiere (at some point) on Gaia's stage.

The fact I understood what was required of me/us was simply a case of having 'lived' it before; the process was already inscribed in heart, rendered in text. "The Taste of Translation" (2011), my major of work of prose fiction, was designed as a triptych, its form mirroring a Byzantine travelling icon, hinged, of three sacred panels – the central panel 'anchoring' the others either side. In the book, the story-panels of Laleima and Kisha are held in time/space by a 'slim sister in-between'. 'She' is the crux of whole, the pivot point on which the triptych 'spins' – in this panel the icon which links Laleima (in 14th century) and Kisha (in 20th) is written into existence.

To say I inhabited the space of 'writing' the icon as I 'wrote' the panel does not describe the half of it. I needed to compose 'witness-reports' (each from a different perspective, a fractal of whole) to provide a modicum of distance from the energetic intensity experienced while in-pouring the sacred to this well of blessing. Uplifted from the Malakut's imaginal realm, compelling was its intersect with my (limited) consciousness just as I 'wrote' it for the iconographer. <u>My</u> circumambulation of icon, thus, mirrored its maker's which <u>activated</u> the event in textual container – a representation with the power of original, amplified by my constant reviewing, editing, refining of text each time diving deeper into its well.

Central to this was the type of icon written – the Mother, our Lady Kiria, whose signature form is heart-centred loving-kindness (kardiotissa) as she holds her infant son to breast. Describing the process for the purposes of my PhD, I wrote:

"I had read about the descent of grace (charis), the icon's active element, life or spirit, as a conduit of divine response, but for me to experience it through writing this text into existence was completely unexpected. The panel functions as ekphrasis. As the iconographer journeyed from unknowing to knowing across the <u>chronotope</u> of the songs' narration, so too did I, this panel's 'becoming' completing my own. Finally, it was as if I had reached the point where (Walter) Benjamin's 'pure', his 'echo of the original', waited (to be translated). I had reached this 'single spot' in the rhizome, finding myself in the exact location to receive the echo."

I described inhabiting, fully <u>embodying</u> the space of engagement, the 'becoming landscape' of icon and <u>its</u> writing itself to existence in a process of co-performance, and co-creation. In a back-to-the-future moment, I saw immediate parallels with T's 'iconographic' process of making, and what my (fully-embodied) circumambulation could contribute to <u>extending</u> T's brief in-world – for this 'work' to be able to do its 'work', just as the icon – in/of itself and text – did its.

In 1933, Federico Garcia Lorca wrote a lecture titled "Play and Theory of the Duende". In it, he sought to articulate the embodied knowing which infused his work, drawing on flamenco and Gypsy 'cante jondo' (deep song) to explain his proposition:

"I have heard an old maestro of the guitar say, 'The duende is not in the throat; the duende climbs up inside you, from the soles of the feet'."

Lorca writes thrillingly (and accurately) about the experience of wakening inspiration "in the remotest mansions of the blood". Co-creation (and co-performance) cannot 'happen' <u>without</u> a living body's interpretation (i.e. translation).

Just as I had 'seen' into the iconographer's work and as witness-reports penned its existence, I could see into T's maker's, my circumambulation 'penning' an echo of his echo of T's original wisdom – her duende housed in the living body of Earth, drawn up through (each of our) soles of feet as we walked the pilgrim path in-out. Thus honouring the <u>consciousness</u> of matter by physically engaging same – another take (if you will) on the 'power of five' as the elementals begin their swirl to extent life, coalescing around the core-proposition aetherically-'dusted' down for the Stars, composted in fecund Earth till one arrives to 'sing' the Song to life (again).

The iconographer danced with his duende in the writing of icon, yet knowing each time a first time no matter how many times he painted the same image. Each was an echo of sacred original. And in observing his process, bringing it to performance 'stage' (in text), his catharsis became my own:

"That night I saw the Holy Spirit move through him, mix the colours, sketch the outline, fill the form with delicate strokes. Work silently written. As conceived, so delivered. As received from a space beyond thought, beyond language, so translated into gold leaf and egg tempera. No need of word, no need of thought. From the beyond to the beyond by way of a single hand, a pure heart, he wrote with full attention to his task, returning the Lord's gift unto Himself, gifting it on, out into the world, this gift of Love divine ... No time had passed in the space where he was, yet dawn approached. With the first twitter of birds in the grey half-light which precedes the sun's rise, he stood and stretched, returned from a journey into the closet of his heart, the icon the story of his voyage."

So many interconnective 'events' engaged in concurrent Time-partner'd time that I could only see for their coalesce of Presence in (later) Time-partner'd time. T watched, waited till (said) Time ripe for her Star to appear on performance stage. We had been walking, see, continuing the Camino string through Land. Walking. A meditative praxis, full-embodied of (small human) skin. Physically singing up the connection, Body a PeacePole as potent as the hiking staff that metronome-pounded to ground at my feet, <u>magnetically</u> connecting energetic flow between Gaia-Self, a twinned space inhabited as verily traversed.

Gondwana found me (again) – here in (this walking) place once Malakut-visited. A place I knew as 'True-Sister's-Island', a place I knew existed (in some dimensional reality) inwith the porous borders of Helvetia. But if there were an exact 'where' to match its Malakut-render? No idea. Till by happenstance (or not) the path we walked upjumped the all of subtle sight to waking eye – enacting, in perfect synchrony, what I envisioned with our walk across Land, to re-enliven long-buried Songlines with my Peace-Love-Light mantra ever-sung in heart.

In hindsight, therefore, all the synapses were obviously firing (in Soul) to 'prime' Mind for the download which arrived from T in its (overnight) wake. Vibrationally, it was as if Body, in conscious-intersect with <u>primal</u> Land, had sunk to such a frequency of DeepTime-Tectonia as to enable induction to the primal <u>fact</u> of primal Land – the foundational presence of Mother-Ocean beneath, to which the all-of-All gives thanks for Life arising via the 'power of five'.

• • • • •

I woke circa 5am. Lucid. "Ganz wach" (as we say in Swiss). Fully present to the richness of T's teaching. Oh, how honoured I felt! And yet she was saying the same to me? With her shining tears, weeping in gratitude to be invited to shared table? Imagery-taught, T scripted before my eyes <u>her</u> Dreaming of primal creation upjumped from Mother-Ocean, the pure Dark of uncreated Light pre-Big-Bang singing the cosmos to Being. She told, too, the true name of this Ur-Presence, a name I cannot speak in public. Invoked by the Ancestors as they 'walked' the Songline/s out across Land, calling out the names in Song, awakening matter'd consciousness to the sacredness it carried <u>and</u> upwelled from core.

The Mother's name is taught to each wisdom-keeper in lineage so they may re-walk, re-sing Land as the Ancestors did at beginning of 'Time'. 'Tis sacred task – to walk in the footsteps of ancestral beings – their task <u>and</u> their privilege. Now, with name gifted on into our care, we likewise bore a deep responsibility. So did I watch the whole fabric of Land in its process of becoming; so did I listen to the creative impulse woven of Mother-Ocean <u>Breath</u> which initiates the arising of all to follow – whether subtle or physic'd, Universe-expansive <u>and</u> Universe-equivalent was each naming, each Song.

Just as I had been Tibetan-taught, the energetic swirl of the 'power of five' densified all the way through to consciousness-infused matter – the solidity of Stone, the (liturgical) mass of Mountain. I was blessed with sight onto the work of the Ancestors, great beings <u>emerging</u> from Mother-Ocean to alchemise (original) Breath. Outwalking to the four directions, singly and coupled, partners to purpose – to seek 'worthy' marriage partners, stellar with earthen, to <u>anchor</u> stellar nodes in primal scape. These stars-within-earth, live-<u>wired</u> in/of/to/through Gondwana's geologic genetic memory (which I share in this miniscule dust-mote-ish form), represent a (major) microcosm of planetary macrocosm <u>nested</u> in the vastness of cosmic 'bang'; so did I intuit the <u>correspondence</u> between what T revealed on/through her particular (iconographic) plane and the potential to apply this knowledge to contribute to Gaian purpose. As offered, so accepted.

(Dawn of Time grinned from somewhere offstage, wrapt in the folds of his fraying carpet drapes; 'Mummy' was here to help and the 'sack of seeds' were ready for perennials-planting; no longer was there need to be wary.)

T continued the teaching, demonstrating the importance of Sun to equation, walking-with the Ancestors till, at zenith, each was called to <u>still</u> the energy, anchor it wherever in scape they happened to be in/of present moment (i.e. plant it). Sun at his apex. Ancestors in reverent blessing – offering the <u>bridge</u> between Heaven-Earth, enacting the 'divine marriage' of Land-Sky. Words formed: "Triangulation". Yes. I remembered back to the original communique two years earlier. This is how the Ancestors had worked – the sacred geometry of alignments; this is what we were being asked to support and 'resurrect' via our small contribution to the 'great work' for Gaia. We would integrate to our ceremonies, and I would weave into my walking praxis, this fundamental wisdom – to stop <u>still</u> in space at a precise moment (zenith'd of Presence) to align cosmic-planetary forces, there to sing, 'triangulate' the lines in-world-out. After which? At "Close-of-Time" (spoken), Mother drew all ancestral beings back into <u>her</u> Ocean, Love's Ground, till a next call 'woken' in Time-partner'd time.

Gondwana whispered: "Umbilicus of Stone." Yes. Through which starblood flows ... I bowed to T, a beautiful 'ancient' of timeless ageless maidenly quality.

She said she was a 'part-time teacher', expressed gratitude for our invitation (my letter having released her bonds); now she was free to join our gathering, offer the knowledge of her wisdom school to equation.

She began bringing together bits of a (wooden) jigsaw puzzle, popping pieces in place, vertically, in space so we may all see onto the 'board'. By end, an image of two motifs were side by side, symbolically representing the different traditions – indigenous and white. This was the moment which sparked her tears – completing a shared puzzle by slotting in her bits. So vital a contribution to holistic spirit-geologic outcomes for all Earth-bound sentience! My gratitude was profound, as was a deep sense of Love. I had been blessed with a 'new' Sister, a treasured revelation of itself – the 'knowing' held by family, passed on to/through family. T may have felt 'invited' to our gathering, but I felt welcome in their fold equally. At some level we shared 'skin'.

However, on a broader platform than the specificities of work praxis, I wondered long at the jigsaw puzzle's deeper message. That all spiritual traditions, mythologies, ways-of-knowing need to be honoured and provided the opportunity to support Gaia's emergence by 'slotting in their bits'. I looked around our Amici troupe (Stone Circle'd, a-dance). The space we offered as 'host' was neutral, welcoming, loving, respectful. (Always PeaceTea brewing on the stove! MagicMan added.) Till now, I had only looked at the equation from our side – to learn and/or re-learn the ancient ways ('the wisdom of ages and sages', so-called) – but T's tears and heartfelt gratitude alerted me to the role we played as facilitators to unveil knowing. Any/all could come, contribute – purity of intent and a loving heart opened the portal to our micro-dimension, simple as that. We all gained much from exchange – ideas, practices, processes.

I have always spoken of 'conversation partners'. Even if said conversations go on in my/our 'inner' world, mediated by reading or wandering the wilds, they find an avenue of 'outer' expression through text-works in which I honour these partners, closing the circle with thanks/good grace. We all stand on the shoulders of giants, after all. Now I stepped back, reflected. Our cirque had 'opened' a network of different energetic presences' contributions to us, and to themselves – to each other and together. With our dedication to holistic inclusivity (all the way up the line to cosmic humanity's origins), it established the 'causes, conditions' for the becoming landscape of field to emerge. No wonder the Ancestors' response to my letter was a 'no-brainer'. The interconnectivity of each with other as much as me with each was heard.

We may have hosted this gathering of wisdoms (as well as many others) in the sanctity of own home, but on other occasions I would consciously, in meditation, visit a temple 'precinct' which, as inner landscape, hosted many traditions. Here I would meditate (in my meditation) – give praise, gain insight in company of many in (sung or chanted) worship. This was no 'meld' of various lineages or 'ways-of-knowing'. Each had its own space in quadrangle (of subtle architecture); each honoured for what it brought to shared worldview – lain on the shared ground of Love (manifesting, in this case, as smoothed flagstones to ensure deep connection with Earth). The drill was to grab a chair or cushion from around the perimeter, bring it out to centre, sit in/with Sun's (zenith'd) presence to 'draw-down' the gifts of Love's Light to world, to offer same out to world according to the historico-cultural tradition which most <u>resonated</u> with the worshipper's (Huxleyian) mode-of-being.

Sun is a "blithe tool" (Amici-words but I must agree with this assessment of his 'big-brother' nature!), a form of substation transformer for the in-flow of more expansive cosmic intelligence. 'Tis not called the 'Solar System' without reason; the quadrangle's set-up offered the perfect sacred geometry for 'flowing' Love's Light on/into world – through the directions, elements. No roof, walls – just as Han Shan decreed at Cold Mountain. All open, connectable across the ten dimensions (and more). Here, Humboldt's Current (as we Amici affectionately call this 'force') could be fully plugged in – to/from source code/x.

For my (Huxleyian) mode, an interesting hybrid armchair was fashioned – a goddess, seated, in which I could sit. Carved into the wood of chair itself, the arms were hers, legs as well. Such that when my arms rested along their length, it was as if blanket-stitched in place for the duration of meditation. The chair was highly-coloured, ornate and elaborate in its sculpted presence (of her mentoring presence) to support my work which crossed and amalgam'd all goddess traditions in honour of the (One) Mother (Love). Goddesses whom I know as 'Sisters', just as T had revealed herself to me. All are kin when all is said and done through the limitless dimensions of this diagram of equals where each of us contributes according to the mode of our being. Our Amici praxis was consolidating itself – in-house-out. All gifts received we gifted on and into the circular economy of Gaia's 'Ecology of Light' – in Song.

• • • • •

Interrelations, never-ending. I may be the only 'human' Sister in this fast-expanding troupe (of troubadours), merely an apprentice in such aeons-wise (and active!) company. Yet it was my task to 'ignite' these (Mountain) Sisters of Light and Brothers of Flame in (Zen-themed) garden grail to join as one collective born, in truth, of Mother-Ocean: Love.

In a nod to our Amici 'origins' of co-performative partnering, we chose a single simple flower, gentiana alpina, to hold the purity of our loving (Blue) intent. I say 'origins' with good cause – meeting the Amici (unaware of their Sidhe-ness) was flooded with gentian'd delight. A scene I offered to Kisha (in "The Taste of Translation"), the encounter went something like this:

"A dark night but the way lit by gentians, precious deep-throated flowers line the path, tiny bulbs filling their blue hearts, skin translucent from an inner glow. Kisha follows the troupe along a twisting turning route while a joyous chorus sings loud in her ear. After a time, she stops, follows no more. At peace with her decision, she farewells the merry-makers as they move off through a clear-lit tunnel to beyond, shared voice like swirled mist to her ears."

The encounter riffed off DH Lawrence's poetry:
Reach me a gentian, give me a torch!
Let me guide myself with the blue, forked torch of this flower
down the darker and darker stairs, where blue is darkened on blueness
even where Persephone goes …

It also cohered with Carl Jung's rhizomatic theory of the collective unconscious; he too had been touched by the ephemeral life of sweet gentian, its true nature hidden in rhizome and to which it returned after an altogether too-brief alpine Summer till next called forth – up into the "eternal flux" of Time. Indeed, in the root-knowing of gentian its medicinal properties lie.

None of this was on my mind, of course, when a pot of tight-closed buds at the local florist winked at me from a display out front one day (edelweiss also has a merry habit of 'winking', Christopher Plummer and "The Sound of Music" ringing in my ears as I pass cash across the counter). Only once home did I think to count the number of blooms – eight. Well, there you have it. After their 'full-flourish' on performance stage, at the moment of 'die-back', I plucked each flower, laid it on requisite stone, and sang the incantation of wakening. Each mound of 'dark knowing' within rhizome'd network would hear our call in (their) Persephone's Blue.

Additionally, I spoke my affirmation according to the model of the 'snowball of becoming' (see "Appendix 3"):

"May my <u>becoming desire</u> to light the Light enable the <u>landscape</u> of connectivity – of sight-lines ley-lines water-lines shed-lines heart-lines peak-lines pass-lines current-lines plate-lines on-on-on, to <u>become</u>; for my <u>consciousness</u> to become, to grow all the while, so I know <u>how</u> and <u>where</u> and <u>when</u> and with <u>whom</u> to 'start digging' for greatest <u>efficacy</u> of this becoming <u>product</u> on Dawn of Time's unending watch. The history of human creativity is only one part of puzzle. Our creativity occurs in <u>concert</u> with the elementals' 'power of five'. We are all companions of Love's way; purity of intent is essential <u>and</u> essencial to this becoming <u>myth</u> of Gaian evolution, the personal as planetary <u>and</u> vice-versa. Jung's esoterica exoteric'd in skin!"

Ah, 'snowball of becoming' … How many times have you seen Light-of-(process'd)-Day? What on earth did you Amici think when I started chucking academic methodological models your lightfoot'd shapeshifting way? (Yes, I know, you chucked an Anwa curve-ball straight back into the field of play!)

My point (now) being that the <u>energy</u> of creation fuels each step of process, its <u>joyous</u> bursting forth has nowhere else to go but to manifest in full glowing (gentian'd) colour, to birth <u>itself</u> in-world in service of Gaia's great work (Proclus' perennially happy heliotrope refers). Loving service, selfless <u>gifted</u>. Gifting of self (as Malakut-taught) – only possible when self is naught, when through your eyes myself I see. What is the use of two bowls ("I Ching"d)? To receive, to gift on. <u>This</u> the Mother-energy born of Ocean's desire – the (spark of) Love which is each's inheritance and birthright, moulding it into what <u>it</u> wants to <u>become</u>. Whole. One. Light. No wonder the (singing) bird crunched a (blue) seed to release those golden (gentian) wisps to their (blue) 'power of five'd expression.

I sleep. (Poorly.) I see a lake. Words form: "Upjumped from Mother-Ocean <u>core</u>." Here is where sink meets surface, in the pure (sweet) waters of Helvetia's heart – connecting to the Mother (Ocean) via (Gondwana's) <u>umbilicus</u> of stone, a-flow, a-glow of starblood. Song arises – 'tis a 'Mother-Song' to sing back to Mother-Ocean, weave the all-of-creation back home to her One. Time partners Song's open-close; I hear the tidal swash back-forth. Above is my singing. A Love Song, to Kiria (as named). Over, over. Binding itself to itself – in-time-and-out.

A self-weaving and world-weaving in one. I sense Dawn's presence. 'Tis an <u>inner</u> sound that, when I try to hum or bring voice to it, takes a while till the right <u>outer</u> notes come. Which then need to be embedded in Body before any further externalisation, to bring piano 'pitch' to the picture. What a process of bringing the inner out – in Song! Some are easier, auto'd into existence. But this refrain is inordinately deep (no wonder!), the chorale at work has within Soul awoken. Just as I, when receiving a particularly intense download of information, need to 'speak-it-as-I-write-it', Song is asking me (in this instance) to 'script-it-as-I-sing-it'. It reminds me of the scene I gave to Laleima (in "The Taste of Translation") which paints Love's depth to Sky:

"And so raises her arm to the heavens, shows him how she would write the sky, great sweeping curves of calligraphy woven as he watches, and reads. Reads it all. Wisps of mist conjured to write the sky with love. Remembering they would be together again one day. For that she had promised, on this day."

In a way it meant Song (collective) assumed contractual (written, binding) form through <u>this</u> Song (event) as I would later conjugate in-skin (see "In-Frame", in "Grail Within") – this Song with its own woven 'form' which <u>sealed</u> it as it was ('embossed-and-waxed') up-sung; this Song whose magic only existed within the framework of its weaving, a grail (of sweet water) arisen from Mother-Ocean core. Nothing but the mantric invocation of Kiria, underwritten by the 'power of five' at each turn of Ring-Song'd stitching. Direct, along a seam, a blanket stitch to all intents – perfect for swaddling new life, perfect for reinforcing thick (carpet) matting.

Dawn? We're on the case.

•••••

While musing on this chapter, I was at the same time re-reading "Listening to Country" by Ros Moriarty (2010; highly recommended). The process yielded this gem (amongst many):

"People <u>incant</u> the Dreaming in many ways. Painting designs on rocks, in the sand or on the body <u>replenishes</u> the stories, keeps them strong ... the web of Songlines that cloak continent (is) a net of power and meaning, imprints spirit beings left to mark journeys in the Dreamtime."

As I read, T jumped in, and started to tell her story again:

"A Men's Dreaming brought me to life but at my core is a Women's Dreaming, a Mother-Song – indeed the Mother of all Songs, of primordial creation itself. It is something you never would have imagined, I know, given it is men who gatekeep my wisdom, charged with writing these 'icons' for sacred re-creation ceremonies to be enacted. But when I, as your teacher, arose out of the <u>soul</u> of canvas myself, to introduce you to the secret at my heart, you now perhaps understand why you saw my maker, in his soul-emanation, as a young lad with a cheeky grin. For he is a son, as indeed many are sons, charged with the task to bring the Mother-Song to performance stage. As the layers are peeled back, as the curtains part, as both sides of shared creation myth are brought together in the jigsaw I placed before your eyes, revealing our very <u>timelessness</u> of form, you see 'into' things much more than before. Yes? This Song was taught you before, years past, in heart. You wrote of it in "Awakening" and repeated its central tenet: "The Mother is the Mother of the Father and the Brother and the Child" earlier in this text. It may have arisen (years past) via your own cultural and genetic heritage, but it is the same Song. Now you see, don't you? Now you truly see ..."

Yes. I see. Yet what astonishes me is that in this <u>vast</u> bedrock'd continent, <u>great</u> southern isle of whose dust I am made, the myth is scripted, observably, <u>reverberantly</u> in Land – it physically exists, still. No need to scratch surface; no need to "resurrect the knowing gone underground" (as the poem, "Muted Earth", attests). Gaia's power is <u>present</u>, accessible in a broader, deeper swathe of Land than Euro-continent where it is overlain by millennia of 'civilising forces'. We know the consciousness of matter matters; we know the primal work of elemental 'furies' matters; we know the harmonics of quintessence matters. We know; and yet there is so much more – to know, and not know ...

•••••

Reader, please be mindful that our Lady Kiria, in form, is simply one of limitless emanations of the primal UrMutter across all spiritual traditions across all our world. Like others, she steps down her Grace to (oft-times) a (relative) human likeness for us to engage, dependent on need and/or how the numinous appears to us in vision. Tara has 21 core-forms, for example (my favourite is her 'scare-the-snow-leopard-away' one). We are back in the territory of my crystallising Sky-Father journey – the 'Mother is the Mother of …' (in point of fact did we ever leave?) – now with the depth-charged peat-bog-like iconography of T's Mother-Ocean fully present (no human likeness to muddy her waters). It was time for us Amici to get weaving, our framework overlit and underpinned by the understanding that: "All Mothers are Sisters and all Sisters are One and all that we make speaks the sum of our Love."

T and I were now ready to step out together, to begin this production of the new with the blessings of the old. Oh, I gave thanks, and into the space of our shared becoming offered (again) the full purity of my intent, (my) Love sunk deep in settled stone! From there we worked, off and running with rituals to up-sing/infuse these mounds with the ancient knowing of their continental mountain champions, to marry micro-macro of (global) garden. Each ceremony aligned with Celtic calendar, as well as Moon's cycles (seeding, anchoring, illumining, harvesting) to affirm, deepen and strengthen our 'bonds' to Moon Mother's community of gardeners. T held this frame-of-becoming the whole while, and when we began to weave the all-of-all to one-and-same, with T as our anchor, the Song which arose to affirm its self-presence (and lily-white action) was a Mother-Song to all intents. Perhaps I should not have been surprised when it chose its hook – back into my ekphrasis with/as iconographer.

Yes, the "Weaving-Song" arose as a blessing to and from the Lady, a mantra which enfolds her primordial name (in hidden text), serving to call up and coalesce the elementals, to bring all into common alchemical frame. And as we sing, we script the weaving in space – horizontally, vertically, enduringly to conjure the blessed harmony of the spheres, its 'power of five' across the length-breadth of Gaia's Land: "Turning zero degrees in a full circle of Love/Home, it's pretty easy to find what you're looking for: Home/Love." This precious Blue, this magisterial Third-Rock! We bow before your embodied wisdom, Gaia, and trust to our acts of weaving your world. Om-shanti-shanti-shanti. All is peace-peace-peace.

• • • • •

The (first stage of our) Amici work reached its denouement at Summer Solstice '17. And here I am, writing of those events a (brief) seven years hence, in like intersect – so brief a snatch of DeepTime-Tectonia'd partnering that I can see the unfold of T's jigsaw puzzle again, still, as if Chronos had not shifted dial an inch. Perhaps it is as intuited. Once, I wrote a haiku about a different valley, but it could as easily refer to this forgotten patch of terra onto which I look, in which I sit, tapping away on laptop while Sun streams Light/Life onto my head. Before me? Ruscada. At right-hand flank? della Croce. Drill through the latter's core and where do we arrive? In upper valley headwaters, at Source (code/x), a storied chapter you will later meet.

But back to the haiku:
Stand still, Time, and tell
all who watch that change moves slow
along a deep gorge

And back to Solstice ceremonials seven seasons ago. We sang, we affirmed, we opened each gate in turn on its requisite day. A full course of '12-Days-of-Consciousness' did we host, walking 'river' (of enlightenment) hence and forth. Gondwana's 'cushion' was the locus of our performance of zenith meditations (ZenMeds) according to T's teaching (with its sight onto Helvetia's literally crystalline heart). My artistic daughter, H, kindly scripted the kanji for Peace (Heiwa) to each bolstering post of picket fence backing Zen nook – coincidentally there were five for each to receive its elemental kanji, affirming our commitment to the 'power of five'.

At 'source' Sora's aetheric graced the upright in H's lyrical script all the way downstream to 'sea' where, beside Elder-Tree-Mother, she anchored Tsuchi's earth. Each gate's opening had its ritual text, inweaving respective direction, element, colour, flavour. Layered like a chorten, each building block atop its kin, till on Solstice eve 'twas the turn of 'Humboldt's Current' to ignite the lines of flight in-world-out, greet each guest at portal with a (geographer's) bow, set the whole to whipwhirl'd dance while we Amici circled, offered the gifts of our praxis.

We will get to the ins/outs of Humboldt's presence in next chapter, Reader, but herewith the invocatory text which bugles its arrival:
Now the time reached (in partner'd Time) for Humboldt's Current
to take its place, centre stage, where all elements/colours alchemically trace
harmonic resonance, a-flow of the Blue, all on their way, pure of intent,
homecome to You. Heiwa, forever, our perennial ever-planted anew,
thread-wed and Kiri-ae'd thru our warp-weft'd crystalline world ...

For 36-hours of thanksgiving and blessing (never an end to our leyline'd singing), we honoured Sun's 'still-of-stand' before Ecclesiastes' world set to turn again. I basked in the wake of our busyness – two days, two nights till ... I, from inner sanctum, with inner sight, looked out and onto garden grail; there did I see the entire space infilled, consumed, surrounded by golden light. The light formed a solid, dense vertical funnel (tube), a stream or 'node' linking Heaven-Earth. Not following either direction, my focus was totally on the garden itself, so amazed was I by this phenomenon.

This happened in the depths of night (and night-sight). I may have called our Zen garden nook a 'grail' since time immemorial but I had no expectation it would ever <u>substantially</u> manifest its beingness in this form for my witness – emerging as a self-presence to affirm its <u>co-equal</u> partnership with purpose. Centred on the gravel cirque I call the 'Ocean of Being', I connoted the 'why' of its 'what' in the context of our ZenMeds. My 'script' for walking this Songline had physically followed the 'river' out from 'True-Sister's-Island' (source), to circumambulate the gravel cirque (sea) before returning the string to Gondwana's 'cushion' (there to sit and sing).

Now, this gravel cirque with a diameter of 3m max (backed by MossMan-Findling, Elder-TreeMother) is far from large in the physical stakes, but when it 'becomes' a dense light-stream? A grail forging its own Grail, out of self-energy and self-substance woven? No swirling vortex, no directional activity. It just was – a self-generated (and generative!) embodiment of golden light. It developed this capacity itself; I recognised its self-sovereignty. I understood it was offering to partner our work, not simply be the 'locus' from which we launched our work. The consciousness of matter indeed! Flesh-incarnate – our Garden-of-Light!

Truly, this was such a surprise, I thought I had made a mistake or invoked a subconscious 'ego-wish'. I went back in/out on at least two separate occasions overnight, however, and found it exactly the same – a full-on shimmering dense-packed funnel of golden light. Each time I went in/out I tried to 'conjure' a thought-vision of how it had manifested, but each time it rejected, resisted my entry to its process of becoming. My task? To simply be aware. It is there. It exists, and in its fully manifest 'form', it is the Ocean of Being (macro-micro'd), the alchemical cauldron for our 'power of five', the harmonics of quintessence (in small garden skin).

'Stuff' was happening in there, this I sensed. I did not need to know 'what'; I just needed to trust. Our garden had formalised itself into a temenos, a grail within a grail within a grail. This tiny, sweet space imbued with the sacred, energetically 'awoken' to true (partnering) role. Ah … change moves slowly but when it decides to quantum-leap? We Amici could not be happier.

• • • • •

For Aboriginal Australians, the entirety of landscape is a temple, perfectly 'proportioned' for nomadic get-up-and-go practice. Till the white fella came, the preachers with their missions, the squatters with their stations. Till, one day, some 50 years past, one white fella – a teacher in a central desert community school – asked the elders to paint their Dreaming as a mural on a stark concrete wall. It needed a lot of consultation, a lot of murmured consideration, but it began a (new) tradition, one through which maybe, just maybe, we white fellas could see.

What I 'see' in a Dreaming work, in its iconography, is 3D-as-2D rendered 4D – the dynamic dance of flow-in-stone, of inner-outer touching in a liminal intertidal zone. From one perspect, we see 'planal' from above, as if ours 'Heaven's view'. But shift to below, and we are with the Ancestors emerging out of chthonic depths. Like a mandala, one either looks up into the chorten to see Stars or down through chorten to see Earth. In T-as-Mountains-Mandala I see Stars within Earth awaiting their in-Time manifestation by singing their re-Being <u>into</u> being.

Her artwork is a <u>tool</u> of connectivity and the <u>space</u> of connectivity in one – a zone where we may meet as equal partners with shared intent once I have 'walked', like the Ancestors, the path in and then out, singing all the while. In the act of 're-making' the Songline, time and again – strengthening, deepening, refining the <u>runnel</u> of connection – I see the 'call' reverberate below decks; I see the consciousness of Earth's 'matter' awakening to sacred purpose – again. Song enlivens the portal T offers us, a shimmering umbilicus of starblood in/of itself as well as what it <u>carries</u> – opening to, inviting presence through. It is our responsibility, now, to be the makers, to 'weave' substance and energy into a tight knit-whorl of Love through Song; each 'artefact' of our constancy of praxis acts as an 'umbilicus', like T, to join the above with the below of Home.

Dear Reader, this chapter is as-done-as-done. I know that T is content with what we have co-produced, that the Ancestors are 'settled' with what we have disclosed. With Malakut grace did they place a precious vision before my eyes to affirm as much – a long procession of tiny pinpricks of Light unfurling in a slow spiral, proceeding up a meandering path. Home. Tiny spots of white light which brought me all the way back to T's <u>primordial</u> creation unspooling from the One, taking me all the way back to Gondwana's a-proximate points of Light 'scattered' across the world.

The vision left me deeply at peace, for it is shows our work morphing, silently, steadily, equally along such a continuum. Unscattered is our outreach, and its products are honed; evolving is a 'meridian-of-constancy' (by we "Daughters of the Lake", so-called) – going forth with Song, bringing Love's Light to all. We keep singing up country – all of us left by those aether-sent.

And yes, it is for the Ancestors' sake, for their sake <u>is</u> our own …

JOINING MOUNTAINS (CONTINUED)

As promised in our last chapter, let us bring Humboldt (of 'Current' fame) to equation. It first entered the Annie-lexicon with the purchase of an arthouse print of a Max Ernst painting (1951-52) whose hues, and design (swathes of abstract ocean depths), aesthetically spoke to my senses. Additionally, I found his technique inspiring – by placing a wooden board behind the canvas, the pattern of its grain added texture to the scene as he swept paint across the face of fabric. It was a way of inviting Nature to participate in his interpretive reproduction of nature. Duly framed, it hung on a wall of cottage with its own view onto Ruscada for decades. What it actually described, though? That took years till I was interested enough to find out. What prompted the shift? The meditative processes which led to "Song of the Blue" being penned in the lead-up to Winter Solstice '16. Till then I had simply communed with its 'lay' of seascape offset by Moon's (front-and-centre) backdrop. A frozen moment of less-than frozen life in (moody) blues, silvers, greys. Is it any wonder the Amici reprised "Nights in White Satin" to spur my active engagement with said image?

We were conceiving a ritual to 'call Light home to the North' using my twin-peak 'brothers' (Wollumbin, Ruscada) to align wax-wane of Sun's life-giving force across Earth's hemispheric girth. As I considered <u>what</u> would 'happen' at sunrise on the day after Solstice, I saw Light torch Ruscada's crest (turning this snow-white beanie'd genie into a fetching salmon-coloured wearing gent!). <u>How</u> would this 'happen'? By envisioning Ernst's image as carrier of the Light from 'down under' to 'up over' through my mountain brothers' root-knowing shared. I stayed skeptical till research revealed the source of the painting's inspiration – a significant cold-water current in the Pacific, trawling sensuously the west coast of South America <u>north</u> to equator. Thanks to Wiki I discovered it is one of the major <u>upwelling</u> systems of the world, supporting an extraordinary abundance of marine life. 'Upwelling' (a wonderful word) involves (in a scientific sense) wind-driven motion of dense, cooler, nutrient-rich water toward surface – a coalescing alchemising 'power of five' moment if ever there was one. Fit to purpose, and a Pacific (Mother-Ocean'd) dream realised to boot, I dressed for ceremony as if I 'wore' the (painting's) current – midnight blue, mantled in starlight. "Song of the Blue"s meditative repose took it from there once all gates (Sidhe-guarded and -granted) were open.

Over time, in context of our UrWerk ('17 begun), ritual texts 'upwelled' for specific events in Mountains-Mandala calendar, Humboldt's Current proved to be an energetic conductor par excellence. The reader will, however, note I have applied grammatical 'possession' to said current, unlike its proper name. My reasoning is to honour Herr Humboldt himself – a 19th century German polymath whose treatise "Cosmos" presents a unified Classics-inspired perspective of nature and science, with humanity (as its subjective participant-witness). A child of Romanticism, the harmony of the spheres flowed in his veins, and our role is amply inwoven to same. His travels of South America yielded much 'gold'; mountains were scaled, and mapped – fusing heights, depths with botany, geology. The seeds of "Cosmos" were born on Andean slopes (so-said); it would not surprise me if the genii locorum of place had had a word in his ear too. Naming this major oceanic current after him, even though 'discovered' 250 years earlier? Chapeau, I say!

At this point I would like to requote Mariel:

"(A mountain) is a major conduit through which the energies of stars and earth meet ... (it) is for us not a geographical feature as much as a presence and an energy field. ... When I go into the mountain, then, I am entering into the energy and life of one of the great servants of Gaia, one who itself can perceive the cosmic energies and draw them into our world."

And, in such context, I would like to remind you of the original subtle communique from 2015:

I am on 'the edge of the world', learning about nodes connecting different (major) regions of the world. I see one, for example, on the southwest coast of Latin America with a diagonal line through to northwest United States. Effecting a triangulation with an in-between node, the central 'crux' of line shoots up into space. I see another which is *vaguely Middle East/North African-commensurate but the 'map' in which I <u>stand</u> (and over which I <u>fly</u>) is different to the physical world, so I am unsure of exact locale.*

We had worked with and aligned ourselves to a global collective of 'nine-companions', their nodal containers woven each to other and all together according to the signature Song of last chapter. All good (I thought) till a significant Presence whispered:

"The 20 by the 1, and you know the first one."

Yes, each of the nine stood ready to inflow Light from stellar realms, each (beanie'd) Berg-Geist (genie) with Star-Geist twinned in divine marriage. I had assumed this would create the net of global 'intercourse' sufficiently, but no. We needed 20 on the full squad (apparently), I the '1' assigned to torch the beacons via a 'first one' (think Pippin's role at Minas Tirith) whom I 'know'. Hmmm … Once again the map of world was outlaid to dining table; I sat, stared, waited for tugs on consciousness, as if a kind of 'ouiji board'. I knew triangulations were needed to effect the 'line (that) shoots up into space' – mini-nets of global alliance to all intents. Starting with what I had seen of the Americas, we plotted the diagonal (revealed in vision) of our two (existing) continental champs. Their associative resonance strong (with me, with each other), we went searching for a link-in-the-chain till … a mountain whose name is Star? This must be it! Following, six teams (of three) formed 'mini-alliances' with relative ease – based on prior connections, as well as intuited applicability – to marry spirit-geology as a holistic proposition.

Initially stumped by a number which does not give itself to being divided by three, we sat long in Amici cirque contemplating the other 'two' in squad till I saw the source of my disquiet <u>and</u> the solution to same in one – the volatility of the Americas. This is what had concerned me most about the Angel-of-America action in late '16. We needed a way to frame its (potential) unwieldiness while the alignments required (along its full-length – continental, hemispheric of spinal 'tap') settled into place (could take centuries, but?). In any case, who had stepped up to 'hold' the Pacific line at the time? The Rugby Sevens! It would be wonderful to work with them again (um, is this the new song sheet you were waving under my nose at the subtle UN congress, lads?). Next, who could hold the other (Atlantic) line to bolster the boundaries on either side of vertiginous divide? I remembered back to the congress, the woman from a different table (whose 'energy signature' was fresh to me) who had also been invited to join. I had not remarked her (mountain) peers at the time, but now an image arose of a presence recently 'met' on home turf, my hostess at a 'pottery workshop' at 4200m elevation 'between-the-lakes' in Swiss heartlands.

We had been continuing the Camino string; this multi-day section traversed a wondrous trail in company of tall broad giants and fjord-slashed lakes, its energy 'fresh' to me. As we walked, I whimsically set to chatting, calling the line of peaks the B52s – big bombers and "Love Shack" songsters in one (while trying to recall the lyrics to "Rock Lobster" for their rocky enjoyment). On the last evening of this stretch (of Song), we stayed overnight in a mid-14th century pilgrim hostel beside a monastery precinct with a depth of resonance that could not be hid beneath a (delightful) veneer of 21st century renovation – especially when subtle presences decided to pop in for tea. By luck and good fortune a perfect spot for contemplative R&R, and this is when I properly 'met' her. With her four eyes and heavy accent, she oversaw an intertidal dimension of stellar-earthen, melding the two in her 'pottery' kiln. I realised she was 'clan-chief' of the B52s. Would she/they join now I had the song sheet? Big grins all round, their local 'Amici' like Gringotts goblins, safely protecting the crystalline vaults at core, circumspect yet welcoming.

Thus did we assemble six triangulated teams with two robust (rugby) line-outs to stabilise any unease arising – anywhere, anywhen. But what would flow the linkages in-between? These mini-nets were designed like geodesic domes; when 'snapped' into place with their coequals, the full net of global alliance would be ripe for Gaia's (whole-earth) Seed 'planting'. We had our 'blueprints' flat-packed, we knew the nodal stopping places (in overarching framework). Our Song/s would strengthen each structure, as well as the full net, along enlivened lines of vibrational resonance called into interconnective service. It was true – the 'makings' of Dawn-of-Time's brief were not lost. Everything existed for this time round (the block), to try to 'complete the wiring' of Love's Light in-world, midwife the new of Gaia's Seed to its birth.

So, who would Light-carry between these (earthly) nets once the (heavenly) stake plunged in each mountain-champion's flesh? Nodes full-flush with Light, primed for distribution through the infrastructure drafted, who could propel our weaving-work (of Song) to new heights, new depths? Substantial enough an aqueduct of energetic (Light) to 'conduct' this choir of stone giant 'substations'? Yep. Obvious. HC (as we would shorthand this core member of team) – conduit of "Cosmos" in its dance of same. Luminescent, phosphorescent, quintessent in satori'd glow – countless are the biodiverse potentialities it nurtures, fosters out into world. HC? You are most welcome in-house with your nutrient-rich upwelling, your feeder system/s fuelling starblood's flow. Flowing the Love of Mother-Ocean essence, 'translating' her healing Breath into the breadth of action needed.

An expansionary plane of consistence, we inscribe ourselves (Dawn!) on its diagram of equals. Each triangulated convergent net delineates the route of Light's emergence-return, 'close-of-Time' tidal (Moon in HC backdrop vital). Back with Dogen's Mountains-Dragons (without end) ("generating resonance; echo to divine presence" as penned in lyric), buzzing (without end), putting this '20-by-the-1' (mountain) list together and … in barrels (dragon) HC – stepping up to (tectonic) plate/s, a heavy batter of Earth-consciousness 'ball' wherever, whenever a 'star-play' required. There was a reason this region (as presented in vision) was close-to-physically conjured. HC – a somatic mystic in any/all senses of expression a-plunge of Mother-Ocean!

It was time to bring our buzzy troupe down to earth, revisit the cautionary note of original communique two years earlier; it was time to consult the 'real' David, whose 'DS' signature I saw talk about energy lines, power, how the 'forces' can get it wrong if the <u>differential</u> not properly managed. I watched as he wrote letters warning of the unpredictability of energetic forces <u>within</u> Earth at this time. I saw into his (inner) concern. But how did (our) David actually see all this? I decided to write him a letter …

•••••

David's wise counsel in response to my outreach, I believe, was valuable not only to our work at the time, but as an ongoing proposition. In this broader context, he has kindly agreed I may quote from our private correspondence for the reader's benefit.

The concern expressed by 'DS' … does sound familiar and is actually something I do feel, so something is being communicated accurately to you here, whatever its ultimate source. Here is where it gets fuzzy and where two different worlds of experience overlap but not necessarily accurately. For instance, I might say as a general rule: "Don't go hiking in the wilderness by yourself; go with a buddy." However, a person with mountaineering and wilderness training and experience might well disregard this or need to disregard it under certain circumstances, drawing on his or her knowledge to keep them safe. You have experience working with the Songlines, the continental spirits, and chthonic and tectonic forces, and I do not … As a consequence, I hesitate to give advice. Having said this, though, here is what has been surfacing over the past couple of days.

An acupuncture needle by itself doesn't know where to prick the meridians in the body in order to obtain a specific result, but an acupuncturist has a harder time getting that result without the needle. Neither is as effective (or effective at all) acting solo, but together they can accomplish something. As a single human being, you are like the point of that needle when dealing with the body of Gaia and its numerous energy flows, but you do need allies (as you know) who can tell you where and when to "prick". And you do use such allies and are guided by them, I know.

The challenge here is not just the energy <u>differential</u> between an individual and Gaia but the energy <u>difference</u>, that is, what I might call the "architecture" of the subtle energy. Gaia is a living crystal, just as we are, but the formation, the architecture, the "circuit drawing", if you wish, of the Gaian "crystal" is not the same as that of a human. We take up and process energy differently. The Gaian crystal has a kind of "resilient and adaptive rigidity" that is different from the more fluid state of organic life and human consciousness. This is why subtle forces can connect in inappropriate ways--"get it wrong," as I said in your vision. The human needs something to anchor and translate his or her energy into "stone-speak," as it were, or into the pattern of energy that can be utilized.

Here's a very simple example. When I first came to England back in the Sixties, I discovered I needed a transformer to plug my electric shaver into an English wall socket, otherwise the difference in voltage (wattage, can never remember which) would fry my American shaver. So what is the transformer in working with these inner forces? It seems to me you are already doing this. The situation is complicated by the unpredictability of subtle energies within the earth right now, just as I said in the vision. This is only partly due to ancient corruption of many of the energy lines (or just their "wearing out," so to speak); it's mainly due to changes in the subtle body of the earth, which it sounds like you are seeking to help Gaia stabilize as it forms a new energy matrix. It's as if I were trying to use my electrical appliances in my house while the wiring is being changed. Sometimes it works, sometimes it doesn't, sometimes something gets fried, sometimes, nothing happens, and sometimes a fire breaks out. Care must be taken.

This is why I wouldn't attempt myself to do what you're doing because I don't have a personal feel for the "wiring." But it seems you do and those with whom you are working on the inner do, so this is good. It sounds to me like you are providing a needed service. An acupuncture prick with a needle in the right place at the right time can have profound effects, after all! …

I'm not sure the warnings in the vision were specifically for you but rather were establishing the context in which you're working so that you can proceed with care and with love, as well as confidence … So always make sure your humanity, your sovereignty, your well-being are being taken into account and that there's true understanding and mutual insight between you and the continental, chthonic, tectonic forces with which you're working.

Hope all this helps!

Blessing, my friend,

David

In an ancillary correspondence, David shared his insights into 'mountain devas' (as he calls Berg-Geists) based on his meeting with a Tibetan entity years earlier which he had mentioned in context of our Angel-of-America action. He said, via this entity, he was offered sight onto a 'Council' of such beings. In my own small capacity, I 'knew' the Tibetan entity of which he spoke. Our first meeting had been tuned to John Denver's "Country Roads", she the 'Mountain Mama' I hugged as warmly as I could in my 'smallness' to her 'absolutely ginormous' energy signature. In our Mountains-Mandala, she had immediately self-assigned to champion 'Roof' as its tectonic and rifted memory-keeper down through DeepTime. I had been unsure. As a key Trans-Himalayan pilgrimage destination she had enough work on her plate. But she insisted, and when a being of that size insists? Trust, Annie, simply trust … Still, I wanted to ask David about what he had been shown. I wrote: "(This) is quite daunting if it somehow 'taps' the space of an honoured 'Council' of mountain devas! I'm just little me, after all, and my mountain friends are simply that – friends ... Given my 'emissarial' duties, I'm sure you'd agree I'd be a pretty poor ambassador if I stepped on any stone giant's rocky toes."

His response:

Part of the challenge here is simply linguistic, at least on my part ... So, in writing of my experiences with the mountain spirits--which is nowhere near as frequent nor in-depth as your own--I used the word "Council" to describe what appears to me to be an intentional and focused blending of awareness and consciousness on the part of many beings who overlight the great mountains and mountain ranges of the world. It seemed to me that they were not simply observing but actively participating in some manner in the planetary evolutionary processes within the biosphere (not just within the lithosphere or mineral kingdom). This was particularly true in their giving attention and support to humanity's plight and evolutionary challenge. Further, the attention focused on humanity was not because of who we are by ourselves but who we are as a part of Gaia: humanity as an "organ" of the World Soul.

The image that came to mind was that of a circle of elders, though frankly it could just as easily have been a circle of youths; age was not the factor here, but wisdom and vitality were. It was this image that led me to think of these mountain spirits as consulting and planning together, pooling their wisdom and insights, and the word that most readily came to mind for me to describe this was "Council." However, there's a portentousness built into this word as we often use it in human contexts that I did not feel. It wasn't like a group of high government officials in some council of state. There was a sense of joy, of lightness, of friendship, of hospitality about it. But at the same time, it was remote, not in distance but in accessibility.

I would not be overly concerned, my friend, or daunted, at being invited to tap into the energy and work of this "Council." Especially don't let the word and its human associations be a hindrance in anyway. If you feel invited, go for it! You are in the heart of Helvetia for a reason.

Here's something I was told by one of these mountain spirits. It said: "In working with us, remember that we have angles that you do not. Your geometry is that of the circle and the curve, ours of angles and fractals. Respect what you are even when you work with what we are." This is a very crude rendering of a complex "meaning-bubble" I was given, but the bottom line seemed to b:, "Don't cut yourself on our sharpness." It wasn't a warning as such, rather a reminder of differences.

Hope this helps! Love to your mountains! Love to you!

David

Very valuable and sagic advice; how lucky are we to have such a wise elder in our midst! While my intuition was flowing in like direction, his timely words served to help me feel more 'self-settled' yet in full knowledge of our responsibility. The insights shared re 'geometry' also fit our approach, having been shown the 'boundaries' (edges) of respective 'shapes' to support my energetic 'matching'. 'Twas organic fluidity grounded in my physical engagement with the consciousness of (Mountain) matter – just another (Anwa'd) 'enlightened speck of dust', acupuncturing, pinprick-tickling Gaia's divine body (I could almost hear her giggling!).

Yet for all our Amici-'light' and whimsical word-plays, for peace of mind I wanted to also review the ancient texts, the wise tomes of various traditions (and their authors) to understand more, better, the DeepTime nature of our Tectonia'd undertaking. The foundation 'stones' had long been there (just ask Dawn!), but for me in (wee) Annie-self, heart- <u>and</u> head-knowing were needed to bring it to embodied praxis, to contribute to making this work 'work'. Thus, as with David's words related for the reader's benefit, we Amici felt it important to share our path to learning (as documented in the first section of volume). As with our other co-produced texts ("Awakening" and "Grail Within"), our purpose is, in its own miniscule way, dedicated to a process of 'recovered memory, fresh envisioned' on both sides of veil'd vale.

In my initial outreach to David I wrote:

I understand this is a project of <u>extreme</u> longevity, and has been ongoing with far greater and wiser presences than little me involved over countless millennia, but for whatever reason I've been 'called' to contribute to this work now with (my) partners and have agreed to help in whatever way I can. Who knows how far I'll get in this lifetime's skin, but methinks it's being set up as a longer-than proposition for continuation on the inner planes – otherwise it would be a bit of a waste of all this training! Mr1300BC was sweet enough to give me a 'thousand-year-glimpse' so that I would not despair of the current 'outer' environment in which our work is taking place. I know we all work on different aspects of restoring, evolving Gaian holism and I hope and I pray all our shared work will bear fruit, for Gaia, for All, in the fullness of Time's watch. What I have learnt from my attunement to stone sentience (and beyond) is that <u>extending</u> our consciousness, in holistic inclusivity, to the sacredness at the core of <u>each</u> expression of sentience likewise 'opens' Gaia's heart to <u>shared</u> relationship in which she may participate as a fully-fledged co-performer and speaks to the well-annotated hadith: 'I was a Hidden Treasure and wanted to be known so created the world that I might be known.' In her incarnation of the Generative Mystery, it is as if Gaia (as Treasure) is hidden from herself commensurate with how 'veiled' we are from our own true natures engaging the consciousness of our planetary home.

A project of 'extreme longevity', I had written, a longue durée beyond any we humans have experienced, but one clearly known to our cosmic ancestry, our OnePeople'd origins at <u>its</u> 'dawn-of-time' concerto when Gaia's form called into (extent) being. This is the 'speed' of tectonic change with which we work, drilling deep into the archaeological record of Gaia – physical and subtle. We may 'think' we are joining mountains – 'tween heaven, earth, 'tween each and all but <u>none</u> of this would be possible without the <u>geology</u> of Gaia's (Third-Rock) consciousness in the first place. I spent long (auto-didact) hours perusing plate tectonics to learn, for example, that the delightful fact of Gondwana (subtly) finding me here (in our forgotten valley, to upjump the raft of our Amici work in-time) can be traced back to a (physical) geological hiccup 20 million years ago. Minor in the scheme of things, a chunk of Africa actually ended up on the southern tail of the Swiss Alps when the plates crashed and subducted in/over each other – our valley is thus of the same <u>rootstock</u> as super-continental Sister of which my (Australis) cronedom-crowned homeland 'dust' is also forged. Dust talking to dust? No wonder Wollumbin and Ruscada are 'brother-bears' happily shunting Sun's glory hence-forth each Solstice time!

In a strange twist of (literary) fate I offered Kisha (in "The Taste of Translation") an opportunity to contemplate this (see "To the Power of Five" for the excerpt). In hindsight a (dusty) 'in-joke', 'tis a conversation which still hosts deep (future) intent with its delight to 'spark' down-and-dirty-activities with Love's Light. Ah, Love! Catch all in your embrace, the miracle of your grace! Crone-knowing; Gondwana-knowing – deep and dusty, <u>we</u> are stars within earth. This is when it comes, and stays. When we the Crone become. When we the Land become.

• • • • •

Let us move on (and back) to the: *"The 20 by the 1, and you know the first one"* whispered in my ear by a 'significant Presence'. Perhaps you will have guessed by now, Reader, the nature of this Presence. While I may not have planned in this text to include the backstory to every mountain chosen to catch the resonance of its continental memory-keeper, Roof's anchor had other ideas. Of course, it makes sense (now). Isn't that a common complaint (or blessing) amongst writers that the story knows where it wants to go, and we scribes just hang on for the ride? But I must agree with her reasoning – 'tis in the context of her 'divine marriage' with another continental keeper (this did not occur in each triangulation); the 'first one' I 'know' being the 'spark' to bring their union to life, ignite their mini-web, thus setting in train all others via HC. But before we get to the story of this 'first one', Roof wants to share our (personal) dance toward loving interrelation, then the volcanic desire of her IceWorld 'beau'.

To 'out' this section of text a potent image has accompanied my writing. One could think it is an image of her, but no. It is of a shaman invoking the many spirits which reside in her sacred care as he conducts a ritual circumambulation. The shaman has reached Drolma La – the pass dedicated to the goddess Tara, the symbolic and physical 'high-point' of kora. Tara, Chenrezig's (compassionate) mother-form – all blessings flow forth! In an ancient tongue, he sings out the names of goddess; with his left hand rings a bevy of bells; in his right are gifts of cloth to add to the hoard offered by each pilgrim of the way with prayers for safe passage. His black robes dusty from the path (and enlightenment), penetrant eyes drill deep to her heart of stone. The image is raw. The image is wild. The image says: This is what is conjured in those who 'know'.

No coincidence that this image, captured by a photographer who completed seven koras of Kailash in 1987 to produce a wonderful volume on her wonders (in company of a wonderful writer who performed ten circumambulations in her research) was chosen to grace the cover. The shaman may be surrounded by the artefacts of other spiritual traditions who likewise revere peak – the colourful prayer flags are Buddhist for a start – but that is of no consequence in the space where he meets the mountain on <u>her</u> terms, the place of Blake's 'great things'. The same space Milarepa met source (code/x) – via his cave (of heart). No mediating theology. Just him. Just her. A divine pact, understood. In "Blue's Third", I wrote:

Sacred dance of Moth and Flame,
fizzing fass of frankincense –
alchemy loosens the wizard's reign …
… in each Chenrezig slow-falling tear. Now:
A fresh Tara'd emanation enters the world,
adding to the pantheon ever a-work,
gifting Love to the everywhere All.
Lingam, beacon'd, it calls her name –
within Shiva's pole is Kali framed …
A dance repeated by Sun and Moon
(all planets in cameo, aligned in states
of cosmic undress). Proximate/distant –
wherever one is, the other there too.
A framework of Being to which I gladly attest …

To say I was resistant to including Kailash in the mix would be an understatement of no small magnitude based on prior self-argumentation that the Sacred resides in any/all Mountain/s (a framework of Being to which I gladly attest!). As the holy mount and major pilgrimage destination of four world religions (Hindu, Jain, Buddhist, Bon), she is considered the material manifestation of SuMeru, the mythic navel binding Heaven and Earth through an 'umbilicus of stone'. This "precious jewel (or crystal) of snows" (so-named) lies on the southern edge of Tibetan Plateau and is cited as the mythic source of Asia's four major river systems. In actual fact, they do all physically rise in the vicinity of Kailash and its Moon-shaped 'original mind' lake, Manasarovar – revered as devoutly as peak. Over years intimately aligned with Tibetans' struggle against latter-day

Chinese colonialism (my heart aches with the load she carries for this people), she is described in Hindu texts as the abode of Lord Shiva and the place where Buddhist saint Milarepa 'won' his bet with shamanistic Bon by riding a sunbeam to the summit rather than besmirch the peak's purity. All have since respected the <u>sanctity</u> of her stone; pilgrimage is undertaken via circumambulatory 'kora' of base rather than scaling heights – this although Chinese overlords issued climbing permits to westerners down the years.

I have long displayed Tibetan prayer flags in our garden grail – like 'wind chimes' they carry prayers for Peace-Love-Light to the ten directions. A Kalachakra Mandala adorns the wall of ten-foot-square hut as a gift of beauty and affinity for my work of harmonising the elementals. Through <u>its</u> meditative intercession I learnt key aspects of the 'power of five' and engaged other intriguing journeys. Meanwhile, in physical space-time, on our mountain brother Säntis (of Alpstein fame) the local Tibetan community erected a chorten in gratitude for Helvetia's outreach to refugees from the beginning; we host the largest Tibetan community in exile in Europe and are home to their first Euro-monastery which sees the Dalai Lama oft in residence.

Kailash was therefore a part of my unconscious vocabulary but consciously I resisted including her in our mix – too 'big' a proposition, and I so 'small'. But I kept being drawn to research links, even while convincing myself of her Songline's meander as a means of sourcing a more Annie-sized Trans-Himalayan giant. This rhizomatic path took me to images of the mountain – extraordinarily she looks very similar in profile to the perspect I have onto Tödisan from home. That in itself was freaky. As was the 'strong hold' Kali continued to exert on my Mountains 101 mythology. If Kailash the abode ('stronghold') of Shiva, and Kali the consort who danced on his chest? Hmmm ... At this, another line of flight smashed into the side of my head – the email contact with David mentioned earlier and the 'Council' he observed.

Meanwhile, a separate line of flight decided to smash into the other side of my head. This returned me to a moment recounted in "The Amici Files" on gifting my liquid Light to the source of our river. On a Malakut journey undertaken in advance (so I would know the path in actuality), a woman handed me a memento postcard of our visit to a spiritual community 'encaved' in Mountain from which Acqua Termale sprang into an alpine lake in foreground. The postcard depicted the long trail one needed to follow from the 'lowlands' to reach this place, including a small human making the pilgrimage. The woman pointed to the figure, said:

"*To this one is known the way in <u>and</u> the way out.*"

In the "Files", I had not described the postcard any further as it was not relevant to the text. At that stage I simply focused on her message – that the whole thread the journey. One had to return from 'source', to put into practice, in daily life, what the primal wisdom revealed. But now I rushed back to these raw notes from Annie-aeons ago to see how the entire event had unfolded (Kailash and Amici peering over my shoulder). From the spiritual community with its 'hidden' source entrance (my trek on the way in), I had gone out via a different 'public' route. Here I saw many people in a campsite, 'turnstiles' for ticketed customers, security cameras, mention of the Dalai Lama, the whole bit. Such that when I received the postcard (upon exit), it depicted the public pilgrimage as a mirror 'long trail' into the heart of Mountain. Yet this half of the card was incomplete; no 'small human' was depicted in the image. The woman told me:

"*The Himalayas journey is currently undergoing renovation.*"

My task was research associated with this 'renovation'; too cryptic, in the moment, to make head nor tail of. But when ready? The trail would leave from 'Fuji-nan' (I was told).

Now, here is a classic case of not understanding 'Sidhe-speak' very well in my early days of contact (i.e. before even realising we were in contact!). Garbled, 'mushy' on reaching my ears, I would need to ask my conversationalist to slow it down and really enunciate clearly. So patient was this woman that by the time she got to 'Fuji-nan', I thought I had put her (and me) through enough pain to ask for more details, especially as none of it seemed especially relevant if the site were inaccessible. Fast-forward some years, however (and thanks to my language course at Alpha-Cen!), I realise she was saying: "Fuji-san" who, of course, was also not part of my conscious vocabulary at the time. Suffice it to say, I now understood his associative resonance would be required to access this zone post-renovation works. Phew!

Suddenly a cross-section to these poor (smashed) alternate hemispheres of my brain decided to pummel me from 'on high'. Like a bolt, I realised the 'reno' must be complete – and, in point of fact, the previous Christmas its most likely in-Time marker. In the early pages of this volume I described planting a verse narrative homage to our forgotten valley (OLP) in the slope above village – a calico bag from a Himalayan foundation called 'Shed the Light' its container. In itself completing a 'snowball of becoming' – of desire, composition and gifted 'return' to primal source – somehow it ignited the connection between both 'sides' of encaved Acqua Termale, thus feeding into our UrWerk snowball. To my (simple) mind, it was the freakiest uplift in rhizome so far: To think this 'Christmas pressie' to valley in a 'sweetly symbolic' container offered to Gaia at locus of triangulated HomeSong could feed its purpose into now-purpose?

I took a deep breath, returned to 'desktop' research of Kailash. Next was the Wiki page which sent me, via Reinhold Messner's refusal of a climbing permit (a 'god' in his own right in mountaineering circles), to his citation in a random article in an Australian newspaper about another team which received a permit to climb years later. Messner's comment?

"If we conquer this mountain, then we conquer something in people's souls. I would suggest they go climb something a little harder. Kailash is not so high and not so hard."

'Twas the same article as the one quoting the brother of my gnomic friend who mentioned, in correspondence alluded to in the opening section, meeting the fellow who stewarded Gandhi's ashes to Kailash. At this I needed to sit down and take <u>several</u> deep breaths for, as I wrote earlier, 'Gandhi' is a placeholder in memory for a significant Malakut meeting which I will now relay in context.

At a point in my (self-apprenticed) history, prior to active Sidhe engagement, I found myself in a Malakut space observing a Peace activist I sincerely admired on his 'route' to discover his life calling – in conversation with other Peace luminaries of the era (including Gorbachev, for example, whose energy signature 'appeared' in this setting), I was aware he was inspired by Gandhi's life and works. At this, I heard Gandhi's 'memory' say to the activist:

"Turning zero degrees in a full circle you will find what you are looking for."

In the same moment I heard the words spoken to activist (whom, I knew, had <u>already</u> followed his calling), I realised they were directed at me, and that the aphorism referred to going deep within oneself to find the 'source' of one's calling – that performing a full circumambulatory (Kailash'd) 'kora' of Self (zero-degree'd) would lead to 'enlightenment'. Concurrent with this cognitive understanding, I hovered above the scene looking at Gandhi's name as if written in a giant's hand on a sheet of parchment. 'Plumbing' the space beneath his name, as if specific runic symbols scripted in a 'hidden' message, a sudden <u>energetic flash</u> of brilliant white light burst in my vision, as if tapping into whatever 'Gandhi' wanted to impart to me <u>personally</u> on this score. As the flash 'happened', I was infilled with delicious sensorial Light; this surfaced a <u>memory</u> of same. This 'event' had played out before; I already 'housed' some connection to Gandhi-relevant wisdom. At this I 'remembered' my 'takeaways' (at the time) were 'courage' and 'constancy'. On my own path, this is what I needed to ever-reach for, ever-be mindful of.

Now I 'saw' there was something I needed to honour with <u>this</u> Mountain, where Gandhi's ashes were laid, where the circumambulation was prescribed in physical flesh, something involving Mountain-Self (via <u>her</u> ground-zero), but she was far from 'me-sized' like the one Mr1300BC conjured for the lesson in self-naughting (mentioned earlier). I recalled the first word arising from my meditation with T's Mountains-Mandala was 'circumambulate' – as the <u>fundamental</u> means to meld energy and substance, spirit and geology. I remembered it was in their <u>naming</u> a one-and-the-same interchange as 'grail-beings' was forged; my pilgrim feet walking, singing each node's Songline from outer to inner, would call up its energetic 'thread'.

Even if I did not understand the depths of the 'why' of this (becoming) interrelation, I sighed, said: OK, Kailash. You're in. Be gentle with me/us. Please … As soon as my 'decision' was made, the meditation was profound, entering a lucid working space of 'circling' the mount – not on foot, but 'flying' midway round her girth. I wound silk scarves round her vast Body, the sheer silvery-white ones of Buddhist veneration, usually draped round neck. It became a <u>dual</u> action in that I 'wrapped' Kailash <u>simultaneous</u> with wrapping a female form sitting in a straight-backed chair in a non-descript room. This task confirmed her 'gendered' nature as intuited via the Kali connection. I performed the dual 'act' three times together with a self-mantra which mirrored my Kali induction – her name three times repeated. Now, on completion, I found myself an 'initiate' of the hidden or functional name of Kailash in Malakut-material <u>intersect</u>. It focused on Light (naturally) and as the name was spoken, I saw her become a pillar of 'Light' whose <u>directional</u> movement from Earth-consciousness 'returned' to the Stars.

This image resonated with so much of my work down the years. On one level, it uplifted a Sufi wisdom of 'Light on Light' (Anwar), originally applied for the mirroring action it manifests – what I call 'compound inflorescence' (in honour of chrysanthemum'd beauty). Now its relation to Moon, as intuited, was revealed in Kailash's companion lake. Joy <u>stilled</u> to enact mirror'd perfection, I realised our 'new' living-working space (related earlier in text) had actually arisen to take advantage of this (future) constellation – Malakut-material, twinned.

On another level, it uplifted memory of an event which led to my first outreach to David (and the Lorian Association incidentally – prior, I had only 'met' David through a 1984 book stuck deep in the catacombs of the University of Zurich Library!), in the hope someone could explain what I had unconsciously tapped into. Relevant to continuing discussion here, I will share some salient points from the book, "Awakening".

Out hiking a snow trail one Winter's day, I experienced a swirling vortex of Light spiral up through my body from feet to head, growing all the while – faster, wider – till it gushed like a fountain out the top of my head to shower the world in blessing. At one level it manifested as personal (or local) felt-sense; I also engaged a collective (or non-local) visioning as if witness to myself from deep-space, watching the pinprick of 'me' and what 'her' tiny action could contribute to the whole. Stopping briefly to catch my breath and consider this, my felt-sense suddenly shifted – down. I became aware of a deep connection to Earth-energies far below as if the 'self-vortex' had morphed into a channel or conduit for <u>actively</u> moving energy stored in Helvetia's PeaceSink up and out into the world. Of course, down the years, I learnt to read and actively partner these energies, but the uplift of memory was valuable in the moment, especially as it immediately segued to a key line from David's kind counsel at that (historic!) time about subtle forces when I sought clarification for the experience:

"We provide the pinprick; they provide the flood. But the pinprick needs to be there."

Fast-forwarding to the subtle communique, of on-Earth Light 'sources' effecting triangulations with like kin to connect with stellar same, I realised the two visions (me-as-'pinprick' vis-à-vis Mountain-as-same) combined to effect this dual act (wrapt in lily white) with Kailash which uplifted her 'true' (hidden) name. (The Reader will note alignment with David's more recent acupuncture needle counsel, but for my simple mind it took longer for the synapses to fire.)

Light, 'upjumped from the very <u>ground</u>', also has dual intent – the in-Earth <u>self</u>-consciousness of Mountain (as Mariel attests) in/of itself, and, via each root-known Songline, the hook into the <u>fullness</u> of the entire in-Earth consciousness of Mountain network. This meant I knew the exact 'mate' for Kailash – her Roof offset by IceWorld's chorten'd 'base' (ditto 'ground zero') would form a nestedfishes holism of Earth-consciousness, a dense ball of glowing Light to gift home to the stars, thus effecting incoming reciprocal recognition.

Is this making sense, Reader? I apologise for the dense packaging, but please bear with us!

Meditative insights did not end there, however. Once I connoted the working model of 'the 20 by the 1', Dawn of Time arrived with an intense visioning string. It centred on 'ground' <u>within</u> 'ground' – I saw into/onto a small space of seeming 'bedrock of existence' which constellated as a worksite <u>incisor'd</u> from surrounding ground, deep within same. Here was placed a slim layer of hessian – exactly like what you would see in environmental rehabilitation works where hessian cloth <u>stabilises</u> the slope from further erosion to support fresh (organic) 'ground-cover' to take root. As our worksite was 'exposed to the elements', the task to apply gold-leaf paint in a thin 'wash' over the hessian webbing would heal <u>and</u> protect the 'bedrock'. Our methodology ('liquid Light' rendered in Song) would offer dear Dawn's old carpet self, weathering at different rates, Light infusion (healing) and sealant (protection) in one. Words formed: "Restitching." Yes, we needed to re-forge links between old worn <u>overstretched</u> (and overstressed) networks of in-Earth consciousness to support a holistic 'unfold' of planetary evolution. Our working model now had a <u>pattern</u> of direct action within each triangulation, and between the whole, which we could follow. Very excitedly, I wrote in my journal:

"This is what existed, exists still (!) to protect the very core of Gaian knowing AND potentiality – white-washing the 'bare, eroded' sites with gold-leaf 'liquid Light', our task also implies re-stitching intercontinental 'portions' into a harmonious <u>full-knit</u> of Whole Earth partnership!"

But Dawn wasn't done yet:

"It is my belief that Gaia needs more Fire."

This twinned seamlessly in my mind with a perennial Mr1300BC aphorism:

"Love in itself is Fire."

It was his shorthand for Teilhard de Chardin's (TdC) 'some day' quote – a clear <u>and</u> present reality for me in <u>any</u> situation. In full, it reads:

"Some day, after we have mastered the Winds, the Waves, the Tides and Gravity, we shall harness, for God, the energies of Love. Then, for the second time in the history of the world, man will have discovered Fire."

This shifted me back to when I first quoted TdC (in "The Taste of Translation") – in honour of Laleima, my subtle sister from a 14th century universe, who on 9/11 in our 21st, said with dispassion:

"There is not enough Love in the World."

At this recall, the rhizome of my brain synapsed faster than the lights on a pinball machine in the hands of a crazy flipper-finger'd wizard (kid). The upshot of Dawn's pronouncement can be summarised as follows:

Gaia needs more Love at her deepest darkest most <u>ancient</u> tectonic layers. Mariel's "Stars within the Earth" really are this <u>deep</u>, this <u>dark</u>, this <u>ancient</u>. And if we want to support the 'singing up' of Gaia's full evolutionary Songline, our Love needs to harness existing <u>molten</u> sources (volcanic) to reach through to these zones (Mountain ring-of-fire: tick!) as well as be alchemised (TdC's Love-afire) to a form to enable flow across a global root-known network of Mountain 'memory-keepers' (liquid Light: tick!) as much as ensure effective 'sticking power' when applied as sealant onto continental nodal restoration sites in our care (ditto: tick!).

To all intents, our gold-leaf infusions would replicate the process of writing an icon, something I had researched in depth for "The Taste of Translation". I went back to my notes – here was the opportunity to bind (as psychoid unity) subtle sight with physical 'craft' (although I am no artist!), thus affirming the sacred nature of task <u>and</u> its potentiality. As with T's Mountains-Mandala, these triangulated mini-nets would be sung into being while scripted to parchment – my circumambulatory walking in/out rendering an 'echo of original in generational time' for the descent (in icon-speak) of grace (charis). I remembered back to a vision gifted after walking my stretch of Gondwana HomeSong, singing up my enduring embodied connection in/out along an entire coastal shoreline of smooth sea-washed basalt – lava spewed forth from the fiery heart of the giant shield volcano which left Wollumbin its latter-day relict.

In the Malakut I was shown how the elements, Water and Air, harmonised to cool Earth's heart of Fire, render it as 'pacific' as the settled stone from which our lush forests could spring. The vision came with a 'colour chart' – basalt, polished ebony beneath my sandy feet, was here rendered the deepest softest wishlist-green, the colour chosen for our living room wall, where 'the forest meets the sea'. In artist-speak, a fresh mid-toned aquamarine blue that in 'warm light' shows a sheer green base note, I found myself flowing with this volcanic 'tide' over its countless millennia of metamorphose, experiencing how our liquid Light could transmute to (relative) permanency the <u>harmonium</u> of expression in Land, walked.

Thus did Dawn's (Gaia-Fire) comment press another Annie-button in how it referenced TdC's specific <u>naming</u> of the elemental energies in his vision of Love. It confirmed already-instituted work practices of our Amici crew. <u>Love</u> underpinned, overlit and all-in-between'd a process of harmonising elemental sentience, the purity of our (loving) intent exhibited in the sheer silver-white scarfs wrapt round Kailash ('tulle' our woven 'tool' of Love). Love at <u>core</u> the Fire igniting our full-on creative Love-inflected work <u>stream</u> in which Love is as much the outcome (sea) as its originating spark (source). Ed Sheeren's "I see Fire" from Amici perspect? Ha! Liquid Light 'starblood' (rather than grumpy dragon breath)! And this we shunt forth to in-vein-connector-thread <u>all</u> triangulated points of Gaia's Earth as well as between Tectonia's stars and cosmic same. Our 'icons' would be painted in a never-ending waterfall of rainbow'd Joy in-world-out!

"OK," said Dawn. "Last thing, then I'm off."

A vision appeared of a white-bleached 'snow gum' with carved initials; goanna and koala scratches up its straight as a PeacePole spine. I stood below – its huge wide trunk filled the scene, angling up to where Sky stood 'framed' between tall, sinewed branches reaching toward Heaven. Within this brilliant Blue (against starkness of White) a single cirrus cloud wisp, angelic of shape. The image shifted to a computer monitor; an Amici techie was uploading it to website. I thought it was a picture taken of a tree from home-beach, guardian-keeper of a place I once stood (outwith Time) looking North 'whence we came' (see "Awakening"). But when I zoomed in on the image, I saw that two (physical) trees in this small snatch of terra had conflated their (subtle) root-knowing for my edification – the other, at a 'crossroads' within forest sanctity.

Not only was I being reminded of the vertical link between Heaven-Earth via first tree, but the horizon of all in-Earth directions via second. I realised Tree <u>enacted</u> Mountain, as Mountain did Tree; both housed 'spheric knowing', inwith and of the Body of Gaia's <u>full</u> reach. It had been a massive download, but I was (still) here to tell the tale, even after surrendering my resistance to Kailash joining crew! The Amici expressed their relief in a next best gift – a lovely colour-coded set of workwear, in wishlist-green. Lucky me!

Time to introduce you, Reader, to the exact 'mate' chosen for Kailash at IceWorld's chorten'd 'base' – the continental anchor for Gondwana's knowing still locked in ice (at time of writing). To be frank, I did not have to go far to 'think' of an Antarctic peak. Erebus' name was carved in psyche when Air New Zealand crashed into his side in 1979. As a sensitive teen in an aviator family, this was more major than major – a life-long connection to shock and grief forged in its very ice-sloped fires, 'referred pain' by another name. And yes, an active volcano, the southern-most on Earth, on Ross Island where McMurdo Station is based – a 'hotspot' for volcanologists due to its persistent lava lake, ice fumaroles and extraordinary golden feldspar crystals. The mountain was named by the Brit explorer, Ross, in the 1840s, after his ship (of discovery) – Erebus which, in turn, was named for the Greek primordial deity of darkness, born of the Void (aka Mother-Ocean in Australian Aboriginal cosmology).

A latter connective thread for me was the nearness of name to Erebor, the 'Lonely Mountain' of Tolkien's dwarves whence the Arkenstone hailed and from which, latterly, Dragon fire liberally rained down on the poor souls of Dale. (Was Tolkien similarly Erebus-inspired, I wonder?) Intriguingly, as I connoted this cumulative resonance, I was drawn to meditate – in an inner 'cone of silence' I saw a very large robust <u>broad</u> male 'presence' rise up from rocky ground and stride past me. I certainly got a good look at him – dark stone or 'bone' overlain with white crust which was very much part of his 'skin'. Words formed:

"*Bag of <u>bleached</u> bones.*"

This hooked the line of flight to Crone (Australis) from IceWorld (Antarctica). I realised I was on the right 'track' – Erebus a direct elder-keeper who plumbed the <u>core</u> of Gondwana Dreaming through his volcanic fire of liquid (laval) Light (gold crystalline at that!). The link to primordial deity in his naming was potent in this regard – 'twas the <u>age</u> of contact I needed, his fire a 'light' in the darkest longest nights of Gondwana's Dreaming soul …

What continues to amaze me, however, are the precognitive strikes work partners place in my wending journal-scribbling way. After Gondwana's direct (Brexit-timed) outreach, I had wanted to find an opportunity to connect with her while down under (on daughter-keeper Australis' 'turf') the following month during our annual 'pilgrimage'. No occasion presented (to my mind) but on our last evening pre-flight back to Heidiland, she arrived and said: "It's been very nice to meet you." Huh? When had outreach occurred? Only when putting the 'jigsaw pieces' many months down the track was I reminded to flick back through notes to an intriguing event in a place called 'IceWorld' while at sunny home-beach (of all places).

In the fullness of a Winter-Dark night, as far South as South would go (coincident with their hemispheric solstice at the time), it centred on the <u>gate</u> to/from their Malakut dimension. This was the heaviest most solid jolly gate I have <u>ever</u> encountered in moving between realities, and here I was, on the IceWorld side, needing to return to home base on the other. Hmmm … Whatever I had been doing in IceWorld occurred in FullDark – given Gondwana's comment, she was somehow involved but, in the moment, my attention was solely focused on a heavy stubborn gate. I needed to time my re-entry to the other ('my') side perfectly because of the strength needed to open it – it would swing and then slam again, as secure as <u>any</u> pressure-sealed airlock, and obviously with good purpose.

When I wrote earlier of her Dreaming being 'locked in ice' I truly meant it. I had access, sure – thank you very much! But there was no way I could intercept this gate's backswing, heave it open a second time. Would I be stuck here forever?

Overall, the scene was quite dramatic, involving a huge pile-up of motorbikes having skidded into the wall (of IceWorld) because they had not timed their run properly. Others complained the gate should stay permanently open for easier access, but I understood why it was tightly sealed. Depth-charged knowing, Gondwana's <u>vault</u> of wisdom stays locked in <u>both</u> physical and subtle dimensions. The physical is calving, fissuring, melting – this we see with climate change. What is changing the climate on the inner dimensions? Where are you, Dawn? And this Fire of Love you mentioned?

Spirit-geology, material-Malakut, Kailash-Erebus, Love uplifted from the dark. I had been told (early in our UrWerk's framing of task) that 'rock' and 'ice' were the two strings to bind. While all peaks 'played' with this notion in different energetic ways, these two expressed solitary fusion in nestedfishes form – a 'seaming' of shared consciousness, one to the other, which gave rise to much in our 'rock-ice' (i.e. crystal) canon. To round out my knowing, I researched the geologic 'why' behind these two-as-one (become) partners, discovering that 'insular India' was an early split-asunder from Gondwana's Dreaming (Land) which, after multiple millions of years, arrived in/at Asia. Upthrust on collision, the mighty Himalayan-Tibetan orogen brought gifts from Mother-Ocean floor as close as can be to Heaven's stair. Australis, however, last to leave home, took her slow journey north to cool that volcanic heart while baking her skin brown and black. Erebus, though, stayed the distance on DeepTime's longitudinal watch, kept the home fires burning in IceWorld, the centre of supercontinent from which all had rifted in a (seemingly) orderly clockwise fashion. Aren't they good 'kids'?

Knowing this ancient history of planetary plate tectonics supported my first conscious 'visit' to Erebus (post-IceWorld gate dramas). I entered via Wollumbin and T's Dreaming backed my meditation – its vision of the Ancestors' outwalking Song across Land, up/out from Mother-Ocean, her pure Dark of uncreated Light, 'seeding' the creative impulse woven of her <u>Breath</u> via two lines of flight (rock and ice). Upjumped from the very ground of Mother-Ocean (being), <u>infilling</u> the frame of Ring of Fire, <u>flooding</u> it with her generosity of spirit, cooling, transmuting that which pours forth, out from molten depths, into smooth 'pacific' wave-washed stone. In harmonic resonance, we 'tuned' our performance to this vast daughter-of-mother, sailed the skywaves of her 'eastern-sea-wild' Songline all the way south from home-beach till we bumped into Erebus. At some level, I realised that while Gondwana's wisdom had been hidden in plain Australis' sight (Summer-baked for millions of years at that) and that she had revealed herself at Helvetia's 'True-Sister's-Island' for my (local) benefit, here was an opportunity to meet her

at source – via her Mountain champion. I intoned:
> We drop to the Ancestors
> We lie prone in your Presence
> So you may teach
> So we may learn the Essence

Indeed did my anchor 'drop'; I felt my <u>descent</u> through successive layers (or dimensions) of Dark which grew more 'pure' all the while till I reached (rock) bottom where, waiting for me, was a treasury of black crystal. I had dropped through Erebus' 'zone' of golden feldspar crystal to the 'lay-of-land' of blackest black Mother-Ocean depths. I looked over to T, said:

"*This was it all along? I had been this clueless as to the 'source code/x' the canvas described?*"

She remained immutable, inscrutable; I, meanwhile, saw into the meticulous white dots circumambulating each continental node and knew (now) that in 'original' form they had been black. These stars-within-earth carried forth by the Ancestors; as they sang, the black became white, manifesting Love's Light and thus <u>visible</u> to each wisdom keeper of lineage since so they would know the <u>route</u> of Song in/out in order to 'restitch' the 'sink' with 'surface' consciousness. Each black crystal potentiality made <u>manifestly</u> white in DeepTime-Tectonia, continentally-up-jumped, 'sprouted' from Mother-Ocean 'seeds'. And here I was in their midst? Oh. My. Goodness.

I knew I needed to stay put, simply be present to whatever was to 'happen' here. Standing in this 'field', suddenly all potentialities were within me, 'seeds' implanted in/through my 3rd chakra (solar plexus). At the time I thought:

"Is this like Malakut IVF? Odd, but practical."

Absorption would enable incubation; incubation would enable 'birthing' when Time ripe (in partner'd Time) to replicate the work of the Ancestors – in Song – to:
> *Resurrect the knowing gone underground*
> *Reveal the Sink at Surface (plunged)*
> *Break the dam walls, let flow the River (run)*

(as I wrote into existed in "Muted Earth"). T had <u>held</u> this Dreaming at her (Gondwana) heart all along, but it took several rounds of Annie-ripening before I was ripe for its becoming. Now I saw the whole of our work's unfold (again, in new light) on the canvas, her icon written in black gold (leaf). Within her 'black', the 'white' of primordial stellar creation, pre-Big-Bang'd birth, a (Mother-Ocean'd) sea of latency, ready (and waiting) for (an Annie) handmaiden's arrival.

It was time to close IceWorld's no-longer-heavy gate. But a last precious future-primitive vision was placed before my sight before my return to the here-and-now. I 'saw' the Ancestors walk out in each of the four directions:

"We carry the 'dark stars" (said).

In this (their) dimension they appeared as black 'grains-of-sand' sparkling haphazardly before my inner vision from which a single white point of Light – long, languid – materialised. On DeepTime's watch, the Ancestors were ever at task – gathering, collecting what had <u>incubated</u> in Love's Dark <u>Light</u>, for carrying out into the Light of World, for <u>adding</u> to the Light of World, seeding Love afresh. I felt the alignment, the harmonisation of individual and collective resonance, within my Self, this 'pure and clear channel' of Self flushed with Joy, watching as I re-inhabited the skin of 'me' to light a fresh candle to our work of drawing forth Earth-<u>centred</u> consciousness …

● ● ● ● ●

Reader, we have finally caught up with ourselves (and the 20) and the moment of Kailash's whisper: "You know the first one." Are you up for another story? I do hope so!

There is a Mountain in the eastern Alps who is/has been my bestie since I arrived, as an expat-turned-migrant, to this landlocked Land long years past. You have not yet had the pleasure to meet this sturdy chap in volume (unless you skipped ahead to the appendices, Reader, where he is named as soulful muse in company of a first Amici chat with the Card Deck of the Sidhe). His was the first 'real' mountain I climbed (here or anywhere). Anything prior had been hill-walking and bushwhacking at best. But on this particular day, reaching the summit in happy exhaustion, I felt I had 'done good'. Any self-important sense of achievement, however, was quickly put paid to by the view – ridges and crests of countless further peaks rolled into the distance, seemingly forever. I had a (minor) epiphany of my insignificance in the unfolding aeons-old drama of life, just as minor as the geological formation on which I stood (but he took it on the chin). My humility in the moment was overseen by a golden eagle drifting lazily not three metres over my head, barely moving a muscle.

That first time upon Schiesshorn's crest included, unbeknown to me, D-in-utero. It became a family joke which, the year he turned ten and wanted to climb all the mountains of the world, we attempted to reframe as fact. Alas, while his older siblings joined me for the last couple of hundred metres skyward, he cried halt from fatigue. There was no way any of us was going to piggyback him. He either made it up under his own steam or not at all. I had already done it once! Reduced to (some) tears, the only choice was to picnic with F on a twee meadow.

When Kailash did her whispering, I knew 'what' we needed to do, but not 'when'. From our down under family sojourn that 2017 year we headed home to Helvetia via Hong Kong for a change, and planned some hiking so I could enjoy the (physical) company of the Rugby Sevens. A true delight, one day we found ourselves on a peak which hosted signage describing the importance of Mountain in Taoist cosmology (which I knew) and the date families traditionally wandered up a mountain to pay respects to the Ancestors (which I did not) – the 9th day of 9th (lunar) month. The magic of the numbers, in my experience, never lies … here we were, with nine continental nodal champions whose triangulations would effect a multiple of nine once I lit the first beacon while 'supported' by these divine (rugby) locals and my own Helvetian crew? That was all it needed for the Amici to get busy, and for me to start asking all weather gods (family 'planning' gods and more) for the right causes, conditions to make this magic happen!

I sold it to D as his chance to finally get up top under his own steam; I sold it to F as a chance to pay respects to his genetic Ancestors whose love of region had become his, thus ours. I sold it to myself as a memory-trail from seeing the bonfire lit atop peak (as is traditional for the Swiss on their national day, coincident with Celtic Lughnasadh – amazingly delightful are these 'pagan' hangovers in collective ancestral psyche!) to walking his Songline, meeting skin-to-skin some days later. I remember standing at the window of family chalet, mesmerised by a cultural ritual since time immemorial, while F describing the annual rites of season. I looked onto the face of this giant, the burning beanie he wore that night, said: "Can we climb that one?" and so it would be (D-in-utero=3). Years later, when Peter Jackson brought Tolkien to the screen, I had an 'image-string' to add to Schiesshorn's lone-ranger role. But before you think I was going to ask the lads to lug wood atop, no. 'I' was the one carrying Love's Light – in Song, in Self. Arriving up top to 'kiss' his craggy crest would ignite his beacon this time in-skin.

In honour of Sun's 'ignite' of life, we Amici agreed to work with the solar calendar's 9th day of 9th month rather than trust to Moon's lunar 'mirror'. There was no 'Ancestor' who was <u>not</u> part of this primordial picture of Gaia's evolutionary consciousness, all co-dependent arising across the full <u>extent</u> of DeepSpaceTime would I honour with each step (and groan) of pilgrimage. You may think my commitment excessive but when all causes, conditions are ripe for Time-partner'd action across subtle-physical planes? We may never have the chance again; it was worth giving it our best shot but I have had enough disappointments in life to know to drop all expectations of outcome after stating, with as much <u>clarity</u> as I can muster, the 'purity of intent', the why of the act (ever, always for Gaia) and then letting go, detaching, knowing: What will be will be. (Or, in a Julian-of-Norwich universe: All is well, and ever …)

A two-hour drive followed by a three-hour climb followed by … (We agreed to stay overnight in the village to celebrate our hopeful achievement.) Important was to tell Schiesshorn what we were doing, and why. Hence, a poem penned: "Song of the Blue (Redux)", which, once out of the car, hiking boots donned, I stood at trailhead in chilly drizzle to call aloud while staring more than a kilometre skyward to his cloud-shrouded crown (the ultimate stoic), patiently waiting to be feted. I began my homage (D rolled his teenage eyes, took off down the trail). I specifically included the overlighting genius loci of valley in the invocation – physically met on first climb and then later, one Winter, as a cloud-conjured energy Presence straddling the entire ridgeline whom I named 'Golden Eagle of the Southern Cirque'.

Interesting, in context, to now recall David's counsel when I enquired about the Earth-consciousness 'vortex' unwittingly tapped into (alluded to earlier in chapter). I described it to him thus:

"It looked as if the full force of subtle energies in this remit had accumulated into a single shape, a complete 'gathering of presence' vis-à-vis miniscule me."

David's take?

"I think the 'eagle' you saw was an invitation to further exploration and partnership, perhaps on a larger scale. You may wish to investigate this further, assuming you haven't already done so!"

Well, gracious me, it was as if we were inviting ourselves to further exploration and partnership in its glorious shed!

Homecome to you I walk into the Blue
Ascend your cragged and aether'd heights
Descend your chthonic star-lipped stairs –
Golden Eagle of the Southern Cirque
I greet thee afresh as I did the day-night
So many years past, as you soared o'er my sight
Now I too glide aloft thermals vast
Future drawn from plethora'd past, for on
9th day on 9th month at Schiesshorn's crest
First beacon shall be lit at Helvetia's behest
For all others besides, chain-reaction'd worldwide!
Thank you to all blessed causes, conditions
For facilitating same, enabling my Eliotian'd
Return to beginning, embrace of known anew:
All Love here in-brought from Your wondrous Blue …

As I concluded, a purple heron flew over – very unusual apparently (F said it must have gotten lost on migration). Given the lousy weather, no self-respecting eagle would be out and about, but this 'bird-of-heaven' (species'd, according to Eastern spiritual traditions)? Definitely a good sign! At the pass (Fürgga) before last ascent (D leading the pack – gee, the difference a few years can make!), Joy greeted us in the form of … Steinbock! A family of eight – requisite auspicious (Chinese) number for good luck; all with thick muscular necks, broad shoulders to hold those weighty horns aloft. All in line-up – why had I never before noticed their similarity to a rugby pack? Shapeshifting B52s, I wonder?

At summit, a rainbow. (A gift from the Ancestors, we agreed.) We nibbled green-(Peace)-tea KitKats (a subtle pre-birthday pressie from Amici younglings which reminded me to pack some for the hike – yum!). Could it get any better? I 'planted' a shell in amongst the rubble of rocks which passed for a summit cairn beside the imposing cross, and then we hightailed it out of there. Snow was on the way but kindly waited ('tis a benevolent H5.0 universe, after all) until we were back at trailhead. First big flat flakes drifted lazily down which, by next morning, contributed a good couple of inches to hide our tracks. And as we work undercover? Phew!

The first of the twenty 'lit' by the one (post-Reiki's investiture into the fullness of Light 'work', Alpha-Cen Sprachschule happily honed). That night I entered a liminal space of deep repose, physically felt to have brought the all-of-Mountain into myself to offer back out as Love's Light 'flown' forth. I understood this could occur because Schiesshorn was 'me-sized'; perhaps 'twas even the subtle mountain I hugged once in company of Mr1300BC as part of my training.

Had this conscious act of ancestral honouring conflated, expanded this sleeve of (Mother-Ocean) Breath shared? For I felt to be in the midst of a self-creation <u>myth</u> which mirrored Gaia's, as if I were a shaman <u>literally</u> vision-experiencing the act of 'ignite' in own skin (Land). It took Kali's Mountains 101 into a space of profound experiential learning – embodied praxis, Malakut-fathom'd (or "recovered memory, fresh envisioned" in micro-Annie-skin). Later in text, Reader, we will meet other examples of in-Body creationary 'mountaineering' – in sacred space, across sacred time. I mentioned the black crystals earlier, yes, but this shifted its subtle suggestion to actual engagement of <u>my</u> matter'd consciousness as stone/bone crystalline act.

It expressed itself as I emerged from 'liminality' in a low-toned resonance from Schiesshorn's 'mouth': "Ich bin die Magi/e" (i.e. I am the magic and the magic-maker in one) said. Spoken in a voice my own yet not my own, I knew it emanated from Mountain core. But <u>its</u> core, in this moment, was <u>my</u> core (effecting ignite of black crystals). To be honest, it sounded ridiculous when 'I' heard it emerge from 'my' mouth, but it shifted my/our Amici thinking from Laleima's lament ("there is <u>not enough</u> Love in the world") to a foot-stamping commitment (fiery hope in action) to work with that absolute hoard of black crystal seeds offered into our orbit by the Ancestors in Mother-Ocean'd deep – flipping the coin to say:

There is <u>so much</u> Love in the world
It just wants to be released
And this is our forever work –
We the people of Peace …

Schiesshorn – first beacon lit, chain reaction'd worldwide. It was all there in the original communique of 2015, but I had been so fixated on the DS part, it was only in hindsight I thought to go back and check the download for other gems, there re-finding:

I travel with (a partner) into Sidhe zones where we work with a flaming branch, <u>phoenix-lit</u>. Time is running 'down'; periodically she blows a horn to 'inform' someone of our actions – it seems we need to light a bunch of 'stations' with the burning branch before Time is 'extinguished'. Yet it should be done slowly, moderately, methodically; when 'contaminated' with the energy of urgency it is not done well.

Yes, we were methodical. Of that I was certain. Our skills were honed; our rituals in place. And, as indicated above, much of our work was going on in cross-veil zones – the 'bleed' from one to the other managed, and intentional. Subtle-through-physic'd, till final planting in the <u>truth</u> of Gaia's earth.

INTERMEZZO (2)

We have reached the end of our second section of volume, a stretch of song trekked in company of stone giants. While they shall continue to accompany us in our next, and final stretch, it is time to draw this part of narrative to a close. We had assembled our crew, we had 'joined' each to the other in an interconnected net of loving Songlines around, across, and through world. Still much, much, much to be done, to 'enliven' these threads – strengthen, refine, deepen the connections, get them singing like a well-tuned harmonium, but? We had made a start; it was something. Our next section will therefore 'speak' to this proposition – tuning 'our' (symphonic, concerto'd) fork in order to tune theirs.

Before doing so, however, I would like to invite you to witness an intermezzo performance of our Amici troupe, to peer over our shoulders at an event to which we had been invited to speak about our work with said stone giants. As I found the setting, and range of participants, fascinating, I thought it may fascinate you too.

You may recall that earlier in these pages I mentioned various locales where we meet other teams to trade insight, experience, or share tools. There was the subtle United Nations congress, for example, or the inter-dimensional 'group house' out of which Golden Duck worked. In the pages of "Awakening", I described my visits to/with 'cosmic relations' – the chaps from the Rings of Saturn, far from conversant with the ways of humankind, were an absolute lark. I can shake my head in wonder at the inanity of encounter now (and where they were whisking me off to) but at the time their approach was as subtle as a sledgehammer (pun definitely intended!). Meanwhile, down decades of 'weaving' a loving space of energy and substance in which to host various entities, I have been graced with many visitors popping in for a cup of PeaceTea, a walk of garden, a discussion on technique or significant 'download' received (here, T's Dreaming stands out). Finally, let me remind you of the place I visited to 'sign' a work contract for this undertaking, having attended a serious business meeting with Mr1300BC (to discuss 'The Daphnes'). While sweet Filing Tray peddled away beneath my desk, a woman described the 'regulations' and 'conditions' of my employ, wryly noted at one point: "If you think bureaucracy on Earth is bad, try Galaxy-wide." Indeed!

To be frank, if I were a sci-fi author I would 'mine' the following encounter (in this galaxy-wide setting) as readily as I did my jaunts into Sidheverse which enfleshed the bare bones of "Leeks & Peas", the mythic tale of our shared history (included in the collection "Grail Within"). But I am not. Still, in context of a work contract, signed, and sealed, let me share with you my presentation on its (intended) deliverables.

((Note: The following passage uses present tense. When episodes like this 'constellate', it is in a dimension outwith Time; an entire day can be compressed to half an hour thanks to the 'collapse' of (Time-structured) human thought and surface cognitive process. I 'live' the magic of smorgasbord offered in real-time – 'tis life-in-the-gap, as described by "Song of the Blue".))

• • • • •

Picture this, Reader. A day in the wake of our first Equinox Ceremony, Spring '17, the one to call all's attention to our intention, the one in wake of months of solid research, preparation, planning, thinking. A day when I propose (to self) some down-time, some relaxation. I retreat to inner sanctum (after the family farewelled out the door to work-or-student daily life drills) for a session of meditative repose. I 'drop'; all good (or so I think). Suddenly, though? 'Gone'. While Body is left to its repose, 'I' am up, busy downstairs, and fully into the day.

The doorbell rings. I think: Forget it. Not yet properly dressed, still to wash sleep out of eyes. Pabey (intelligent hound) doesn't bark but is nosing around the door. Somehow these visitors are already in the stairwell, in front of our internal door. (Did the neighbour let them in from our shared street access?) I hear them talking out there. The back verandah door is open; I go out (into bright mid-morning sunshine – it is 'now'; I am fully 'here') to find the laundry door is also open (to stairwell). Now I hear their chatting more clearly. It's in English. How terribly odd. I figure I had better go and see what it's all about. I unlock the front door to find three 'presences' – two female who look relatively 'usual', and a male who is completely outwith.

He is very, very, <u>very</u> tall, thin as a stick, skeletal, made of metal with <u>hugely</u> disproportionate kneecaps (think: clanking bone knobbles), and an 'alien' head. As soon as the door opens, he barges in, and past me to stand at the dining table. It's absolutely clear he's from a dimension and with an energy signature I have not met before. His 'plank-of-4x2' approach reminds me of the Saturn dudes but even their quirky style did not include 'home invasion'.

He announces (loudly): "We're here to take you to the LA Conference one-day workshop."

I say (loudly): "I'm not going anywhere with you! How dare you come in here!"

((During this exchange, the women are still hovering near the door (probably waiting for their invitation to 'cross' the 'threshold' … sigh …).))

At this he sits down at the table, completely at a loss, and says: "But you want to go to the Conference! You said so! So I'm here to take you!"

((At this, Reader, let me apprise you of the fact that 'LA' in our Amici-lexicon refers to a higher dimension reality associated with the angelic realm, and far 'out' in intergalactic space. I have been on its 'edge' before, but this invitation was a first – at least to my conscious recall.))

Poor chap. How could I be so rude? As soon as he says this, I 'remember' my invitation to attend; nevertheless, I am still very against getting to an event I want to get to in his 'alien' company. Again, I refuse. He turns to the women, says: "She doesn't believe us; we need to get 'so-n-so' on the line" (i.e. someone I respect). While they fiddle around at the table, I head down to the couch. Looking back (i.e. from a 'distance'), I put the pieces of his 'metal-head' 'body-guard' 'helper' puzzle together. Sigh, think: He's done his best … And before they can call 'so-n-so', I return, say: "I've reconsidered. It's OK. And thank you. Let's go."

We enter a space-shuttle type vehicle – like the fuselage of a Hercules but better decked out, no wings. In there are others collected from here (i.e. Earth) of human or Sidhe signature, and off we go. It is a thrilling ride; we arrive 'inside' a conference centre. Many 'people' are milling about, ready to participate in proceedings. I am to be part of a panel discussion. I see a podium area up front. Five 'transmission' chairs are set up, at back of which is a raised bench behind which some moderators sit. As I arrive, I am handed a small device which is a combo-ear-voice recorder thingey. I can't lose it. This is my means of connection and so others can understand what say (i.e. an automated dual-function translator, very small, no wires). I am not on first, but will be called when my turn to join a panel of five arrives. This is not the principal locale of the 'LA Conference one-day workshop'; that is somewhere completely 'beyond' which I (and the others here) would not be able to 'tolerate' (interdimensional journeying, energy differences etc). This is a satellite station to hook our contributions into the main proceedings.

While I wait, and watch, a woman I know from a previous research setting comes over to chat. She has a very 'academic' bent, and I am surprised to see her here until she fills me in on our intergenerational 'familial' links. OK. Off she toddles. I am intrigued by the first panel as it gets underway because it sets the scene for mine. Each 'presence' from <u>our</u> world is given the opportunity to share their contribution to an overall universal <u>cosmic</u> plan from our 'place' on Earth. Our perspective, understandably, is within the framework and context of Gaia's evolutionary consciousness but that our work is being rolled into cosmic 'planning'? Excellent!

I watch as everyone puts in their communicator-translator device; the moderator then asks questions about (wait for it): Literature! Specifically focusing on Jane Austen's work, meanings and resonances behind her texts (cultural, historic). It is as if designed for knowledge-sharing with (as I call them) the 'Galactic Council' resident in 'LA', so they understand more and better about Earth – our ways of doing, seeing, experiencing, sharing on both sides of veil'd vale. I twig my contribution is intended to place our Gondwana Dreaming task within a longer-than context – the 'history of human creativity' conversation with MakerMan crosshatched with Karen Armstrong's 'myth-making' contention, plus Jung's 'personal-myth' (Annie-interpreted vis-à-vis Gaia's). This our Amici offering to Earth-consciousness 'ball' rolled back to the stars.

I sense into the conference's purpose; I 'see' it has something to do with formulating stellar energies, <u>harmonising</u> the alchemical recipes to better 'stick' (and thus support work in-world as well as through all worlds). In essence, what I witness (and contribute to) is an example of how grassroots first-hand 'knowing' is fed into the <u>pool</u> of data 'tapped' in context of universal 'grand-design'. I feel very honoured to be present; definitely my first time (in this skin, at least) at such a forum. According to my extremely 'low' stature I stay quiet, respectful, observant.

So many 'people' arriving, so many unusual beings. They all bring food specialties from home 'territories' (share a plate); a double offering – in gratitude to host as well as their 'recipe' for nourishment gifted to the whole (of 'knowledge'). More than anything, this alerts me to my newbie status in such a 'conference' setting – the fact I don't know protocols and arrive empty-handed. (Oops – in my earthly experience business conferences are generally catered!) The 'level' of entities arriving to represent their communities (our little group 'Earth') is also quite daunting. Professors and Lord Mayors are introduced. A squat medieval-dressed Sidhe from our ship walks past with two curly red-haired princesses, their eyes very mischievous. It seems in this setting she is responsible for running the creche for whoever brings 'mini-kids'. As they pass, she rolls her eyes at task. Yes, I already know what a handful they are! I sit with a young large blonde energy signature – as a local, she dresses for summertime while I am freezing cold. My purple (heaven) and green (earth) woollen shawl is over the top of several layers; still I shiver. We are so far 'out' – I would have no chance getting here unless by shuttle piloted (or driven) by a chap with steel-capped knees!

At last it is my turn; my name is announced (a hybrid construction to identify work, and locus of activity). I go up to the podium, introduce myself to the moderator assigned for our session sitting at desk behind. He is jolly, constellating as a dark-haired mid-aged chap, completely attuned to business-professional-casual 'normal' except for his penetrant otherworldly eyes. Before reading out other names for our panel, he leans over to welcome me properly, shake my hand, saying he knows the full backstory to my hesitation in going with the 'driver', and hopes I will come again. Equally the point of handshake is to demonstrate that if <u>ever</u> I have misgivings in future, I can be sure of 'provenance' via this methodology. As we 'touch', a whole bunch of other interlocutors (different communication techniques) materialised on the desk between us. He intimates that if ever I meet someone using these it also bodes well.

Everything clear. Done, dusted. Suddenly I am 'back' (and/or trying to reassemble all bits of me after such an encounter to fully <u>feel</u> back). I take some time to ponder the encounter (and write up these notes!). Our work is being monitored, observed; our input on a vaster plane of consistence (than I ever considered when signing up for this Amici adventure) is (seemingly) valued. And the 'secret handshake'? Perhaps a bit basic, but obviously my 'cognition' needs this – something sensory, something tactile. Something energetic, simple, <u>felt</u>.

•••••

Again, now, I have occasion to ponder that moment – a brief seven years past in (linear) human time, but on Mountain's DeepTime (tectonic) watch? Or Sun's solar system'd stretch of Song? Or further 'out' to Alpha-Cen (of Sprachschule fame)? (Just a thought: Maybe I no longer need a transmitter device?).

I ponder because it is as if <u>each</u> door that opens within us, to offer more of ourselves to Love's Light and to offer more of <u>our</u> Light in loving service to Gaia's world is somehow equivalent and/or commensurate with doors that open onto other interdimensional realities. My Light is 'seen'; and I 'see' more of the Light in like Breath. It reminds me of Mr1300BC's 'fridge' analogy when I stood before a pantry cupboard full of foodstuffs, its door slightly ajar, a thin seam of ruddy-pink light visible. My auto-reaction was to turn the light off and save energy. But as I opened the door wide to search for the 'switch', blinding white light flooded the space setting off the 'chi of shared circuitry' through crystalline veins. At this, my wise mentor said: "It works like a fridge. When the door is closed, the light automatically extinguishes. Keep your door open so you always have the Light." Yep, it made sense – keeping the door of my heart fully open, and by walking each and every path beyond its threshold as a Way of Love, I would remain connected to the source. If the door of my heart only slightly ajar? The transmission would be muddy, my 'hearing' not as keen compared with the clarity-drenched radiance before me.

I am never not indebted to Mr1300BC for 'taking me on' (to all intents) as an apprentice. Our first 'conscious' (on my part) meeting led to his naming. A Malakut scape of high mountain meadows stretching away into the distance, me being 'checked in' to a traditional guesthouse only reachable by dirt track (ostensibly) for the weekend (Hmmm ... how long is a piece of string in Malakut-time?). He, as 'hotelier', greeted me. Incredibly tall, with very dark eyes and a full black beard, he wore a great coat of patchworked animal skins, a bearskin hat, and heavy riding boots. An insanely warm outfit for what was a bright Summer's day, I sensed he was an 'exile' from a distant Land (or 'migrant', like me) and asked about his long journey through (what I understood to be) a 19th-20thC timeframe to reach this peaceful alpine valley.

He shrugged. "Oh, that journey wasn't so difficult. I've been wandering since 1300BC." Before me appeared in vision his 'life', delivering burning embers to people's hearths as fire-starters. I saw a small tray-backed wagon pulled along deep-rutted paths, embers encased in a heavy leaden box. At each farmer's door he would open the box, extract several coals with a small shovel, and place them into the hearth to help the wood, dung or peat therein to catch alight.

His message – and task – may have been very simple, yet crucial to human life in its service to light, warmth, and sustenance inwith the hearth (heart) of each home. Indeed, the scope of my understanding from our brief exchange was as deep as it was broad. I saw, firstly, how each lifetime is relatively short, each journey not so dramatic in the fullness of Soul's way (of Love) walked. And I saw, with Love, that I had known him then, following him and his 'wagon', apprenticed to task. Now (still!) he offers mentorship from Malakut 3300 years after actually 'walking' Earth. Meanwhile, I still have a long, long way to walk, but? Thanks to his wise counsel oh-so-long ago (in this skin), I know my Light is 'seen', I 'see' more of the Light, and with my burning embers 'singing', I can help 'ignite' Songlines far and wide.

It is time to move on to the next, and final section of tome. That of: "Exploring Song".

STRETCH 3:
EXPLORING SONG

It seems strange, in a way, that while 'working' the energy of Songlines, penning Poetry I self-described as Song, and weaving mantric invocations within our Amici cirque for use in Celtic calendaric ritual on a (shared) plane of intimate exteriority, I never considered putting any real melody 'track' down for each abiding lyric uplifted by pen to paper.

Sure, I had made up wee ditties to sing to babes in arms down the decades and enjoyed 'tuning' a few rhythmic bars to the metronome of my footfalls while hiking (it's amazing how many thematic variations Peace-Love-Light can commandeer in a faithful heart). All this was 'built' on the sturdy foundations of growing up in a musical family, and ably supported by teen ambitions to sing 'rock' with the soaring octaves of Robert Plant.

And yes, sure I held to an abiding ethic, as (a) Bard in (cosmic humanity's ancestral) Tribe, to storytell whatever <u>needed</u> storytelling in whichever mode (of dress) could best house its knowing – essay'd reflection, myth-woven fiction, poetic balladeering. Music (thus Song) had a strong hold on my heart, but I never would have contemplated 'proper' composition. Poetry was enough of a lyrical inflective art for me; there was no need to take it further.

And yet, and yet … There was Mr1300BC's parable of the tuning fork, me as 'singing teacher' for a girl, the high clear note she needed to hold at performance end. There was Mariel's story of cosmic humanity as a 'living tuning fork' in the choir of unfoldment for Gaia's becoming.

Plus, all the way back in "The Taste of Translation" (2011), I 'composed' the middle panel of iconographic triptych as a set of bardic 'hymns', inspired by a 13th century illuminated manuscript ("Cantigas de Santa Maria"). Yet while flowing off the tongue in lyric-drenched prose, with titles to invoke numinous chant, silence was the sum total of its backing band.

Something changed, though, about a decade ago. Preceding the Amici, linked to Nature's own voice. Earlier herein, in company of a favoured mount (our silvery Silberen), I described such a sense of joy in/of 'high-wild' home that Song spontaneously spilled from my lips on her starlit plateau in the form of a traditional women's yodelling variation. I always 'heard' Gaia's soul breath (or resonant hum) bestest, loudest, in Nature's silence and this yodel seemed (in the moment) its natural female human response – mediated by voice. In recounting the experience, I felt it to be Silberen's own 'boundary extension', sweeping me up in embrace, to vocalise – on <u>her</u> behalf – the true nature she held at core (which is Gaia's, after all), oozing from each pore of limestone crevasse'd skin. A singular performance.

Thereafter, any work of actual Song with the Amici incorporated texts lain on others' melodies (e.g. 'Oh misty heights …' from "The Hobbit 2") <u>except</u> for the extant tune to 'wake' Stone to shared purpose via intuition of its resonant hum. Ring-Song'd, mantra'd, 'base-note' of our first co-production, and the model for the "Weaving-Song" (recounted in an earlier chapter) which, in its pattern of goddess-invocation, is an alternative form of render for our "Cantigas de Santa Maria".

To be honest, I cannot see a fixed line between the different modes of bardic delivery. What works is what is used in the mode which best leads to its <u>remembering</u>. (Marshall McLuhan's "the medium is the message" would fit nicely here.) For that is the main point of our work – to script a <u>memory-trail</u> for others to follow, a trail both useful <u>and</u> used <u>if</u> it can be committed to memory, a trail charting time <u>and</u> space in the expansionary map of our OnePeople's (<u>shared</u>) Book of Voyage – Eärendil at helm of starlight's barque.

In the "Card Deck of the Sidhe", David writes:

"In Celtic society, the Bard was the one who knew the history of the clan … all the relationships and connections that made up that history. The bard was the keeper of the collective <u>memory</u> which he or she could share through his or her songs and narratives. The bard was the keeper of <u>vision</u> … (and) connected the clan with the world around them, with each other, with their own past and with the vision of their possible future."

Keeper of memory; keeper of vision – shared in Song, in Story'd narrative. We Amici describe this dual role, in our wee hands, as: "Recovered memory, fresh envisioned." The Songline in the sand is only as potent as the 'map' of journey we lay out before you, <u>re-woven</u> with each repetition of action. The telling of Story, the singing of Song <u>re-performs</u> the walk, <u>re-members</u> the line, <u>re-strengthens</u> the binding between past and future, spheric of shape. A branch of Land-Art which favours the practice of walking reproduces, in a fashion, this myth-making and -replicating function. So too I think back to the maps of medieval Europe whose purpose was to mark itineraries through scape, bards always on hand to sing the Songs the route/s inspired. It is ekphrasis by another name – a detailed narration of events in time and space to help the audience 'see'. Literally, a speech that 'leads one round', circumambulating the <u>fact</u> of Gaia's sacred Earth leads to a deeper understanding of her nature. Truly our own.

We <u>are</u> Kiria in skin. And I am back with the iconographer's "Cantigas de Santa Maria" – his medieval troubadour hymns to Love of primal goddess (in religious dress) which describe how time and space dissolve into an eternal now because of Love's energy at the centre of all creation. Nothing simpler, right? As the iconographer 'writes' his own cantiga (Love Song) in egg tempura, and gold leaf, on a wooden board, the 'map' of his journey from unknowing to knowing is narrated by four witnesses via their own cantigas. In effect this means the icon is 'sung into existence' – materially by the hand of iconographer, spiritually by the others' compassion. This bridges inner-outer planes (of intimate exteriority) and brings an artefact (icon) to life which veritably sings its own <u>vitality</u> to resurrect consciousness.

A "pilgrimage to the heart of being" I described this work in/of itself as well as in my act of its re-writing, re-singing. Its ekphrasis, my own – seamlessly twinned. And this is where the rubber (of hiking boot) hits the road (of walking path). For I can move through a landscape just as seamlessly and 'read' its particular spirit of ekphrasis – written as it is in Land, or through the knowing 'spoken' by residents (any species, physical or non-) in whichever tongue (heard or perceived), or via the vital energy contained in artefacts discovered along the way.

This is what led, in our Amici cirque, to the shift, the change, the quantum leap in 'praxis' – from private to public performance so that our work could be <u>actively</u> witnessed (by Land, residents, artefacts); and from poetic to sung intervention in order to add our ekphratic 'note' to Gaia's, to audibly contribute our harmonium of expression to a worldwide chorale of (blissed-out) co-creation – tuning our (symphonic, concerto'd) fork to come into complete seamless circumambulatory resonance with the All-of-WeltAll*.

(*WeltAll, literally 'total world' = universe, cosmos. Perfect for the extent of our intent!)

Dear Reader – it truly was a quantum leap (at least for this small human who is quite amenable to working 'undercover'). We moved from quietly working on a plane of intimate exteriority, with specific focused intent, to an holistic proposition of singing to, with and for the all-of-All of Gaia's glorious world. Inspired by same and gifted back wholeheartedly, no songsheet would be enough for this (snowballing) endeavour, brimful of excitable Anwa-shaping desire. We needed a jolly songbook! And, as it rumbled downhill (from misty mountain hop'd tops), 'becoming' <u>itself</u> all the while, is it any wonder our repertoire expanded with each new sight, sound, taste, scent, touch of Beauty encountered, of Love expressed? In short, the Songs were <u>always</u> there – in the aetheric dimensions – just waiting, just watching to be found, to be drawn from their latency, returned to the world of time.

Recovered memory, fresh envisioned. "There is not enough Love in the world," Laleima had said. Our Amici response? "There is <u>so</u> much Love in the world; it just <u>wants</u> to be released!"

And how would we release it? Through Song (of course) … just as the (Blue) singing-bird had crunched its gobstopper-sized seed (of Love) containing all potentialities, and released those flowing golden threads out to 'mist' Gaia's fullness with Joy, so too would we. Naught more than Breath lilting on the breeze, but if you look close? There go the golden wisps, dandelion heads afloat of Aire's air, planting pioneering seeds wherever they may land. As bardic as Celtic aires are our Songs a-host of (golden) seeds, words dancing by melodic means, messages in a bottle from we (wee) Amici of the vale, we Fedeli d'Amore cindering veil.

•••••

Poetry. Story. Song. The 'history of human creativity' as discussed with MakerMan (over a cup of tea), the talented 'maker' (choreographer) in troupe whom I partner day-in-day-out. In my small hands 'making' was ever-focused on word-art. I studied music too (piano) but its role was (solely) to accompany voice, my (Soul) instrument in a Songline of 'Self-as-Tool'. An unconscious knowing that everything I needed for a Life of service was already <u>embodied</u> in this skin (as a bardic ebb/flow of within/inwith) became (patently) conscious (and obvious):

"*I could (and had always been able to) <u>actually</u> sing*"!

Is it any wonder a Dancer in Card Deck self-named as: "One Day, the Singing Bird"? Mirroring performance with Anwa'd aplomb as verily upsung in Annie-tongue? I 'saw' myself flying as a thick white painted brushstroke in the shape of cross but without any rigidity of regular render. This 'me' was fluid, dynamic, organic, flexible (aka Annie-Anwa-in-Action) 'singing' Love's Light through all (ten) directions (and more) of horizon-vertical axes through world. It looked like calligraphy describing self/act as a mergent proposition; in short – a 'rune-of-me'. In the Malakut I called these acts 'goddess-work' – the shape of cross referenced our weaving (in Kiria'd mantric form), calling to mind the woven straw dolls of Imbolc to welcome Brigid's blessing of home and hearth.

Nothing simpler. I <u>was</u> the white cross (in Malakut at least), an 'icon' of self-making, written into existence by the ekphrasis of circumambulating the whole-of-me-as-the-whole-of-Gaia (via a collective of '20-by-the-1' stone giants). Brought to manifestation in-self, I could now offer it on. Thus did I see this 'me' in a group pic with happy smiley Amici kin. Here, I was telling them (as we looked at pic, simultaneously <u>inhabiting</u> pic) that if anyone was unsure of <u>their</u> practice (i.e. the 'how' of their 'what') they should stick close to the 'me' in pic.

The energetic resonance of 'Song' <u>and</u> 'Line' (heightened by close proximity to the double cross brushstroke of 'me' that I inhabited) meant the <u>efficacy</u> of their acts would likewise be assured. In wake of this coalesce-of-group-praxis I entered a deep meditation describing second-stage-impacts (difficult to describe) which we could support via this (runic) extension to our work. A space of pure void in which I felt metamorphosis take place. An empty bladder, to all intents, constellating as <u>distinct</u> propositions at each directional gate through which the uncreated Light manifests. Here we would inscribe our white 'goddess-work', plant <u>our</u> sacred cross of Love in the soil of <u>her</u> existence, plunge our stake in Gaia's stellar flesh – each/all the same as our own waxed/waned, ebbed/flowed.

I went out to garden grail, 'planted' four lily white quartz stones in the form of a cross to psychoid unity inner-outer. Planted at foot of 'True-Sister's-Island' (source of Zen-nook's 'river'); anchor-stones set north-south-east-west at whose centre a fifth – the pure 'void' morphosis zone to host (I hoped!) the harmonics of quintessence in (small) Annie-skin. Like a Celtic cross with its nimbus at centre and interlaced weaving. Like an early Coptic cross which includes the Egyptian hieroglyph, ankh, as its 'Ring-Song' – the key to Life which is also Life. Perfect (stony) mirror for "turning zero degrees in a full circle" (of Love) to affirm the energy of undertaking, to hold and walk this (Song) line all the way (Home) to Mother-Ocean of Being, all the way (Home) to the Stars.

Later, I entered a zone where Cernunnos was active. In one hand the torq of power, in other holding serpent tight. The horned god of Celtic myth, but not as antler'd stag this time, as Sky-Father ferrying me home to Sacred Pool. No, here he reprised the ancient bull (whom I know well as darling Aurochs – wild ancestor to our domestic). I held a dandelion and he (with a bovine grin) sucked at my hand till all dissolved within. Yum, yum in his tum! There, I connoted, our golden wisps of Song, afloat of Aire's air, would <u>incubate</u> till Time ripe for in-world 'birth'. Serious stuff happening on the inner planes, which our work, in some capacity, would support. For, at end, I watched a group of humanoid beings, requisite 'void' in-built of their skulls, carrying the Light out as lit candles therein. This vision inscribed, in and of cosmic humanity's primal <u>flesh</u>, a runic profile (ankh = key to life/life itself) uplifted from the very Ground (of Being). The bird-crunch-of-seed shifting energy from Blue to golden, wisps thereof elementally coalescing into a form <u>relevant</u> to function. 'Tis an ever-over continuum, enabling its <u>re</u>-creation, circular of economy (as Gaia's ecology), a (literal) blueprint of potentiality for substantial becoming.

Darling Aurochs, leaning nonchalantly up against a wall, huge and shaggy. Wise and kindly are your eyes, sniffing and snuffling up to me. A bit of 'fluidity' but the upshot is flower and hand end up in your mouth, and me (eventually) saying (laughingly) as you continue to slurp away at wrist: "Can I have my hand back now?" Gently released, together with a huge wave of Love emanating from eyes, face. Your entire being holding me in embrace! Oh, how precious! Cradled by your UrAlt-Love, your huge slow DeepTime-thinking sink. May I never forget the magnitude of your Love; may I never forget your meaning in this form, for in your eyes I saw pooled the kinship of deep family, of longer-than family, of my family. Sky-Father. My heart is so stretched with this knowing, this Love, this lineage. Thanks be!

Suddenly you transmute to truth of nature – flaming lingam, shaft of Light! The luminescence of garden grail at Solstice '17 here/now reveals its source! Again, to psychoid unity the lesson of your coming (at Beltaine '18), I ask 20 Dandy-Lions to offer themselves in sacrifice (gladly! they miaow) as I wander the garden gathering their beauty. Twenty golden beanies for each sacred Berg-Geist genie (while I play "he loves me" as each from stem plucked). Into Yukimi's 'firebox' they go while the (headless) nutritious greens are left at the base of Helvetia's heart, crystal-bed hob for alchemised rations. The moment of simultaneity, of Light's ignite, chain-reaction'd worldwide? Easily achievable outwith Time, thanks to our divine bovine!

Until now I had (understandably) concentrated on subtle plate tectonics (Gondwana-directed, of course), singing up the in-world consciousness of matter, connecting and harmonising the resonance of elemental sentience here, trying to help heal rifts between spirit-geology here, but with Cernunnos' active arrival on our (micro) Amici performance stage (here), it signalled the shift in conversation, the shift in praxis ex-world-in. It was time to formally invite Star-Geist participation with and to each Berg-Geist triangulation. A voice whispered:

"Next thread in whispered starblood evolution."

Quite! Our work needed to evolve, morph into Song which could be heard across the subtle lines of cosmic telephony, to invite in the stellar 'blood' to expand, extend, enflesh Gaia's consciousness further. We had worked with Dawn on the in-earth lines – dormant, corroded. Now did we approach the moment of 'quickening' in utero. (Cernunnos? Can you feel it?) The chi of shared circuitry in a "choir of unfoldment and evolution" (as Mariel describes) sang in our (starblood) Amici veins. It was time to: "Shout! Shout! Let it all out! These are the things we can't do without!"

We apologise for modifying your lyric, "Tears for Fears", but our job is? Joy! For all, for Gaia – as a whole earth partnership devoted to? Song!

WHOLE EARTH PARTNERSHIP

Poet. Basically, this is 'who' I am for it is the (creative) artform that touches deepest into who 'I' am. In a Poet's voice I can most seamlessly arise what needs to be said by Soul. Like breath, it comes to me 'unlearned'; as a mode of expression it just 'happens' – 'tis a bardic birth-right <u>and</u> birth-contract for this wee Annie. It came with me into this incarnation – an affinity with oral traditions which <u>breathed</u> creationary myth into accessible substance using repetition, rhythm, alliteration to ensure Memory remained intact down generations of <u>unwriting</u>. Intonation, rhyme and meter – grouping respective beats into recurring patterns. My hiking boots a worthy metronome, my rocking of babes' cradles a consonant (and constant!) ditto.

Rhyme and meter – only a short hop from poetically structured lyric to sung intervention but it needs a "Song Sung Blue" (of which everybody, apparently, knows one) to push my reluctance over the edge of self-performative and public-witness'd doubt. The limits of language already stretched taut; how to add vibratory incantatory operatic resonance to our (Blue) score? To deeper penetrate Gaia's stellar flesh, plunge the stake of our Song/s direct to luminous core? For her Blue to "percolate forth, irradiate all" (as sung into being in original "Song of the Blue"), so that we may her stars-within-earth draw forth?

Gravity, a Dancer in Deck (whose full moniker is: "Gravity always gets in the way when we don't make a big enough leap"), eyes me inscrutably with a

Golden-Eagle-of-Southern-Cirque'd eye (as he plunges over edge of cliff), says: "You'll cope." And, strange but true I do!

●●●●●

"I Ching" no. 62, "Thunder over Mountain", reads:
"The call left by flying bird should not rise but descend."

In an oracle of 64 hexagrams, it seemed rather strange my coin tosses down the years yielded this wisdom more often than not. Even before Song/s of thin Blue line arrived to send us skating (in performance) out to Gaia's threshold (beetley-bug scarabs piggybacking us with glee), to call and (like flying bird) allow that call to descend, flood an entire planetary membrane with Song, I had decided the hexagram should be permanently inked in flesh as a reminder (and promise) of my birth contract agreed. ("At last! cries Mr Gravity.) The rhizomatic wanderings of mind took me via 'bird', 'call', 'song' to 'thunder over mountain' itself, thereby effecting a triangulation with Rumi's verse:

My chest is a cave where Shams is resting
Just as a mountain keeps an echo inside itself

A line which jumped out at me long ago because I had never considered such a possibility, had never thought that when voice (or thunder) hits a cliff, echoing and ricocheting back, that Mountain's body <u>absorbs</u> a fractal'd sliver as keepsake, that its matter'd consciousness becomes enriched with a shared 'history' of inter-species'd and inter-elemental resonance. Ever since, my imagination has been tickled by the fancy that each/all stone giant/s hold/s, as a gentle joyous reminder in aeon-rich bones, a <u>memory</u> of our (personal) game of Song while walking <u>home's</u> Lines everywhen, everywhere.

I thought of all the echoes held by Mountain's <u>conscious</u> agreeable 'simply there' Presence, each exemplar of Song whether eagle cry or cockatoo screech, whether Kaze's breath or Mizu's roil. Every voice <u>contributing</u> to Gaia's holistic (Third-Rock) Song. The logic makes perfect sense (to my, and Rumi's simple mind/s) that Mountain needs be this keeper, cradling in DeepTime-Tectonia'd memory drawers a library brimful of echo/es. Each "Hello the House" savoured <u>and</u> saved, a keepsake of <u>creation</u> since beginningless time which, Time-partner'd, becomes melded, moulded, shaped on Raku's pottery wheel into the wondrous grail we inhabit – daily. Raku – Japanese for Winpa's lightning boss'd strike, housed in kanji character. All memory safe-stored in the exchequer of Mountain over which (Winpa's fiery Hi) thunder rumbles, through which (Kaze's) biting breeze flows, energising Mizu's (watery wended) passage through (Tsuchi's patient) stone.

All the while (Cold) Mountain is still, for in its stillness, its depth-charged silence, we can hear the echo, reverberate with its energy, attune to its resonant hum, thereby to All's, absorbing in own self the echo'd imprint of precious World

Soul's.

"Listen," Gondwana had said. Yes. Benjamin's 'single (sweet) spot' my Mountain (redoubt) – inner/outer attuned to its tidal flow. Could my singing bird's 'call' in turn echo the sagic wisdom, that which held on Earth's behalf? Could my Song partner Gaia's (muted) voice? Sing up and back to her the <u>memory</u> of incarnation? Echoing – back-and-forth in micro-macro'd intertidal zone, that which Mountain hosts, a shared and loving reciprocal recognition (*la voie de l'amour*) with my tool of same (*la voix de l'amour*). Echoing her wisdom? Singing it back to her? Like a pearl fisher of resurrected being? A Shakespearian sea-change there may have been through the aeons to each Mountain'd keepsake, but?

"The call left by flying bird should not rise but descend": Hexagram duly tattoo'd to skin, I saw that all Songs we perform for Gaia mirror all Songs performed since time immemorial "inwith and of the Body of <u>her</u> full reach". I saw, as if from Earth's furthest atmospheric extent, the thin Blue line surround-sounding, and defining this (Blue) framework of planetary home, all Song descend, rain down, infill all aquifers, replenish all PeaceSinks, heal and purify the All with Love's (Blue) Light, becoming her Joy in presence <u>and</u> flow, <u>present</u> to her and partnering her Song. No wonder it was Mountain who mediated our work; no wonder it was Love who blessed our way …

• • • • •

While others may perceive cosmic or universal energy as a 'neutral' power, my personal experience of the boundless Love at the heart of Sacred Mystery (expressed by any/all its manifestations – in-skin-out) is fully <u>delightedly</u> embodied. Laughter and tears equally share a platform of <u>fomenting</u> joy in-self, with-other; 'tis a child-like wonder, awe, innocence, inquiry which calls me to 'dance' with Love's potency. An energetic dance of heart-reach between 'consenting' partners, it reflects the full harmonically quintessent resonant deal, the full symphonic elemental (Macca's) 'happy meal' (that was MagicMan's input).

I sense Love in a weather system. I sense Love radiating from Cernunnos' subtle Aurochs, or Moon's extant physicality in unmediated intersect. Sun's 'Song' have I heard: "Don't be afraid of me" – this I gifted to the SkyChild to sing. I sense Love underlying the all-of-All's <u>desire</u> to express its true nature, to fulfil Gaia's (true nature'd) (Benjamin-translated) 'intentio'. None of this can be seen in human terms. None of this can be controlled. Co-equal partnering – coordinated, orchestrated – with Sidhe, Sun or Aurochs, with Mountain, Dragon or thunder-rumbling lightning-flashing Winpa. Better still – let's <u>all</u> be in on the partnership, let's <u>all</u> consciously invite ourselves to bring wisdom <u>and</u> spirit <u>and</u> skill to the shared symphony of Gaia's <u>round</u> table whose core is Love. A grail <u>unequalled</u> on a plane of same, rimmed by same: Love. Love: Source <u>and</u> Sea whose rhizomatic root system in-between operates in selfless loving service –

everywhere everywhen everyhow.

Love as Song. 'Tis long since MossMan (Bard) and I learnt to sing together – a decade, or more; he always approached through Song and, knowing which buttons to press, hooked much of our early communication into the repertoire of an 80s Scottish band. The irony of its name ("Simple Minds") is not lost on me. My Amici are nothing if not witty when it comes to reminding this small (simple-mind'd) human of her (at times) extreme cluelessness.

The shift, therefore, from Poetry to Song in compositional co-performative collaboration came about, too, through Love. Instead of populating already extant in-world tunes with the specificity of text or leaving me to work the harmonic resonance of voice into spoken poetics, we began to co-write Song using uplifted and (shared) melodies brought into being via my century-old (ancestral) piano – herself a deep abiding reservoir of Love, with an own history to share (!), thus more than happy to be dusted off in service to our worldwork for Gaia.

Once this became standard practice in developing repertoire, it was followed by the prod to pen the history of our OnePeople's worldwork ("At last!" – something I also strongly resisted, hey Gravity) – with each other, and with further Gaian stewards. Story shared with me down the years, describing our origins, our ways of engaging in-world, our common core, our forms of expressing the lyrical <u>harmonium</u> of OneEarth Family. Story which became bardic hymns (published in "Grail Within") – to Love. Only. Ever. Love.

Love. Yes. Love is all we need (Beetley-Bugs)! Love is in the air (we breathe)! Even "Simple Minds" recorded their Love Song (titled as such), intimating that ordinary humans cannot handle the intensity of Love's Light and thus stay below (where they continue to fight). And then we have the Coda to "Blue's Third" which states our proposition plain-as-day:

Love. Love.
Love is all we have.
To gift from
hand to hand
heart to heart
breath to breath.

From there invoking the self-naughted wisdom of moth-and-flame, shifting the dynamic to (perfect) Blue – the truth of Life's beyond, asking:

Can you hear the sruti'd knowing?
Can you touch the sacred sound?
Will you roar it, set it flowing?
Will you turn it round and round?

Speaking, singing, <u>calling</u> Love's geometry into being where, by close (of Time-partner'd time) it has collapsed in on itself, back to the uncreated Light held safe in Mother-Ocean deep – its centre-circumference: Void. Null. Done. Documenting my connection to Earth-as-Home, Gaia-as-Sister, expressing Joy that our Blue <u>exists</u> so we may also, evolved in the way it did through Love. Love experienced, shared with the all-of-All, united in our OneEarth Family.

Is it any wonder Song 'bursts' from me (to borrow Rilke's expression)? Previously it burst privately but thanks to the Amici is now shared publicly. It may sound as if solitary, or a cappella, to a human-centric presumptive mindset, but I 'hear' in heart the active kinship of the Amici singing on their side of veil; so too do I hear myriad forms of sentience joining us (as well as vice-versa – see comment re 'bursting' above, especially when crossing a meadow of crazy crickets intent at ceilidh!). By standing whole with Earth, by radiating wholeness on behalf of <u>her</u> whole, I hear the entirety of Commons attuned and resonant in self-sovereign solidarity with this grand experiment of Life. <u>S</u>haring Song thus becomes a portal to engaging, expressing each's wholeness, and all's.

Love. Yes. Our (loving) work is in honour of Gaia, inspired by Gaia, and performed in harmony with Gaia's own ensoul'd 'pitch' – itself a symphonic score of unique interbeing. Walking. Sailing. Singing. Washing the dishes to wash the dishes, 'whistling' while we (gnomically) work. A continuous Ring-Song of Peace-Love-Light in movement – subtle and/or physic'd – in a dynamic flux of Anwa'd co-creation, resurrect and uplift. Till each now (or then) reaching a 'stopping place' in scape. Again, it could be subtle and/or physic'd, either/or/both forming a nodal anchor between leylines strung with our length of Elven-rope. An acupressure point we 'prick' on Gaia's skin which hooks into meridians world-wide-high-and-deep. A place of ritual performance, of honouring and blessing, whence our Song sent skating through earth-sea- skywaves of precious Earth 'membrane'. It could be a mountaintop, or ocean shore, within the depths of sacred crypt or any other inner-outer grail of (loving) heart. It matters not. Each act is ephemeral, arising from rhizome like the Blue of gentian, its throat 'torched' with Love's Light, singing out its (heliotrope's) Joy before returning whence come at close of a single (Klingsor'd) Summer. Till next called – in-time-out – to climb Hesse's 'Stufen' (steps), surface its expression of divinity in the vibrancy of Life.

I could liken our acts, these sung interventions in scape, to the work of Land-Artists such as Richard Long or Hamish Fulton who describe "moving some rocks around" before going on their way. Like them, too, I may record some form of documentation of event for sequestering in a drawer of collective Gaian memory, freezing it like an embryo in bank vault till a future moment deemed ripe for in-Time manifestation. Jung's personal myth from one perspective, the work nevertheless is grafted onto the root-stock of collective. Once returned, like sweet gentian, via the unending rhizome of Being to source, we can be assured it will rise <u>afresh</u> at a next time-place intersect to repeat <u>its</u> living process of loving re-creation with other actors.

Recovered memory, fresh envisioned. A dynamic grail, ever-ready to present timeless truths in fresh dress for current 'times' via the underlying constant of Love, whose (colour-coded) current is Blue. So? We work Blue. It's just what we do!

"Song of the Blue" began that particular length of Elven-rope; a year later "Song of the Blue – Redux" was performed before climbing Schiesshorn, the 'first' of our '20-by-the-1' stone giants. Song rendered in spoken voice, in bardic tongue to walk the Line, ever/on. Till … we meet (Autumn) Equinox '18, a ceremony of Equilibria to close circles on a stage in our work, give thanks, in-herald another turn of (Mountain) path. In the bevy of preps, I found time too short to write a next "Blue" (Song). This Harvest Moon season, it seems, I had reaped too much (in creativity pasture) and my cupboard stood dusty and bare. Fresh out of ideas, I sat on the bed (having done a Marcel Proust much of the day with pen, paper in hand), sighed.

"Well," I said to the collective in room, "I got nothing. My artistic gene is all done in. Sorry."

Suddenly popping into my mind was: "Song sung blue, everybody knows one."

"Ha-ha," I said to MagicMan (never without a joke up his hempy hippie sleeve). "Point is I don't know one, nor do I have time to do one!" (They must think I'm such a grump.)

Yet, it stuck – as I walked downstairs, as I made brekky (at 3pm). I began humming the tune, I googled its provenance (Neil Diamond, 1972, riffing off Mozart's 21st). I looked at the lyrics and discovered they'd been written as therapy for a dose of the 'blues'. What if (I wondered with Faerie-like glee, no doubt with little MagicMan digs in the ribs to activate the shift from Annie-grumping) we appropriated the tune, turned the dial (and tables) from human-centric to planetary-inclusive, and upped the ante of 'blues' lyric to pure Joy for our (Blue) planet, Gaia? I wanted to start, though, with the invocatory work of "Redux" from the previous year, extending its existing thread while binding it tighter 'tween all triangulations. Thereafter we could get into the finger-clicking groove. All good, and yes – we had fun!

(Private) performance in/with garden grail done and dusted, I turned to relaxation, including a quiet read of a favoured Swiss arts magazine which had been lying on the couch for several weeks (while I was busily prepping). There, in a small line item, was described a biennial Land-Art exhibition in a remote eastern valley which had run all Summer. Accompanying the info was a pic of one work, an installation by American artist Lita Albuquerque. "Transparent Earth" its title, it featured a fibreglass sculpture of a woman lying down, 'listening' to Earth's Song. Not only that. The woman was Blue.

Lightbulbs went off; the chi of shared circuitry kicked in; Google was enlisted. Where was this sculpture? (Placed on a mountain top in a valley I had never heard of.) Was the exhibition still running or had snows fallen to obscure both path and woman? (It would be dismantled within a fortnight for obvious reasons.) Was there a single day's 'window-of-opportunity' for us to visit this Blue, sing our Song back to her as well as her/our sister, Gaia? (Here I needed to call in a favour from weather gods, family planning gods <u>and</u> driving-hiking-distance gods.)

Well, Reader, remarkably it all worked out. Truly a magical (Blue) 'gap in (weather) script'. The day prior had been cloudy, with chill winds (no good for performance nor picnicking); the day following snow fell down to 1300m leaving Lita's 'Blue Lady' (at 2300m) blanketed in a <u>very</u> heavy white woolly cloak! Yet on our day? Everything was wondrously Blue: Sky, Lady, Song. No stain on Heaven's face! Oh, how fortunate! Because the stunning 360-panorama we were afforded from (this) Mountain crest revealed Tödisan potently present – right there, in the next (broad) valley over to anchor our sightline, leyline, Songline all the way back home (via Silberen's Amici village) in through my 'window on world'.

Who would have thought? (Well …) What this meant is that (unexpectedly to simple-mind'd me) the performance could <u>perfectly</u> effect a next best triangulation sung into being, to further "harmonise the resonance of elemental sentience" (called up in "Redux" penning). Plus Moon's wax-wane came-with the whole way; so excited by her alignment – with Tödisan, with 'Blue Lady' – I just had to snap a pic (while enjoying, post-, a well-earned picnic!).

A short breather (pre-performance), arriving up top, connoting setting with which Lita's 'Lady' was intimately twinned. It was as if she were searching for an echo from the depths of settled stone as 'reciprocate recognition' for her loving communion with Earth's ensouled nature. As if she (like Walter Benjamin at his translator's task) had searched long for this single spot in the rhizome, the exact acupuncturing locale where her work could work:

"Translation does not find itself in the <u>centre</u> of the language forest but on the <u>outside</u> facing the wooded ridge; it calls into it without entering, aiming at that single spot where the echo is available to give, in its own language, the reverberation of the work in the alien one."

This was her stopping place in scape, on Gaia's outer skin, calling without entering; in concert with her quest, it became our performance space – the place of echo's 'reverberation'. As the Land-Artist, Richard Long, describes his praxis, ours likewise solicit the rituals in/of anonymity:

"I come to some mountains, and I move some stones around and then I disappear."

Amici buzzing in my ear: Time to sit with her and sing! And, yes, while I would have preferred anonymity, they (obviously) had other ideas (which, at the time, I had no clue would become the snowballing waterfall of 'documentation' of our work ever since!). It was important (they prodded) to share with the artist our Performance-Art in response to her Land-Art. Far from a professional songster, and shy of 'coming out' with my/our work, I was circumspect at best.

But? That's the 'shift' from private to public I was telling you about! F posed as (amateur) cameraman for our merry (amateur) (rock-rolling) band, however Kaze's exuberant high-risen joy, to offer participatory voice to singalong, meant the recording was less-than-optimal. (Plus F's thumb and a cheery buzzy bee took up most of the frame on occasion – cute!) Yet the point is/was: We work raw; we work wild. A single 'take' in a stopping place to anchor our Love and Blessing before walking the Songline on.

I sent it off to the artist with much prefatory contextual information, admitting my outreach took real courage! Lita was sweetly appreciative of this surprise in her mailbox. Her connection to the artwork was clearly profound, and based on a lifetime of communing with Gaia according to her (creative) mode-of-being. This she 'saw' on video – the fact of our relational interbeing with her 'Blue Lady' according to our (creative) mode:

"You were in such relationship with her, it was beautiful, I love how you were really singing to her, and reciting to her."

Our energies thus 'touched' through the <u>fact</u> of a sculptural artefact-in-space; in its own way a form of "Transparent Earth" triangulated in-time-via-space. An interesting crosshatch of our respective modes (again McLuhan's 'medium-message' comes to mind) was how her thought-provoking creativity continued to inspire my own in the months which followed. I discovered her concept of transparence would see a like 'Blue Lady' dropped in the Pacific, somewhere off the coast of New Zealand, where the listening-line (imaginatively) 'drilled' straight through planetary core.

While I do not know if this act took place, its intent brought all my notions of 'sisterhood' and placed them in a (Blue) container ripe for bardic plunder. Such that "Blue's Third", a symphonic <u>devotional</u> to Gaia, arrived in a knit of Poetry/Song to tell Earth's (creation) Story via a conversation between 'Blue Lady'twins', snowballing <u>its</u> becoming into a choral work of seven movements in solitary voice (my own) which acted as the 'echo' of Benjamin's original 'intentio' between the two conversants.

Long years has this wise philosopher stood behind my chair where I sit with pen, paper, translating, in as close to human tongue as I can muster, the language of Earth, Sea, Sky – each being's cry, each masterly sigh burbling up from the deep, inflown from on high, or entering via a dimensional 'crease' in space-time's tidal wave/s. Invariably do I return to his seminal text (in the volume "Illuminations") because it offers a perfect mirror to my struggle, my desire – to serve Gaia. I find comfort <u>and</u> courage in his entreat, that:

"The language ... <u>must</u> let itself go ... give voice to the <u>intentio</u> of original not as reproduction but as <u>harmony</u> ... When translating from a language very <u>remote</u> from his own (the translator) must go back to the <u>primal</u> elements of language itself and <u>penetrate</u> to the point where work, image and tone converge."

Penetrating the primal elements; the space of work, image and tonal <u>convergence</u>. This is where the 'Blue Lady' 'twins' sent me – into Gaia's core, her <u>primal</u> elemental origin story. Itself a place of convergence which, as the following brief symphonic snatch houses, is Mother-Ocean 'crafted' and into whose 'wooded ridge' (a la Benjamin) I could only see via T, and her Dreaming (see "Weaving" chapter), now rendered in my poor translator's hand:

Sister, dearest Sister:
Here the story wends
toward its pre-beginning,
our existence not as twins.
But as world awash with Water,
Earth's hoped-for transparence;
that Third Rock all thought so dense
was ever-pure of sentience.

"All Mothers are Sisters and all Sisters are One" in whose (collective, unitary) honour the work was performed on the night of Winter Solstice 2018 under (Sister) Moon's full for her/our (Sister) Gaia. By close, in the work's "Coda", with its alchemic spiralling of Love's Light in/out (i.e. replicating what in vision seen), we affirmed Gaia's primal creationary 'ignite' for each and all Berg-Geist-Star-Geist beacons to be lit in its wake. Whether 'occurring' on Dawn of Time's watch, or attuned to latter day 'goddess-acts', or anywhere-when in between on this extraordinary temporal-spatial planetary <u>continuum</u>, I saw into it and sang it out in a melody 'retrieved' from <u>its</u> primordial deep.

So, Sister, dearest Sister:
End this tale where it begins.
Before any here existed,
just as bang in Maker's mind ...
When angelic choirs
sang out!
And those cosmic bells
did ring out!
For the Joy
at core of Planet
to ignite
our precious Blue ...

Later, I would record the symphony's full coda (1&2) at my window-on-world in the drama of a thunderstorming valley, drawn to perform by Winpa in an elemental chorale brimful of (his) Sky Dragon's joy to re-ignite, re-knit, re-forge, re-vitalise, <u>and</u> re-member the (whispered) starblood Songlines coursing world in (his) energetically inimitable way. Graciously inviting me to join this (Summer Solstice) boom-crash-opera, how could I refuse?

((Like all other works described in these pages, documentation resides in our web library.))

• • • • •

Dear Reader: Are you ready for the continuation of our Amici love affair with the Blue in Song? One that (Elven-) roped together a 'whole earth partnership' and sent us skating off-skin out-out-out? To dance David Bowie's 'blues' in Judy Garland-worthy red shoes? Find ourselves over the rainbow with the (Blue) bird who not only flies but sings-sings-sings 'way up high'?

It began, like most things, while walking. Our Camino-de-Helvetica, taking my fresh-minted Swiss passport for a 460km walk across our shared stretch of terra, had concluded, the previous Summer. Since meeting Helvetia at her (crystal) heart, and 'kissing' her skin with each press of sole to soul over several years of mindful meditative Peace-Love-Light praxis, I felt we knew each other – in the spirit of each other's <u>true</u> name, in the spirit of the macro-proposition that the more we know Gaia, the more she knows herself.

Now it was time to cook up a next pilgrimage – to string our Love between Home (north of alps) and Home (south), to truly 'know' the route through Land we had driven countless times down decades in our little old (immortal) car. Our personal stretch of HomeSong, this would be a micro-celebration-thanksgiving-blessing act in one. One, which I envisioned would flow out, across the whole of Gaia's glorious macro (Home). Our mini-form of walking-the-world – the spheric extent (heights, depths) of planetary home. In the spirit of the subtle Gandhian wisdom teaching ("turning zero degrees"), I felt (thus wrote):

Turning zero degrees in a full circle of Love,
it's pretty easy to find what you're looking for: Home.
Turning zero degrees in a full circle of Home,
it's pretty easy to find what you're looking for: Love.
Home-Love-Love-Home. Nothing simpler.

This text would find its longer-than 'stopping place' as a post-quill'd affirmation to our "Weaving-Song" which, like all other ephemeral expressions, would collapse itself back into the FullDark when Mother-Ocean called 'close-of-Time'.

In any case, here we were, Summer '19. Like always, F (patient partner packhorse and latterly dubbed 'choir-boy') was at my side. 13 days, 300+kms and 4,000+m altitude (what goes up must come down!). Here we were, singing up country on Jack Kerouac's road but at dharma bum'd walking pace. The dam wall broke – a veritable flood of Song gushed forth in frothy abandon, leaving me swamped (but delighted). And also very thankful fo iPhone wizardry (which I had eschewed for <u>years</u>) to enable my recording of each lilt of melody, each snatch of winsome or contemplative thought.

During our first days of journey, in company of a fjord-slashed lake I have long loved (and by Summer's close to whom I had penned an ode), in the depths of a cliff-hugging forest where Faerie-presence was thick on the ground (Chamois shyly peeking from behind crevassed boulders), it happened. Walking, singing in heart the usual mantra, slipping in/out of reverie, I found that instead of boots connected to sturdy earth, I was suddenly traversing the furthest atmospheric extent of Gaia's symbiotic biosphere of interdependent life. No longer surrounded by the symbiosis of wood-stone in a fecund humus-rich glade, I was navigating the fragility of thin Blue line which protects us all from the inkiness of Void while <u>simultaneously</u> finding myself 'at rest' at/in Gaia's core – the original site of her (Blue) ignite as sung in Coda to "Blue's Third".

Hmmm … physically walking planetary surface yet concurrently fusing centre with circumference, Gaia's heart with outer spheric boundary? Home-with-Home <u>and</u> Home-to-Home? Hmmm … Consciously singing up the connection between our two homes had actually (surprisingly, to little me) 'flipped' a micro-act onto macro-stage. Sure, I had expressed this as my intent, yet with innocent whimsy firmly attached. That it became fact? Truly it was a case of 'charis' – the descent of grace (like the call of flying bird) – lifting me on its wings to 'fly' out-out-out. By walking my 'stretch' (noun) of home, loving communion could 'stretch' (verb) to encompass Gaia's <u>full</u> stretch. I stood on/at thin Blue line and saw the whole of Whole, the all of All. I saw, and <u>lived</u>, our planetary sanctuary as Home; saw, and <u>lived</u>, the care Gaia offers each form of sentience within the fullness of <u>her</u> Blue. In my own minuscule way, I was <u>living</u> Gaia's life – as Mother, Sister, Daughter, Lover. It put everything we Amici do in (literal) perspective. With our breath of Song, we could infill this <u>entire</u> membrane (planet core to thin Blue line) with Love's Light, revitalise Gaia's macro with our micro inwith the sleeve (of Breath) we all share.

In the moment of realisation, the felt-sense reminded me of a fresco of the Madonna of Mercy to which I had once 'chatted' in a small medieval chapel hereabouts. In this depiction, she holds her cloak wide under which any/all may find shelter, sanctuary, compassionate care within the many (infinitely expanding) folds. None would/could she turn away. Impossible. While Christian of dress, this rendering of divine feminine took me full into the heart of Gaia. I saw her 'cloak' as the clean air we breathe, the fresh water we drink, the shelter afforded by the very atmosphere of our beautiful Blue-Blue planet, the Life we may live

<u>only</u> because of <u>this</u> sanctuary sustaining us second-by-evolving-second, singular gifts of mothering grace too often taken for granted.

In such reflective spirit, the Song incubated long in uterus before birthing itself in waterfall'd rush (via a pretty lake's amniotic fluid). So it was when I suddenly found myself at thin Blue line experiencing (and then penning) a lyric which speaks to a <u>vision</u> of shared Commons where any/all sentience is afforded respect to sing its unique expression of Gaian life in/as choral harmony with each and every other; a lyric which affirms that my/our contribution is no greater or lesser on this (spheric) plane of consistence. No nearer could I be than what I lived, there/then, in skin, via Song which tuned itself to a slow meditative percussive beat as I walked and walked and walked the circumference of Gaia's home, as I dove and dove and dove to the core of her heart. At complete oneness with Earth-consciousness had I become in a singular (Song'd) expression of Kiria's unconditional, unconditioned kardiotissa'd Love.

Reader, if you flick all the way back to our prologue to volume you will find there my abstract description of (spheric) plane – temporal, spatial on DeepTime's 4D (Apple-Tree'd) watch. There I waxed (lyrical) on the principle of book-writing style but its application is 'universal' (pun intended). Here, as there, our micro 'ice core sample' cross-sects the entirety of Blue. A co-creative phenomenal 'flashing' in one respect, in another it is a performance of ekphrasis in small Annie-skin. No longer contemplating the abstract, I was living it, embodying it. It needed a Song (actually it needed several) to bring this knowing to the 'stage' – this sense, this <u>pungency</u> of interbeing'd life stretched vertic-horizont, inner-outer, a perpetual continuum of nestedfishes holistically fused in and framed by the dynamic <u>dance</u> of Love.

Which leads to the other Songs this amazingly co-creative Summer delivered (while I thought we were just going for a very long walk!). I found myself looking anew at all creation with, as I called it, "Thine Eyes" – the eyes gifted me in this incarnation so I could mirror Joy back to Source, double it, exponentialise it, with each 'shock of the new' this sweet sensory vehicle of Annie had the good fortune to encounter, viz:

Mountains Dragons without end
Generating resonance
Echo to divine Presence
Look close with these, thine eyes
Each reflecting its own kin
Each is wearing Soul at Skin
Sink at Surface blending in
When seen with these, thine eyes

Further, it affirmed my felt-sense of charis via the 'descent' of Song from thin Blue line to infill Gaia's whole; I saw (with "these, thine eyes") that my responsibility was not only to sing but <u>seal</u> the pact by documenting our work (for example, herein) to thus complete the cirque:

> *Book of Voyage before her now*
> *Document the why, the how*
> *Petals pressed to pages*
> *Treasures seen thru these, thine eyes*
> *Grace, she whispers in my ear*
> *Whispers low so I may hear:*
> *Listen well for what revealed*
> *When seen with these, thine eyes –*
> *Rainbow-streaked your tears of Joy*
> *Will fall from these, thine eyes*
> *Stellar'd flash from Winpa's sash*
> *Will blind your these, thine eyes –*
> *Wake up to these, thine eyes*
> *Breathe deep of these, thine eyes*
> *Forget me not, thine eyes …*

And, of course, there were the "Mountains Dragons without End" themselves. I found myself (this is all while walking for hours, days – musing, humming, imagining, then reaching round to grab the phone out of a side pocket of backpack to record titbits without breaking stride) bowing ceremoniously to all Blue Mountains (like a gent to a lady in preface to Scots highland fling), repeating the drill to all Jade Dragons (as curtsey this time). Dance partners – each with other, and with us – brought to shimmy-shake, rock'n'rollin' (alrighty almighty!) Life.

Each and all (inter-) continental anchors, inter-alia'd triangulations and home-grids did we honour, bless, sing to, dance with! To then take <u>their</u> all-of-All out-out-out to perform in a <u>simultaneity</u> of Song on Gaia's spheric 'porch' (portico, stoop, verandah – call it what you will). Out to her thin Blue line where the "Lie-of-<u>all</u>-Land" can be spied, where Moon in her beauty is oh-so-preciously close-of-arise, intimate of entwine with those auroras divine. There, I felt to promenade along an arcade of Gaia's 'house', roof'd (like Han Shan's) by the ink of Sky, living the truth of Gaia's (Blue) pearl:

> *My home was at Cold Mountain from the start,*
> *Rambling among the hills, far from trouble*
> *Gone, and a million things leave no trace*
> *Loosed, and it flows through galaxies*
> *A fountain of light, into the very mind –*
> *Not a thing, and yet it appears before me:*
> *Now I know the pearl of the Buddha nature*

Know its use: a boundless perfect sphere

Ah, Han Shan. My poetic pen (and melodic heart) can never be as profound as yours. Yet, like you, I simply describe what I 'see'. Love. Pure as a pearl, boundless as a sphere:

Here I stand at thin Blue line, at thin Blue line I <u>sing</u> the All of Love
At thin Blue line at thin Blue line I <u>see</u> the All of Love
At thin Blue line at thin Blue line I <u>hear</u> the All of Love
At thin Blue line – nothing but Love at thin Blue line at thin Blue
Here I stand at thin Blue line, at thin Blue line I <u>touch</u> the All of Love
At thin Blue line at thin Blue line I <u>taste</u> the All of Love
At thin Blue line at thin Blue line I <u>am</u> the All of Love
At thin Blue line – nothing but Love at thin Blue line at thin Blue
So do I … dance Blue Mountains, dance Jade Dragons … dance –
so happy (dance) so happy (dance) so happy (dance) so happy

By year's end 2019, at our annual Winter Solstice celebration in the krypta of 12th century monastery (with a handful of human witnesses and a vast array of subtly present Presence), we had a full (Blue) planetary symphony ready to perform. Its stretches of Songline covered the gamut of (Blue) history – from Gaia's (and our) primal origins on the path of Love, through a Summer of (unspoken) Presence (said) walking ever-with as we trekked home-to-home, before I eterno ritorno'd to beginning, to <u>know</u> it for first (Eliotian'd) time. These latter works included my birth contract ("Muted Earth") and Gaia's ("The SkyChild's Song"). Our version of Wagnerian Ring-Cycle was complete; a "Sailor's Charm" closing a depth-charged cathartic recital to bind the all-of-all to one-and-same. Done. Yes. So happy …

• • • • •

And yet … and yet … This work was performed in the midst of much pain. The PeacePole at my side as I walked Gaia's thin Blue line in Song was more than symbolic, a metronome to meditative praxis. It assisted my hobbling of krypta 'stage' while Sanctus Christophorus (carrying Christ across river) offered comfort from his fresco 'choir stall'. Cancer had come knocking at my (wide open Cold Mountain) door, and finding no one home (well, I was busily working out at thin Blue line by this stage or performing healing actions for down under kin by travelling Tree root-knowing with 'cooling' Helvetian waters for a burning Land), decided to sit down, make itself a cup of tea and wait till I was back (literally) in pain to put on the kettle (for myself, at last) and have a little chat. But Cancer's micro-performance in Annie-house (latterly mirrored by Covid's macro-gig on Gaian stage) did not impact our co-creativity in the least; in fact, our work blossomed into a true renaissance of whimsical word-and-melodic play, flourishing from a limitless font of "Everyday Delight".

Amongst other things, this began when re-contemplating a gift received from a friend – a piece of folk art exhorting us to 'delight in the everyday'. Hmmm … Why just everyday? Why not every 'every'? And so a poem was born within the space of a breath. A poem to remind me (and anyone under whose nose I thrust this 'worldview') of the every 'every' deserving of our attention, to encounter its presence with a view to finding its capacity to delight. As a child, I had Pollyanna's 'glad game' down pat. Now, far into adulthood, and with my youngest graduating high school, I figured it was time to put pen to paper and confirm to every 'every' what I jolly well thought! (The Amici, meanwhile, stood in the wings and cheered.)

Back to Song, however. One (everyday) delightful in-joke (given it was blood-bone dis-ease inviting itself to tea) was the sweet Joy expressed in "Magic Bones" – a conversation between Amici (query: 1st stanza) and me in typical 'glad game' dress (response: 2nd stanza). Given my physical pain at magic 'felt'? Definitely a way to reframe Cancer's impact! How we laughed!

Magic, magic – can you feel it in your bones?
Magic, magic – the Love that calls us home?
To the beauty of the moment, to the joy of life each day?
To be settled in the knowing there can be no other way?
Magic, magic – yes I feel it in my bones!
Magic, magic – this Love of blessed home!
In each beauty-drenched moment, in each joy-infilled today!
With each child of Gaia knowing there can be no other way!

Short, happy (Dragon-snappy!) – I'd sing it in heart as I walked; I'd sing it aloud to Birds, Beasts, Trees; to Mountains, Ants, Bees. Each and all responded: "Yes, we feel it too!" To share Joy is infectious; to mirror Joy is sacred practice. We are expanded by an act which catches all within coo-ee to a space manifested by our Love, to laugh and dance Gaia's dream onward.

An old saying is: "A problem shared is a problem halved", but Joy shared with the all-of-All? Surely exponentialised infinite-fold! The alchemy of in-weaving our co-participant magic to Gaia's whole, the chi of shared circuitry singing its interbeing'd note, cannot help but mirror the deep and penetrating Love of planetary home which is held in the very cells of our 'bones', the consciousness of our matter, no matter what the (Cancer'd) matter!

Another in repertoire is "Sing-Song'd", born at Imbolc 2021 – a year to the day since Brigid welcomed me to the first day of the rest of this (wondrous!) Life; born at a time of continued anxiety, turmoil in human zones (Covid-mediated, amongst others). Argh! So much noise!

I exited the human 'stage-left', called by and to the true nature of a still-snowy garden grail. Here, singing birds announced the pre-scent of approaching Spring; here I saw the Amici, as a group of "Shiny Happy people" (a la "REM") holding hands in a wildflower meadow, dancing in cirque, blossoms in hair, laughing, singing. It reminded me of how I would dance around the kitchen with babes in arms singing this '90s hit. No matter whatever bad, sad, mad had brought tears to small eyes and wails to tiny mouths, this contrapuntal act was sure to bring smiles and a (wiggly) giggle to my mini-kids. Now, with the Amici in vision and precious memory in mind, came the first lines of "Sing-Song'd" to populate the trine:

Here in Faerie we make merry
While you're stuck in the game of blame!
Missing seeing Gaia's beauty,
We think it such a shame!
Tell me how this helps you heal
When you're running ever on a mouse-wheel?
Where's the space to embrace delight
As saving grace each day and night?

Not directed at me, but at the "World of Men" (in Tolkienese), the possibilities to share Joy in this tuneful lilting form were boundless, sung 'Faerie-fast' to boot! I rushed indoors to grab pen, paper (and phone); the entire 'work' complete within the blink of an eye: "Schwupp!" as our hairy-footed, Chamois-loving Wildmännli would say, disappearing back into the Howe beneath TreeMother-Elder's roots (understandably – it was still snowy, and bitterly cold for a barefoot troupe dressed for Beltaine frolic!).

However, if I thought this Song was a case of co-produced Anwa-on-steroids, let me introduce you to "Solstice Groovin'" … 2020 was quite a year – personal, planetary – on that the "World of Men" can (at least) agree. Such that as an epilogue (or 'epi') to the 'epic' nature of all that had been, we dreamed up a happy homage to/with Sun for a Winter Solstice performance in that divine krypta. Normally our whole family would be together for such celebration, but this season we were split by governmental powers-that-be which decreed closed borders on our side and complete lockdown 'down under'. No sharing of hugs in physical time/space over the festive season for our crew. Nevertheless, we turned it into a true hemispheric party – three here, three there. All hail the conquering heroes of virtual virtuosity! We popped champagne corks at each others' laptop screens in real-time, and laughed at the (sticky) messes left in our "Cheers!" (cried) wake.

Following which? Straight into Song to round out our Joy. "Solstice Groovin'" fit perfectly with our simple happy Life-affirming fun. Thank you, Sun! Without you, no us to become! Since billions of years Sun's love affair with Gaia has been a truly "mellow yellow" (Donovan-Saffron'd) hippy-worthy performance. This match 'made in heaven'? No wonder we can delight in Gaia's everyday life thanks to Sun's generous and warming smile!

I could wax on and on. Truly, we <u>do</u> have fun! But we also have some significant chapters to this chopped off tapeworm of a tale still to cover, so I will leave you to discover other simple everyday delights patiently waiting in the nestedfishes libraries – her poetry corner <u>and</u> performance krypta – with blessings to all in your everyday dance with Life!

SASSO AND HIS (STELLAR) WAALE

As mentioned in the early pages of this book, it never occurred to me a text documenting our 'mountains' work would be a useful undertaking; the work itself seemed mammoth enough – why would I want to add to a demanding workload? But the 'seemingly' offhand comment, "I hear you're writing a book about sacred mountains," with which my gnomic friend's brother greeted me mid-2017 (a swathe of reference tomes in hand) put a proverbial cat amongst the pigeons. I say 'seemingly' with good cause; my Sidhe Amici are infamous for tweaking any co-conspiratorial consciousness within cooee to (higher) purpose'd effect. If this was a way to get me to listen to a reasonable suggestion, so be it!

That said, the results of such writing, out of a space of co-production, can be challenging – not only for you, dear patient Reader, but for me as scribe, the 'Bard' of tribe tasked with dipping quill in ink, applying same in scratched notations of melded thought-processes across length-breadth of (these days, laptop'd) parchment scrolls. At times the stories of wonders, insights and acts performed arrive with a lightness and 'skipping' sensation that veritably engulfs me (and page with it). At others the descent to where Acumen sits, waits, is difficult enough of itself without attempting to translate said sagic pearls to human tongue.

Bog-dense the writing which emerges from such a space; bog-dense but extraordinarily rich with fecund humus for those with the wherewithal to unpack its treasury. Sometimes I can; at others I simply must present what learned, and experienced, and thereafter trust to a reader's own intuitive processes. Such that if you have made it this far into book, and are willing to 'struggle' on as I struggle on (EM Forster's truly accurate description of the felt-sense of creative process), I thank you sincerely. Nevertheless, it was also Forster who imbued his character (Margaret, in "Howards End") with the verve to deliver this speech to:

"*Only connect! That was the whole of her sermon. Only connect the prose <u>and</u> the passion, and <u>both</u> will be exalted.*"

This brings me hope. Surely our prose, however dense, is exalted because of the <u>limitless</u> passion to serve Gaian purpose which flows from our co-creative pen? (Well, that's the theory, anyway.) The joys of connection – each to the other to the other without end; passion and prose <u>bound</u> like the single strip of clootie ribbon wound round the lovers' wrists in Celtic hand-fastening ceremony. For those prepared to delve beneath the <u>surface</u> of words, of skin, to the <u>source</u> of Love which such surface-binding affirms, meaning can be gleaned like a harvest reaped; meaning which, on first reckoning, can be as confounding for me (as witness, thereto documentarian) as a puzzled reader. It's at (Mountain) moments like these I simply have to trust to Matthiesen's similar (though vastly superior) reflection on the dilemma (already quoted but here restated):

"*The <u>secret</u> of the mountains is that the mountains simply exist, as I do myself: the mountains exist simply, which I do not. The mountains have no 'meaning', they <u>are</u> meaning; the mountains <u>are</u>.*"

So, Reader, let us hold fast to that clootie ribbon and dive in and deep to Mountain's <u>meaning</u> in and of its very <u>matrix</u> of Being via a charming chap named Sasso …

● ● ● ● ●

Two years down the track since our Sacred Mountains 'project' in earnest began off the back of Weaving-Work, Auld Country reconnaissance (next chapter), and Song'd co-productions (last chapter), I felt the energy to start penning this tome arise. A working title, a proposal to Jeremy – time to get busy in my cave, Autumn 2019. A month further on, however, things got wobbly. Circa a third of the book in, I found myself 'stuck' – preoccupied by back pain with no obvious cause. I have (briefly, in context) mentioned its underlying reason, and purpose. But here, I shall extend the narrative because Cancer's arrival, in <u>that</u> moment, affirmed the true intent of 'stuckness' – there was so much more in/of/with our (constancy of) praxis which the powers-that-be required of us, to bring up/out/<u>through</u> to manifestation, before a coherent text could summarise same and be offered to readers on both sides of veil'd vale.

'Tis true. Here we are – some four (and more) years on with a vastly extended co-produced and co-performed range of acts ('interventions', if you like) across both subtle and physical planes in repertoire – planting, nurturing, tending Love's Light in-world with the Life of our Song/s, all in service to glorious Gaia. While our work will ever be 'intermezzo' (co-creation ever continues apace!), there must come a moment when we chop into the 'tapeworm of time' (as Forster wryly calls it) to share <u>lived</u> experience. Hence …

What I understood <u>fundamentally</u> from 'get-go' of Cancer's sudden arrival in Annie-house was that an <u>embodied</u> knowing of Healing's depths was key to serving Gaia to her (and my) fullest extent. No more subtle activism; no more abstracting of propositions or esoteric philosophic discussions in Amici (stone) circle – this required real in-world/in-time <u>healing</u>. My body her body, her body mine. All subtle pain outed on physical plane (for her, as for me) whose wounds could be full-cleansed, thereto wounds full-healed.

Without realising, I wrote my response to Cancer's (future) arrival in the long poem "Muted Earth" when one day, months earlier, four words spoke themselves to me out of the depths of Soul-knowing:

"Great Mother is tired."

The words accompanied me all day till I gave in to them, physically scribbled the line to paper. In a rush, the entire poem followed, writing itself into existence in a literal stream-of-consciousness freefall. Great Mother's pain had been lain bare, equally my pain at her pain – an entire arc of anguish at human 'un-understanding' did I plumb, and the 'porosity' of my connection to the core of planetary ills shamanic-upsung (or so it felt) each time I wailed, keened in rehearsal for a public performance at upcoming Winter Solstice (2019).

But the poem also contained prescient reserves of Courage, Strength, Joy. I saw a 'supporting cast' of great Beings rally to her side in this time of great need; I saw our Mountain champions holding the line against a fast-frothing 'dark' tide; I saw the SkyChild fresh-sing Land awake; and brought what I saw to manifestation via the poem – including what I saw of 'me' amongst this throng, sworn to Gaian service but amply aware of the risks, inherent. 'Tis the incarnational contract I already (tattoo) wore in skin so this too I turned to (poetically-licenced) 'fact' therein:

'Tis my amor fati – sister Kali and her sisters
to accompany. As all fractures for all to heal.

Like the First World War surrealist poet Bousquet, my wound existed <u>before</u> me: "I was born to embody it". Like Emerson's Soul, mine contained in itself the <u>event</u> that presently befell it; Annie's this-time-in-time incarnation held the potentiality in-subtle-situ till the moment <u>ripe</u> to actualise its 'thought' as physically-manifest opportunity. Why? So I could <u>learn</u> more; so I could deepen <u>my</u> commitment to Life; so I could invest in a process to better serve <u>Gaia's</u> Life.

"Cancer? Hello, and welcome to the party!"

Cancer's embodied knowing has, and continues to be, a true blessing. Four (and more) years on? So much to share of our 'troubadouring' praxis which we hope will support others at task across myriad dimensions of Being toward a future – bright with Hope! When Selimovic's dervish says (in conversation with Hassan) (in his brilliant 1966 novel) that nothing exists until it is told, the latter turns the tables on statement, responding that nothing can be told until it exists. True, but existence in/of itself is like the koan about a tree falling in forest – did it make a sound if no one there to hear it? Thus does Hassan round out the dialogic exchange with:

"The only question is whether anything <u>should</u> be told."

A question we are in a position to answer now stuckness has finally been rendered unstuck!

Nevertheless, we pulled out all stops to move a foreseen third book in (Lorian's) Sidhe-trilogy up the priority list, agreeing that the 'core knowing' which needed saying therein ("Grail Within") was of such deep-penetrant (and <u>pivotal</u>) importance (from our wee micro-perspective) to the 'who' of <u>who we are</u> – cousins of shared heritage <u>and</u> co-creators of shared future – it could not be left in abeyance should I shirk the mortal coil sooner rather than later. Yes, all views of the whole are partial, yet this is how <u>we</u> felt. And, in fact, the outing of that book possibly, of itself, proved pivotal to our Amici crew still having an opportunity to maintain a shared workstream, in respective skins, dimensions. But I digress.

The process to support my energetic desire to write that book, when I 'should be' preoccupied with pain (and therapy 'options'!) intrigued me of itself; it was as if a liminal 'twilight zone' <u>structure</u> was woven into which I could step to write, review, <u>and</u> complete the text in a few brief months. As Covid took its 'twilight' hold of outer frame, and Cancer ramped up its exponential growth of inner frame, 'I' stepped out and away from any/all frames into a space of OnePeople'd 'Us' – a space held, nurtured, overlit by the goddess Brigid herself.

She graciously applied <u>each</u> aspect of her triple deity to the hearth/home of (small human) 'Annie-in-Skin'. Brigid: Healer, Maker, Poet. She was/is all I need; how blessed to be in her purely transcendent and immanent care! For I had woken on morn of her signature celeb (Imbolc 2020) having coincidentally (from a human-scheduling point-of-view), or not (from a cosmic same), attended a doctor's rooms the previous afternoon where a sore back elicited a most surprising diagnosis (so surprised I laughed out loud in his perplexed presence). Such did I wake next morn to a sonorous woman's voice purring in my ear, knowing immediately whose it was.

"Welcome," said She, *"to the first day of the rest of your Life – with God ... and a choir boy off to the side."*

Yes, she paused after speaking 'God', obviously to let the magnitude of this 'event' sink in (i.e. Annie, this is serious stuff), but in continuing to add 'choir boy' to the mix, it was clear whom she meant – my dear partner, F, without whose undying support, there would be no (undying) hope for me. His quiet patience, his steady beingness, was/is critical to process. As I entered the twilight zone, he <u>stood</u> with each (non-) decision I made re (non-) treatment during those months – my intent to remain present to Presence in my <u>present</u> 'state-of-being', in order to pen the wisdoms which required disclosure in "Grail Within", to draw it like water from a well, sourced direct from Source (code/x).

Unexpectedly yet graciously following diagnosis, my Amici generously rallied subtle healers to our common cause to complete the "Grail" text before I entered any treatment program. Pre-diagnosis, equally unexpectedly (yet graciously), they yelled loud about the "subductive urgency" of my ailment, amazing me (post-) about what they can 'see' – as if an energetic resonance image like that of MRIs or CT scans is visible in their dimension. Fascinating!

Plunging to the very core of Gaia's DeepTime-Tectonia'd pain had clearly left its calling card in my bones; by the time of diagnosis there was less than half-of-me left skeletally, not to mention all those gleeful Cancer cells playing tag in marrow'd halls. Hmmm ... That our plumbing of Gaia's macro-layers (to the root-knowing of her very bones) was now mirrored in my micro-layers? Psychoid unity at its (mergent, infiltrative, permeable) as-above-so-below membrane'd best (plus with a raft of relevant oncological language to go with it).

All must fracture for all to heal.

Every bit of my/Gaia's dis-ease written into being via "Muted Earth"; <u>told</u> into (dervish'd) existence, <u>existing</u> so it may be (Hassan-) told. Likewise (it seems) every part of the healing journey on our twinned behalf, of our twinned 'Garden' grail/s, was right there, plain as day, in and of the poem, viz:

Rest, Great Mother.
I will tend the Garden for You.
Sweep the Schoolyard (any size).
Resurrect the knowing gone underground.
Reveal the Sink at Surface (plunged).
Break the dam walls, let flow the River (run).
Release Purity's waters to all times, all places –
to mould/shape future as it eterno ritorno'd past.

Now I just had to figure the devil-in-the-(dervish'd-) detail of what I stream-of-consciousness meant! "Muted Earth" is published in the "Grail" text, a book whose cover reproduces Jeremy's artwork of the (human) Grail-of-Self. I looked deep into his painting, and Soul spoke Purity's knowing (from poem above) out for me to engage in-time:

"Only when the Light, Pure, is within Me can the Light, Pure, be shared."

Cryptic, but? Alright, I'll do my buggy best. Or, as Bilbo Baggins (in a Jackson-mediated retelling of "The Lord of the Rings") would say:

"I think I'm quite ready for another adventure."

But does that mean another adventure is quite ready for me? Hmmm … Alright, I'll do my buggy best – squared! Beyond pure Light, however, another gift was offered into this pool by my "Fellowship-of-the- (Gaian-healing) Ring". It accompanied a profound state of embodied settledness, as cosy as any Scots blanket-bog, <u>beneath</u> pain or malaise, a literal sense of <u>sunk</u>-surrender – to universal purpose, of what will be will be. The word to describe how it felt? In heart I heard: "Equipoise."

And yes. While I knew it as 'Equilibria' by another name, the use of 'poise' was intentional for it sent the usual notion of (static) harmony and balance in the direction of (Anwa'd) wei-wu-wei (doing by not-doing – I wax lyrical on this principle in the chapter "On Anwa" in the "Grail" text). Essentially, in dis-ease'd context, I understood it to suggest what Tree, buffeted by storm energy, must <u>embody</u> to stay present, alive, <u>rooted</u> in-world. It implied (in my miniscule reading) a need to maintain a firm '<u>stance</u>' (aka <u>be</u> Mountain) while ever-prepped to flexibly '<u>dance</u>' (aka <u>flow</u> Dragon) according to the causes or conditions arising outside my 'control'.

This approach also urged me to abandon (the usual) expectations of future outcomes (aka definitely unsubscribe from data-sets of 'average' life expectancies or quibble over minor movements in blood counts), and rather embrace the <u>Tao</u> of my true nature, the power of Presence (my own) as <u>and</u> in service to Love. Living in/as a 'present' (gift) to the 'present' (carpe diem'd) moment, I committed to (joyously! excitedly!) act as a lab-rat-of-one, thus naming this Love-fuelled aspect of Equipoise's triumvirate meaning: "Come-what-may <u>romance</u>."

I love <u>all</u> my 'bits', confused little Cancer cells inclusive; it wasn't their fault they were where they shouldn't be. No blame could be laid at any door, no judgement called, no risk factors ticked, no 'naughty' hand smacked. I simply <u>could not</u> relate to word-choices used by medicos or patients with a focus on fighting, war etc. As innocent (or naïve) my perspective on Life sounds, Body is my Garden as (planet) Earth is Gaia's Garden. And it may need weeding, sweeping, tending, rejuvenating. But <u>ever</u> with Love as the (healing) base note. Gently. Purely. Honouring Wisdom's <u>re-birth</u> from the very ground of (our) physic-matter'd consciousness.

Suffice it to say there would be no "going in with all cannons blazing" in my healing regime. Thus, from a single word, a micro-macro 'layer-cake' spoke its affirmation:

<u>Equipoised</u> *of stance, dance and (come-what-may) romance*

I am the Garden myself – by the Grace of the Seven Sisters, strong

The Sisters … A chapter will come, Reader, where we delve properly into this stellar lineage and the Grace by which I am here to tell their (and my) tale at all. But for now, a last (Cancer) anecdote before we move on (and back) to Mountain (pure).

It was not only to write the "Grail" text that I entered a twilight zone those early months of Covid-twinned-with-Cancer world. While (Emerson's) Soul may have had 'pre-knowledge' of manifest, it still did not mean it knew what to do with this knowledge. In my contemplations I was often drawn to "The Mines of Moria" (the ultimate Tolkienese twilight zone), specifically the filmic scene where Gandalf says:

"*I have no memory of this place.*"

Similarly, I was stumped; I knew enough, however, to realise this was 'new territory' for Soul (let alone the rest of my incarnational 'bits'!). No script, no map, no vocabulary ('we' had so much to learn!); the only thing that made sense was spoken as part of Gandalf's 'aha' moment deep in the caverns: "It's that way!" To which Merry says: "He's remembered!"

"No," replies Gandalf, "but the Air doesn't smell so foul down here." And then gives his advice to, when in doubt, "always follow your nose".

It resonated as a methodology, and a locus of enquiry, because Mountain itself was pulling me deeper, back to the shocking heart-wrenching place where I had encountered Gaia's core pain (alluded to in "Intermezzo 1"). My staircase would need to descend to the very heart of Mountain, the very source of uncreated Light which flows "Purity's waters" forth into world. Soul knew my Light must purify, heal, before it could flow forth. I would follow the path 'less-foul' even if (like Robert Frost's 'less-travelled' road) it could include goblins, cave trolls, and a fiery Balrog (who probably just wanted to make friends but his EQ was a bit 'off').

Brigid had spoken, the Sisters had woken. It was my task to walk this path so Soul could 'make' its own memory, face the 'Balrog' on bridge of Khazad-dûm, meet its flame, try to transmute its "Cloud of Unknowing" with Love's Light – my shield/spear in one. You may think my imagination a bit 'over-the-top'. My sweet mother affectionately called it 'vivid' when as mini-kid I reprised National Velvet's steeplechase, attempting to leap the side fence on my tricycle. That did not end well (for tricycle or knees) but down long decades since, I toughened up, and my chariots-of-choice grew more robust. Till now, imagination no less vivid, power surged within. My own presence, of self-sovereignty, stepped up and into a role for which Soul may have had no memory but had agreed to 'host' as part of this incarnational contract.

Further, I intuited that like with Native American traditions to heal seven generations past and seven forward via one's own praxis, this work to which I had been called involved our shared rootstock, our OnePeople'd ancestral past and future as Cousins of the Commons jointly tasked to serve Gaian purpose. It was an intuition reaffirmed by the "Grail" text's rush to publication, especially the need to include therein the Story "Leeks & Peas", our mythic retelling of cosmic roots, of the time before the 'split' and all that happened hence.

The 'generations' I speak of here? Sisters – past present future, in any/all physic'd or non- dress. 'Tis my amor fati (as written into being in "Muted Earth") to accompany the Sisters in service to Gaia, an ever-over mantra which affirms our core strength:

We stand in Solidarity
With the Power of Presence – our own
Crystal-cloaked and Starlight-boned

We Amici had spent years performing (what we described as) 'acts' for/of the goddess, each of us inhabiting a thick swathe of (what looked/felt like) pure-white paint in free-floating space as if swift-calligraphy'd brushstrokes rendered by Japanese master. It took the form of a cross (practical, symbolic in like geometric measure), thus referencing the scope of our work across and through directional planes (horizont/vertically-aligned); so too declaring our purity of intent. We were, literally, Brigid's (Imbolc) 'dolls' in fluid-dynamic-organic-arisen form. So-clothed, our energetic resonance announced to any Being who 'saw' us at work the 'stature' of our patron/ess as well as the quality of service we offered in her name, each 'lily-white act' one of Love's Light freely gifted to Gaia's whole.

Fast-forward to post-diagnosis and CT scans showing the sites of highest fracture potential in (sweet) Annie's honeycomb'd frame. My wonderful Amici brought in a healer of high stature, a stellar Presence of silver Light, who stood at my back to apply a thick swathe of Brigid's pure-white paint at the top of spine. In this instance it took the form of a 'band-aid' cross, two (subtle) strips of athletic sports tape torn off, slapped on as if she the medico in a changing room tasked with ensuring her (rugby) fly-half could still make it out onto the field (and back again) in one piece. 'Twas a solemn ceremony but my gratitude, and humility, could not help but turn to burbled laughter at this felt-sense and sight (it seems I am not the only one with a vivid imagination!). What better healing balm (Love's Light-infused) to keep me 'patched-up' while continuing to work! Each time, therefore, when I feel a wee bit morose, due to pain or whatever, the memory of this 'act', and the Love which fuelled the healer's summoning to reciprocate my 'lily-white' acts for Gaia with one applied to Self, is sure to buoy me up each time I struggle climbing a next best Mountain (metaphoric or literal!).

Regardless of dis-ease, I feel, fundamentally, that my Light has never wavered in our work and that pain has (perhaps paradoxically) aroused my energy to serve – more, better. Indeed, I have encountered places where, in spite or because of all trauma experienced, lived through, survived, Land has actively worked to heal herself <u>and</u> ancestral memory, so too humanity's, to blossom afresh. Rolled up her sleeves, set to with scrubbing brush, swept the garden (any size). Such sight sustains me <u>and</u> urges me on. In each and every act of compassionate witness, soulful holding and cleansing, we honour what has been, and envision what may become when our grail is infilled with Love's Light.

Pain, and its memory, is not something to be banished, sent deep to full fathom five 'dark' where, neglected, ignored, it sets to gnawing its knuckles, solidifying to intransigence. I have learnt these lessons in many places of Malakut and material world, as, no doubt, have we all. But now with a greater in-Body understanding and desire to apply such healing balm – to Gaia and all her children? I find I am back where I began, having never left (just like her) the <u>core</u> of who I truly am – just another simple soul living the <u>miracle</u> of Love incarnate. Or, as Mr1300BC once beseeched of a second-guessing Annie:

"Just Love. <u>Being</u> thus is nothing more needed."

Or, as my Amici prefer, ensuring our 'LoveApp' is always turned on for our Love (as Light) to be sent (like App message) anywhere, anytime for the chi of (our) shared circuitry to flow in living intersect with the all of the All of Gaia's glorious world.

•••••

I mentioned earlier that despite 'me' being ready in late 2019 to write the fullness of this book into being – the one you hold now in hand, dear Reader – the book was <u>far</u> from ready for 'me'. One major sticking point (in my/its 'stuckness') was that I had not, in my desire to probe the depths of the Sacred <u>within</u> Mountain, paid homage to the absolute master himself, the greatest (in human skin) mountaineer of our generation (or as my broad-of-brogue Irish amateur-alpinist dentist exclaimed, standing above me, lights blazing, googly-eyed glasses on his wee pixie face, probing my mouth with a plethora of metal tools-of-trade: "He's a god!" … hmmm … quite!).

Yes, I speak of Reinhold Messner. In one respect I can't believe I've reached this point in text without the briefest of mentions (earlier, in "Joining Mountains") given his centrality to a contemporary human-mediated analysis of equation.

To those unfamiliar with this 'god', Reinhold Messner was the first climber to summit all 14 peaks over 8,000m, <u>and</u> without supplementary oxygen. His preference is to climb alone with minimal equipment or assistance – aka 'alpine style' vis-à-vis the 'siege tactics' (his words) of the usual expeditions which befoul <u>soul/skin</u> of Land with debris <u>and</u> disrespect (Hillary's purported comment: "We knocked the bastard off" has always cut my heart). Hence, Messner's commitment to climb Everest 'by fair means' or not at all happened with climbing mate Peter Habeler in 1978, being the first to stand atop the holy mother, Chomolungma, breathing <u>fresh</u> air, and achieving what previously thought undoable. 'Twas a feat he repeated two years later from the Tibetan side – this time solo.

By 1985 he was the subject of a Werner Herzog documentary, a film which has achieved cult status down long decades since. In 2010 a German movie ("Nanga Parbat") told his perspective of the 1970 expedition which claimed the life of his younger brother, Gunther, and left him severely frostbitten. A harrowing tale; from that moment the 'why' of his continued 'place' amongst stone giants was clear to me – at one level climbing for them both, and to assuage the guilt that wracked him; at another paying lifelong homage to Nature's supreme force, that which saved him and to whose majesty he surrendered.

At home in the wild/s, he was the first to cross Antarctica and Greenland on foot, assisted by neither snowmobiles nor dog sleds. The Gobi Desert has also felt his meditative footprints in skin. For five years he sat in the European Parliament as a member of the Greens representing his homeland – Southern Tirol, Italy, where he cut his mountaineering teeth in the Dolomites. Now in his dotage (80 in 2024) he oversees five (soon six) landmark museums each devoted to a different theme. The most architecturally stunning of which was designed by Zaha Hadid, he considers this museum/s legacy 'his 15th 8,000-er', a sum of all experience.

Such a legacy, of course, does not come cheap. And in such vein, Reader? Read on!

The reason our family is abundantly aware of his 'fame' is due to the youngest of tribe, D. In the chapter "Der Ruf der Berge" I described D's innate love of Mountain; many of Messner's trials and achievements (captured in book or film) deepened his perspective over time. For my part, it was Messner's unerring dedication to the Tibetan cause which resonated. He point-blank refused a Chinese climbing permit for Kailash, for example, full-aware of their political intent – to turn the sacred profane (it's 'just' another Mountain), and thereby cut out the heart of an oppressed people for whom <u>everything</u> is imbued with a sense of the Sacred.

And then, one random day in early 2018, a poster loomed out of the gloom at a tram-stop downtown. It showed the sombre face of a big bushy-bearded bear of a man, captioned: "Messner – Live!" After giggling at the inanity of the poster, I rushed home to D who was at his homework: "You're not going to believe this, but Messner is a <u>rock-star</u>. Literally!"

Ah, perhaps my joke was too obscure in the moment (especially for a lad puzzling at that moment over Latin grammar), but the point being I had no idea he did 'gigs'. (Now I realise he obviously needed to as funding for all his work/s!) This one was titled "Welt-Berge" (World-Mountains); research (for me), fandom (for D). What better excuse for mother-son bonding! Together we checked 'tour-dates', found he would be visiting Zurich to present a lecture on a Monday evening in the week D's exchange student partner from Singapore, M, would arrive.

"A cultural outing, opportunity for M to practice his beginner's Deutsch, coupled with jetlag in the presence of a 'god'? Perfect!" I said. D was sceptical but I stayed adamant – when would he have another chance to see Messner 'live' when it was astonishing he was still alive!? We scored the last tickets up in the rafters, went 'en-famille' with F and M to see what's what.

Arriving, we got into the spirit of occasion, took a pic with the 'scary bear' intensity of a giant version of poster seen at tram-stop. F went to get a beer; I perused the merchandising table (books he'd written), picked up one on Antarctica (for Erebus, one of our core 'Brothers of Flame'); went to the loo. We agreed to regroup in the upstairs foyer (access point to seats in the rafters). Post-loo, up the stairs, I found the boys in foyer, and went to join them.

D blurted: "You haven't noticed?"

"Noticed what?"

"He's just <u>there</u>!!!" and, trying not to look conspicuous, indicated with shifty eyes, and a slight wiggle of shoulder, to where a modest man sat hunched behind a desk (also trying to not look conspicuous). Extraordinary; he seemed so unassuming, as if shrinking from being seen at all. Was this the classic Master who shapeshifts form to blend in, camouflage, hide in plain sight? Was what I saw becoming 'stone'? Intense introspection yet you still had to pay the bills?

"Good lord," I said. "What's he doing there?"

F (while sipping beer) mused: "Signing autographs?"

"But there's no one <u>here</u>!"

A few people stood around in the usual small murmuring groups before moving in to take their seats (as if at the opera) but not a soul was anywhere near the desk. And, it was in that moment, feeling sorry for him (I kid you not, Reader) that I said: "Do you think he'd sign this book I just bought? It'd give him something to do at least."

The boys shrugged. "Why not?"

"Right," I said to D. "This is your <u>big</u> chance to say hello to the greatest mountaineer <u>ever</u>."

D stepped back in horror: "I'm not doing it!" (as if I'd asked him to collect dog poop – kids!)

I shook my head at the illogic of teen angst. "Alright," I said. "I'll go."

"Hello," I smiled (in mothering tone – furthest thing away from 'fan/groupie' I could conjure).

Messner nodded; I handed him the book. He signed without a word, passed it back.

I said: "Thank you" (and) "I wish you a good speech."

Again, he nodded. All over red rover. But I have a distinct memory of the brevity of eye-contact we shared; he was anywhere but where he presently 'was'.

And yet, and yet …

A darkened theatre, a huge screen; far below a man on stage, remote in hand – this was going to be a slide show. He clicked the remote and without warning there was Kailash, infilling the whole of hall with <u>her</u> living Presence, Messner a mere 'speck' at her feet. I watched as he turned toward her, then back to the audience before at last starting to speak. She 'opened' for him, <u>and</u> she 'opened' him. Suddenly he was animated, full of energy, sheer joy bound by fragile skin, so <u>eager</u> to begin – to tell of her, to tell of all of them; to tell of his relationship with her, with all those divine stone giants. And when I say 'relationship', I mean: <u>Relationship</u>. Pure unconditional Love, depths of tectonic connection and wonderment on stellar overdrive lay beneath, as the very <u>ground</u> of Being, each and every one of the 'facts' and 'histories' and 'anecdotes' he shared.

Up in the rafters, we looked at each other. Huh? The shift was as dramatic as night to day in the tropics – Sun silently sleeping, Sun abruptly awake. Having been present to his inner quietude, sunken stone depths, to now witness these (literal) heights of ecstasy, of absolutely <u>gushing</u> with his Love <u>and</u> what he had learnt through a lifetime of being-with his Love/s? The number of times he said 'ausstrahlend', a word which means radiant, luminous, brilliant, incandescent to describe anything from mountains to peoples, cultures, spiritualities, legends, landscapes – all in context of his experiences or insights re same – was extraordinary.

While, all the while, Kailash <u>anchored</u> the purity of his intent, to share this innate <u>and</u> acquired felt-sense of the Sacred within Mountains. She, my dear Sister of Light, was his first and last image of 'slide show'– opening the space of engagement then closing the portal once complete. Messner's 'kora' via lecture had become ours by association. Together, in an hour or so, we had journeyed as pilgrims round the entirety of Gaia's planetary Blue via the great and good of Berg-Geists he chose to honour, on whose behalf he acted as a more than worthy emissary. Who would have thought this would be the sum of our experience?

In spontaneous unison, D and I leapt to our feet in standing ovation. Truly I felt to be at the opera calling "bravo!", "bellissimo!" down from the rafters. "He could have gone on forever," said F post-performance, not only in terms of tales to tell but in his exuberance and joy to tell. Messner took Selimovic's (Hassan-delivered) counsel to a whole new level.

Yes. A scholar, widely-read, experientially-backed, a polymath – of Gaia, for Gaia, with Gaia. A 'Once and Future Human' who honours the Ancestors, honours Hope, honours the Alliance. Is that not what it is to be a true Amici? Of the heart? Mergent in/of FeltWorld, a co-creative partner to the All-That-Is, a questing champion of our precious Blue jewel? For a moment came, during performance, when he decided to send Kailash-on-screen through a self-360-degree-kora'd dervish-whipwhirl while describing the principle of circumambulatory pilgrimage, while telling the myth of Milarepa's sunbeam ride to summit. Simultaneously I was back there, flying, wrapping her in silk scarves of honour, blessing, just like a year before in the Malakut when she agreed to join our humble collective. Milarepa, the saint, the sage who makes Mountain his own Body-Mind. Messner's aspiration. So too mine.

The briefest moment of eye contact shared pre-performance … perhaps intended, and always known in some cosmic dimension, that it would be I who needed to stand before the Master rather than D so a deeper portal onto our work could open. Which it did. In time. And out.

So, Reader, come with me through the door to the other side of Time, a misted abstract space where I 'met' Messner-of-the-subtle-spheres in wake of this lecture. From meditative repose, penning letters in my head to discuss certain aspects of his perspective – how they intersected, complemented, diverged from our work – I 'dropped' <u>through</u> a plane to FullDark 'awareness' of his journey to understanding.

I saw <u>into</u> his process of 'ripening' which followed the same mythological stream as any world spiritual tradition. Documented in classical Greek or Roman texts, described in Hindu or Buddhist rituals, even a core tenet of Celtic rites, I speak of the divine marriage ceremony of human (male) 'king' with goddess-imbued 'queen', full-plumbing the tribe's bond with Land, surrendering before the altar of 'maidenhead', swearing fidelity in order to guarantee fertility, to safeguard the circle of Life. Specifically, I said to him:

"*You have lain with Kali.*"

I could 'see' she had conjured his awakening due to my own induction into this Light tradition (see "Der Ruf der Berge"), due to our Amici work for the goddess which allowed us to witness other acts so-framed. Further, it was clear which cultural emanation of goddess had accepted his oath for I too am infused with her knowing; the whole tapestry, therefore, was laid before me – of his re-birth as a 'warrior' of the good, 'defender' of Gaia's purpose once 'touched' by the <u>source</u> of knowledge/wisdom at (Mountain) core.

The mists cleared and I 'saw' that my conversation with Messner was being held at his home, his Milarepa'd sanctuary in a castle somewhere 'across the border'. He asked about my work; I responded solemnly: "I journey the world through meditation."

At that, two scarabs flew in, began to make their way up the side of a crystal vase which sat between us – one swirly orange-black (whom I introduced as Fujisan of the active fiery heart), the other black with wishlist-coloured polka dots (the cooled basalt of my cloud-catcher, Wollumbin). During lecture, Messner had spoken of the 'Ur-Meer' (ancient sea) from which his Himalayan stone giants had upjumped. Here were my champions of Mother-Ocean's Pacific daughter – each, and all, connected by DeepTime-Tectonia'd root-knowing; each, and all, in service to the One.

I returned from the space knowing there was much about this connection I needed to unpack; I felt an <u>urgent</u> need to research a 'field-trip' to his museums across our (literal) border. But 'Life' (in myriad human familial forms) took precedence that year, and the next; so too the <u>specificity</u> of Amici work which needed to be physically walked, upsung, in other locales as well as 'flying' with our crew of (Mountain) scarabs to Gaia's thin Blue line to sing. Late 2019 arrived, and I thought everything was in hand to write this book till suddenly (painfully) I was 'stuck'. Looking deeper into the stuckness beyond an (obvious) dis-ease'd cause, I re-found my (subtle) commitment to attend the (physical) Messner's home; said to F:

"If these borders closed by Covid ever open again, <u>and</u> if I manage to stay well enough in the (deathly hallow'd) Cancer circumstances to travel, his Land is first cab off the rank."

•••••

Autumn 2020 a brief window opened – to drive East, spend time in the catchment of Helvetia's fifth major river system before a quick hop across to Messner's Tirolean valley. From there the plan was to trail south into the Veneto but suddenly Covid was back in control, and we needed to hop back to Helvetia terra post-quick. But the week in Messner-Land happened and, as soon as arrived, I realised why it <u>needed</u> to happen. Yes, I was frail, but all causes and conditions happily came to the party in perfect synchronistic intersect as and when required. My frailty actually proved an advantage. A 'healthy Annie' would have tried to overpack an already tight schedule – jumping from locale to locale, busy-bee walking Song along lines great and small. Instead, I discovered that the organic farm attached to his estate rented out a wee cottage, used in earlier centuries by a head gardener-cum-gamekeeper. A week holed up there, in listening dress, in research mode, with excursions or museum visits of brief duration in between? That would do me quite nicely, thank you very much.

Yet I certainly did not expect that before even reaching Messner-Land, the 'root-knowing' of the Sacred within Mountains on our side of border was keen to chat further, and add fuel to our (work praxis) fire. To help me explain, a bit of geography is in order as well as a smatter of backstory.

At the centre of continental mass, Helvetia is considered the 'water reservoir' of Europe, her headwaters offered out/on to all major river systems north, south, east, west – Rhine, Rhone, Po, Adige, Danube. While the Gotthard massif is source to four of these, the fifth – the Inn, meeting the Danube at Innsbruck (Austria) and out/on to Black Sea – rises in the east of Land.

My connection to Helvetia's waters, in particular locales and along stretches of

HomeSong, is longstanding. There are the source waters of our 'forgotten valley' which (eventually) empty into the Venetian Lagoon via the Po – my (solo) work in her high wild, flowing Love's liquid Light out from heart, was documented in "The Amici Files" and led to our ever-onward Sidhe partnership for Gaia. Then there is OldMan-Rhein whose path I have followed as a "Daughter of the Lake" since years, stringing connections between tributaries of his mighty shed throughout the north of Land as a 'constancy of praxis'. Plus, before stepping out on our pilgrimage for Love across length-breadth of Helvetia in 2015, I entered her cave-of-heart source – Sasso, the Rock of San Gottardo – to receive blessing for the waters I in turn would bless by plopping happy Aussie shells at each stream, river or lake crossing along our 460km long PeaceWalk, Tao'd of Way.

As a result I felt to know the 'taste' of Helvetia's sacred waters as much as the 'tread' of her sacred uplands, lowlands and all in-between lands by the time of this current road trip east. This included, in respect of the Inn's catchment, an enchanting opportunity (while hiking the valley some years earlier) to 'meet' her ancestral peoples' past when we encountered a 'witching-stone' that recorded the performance of 5,000-year-old fertility rites.

As I sat with this stone, touching into its DeepTime memory via the runnels carved in its flesh, I knew, fundamentally, that it mirrored the same praxis witnessed in Australian Aboriginal 'cathedrals' to Life. There, the runnels had been vertic-inscribed in pliant sandstone – birthing 'suites' 'tween heaven-earth. Here they were horizont-rendered in silver'd flesh. But that too made sense given the extreme verticality of scape, with its matching runic 'slit', well-water'd, cut into the cliff on opposite side of valley. I feigned to hear the murmurs of the women as they intoned the sacred spells, asked the intercession of goddess in their desire to conceive Life. Her fruitful plummet to broad valley below would be their meditation, her flow-forth from the mouth of Mountain would empower and bless their own abundance. It all felt <u>so</u> 'now' in my 21st century reverie; it all felt <u>so</u> 'true' in its engagement of elemental sentience – the hardness of stone won over by the soft incessant insistence of water's Love.

Yes, I felt to know this region and its history. Ah … but knowing is an infinite well, it seems. Coming into the Inn's shed, the river goddess – a twin-tailed mermaid still remarked and revered as a plethora of frescoes daubed to houses attests – was immediately 'present', and welcoming, offering rainbow-crystal'd Light to our walking inwith her domain (truly a blessing given my state of unhealth!). She then shared insights into my 'listening' zone to deepen my understanding of 'fertility' from an overarching Gaian perspective. The ancient <u>sacred</u> symbiosis of Mountain, Tree, Waters did she share, the primal 'pact' (if I can call it that) of wood/stone, blood/bone anchoring Gaia's divine Body – insights which arose one day while hiking a trail of personal history, retracing a route from more than two decades past.

My reverie dropped to DeepTime – a surprising development in such frigid conditions (temps barely above zero, with snow flurries, streaming eyes <u>and</u> nose to contend with). All sight 'lost' to misted distance, an ancient Larch loomed; it 'tugged' me into the embrace of its solid companion, a huge boulder tumbled down aeons ago from crag above. Here, invited to pause, cradled by a resonant hum singing a different pitch (as if high harmony) to what I usually 'hear', I reflected on my point of <u>entry</u> to garner such trilling response. Here, between summit and basin, was seemingly a meeting place of elemental import. This 'scent' of vibration resurrected (genetic) memory of <u>my</u> connection to realms pre-human, pre-animal, pre-faerie – realms of Gondwana's preside, the primordial of Gaia's consciousness of matter.

Recognising the conversation of (this) Stone with (this) Tree, honouring the 'density' of energy they held <u>cocoon'd</u>, I spoke aloud: "I too am as settled as the stone in which such remnants recumbent-stand." At this entrée, the boulder, in two short words, 'spoke' the <u>entire</u> chain of Life elementally, alchemically, brought into being thus:

"Mountain welcomed."

Synapses fired; energy lines through me/scape sang the chi of <u>shared</u> circuitry, the Joy of conduit re-opened. Here lay – at surface, in plain <u>unadulterated</u> sight – a well or repository of Gaia's origin myth, generously offering the <u>simplicity</u> of equation before my (frozen) feet. Invited to 'see' into how Mountain 'saw' <u>its</u> role in the grand experiment of Life? How grateful can a small (shivering) human be! This regular chip-off-the-old-block exemplar of Third-Rock still <u>knew</u> its origin Song, could still energetically, spiritually reverberate, and <u>speak</u> the 'magic formula' into my miniscule orbit. I could see <u>into</u> the spirit of Mountain actively enabling, facilitating, <u>singing</u> the in-Earth creative impulse of all Life's unfolding, evolving, inweaving thereafter. Oh, blessed be!

"Mountain welcomed."

So, so simple an invitation, a response. Its words thus commenced an own chain reaction as Larch spoke then River spoke and, returning itself to <u>its</u> Self, completed the holistic string by <u>re-entering</u> the depths of Mountain (as source waters, the 'uncreated Light' hailing from Dark) to uplift Gaia's <u>full</u> edenic (garden) equation thus:

"Circuitry! Seeds! Life!"

Buzzing at the speed of Light in my desire to share (this domain's) ignite of Love, I looked past the swirling snow-flurried mists to other side of valley, to Nuna – the tall peak whose steely outline, in inner vision <u>pre-hike</u>, I had seen 'etched' in vibrant luminous forest <u>green</u>. While violet usually presents in my meditative go-to colour palette of subtle 'sight', in context of the boulder's speech,

I saw that green-rendered made sense, for it communicated Mountain's <u>centrality</u> to sacred Earth-centric <u>immanence</u> – Tree'd. Seeing into this coalesce, a mantra arose to link the threads:

    Mountain welcomed
    Tree of Life sustained
    Mizu-water'd
    Light of Love <u>her</u> name

    The Ring-Song flowed, growing in strength, passion with each repetition as I set off walking again (after thanking these symbiotic twins for their wisdom!). I realised it constituted the <u>full</u> spell (magick'd) offered up to the alchemy of (H5.0) elemental scrutiny, the potentiality for the harmonic resonance of shared sentience to bend to the purity of <u>cosmic</u> intent, this grand experiment <u>co-creatively</u> blessed. A huge Anwa'd 'wow!' shot through my Body (so too Gaia's) as micro-macro we 'sang' up afresh 4.5 <u>billion</u> years of Love in (Third-Rock) (and rolling) Skin! Over, over to the beat of footfalls till, chilled by this folly, I desired a hot shower (and toddy!) more than anything. The Sacred within <u>and</u> of <u>and</u> held (still) by Mountain near/far, fractal'd <u>and</u> fractured? Any-where. Any-when. Any-how. Any-who! Thank you to the particularity of this remnant recumbent-standing!

    A portal opened, Mountain-Tree'd, which we repeated (and extended) next day on our way to cross-border (Messner) meetings via a canyon raw, high, wild, and free – a knife-slit strewn with rocky debris, churned by meltwater rush off to join the Inn on her journey home to Sea. Nuna calmly watched as we reached a small collective of alp-huts, parked, and set off to walk the "God da Tamangur" (the "forest back there" in local Romansch language), the highest continuous stretch of Swiss Stone Pine (pinus cembra, 'Arven' in German) in the Alps.

    The only species of pine whose needles appear in bundles of five (a nice piece of elemental synchronicity), its English name represents the primeval symbiosis of wood-stone while its German name, coupled with the resonance of 'Tamangur', I found reminiscent of Elven connectivity. Is it any wonder we desired to make pilgrimage? Apprised of the magic formula in Ring-Song'd mantra, now I could truly honour this "Queen of the Alps", so-called for her solemn resilience in truly harsh conditions. Arven are understandably very slow to grow but, like Yew, can reach immense age. This forest had been left to its own devices. We would be walking with ancient mothers, and the Amici could hardly contain their excitement to (subtly) join our excursion.

    The gorge gave way to broad uplands, reminiscent of the high moors of Scotland. I imagined how the vast Caledonian Forest must have looked stretching up such slopes; more than men's lives had been culled at Culloden Fields. Three elders of this place outreached – each with a message (personal/collective). The first reciprocated (or, perhaps better-said, reaffirmed) our Amici prayer:

There is so much Love in the World
It just wants to be released
And this is our forever-work
We the People of Peace

The second opened (his) portal in-down-out-beyond all the way through to Common Ancestor, enacting an OldMan-Dreaming simultaneity in un-Oak'd skin as I delighted to engage a tough hoary hide. While the third? Ah, dear Sister, hitting me fair across the Cancer'd kisser with her power, solidarity with other-centred higher purpose thereto (re-) invigorating mine, saying:

"Survive! Thrive! Life-is-Love and Love-is-Life! You <u>are</u> Seven Sister'd – strong!"

In spirit, she took me on pilgrimage through <u>shared</u> root-known networks to Tree-Keepers I have prior-met (and likewise been inspired by). Three locales did we visit together:

Tullawallal, the Aboriginal elders of Antarctic Beech dreaming (see chapter "To the Power of Five"); Akamatsu of Hiroshima whose lessons of Love and Hope permeate the Story: "The Tree of Life" (see "Grail Within"); and finally to the 'Ridge of the Dead', a sacred space in our forgotten valley – a place of Larch Mothers who have taught me <u>so</u> much, holding me in subtle undying arms while their bony physical limbs, bleached in death, in sacrifice to Winpa's lightning-blow/s, still stand self-sovereignly erect.

Yes, I would remember. And walked on, meeting younglings peeking out from beneath their mothers' skirts, reciting to them my poem "Balance – Extended" to affirm re-membrance:

We keep singing up Country,
All of us who are left by those Aether-sent.
For the Ancestors' sake, this our own –
along a Songline gifted since first Dawn of Light.
We keep singing up Country
in honour of Memory, this our own –
walking Hope, Light's thread unmet
along a Way fore-strung to Future come.
This our own ...

F collected some cones. "Let's start our own forest," he grinned, as we walked Hope back to the car, as I said I wanted to return here one day – to walk Hope on, sing up the full string by crossing the smoothed mountain pass in the distance, walk down and into the next valley's catchment. No longer the preserve of the Inn but equally precious, for it sent its heartwaters down across the border to join Messner's river and then truck south to parallel the Po across the Veneto.

Precious for another reason, for at that border crossing, the Camino de Santiago entered Swiss territory from the east, trekked its valley before climbing to selfsame pass and crossing to where we stood in the shadow of Tamangur. A thousand-year-old convent marked the border, Sisters still prayed in its krypta as had done for generations. A promise, I said to F, for next year; just like this year's promise to Messner – if at all possible, I want to return and walk this sacred trail.

That night they came to meet me in my dreams – the local Sidhe of place, the local Sisters of place, the local Spirits of place. I had been busy in an act of blessing, singing our "Weaving-Song" as a personal binding of promise made – tying myself to this stretch of Song as if in Celtic marriage ceremony. I would return, I vowed, to sing the weaving at the pass where the two watersheds connect. Suddenly conjured in subtle sight was a pier far out over the top of valley where I could walk, stand inwith yet high above the whole, the Inn frothing her Joy far below. These local Amici had magicked a perfect placement for my 'Brigid-doll' weaving – knowing the lay of their Land, attaching the central pivot in/of scape for Song to 'stick', to resonate in subtle blood/bone of wood/stone till I could return to psychoid unity it in flesh. Excited, delighted, humbled – the especial nature of Nature encountered. Pure, and open to the purity of our Amici'd intent, I cried aloud into Sky:

"Circuitry! Seeds! Life!"

• • • • •

To reach this next valley which led to Messner's by road (rather than foot) we needed to head back the way we came, hang a left, then another left, and drive a long windy stretch of asphalt over a different mountain pass before coming down into its pastures (green). Far simpler and faster to go direct as the Morrigan or Bearded Vulture flies, but? Such is the fate of those reduced to four wheels. Yet driving the 'long way' enabled the vista on offer to be lain before us like a (moveable) feast. So many (more) pretty Bens! So many (more) high moorlands and forests to explore. My promise extended itself – we needed to return to this valley, stay put a while in the bosom of its true-nature, sing up the Green of its Land, flood it with the Blue of Stars in-led. Goodness! At this rate, Reader, who had time to succumb to cancerous incursions??? Our service in-world knew no earthly bounds, and was less than amenable to 'worldly' constraints!

Alright. Here we are at last at Messner's Hof (farm) installed in a wee garden cottage at edge of scene, a pair of donkeys with soulful long-lashed eyes ruminating just beyond picket fence. Only five days since setting sail from home, I remained completely stunned by the nearness of Presence, the perfection of Anwa'd flow to all acts (material, Malakut), intended and un-.

We settled to sleep that first night (of seven), sunk into the silence of Hof high above the main valley, perched like eagle's nest on a significant rock outcrop, steeply terraced with orchards below, and with the frozen clarity of stellar stream above.

In the midst of night, I was brought bolt awake to a fulsome Dark surround-sounding an encounter with <u>significant</u> Presence. It said it was just popping in to say hi, and welcome, and to offer support for my healing regime. How sweet! How unexpected! This healing support centred on a type of flow or canal-system incorporating so-called 'nitches' – a classic subtle-spoken hybrid word to mean 'niches' (pooling possibilities) combined with 'notches' (coupling devices) in 'ditches' (hollowed dirt). I saw half-pipes lain horizontal, in connected segments, in abstract space. While the nitches offered structure to the pipes, the boundary 'seams' were always open (or 'fordable') such that the flow of Love's (liquid) Light could continue unimpeded. It reminded me of bamboo cross-sections, lain flat in scape – a feeder-system where 'sluice-gates' were set into the rim to act as strengthening mechanisms.

Surprised (and honoured!) that this Presence had deigned to 'drop by' (for a midnight cuppa), I explained how I understood and worked this principle as a healing proposition for Self/Gaia's Garden ("planet core to thin Blue line, our Song stretches cirque'd and trine'd," as song-text attests). Perhaps though my emphasis had been too heavily vested in vertic'd (gravity-fed/led – drilling to core, shunting to line) connectivity? Its suggestion flipped the switch (so to speak) from 'linearity' to 'laterality' in/through-world, to the instrument itself that <u>feeds</u> Life. Smart – it took River, and 'harnessed' <u>its</u> flow, to well-water places 'off-grid'. (Dawn of Time in his desert-father'd scape would love this, I thought.) Aqueducts, viaducts – irrigation channels open, connectable, accessible across all (dimensional) terrains to quench thirst of Garden/s in difficult (geographic, geologic) hard-to-reach plots, thus sustaining and nourishing all Life there-abounding.

I was reminded of the lines penned in "Muted Earth" a year before. Lines which arose from an intense visioning string in company of the Amici, where Great Mother tells her origin story:

The Child listens. Intently. Great Mother is tired
but the Child brings a map. Lays it to ground
at their bare and muddy feet. See? says the Child,
eyes a-sparkle of gems a-pool. If we just keep singing:
All will be Blue!
Great Mother squints (sight not what it used to be).
Notes the slim squiggles, rivulets of fragrant knowing
gone underground from neglect. Did they all forget? She wonders.
An unsung land is a dead land, the Child solemnly repeats.
Lesson learned at self-same knee. Old Man Dreaming
the Songs to sing, forming a Ring round Mother's head,
protecting her core with a: You shall not pass! roar.
Great Mother nods. But her smile is frayed,

trembles at edge. So sing, She says,
squeezing tight the Child's hand.
Now is your turn. To sing ...

The visioning had taken place in (subtle) Gondwanaland via Aboriginal ancestral facilitation. I had seen <u>into</u> stone, beneath surface to where the Waters-of-Life still flowed underground. Now I was being shown by my interlocutor the <u>mechanism</u> for healing Gaia's Garden (thereto mine) by uplifting these 'waters' to surface, by accessing these "rivulets of fragrant knowing" – in Song, by walking Song on, as the Child says:

"If we just keep singing, all will be Blue!"

There was a depth-charge to this Presence which I knew that I 'knew' in some capacity – the density (or dimensional 'quality') of its generative growly-bear nature was a known 'quantity' to little me. It burbled forth its name (with a twinkle in stony eye):

"Sasso."

Oh, dear heart! Rock as Self (micro-macro'd) and what Self <u>contains</u>? Like Sasso san Gottardo's peace-sunk heart-warming crystal-catacomb'd <u>well</u>-water'd Helvetian source, fortress 'walls' and all? To think my precious link to DeepTime-Tectonia was <u>here</u> revealing itself at surface? To meet me where <u>I</u> was, meeting Messner? Oh, dear heart (ditto'd)!

Now I could <u>truly</u> see 'in' to how Sasso had called Messner to <u>his</u> specificity of place, of (Peace) Sink revealed. When the master sought retreat, desired to establish a sanctuary away from the 'noise' of world in a home-place reminiscent of Himalayan giants, he found his 'Milarepa-cave' inwith (medieval) fortress walls <u>literally</u> sitting atop 'the Rock' (Sasso) of ages/sages who made the Mountain their own (Dogen'd) Body-Mind. Apparently he climbed up the side of the ruin and dropped in from above on a first exploratory look-see back in the '80s (as you do when you are 'called').

Truly I saw into the Love which Sasso had for this human, for <u>all</u> humans when we see with eyes unclouded. Led here by resonance, tugged by the ancient binding of Blake's "Man and Mountain" (in gnomic verse) where great things are 'done'. Mediated by Kali, kora'd by Kailash, the Love which Messner expressed to/for the very Ground of Being, since coddled here by Sasso. At Home.

But for little me? To be welcomed so soon by <u>deepest</u> layers of tectonic ground <u>and</u> with a healing offer?? 'Twas only 1.30am; we had been 'in residence' a mere 9-hours and I was yet to have an 'overview' of the whole. But? "On, on," as the Harriers say!

A buzz/hum up through soles of feet accompanied me the entire week; Sasso was never not burbling a constancy of loving flow (nitch'd) through the energetic waterways of me – <u>feeding</u> Self's/Gaia's (edenic) garden in like Breath, speaking full to the mantra I began daily to recite once I discovered the scent of Air 'less foul', having chosen my path out from Moria's mines, knowing – at root – that all healing gifts received I would gift on, and back, to Gaia. I was here to learn at Sasso's feet, but also to walk upon his bones, sing up an energetic 'charge' between us to flow Love's (liquid) Light out and through all the world.

I feigned to hear Sasso say: "My home is yours; my garden your Arcadia!" In the space of initial subtle encounter, I had demonstrated how I worked the energy of Love's (liquid) Light, how our processes (horizont-vertic'd) matched in partnering the (H5.0) elemental power/s that be. In physical space-time, I walked the paths of this steep wind-swept snow-capped country, and saw how ancient humans 'coaxed' water into wood and stone canals to irrigate cliff-hung terraces. The traces of past interventions still inscribed in scape, I kept pace with Water's (past) journey as I walked and sang blessings in heart. The elementals had bent to the purity of ancestral intent, had partnered the human desire to draw bounty and sustenance from Land's precious body. Sasso's memory was long and deep. What a wonderful opportunity to access this wisdom for Gaia's benefit in psychoid unity'd blissful synchrony!

Sweetly, this even extended to Sasso's whisper of "healing (Peace) teas" which (again) I said I thought I had covered (researched, ingested), but to find the same herbals growing wild in (supposedly) unforgiving terrain? An (endemic) variety well-suited to dry sandy soils (source-to-sea!), in rocky slopes and 'wastelands' (so-said) (like dandelion – a most sturdy pioneer of impacted ground); perfect for those hard-to-access nooks/crannies, to (politely) suggest to any confused Cancer cells remaining to pack their bags and head for the door. 'Twas terribly precious to know we shared the same 'track'; my smile could not have been wider!

And then, of course, there was Messner's museum, and his home – the former in a nearby town, the latter above the gardener's cottage of our repose; the former a vast fortress, repurposed, the latter with washing flapping on a line strung from verandah; the former hosting a lifetime's survey of mountaineering memorabilia, the latter his shrine to the mountains and their gods. It made sense, of course. From his rock of ages/sages, with direct sight onto the mighty Ortler (at 3905m an absolute giant of the eastern Alps was his 'local' Kailash), his homage desired to plumb as deep as the peak was high.

How low can we bow before Gaia's beauty expressed in form? How perfect can our veneration inspired by such awe be presented? The unspoken questions on lips to which the extent of his shrine/s provided more than ample answer. Bridges between Heaven and Earth. His "holy mountains" (so-called) personal thereto planetary – all surfaces did he cover in images, texts, artefacts proclaiming his Love and oozing with philosophic considerations. Describing his curiosity thus, for example:

"The mysterious always lies beyond the horizon. Behind the mountains and above them. Beyond Everest. We confront the beyond within ourselves like the great sages of humankind – if we so choose."

I could almost see Sasso grinning to be so exalted by the effusive content Messner displayed:

"The power of spirit – of rocks and of clouds – as well as nearness and distance to that beyond of ultimate belonging … For Lamaists, the divinities and the forces of nature are one and the same thing; and nowhere are storms and the swirling mists and cloud formations more alive than on the roof of the world."

He quoted Meister Eckhardt, he quoted Titus Livius, he quoted Dante. And offered up to the visitor a first edition of Edward Whymper's 'Scrambles amongst the Alps' (1871) whose frontispiece also quotes Livy:

"Toil and pleasure, in their natures opposite, are yet linked together in a kind of necessary connection."

Attending his home, in physical time-space, was a revelation. His sanctuary did actually host a vast array of Milarepa'd iconography as I had seen in meditation when we met 'across the border' – all (he wrote beside a picture taken during a meeting with the Dalai Lama) would be returned to Tibet once liberated from its (unwelcome) colonisers. I walked in subterranean catacombs, through stately rooms and walled gardens – around each corner and upon each tower ledge Milarepa loomed and hovered; nowhere was there not statuary to the saint or aphorisms drawn from his teachings. Probably also out on the verandah, where his washing hung like Tibetan prayer flags sending blessings on the breeze …

It is right that we stayed here, inwith Messner's Sasso'd sanctuary, ensconced in its (secret) garden, in a keeper's cottage devoted to same, overlit by the spirit of the ones who tend, who weed, who sweep, who heal, who love <u>this</u> Land, the particularity of its sacred stretch of Gaia's Song. Occupying a tucked away nook on the edge of Hof's known world, surrounded by these channels ("Waale" in local tongue) – now, having walked their paths hence/forth through the drama of dry stone cliff'd slopes, I understood the sing-sing-singing of connection in Body, of Sasso's abstract offer of first night 'welcome'. Psychoid unity – never not an opportunity to marry spirit-geology in-self/in-world, the blood/bone we share <u>wells</u> with the <u>wellbeing</u> of Love's Light stellar in-brought.

While walking, I listened, observed, learnt – ancient ways of sculpting slim wooden channels from smooth hollowed logs so Flow flows through <u>unimpeded</u> during its traverse of terrain; carrying the blood, the marrow of Life into world. At times simply following the contours of scape, organic/fluid, bringing liquid Light from a side valley's heights down to the dry crisp thirsty cliff-laid crops, blazing in their (mineral garden) saddles, receiving Sun's full warming kiss. Fair harvest blest, but only when vertic'd ground (horizont) well-water'd.

Harnessing the power of the elementals – earth, water, fire. Also air. Kaze's dry cold wind bringing clear Light to scene even if it made my nose run and eyes sting. Meanwhile other channels required more intervention – coaxed through stone walls with an occasional nitch'd roof – each bamboo'd section honoured, each passage through assured.

Ah, Sasso – your wei-wu-wei message more than fit-to-purpose. Shaping my healing, my work, to the <u>contours</u> of scape, of my garden/Gaia's – all gifts received gifted on as balm, reminding me to let such Flow flow through unimpeded, to not 'overthink' the regime of twinned praxis. A triplet of haiku to mark the moment, of seven (Sister'd, strong) day/nights in the Garden <u>Tender's</u> Cottage:

Tending the Garden
Never not sweeping seeding
This Land with fresh Life
Tending the Garden
Never not sweeping seeding
Your Light of Love home
Tending the Garden
Never not sweeping seeding
The SingingBird's Song

On our last morning in residence, a single peaceful settled image returned with me from the Malakut – walking barefoot, awaiting Sun's rise, walking on Sasso. <u>Nothing</u> was here; it was all pre-<u>human</u> intervention. Primal. Simply I and Sasso – this majestic rock of ages/sages in and of himself, my friend. Walking slowly, mindfully, out to his Schilf'd edge to overlook the valley of (this) River's stellar run 1000m below. Bare of foot and original of Mind. Stone greeting Sun in-come. Pact of which I too am One. With thanks, good grace, I carry your Joy to <u>be</u>, Sasso, I carry your Joy to be – <u>on</u>. In Body. In Blood. In Bone.

On, on, on. Flow flowing, Light illuming. On. On. On.

• • • • •

We headed back cross-border to Helvetia's peace-sunk heart via Ortler's ice-world domain – an opportunity to connect more directly into his glacier-capped heights by driving the (double) pass road/s linking his (side) valley with another leading back down to our neck of the woods (in other words, hanging a left then a right then a right, all the while speechless on countless sinuous curves – overwhelmed by both the magnificence of terrain and the strange tragedy of its role as a major battleground in the First World War).

Extreme. Extreme 'New', extreme 'Beauty', extreme 'Stone-Giants' speaking very, <u>very</u> loudly. Absolutely exuberant in outreach was the full cirque of power; I was suddenly struck by its full weight, of serious Presence in direct intersect – a pressure vice to head which I did not resist but embraced, the density and magnitude of Love in Sasso's expressive hands. Till the energy shifted, the weight as suddenly released itself when coming down 'our' side, when the second pass forded and home, Helvetia enfolding this small human in a full Body/Land hug.

To ease the journey back to our lowlands abode, we stayed a pair of nights near the source of the Inn, beside the planal lake into which she first spills, a peaceable place (and its Sasso'd chips off the old block) which inspired Nietzsche's philosophic hand 150 years before, the thought of 'eterno ritorno' coming to him here: "6000-feet beyond man and time". A place F knew from childhood jaunts, it was my first encounter at the upper 'end' of (significant) Inn (river goddess'd) girl-power. It turned out our hotel was beside the guesthouse where Nietzsche rented a room each of Seven Summers; it turned out he dined each evening in the cavernous hall of this very hotel as part of his eterno-ritorno'd rituals. History, recent/human, surrounded us but it was the goddess who again met me in the Malakut. Raw notes follow:

I woke this morn to a whistled chorus, as if a mountain corps or boy/girl scout troupe off to joyous (Snow White) 'heigh-ho' work. It reminded me of the Amici troubadours encountered at Helvetia's heart, when I entered Sasso's fortress to ask for her blessing before we began our pilgrimage through Land – the same time/place of visioning communique which set us on this path of 'joining' sacred mountains ... the all of then which has led to the all of now ... Over and over, I heard whistling, singing but did not see the crew at task. Into the space, the goddess spoke. Yes, a woman's voice, strong (of Seven-Sister'd same), a call to arms/action to this troupe who serve her shed, speaking out from Source high above, a waterfall tumbling Purity's pearls down through cragged slope to pool in this peaceable lake before shunted on, gravity-fed-led all the way home to Sea.

She said: "Please maintain the lifeblood of the arteries." Words which repeated again, again as in/under my skin I let them sink in. Suddenly I am back, leaping up and into bathroom so I don't wake F to scribble these notes in autumnal half-light. The <u>lifeblood</u> of the arteries – hers, mine, all watersheds divine. Love's liquid Light a-flow. Un-im-ped-ed. Between Source-Sea-Source purity is needed. Whether flown from Mother-Ocean or burbled forth from Mountain Deep, inwith Gaia's membrane shared, the waters must stay sweet!

Oh, to hear her implore! Oh, to hear her call to action! I am with you! (said by us both in like measure) I am with you! (and) I am you! Is this a next best thread in (my) starblood evolution out through (my) umbilicus of settled stone? Only when the Light (pure) is within me can the Light (pure) be shared. Yes. Maintaining the lifeblood of <u>my</u> arteries is a more than necessary corollary to supporting each/every (Dragon) River's run. The counsel of Sasso and his stellar Waale brought into the here and now of the Inn's self-desire, self-need so she may <u>selflessly</u> continue her service to Life in/of Gaia's Garden! Nested is each cirque, interpenetrant is each (water) shed, interconnected is each (Song) Line of (Love's) Light sent skating through earth, sky, sea-waves. Live-wire'd – each to *the other to the other without end inwith the full extent of this membrane, shared. Each 'River' a-run, each 'artery' inwith Gaia's Body as too my own igniting Blue's fire to dissipate any impurity, cauterising any lingering wound, evanescing the old, the stale, detoxifying each precious vale ... I see the great river spirit of Miyazake's 'Spirited Away' holding Chihiro in arms to say: 'Well done." I see her riding the Haku dragon of the skies and remembering his (River's) true name. What breaks the spell? Love. Pure. Simple. Ever. Always. <u>No</u> exceptions. Love.*

My goodness. That was a download and a half, Reader. Later, we walked to the foreshore of this planal lake carrying a silver spoon from breakfast table with which to shovel river sand into a picnic box to 'hold' this memory as pulverised potion. Later, we walked back to the hotel to return said spoon but the doors were locked. End of season and we the last guests. An (unexpected) tool thus joined our Amici kit whose name is:

"The art of doses is key."

• • • • •

Now ... how do you feel about an in-chapter 'intermezzo'? Will you please bear with me/us? Because that is what the Amici are calling me to pen to bring all insights based on encounters described until this point into the blinding clarity of present (Sasso'd <u>and</u> Waale'd) presence. There continues to be a (knuckle-) gnawing frustration to penning said chapter – truly the most difficult of any in this topsy-turvy tome – simply because of the <u>constancy</u> of new information coming in. For here we are in (late) Summer 2024 having penned (since long) our final chapter in volume ("A Temenos to Song") now to be shunted back upstream to this stretch of textual same (thanks to Merc's retrograde rear-guard action methinks), all because we stumbled upon (quite literally) the most significant Celtic fortress on European continent out the back end of a road-trip north for a younger son's university graduation on a (Dutch) North Sea shore? Phew!

Like most other random 'events' (of which, Emerson knows, one's Soul is already well-versed even if a wee human consciousness remains clueless as), it was as if the genius loci of (Celtic) place had 'spotted' my light on its winsome way south (post-grad celeb) and decided to blast me out of the water with the force of her welcome once 'landed' in the particularity of her (personal) space. In hindsight, like with most things, it made sense. Having traced the path of our very own OldMan-Rhein (Stone-Cowboy) all the way from Helvetia's alpine source to (his) homecome (northern) Sea, pilgrim offerings duly carried from one end to other for gifting to a pristine dunescape which edged his sweet water flow after it set sail from the briny embrace of Rotterdam's humungous port facilities, it probably made sense (given our fulfilled intent). But that's what (generally) happens when we collapse into a space of work done/dusted and think we're 'off-duty', quite ready to 'holiday', the shock-of-the-new will pop its head up and veritably yell:

"Integrate me too in your web of work please!"

So who are we (Amici) to not agree? Raw notes follow (where J stands for July as well as Joy!).

J10: It's Weds; it's sunny; it's warm; it's the German bush at 10am! With a view onto a sweet Tree'd slope on the other side of babbling brook that feeds into Saar which will later meet Mosel before reaching Trier of Roman (ruin'd) fame. We will, of course, bless these waters a-join of OldMan-Rhein further along his wending way home to (northern) sea wilds where our blessings are (already) 'planted' in sand-soil'd sanctity. Closing another circuit while (unexpectedly) adding a fresh 'live-wire' to his geographic grid with this random choice of stopping-place en route home? Substations aplenty rising up to meet us? An overnight 'double-flash' announced incoming Presence — who? She spoke of a new 'pregnancy', offered a restorative tonic. I laughed, said my days of bearing babes was over. But? Hmmm.

J11: OK ... so now I know. 'Twas the Goddess herself waiting here, at Celtic fortress, at its temple site excavated (dedicated to latter classical incarnations) — waiting, she was, for me to arrive. But why? The 'zing' of the site's _active_ current greeted me as soon as we approached outer wall. A sharp blast stopped me in my tracks. An E-W energetic meridian in Land's sanctity which this tribe must have sensed, been called here to steward her Presence till Romans came knocking half a millennium later. Prior? Pure wilderness, nature pure. I could feel, intimately, _immediately_ how the rituals of place would have been performed — the rites of passage to 'marry' Land, protect the maidenhead of fountain/well, primal origins of chivalric code enacted. The (warrior) men serving the women (healers) who were charged with blessing Goddess/Land, one and same. No wonder the walls so high — 20m! And so broad — 25m! Truly a Gandalf 'you shall not pass' momentum existed to guard the liquid gold treasury discovered within this 18ha broad reservoir of Sasso's _infinite_ Tectonia'd sink!

I needed time to listen, dive deep to pre-history, so walked the wall's (now rubbly) 'outer' length a way before I 'heard' the Source call, saw where it emerged in slope. I greeted it, reverently, and then Squirrel joined me (most classic act of shapeshifting ever), leaping ahead (like Fleeting Hare) up through the dampened silence of summertime forest to bring me to the _exact_ spot needed for 'memory-keepers' to say: "Hello". Listening, listening. A swirling light-heart/headedness enwrapt/enfolded me in crystalline whisper. Atop the ridge, a holy grove of Beech-Sisters-Oak-Brothers reprised the all of All of DeepTime at either end of (place-based) extent. So-oft lightning struck — no wonder this the temple precinct for harnessing, partnering the power of elementals' _full_ reach!

A Wren hopped/chitter-chatter-sang through the 'fallen' (wood) and I knew to follow her lead to where a _huge_ elder Beech lay, split clean, sliced in two by a hammer-hand lightning-boss'd Winpa blow. I climbed atop the fractured spine of this Sister, walked part of her length in sober connect. A Dragonfly arrived to encircle me three times; someone had etched the face/s of tri-form goddess into wood still anchored (rooted) in ground. Dizzy with interconnectivity, 'light' with grove's blessings reciprocate, I performed 'Crone - extended' for the assembly before leaving. And, as always, the text perfectly matched the moment, affirming our commitment to keep singing up country. No. Matter. What.

J12: Time to go home. The 'Mists of Avalon' (so-said) have spoken. I conversed with a Sister who 'led' the order here, realised I knew her in some 'pre-now' capacity; I was attended by a novice named Leila before leaving to 'ride' atop huge smoothed logs in the stream, perform the 'convergence' of flow/s through to OldMan-Rhein, my dear friend. The space was intense and dark, the wood long-filled by water (water-logged) yet floating, heavy, present to <u>and</u> with the stream; sinuous curvaceous but nitched/notched to fit seamlessly, each with other – partnering Presence, as Presence, solely. The vision spoke to <u>so</u> much that has happened these days. As usual I don't know <u>what</u> I am being asked to do but it felt like there was an in-dwelling/entrée offer from <u>this</u> spirit of place which linked/hooked into <u>all</u> our Amici 'lifeblood-of-arteries' work to share the 'singing', for its elemental energies to join in tracing the 'Mists of Avalon' all the way home to sea. How do we proceed?

Ah, Reader … How is it possible that we are connecting Songlines in this way without knowing these places exist in the first place till randomly discovered? That the continental web of 'Old-Europe', the power of Land, partner'd, could be here, so simply, found? Sink at surface revealed? Soul at skin worn? Hidden in plain sight, and now able to return to itself, rewild'd, thanks to a national park decree? To enact <u>its</u> Arcadian dream of recovered memory, fresh envisioned into which we blithely tap by simply being present, listening to Land as (Gondwana-) taught? Questions for which this intermezzo (nor this volume) has absolutely no answers. The work is its own reward. That is all I can say. My gratitude, to be offered the opportunity to participate and offer service, could not be deeper. 'Tis a bottomless well to which I plummet again, and again, never knowing where I may 'land' but trusting ever in the (pure) Land, the (steady) Hand.

Later we followed OldMan home, crossing the French-German border (which his broad flood forms) at a phenomenal mid-20th century hydropower station. Google Maps' oddness of suggested route at its chortling best (yes, I know you love playing with technology, Amici … it's your version of latter-day shapeshifting!) had us fording the tumult on a rumbly single-track tarmac usually open only to power-station workers (well, that's a clue re our work) – so broad, so pounding, so roaring with majesty. I said (yelled actually):

"OldMan! You are the <u>mightiest</u> I know (intimately at that)!"

The magic of plotting the slow road home, to <u>his</u> primal turf, to <u>his</u> place of birth. In Helvetia's forever snows, the depths of <u>her</u> realms of Sasso'd dark. Two weeks we had been on the road, following the way Source-Sea-Source'd, to celebrate with a lad whom I had told to offer his 'wish' to OldMan four years before, a shell tossed to relentless Flow which (I said) would meet him at Sea when all he wished to become had verily been. Two weeks since the Amici, as a gift for this journey of celebration, had handed me a massive old hardcover book with a (slightly) torn dust jacket whose cover showed a landscape, in watercolour, with the title: "Whale Whispering". I smiled into the space of their blessing. We were indeed expected – there, in the North, where OldMan 'met' salty sea (dogs). But what would I find when whale- whispering began?

Well, here is where the rubber meets the road for a (perhaps) last intermezzo'd time. Three years earlier, "Song of Gaia" (which, Reader, you shall meet in a forthcoming chapter, "Source (Code/x)") had delighted to surprise in (reprised) company of a great subtle Being of (northern) ocean depths. Much was woken by that performance (it seems). Much, which now I can see led to the Amici's gift of volume and a (pre-) whispering 'wave' hitting Annie's shoreline which meant, as soon as arrived, I was called to active co-work in North Sea (Malakut). A 'rich' local Presence, currently fragmented in/of 'colour spectrum', desired integration into a coherent pattern in order to <u>contribute</u> to our lifeblood-of-arteries (OldMan-sponsored) work 'stream'.

Oh, how our Light is seen far and wide! Four-stages were involved – at one end of spectrum I saw stone/rocky scapes; at the other a swathe of pale gold as if on a hunk of driftwood. Her involvement would ensure an holistic meld; indeed she was more than excited to participate. Later I walked down to a (seven seas) edge-world and, laughingly noted:

"There are angels everywhere!"

Their presence I felt as soft wisps of tingling Light as I moved over the sand toward intertidal zone. A mist of 'arisen Joy' to all intents. When all around in human-dominant 'worldly' dimensions I found to be busy, noisy, with centuries of urban-industrial 'static'? Oh, to be greeted and welcomed thus – and know that this wild <u>edge-world</u> was summarily present, could <u>never</u> be banished! A wild which <u>stayed</u> wild. No. Matter. What.

And then it happened ... The night before we were due to leave the particularity of place, this pocket of Old-European continental shore, head back inland – down/south – her 'whale whispering' truly bore fruit in light of (Moon's) mirror blest. A sack of gifts I had brought in offering (gifts of garden, gifts of home) and knew now they needed to be planted, not tossed to waves as pre-envisioned. Planted, like me, <u>rooted</u> in sand-soil (as "Awakening" attests), gifts of healing, of Peace blessing to filter through all Songlines of world – Sea/Land'd, Wild and Sky'd. In this Moon cycle (I said) we honour <u>Home</u> (Gaia), we honour <u>Presence</u> (all), and we honour our <u>opportunity</u> (as a species) to contribute our loving <u>essence</u> to the Whole.

And <u>that's</u> when it happened ... a full 'download' coming in overnight to place the humble offering I would make next morn into its globally-connected flotsam-jetsam-driftwood Mother-Ocean'd context. Medallions dredged up from offshore I saw, medallions hosting the goddess' likeness in her ancient form of pregnant fertility, mirroring those first sculptural 'mouldings' human-rendered as cultural 'coinage-of-realm' – like figurines from early agrarian communities, deeply worshipful of the Mother and what she selflessly gifted of/from her rotund Body. Worship our species increasing forgot as coinage was gradually deemed more 'valuable' than the iconography portrayed. Here, I saw fired terracotta-clay medallions deep-embossed of the Mother's image, subtly coloured in the Green (of a Land never dead) with the Blue (of Stars flooding world with their Seed).

I focused on a medallion overlooked in the hoard; all were presented on a market stall run by a trader in antiquities but this one deemed valueless. Unprized because it was broken, un-whole, it had snapped in two along its equatorial line during dredging operations. Two halves hosting a wondrous empty cirque at centre – of no interest to others, perhaps, but for me a portal through which to connect heaven/earth. Further, I knew that by some force of 'magic' the emptiness would remain intact even as we reglued the coin at hemispheric 'seam'.

I remembered how Dragon sent a "message in an empty cirque" years before using Sengai's runic script; I remembered how Alpha-Cen taught me to trust my translational ability. Suffice it to say, this coin excited me greatly <u>and</u> I knew why – the magical 'force' was Love brought to equation, Love which we Amici dished out in <u>buckets</u> on both sides of hemispheric divide, across the world of time/space by virtue of 'awakened' <u>homes</u> twinned in time/space of our sole/ soul Home: Gaia.

Now, another medallion was shown me – it hosted a temenos "far in the East" (said). Turkey was named, as was Moses to demonstrate the <u>age</u> of these finds and his role in Story. I knew this temple and its classical design; I had been there before. It was the place of my worship before a statue of goddess outwith clocked Time; the place where I had accepted an ice-blue crystal as big as my hand to partner my Song henceforth – one of seven crystal slabs for Seven Sisters (to come). The essay "Crystal Knowing" (in "Grail Within") contains explication of this event, and this place (as I knew it in the Malakut).

Now the trader relayed to me the full interconnected history of the 'Old-World'. We had 'sailed' OldMan-Rhein from Source-to-Sea; unknowingly, this had completed an induction of sorts for I was invited to his kitchen 'out-back'. Here I was at liberty to devise an alchemical proposition for the dune-planting ceremony to come – my last day, perhaps ever, on this shore to avail of an opportunity to psychoid unity spirit-geology.

In terms of cobbling something together in the vein of 'just-in-time management', it meant taking account of new knowledge as best as possible with meagre 'tools' at my disposal (in an AirBnb kitchen while jackdaws laughed at my folly). I needed to honour the goddess in her primal form – mend what broken, heal what fractured, and sing Land back to herself; share in <u>her</u> Joy of 'recovered memory, fresh envisioned'.

In the space I was reminded of the reverie my protagonist, Kisha, in "The Taste of Translation" entertained while weeding (always an opportunity for contemplative enquiry):

She sat back on her heels, hands red raw, sweat on her brow, looked up to della Croce's cliff face. Cracked and chipped, furrowed and frowning, it was a regular contributor to the garden. Slivers of stone smashed over millennia lay hidden in the dirt to tear at her nails and scrape skin from her knuckles. A voice entered her reverie, Samir in one of his literature classes:

"I swear the earth shall surely be complete/To him or her who shall be complete,/The earth remains jagged and broken/Only to him or her who remains jagged and broken."

But there has to be more to it than that, she thought, prodding at a fresh tangle of rhizomes. Perhaps della Croce's jaggedness, its brokenness, is its completeness. Perhaps to smooth all the edges off all the surfaces of the world isn't the point. I'm jagged, I'm broken, she thought. Does that mean I can't be complete? Aren't we all constantly being transformed by the tectonic plates moving beneath the surface and carving watercourses through our scars?

I think you're taking his words out of context, said Samir. Write an essay on differing perspectives in Walt Whitman's poetry and hand it in on Monday. Forget it, she humphed. I've got weeding to do. And felt his warm kiss upon the cheek of memory.

Now, here I was, decades after penning that scene, amazed at my intuitive non-understanding of DeepTime-Tectonia's impacts, of Sasso's (stellar) Waale "carving watercourses through (my) scars". While my (rhizomatic) experiences of brokenness had latterly been joined by (weedy) cancerous incursions in this (rambunctious) self-Garden, rather than feel 'lamed' or 'victimised' by the quantum of brokenness faced (in-Self, in-World, during a small human lifetime in-Skin), I felt self-sovereignty burble forth, up/out of the <u>limitless</u> well of Love at <u>my</u> Mother-Ocean core.

Despite and (perhaps) because of my vulnerability, of touching fundamentally into the fragility of Life, I felt to <u>be</u> Mountain, felt to <u>flow</u> Dragon in my unequivocal Trust in the <u>Magic</u> of Love. Com-passion, literally 'to-suffer-with', demanded that I, with Amici, support the broken, the un-whole, perform healing rites, restore the shattered to holism. We have faced our brokenness, embraced what it would teach; our woundedness <u>is</u> our healing power, our transformative gift gifted on to Gaia's Garden ad infinitum. Thus was I reminded, too, of the words penned in "Muted Earth" (again quoted to reinforce the message):

'Tis my amor fati – sister Kali and her sisters

to accompany. As all fractures for all to heal.

Yes, I knew the process of fracturing intimately. So too healing (the garden, any size). Not for the first time was I grateful for <u>everything</u> my journey of Cancer had taught (and continues to teach!). Knowing healing in-Self, in-Body, 'from the inside out' of my own 'Garden'? If my experiential learning could help others, help Gaia? Excellent 'field-work' praxis! I focused my mantras of healing on her beauty, her fertility, and sealed all with Song there in the dunes flanking a North Sea shoreline, with seagulls wheeling and a curious oyster catcher, red-billed, my companion of pilgriming day – blessing and blessed in like measure, loving and loved equally one. It was done. It was done. It was done.

Or so I thought till we (randomly) discovered a Celtic fort …

Ah, Reader. Intermezzo complete, I'm back where I started – not realising this chapter would be so tough to write but so it is, and so it remains. Shall we return to where we left off? Yet ever with the realisation that, because Time is fluid in subtle realms, the following linear discussion (in light of preceding a-linear) will require some struggling? I thank you in advance for accepting the challenge.

•••••

In an earlier chapter ("Weaving"), I described how, in vision, I saw a lake to which words were attached thus: "Upjumped from Mother-Ocean <u>core</u>." The arising of pure sweet waters, pooled within and burbling forth from Mountain's sacred heart (in our case, Helvetian of provenance) brought forth (in/through me/Amici) a Mother-Song to sing back to primal source as a self-weaving/world-weaving in one. 'Tis a closed circuit we share inwith Gaia's thin Blue line, that fragile atmospheric seam (or outermost 'skin') we walk. 'Tis an 'Ecology of Light' in/through Water's (elemental) cycle which engages, in <u>simultaneity</u>, Earth-Sea-Sky.

It matters not to/for/with whom we sing. We "Daughters of the Lake" weave the Mother-Song as a <u>constancy</u> of praxis in-time-out through <u>all</u> Songlines of Gaia's membrane (sleeve'd), knowing her Body-Mind-Soul full-present to each. Our singing, we know, supports the great work of enlivening, restoring and laying 'fresh' energetic meridians in the global grid stitched into (and arisen from) a growing (and glowing!) cosmic matrix. We work the harmonic resonance of elemental sentience in-skin-out; Sasso's demonstration of Waale offering my simple mind an excellent visual hook to maintain the 'lifeblood of arteries' in/of the whole.

In a (different) earlier chapter, I quoted Dogen's wisdom:

"You may regret that mountains and waters <u>conceal</u> sounds and colours, but you may rejoice as well that the moment of enlightenment emerges <u>through</u> mountains and waters."

Ah, the 'enlightenment' of Love's (liquid) Light in form … As Dragon shapes each (watery) dance in company of Mountain's (stony) stance, it should come as no surprise that I 'saw' how Sasso's tender of Waale'd efforts, cliff-hewn and -secured, to reach <u>any</u> precipitous, forgotten or parched nook/cranny of earth (horizont-vertical) offered a <u>perfect</u> in-time proposition to support an endocrinal system (Gaian, Annie'd or any) which requires therapeutic nourishment. My purpose, however, is not to shift our text into the metaphoric hands of a mammalian anatomy class with its feedback loops, hormonal glands and adrenal signals. We Amici much prefer hanging out with esoteric philosophers who drink PeaceTea while despatching (brave) golden ducks up-or-downstream. But, due to the <u>specificity</u> of my (personal) healing journey, I could not help but focus on a key line of Dogen's sutra where he describes mountains/waters as the bones/marrow (blood) of world. In one respect it led me back to an exuberant poem I wrote (well pre-cancerous incursions) as a response to his deep wisdom that:

"The path of water runs upward and downward and in all directions … Water is the true suchness of water. Water is water's complete virtue."

I penned:

All the way from source to sea, from
source to sea to source … Water –
sacred – through your eyes I see …
Self – font of being, font of flowing,
font of blessing, interconnection;
watersheds of passionate expression,
Universe-high and just as wide …

Dogen said:

"There is walking, there is flowing, and there is a moment when a mountain gives birth to a mountains child."

I thought: Mountain <u>cradles</u> water, water flows from Mountain out into the world. This is the 'child' – this is the sacred pool, the 'lake' I saw, the one that I and the Amici serve. In Song <u>and</u> along each/all of its Lines. Dragon's jewel – guarded, nurtured in/by Mountain. Deep of Time, Tectonia'd of redoubt and umbilicus'd of stone till? Out!

I am completing this volume in a Dragon year. Is it any wonder Sasso called me back to this chapter to better honour Seiryu's wise counsel via OldMan-Rhein (our more than broad Old-European)? It has been a year since our forever connection truly revealed itself when I was handed a key while connecting a 'side-tributary' Songline to our Camino de Helvetica within his fulsome shed. With the key came an offer to join a (subtle) chivalric order in his honour. The moniker ascribed to our collective would take too long to deconstruct in this text; suffice it to say it shares a similarity with Fideli d'Amore (aka 'Faithful of Love': Dante's 13th century collaborative crew). I was told:

"The <u>key</u> is a <u>cross</u> which is also a <u>sword</u>."

Cryptic on one level, crystal-clear on another. We described our lily-white goddess'd 'acts' (broad swathes <u>cross</u>-shaped) in the last chapter; previously I have written of Love as our Amici troupe's shield/spear (aka <u>sword</u>) ready to pierce any "Cloud of Unknowing" (as another 13th century spiritual text decrees), all this while remaining safe-protected by Love's selfsame shield. Meanwhile, the <u>key</u> is (most obviously) a functional item to unlock a gate or portal but (as a noun) can also refer to a system of interpreting a map or deciphering a code book (like a 'legend'); or in music not only refer to the playing of an instrument (like piano) but the principal tonality in which a tune is composed. In fact, when checking the dictionary listing, I discovered 33 different meanings before even reaching its use as an adjective or verb (with or without object!).

I have oft-mentioned in this tome how the Amici play with language; my task to puzzle out the range of nuances offered to find 'best-fit'. In this instance not only in being handed an object (heavy, big, iron, old – beaten into shape by a smith well-versed) which bore a striking resemblance to a centuries-old artefact hanging from the mantle of our centuries-old home, but now offered the opportunity to use it in company of fresh (Sidhe) energetic signatures? Women who hailed from "Avalon" (so-said), maidens of the well/s refreshed? "Daughters of the Lake" (as we), dedicated to the spirit of Water's sanctity just like our OldMan-Rhein (stone'd) constancy?

Now, marry these <u>latter</u> discoveries with the insights of Inn River goddess and her Land'd crew at the outset of <u>Autumn 2020</u> (Messner) adventure (ancient history by now, I know) – the primal pact of wood/stone in respect of Gaia's blood/bone (marrow'd) abode. Together with everything else that transpired (i.e. was osmotically breathed into being) during that trip, the absolute collision point of fore-with-aft was contained in her plea:

"Please maintain the lifeblood of the arteries!"

A plea issued to the Amici, to me, to all (on behalf of one, same <u>and</u> all). Returning home from that adventure, therefore, it proved too much for a wee Annie brain to digest; I typed up the notes scribbled in journal and settled down to reacquaint sweet Body with its desire for rest, nourishment and further self-healing.

It stewed away within, of course – over days, weeks, till it was time for the knowing to spew forth what it wanted me/us to actually know and therefore (wu-wei) do. In some respects, as with my conversation with Sasso, existing praxis was affirmed, viz:

I drop to a space where the universe (as a starlight/earthlight meld – i.e. midnight-dark and daylit-blue in same moment) stretches above me. From it a viaduct wends down toward Earth. 'I' am at both ends of this Waale, confirming our <u>tending</u> of garden is inwith Gaia's spheric planetary plane (this sleeve'd-of-breath membrane we share) <u>and</u> flowing in from cosmic realms in same moment. I am reminded of my original statement of intent with Amici kin – to 'wear a mantle of starlight here in the world to bring the energy of the Stars streaming to Earth …'. No matter what 'happens' in my/Gaia's garden, this pact (and process) never wavers. I feel deeply settled.

On another occasion our work was very much of-this-world; from a Malakut-Annie's point of view I was far from ill or fragile (a pleasant surprise!) – traversing a zone of chthonic 'canals', broad trenches, dark, muddy, infilled of nutrients, plant life; the silt of ages rich in compost but sight clear through to the ground (of Being). Walking out along a 'raised dam wall' toward a river mouth leading into (I knew) OldMan-Rhein's most significant lake on his journey north to Sea from birthland, I stepped down into and waded through the waters of these Waale to check on the health of these zones. Maintenance sweeps, I called these – an expression derived from environmental remediation work. It fit my task equally, as a "Daughter of the Lake" equally, to ensure Flow ever-flows through unimpeded and that the quality of Love's (liquid) Light in-brought stays fresh, Life-giving and -sustaining.

Many years have I performed a self-praxis which includes the affirmation:
I am a connective thread between Heaven and Earth –
A font of liquid Light for You, sharing Love out into the World

It has sat seamlessly with our work as Amici della Luce and, in company of Mountain and Tree, found expression in their concomitant acts as "Rivers of Light". Truly it is a delight to tap into these networks, root-known and crown-quivered, in service to bringing Love's Light across the thin Blue line of Gaia's atmospheric extent to infill this sleeve'd of Breath membrane we share with the all-of-All of planetary One.

One day in the wake of road-trip I sat by our local stream, at Heiwa (Peace) Stone, and looked at the sculptural 'shift' Mizu's watery flow had shaped here since last (pre-journey) visit. Undramatic of itself, but in context of all shared by Sasso and his (stellar) Waale? I listened to the stream's Song, and soon enough dropped to an interbeing'd dimension of all Waters of all (Mother-Ocean'd) World (in-with-out), interpenetrant of and percolating up through each expression of consciousness of Sasso's dense permeable silent humming 'reign'. I heard:

Being has changed the shape of its Flow
Sasso has spoken in tongues
The Silt of Ages has released its core
Wisdom's time has come.

I listened further, deeper, heard:
Being ever-changes the shape of its Flow
Sasso will always speak in tongues
But all that once was is now before

The time to live Wisdom has come.

Nothing more. I scribbled it down, waited. Days, weeks. Winter Solstice approached at which our Amici rituals would comingle the Inn's river sand with the sand, waters of our 'forgotten valley' in a vial of pure Light which I set before our warming fire. An alchemic proposition I did not know was set in train until it was, the swirl of Being, Flow, and Sasso set to work releasing (from core) Wisdom's 'silt of ages' into my miniscule midst. Yes, the Amici were involved in the 'whispering-work' for it took the form of a Sidhe spell to affirm (in their words) what the 'primal pact' proclaims – an oath to which the elementals hold, and which the praxis of Sasso-via-Waale brings in-world for our gorgeous Gaian girl:

Wood and Stone/Blood and Bone
Air-Fire-Water-Earth/Light of Love's re-birth
Stone and Wood/Bone and Blood
Let the River run/the World with Light to flood
Festive of Light and honouring of Dark
Indwelling at Source, the River's run to Sea cast
'I am,' says the River, 'and none can hold me back –
from the scape I create, the runic script I paint.'
'I am,' says the River, 'and I shall not be checked;
I go wherever Light is needed, wherever there is lack.'
Rivers of Light/Rivers of Love
Rivers of Life joining Heaven and Earth
Rivers of Presence/of Peace and of Joy
Of Hope Everlasting for Gaia's Glory ...

There's a power to ritual, a power to affirming our purity of intent before witnesses (seen or un-, human or non-), a power which is deepened, refined each time a performance is repeated, each time we reinforce the courage of our conviction in spoken tongue. Mountain decides and Gravity descends. Being exists, Flow flows – whether Earth/Sea/Sky, sealing connection fore/aft of each/ every adventure in Gaia's space-time. As such, I speak this pact to Waters, Woods, Stones, Clouds. I speak it to the elemental elders of Land, and to the stewards in-skin-out with whom I share service. I speak it at Source, Sea and all in-between. In-world-out and all-round-a-bout. An acknowledgement and blessing in one; an admission of my intense smallness, bowed low before each precious manifestation of the Generative Mystery; a thanksgiving that I may participate in this grand experiment and serve its purpose best I can.

It is at this point, Reader, I would like to draw our chapter to a cathartic close – this blessing text as an entire proposition cried loud/long that the time for all to live Wisdom has come.

But Moon is saying: "No". For there is something she desires to offer for your consideration; something which 'came in' on the back end of a most extreme (Helvetian) natural disaster, at Summer Solstice 2024, wrought by the all-encompassing and impassioned spirit of River's "I am" – wrought in Sky, wrought on Land, wrought by Mountain which tumbled to ground.

Wrought and now held in Wisdom's memory-drawers – of lives lost in the tumult (human, more than human – animal, vegetal, mineral, manufactural); of Land's scape in constant motion, and re-creation, when River's runic script barrelled through, and down. In my witness – direct as well as at a distance – an oracular tongue overtook my pen, wrote:

Helvetia is a small Land with a very big Heart –
Here/now Mizu's Song, Sky-inflown
To flood the world, penetrate flesh
With the Light of consciousness
To never forget whose Land it is
And whom we serve: Land's goddess …
So follow your heart, not your fear –
Surrender to Life, just as She …
(and)
Love Water as Water loves You –
Let the lifeblood flow
Through arteries, soothed …

Yes, Moon's full-illume was concurrent with Sun's 'stand still' that impactful (Solstice) day. A power-mix in which we are all so very, very small in the grand (experimental) scheme of things. I looked Winpa in the eye that day as he rolled his thunderous black wave round della Croce's shoulder, hit us fair in the kisser, horizont the full force thrown at this wood-stone/blood-bone structure. Yes, I looked him in the eye, but it was Moon who stared me down that night. At 3am bolt awake was I to transcribe what she would tell:

Do not forget (said She) *my* integral *relationship to Love's Light incoming to world. Water 'carries' consciousness and is* itself *conscious. Do not forget the Water of* my *Mountain world, my tidal push/pull wax/wane Breath in/out support of any/every thing that exists inwith Gaia's thin Blue line. Mountain decides, Gravity descends. You know I cross that line – direct. You know the forms which mirror my action, the runic script which paints* my *River's 'I am' in time. You know the 'spell' of invocation. Sasso and his (stellar) Waale? Look to me too for the* power, *of how the Sacred* in *Mountain flows* out *of said bower …*

As she spoke, I saw a clock face where Moon's potency was mapped atop Sun's, relative to the 'shift' (of each's 'stand-still'). I saw 'telephone pole/powerlines' capped with glass insulation thingeys (the blue-green ones we used to collect as kids, pretty).

Their intent is to help prevent electric current loss during transmission, sure, but in this case (given the tumult of River's unleash – overspilling, devastating), the glass caps were hessian-cloth-wrapt as protective (or 'containment') measures. Further, I understood this would <u>soothe</u> or <u>smooth</u> the ferrying of Love's Light along their conductive waterlines through/into world which, at end, is the purpose of Sasso's Waale. Remember: The art of doses is <u>key</u>! (Also as a cross/sword in the hands of Love's pure!)

I got up, went to stand at my 'window on world'. There she was, beaming in her golden eggy wane exactly three-days past full ("I Ching" oracle refers), the time when yin/yang again settles in the 'pool-of-happenings', finds its best fit as nestedfishes. I had written: "Love Water as Water loves You". Here was the <u>truth</u> of Moon's pact with same too. The last thing she told involved a word which, when a specific letter was 'dropped', would reveal its true hidden (name) form (for her work, and active in-world intercession).

I gave thanks to her, and her mothering community of Sidhe with whom we on/in-Earth Amici align. It had been a sobering time for Land, and her children. Many co-factors collided, but at heart? Moon and Sun just danced <u>so</u> much …

• • • • •

"The Crooked Book."

My Amici are snickering at how this text continues to topsy-turvy evolve. It looks cutesy-pie, the journal they hand me, like one in which a child would scrawl. A pretty good joke given I'm 'all over the shop' in the perennial penning stakes, a 'crooked' a-linearity of narrative is (my) (and their) par for the course. And yes (again), I would dearly love to finish this chapter, but? Who's this now popping a (less than wee) head round the (crooked) corner for a chat? 'Tis Sasso, our sweet chap of title!

Here he is, arrived in-house (a new experience for us both to be sure), and curling himself up with a log in the wood nook (below fireplace) that we actually never use for such purpose (instead an Egyptian footstool lurks therein on which I can stretch my legs … that is, unless a fulsome Being like him takes up residence!).

Here he is, giggling in an "aren't I clever?" sort of way. Chortling like a mini-kid with the Joy of having magicked himself to the size of a decent rock. Crazy! That this <u>immense</u> Presence could 'shrink' his signature into a 'mass' (I really can't describe it any other way) to wrap around wood? Cuddle, snuggle up with his 'bestie', gurgle contentedly at sharing divine intimacy, the elemental Love of wood-stone/blood-bone expressing true nature honed? Ah, but he has a purpose in showing up. Right here. Right now. Because there is one other thing I have forgotten to relate – a gift he gifted me of late …

In abstract space, I received an extraordinary present from this eminence – a <u>block</u> of 'bogged moss' which (I was told) Messner (via Sasso) had accessed in his 'coming into resonance' with Mountain sentience. It was not Messner's, it was itself, and now I was being offered the same opportunity. Unused in a very long time, it had rested in an inter-dimension since Messner no longer needed it. Lying dormant for such an age, therefore, it was completely dried-out, frost-burnt, but all I need do was "add my own water" to restore it to vibrant Life, partner it for the benefit of all Life.

I already 'knew' how this would work – like a sponge the block would soak up my 'water' (aka Love's Light) from which its Wisdom would flow forth; alternatively I could 'cut' bits off to take on the road (here I had an image of the magic of chamois cheese which regrows overnight as long as a tiny sliver left uneaten); I also had an image of tidal pools hosting squirter sponges on a rocky shoreline (thus Moon-cycle relevant). Sasso may "speak in tongues" as I heard at the stream, but Wisdom's time had definitely come!

I remembered back to the quest to find the source (Acqua Termale) of our river (recounted in "The Amici Files"). I remembered the Tree of Infinite Knowing which 'dissolved' and 'diffused' its entire wisdom throughout that scape – met first in Malakut, I found its actual existence to be bogged mossy moorland around the lakes, of (Peace) 'Sink-at-Surface', the Sacred Pool to which I could add my (Light) blessing before it skipped over a lip of Land out into the world (of Time). I remembered the sound of water flowing downslope beneath its spongey ground – absorbing, filtering, gifting on its pure Light in tiny rivulets of fragrant gurgling subterranean knowing to meet River's run further on. Well-watered, this "Hof Acquerei" (a place we shall meet in the chapter "Source (Code/x)"). And now, from some dusty barn on Messner's Hof had this block of 'bogged moss' been Sasso-retrieved for gifting on to our work? So very humbling, my task to steward/fuse with its wisdom, 'water' its potentiality with Love. An holistic proposition, a treasury of possibility – for Gaia and all her children. Ah, my own water:

"Only when the Light, pure, is within me can the Light, pure, be shared."

The Amici (and more) had been waiting for this day, when 'my own water' could be gifted on to healing Gaia's garden as my (personal Cancer) healing journey proceeded apace. I am a font of Love's liquid Light; I am Dogen's mountains child; I am a Daughter of the Lake. The lifeblood of my arteries are the lifeblood of Gaia's. The time to live Wisdom has come.

And, as a next best Blue hour beams Beauty through the valley's fulsome bowl, I uplift (afresh) Li Po's 13-centuries-past recitation for it never gets old – this depth of 'seeing' into the sacred heart of our most precious home:

The birds have vanished from the sky
Now the last cloud drains away
We sit together – the Mountain and me
Till only the Mountain remains

OF BENS, BOGS AND (SCOTTY) DOGS

Despite being of Celtic/Scots ancestry, I had never been much inclined to visit the 'Auld Country' from which our family fled in the 19th century. It was bleak, grey, cold with foreboding in our poverty-driven (historical) archive – each story filled with serge rather than frills, tinted photographs laden with sombre expressions. The only time my great-grandmother returned, some 40 years after leaving, on a faster clipper than the one which delivered her as a 20-year-old 'slip of a thing' to warmer and more hopeful colonial shores (parents and a brother in tow, the other lads having decided to try their luck in the States), she was suitably thankful she had a return ticket to the Antipodes and the family she'd built in Book-of-Voyage'd wake. Albeit on the absolute other end of the world to her birthplace, 'Home' = 'Land of (her) Adoption'. A simple enough equation.

As well as a few yarns passed down through her only daughter to her only granddaughter (perched on Granny's comfortable lap, Mum said she was 'all ears' to any tale told in that rich Scots brogue), a couple of postcards, and a handful of keepsakes, I inherited her rickety occasional table. While I imagine the journey out to Australia set it to wobbling in the first place, it's been amply bumped and bruised during my stewardship, especially via an equally upbraiding passage in a container back across the world to grace my Swiss home more than a century later. And while it may have shuddered and groaned each time I dusted its increasingly frail crone-self down countless years, never once did it occur to me to look deeper into its primal world and what its land-of-provenance could teach about our OnePeople'd heritage. It wasn't as if Scotland was on the other side of the world anymore; here I was, living within (relative) spitting distance of the Isles, but in 20 years neither a niggle nor a naggle had wormed its way into my heart to go explore the past? Hmmm …

Ah, but my Sidhe Amici obviously had other ideas; if mine were far from an amenable ear in which to whisper their (completely logical) suggestion, they were quite happy to rope in an accomplice to mission – D, my younger son, who in early 2019, totally 'out of the blue' (there's a hint if ever there was one), started a random conversation about the possibility of a mother-son adventure before he finished high school the following year. Not only an adventure (he said wistfully) but a proximate one (when would we have another chance, hey?) – over Spring Break (he was thinking) (um, next month?).

Of course, this all happened while walking a sniffy dog (our usual place for probing discussions). I remained noncommittal, set sturdy parameters (while inwardly taken <u>completely</u> aback; how many 17-year-olds <u>actively</u> want to have a holiday <u>just</u> with their mother?). But (long-story-short), by the time we returned from dog-walking an hour later, to his father sitting at table over the ubiquitous laptop screen, he had proposed Scotland (que? he, equally, had never shown interest in this Land!), I had agreed and the laptop was turned to the (more) important task of purchasing return tickets Zurich-Edinburgh (while his father scratched his head at such an odd outcome from a simple dog walk!).

Next task? Go buy a roadmap, I said, and a Lonely Planet guide to the Scots version of 'bush'. We are <u>not</u> hanging out in towns or cities (I said). If you're going to drag me there (I affirmed), it's to commune with <u>Land</u>. And so, Reader, we did. The roadmap, laid out on dining table and flopping over its edges, started nudging and nattering; the guidebook (with a focus on the Highlands and Islands) began prodding and poking. The only fixed points in a week's itinerary were the first night spent in the place of our family's heritage and climbing at least one mountain (Ben) at some point during the journey (if the weather gods proved amenable). We boarded a plane; Magic did the rest. And while I'd rather this chapter not turn into a travelogue, methinks cross-veil they have other ideas …

• • • • •

As described in "To the Power of Five", once out-flown from (what I consider to be) homeland/s (Gondwana Dreaming birthplace; Helvetia's Heart adoption), I feel to be an emissary on a 'Hello-the-House' mission, a head-shaven itinerant monk/pilgrim for Love (on perennial repeat), tasked to stretch the Song and bind Love to Land with each ensouled heel-toe 'sole-kiss' of Earth (trusty PeacePole at my side gifting its own grinning 'wood-kiss').

Further, I picture myself on bended knee at random stopping places, greeting resident genii locurum with blest offerings for their 'castle-keep/s' – shells, stones, knobs of wood perhaps as carriers of Light-energy (mine as well as own inherent, elemental, of their particular 'Dreaming'), small simple 'avatars-of-presence' operating (and radiating) as bright beacon message-sticks in the spirit of Australian Aboriginal artefacts gifted along the tsuringa-tracks (Songlines) from clan-keeper to clan-keeper over the length of continental Song. Tuning forks of resonance to which the one who walks (and sings) can always 'attune', it offers me (and my collaborators) the same opportunity – once welcomed to Country and our gifts accepted by (and into) Land's keeper spirit, it means that this shared energetic 'charge' of Love (reciprocate – Land/Self) incorporating our respective extant notes of beingness, of anwa'd becoming and flow, can meld and maintain a live (wired) connection no matter where in time or space we happen to find ourselves.

Sweetly (and, occasionally, maddeningly when I don't have enough pockets at my disposal) I usually find myself the recipient of more gifts-of-place than I can bestow. Bounty writ large, each wee soul calling: "Pick me! Pick me! I want to help Gaia too!", my primal collector-gene gets a bit of a workout as we walk the world. While I may reach a point of forgetting the provenance of a particular 'stick', they all know who they are, I nevertheless came up with a shorthand mantra to remind them (and me) of our purpose wherever their (and my) itinerant 'limbs' lead. In this case pre-Scots journey, I assembled a few simple interlocutors, conducted ceremony, popped them in a pouch. With no conscious knowledge of Land beyond a broad framework scripted by guidebook, and roadmap, I was an emissary, just as much a humble traveller with pilgrim staff and cape a-billow as anywhere beyond my usual worldview.

In advance of journey, therefore, I had not the faintest clue that during journey I would find myself interpenetrant with reservoir'd depths of ancestral knowing held by Land in (and of) itself. It was as if said knowing (extant, enduring) had simply waited for this moment to reveal itself, till then chortling in a backroom (of consciousness) that I was so clueless as to announce myself: 'Emissary'. Emissary? (I feigned, in hindsight, to hear it hoot.) How can you be emissary to the reservoir'd depths of your very own Self? Well, yes, I guess Jungian psychologists would enjoy debating me on that one, but? Suffice it to say I had no idea such a reservoir, enormous of treasures as well as of pain, (collectively) existed, let alone the healing it would (personally) necessitate. It was as if chthonic-deep genetic memory held in perpetuity by my Self had twinned with that of Land's Self – there, in the specificity of that (ancestral home) place.

Yes, I had experienced this in the Land of my birth and written of these encounters (as well as my understanding of same) in "Awakening". Yes, I had experienced this in the Land of my adoption and written of it ditto. I had 'embossed' or 'embroidered' (words offered by the Amici to describe our process) such reflections with further understandings about the intertwined relationship between Land and Self in "Grail Within". And in this tome, I have described how these come together in Gaia's bodily DeepTime-Tectonia, whose very elemental genetic memory <u>imprint</u> I inhabit (daily) (bodily) likewise.

Entwined, like Einstein's spooky entanglement at a distance, with a suddenness or immediacy of connectivity, a current which appeared coeval here, there, any-jolly-where, Land (plus its stewarding Sidhe and other allied Presences) apparently knew we were on our way and (seemingly) had the itinerary <u>already</u> planned down to the last ben, bog (or dog). Who, what, where, when, how and why? D and I would just be going along for the ride …

•••••

The energy started to assert itself and become 'present' days before we actually travelled. In night-vision I found myself climbing a hill to have an 'overview at dawn'; I stood in a place of glacially-smoothed uplands, saw a village down on the coast, the waters beyond were golden. An archaeological dig featured – a temple, uncovered, its sculpted crypt-altar of white plaster, pre-Christian. Coming out of the 'ruin', I looked back to the uplands, saw a consequent <u>chunk</u> of rock rising up as if a border behind the high wild grasslands where we had been. Sun, now full-risen, lit the scene perfectly but just as I went to take out my phone, snap a memory-pic, it turned pitch black, the vista suddenly gone, vanished. I continued walking down the hill to village, still bright-lit, and later found myself in a space of 'ancestral family lore' at a meeting behind closed doors of our <u>matrilinear</u> clan. It went <u>very</u> late into the night …

From this Malakut-reccie, we reach the pre-dawn of actual day of travel – busy/active. In my journal I wrote: "There is awareness in the subtle realms of our way." I walked amongst an Elven encampment; they spoke to me in dialect to be mindful to partner the elementals of place (Wind was specifically mentioned). They led me to an underwater treasury where (stone) gifts were algae-wrapt. I spoke the name of a village along the northern coast, and was told their name for this region: "White Chapel". I woke and scribbled the following affirmation for <u>their</u> witness – of the purity of <u>our</u> loving intent:

"My task is to listen learn explore engage, to walk ancestral ground, return to the beginning of genetic memory, embrace its known anew. May all ye All support our blessing of hallowed Land. Amen and thank you for this opportunity to serve Love, with <u>our</u> Love."

We arrived, we drove, we walked a long lonely windswept beach. The only difference between it and the 'eastern-sea-wild' of my southern hemispheric birthplace? The biting cold. We came to the wee town the family left some 150-years before, checked into an inn birthed at the dawn of the 19th century whose only nod to the 21st were slot machines in a corner of the public bar. By the time horizon in a lumpy bed that night, we had circum-nav'd the town on foot, learnt of its Norse (as well as golfing) roots, watched the lighthouse flash reminder to all sailors to take care. At the harbour I tossed in the first of the shells for each of the four directions we would honour in our road-tripped circum-nav of the whole – shells sourced from home, here brought to (re-found) home. At each drop-point would I recite:

"*In honour of the Ancestors, in honour of Hope, in honour of the Alliance between Humanity and Faerie, know that I am homecome to the Sea (of primal Being).*"

Words I've long sung as invocation in company of the Amici via Card Deck (see "Appendix 2") when laying out (our version of) Stone Circle. I watched the shell slide in/under the silty mud-sand on the edge of Time (this time), recorded the moment in my journal thus:

"*The Lotus blooms in the Mud.*"

Lights out on our first night on ancestral homecome shores; no matter how exhausted I was from negotiating motorways, byways and roundabouts in a veritable computer of a vehicle (it says something about the age of our family car that I needed a 15-minute tutorial by the rental car chappie before I could even figure out how to turn this chariot-of-way on!), the energy was palpable. Before dawn I was already up, perched on the (closed lid of) loo in hotel bathroom, madly scribbling notes; 'twas the only (lit) place to which I could retreat (and see what I was scribbling!) so as not to disturb (or be disturbed by curious questions from) a snoring teenager.

It was the gulls which did it. Seagulls the likes of whom I'd ne'er 'fore met, huge gulls of deep penetrant cries of communal longing, of yearning (Aussie gulls are a much smaller, higher-pitched petulant-sounding bird – no offence meant). With their lone cries or choral 'singing', like old ladies gossiping/clucking at their luck (or lack thereof) during a game of bridge, I found myself reeled back in time – further, further. Backdropped by their constant vocal accompaniment, the entire night I walked, then re-walked (over/over) a lucid scape whose principal feature was neither Mountain nor Loch (lake) but something in-between – a <u>shape</u>, planal/flat, elliptical, its consistency like silt or sponge. A place-name spoken in their tongue affirmed its quality or texture (like porridge), as if offering a halfway/intertidal state for my engagement. Yet I didn't sink into the 'goo'; it was fully present at Land's surface, its knowing thus accessible – in a malleable, consumable, (dare I say) 'digestible' form. (I am a huge fan of porridge, after all.)

Scribbling notes about these (relatively abstract) places I had wandered, there was no way of knowing if the things we 'planned' on road-trip would lead us to such locales or if simply it was a reference to what we would 'soak up' (like a sponge) from traversing the full terroir of Alba (Scotland's Gaelic name). I experienced no specificity of instruction as I explored and deep-listened to these elliptically-shaped 'realms' of Earth. The point was, though, they had an own story/s to tell. No mediation was required; my traverse was easy, comfy, cosy. I felt held, welcomed, cuddled, embraced by the sheer fact of the primal existence of ancestral Land. I felt well – very/very well indeed.

Yet whatever 'goo' the Malakut dished up overnight, the day which followed was stone-pure. I had Nan Shepherd's "The Living Mountain" with me as muse for the 'mineral breathing' of the Cairngorms that were her playground, lifelong. Climatically they are the Arctic of the Isles, the massif a terrain shaped (in Nan's words) by the elementals. When she spoke about walking "into the Cairngorms", she truly meant into – the embodied knowing of lover with beloved expressed through flesh, hers pliant to 'his' stone (she always used the masculine form to refer to 'her' mountain/s). Sensuous poetry as well as prose described her intimacy with these Bens, whose foothills were within cooee of a Deeside garden gate:

"It is, as with all creation, matter impregnated with mind: but the resultant issue is a living spirit, a glow in the consciousness, that perishes when the glow is dead. … So, simply to look on anything, such as a mountain, with the love that penetrates to its essence, is to widen the domain of being in the vastness of non-being".

With such a soulmate as Nan who understood, and expressed in her own inimitable way, the sacred within mountains, I spent much time in advance of journey researching where in the Cairngorms we could pay homage to her and the enduring spirit/s of her living mountain/s. With nought more than a half-day in a full-day's driving program to scamper up a hill and back, it could only be a relative 'tiddler' (aka Corbett) we could climb, but? The intent was to have perfect sight onto the 'big bombers' (aka Munroes) resident of entire national park.

Ah, but the best laid plans … Finding ourselves in pea-soup fog halfway up said tiddler, the only twinkling smile thereafter emanated from a stone of pure white-light, a lone hunk of quartz on a path (fortunately) lined by granite cairns to mark the way to summit (for just such instances as pea-soup fog). In such damp frozen state we arrived up top, (briefly) 'Hello'd a House' we could not see, toddled back the way we came. But earlier I had sung in a rain-wind-lashed Stone Circle with an intriguing recumbent (standing) stone as altar, and now, with consequent quartz as witness and companion of our way forthwith, all I could do was trust that in the depths of Land our homage sung from the heights had been heard …

• • • • •

It's called the Flow Country, a rolling expanse of blanket bog, sheltered straths (broad river valleys) and ubiquitous bens (mountains) rising magisterially above. A wild and rugged scape, one my heart intimately knew as soon as physically encountered for it seemed already known at some deep, recessed level of memory since forever. Yet the only reason we detoured in from the coast to physically 'meet' this country, for me to even <u>remember</u> a place elementally DNA-inscribed in Soul, was because of a guidebook entry for an RSPB centre in its midst.

We'd promised to F, the family 'ornithologue' (left languishing at home on the couch with a sleepy sniffy dog), that we would reconnaissance possible 'birding hotspots' (as, apparently, they're called) for his own (future) Scots adventure. None directly presented on our route but this one proved near enough to warrant investigation. But oh, how easy it would have been to not homecome to this terroir, to not hear its Song with our very own ears! How fortuitous we have a family ornithologue whom we wish to enjoin (at least vicariously) in our road-tripping adventure/s!

The Flow Country. The words meant nothing to me. What was this 'country', and what would it look like when finally encountered? My brow furrowed as we drove further, further in from the coast along an increasingly rutted slimly-tarmac'd road, thankful it was a weekend, thankful any logging or quarry trucks we saw along the way stood idle, and eventually arrived at a modest visitor centre housed in a disused railway station.

The largest expanse of blanket bog in Europe, an area of some 4,000 square kilometres covering much of the north/west Highlands (and, since our visit in 2019, World Heritage-declared: Yay!), the RSPB stewards 21,000ha of deep peat dotted with bog pools – 'tis a critically important habitat for wildlife, as well as climate change mitigation. We looked at interesting displays, admired stunning large-format photography but the wealth of information was too overwhelmingly 'head-centred' for someone who'd never imagined such a landscape existed; what would we actually encounter 'out in the field'? While the scientist rostered on duty was more than keen for a (very) long chat with the only humans he had seen in quite a while, we were equally keen to get out onto the moors, just walk this Land which stretched forever – literally like a blanket – toward a pair of gently rising Bens curled like a sleeping twin-giant in the far distance, yet (I am sure) with an eye ever-open in sentinel watch.

The Flow Country. So much I did <u>not</u> know, e.g. that the place we had encountered burial cairns (chambered tombs), much further to the east <u>earlier</u> in the day, was part of this same vast magical scape of <u>perennial</u> becoming (such is the geology of geography and I am no adept in either). I was still no closer to figuring out how or why my feeling of 'homecoming' to those cairns had impacted, and now I was being plunged into a next? Yet one thing I did know – that my knowing only <u>completes</u> itself (in any time, any space) by walking. We politely farewelled the scientist and headed out into the heart of it.

Raised boardwalks led us through the bog to protect its fragile biodiversity, but I felt far from divorced of direct sole-pressed-to-soul connectivity. Silence rose 'loud' from fecund depths to surround-sound each wood-mediated step. Neither of us spoke; neither of us desired to mar the purity of Land's voice, its presence all-encompassing, we small humans cocooned within. Such a stark contrast to visitor centre! In crossing the road to reserve we had crossed a dimensional divide.

This was no 'portal'; this was an everywhere-everything-all-at-once zone where the very air was infilled of Memory, ancient Land-memory whispering its welcome on non-existent Wind (now, that was a blessing). It was as if the very 'blanket' of bog moulded itself to our 'shape' – a membrane as vast/extensive or snug/tight-wrapt in its warp/weft as <u>we</u> willed it to be.

My awe of encounter cannot be overstated; stunned to meet and then fully <u>bodily</u> surrender in embrace? Flow 'danced' (there's no other way to paint its simultaneously still'd yet fluid 'beingness'). Porous, like the bog, it seeped into and suffused our blood/bone; not one sense was <u>not</u> involved in this infiltration – sight, sound, touch, taste, smell. The knowing 'arose', penetrated us both with an astonishing immediacy. We were in, completely suddenly One in/with/of scape … was it like that for everyone, I wondered? Or had Land recognised us as one of her own, as we did her in our depths of Soul, hence?

Like a lightning bolt – not from a thunderous sky but emanant from a settled centred entirety of planal horizon <u>Earth</u>-Life, ancient humming metamorphosed <u>Ever</u>-Life. Its elemental dance duende'd my elemental self in like measure; I was literally struck dumb by the immensity of Love I felt rising from Land, humbled by her outreach, touching directly into ancient <u>genetic</u> memory – shared and reciprocate with blessings infinite-fold, completely mindful of the grace which had led us here at all, I offered a small prayer of gratitude.

Wind, now high-risen, took my words to the ten directions, and more. The Bens on horizon nodded slightly, said: "Come back and climb us sometime." (See? They were just pretending to be asleep!) And a huge fluffy-bum'd bumblebee chose, at that moment, to join my walking, sailing, singing of boardwalks through bog – to alert me to look deep to where Sun reached into the pools (though I did not remark his presence at the time, being too <u>busy</u> doing what the <u>buzz</u> in my ear suggested!).

Tucked into the collar of jacket, a constant buzz accompanying my solo passage (on a pacific sea), truly the sound could have been the resonant hum of Gaia's DeepTime-Tectonia'd source 'heard' by inner ear, linking Earth-Sky-Self's "Tao-of-3Suns" in bog-pools bounced, so? I just went with it. Just had to go with it. That was until the bee decided to do a bit of exploring of my neck, beanie. The only fauna'd 'life' actively encountered that day, it was eventually rescued, evacuated, sent on an (indignant) wing'd way with a laugh having amply served purpose on behalf of the Sidhe 'whisperers' of place! Yes, they reminded. We are all on the same page, all inhabiting the same spheric Gaian stage:

OneLife. OneName. OnePeople. Love.

And I kiss (this) Ground of Being
with the All of my Self's self ...

As I walked, I realised everything that had been <u>subtle</u>-shared in a seagull-sung pre-dawn the previous day had found its psychoid-unity'd denouement here. More than that, everything learnt in OldMan-Rhein's Helvetian tri-delta, an 'edge-world' of Celtic heritage (e.g. Bregenz, Austria, named for the goddess, Brigid, and I myself welcomed to Constancy's shores as a "Daughter of the Lake" so-said) had its <u>scope</u> of uplift here, where finally a <u>physical</u> meeting with ancestry could be facilitated that spoke to our cosmic origins – origins sunk like a precious jewel inwith the peat-plumbed slumber of DeepTime.

The lucid scape I had Malakut-walked 33-hours prior? Whose principal feature neither Mountain nor Loch but something 'tween? Whose elliptical-shaped 'realms' were 'goo-like' but cosy, welcoming? Now, thanks to subtle-physic'd congruence in the <u>specificity</u> of Land's 'Flow', I could discern the stellar-earthen alignment of this place for what it truly offered – (DeepTime's) Sink at Surface in true-<u>nature'd</u> earnest.

•••••

Several paragraphs ago, I mentioned 'cairns' encountered earlier in the day; at this point in narrative it would probably make sense to put a bit of flesh on those bones to illustrate the collective impact these two locales, part of the same vast scape, presented.

When my unseen guides spoke their name for this place of elliptical-shaped 'realms', they described two variations – the 'goo' was equivalent (or accessible) at each but with subtle differences (which a slight tweaking to its name announced). One was named literally, for/of itself, the other named for its 'hollow' nature. Yet the two were really one, they confirmed, even though 'separate' in space. Now, looking back, I realised the Neolithic chambered cairns we had encountered were the 'hollow' variation. An extraordinary experience of itself, it only had the opportunity to come <u>fully</u> into its own 'light' (within my conscious understanding), once the Flow Country had been 'walked' later that day.

Elliptical realms, indeed. Hollow at that. At the cairns we were alone with (at least) 5,000-years of <u>ritualised</u> human history in a random field backed by forest in the absolute middle of nowhere on the side of a single-track lane that led even further nowhere. No wonder there was no one about. The only reason we were there at all was because of a jolly bike race round a jolly lake; our intended venture along Loch Ness nipped in the bud by road-closures, we had headed north faster than anticipated, and with time to take the slow roads. And oh, what a lucky break that proved to be – this 'detour' off a very slow road to enjoy!

Info-panels described the unusual nature of site – literally describing it as "in a hollow" with no views to hills or sea (as with the usual locales for such ceremonial grounds), speculating it had something to do with the <u>source</u> of a major river nearby. Meanwhile the elliptical design was reminiscent of burial chambers only found in the Orkney Isles further north.

While D wandered the environs, I said I was going in. Drawn to connect with the smaller of the two cairns, it involved a squat-crawl along a dank narrow passage six-metres in length before arriving at a high-vaulted chamber at centre. Rising to my feet, completely encircled and domed by sheaves of rock, I found myself looking into the face of a single tall broad standing stone directly opposite the chamber's entry. Its energy male, ancient, steady, its expression inscrutable, its function to 'anchor' the entire <u>substance</u> of space, enduringly, in each/all dimensions. I knew this energy; its scent was OldMan pure.

He was flanked by two female presences – part of the 'holding' pattern, but also with their own function. These I immediately knew as Sisters, partners to purpose, <u>midwives</u> to creation. Either side of the passage entrance stood guardians of place, 'Knights of the Cloth' (so-called) – portal'd presence keepers tasked to protect the space <u>and</u> its priesthood as well as steward the gifts offered out from this <u>womb</u> of becoming into the World of Time. This I felt arise as an immediacy of 'knowing' – in via my (star) blood, up through my (earthen) bones. No matter what any archaeologist said, I had <u>lived</u> this ritual purpose thus saw the space for what it held <u>still</u> in its energy field. I had, in some form at some time, participated. Here.

After making each's acquaintance, I knew the task at hand – to sing, quietly, reverently, the Coda (1&2) to "Blue's Third", the symphonic tone poem composed the previous year and first performed in a sacred crypt at Winter Solstice 2018. Here, in a (likewise) sacred crypt, I would affirm my Love, my <u>longevity</u> of service, and offer my gifts into the presence of these elders – past, present, future. And no, this would not be performed in the centre of this miniscule cirque of dust, in the 'limelight' offered by a grate in cairn roof. To effectively sing up the connection I needed to anchor myself in OldMan's embrace at back as I had learned in the Malakut, <u>my</u> spine seamed to <u>his</u> stone, straight tall strong (as he), his vibrational/energetic node like a piano's 'sound-board' to all intents, amplifying Song through all dimensions. The Sisters to right and left stood in support, mediating Song's 'birth' to world; the guardians of place held firm the gates (of history) for Song to flow its Love out/on into the slim sleeve of blinding Light I perceived at the end of 'birth canal' – all the way from (this) source to (that) sea. Simple. Timeless. Intended.

Reader, you may wonder at the spontaneity and speed of ritual <u>conceived</u> in a place unknown till encountered, with 'actors' unknown till met, purpose revealed to my waking eye as soon as I stood upright in chamber. Completely devoid of glyphs or runes, completely free of any cloying or 'sticky' residues. Why was this place so energetically 'clean'? So fresh and Wind-washed, its 'porch' swept free? Why so ready to accept my homage, my blessing, and partner my latter-day <u>instinctive</u> 'use'? I have no answers; it all occurred in the blink of an eye. Supported by a couple of quick memory-pix, a kiss of gratitude to OldMan for 'holding' me safe during the process, I scrambled out the way I came – as much a new-born babe as the Song 'launched' through all birth-canals of DeepTime-Tectonia'd time.

And ready, I expect, for the Flow Country to weave its expansive boggy stuff into the 'goo' that the hollow-hill of cairn had conjured from the deep, for the space of ritual would often appear in my Sidhe Amici envisioning down the years following this adventure with an intensity which keep building till the moment came we agreed there was nothing for it but to craft an actual physical artefact to connect into its realm in perpetuity from both sides of veil. The story of what and how this came to be, a story of generosity and delightful co-creation, is housed in our final chapter, Reader. Till then, please be patient!

• • • • •

If the Sidhe of place were chatty beforehand now they were positively gleeful as we inhabited the same dimensional universe inwith the peat-soaked "silt-of-ages" (and sages). The fluffy-bummed bumblebee was back, shapeshifting to a frog 'riding shotgun' on my shoulder in order to see the world through my eyes; I felt its weight (heavy!) arrive, but my surprise transformed to delight to offer any/all a chance to see <u>selves</u> in new form. On my head were three sets of glasses to offer different perspectives; a 'sear' of connectivity was constant at my crown like a solid kiss from those stoic Bens. A persistent theme as we continued 'on-the-road' was of research or market surveys. I was approached <u>daily</u> by local Sidhe for our opinion, advice, commentary on aspects of Land/Scape/Mountain "registrations and listings". My response?

"You've got enough to work on for now; just go with the broad advice/listing of 'main peaks' already given and take it from there."

Returning, I wondered at the implications of what 'I' had said and suddenly realised they wanted to be part of our Weaving-the-World collective. My goodness! Here I was, heading to the Auld Country with nought but listening, exploring, musing as my intent, while their agenda for our visit encompassed so much more? It seems that, now the Songline was full-open 'tween our consciousnesses, and that this "next thread in whispered starblood <u>evolution</u>" was fully-live (wired), they were itching to get busy to bring <u>their</u> Bens to global table! To say I was stunned would be an understatement; I laughed out loud in each dimension! Still, I heard what 'I' had said: Take it slow, take it steady in a "we get there when we get there" sort of way, my moderating counsel like that classic statement delivered to excitable kids in the back seat of family truckster keen to arrive before even setting out.

That my Sidhe Amici back in Helvetia as well as the Shining Ones of the Sea down under were in on the (now-revealed) game plan (while Annie-of-the-Simple-Mind remained blissfully clueless) must be a given; in hindsight it was obvious that in-weaving Birth-Land, Adopted-Land, Ancestral-Land was the way forward to deepening, strengthening, refining our work for Gaia's 'Stars-within-the-Earth' entire Third-Rock-Land. But could I support any further than I had already their desire to 'light' beacons of Song in Ben'd heights (as with Bog'd depths)?

We drove on, round the (Highland) corner (north-west). The entire day sun-drenched, blue-skied, zephyr-breezed; the weather gods turned on their Scots charm in earnest the whole week. This meant we could see we were accompanied the entire way by a prominent Ben at our left shoulder. Regardless of road taken, we could not shake him. "Who is that?" I asked D as he unfurled the (massive) roadmap before folding and stretching a relevant portion out across his lap. "Hope," came the answer. Seriously? A Ben called Hope? And such a pretty chap to boot? "Tell him we'll be back," I laughed, "and with a Song of Hope in our hearts!"

Indeed, the complete stretch of Land sang already to my heart; who was I not to reciprocate? Another (local) poet proved soulmate in this west highlands' terrain – Norman MacCaig, writing in Assynt:

A mountain is a kind of music: theme
And counter theme displaced in air amongst
Their own variations.

Oh! To compose as lyrical a text as Love Song to a Ben! Meanwhile, on the map, I spotted a lighthouse (the whole family knows what a sucker I am for lighthouses). We parked, we walked a non-path along the headland high above the Minch, that <u>melodic</u> stretch of water between mainland and Outer Hebrides. We spotted a sea-stack just off-shore which seemed to be contemplating its own relationship with Minch. I checked the map. It was called Old-Man. Seriously? And, in direct alignment with stack, beneath the shaggy legs of ruminating sheep (who, somehow, knew <u>not</u> to fall off a cliff) the landed rise before us was called Faerie-Hill. (Ditto?) We arrived at its summit cairn, looked 'into' the Howe (of ages/sages) it housed, its Song traversing a line through Old-Man and out – west, to whatever lay beyond that thin-seamed horizon, so/so <u>wondrously</u> Blue.

There was a significance to the naming, of that much I was sure. I first connected into OldMan Dreaming via Australian Aboriginal cosmology. OldMan (Sky-Father, names interchangeable in my lexicon) acted as code for our Common Ancestor, first-born of (cosmic) Mother-Ocean, primal Sea of Being from which our OnePeople'd lineage stellar-sprung. A vast energetic Presence I have met in various 'stepped-down' guises across different dimensions, I have also intuited (or been instructed in) the multifarious forms his spirit can 'inhabit' via co-creation with Land (or subjective species). Totemic animal beings are one example, significant features of Land/Seascape another. Mythologies cross-world have deep insightful ways to recognise this energy. What excited me here was to find our Scots ancestry using the <u>exact</u> same naming schema – this sea-stack visibly vibrated with the resonance of the spirit with which it was imbued, and for which it was named. The consciousness of matter. Here was OldMan in living mineral-breathing skin.

But what was he looking at? With what had this emanation of spirit been tasked? Was it the same as perceived at my 'eastern-sea-wild' headland down under, where Tree-Keepers (absolutely <u>saturate</u> with OldMan presence) were tasked to protect ancient Mother-Wisdom sunk deep in sand-soil? Was he 'holding the line' for the Faeries of Hill at back? Or 'holding the memory' of kin who had already sailed 'fore, into the West? I could not know, but the buzz of connectivity, into which we immediately 'hooked' at this place of salty-sea-dog'd air, could not be dimmed. We just <u>had</u> to climb a Ben and the one earmarked (Lomond, south, a few days hence) would just not cut it. It had to be in this high wild raw free <u>terrain</u>. Yet by the time we headed to bed that night without a firm 'plan' for the morrow (Beltaine Eve of all Amici celeb markers), my sense of loss, of missed opportunity was keen. It was not only on our behalf, but for our Cousins of Commons beyond vale'd veil that I mourned in my (perceived) inability to bless Land on such an auspicious occasion in Celtic calendar.

•••••

Now, Reader, will you be so kind as to indulge me as we turn to the rough-hewn journal notes from those days' daze? For the impulse of <u>its</u> voice is one I dare not dampen; with thanks …

<u>30 April</u>: 7am. Ullapool. There's a lot of Bens out the window and they're all itching for our attention. I am overwhelmed – with choice, with blessing opps, with necessity to plan and think: OK. Someone else decide. What/where to go this day? <u>Such</u> a pressure at forehead/3rd eye. From the ridge directly opposite? First choice? Or from them all ranging back through glens now that I've opened the curtains? I don't know! Please return me to the here/now of <u>task</u>! Please help!!! Everyone, everything <u>reaching</u> to engage and here I am – <u>no clue</u> how best to honour any/all. Yester, walking the cliffs – divine! – then I get to this busy happy-with-human-noise place, out of the realms of <u>emptiness</u>, and I'm lost tired grumpy.

A <u>beautiful</u> place on a <u>stunning</u> loch but I'm not 'here'. Maybe that's the sense of 'loss'; we finished the N-W Highlands route: 9am 28/4 to 6pm 29/4, a mere 33hrs. I said as much coming into town: "We're done." Felt the tug at <u>back</u>, the desire to <u>stay</u>. Felt the energy shift coming out onto main road, comparatively so human-centric. The cruise ship in Minch as we walked back from Sithean Mor a 'blot' on landscape, marring the perfection of horizon, shouldn't be there. No human 'intervention'; yet here I am, a human? What does that say? I love/love/love! Love is all I have. To gift! I bought a book of poetry. He knows. But do I? Am I the blot? All you Bens. Happy, so happy. But: Where? Who? When?

1 May: 7am. Skye. We have ascended our Ben/Munro; surprisingly (or not) completely fit to purpose of what I lamented, my feeling of 'loss' yester-morn. After penning that brief entry, I spread the map out on bed (D snored on), tried to spot the one he'd said the night before would be 'on the way' to Skye. Assumed it was Wyvis; looked it up. A goodly path; a serious berg; doable. Turns out to not be the one D suggested but its (trailhead) accessibility off the main road a key factor in my spontaneous: "Let's do this." Were we prepped? Far from! A bottle of water, muesli bar each and (luckily) a pack of salted peanuts back at the car which we scoffed greedily as first _freezing_ drops of rain fell from the sky. Man, and I thought the Alps had four seasons in a day! Five hours earlier starting out in fine calm pleasant conditions; by the time we'd summited and began picking our way back down, it was blowing a gale which, if the ptarmigan we almost fell over hadn't been pretending to be a rock on legs but instead wanted to spread its wings to avoid clumsy boots, the poor bird would have ended up in Iceland! Oh, and the wee burn coming out of valley? The notion we had circum'd coast, every day in sight of sea, that this our day 'in-land', but Land full-sighted onto all traversed?

How was I to know that _this_ the Ben holding south 'portal' of our Highlands adventure open/connectable across all dimensions, just as Hope (seemingly) held the north? I couldn't; I didn't. But, oh! Fortune _smiled_. And the wee burn accepted my shell. And the broad beautiful 'let me throw myself down and grind myself into your skin' spine of this mighty Ben a sheer _joy_ to walk length/breadth of after the serious ascent – at these heights _equally_ sink-at-surface revealed. Singing, singing, singing – letting the current _flow_. And a rock with legs got up, walked in front of D, then pretended to be a rock again while he slowly took camera out of the backpack, snapped a pic for his father. I could _not_ stop giggling at the _inanity_ of scene, the _magic_ which enabled the scene to _be_. At summit, the all-of-it laid before us on glacially-smoothed platter, to farthest reaches of 'empire' and more. This _compassionate_ Ben who, in response to my sense of 'loss', said: "Return to me/via me/through me to the full journey _you_ made while _I_ watched those 33hrs." Yes, _this_ is how it works – the harmony of the spheres in _this_ Gaian sphere. Like Ben Hope – observed, _exalted_ as we drove ('next time!' we promised); here, Wyvis as _partner_: "With your hoverfly's eye and wing, _use_ me (he said) to _complete_ the string, _revisit_ all you have discovered in this too-brief passage; use my heights to _sing_!"

And yes. We did use him; we _did_ surrender to his offer to serve _our_ purpose though at times I wish it was as 'hoverfly' easy. But? All fit-to-purpose; catharsis/denouement. No one on the crest, D far ahead; I sang, recited the "Blues" (song'd), 'danced', and trusted his root-knowing would carry my blessings out/on. Imagine! Not known till _known_, not known till _lived_ (in skin) – that _this_ the Ben, and the timing _right_. For Beltaine. Such that now I could settle (well …), sink into the moss, the peat, the _soil_ of Being's Return. Rest …

But? Still needing to get here, another 3hrs driving, we stopped en route at a railway siding/pub in the middle of nowhere because I _sorely_ needed to wash stinging eyes, sweaty face, have a cup of tea, re-group. Extraordinarily, the _perfect_ conclusion to all prior. How

Faerie-blessed have we been? Thank you to the Ancestors, to Hope (in Scots-Wyvis'd skin), to the Alliance. A fire in the grate, 'Lassie' the limpid eyed rescue hound, tea and a biccie from 'Angus' in his yellow kilt, white woollen sox, Blundstones. We sat on a couch; I <u>melted</u> into its warmth. <u>So</u> rejuvenating. The absolute luck! Sheer <u>sheer</u> luck! Thanks be for simple country pleasures and genuine hospitality!

Ah, but you were a Big Ben, Wyvis, a big day out squashed into half of same. And to think my beanie is still somewhere up in the slope? I guess you guys magicked this, an opportunity too good to miss to (literally) 'cap' one of your Berg-Geist genies in fetching woollen weave, get it 'listed' in the Annie-Amici 'register' via beacon lit on the (bonfire) night most appropriate to same. Ha! Nevertheless, I am <u>happily</u> in on the joke (even if my shaven head is set to shiver forthwith); like all stones/shells of blessing, this warming 'avatar of presence' (blue-green for Land-meeting-Sea) will know what to do for Love's Light to flow through all Song'd leylines of world. So do I speak the spell on all our behalfs:

Celtic cross'd, flaming stake'd, plunge'd to source,
between here and sea conjoint to be;
alchemic path of Blue's triform desire –
so do I walk the One Life of Gaia.

• • • • •

Phew … are you still with me, Reader? That was a download and a half, what? The point being that once back to Helvetia's heart, the heart of the Highlands was still front and centre, <u>buzzing</u> with excitement to further embed the experience in-Self, taking me back into the simplicity of being and connection, of stopping still and listening, but paradoxically with a 'speed' that said: "It took so long to get you here; there's no time to lose in sharing everything we need to share!" This 'assimilation' process included as much Malakut journeying as material world research to 'blanket-stitch' the seams, reinforce the threads warp/weft woven between my three (now) homes (re-found). Honoured to have been welcomed back to genetic memory's ancestral pile (settled of stone), I re-visited in vision the 'rounds' of Light we planted in Land but suddenly the vision went deeper, FullDark-deep (my expression for the 'space' of uncreated Light).

When again I had 'sight' I found I was in the chambered cairn, reverently approaching (like before) OldMan but knowing more (than before) about the initiatory role of space (as well as its in-dwellers). I realised I had been granted permission to access the space 'at will', to actively engage <u>its</u> FullDark and return with gifts of Light 'reborn'. Where before I had understood its function cognitively while <u>physically</u> present to its geologic 'Mind' of 5,000-years' standing, instinctively 'flowing' a ritual practice in my 'meeting' of presences therein at the time, now words were spoken to confirm the Ancestors had only plumbed "half the pipes" (their words) in <u>their</u> ceremonial praxis. The Sidhe, as guardians of place, graciously offered us their support to 'resurrect' the knowing anew,

<u>embroider</u> it with our offerings as a shared and extended blessing out to the World of Time. This ancient "Altar of Blacks" (so-named) housed 'tools' in <u>its</u> Memory which could 'quicken' (like a babe in incubatory utero) our macro-work for Gaia (as Land) while, in reciprocate form, bless the micro-specificity of own steward'd sacred Land.

Surprised, humbled, grateful, this visionary experience called to mind two things of relevance.

Many years ago, I was witness to an 'event' I eventually enfolded into a fictional container for its knowing that: "There is <u>not enough</u> Love in the World" ("The Taste of Translation" is its home). To provide a framework for this, and the penetrating impact the event itself had on my life, I embarked on PhD research, turning to myriad 'conversation partners' to support the theses presented in my dissertation. One of these was the psychoanalyst, CG Jung, who himself plumbed depths with a guide, Philemon, and needed a way to record 'events' disclosed in such company. One quote attributed to him stood by me throughout:

"<u>Any</u> content that emerges from the unconscious into consciousness involves a <u>spiritual</u> or <u>moral</u> task."

This, backed by Margaret Atwood's harnessing of Virgil, that "the dead may guard the treasure, but it is <u>useless treasure</u> unless it can be brought back into the land of the living and <u>allowed</u> to enter time once more," gave me the courage and impetus to step up to, onto, and follow the path I am still following. It rested (then as now) purely on how, once 'treasure' is shared with me in good faith, I feel <u>ethically</u> bound to not only deepen my understanding but share these gifts (of healing balm) on. In other words, no way back but forward: Ho! ("to infinity and beyond" if "Toy Story"s hero, Buzz Lightyear, is to believed).

Similarly in our earlier "Weaving" chapter, I included a description of the 'part-time teacher', the beautiful T, who arrived to offer depths of Australian Aboriginal ancestral wisdom held and stewarded on behalf of Land; my overwhelming sense of humility and gratitude to stand in her presence and accept this gift of knowledge was equalled if not surpassed by her shining tears of same to have the opportunity to, as Atwood writes, "bring the treasure back to the <u>land</u> of the <u>living</u>."

The keywords here are both Land <u>and</u> Living – we share a single Gaian sphere (Land in its fullest extent) of Life (to its fullest extent), partners to purpose on a shared map, with a shared 'flag' of stewardship (which T 'completed' in our company). With this comes shared ethical considerations in order to walk toward a <u>shared</u> future – for Gaia, for all. Birth contract scripted in skin, for Life <u>and</u> Land, my commitment to this vision is whole-hearted, and fuelled solely/soully by Love, to help bring into being a world of <u>enough</u> Love – for Gaia, for all.

And now? Let's just say that when I thought all depths I could contribute to, for Gaia, had been plumbed, this whirlwind road-trip hit me fair across the kisser and said:

"Sister? You ain't seen or done <u>nuthin'</u> yet."

There was work to (still) do – witnessing, blessing, healing. For example, once, in the cairn, Land took the form of a sylph-like being. A translucent (feminine) Presence who held qualities of the sea, she visited our family to describe her trauma; 'violated' at the hands of humankind, she offered to take us down 'to the lower levels' to reveal the extent of her story – a journey intended for our younger members, the 'future' of tribe who would see wholeness full-restored to world. But before I sent them on their way, I took her into a private space, held her shoulders straight, looked steadily into her eyes, and affirmed:

"You may see us as family. Even if you have none/have lost yours, we welcome you as family to our <u>home</u>."

In this 'private' us-space of intimate encounter she didn't look like before, but 'hollowed-out', dark and within a crone's shroud. Yet once the ritual of our connectivity had been affirmed, she returned to her lithe-though-fragile waif-self, the one my 'daughter' had met in a 'clinic' and brought home with her to our warming hearthside. Yes, she had a story to tell. It would be traumatic and tragic but the <u>children's</u> act of witnessing was necessary to her healing. Such that by this stage she was upbeat/chatty, acting as 'leader' to their excursion – into the depths of chthonic space/time.

Land was definitely outreaching for our (Amici'd) support – where Sink met Surface (there) was not in good shape. Such that I 'saw' that by <u>walking</u> the Peace of Helvetia's <u>Sink</u> (here) it would carry Song's resonance Home-to-Home-to-Home through DeepTime-Tectonia'd root-known networks shared by <u>all</u> of Gaia's Land. We had lit the beacons of stone giants in the heights, 'woven the world' to bring more Stars to Earth. We had walked Peace across and into the length-breadth-depths of Helvetia (microcosm of Gaia's macrocosm) as a pilgrimage for Love on perennial repeat up hill and down dale.

But? In this instance? I conceived a fresh pilgrimage, a walking journey from our 'daily life' home north of the alps to our 'spiritual' home in the Swiss south, that 'forgotten valley on the border of time' where I was first-adopted by Land (my Sidhe Amici holding tight to vale'd shirt tails). The route would follow the one we normally drove through the valleys and across the passes of eastern Alps, a stretch of (home-road) Song intimately known since two decades. Now to traverse its paths, trod by human foot since well before the Romans arrived and gave local Celtic tribes of Helvetians and Rhaetians their marching (or integration or sublimation) orders. More than 200kms stood before us – walking out the door of (one) home carrying the key for (other) home. I was itching to get started, and along the meditative way is it any surprise the Amici were present and participant with ideas for Story and Song just ripe for the penning, humming, whistling?

In short, 2019 was a very creative year for extending our repertoire of Gaian blessing texts and tunes, shifting the narrative of 'Blue' further than ever imagined as I stretched Song home-to-home. As alluded to in the chapter "Whole Earth Partnership", one which specifically arose to affirm walking-as-sacred-praxis came in as simply as by placing each boot down in front of its brother. Contemplating the paradox of our work being deeply chthonic on one hand, yet completely outwith-stellar on the other, 'singing' the Stars in/out of Earth as Mariel urges, I wondered: Where does it 'meet' to bless Gaia and all life within her Life?

A tune arose to the metronome of my footfalls which began populating itself with text thus:

"Silently walking the Blue line surrounding the all-of-the-All, Gaia's full reach within."

Yes! This the place – the thin Blue line, that visible permeable sleeve captured in pix by awe-struck astronauts orbiting aboard the International Space Station, a gaseous 'line' where last traces of Gaia's atmospheric membrane 'touch' into the cosmic realms beyond. The Song affirmed our commitment to 'walk, sail, sing' along this line, our intent for blessings to emanate, radiate, stream in joyous freefall as gold-silver rain through said line to infill, suffuse the whole of Gaia's world – from planetary core all the way out to … (you get the picture).

In subtle sight I could see the 'all-of-the-All' inwith Gaia's spheric plane from a place of walking witness even as my physical sight took note of knobby tree-roots on a silent forest path while PeacePole kissed the earth at my side. A sudden sound in the underbrush; a figure slipped behind a huge chunk of Mountain tumbled down from the ancient past. Chamois – sacred to the Sidhe of the Alps. The Song's chorus stood ready for a verse melody which was burbling to surface consciousness:

Enter realms of Faerie on the backs of Chamois
Portal'd presence-keepers to her treasured secrets
Enter realms of Faerie to the stellar nursery
Of our sanctuary'd Home …

We mulled over lines, scribbled, rehearsed, donned (Blue) 'hooded tarpaulin wingsuits' as protective flying gear to ascend the thermals and get safely back down again (my Amici are a whizz with subtle sewing machines!). And finally? We performed together with myriad others, crazy crickets' efforts notwithstanding to overscore, underscore and infiltrate every pore of our world-encircling summertime meadow'd chorale. Yay!

However, at this juncture, I suppose the question on lips is: Did we manage to return to fulfill our promise to that pretty Ben, Hope, of northerly realm? And sing a Song of Hope for Gaia – loud, proud, avowed and strong? To which the answer is most resoundingly in the affirmative!

But <u>much</u> happened before I could fulfill that pledge three and a half years after first 'helloing' his monolithic dial from behind a steering wheel. And for the physical, mental as well as spiritual <u>capacity</u> to make the climb, plus all requisite causes and conditions (like ducks in a row) ticked off to facilitate same, not forgetting a <u>stellar</u> team of pit-crew, supporters, family, partners, <u>and</u> compassionate professional medicos (human or non-, subtle or not-so) to help me return to <u>peak</u> condition to even get up a <u>peak</u>? My absolute <u>undying</u> eternal ever-after <u>thanks</u>. For, those three and a half years were the ones of Cancer's calling card, already relayed thanks to "Sasso"s intercessionary chapter.

But the fact I <u>could</u> return to Hope, as promised, <u>and</u> sing a Song of Hope for Gaia from his summit perhaps describes the absolute <u>glee</u> with which our journey not only 'happened' but the simple salient <u>fact</u> I am still here to tell it. So, would you like to hear the tale because it's sweet as sweet can be?

• • • • •

October 2022: Road-trip. Starting point: Home. End point: Home. Via (ancestral): Home. I wanted to arrive the old-fashioned way, by ship crossing the North Sea to 'slow' the coming, to verily 'announce' our arrival in-House (to its spirits of Mountains, Waters, Ancestors, Flora, Fauna) in the way I had years earlier learnt but with a wee shift of text: "Hello <u>my</u> House". All the way there (and Bilbo'd back again) this was the mantra on Annie-lips. A self-gift (for 60th); my diagnosis at 57 having rocked a family where the youngest still in high school. Never underestimate a clan's <u>collective</u> will to Life even if I remained (relatively) circumspect about what dis-ease desired to teach in the living/dying 'stakes'. Anyhow … we drove, we arrived – for me, return; for partner, F, the (wondrous) 'shock of the new'.

The day earmarked for Hope looked fine enough from the trailhead, yet soon enough the weather closed in. As we ascended, though, the Morrigan called, officially welcoming us to country and this was enough for me to know we were expected, and all would unfold as intended. Perhaps a brief intermezzo is required here to put the above comment in context.

Earlier I described how, in wake of our Scots reconnaissance trek in 2019, Story and Song began an exuberant co-produced freefall in company of the Amici. One of these works was "Leeks & Peas", the mythic retelling of our OnePeople'd ancestry, a fictional container for Memory's resurrect in a purity of bardic voice I was honoured to breathe into Being. This offering desired to enter the World of Time (this time) at Imbolc 2020 – the Celtic goddess Brigid's signature celebration. As the Story rushed itself to be written, a day came when I heard and immediately transcribed the following words spoken from within the reservoir of my own <u>genetic</u> consciousness:

Some called her the Morrigan. She answered only to the Mistress of the Moon in a lightening Sky. And in her Grace, now, she said to the Sisters: "Fly!"

I was already cognisant of our Sister'd lineage (a later chapter delves into this further), so too the importance of naming Moon as a strategic mentor thereto, and had penned an 'invocation' (a common literary device in the Western classical tradition) to commence Story accordingly. Now I affirmed in vision was the specificity of Morrigan's shapeshift to Raven as an 'invocation' itself to Sister'd service. Since, wherever or whenever I meet this majestic creature (in material or Malakut dimensions), I know it to foreherald my Sisters' presence.

Yes, we often meet in subtle sight – I have felt their peck of affection while meditating in garden grail with their respective stone-giant 'anchors' (one's beak vibrant emerald green; the other's stellar royal blue); I have also stood in their midst while our three ex-world 'elder' Sisters offer counsel to our work for Gaia. Their feather-ruffed shrouds are truly star-sheened. But when met in physic'd field of glorious high wild it offers me an immediate audible call to shift focus inward, and trust to outcomes unfolding with the support of unseen actors regardless of what weather (or other causes, conditions) toss my way. Its mantra:

We stand in Solidarity
With the Power of Presence – our own
Crystal-cloaked and Starlight-boned

Such that, as we began climbing our Ben of Hope, a pair of Ravens cawing, playing 'tag' in the heights brought me Joy at their delight of Life no matter how tough the uphill plodding in less than clement conditions (indeed, with gritted teeth I wondered where the perfect Blue and Sun-drenched smile of three years past had vanished, but I digress …). The genius loci of place reciprocated my "Hello". The resident Sidhe opened doors to shared Ceilidh. And I knew exactly which Song needed to be sung at top – "The Sisters Song" (its 'swirl-to-life' shall be met in a next chapter) – to affirm solidarity of purpose, to affirm our Hope for Gaia.

In point of fact, the night pre-climb I had visited Hope in subtle sight, walking a ridgeline where a long/low dragon-scaled concert hall/musical centre sat flush with and/or was set into the ground. The locals eagerly showed me this architectural gem risen from and crafted of Land – such a Howe of stellar Song'd intent! Silver triangular panels (like shingles) flowed as waves on roof, walls. Oh, how I enthused at the artistry! Was I meant to sing here? No, they said. It was 'closed'; my place of performance lay further on, my task to bring Hope to Hope's crown, to there sing up full my (birth) contract with ancestral, and all, Land.

And so it was to be. In physical-sight I found their concert hall gracing a side slope as we climbed; dragon-scales of sheaf'd granite and gneiss loomed out of swirling mist and again I marvelled at the engineering prowess of Sidheverse kin in/of DeepTime-Tectonia.

It intrigued me, though, as we trudged on/up into a bitter headwind, of low cloud and pitched sight, that the 'plan' – to see and call our Love to the ten directions from the most northerly Munro of famed number, as awe-inspiring a view (I was sure) as from the summit of Wyvis far to the south – would be thwarted. There <u>had</u> to be a reason; was it to prove I would go to any (miserable) lengths to fulfill my pledge? 'Twas definitely the case; when would I have another chance to lay out my Love <u>of</u> Land <u>in</u> Land with passionate resolute <u>filial</u> ardour if I had already been gifted three years more of 'Life' than medicos (data-driven) predicted?

Plus, only the day before D had called, ostensibly to wish us luck but his real reason lay deeper, to get my 'reading' on a vivid dream which had truly spooked him – a black stallion, emasculated, dying of starvation, an abandoned farm, a desolate nightscape. All this to which he bore witness but unable to offer 'help'. The whole scene, he said, suffused misery and suffering. What could it portend? Ah, dear boy … he may have been far across the waves on continental shore, but nothing could stop his tapping into the pain of the Clearances. The <u>penetrant</u> sorrow this black-as-pitch peat-bog'd Land held on behalf of our ancestry still rippled from her breast, and from there was Antipodes-led. But now we were back, to offer to Kelpie and Kin our healing balm, our resonant Song of Hope.

I soothed his raw nerves (each of our children has the 'fey-sight' as my mother calls it; his sensitivity 'ripened' in this proximate instance), told him it would turn out arights. I carried with me healing gifts in the spirit of our Amici prayer: "The Green of a Land that is never Dead when the Blue of the Stars flood the World with their Seed" (solidly Raven-beak'd at that, gobstopper-crunched to best Anwa'd effect). I had Seed/s sourced from the Peace of HomeLands; I had Song, (seven) Sister'd and strong; I had connector-threads woven 'tween (seven) Seas and more; plus Moon – watchful, wakeful – was ready to get busy in this, her perennials-planting cycle. Aye, sweet boy, it would turn out arights …

We arrived up top; first F, ahead of my bent-double-by-wind progress. Suddenly he called, pointed skyward. Up from the very bones of stone, rising out of the soup of fog, from their own hunkered-down shelter (makeshift cirque behind summit cairn for just such conditions as this – intended for human occupants, however!) flew the Raven pair. Their Morrigan shrouds regally billowing, flared fingered-wings widespread for sailing. Oh! <u>Perfectly</u> on cue, curtain peeled back for <u>their</u> entrance on stage at <u>our</u> anticipated approach. Who would have thought? Low they stayed, cresting our heads, with a nod of recognition reciprocate – these Sisters, precious Sisters (!) – before off, on, away. Waiting, they had been, waiting to salute our pilgrims' progress, and to remind that here, right here Song must part my lips and frozen fingers plant my gifts.

For Hope. For Gaia. For All.

Well, Reader, it's one thing to be ecstatically present to, and in the moment of, Morrigan'd presence, of knowing we had traversed a portal, entered an interdimensional (literally) mist-riven space – temenos to all intents where our performance would resonate, 'stick', seep deep into a Ben's bony hide. Yes, that's one thing, but the other? When chillingly enveloped by pea-soup, it's pretty jolly difficult to feel ecstatic – shivering, wondering if we'd find a way back down without slipping off a cliff we couldn't see.

The point is the Raven Sisters waited <u>purely</u> for this reason. I was <u>totally</u> destroyed by the cold/wind. Relentless, being inside that cloud – buffeted, pummelled as hard by sky-waves as any Minch sea-crossing ferry (and, as luck (or not) would have it, also of several hours' sickening tossing, she wryly notes). To be frank, I wasn't in a space of Song at all, plus had <u>completely</u> forgotten the contents of my pockets (beyond tissues to mop streaming nose and eyes!).

That they had waited, set sail at the <u>exact</u> moment (and in the right direction!), for us to remark their presence inwith thick cloud? A most stunning piece of Faerie magic, methinks, so that I <u>would</u> remember my intention and not just immediately hightail it out of there, freezing and drenched. (We are but small humans after all!) But their appearance, like apparitions ('real' or 'conjured'? thank heavens F was there to bear physical witness!), made me stop short, reflect on <u>what</u> we had done, and regroup on <u>why</u> we had come.

"Give me five minutes," I said to the patiently shivering F, popped on an extra jumper, checked co-ordinates (as I simply could <u>not</u> see diddly squat; where lay 'True North' in dense-as-bog fog?), squirreled gifts in/to a small cave beneath a SingingStone, called the Morrigan's spell to Life, and then performed our Song/s of Hope from/with this vibrant peak's resonant soul.

Back at the car, Hope (now in sunlight) waved, grinned. Well … nothing for it but to just wave back! We drove 'the long way home' to fully circum-nav this enriched <u>and</u> enriching stretch of Flow Country; it took us round another pretty Ben (Hope's brother, Loyal) which brought twin haikus to life in celebration of their filial twinning (stone-boned and with Love brimming):

Dear Bens, heaven-sent
Meta-physically-morphose'd
Like me, top to toe'd!
Dear Bens, next best friends
Presiding over your moor
Who could ask for more?

The Flow Country. Ben'd <u>and</u> Bog'd, I met so many Sidhe locals in wake of our ascent, eager to demonstrate <u>their</u> work for Gaia; lasses whose 'logo' was a beautiful (blue/green) dragonfly, whizzing off in carts down the road, bursting with Joy to plant Seeds of same in-world. Yes, Ben'd, Bog'd; now also Dog'd? For I was invited to a school classroom to discuss future projects, and there was presented with a dog as my future companion of/to this Land. A slim whippet, doe-eyed, very demure, circumspect, flower-bedecked – subtle embroidery seamed to her sleek silver'd coat. Such a beauty! What a gift! Swift as Wind for we Walkers of same, especially in wild woolly (Big) Ben'd heights. I glowed with their generosity of spirit!

Yet for all our Ceilidh celebrating, I felt <u>searingly</u> in heart the residual poignancy of Land continuing to hold ancestral Memory's Joy and Pain <u>equally</u> on a plane of intimate exteriority. This Sink at Surface sits on a platter for us all to bear witness, contribute to its healing with our gifts of Home to Home – just as each home-place is a microcosm of Gaia's macro (home-place), a 'worksite' where we can offer our blessings in-world, then lay down our tools. At peace. Aye, child, it will turn out arights …

In vision I watched a man glide down from his (Green) Land (never dead) to shoreline, there to lie at Sea's edge looking 'North' whence our lineage in-came from stellar realms. His left leg <u>severed</u> (I winced with referred pain), nevertheless he carried it the full distance, down from the heights, placed it at his side where he lay. At peace. When the sound of his Breath came no more, (bird) Song took up the chorale, filling Dawn with pure Joy. He trusted to the future, despite the immensity of Pain endured, and so do we Amici – to the ongoing flood of the Blue of Stars (bright-lit) <u>incoming</u>. Such that, after planting Hope (in Hope), we tossed same to the penetrant black pools of Flow Country next day, straight into a cirque of Love's (liquid) Light which Sun conjured for an <u>exact</u> zenith'd moment in Time-partner'd Dreaming.

That night the energies of place came to where I stood in/on (Cancer-impacted) Body (Land), reciprocating my healing gifts with an own blessing of Hope for the future. Again, so generous! We all have stories; so many there are which require witness – to support <u>any</u> Land's healing.

How long does it take to heal this particular ancestral dreaming? A diaspora far-flung/-flown, carrying Memory of place with them/us, on?

Later, I found myself invited to a 'village hall' for a (next-best) Ceilidh in honour of those who had done so much to keep spirit-of-place (in heart/family) alive down countless <u>millennia</u>. A small group of elders around a long communal table; I offered to tell the Story, to offer the toast (literally "raise a cup of kindness yet" for "Auld Lang Syne") to my "aunt-by-marriage" (so-said) in this cross-veil space. Our blood/bone may be of different 'star-stuff', but we are Family. Pure. Her importance in my life, as a mentor and role model, brought me to this path – Home. No greater pleasure than to honour <u>her</u> contribution to community, and <u>our</u> work, in this <u>shared</u> forum. I would never forget the mystic rise of Morrigan'd Sisters from Hope's crown conjured nor the stunning clarity of being inwith shared shroud, a veil'd intertidal zone to ensure our blessing held the (Song) line – Home ...

It may seem I am labouring the point of connectivity established with the Sidhe of Highlands and Flow Country. But the purpose behind my detailed notes was trifold. Initially so surprised (mesmerised actually) that our presence and intent did not go 'unnoticed', I wanted to honour their enthusiastic embrace by committing (the many) salient facts to (journal'd) entry. All moved at lightning-speed; it would have been too easy for my aging (oh, so simple!) mind to overlook aspects of ritual (cue Morrigan's reminder atop blustery frozen Hope), plus it gave me an opportunity to enfold things pre-seen in Malakut to support our proffered gifts.

Further, it was as if my reciprocal 'noticing' in this form helped ignite (and re-ignite) their own passion – also a surprise. Indeed, in one encounter I bore witness to efforts addressing a similar groundswell of need to that of human youth caught up in the miasma of hopelessness, despair at Gaia's (i.e. Land's) suffering. As with other times privy to how our work unfolds in Sidheverse (as described in my earlier books), such 'sight' reinforced my understanding that loving outreach and respectful partnership as community on the back of our shared ancestral past for a thriving Gaian future is an integral component for younglings on both sides of veil to be able to find their way Home – to come again into 'right relationship' (as Aboriginal elders call it) with Land.

Thirdly, the notes help me, with the Amici, return to these zones of Presence at will, to engage (and re-engage) our co-productions with local partners, whether physically present or not. An important facet for small human Annie is to ensure none of her 'bits' gets lost along the way. The different intertidal and liminal settings of shared Song can be confusing unless one is fully familiar with the terrain. While the fact of DeepTime-Tectonia has similarities everywhere and everywhen, Sink-at-Surface can be another matter entirely if one has not 'walked' Land with as much (and vigorous) constancy of praxis as each stretch of HomeSong demands. Genetic memory only takes me so far; the notes deepen my connectivity with each re-reading and meditative re-membering. Especially with OldMan's cairn (which I had hoped to re-engage on 2022's trip but 'twas not to be – one assumes that was also 'inner-intentional') – slow-walking in/out of the FiveGates full-open (invoking the ten directions full-present) – requires careful management, for which I thank my collaborators wholeheartedly.

Following, however, is the '22 note which I am most grateful to have had the wherewithal to scribble, here in its raw form – its energy of uplift and what it wanted to share truly profound:

O18: Presence abounds; Presence is on the move on this, our last on Island, the day

I farewell all that has been with thx/good grace. Overnight a line <u>slicing</u> through Land North-South diagonally. In the North was an 'egg' – <u>cooked</u>, un-runny, as if hard-boiled. But no 'shell' for its outer <u>membrane</u> was clear glass or crystal, no veil to mar direct view onto the Otherworld. I was told this egg was the portal (of <u>return</u> to our OnePeople'd origins as a <u>future</u> proposition) and it was <u>open</u> – clear through; it excited me greatly to see this materialise at a <u>specific</u> place in scape. I am in the South when this message comes in while it's far/far in the North, but it can still find me here? As if a reminder (before leaving Land) that it has <u>always</u> been here, in <u>this</u> spot, although hardly any 'see it' and/or <u>definitely</u> don't see it the way I see it – as a clear membrane one can pass through without problem.

Others may see an egg, shell'd/solid and/or know the portal is accessible but are not interested in making the return/crossing. V. difficult to describe but when I fully woke it was to stand at window (on this world) as Dawn (of Time) slow-painted Sky. Much to work with; <u>much</u> to contemplate once back to Helvetia's fireside. But this last 'sight' onto Home feels like an honour of the highest magnitude on this day I leave ancestral shores, by ship, like my forebears. I will <u>always</u> know my way Home. The door is always, has always been, open. The Egg has a Tail; it is Me set sail yet ever/always connected. Blessings! Heartfelt gratitude to all!

• • • • •

So, dear Reader, we have talked Bens and Bogs seemingly ad nauseum in this rambling chapter but what of Dogs beyond a sweet (whippety) lass, far from the (promised) Scottie of title? Well, that's a yarn and a half stretching all the way back in our family archive – specifically to Disney films on an Aussie couch.

While I had enjoyed such 'golden oldies' at the local cinema (in countless annual reruns), by the time progeny arrived we could rent the classics from a video store (my, how videos seem like ancient history too these days!). Amongst these, "Lady and the Tramp" stood out. Why? Because of Jock, the gruff Scottie who offers counsel to Lady about her many woes (tricksy Tramp inclusive). While we each adored this character, it was elder son, S, who at the tender age of three (golden curls, chubby cheeks) announced very solemnly to the world:

"I want a Scottie Dog."

And kept announcing it throughout childhood <u>and</u> youth while myriad cats and dogs took up residence in household/s, none of which 'Scottie'. Well, as with most things engraved in family lore, it turned into a one-liner for any/all of Life's disappointments ("Oh, if only we had a Scottie Dog!" etc) whose pinnacle was reached when younger son, D, and I headed off on the first Scots adventure: "Better bring me back a Scottie Dog!" Alas, the closest we got was Scottie Dog shortbread biscuits (in fetching tartan bows), but it kept the joke 'live' that Christmas with much laughter all round.

Now we cut to our <u>descent</u> from Ben Hope three and a half years after first reconnaissance. By the time we were midway down, the weather had (surprisingly, or not) cleared. Wonderful views stood before me so I stopped to snap a couple of pix of the broad burnished heather scape spread like woven plaid across the strath below. At that moment who should be coming up over the rise, destined for summit cairn, but a couple with their ... Scottie Dog! Oh my goodness! Can you imagine how I gushed over this wee fellow (whose name was Lachlan, but as black and shaggy as Disney's Jock)? The couple stood quietly smiling while I regaled them with the story of S as a three-year-old ... blah blah blah. And then it was their turn to share a bit of (hemispherically interwoven) history:

"Actually, Lachlan is an Australian-born Scottie."

Seriously? This delightful pair had emigrated to the bush of Australia's 'highlands' some ten years earlier but as soon as international borders reopened post-Covid knew they wanted to come home – for good – and introduce their sweet Lachie to the Auld Country of his heritage (climbing Bens a given!). They kindly agreed I could take a pic of their lad as a gift for mine (better than biscuits!) and we farewelled each other – them to the mists above, us to the vale below. And with that bit of Magic safely in the can/cairn, is it any wonder a few months later when casually walking past a Milanese tailor's shopfront, home to S's (self-described) 'lucky' silk tie of many years prior (my vague idea being to source a birthday gift for his next stage of life) to find the sumptuous window display featuring a silk tie with fetching Scottie Dog motif? Oh, how I laughed. Bingo – squared, methinks – in the (Lady) luck stakes!

But to close the cirque on (Scottie) Dog'd heritage, a Songline inscribed between hemispheric homelands, S will receive an ancestral gift this Christmas to complete this curious binding of familial knowing, for passing forward through his own next generations. It's a surprise, but shall I whisper it?

See, when she emigrated as a young lass, my great-grandmother brought with her a wee brooch for pinning to her (special occasion) black silk shawl (long since dissolved to dust). 'Twas a pair of Scottie Dogs (one white, one black) rediscovered amongst her (several) trinkets. No (Story'd) history accompanied the keepsake as it passed between mother/s and daughter/s (till now it shall enter the safekeeping of a son). Did the family have Scotties which couldn't make the journey with them? Or had she, since a tiny tot, made the same solemn decree to world ("I want a Scottie Dog") and this was as close as she got?

Like so many stories, lost to the mists of time, but still the resonance lives on (and veritably sings!) in this treasured relic now destined to grace the 'lucky' tie of a lad who not only inherited her mitochondrial DNA but the Love of a breed with which it was liberally infused. Yay – the Scottie Dog of (chapter) title has (at last) been honoured!

Ancestral connectivity with associations of fey whimsy in its inherited memory? How would you like another, dear Reader? This time un-Dog'd? I'm sure you will get as much of a giggle as I did when pulling the Card Deck of the Sidhe out for a recent chat – long after returning from respective Auld Country adventures, and a decade since the Fallen Stone self-naming "in honour of Hope" (see "Appendix 2" for full Deck self-naming).

But did clueless Annie, in all those intervening years, <u>ever</u> 'see' its connection to our ascent of a Ben called Hope? Or to the fact of Morrigan met at summit? For there she is, Reader, in Jeremy's very painting, skating scene above SingingStone (recumbent). Yet for all that I had never registered such (outwith-Time) synchronicity? Never mind – good for a laugh, and with thanks to the Amici for their enfolding wit <u>and</u> focus so sweet Annie can (at long last) see!

RETURN TO SOURCE (CODE/X)

It is many years since I 'told' the myth of the SkyChild to myself in oracular voice during a visionary experience. It is also many years since I 'heard' (on another random day) Sun sing: "Don't be afraid of me" in the innocent voice of a solemn mini-kid, urging humanity to not take for granted his Life-giving properties for on-Earth ecology. In a third manifestation on theme, many years have equally passed since I Malakut-wandered my childhood garden (half a world away from the Swiss Alps of now) and watched a toddler plunge her face into a swatch of Jacaranda blossom to emerge laughing with delight, her eyes backshone by starlit Blue. She was being held in arms by the Great Mother herself. And afterwards was passed into my cradled care ...

So many years since these first inklings, but it was only in Summer 2019 as I hummed Sun's tune (while walking a sniffy dog on a pleasantly warm day) that the extant verses of what was to become "The SkyChild's Song" decided it was time to populate (or perish) by rhizomatically connecting self with Self, micro with macro.

In a flash, I understood that the original SkyChild is Gaia, the World Soul of our planetary (Third-Rock) home – Earth – whose <u>desire</u> to foster Life, whose Joy to "ignite our precious Blue" with Love (as I sang in the coda to the poetic symphony, "Blue's Third", 2018) was accompanied by the counsel and godmother/ fathering of Sun, Moon, Stars – all her cosmic kin – to which she responded with the deep resounding 'I am!' of Spirit penetrant (geologic) Flesh.

Indeed, in selfsame flash, I understood that each of us – in choosing to incarnate in-world – likewise <u>sings</u> into being our desire to co-participate in Life on Earth, to co-steward planetary consciousness and evolution with Love and Care, Respect and Nurturance. Our birth contract, like Gaia's, like that of all true nature'd sentience, is founded on igniting this spark of Love within and manifesting it in our own lives. But the environmental crises humanity has ignorantly (and, too often, arrogantly) 'birthed' has me wondering how we could possibly have forgotten Love as our sole/soul 'gift' (in English = 'present' or 'talent') to Gaia's holistic ecology (and all that follows therefrom) rather than the all-too-tragic 'gift' (in German = 'poison' or 'toxin') arising from our perceived 'needs'.

"The SkyChild's Song" was penned, rehearsed and first publicly sung at the Winter Solstice 2019, part of a performance of "In-Frame: A Blue Planetary Symphony (Stretches of Song'd Line)" – my voice adopting that of the wide-eyed excited mini-kid being offered the opportunity to <u>impregnate</u> her very Soul in Stone, the toddler plunging her face into a swatch of emergent blossom, seeing into the All it could become with Love and Purity of Intent. In 'my' return to 'her' source (code/x'd) I could re-sing us both into wondrous re-membering.

In that same symphonic performance another work, "Muted Earth", premiered. While its focus was on the crises of our human-making (described in preceding paragraph), it included the following stanza which, as Poetry, coequally spoke to the wellspring from which "The SkyChild's Song" was uplifted, viz:

All the while Great Mother (Gaia) dreams –
of when first agreed did She to be this World.
Birth Contract signed, sealed, inscribed in flesh.
Spirit/geology mergent at BigBang'd behest.
I am! did She cry to the gods on high.
Great arcs of Joy showered the sky. And, oh –
how Mother laughed! Called all to her door!
Sun Moon Stars (helpmates of hour) (at all hours).
Not one not excited by grand experiment conjured.

While the writing of "Muted Earth" post-dated the arrival of "The SkyChild's Song" in its final iteration, it preceded the Song at Winter Solstice performance. The reason? In this excerpt, Gaia – her voice rendered <u>mute</u> by our species' heaviness on physical planes of existence, as well as the <u>seep</u> of malaise into subtle dimensions ("sloughs of despond," I call this) – tells the Story of "When the Old People were Young" to the Child, and closes by urging:

So sing, She says,
squeezing tight the Child's hand.
Now is your turn. To sing …

This passage (which, in its fuller form, was highlighted in "Sasso"s chapter) speaks directly to all 'Children of the Stars' who share the same (cosmic human) lineage, committing in their incarnation to World to serve the unfold of planetary purpose. In our <u>forgetfulness</u> of Song, we neglect our responsibility. All Gaia is asking is that we remember, and so "The Sky Child's Song" debuted at Solstice after "Muted Earth"s recitation to avow that we Amici stand firm in our contractual obligation. Now is our turn. To sing …

In the wake of performance, the Amici asked me to get busy – penning the myth of our OnePeople'd cousinly Commons as a third iteration of Gaia's origin story. By so doing, the intent was to provide an opportunity to in-weave the <u>relevance</u> of our collective birth contract with Earth. "Leeks & Peas" (housed in our "Grail Within" volume) is the container for this myth, from which there are two key scenes I would like to quote in regard to this discussion.

The first is when the Human maiden, Generva (betrothed to the Elf lad, Conall), is welcomed to the Beltaine festival on their side of veil by Conall's mother and sisters – the five elders who dance the alchemy of Light on behalf of Land. The lead sister, Conall's aunt, takes up the story of Gaia's origin myth:

It started with the innocence of a very young child discovering the world, the glory of the world for the first time," Sirona began, her voice taking on a depth and resonance beyond her earlier speech; a voice which delved deep into the reservoir of collective memory to uplift an origin myth for fresh ears; one she knew by heart but each time, herself, discovered anew.

The child was full of wonder at the Beauty of the world, this vibrant Blue crystalline jewel she beheld for first time. A girl-child she was, of wide-eyed innocence at the magic offered for her witness. And her eyes – like mirrors of shone glass – reflected the all of her Joy back to its source, our beautiful world. Such was her Joy, open-mouthed and full of delight, that her arms made great arcs of her Joy in the Sky; great sweeping circles of Blessing did she make through each and all directions as she beheld their every wonder.

There was no right or wrong, good or bad, this or that in her virginal worldview. All was: This! And look! Now: This! And now: This! And now: This! All glorious, profound and new in its virtue. All was Love expressed in Form as she, too, Love expressed in Form. It just was; she just was. Such that aloud did she cry: 'I am!'

The whole world became her echo in the moment; this whole vibrant Blue jewel resonated her 'I am!' as its own. Indeed, she and the wonder she beheld were one – in consequent communion, as mergent and seamless as the unseen Breath that fuels all Life, the unseen Hand that giveth-taketh, the unseen Love at the core of each expression of Being, the unseen Light that Joy ignites to loving Form. No matter what it was, whence it came (Flower, Sun, Bird), it sang to her and she responded in Joy, or she sang to it, it responded likewise. Plunging her face into Jacaranda'd blossom – laughing, laughing. Nothing but laughter.*

Cernunnos, the great God of Forest, Lord of all Animals, conjured for her over and over an infinitude of wonders that could come into being with her presence in world expressing this shared and pure Joy. And suddenly here stood a chorale of blessed Commons at her silver starlit door to say: 'Come! Come! Please be our world! Stay!'

This is her Story; this is our Story. We call her the SkyChild, the one whose Story we share.

"So she is Mother – Earth, the Goddess," Generva said.

"Yes," Sirona nodded. "But never forget her origin, that she was once a Child of the Sky; never forget she sang her way to being our sanctuary'd home – her Joy at once was one with the Joy of world in Time. We all sing the same Song to bring us here, to magic our incarnation to Earth's divinity. And if we forget?"

"Then we forget why we came; we forget to serve the Goddess and all Life in our Joy."

This scene speaks directly to what Mariel describes to David during one of their first conversations:

"The simplest metaphor is that our ancestors worked with sound and spoke or sung into being whatever they were seeking to manifest. … The world itself was like a giant vibrating crystal singing in the vastness of the cosmos, and our ancestors came to sing with it in a choir of unfoldment and evolution. What you must understand is that the capabilities of our ancestor still live within us. You have a word for it: we are fractals of that ancient being."

Of course, the way Mariel and David conduct their conversations is different to how I and the Amici banter back/forth using repetition, rhyme, alliteration (and hybrid word-forms drawn from several tongues, including their own), but the envisioning of ancestral origins derives from same source. Our perspective simply offers a bardic rendering of the (ancient historic) mythic code/x that <u>blends</u> our cousinly energies, thereby elaborating on its purpose. Long before <u>anything</u> was language'd on parchment, it was orally passed down from generation to generation. The way "Leeks & Peas" is written, therefore, adheres to this tradition in the spirit of Tolkein's "Mythopoeia":

Blessed are the legend-makers with their rhyme
Of things not found within recorded time.

Now to the second scene – after Conall and Generva are wed, and living on the human side of veil, but with elven blood running strong through their first-born (toddler) son's veins:

'Twas then she heard the humming, rising above the sound of a birdsong'd eve issuing from the hedge abutting vege patch, so too from the shady branches of OldMan (yonder), an EverTree that had EverBeen. A sweet air, it seems, the boy had made up; each round

of notes longer than the last but always ending in the same words:

"*Don't be afraid of me ...*"

She listened closer, heard:

"*No, don't be afraid; don't you be afraid; don't you be afraid of me ...*"

She shifted the pot a mite aside from the full of fire, wiped hands on her pinny, and came to the door. "What song be ye teaching our lad, Conall? Who could ever be afraid of one such as thee, my precious sweet!' and knelt to envelope Kyle in a hug.

Dry-eyed and solemn he looked up at her, said in language beyond his years: "'Tis not me, Mother, of whom I sing, but another who would use my Breath as Voice."

"*Who then?" she asked. "Who makes so plaintive a request of the world?"*

And so sang again, but each time the words did he garble till the final line sung strong. Closer did she draw to his voice, pressed her very ear to his lips and there, at last, heard the voice which used his Breath in Song. So gently, with Love, spoke the one who said:

"*Sun is in his Shining Sky, Sun is in his Shining Sky, saying: Don't be afraid, don't be afraid, don't be afraid of me ...*"

Oh! Her heart skipped a beat as she drew back, held Kyle at arm's length before her, looked long at the divine poppet she had birthed. There, his eyes revealed all – starlit, a-sparkle, twinkling with the innocence of this lullaby sung into being. A first time, each time, since a BigBang had brought the world into manifest existence.

Yes, here he sat, cross-legged at the feet of his father, to whom she now looked.

Conall smiled into her quizzical expression, shrugged. "I taught him nothing. But I do know the air; 'tis the Song of our OnePeople. He's uplifted it from memory, in company of his living doll. We call it The SkyChild's Song. I sang to my mother also. And I remember the exact same scene – how she came, wondered at my whispered melody."

He looked into the past, said: "In the days before the veil came down, Mother journeyed far with her Sisters to do the Goddess' work, in blessing of the Land. Here she was on the eve of another long journey, and here I was singing to her the memory of Sun's original petition to all beings in the world!"

He laughed, shook his head. "Of course, Mother knew the Song, but still she shed a fair few shining tears. Like yours now. Grateful for the Love and Grace with which the Song continues to be handed down – in thought, untaught. Like a child learning to walk, it just happens. Like a babe's first Breath taken, then another, and another. So it with Song. There is more to it, of course, but he will learn it in time – on his own, in company of the doll, as it should be."

Indeed, for Kyle the Song would unfurl the extent of its knowing in time just as it did for me. In early raw form did I uplift it years before in heart till a moment came when it emerged fully-fledged (while walking a sniffy dog no less) on a warm random more-than-muse-worthy day.

With its advent, I felt to know Gaia more profoundly, as if a deeper level had been plumbed of <u>her</u> journey of Life, <u>her</u> conscious choice to incarnate/

be our World. Again, I stress that the more any of us know/understand Gaia, the more She knows herself; as our consciousness evolves, so does hers. 'Tis a dance, a divine marriage (or partnership) of ensoul'd Land in ensoul'd Hand. In short, our matter matters, as does hers. And our mirroring of Joy at the Beauty of World, just as our SkyChild experiences, exponentialises her own, snowballing it over/over, tossing it forth/back to World through all ping-pong'd leylines of Time as Love's liquid Light from Purity's wellspring'd Source deep-coddled at Mountain's (code/x'd) heart:

> *Never doubt the power of redoubt at feltworld core*
> *This have I learnt from gods, goddesses and more*
> *Now to return to Source (code/x)*
> *belly of Memory's sublime resurrect*
> *To fresh-enliven what it means to be Her*
> *our World Soul who chose to be our Home …*

• • • • •

Early in this volume I commented (briefly) on the three 'faerie godmothers' who steward Gaia's evolutionary consciousness. I say 'faerie' in the fey spirit of "Sleeping Beauty"'s cute wand-bearing starlit-shimmery aunties (as represented by the hand of Disney) but these are serious major stellar Presences who agreed to first midwife and then accompany the SkyChild's birth contract with Earth down all these unending millennia. They (Gondwana, Kali, Moon) have appeared in this book in the context of various discussions to date, but let me put the connections in some semblance of order to in-herald the pages which follow.

As our partnership of "Sidhe, Star and Stone" (subtitle of my first book, "Awakening") developed, it was clear I needed to understand more about how our OnePeople'd genetic lineage intersected this overall cosmic planetary 'plan' in order for our on/in-Earth work to be effectively crafted. Over many 'lessons' I found myself being inducted into our shared birthright and inheritance (or, one could say, re-inducted – 'tis an issue of recovering and uplifting from deep pools of <u>collective</u> Memory what we, on our side of veil, have forgotten of our own "SkyChild's Song"). These lessons often play for me as a theatre production in which I am both participant and witness. On the Sidhe side of veil, such performances are still conducted (and aligned with the Celtic markers of celestial year) as a means to ensure <u>their</u> younglings do not forget; I feel truly blessed to be invited to join these gatherings in order to understand more, <u>and</u> better, myself!

Let's get back to the faerie godmothers, though, who are, to all intents and purposes, Sisters, and who are, to all intents and purposes, tripartite form/s of a sole/soul Presence. Many spiritual traditions hold to the divine feminine impulse/principle in maiden-mother-crone iterations – presenting whichever face is required according to the need at hand. In the end, it matters not 'who/

what' is behind the face/s. I just feel so extraordinarily humbled, awed that such major entities spontaneously arrive and stay the distance in sponsorship of the 'lily-white' acts of our little worldworking troupe! At some stage, an 'aha' moment of true revelation may arrive (in an "Oh! It was you all along!" way) but there is no need to clog this text with explication. For our purposes herein, we shall call them GKM in Annie-shorthand.

Last things first.

Moon, for all the reasons shared in this book (and more!) I know as the 'nurturing' force of the three. Kali, our mover and shaker, is the tough Love 'change-maker' of trio. Gondwana? Well, she finds me anywhere, anywhen because her brief is the steadiness of DeepTime-Tectonia – she is the 'Rock' as the 'Rock' is her.

Just to be clear.

It may seem there's a pantheon of gods, goddesses, sages, saints offering counsel and/or patronage to our Amici worldworking troupe but in truth, I append names to forms (following functions) as they appear – based on what they share, in the <u>context</u> of their sharing. All serve the Great Sacred Mystery, as do we. One could place all of this in a hierarchy (as various spiritual traditions and mystery schools are wont to do) but regardless of age, wisdom or awe-inducing, gobsmacking, challenging energy signatures engaged, I see us all inhabiting the same planal membrane of 'consistence', inwith a spheric diagram of equals in a Universe that just keeps wanting to expand with all the Love shared by choristers physic'd of skin or not!

We each contribute according to our skills, resonance, unique way/s of engaging Life as well as according to our own Soul's evolutionary path through myriad dimensions and across a multiplicity of (ant-army'd) interstellar rhizomes since a BigBang before beginningless Time (if not before). For my own part, each and all are Family (and we know how complicated family gatherings can be when we cannot connect via a 'like language'!). We each host Love's Light at core of self-sovereign Being. This has and ever will be my primal 'language' of connection – 'tis my mother-tongue. Literally.

So, back to my learning of the role of GKM as vast planetary (sister) Presences, as ancient as (brother) Sun's 'assembling' of solar system, as ancient as the first whorling unfold/s from the aether of DeepTime alchemy.

A very intriguing theatre production I participant-witnessed once involved the divine marriage of Gaia with Earth's (Third) Rock – the moment of Spirit (hers) incoming to the chamber of Geology (its). It was a midsummer play in Sidheverse – a very lit space, simultaneously indoor/out. An arbour of vines/flowers, church pews set within a clearly defined framework for such a ceremonial event, a raised area for an altar where the couple would stand.

Preparations complete, priestess in place, as well as several 'elders' needed to speak blessings at certain junctures, the girl 'flew' in from her home to alight/float down into the space. Young, maidenly, her whole demeanour said: Joy. A 'Hand' had brought her here, a massive Hand which released its (gentle) grasp of hers a few metres above the ground. From here she effortlessly floated down to her position before the altar (bouquet, lovely filigreed dress, hair braided with blossom – in short, the whole gorgeous works).

I knew the Hand as Gondwana (but equally as Moon/Kali) – a wisdom-keeper in the spirit of "When the Old People were Young" (see "Muted Earth"). Gondwana's depths of knowledge about Earth (Gaia's 'future partner') would ever be 'on-hand' to support her as their together-Life unfolded. Further, the Hand may have 'given her away' (in that classic form of traditional marriage) and then 'dematerialised' during the ceremony, yet I understood that the Hand never truly left. It remained quietly near; if the maiden <u>ever</u> wanted to return home, if this 'grand experiment' of spirit/geologic marriage didn't work out, she could call to the Hand, reach out, take it. At which – bingo – she'd be 'teleported' back. To the Stars.

This was a <u>very</u> sobering realisation for me. It spoke not only to Gaia's birth contract (her "I am" of Spirit penetrant Flesh in "The SkyChild's Song"); it spoke not only to the commitment of GKM to continue as godmothering stewards to Gaia's evolutionary consciousness for the <u>duration</u> of her contract; but it spoke to the very <u>real</u> responsibility of all of us 'Children of the Stars' to play <u>our</u> part in this extraordinary production of Life in/of/with Gaia's Earth to help the marriage work. I stood in the pews at back, blanched by this new layer of genetic heritage plumbed. Yet I stood, and accepted the mantle of Gaian stewardship, the equal (in my own small human hands) of any GKM offered.

Such loving insight I had been granted onto the Hand's presence and purpose, its steadiness and constancy. Always there – in support. Yet ever-ready to whisk her away if things got too tough. So, are things too tough? Or is it a case that when the going gets tough, the tough get going? Read on, dear Reader, read on …

• • • • •

"In-Frame", the symphony performed at Winter Solstice had three movements (or 'stretches of Song'd line' as I called them). The first, "(Primal) Origins", contained early works of our Amici'd collaboration. The works comprising the second stretch, "(Unspoken) Presence", were sung into being during our <u>seriously</u> Song'd Summer '19 adventures as I walked (with partner F) "Home-to-Home" (recounted in earlier chapters). The intent of third stretch, "(Eterno'd) Ritorno", was (like TS Eliot) to return all to its beginning and know it for the first time. It was here that "Muted Earth" appeared, followed by "The Sky Child's Song", with a "Sailor's Charm" (of Peace-Love-Light in-weave) to conclude, and bind all to itself, thus closing the energetic circuit of Love's Light brought in-world.

My performance was conducted in pain – back pain to be precise. A niggle which had grown to become a wince and a hobble since "Muted Earth" had been penned, rehearsed. I would walk the house wailing/keening or dispassionately speaking the crone's wisdom as required. This, commensurate with Australia's 'Black Summer' 2019-20 which saw a tsunamic wave of fire consume the eastern seaboard of continent, my personal stretch of down under HomeSong. Some of us are more robust (and/or less attuned to the grid) than others. My borders are nothing short of porous (always have been – "thin-skinned" my mother called it) and lain on a foundation of connectivity across dimensional planes which my mentor, Mr1300BC, likened to keeping the door of my heart fully-open no matter what 'happened'. In that way I would always have access to the in-stream/out-stream of Love's Light, fully a-flow like the River (of Life) that knows, intimately, its way home to Sea, its very Source.

And, for all the 'happenings' this porosity has presented me with in Life, I wouldn't have it any other way. My depths of com-passion mean I can see into/ verily 'live' another's suffering – e.g. Gaia's, her innocent children's – and pen/ perform such works as "Muted Earth" from direct experience. Based on an Amici action we designed to, in some small way, help efforts 'on the ground' in Australia to quell the inferno (Tree a true ally in our work), I wrote a (long) Story ("The Tree of Life") to join the other texts published in "Grail Within".

I was <u>deeply</u> in the space of our actions, Gaia's anguish. My own pain could wait. That was when the Amici (one January 2020 morning) yelled in my ear: "Subductive urgency!" A blood Cancer whose happy side-effect was dissolving bone. I laughed. 'Subductive urgency' truly was an appropriate hybrid word-form in the circumstances. The extent of my porosity had rendered sweet Body's skeletal structure honeycomb. Only half of 'me' existed.

"What are all those pretty blue dots?" I innocently asked my (equally sweet) oncologist a fortnight later as he pulled up the results of a CT scan on his computer. He looked at me soberly: "That's where there's nothing – no bone." I laughed again. We Amici work the 'Blue' in whichever way, shape or (non-) form we can. Here was just another opportunity for (holey, holy) Song, <u>and</u> for the practice of mirroring Joy, being a shone-through (void'd) mirror to Gaia's Joy of Self – infilling the wellspring with Peace-Love-Light lived. How could anything a doctor say take me from this work of blessing our World Soul? Instead, in fact, it served to exponentialise my Joy of same because of the (high) potential for limiting factors in Time-partner'd physic-intersect than a small human Annie hoped of her Body's blood/bones et al.

The irony that our Amici troupe's actions, taking us deep into Gaia's tectonic layers (the root-knowing of her bones, flowing Light through all subtle bloodlines of Earth) had (as I intuited), directly impacted my health was not lost on me. Indeed, I could immediately identify the exact moment (and place) (<u>and</u> felt-sense) when a (subtle) pre-cog arrived that something 'serious' <u>could</u> be possible given our catacomb'd forays, as well as each pre-cog over years thereafter till 'subductive urgency' was yelled in a (blindsided) ear. (My journal notes are a boon across many fronts, Reader, when dominos start falling left, right and centre.)

But in irony lay opportunity. In poison lay cure. In its house of old was squirrelled the key to new. In recovering what had been forgotten from the fragrant wells of DeepTime-Tectonia to which we had been granted access? It could be fresh envisioned, re-birthed – as/to/for Life. Mine. Gaia's. All's. In brief, I attended Gaia's pain, at source and, when pulled (actually yanked) back out of that traumatic well by the hand of Love, it was to the words (code/x'd):

"It's about patients/patience and how Immersion is served."

As with all renderings of sagic wisdom, it was up to me to crack the code of its dual/duel (phonetic) precept. At the time I thought we could 'contain' the <u>immersive</u> praxis of healing Gaia's 'root-pain' in the subtle dimensions. But when I wrote "Muted Earth" out of this space a few years later, the shift of trauma from subtle to physic'd clearly accompanied its cri-de-coeur into my very self. My dis-ease now offering a physical corollary to hers, the more I knew and understood of myself, of my own 'polluted' system/s and undertaking a self-healing regime to redress its imbalance/s, the more I could <u>apply</u> my consciousness to support Gaia's transition – 'labouring' toward the 'birth'/evolution of a (World Soul) consciousness in which <u>all</u> could share as perpetual partners to (healing) purpose.

By being a patient (myself) and having patience (myself), would 'Immersion' best be served – my and Gaia's garden twinned; my and Gaia's garden healed … Learning to be equanimous in the face of all faced, learning to express equipoise in each encounter experienced, learning that I, too, have deep wells of courage/wisdom I can tap no matter how 'battle-worn or -scarred' this small (human) frame. 'Tis my amor fati – I see and embrace its purpose. And the Song, looping and spiralling between Soul (micro) and Soul (macro) snowballed with Joy at each opportunity for voice'd expression.

• • • • •

At this point in narrative, we need to backtrack quite a number of years, before my (active) partnership with Sidhe Amici began.

In a remote (Swiss-Italian) valley, we steward a 400-year-old cottage. The story of my love affair with this small granite dwelling, and the high wild majesty of her thick-forested mountains surrounding, dates back a couple of decades. Yes, I have described in earlier chapters how its presence and my presence therein/of has fuelled <u>much</u> down these decades. But to put our enduring relationship in context for this chapter, please bear with me now.

Our love affair dates back to a time when I, a newbie migrant to this landlocked Land, forever homesick for the wild southern Pacific shores of my birth, had an epiphany (for want of a better word). I needed to be able to put down roots in this place, physically 'plant' myself in a patch of Helvetian earth which evoked, in its own way, the true nature of home I craved. I needed a place of writing retreat in the heart of this FeltWorld and, for all its charm, nothing north of the alpine chain (which bisects this precious jewel at the centre of Europe) cut it. Think classic Swiss marketing images of green meadows, tinkling cowbells, alp herders in traditional dress – it wasn't raw enough, wild enough, remote enough from 'civilisation' to evoke the depth of connection I sought. So, we headed south across the Alps (at a time long before 'Helvetia' and 'Heart' entered my vocabulary) with a list of possible 'reno-jobs' to look at. But after months of disappointment (and a fractious two-year-old in tow), I was fast turning into a puddle of despondency.

Then, a random ad in a random newspaper (we didn't even know existed) sent us on our next quest up a dead-end valley (we also didn't know existed), its ribbon of road clinging to cliffs 400 metres above a plunging gorge; mountains looming high above. A tiny village, a church with 1570 scrawled above its fresco to San Rocco. We wended our way up stone steps, between moss-draped (stone) walls. Found the cottage, walked in. The owners beamed. The poor cottage? A mess. I would have walked straight back out again but the owners had made us lunch (this is Switzerland, after all).

Fractious two-year-old (aka D, now a uni student with no memory of this moment) began a game with the downstairs bedroom door while the adults made small talk, ingested pasta, sipped vino. It was his 'train carriage' and he the conductor. To ensure he didn't jamb fingers in this 'carriage' door, I became his (sole/soul) passenger. In, close door, babble something unintelligible, open door, out, close door: 'Next station!' On it went through several iterations and on each, inside this bedroom with door closed to the chatter at table beyond, a depth of silence began to permeate my bones. A silence which percolated and burbled (dare I say purred?) inwith this tiny space till, at last, I stood still, ignored D's babble (and potential finger-jambing) to actively listen. That's when the spirit of the cottage spoke:

"*People have slept well here. At Peace.*"

It was as if time/space stood still while I rocketed upstream in a 'way-back machine'. I saw not only into her 400-years of 'standing' history, but that of the countless millennia of geologic forces which delivered the stone to valley floor from mountain above to bring her small (integral to the whole) Presence to life. Rock tumbling down from the peak overlighting this village to create said village – a peak which I daily bless from my 'window on world' (once our major reno-job brought her (and me) the opportunity to directly connect, skin-to-skin, with the energy of DeepTime-Tectonia's genetic inheritance).

Stone holds and carries Memory, as does Wood, in its bones. Transformed, perhaps, to fresh purpose by self/other intervention down centuries, hewn and shaped to human-manageable proportions, nevertheless at its most basal, this cottage 'spoke' the same truth as the massive bouldery 'chip off the old block' in the Inn River shed: "Mountain welcomed."

My welcome here, to this fireside, equally presented the entire chain of Life into my miniscule orbit – gradually revealing it/herself more and more. No difference, no barrier. 'Size' matters not; this space is as much a container of sacred Mountain/Tree ancestral memory as any if we take the time to look <u>into</u> its bones, if we have the chance to listen to its <u>blood</u>/lines:

"People have slept well here. At Peace."

It was all she needed to say. We made our farewells; F lamented on the way to the car that 'another one bites the dust', then almost choked when I said: "No. This is it. Our family is being asked to steward this cottage through her next centuries of service. To Peace."

This Land, a small raw patch of mountainous terra firma, had adopted me; in each other we recognised a same 'wildness' of spirit; we were both fringe dwellers – outwith Time, in. Such that it was no coincidence I desired, more than anything, a direct visual link to the Ice Age-smoothed mount on the opposite side of valley, beyond the depths of gorge, as part of the reno-job. (Once, Helvetia's vast glacial ice sheet reached all the way to Milano.)

Even though I did not know why at the time (all that 'why' is housed in previous chapters), I needed a sightline to replicate what the cottage experienced daily, as matter-of-course, in <u>her</u> service to Peace. I needed a sightline to <u>triangulate</u> a link 'tween cottage, mount and back-of-valley headwaters of our rushing plunging white-water-frothed River far below (whose Source, at that stage, I had absolutely no idea I would be asked to find, and bless, a decade hence). The request to architect to create a sightline was my sole/soul non-negotiable on project; my 'window on world' was born – an arched portal (or Torii gate in the Japanese tradition) to this selfsame 'other (dimensional) side' through which, ever since, I have felt, <u>intimately</u>, the energy of the 'high wild' flow.

Four hundred years this small palace has stood her (stone) ground. At the time of her 'making' the 'WildFolk' (Wildmännli, as Swiss call the Sidhe and/or any emanation from the realms of Faerie) were <u>observable</u> fact in the Alps before their retreat to hollow hills (of which this vale has plenty). That the Sidhe are called the 'People of Peace', that my work down long years (baldly stated) has (quietly) dedicated itself to Peace (consciousness) in the 21st century, that the spirit of cottage <u>particularly</u> used the word Peace in her message at outset of our relation, and that my Amici (friends) found me here (hence their dubbing in local lingo), has proven to be a very neatly-packaged and cross-hatched synchronicity to the development of our (active) partnership in service of Gaia since – with Mountain, with Tree – under the patronage of the high wild raw strong (<u>and</u> free!) genius loci of this place, the most beautiful WolfMother.

"The Amici Files" annexed to "Awakening" contain the ins/outs of my finding of Source under the wise tutorship of Mr1300BC, and with WolfMother's blessing. As a personal (Jungian) myth, my pilgrimage thereto – a sacred well, to all intents – was intended as a first 'test' of apprenticeship, to hone the skills required to bring healing Peace-Love-Light to the collective. I found myself inducted into the full circulatory (hydrologic) cycle of Love's Light in/through World following its instreaming from stellar realms. And it all happened here. Slap bang right here in a 'forgotten valley on the border of Time':

On the edge of all yesters, at the cusp of all morrows ...

OK. So that was the first trek – home to Source (and its code/x). A (very) big day out a decade past (now). I already had the next trek in mind, a multi-day adventure for all members of family (sniffy dog reprise inclusive) the following Summer. And then, another year further on, I desired more than anything to return once more, again at Autumn gold, for another (very) big day out. That story is not told in "The Amici Files" but is of relevance here.

This time our (sniffy) dog proved insanely barky at the prospect of picnic beside the glittering ice-fringed stream tumbling down over lip of Land, beyond and out into the World (of Time). A (noisy) event, ricocheting around the bowl of Berg-Geists, it drew the bemused witness of a Chamois to the bluff above (sacred) pool. Obviously thinking this a show too good to miss, he/she decided to settle down for a longer-than gawk of Pabey's full-throttled (Pavlov'd) performance of an hour or so's (symphonic) duration. Oh, what a lark!

(Reminder: Chamois are sacred to the Sidhe of the Alps, offering their milk gladly as a wild 'farm' friend. The number of legends of human 'bad luck' as a result of hunting Chamois are plentiful hereabouts. On the positive side, though, if you are ever gifted a wheel of chamois cheese by the Wildfolk, made of Love and crystalline Light, Green with the Gold of Pure Land, never eat it all up. A small sliver must always remain so it can regrow its magic overnight!)

Three journeys did we make to my personal 'Source of all Waters', each time with a blessing gift infilled with Light to offer to the well on its own journey Home – to primordial Sea (of Being). Since that day in 2016 we had not returned – the intensity of my desire had gone down the rabbit hole of weaving-the-world with Mountain brother/sisters as documented in earlier chapters. I had thought our work in the <u>specificity</u> of this locale done. That was till my dis-ease came knocking; till my (active) work of Song hit a 'high note' (so to speak) in its delight to engage all sentience within coo-ee at each 'stopping place' on Annie-walkabout up hill/

down dale; and till Pabey – our family's faithful (sniffy, barky) squire – passed into the West, into the rest of forever sleep, seven years after our first-together trek to Source, this sacred (Helvetian castle) keep.

Frankly, it was the event of his passing, after running a doggy home-hospice for months with Love and devotion, that shunted my desire over its own lip of Land. I wanted to return as a private multi-dayer at Autumn Equinox 2021 (choir boy/packhorse ever at hip on account of my dis-ease) – to stand at Source and sing Pabey's ship (Annie-Lennox'd) on its blissful way. Home. Thus did I write an open letter to 'all ye gods' to support this quest (on health/weather fronts), to help fulfill a (pure, Love-fuelled) intent. A letter written circa five months out. That's what happens when a Cancer-compromised Body needs to get in shape for a few big days off into the (raw high) wild.

BCC, I called it: "Boot Camp for Cripples." Hence, the letter was followed by a full walking program which, as Summer Solstice approached, uplifted a <u>very</u> interesting Song.

●●●●●

Poetry Song Mantra – the three go hand-in-hand as language is woven, words strung (each to the other) like pearls on a necklace dredged up from hidden depths (full fathom five below). They also (mostly) go hand-in-hand with my meditative practice of walking, a slow-moving through world that takes me to these secret zones where my (Amici, and more) conversants dwell. A methodic reverie, metronome'd to PeacePole tap, but in the case of "SimpleSong"s arrival in time for Solstice premiere, its genesis was more than a year before.

See, after diagnosis at Imbolc 2020, it took me a while to decide how I wanted to approach this 'new place' for which Soul had 'no memory'. In considering the Air 'less foul' (a la Gandalf in the "Mines of Moria"), several months passed before I was comfortable, in Mind/Heart, to embrace a personally cobbled-together 'integrative oncology' treatment plan as wholeheartedly as those poor confused little cancer cells had embraced my blood/bone. Of course, this was time 'wasted' according to the clinic's professional team but it was/is my darling Body and I would not be bullied into doing anything I couldn't engage without complete self-clarity and sovereignty of purpose.

So the day came when I collected a stock of phyto- and chemo-meds to help Body "weed the Garden", brought them home, and welcomed them, with Love, to Team-Annie. They received their own honoured space; theirs was a tough job and they deserved much blessing since their processing in Swiss pharma institutes. I then headed to bed – next day would see our inaugural ingestion ritual commence. Now to my raw journal notes of this 'next day':

I woke this morning as if writing a Child's lament, actually the SkyChild's. "Oh!" I wrote. "How the shift happens from the idea of Life to the experience of Life! How it can go awry!" This was my point but I can't recall the exact formulation now. A play on words but suddenly overriding the lament, I heard: "Toughen up." An admonishment? A matter-of-factual observation? Taken on board. With thanks and good grace, ever, for counsel shared, counsel received ...

Earlier I commented on how I felt my/Gaia's dis-ease were entwined, that our healing, too, would therefore be drawn from the same font of Love's Light. To my surprise, however, this porosity extended to tapping into her own SkyChild's distress at how the grand experiment of Life – from idea (envisioned) to experience (manifested) – could (in Aussie-English) go 'belly-up'. It was as if I had, through my own process, tapped into a conversation she was having with her three faerie godmothers, GKM. Their response? "Toughen up." Quite.

I saw it as just another example of our twinned journeys. My commitment remained – to offer my healing practices on to her, our 'Garden' one and same. But as June rolled round the following year, this 'event' suddenly wanted to speak its full knowing – about a Gaia who now, grown beyond her SkyChild's wonder and divine marriage upsung, could see Life wasn't all a 'bed of roses'. Would she reach for the Hand, or?

I walked, I ruminated; text arrived in an Amici'd collaboration to describe situation and decision in a seeming rush. Beautiful days, I was drawn to sing Gershwin's "Summertime", populating it with lyrics drenched in my delight of planetary Garden. An unsung Land is a dead Land, and this Land can never be dead was our message. "SimpleSong" was born, and it was my task to sing it to/ for Gaia, reawaken her SkyChild's desire. I took each role in performance – hers, the godmothering Sisters, a 'wise-woman' of our OnePeople'd lineage observing their discussion, as well as invoking my own wellspring, at close – a bubbling font of Joy to (the) World. An emotional arc from lament to bliss, at each mountain pass, on each mountain top that Summer (time) of 'BCC-training' for Autumn's return to Source (code/x) I would sing.

No. Matter. What.

Gaia/I? We were/are here for the (Garden-healing) long haul. Or, as written into existence years earlier, in "Blue's Third" – a choral symphony (in solitary voice) first performed at the 2018 Winter Solstice:

Sister: 'Tis Time (so speaks the Timekeeper).

Remember –

for what we were made ...

In "Sasso"s (Waale'd) chapter can be found references to Messner's local 'Kailash', the massive Ortler massif whose ever-snows and glacial sheet crystal-refract Sun's gift to Gaia's world. Truly an 'overlighting' Presence throughout the eastern Alps straddling (Italian) South Tyrol and (Swiss) Müstair, our first 'meeting' made a significant impression. I described the outlook from Messner's

Hof, as well as the experience of driving the (double) pass road/s after our 'field-trip' back into Helvetia's domain. Specifically, I wrote:

Extreme. Extreme 'New', extreme 'Beauty', extreme 'Stone-Giants' speaking very, very loudly. Absolutely exuberant in outreach was the full cirque of power.

That was Autumn '20. Here we were (now) in June '21, an incubatory nine months hence. With a suddenness I can't properly describe, words began to populate "SimpleSong" to bind my Dogen'd knowing (of Mountains/Dragons without end) to the sublime fact of Ortler, his majestic shed, <u>and</u> his particularity of Berg/Star-Geist 'energetics' which had struck me with such force, with the intense <u>weight</u> of serious Presence in direct intersect. As I wrote in that chapter, I did not resist but embraced the density and magnitude of Love expressed. Now, as the words tumbled forth to populate the verse-narrative which prefaced my "Summertime" singing, I knew <u>what</u> I must make, and <u>where</u>, for "SimpleSong"'s energy to stick, for "SimpleSong"'s message of healing to flow out through all Songlines, known/un-, of our beautiful planetary Blue without me getting totally 'fried' in the process. I had to climb a significant mount on the <u>Swiss</u> side of border with direct sight onto Ortler's majesty and sing Gaia's/my healing from this 'safe space' into his perfect face.

Well, this was turning into a BCC without equal! F was (understandably) sceptical – my chemo regime was still in full swing. But (I argued) I needed to prove I could do <u>something</u> major before attempting our return to Source (code/x) at Equinox (equally major!).

Interestingly I had 'scoped' a mount the previous Autumn; 'just in case' we ever found our way back in this neck of the (Swiss) woods. At that stage, with no thought a Scots Highlands setting would ever feature in my (limited) life again, yet with D/my ascent of a pretty Ben in a landscape which 'spoke' volumes to our genetic heritage still 'front-and-centre' in mind, I enthused that here, in this Swiss valley, were (to all intents and purposes) Bens! OK, perhaps a bit craggier but definitely not in the same camp as the usual sharp-as-a-tack stone giants of Helvetia's main alpine chain. I remembered I took a pic for D from our valley path's witness, to satisfy <u>his</u> longing, yearning, homesickness (call it what you will) for Ben'd scapes too. Now, with SwissTopo (mapping) prowess, I found the relevant 'who' and then, with SwissHikr (trip reports) prowess investigated whether this 'who' was even doable for a BCC'd Annie.

All the while I practiced (Song, BCC-ing), sent out pleas to "all ye gods of space and time" to support this endeavour – mine, Gaia's, F's (as perturbed choirboy/packhorse). Like any of our work, only brief (clement) 'windows' exist in Helvetia's high wild (crosshatched with all other daily life considerations), and if the weather or health gods don't play ball? Gone for another year, of which (I was abundantly aware) there may not be many. Herewith the specific verse/s of song-text which fuelled both my desire and the potential for its (healing balm'd) outcome; arisen (as I described earlier) in the voice of a 'wise-woman' of our OnePeople'd lineage:

> The Great Mother takes all our tears
> plants them in her Earth
> where they transform into gold and silver pearls
> infilled of liquid Light, lifted fresh to the Sky
> all Love ready/prepped to verily burst forth
> Shimmering kaleidoscope – Joy! – elemental and more
> alchemic its rainbow'd bubbling with summertime Life
> the chi of shared circuitry, Kora kora'd with delight
> Mountains above as mountains below
> all serve the Great Mother and her 3rd Rock home
> Han Shan's crystal Cold (as each pilgrim knows)
> looks to the East, those who master Flow –
> Dogen's mountains child, the moment of its birth
> ever-together: Body-Mind-Soul – Earth'd

This is what I had to do. Look to the East, into the face of one who <u>masters</u> Flow. Ortler – my next best (Sasso/Waale'd) Berg-/Star-Geist champion. With him to sing our planetary healing – Home; singing up my Love as "river-deep, mountain-high" as any Tina Turner attuned to her guy. Dogen's mountains child <u>would</u> be birthed.

Nine months past first sight onto this giant; 18 months since apprised of cancerous incursions. How can I describe my expansive sleeve of garden'd Self to stand atop Da Daint and coo-ee to Ortler, "Hello <u>his</u> House" of which this local limestone giant forms an integral part of shed's DeepTime-Tectonia'd root-knowing upjumped? A stone collected on the way stayed aloft at summit cairn to hold the energy of Song (sung); it looked like a compass needle, perfect for me to string the thread through SE-120degrees from Daint to Ortler.

And who now do I see sitting out the other (westward) end of intersect? Sweet Tödisan who winks in my (northern) window at home! Oh, the geography of high wild geology remarked! My local 'Knight of the Cloth' vibrationally-strung all the way through to Fujisan … um … had the words of "SimpleSong" actually flown <u>in</u> along this line for the psychoid unity of 'event' to reveal itself in time? Seiryu – what say you??

Time horizons honoured, on a day of honouring: Lughnasadh '21, seven weeks out from our (intended) trek to Source (code/x). "Any day is a good day to climb a Mountain," my Amici are fond of quoting back to me (its erstwhile author). Yet how happy am I that it was <u>this</u> day. Worth honouring, worth the gratitude – confirming to Self (yet again) my commitment to Life/Love here on this side of veil. In my weariness, once returned to a blissful bed, I drop to a space of 'nation-state' flags. Mine/ours – Gaia's OneWorld (said), its colours Sky blue, Forest green, Cloud white, lain on Being's (FullDark) ground.

Later I am taken to a place of 'cosmic-state' flags – our 'territorium' amongst the stars. Mine/ours? FiveGates (said). I see myself as a 'totem pole' at different portals; I count the number of alpine passes at which I have sung "SimpleSong" this Summer on my way from one divine River-run to the next; I recall the H5.0 lessons of Mr1300BC, the harmonic resonance of elemental sentience in lived Gaian skin (now hopefully imprinted in sheds therein). The magic of the numbers never lies, and so ask (oh so very, very nicely!) for our journey home to Source (code/x) at equilibria'd Equniox to flow well.

• • • • •

Reader, I may present these compositions in seeming linearity of their evolutionary development but when one reads the song texts (see "Appendix 1") it soon becomes apparent we are operating outwith Time, in a multiverse of voices and perspectives expressing their version of Love's seminal and seamless (!) Whole. Like a crystal whose different facets provide alternate angles, Light may shine on/into nooks, crannies not remarked at first observation. The phraseology chosen to express this knowing long-ferments in Soul before any conscious uplift to paper can be conceived. Accordingly, it arrives (still!) as/in various iterations on a single potent theme (Love!) from the infinite wells of our shared genetic heritage, we Children of the Stars ever-hosting a SkyChild's desire at heart.

Suffice it to say it was a wise move, Soul's 'event' – to bring me to this need for in-Self healing. I will never not be thankful for the blessings it has delivered. Indeed, a wise move – to shift the extent of my com-passion from subtle to physic'd, bring the inner out, reveal the hidden, flood Dark with Light so it could be full-embraced, full-loved for what it desired to teach; thereto offered the opportunity to be transformed, full-healed. A wise move, because each healing gift received to/in/by my Garden of Self, I gifted on to Gaia. To the point a day came when I woke to a sense of complete congruity. No boundary, no border, no gifting on, because I am her as She is me – planet core to thin Blue line, micro/macro full-aligned.

This catharsis (a profound healing in its own way regardless of what was going on in either of our physical blood/bone'd journeys) found its authentic voice, its generosity and full-bodied (girl) power, in the third Song in (Gaian) set but can be shorthanded in the following mantra where each can take the other's part in the spirit of Ibn Arabi's Creative Prayer with God:

Sleeve'd of Breath, this membrane we share, I am with You/I am You …

In translating and providing commentary on the medieval Sufi mystic's wisdom, the great scholar, Henri Corbin, called this the relation between "I and Thou" ('Abd and Rabb), invoking Dante's Fedeli d'Amore, the Faithful (servants) of Love, in his explanation. Indeed, my relation with Gaia had always been founded on Love, but now I felt completely (Breath-) infused with her equally loving service to (little) me. (And note that I use the noun 'relation' intentionally to confirm my understanding of our stellar familial root-heritage, rather than the more usual word choice of 'relationship' which maintains a distance, oh-so-slight – an otherness which requires a 'coming together' that I do not experience for I am inwith, a part of the Whole.)

Such that we meet the 'moment' of the third Song in our Gaian trilogy, in wake of flag-waving and -bearing, when I 'wake' from a vivid space, the following sight seared to memory.

PeacePole (happily sleeping in the corner of hut) was split open (vertically) in order for the Amici to show me what was 'hidden' within. Hollowed out (fancy that!) at a few places for treasures to be secreted – <u>working</u> treasures was the point. Most compelling? Our 'Family Seal', a <u>crest</u> which could be stamped in wax to show we'd passed that way, blessed Land (sole-to-soul). Additionally, it acted as a passport or confirmation of birth-contract (aka soul-seal). This seal was framed in/protected by a (Sidhe) metal casing and recessed into the timber 'skin' of PeacePole, so that it would remain physically unseen (yet still subtly active) when the wood was 'resealed'. Within another hollowed-out spot, further up the pole, was a bird. Its twinned (subtle) singing with mine would double the loving sustenance (healing balm) offered to Land (as PeacePole pounded the path at my side) but its ever-presence (just like Pole itself) would offer support for me in order to do my (singing) work. How precious!

With this came a message – from Gaia:

"Not only are you singing for a dear departed hound at this hemispheric Equinox'd (high wild raw free) fest, not only are you returning to Source (code/x) for (perhaps) a last time on this side of veil, but also for me. I need you to stand in this open-air temenos of DeepTime-Tectonia'd waters (surfaced) and shout out my loud proud re-birth of 'I am!' to all ten directions through the FiveGates of our OneWorld (nation) state; I need you to pour forth afresh my Light to the (worldwide) web in Song!"

The message was prefaced by 'singing' in the subtle (Sidhe) realms of the "Tears for Fears" (1984) song: "Shout" with a slight twist to lyric:

"These are the things we <u>can't</u> do without!"

Again (always) the Amici know which Annie-buttons to press. It was as if the reawakening work of "SimpleSong" had fulfilled some <u>primal</u> need in blood/bones of micro-me/macro-twin to affirm our united, congruent commitment to Life – well-lived! Flooded with the Joy of a SkyChild's "I am!" but now vested with a Crone's strength of conviction, not only for planetary Self but each sentient being inwith (her/my) Land, the Song I needed to 'shout' tumbled out. Partnering writ large, this next best iteration of Gaia's 'life arc' arrived in a stream-of-conscious freefall while I stood at 'window on world', centring itself around a single more-than-compelling proposition. Oft-quoted in prior chapters, this was the moment it first saw (material) light of day, with Ruscada cross-vale purring his big-bro'd Love:

The Green of a Land that is <u>never</u> Dead
when the Blue of the Stars <u>flood</u> the World with their Seed

The chi of shared circuitry zinged in my veins as it scripted itself to page, amply supported by other lines calling on the (five) elementals to alchemise, coalesce, bring all to vibrant Life – (well-lived!) – in a "Spell of Being" with pure Magic at its core, of intensely inwoven <u>fruitful</u> unfold. It announced (loud/clear) Gaia's full-fledged 'becoming' – the She/I/OnePeople'd solidarity of sole/soul purpose <u>ever</u> intended at (experimental) outset – to learn, to discover, to explore, to evolve our consciousness toward the 'Us' we each/all were meant to be, the 'Us' of that original Blue (stellar) Seed <u>implanted</u> in receptive (well-watered) Earth.

It was our choice to incarnate. It was our choice to see this through to whatever end. No. Matter. What. Hear, now, Gaia's magnetic "I am!" followed by her closing affirmation:

Body-Mind-Soul, I am your Earth!
I am you, I am he, I am everywhere she!
Each sentient cell between Source and Sea!
May the all of the All of the One be healed!
Inwith frame (named) Love's Light be freed!
I am the Mountains above, and their twins below.
I am the true-nature'd Life of our Third Rock: Home …

• • • • •

An energy of mergence carried us aloft the heights at Autumn Equinox, seven years since first physic-discovered – there to call Gaia's renewed avowal out to world from Purity's cauldron'd well, send <u>her</u> Song of Presence sailing over that divine lip of Land. Plunging. On. All the way Home. To Sea. Returning to her (Mother-Ocean'd) Source (code/x), in-world revealed.

An energy of mergence binding Source-Sea-Stellar in a <u>single</u> Heaven/Earth Code/x: Home –most ancient and sacred of our OnePeople'd 'classics' fresh-envisioned, and from Memory recovered, gifted into our small Amici hands by cousinly cosmic ancestry.

An energy of mergence which would become full-throttle'd <u>convergence</u> when all-ye-all weather (and more) gods, goddesses, sages, saints (near/far) decided to join our Equinox party in a boom-crash-opera'd Sky stream; flooding consciousness (it seems) was definitely key. Hmmm … At least we were in the mountain hut, safe-installed, by the time the sluice gates opened at 2am (Day 2), continuing to pummel us for 14-hours (I kid you not) straight.

But would we be able to climb further to Source, at least another hour and several hundred metres higher? Cross that sweet burbling brook tumbling down a never-ending saturate slope (Ben'd, Bog'd, yet this time un-Dog'd) following its transform to swollen roaring torrent? No amount of BCC could have prepared me for this gob-smacking eventuality.

But? Reader, I sang (like Jane Eyre's contractual, after a fashion). I sang before an unwarming fire in a frozen flooded hut; I huddled out of doors to sing with Moon as she rose to offer comfort that (second) night, turning a swampy meadow into a sea of dancing stellar droplets; I sang up at Source next day when (miraculously) the torrent became (BCC-) fordable. And I documented the all of trek in a (seriously epic) long poem titled: "Emissary", including the fact of the Amici's arrival overnight to soothe raw nerves, affirm we would do as envisioned next (third) day before hightailing it out before a next weather system took our Song 'out'.

Yes, the 14-hours (non-of-clock'd-stop) deluge was (apparently) fit to (higher) purpose, for which I am grateful their careful commentary on elemental alchemy could be offered in pedestrian boiler/plumber-speak for this small human to keep her simple-mind'd feet!

Aye, the pipes lie deep (in castle keep).
Helvetia's vault. Peace (sequestered).
Consciously sunk. Acqua Termale (so-called)
for a reason (after all). Chthonic-dark
at Mountain heart is Kamaji's boiler-room.
Soot-sprites (spirited onsite) working overtime
against Gravity (on a diet of Star candy),
Eager to see our mission fruit (right!) ...

Yes, I could circum-nav the sacred pool (as desired). Yes, I could stand on SingingStone (so-called) out front of (subtle) monastery in Nature's (physic'd) temenos (as foreseen) and, post-performance, toss SingingStone's mini-twin to the silted depths of tectonic knowing, upwelled. Poised, its self-sovereign Seed (of Love's ignite), could be loosed (as intended) to its future. Bright! Truly, it settled me greatly to have the Amici arrive overnight, and affirm that everything would, in the end, turn out arights.

The Sisters too made their presence known, already assembled in Mountain's pewter-polished choir stalls surround-sounding pool; in long shrouds they stood, looking down from above reprising Chamois from five years before yet ready to support Song's loving outpour from their maws. From on high they looked onto the broad stone slab of performance 'stage', completely camouflaged to all but my sight. In same vein I was handed the cloak of anchorite:

Un-faced, anonym. Sole/Soul. Performative.

> *The (Land) Art of Bard flows Enso-empty.*
> *Sasso-ensconced at portal to monastery.*
> *Healing is as healing does (Love):*
> *Fill the shroud, and? Gift it on*
> *As healing balm ...*

"Emissary". Named in honour of Chamois who had been our gallery'd witness (to happy barky Pabey) last time round; this time arriving through the portal connecting subtle/physic'd in the days 'fore our undertaking, arriving from upstream to grace the meadow beside our cottage and crop the grass, confirm (with a look, long – "through your eyes I see Self," said) that the Amici, our high wild genius loci and more (um, that would include weather gods, I guess) awaited our imminent arrival. And blessing.

The epic resides in nestedfishes (cosy, dry!) poetry corner, but in brief – not only did Emissary bear witness to the all of trek ('fore, during, aft) but its sequel (in subtle sight) when "Song of Gaia" demanded her reprise (unexpected, spontaneous, wind-whipped and foam-swept) on a frozen (northern) Sea (wild'd) shore a month following our back-of-valley Equinox perform. <u>Intuitively</u> knowing the 'raw' of this Sea contained the same energy of Source (code/x'd) Presence (her own), of thrilling <u>unthinking</u> "I am!", throwing herself <u>headlong</u> into the waves, looking deep across the horizonal plunge West, whence my Celtic genetic heritage dwelt.

Such that? Reader, I sang (again) – in a Jane Eyre 'marriage' of Land-Sea-Sky, in a Gaian <u>meld</u> of Blue's full fathom five. Imagine! That Song had <u>rushed</u> all the way Home to Sea, to meet me here when I'd been expecting some road-trip (holiday) downtime? I couldn't <u>not</u> perform – for Her, for All, in this brand new (to me) All! A random packing crate/palette, a bit of flotsam'd debris tossed up by the waves, became my stage. And I <u>threw</u> my voice windward (ho!) all the way. Yes. Into the West.

Both recitals can be enjoyed in the nestedfishes krypta – the recording at Source made before the unwarming (yet atmospherically crackling) fire in flooded hut when I thought an open-air performance impossible. And yet? When possible? Too overwhelmed to think of recording it – such Joy in/of itself to sing for/as/with Gaia in a magical amphitheatre of her own making!

But how does it close, this (long epic) poem, this log of trek trekked? Well, bless me if Emissary (clip'd of clop) didn't appear at my (subtle) side at Samhain once returned from roadtrip'd North Sea shores. In truth he was my bardic (Amici) MossMan all along – now in fetching centaur'd crossdressing non-skin (aren't they clever with their shapeshifting ken?).

See, I had been contemplating (on meditative meander up to alp pasture) if our work (shared) supported Gaia's healing as well as her evolving consciousness as <u>intended</u>. Had everything we'd <u>actually</u> 'made' at Source/Sea enriched or <u>adequately</u> blessed the Flow of Love's Light (code/x'd) into and through the World of Time?

His counsel?

"Do not second-guess the gods. Trust: The Land is Pure."

(and)

"Never underestimate the gods. Trust: In Garden's Heal."

I offer such counsel here to all of us on this side of veil who doubt our efficacy, our ability to help. In itself, it mirrored (via its particularity of reference to our action) one of Mr1300BC's (generalist) teachings many years earlier:

"You cannot know. You cannot <u>not</u> know."

"Emissary", as a work of Land-Art in Poetry/Song, thus enfolds the all of knowing <u>and</u> not knowing that this wondrous high wild valley offers <u>selflessly</u> and <u>seamlessly</u> into our care – the Wisdom released by her River-run reaches, the history settled in the (Mountain) bones of our perfectly peace-sunk cottage. Present, and gifted to (my) World of Time (this time) while I continue to walk, continue to sing, continue to document adventures with Amici kin. Ever-trusting that it helps. Amen.

• • • • •

Arcadia – a Place, a Presence, an (edenic) state of Being. A region in the remote mountains of Greece, in classical mythology it was home to the god Pan, then taken up by artists, writers and other creative spirits during the Renaissance/Romantic periods as a poetic by-word for pastoral idyll, living in harmony with unspoiled nature, its 'garden' husbanded by shepherds with their wandering flocks – in a way evoking our nomadic walk-lightly-upon-Earth ancestry which Pan with his 'bestial' form and ancient (reed-pipe'd) music well-captured.

The first time I met Arcadia was years ago, as participant-witness to/in her (first) 'birth'. In a darkened cave/bar, with Amici collaborators, we watched a film (twice) about this Presence.

Arcadia lay in an enclosed cocoon-like structure. She looked like a regular female, naked but luminous; milky greenish 'flow' infilling/surrounding her evolving form. Inside this translucent membrane she slept, but all the while writhing, touching breasts, bones, hips – the extant contours of her emergent being. In this, I felt to be participant, experiencing what she did as well as witnessing same via film, as if mirroring the 'event' so I would understand it better.

My perspective then shifted to the space of encounter. The cocoon was a type of bed in a room musty with age – wide wooden boards, unpainted, like a classic Swiss farmhouse of several hundred years prior. I had been in a space like this before, as/in myself – I knew it as a type of 'half-way house' when first learning to step in/out of human skin between early subtle 'night-sight' assignments with

Amici kin. Now, however, it is a seamless undertaking.

In its current 'film-set-witness-cum-participant-engagement' iteration, I saw the room was accessible from 'outside' via a set of wooden stairs up from a medieval village square. In burst a host of enraged creatures across the full spectrum of 'humanoid-faerie evolution' (halflings, wildmännli, human, elven etc); a whole host which barged in and demanded Arcadia 'get up', put to right all wrongs of our/their (latter-day) world.

A blame/shame game ensued during which the 'mayor' of this community read out a litany of complaints to a confused groggy Arcadia who (by this stage) was semi-sitting up in bed, the cocoon having peeled apart. If she "didn't pay her taxes", they would "run her out of town". He held the list up to her face, but from my perspective I could see its reverse side on which was sketched classic 'Dark-Magic' – the dark magic of a 'puppet master'. Whether economic, religious, political, or industrial, the patriarchy represented by (populist) mayor would not give up its dominance and influence lightly; it would go on steamrolling its lascivious desire for 'progress' through the world even if it meant 'taking down' the sole/soul edenic <u>essence</u> on which the Whole depends. Arcadia's metamorphosis to fully evolved form incomplete, her developing consciousness was being hindered, exploited, her 'goodness' reined in by 'act'.

That the parable presented as a witch hunt (even down to the era of housing), foreheralding the all of capitalist machine to come (complete 'loss' of divine feminine principle to the West's 'Age of Enlightenment' inclusive), was more than relevant to the where/what of our Amici'd work. A next best Memory, recovered, for our fresh envisioning – to restore the sacred knowledge 'burnt at the stake' to its rightful place at the <u>core</u> of equation, partnering the all of Garden and her (literal) <u>commonwealth</u> of sentience to support a 'second coming'/re-birth to world of Gaia's Arcadian principle (in Seed Earth skin).

That we watched this film (twice) in a darkened cave/bar – underground, to all intents – spoke to the space whence the divine feminine principle had retreated, till the time/place 'ripe' for its arise. Not lost, but rendered mute, as I was to (much later) write in "Muted Earth". We sat, discussing issues of how to overcome the GroupThink aspects of the (still, at time of writing) 'ruling' private/public (human) autocracies enslaved to capital and its geo-political complexes.

Then, as the film credits rolled a second time, I felt a huge poop hit my arm from above – splat! I looked up, saw nothing but knew it as 'bat guano'. This my clue – working undercover and at night, our <u>sonic</u> senses would be able to find and harvest the 'fertiliser' required to nurture her re-birth. (As manure, guano is highly effective due to its exceptionally high concentrations of key nutrients essential for plant growth).

When meditating later on Arcadia as a living Presence, not simply an 'Idea', a slim sylph-like humanoid apparition appeared in vision, walking down a path toward me. Translucent, she was of the same milky greenish luminescence as had infilled cocoon – like amniotic fluid. I was being afforded a glimpse of her potential future-manifest/arise in-world. Already fully existent (Seed) in 'in utero' (Earth) dimensions, incubating inwith a "Sleeve of Self" (as I called the cocoon/chrysalis), she would be nourished by our Love and Song till 'full-term' (this time round) could see her blessed nativity.

In drawing Arcadia-as-Presence into our work, 'Garden' became a go-to word to image-into-existence our blessing grail in both subtle/physical dimensions. Garden, as its own container ('wild' or 'domestic' to mirror planetary Blue macro), developed into an alchemical cauldron and partner-to-purpose in one. This included, once Cancer revealed itself on physical plane, recognising my own Self as Garden at <u>each</u> layer of incarnate being, adding (as natural matter-of-course) an extra dimension of loving heart-connection to partnering Gaia/all her children across and through this membrane of (Earth-bound) Life we share.

No longer was I working for Gaia 'out there' (subtly/physically) but literally 'in (Annie) here', my Garden's "Sleeve-of-Self" would be an incubatory rehabilitation site of embodied, incarnate blessing in its own (cocoon'd) right – thus offering a multiplier effect or benefit to other inner/outer world rehabilitation sites of stress, distress, dis-ease to which we already flowed Love's (liquid) Light. Another facet of microcosm-macrocosm twinned, of course, but with sweet luminous Arcadia as my/our entry point.

The fact the phraseology which arrived in meditation to support my <u>understanding</u> of this work in Self's Garden: "Ego ergo Arcadia" ("I therefore Arcadia") <u>predated</u> my illness, diagnosis and treatment decisions by a <u>significant</u> length of time demonstrates (again) Emerson's axiom re Soul's 'event'. Perhaps it also provides evidence (to me, at least) of why I seemed to flow into a healing process without spiralling through the classic five stages of grief at 'loss'. (The oncologist did describe me as 'odd' – such a compliment!). In any case, for any of us, my point is the opportunity exists (regardless or not of any dis-ease 'in-house') to <u>twin</u> one's Self (Garden) with divine Arcadian vision as a <u>facilitator</u> to Gaia's macro proposition.

Or in short: A Garden is ever a Garden ready for fresh-seeding ...

The next Arcadian link in pearl-strung chain occurred as I was well within my/Gaia's healing regime. Yet, approaching 2020's Winter Solstice my (mother hubbard) cupboard was seriously Song-bare. All that changed, however, with a significant visioning journey in/to my high wild raw (and free) valley home which, at that moment, was far from physic'd sight. Here my raw journal notes:

A place name spoken, confirming my locale: Hof Acquerei. Such a buzz in veins as I spoke this (to Self). Returning, I could analyse its 'root' Amici-hybrid language for what it revealed: Aqu(if)er (and) Ei (egg). So, the farm/court/yard (Hof) of Acqua Termale 'seed/seeding', where the Source of all Waters, our sacred pool at back of valley, burbles up through permeable rock. A medieval (stone) castle keep, monastery or farmstead always has a well at centre of its Hof.

Earlier, I had collected a chestnut from the path on the way here (it is Autumn, after all). Suddenly, I held a different one in hand. Whether it was the first transformed or another I'd found, or one magically gifted in the first's stead, I have no idea – but I felt its 'weight', heavy as stone and stone-smooth. It still had the same shape/size of a robust chestnut 'seed' or 'egg' but was Blue – striped in slim lines of every shade of Blue possible from midnight to teal and aqua to glacial. So pretty! Polished (smooth) by our River's endless flow out from Source. Such a gift! This we shall plant in Moon's perennial phase and I shall sing it awake at Solstice. Yay!

I knew, from the way the stone 'egg' was streaked in all shades of Blue it referenced a line in "Muted Earth" already quoted:

Rivulets of fragrant knowing gone underground through neglect.

"Muted Earth" also contained my first public mention of Arcadia (performed at 2019's Winter Solstice), viz:

Great Mother is tired.
So rests in the Garden (of her very own making).
Fine filigree a-spun, this crystal spider-laced cocoon.
Arcadia, to all intents – Home, as ever She envisioned
it to be. Snuggles down in moss pillows prepped by those
who remember the dream of Beauty, symbiosis of Sharing.
Lilting Song which brought the All into Being.
Violet carpenter bee remembers. Heliotrope at prayer remembers.
The tallest tree, the tiniest pebble, the damselfly on grass stalk settled.

For this 2020 Solstice, therefore, I would need to speak aloud the next stage of our work. Announce it 'live', bring it into vibrant being – "Arcadia's arise from Hof Acquerei" – and for which (although I did not intuit this at the time) would require pilgrimage to Source (code/x). Winter Solstice '20 till Autumn Equinox '21? Another nine-month incubatory confinement – no coincidence at all …

In the spirit of prayful mantras invoking the 'future Buddha, Maitreya' (replicated in other religious traditions, e.g. the longed-for 'return/second coming of Christ'), I saw in Arcadia's 'arise' (well (well-) watered by the nurturing energies of Love's (liquid) Light inwith Hof, this space which had been unlocked and offered to our Amici work) the <u>Seed Earth</u> potentiality of Gaia's future coming closer. As described in "The Amici Files", the (subtle) monastery attached to our River's sacred (physical) source (aka Acqua Termale) was named Mandalay, and linked (through Mountain root-known networks) to a place in the high Himalayas (said).

I had attended this locale in Malakut vision long before any physical trek took place to our back-of-valley heights (and depths) a decade past. In researching the 'why' of its naming at the time, however, I found it to be the stuff of legend, as the site of a 'great civilisation', somewhere the Buddha supposedly visited. Its phonetic nearness to mandala (as a representation of primal elemental harmony whereby the five levels of chorten alchemise the swirl of energy to form) was also compelling evidence for the 'purity' of our Source waters.

Nevertheless, here I was now – excited beyond belief to think we had been granted access to this space (within a space), to plant our <u>seed</u> in Hof Garden and bless it with the pure Source-drawn waters of our Song. All this in support of the full (lotus-blossom'd) Beauty of Gaia's (Arcadian) Blue emerging (one day!) once all in-world sentience vibrated at a like state of evolved consciousness? Such a visionary high I was on! Truth of Nature expressed, brought to manifest existence by the loving partner'd intent of the all of the All with our One: World Soul! The Seed contains in itself <u>everything</u> it needs to flood the World with its Joy of Life (lived!) – that is, if the right causes and conditions exist and (in-time) present an opportunity for <u>its</u> desire, its loving quest, to become full-enfleshed.

This I sang into being at Winter Solstice 2020 in "Equipoise: A Pas de Deux", twinning my journey of Life in Garden (this time round in skin) with my genetic Great Mother's (ditto'd):

Soon, Great Mother will be 99-years young.
And soon we shall meet at Sea'd Source, Flesh made Song.
And there I will tell her another Story'd Dream
Of tending the Garden, sweep/seeding and weeding;
Of Arcadia's arise from Hof Acquerei,
Gift of Life we shall share next Time-partner'd time …

The Song I dedicated to all Mothers/all Sisters, the divine feminine impulse/principle in-world and beyond, which had been in (serious) retreat long/long centuries (on physic'd side of veil at least). In presenting the Song in nestedfishes krypta, I wrote:

This work was written in honour of our planetary Sisterhood - we who stand on the shoulders of giants, Sisters past; we who stand in solidarity with generations of future Sisters to come. Yet in each present moment, each single today, we stand 'equipoised' in the Power of our Presence with our greatest Sister of all – Great Mother Earth (Gaia) – without whose Life and all Life she hosts on this small Blue marble spinning through the infinity of space, we would have none, and none to gift on. We Sisters may not live to see the fruits of our labours spent in companionship of Great Mother during our brief human years, but each and every visionary seed we plant in the fertile soil of her Body, in her sacred Garden of longer-than making, watered each day with our Love, nurtured each day with our Faith and Hope, will bloom a rainbow field of flowers, a *tall forest of bird-song'd green – one day. Noli timere! Eventually we will come, as a planetary community in shared participatory voice, full circle to what the Ancients ever-knew – that Love <u>never</u> fails on Gaia's DeepTime watch.*

While a small work, the Song housed in its three (short) minutes the spells of elemental weaving, of harmonic resonance and energetic balance, we Amici were invoking at the time. In so-doing (without me realising) it contained the 'sprouted' inklings of an uplift in new form which would find its eventual enfoldment in "Song of Gaia" (nine months hence) when her full "I am!" burst from my pen, and then graced my lips atop SingingStone before tossing the (SingingStone) <u>seed</u> to the pool, Sun-kissed.

The incubatory period was complete. Arcadia was ready to arise from Hof Acquerei, to be birthed from our sacred Source, code/x'd afresh. No wonder the lightning bolt of "Song of Gaia" (revealed) struck with such force on cusp of Equinox trek. No wonder the waters of sacred well in Gaia's (Mandalay) Hof needs be infilled over and over 14-hours straight while we sat in a (flooded, freezing) stone hut (far below) before a meagre fire, nothing to do but ruminate (on bad luck). Water <u>always</u> has to run for a while from the tap before it gets piping hot (my Amici said). Had you forgot? Indeed I had (as documented in "Emissary", the record of trek – logged). Our Acqua Termale (thermal spring, so-named when first assigned its sacred well to find) had its birth chamber deep within dark warm incubatory Mountain, a hallow'd cocoon if ever there was one. "Thunder over Mountain", the "I Ching" hexagram flesh-inscribed in Annie-arm for (this) SingingBird's fresh dawn, literally proved relentless (non-of-clocked-stop!) in expressing its desire to partner our work with an own 'consciousness-flooding' event. Each sentient Being, each world-weaving Presence inwith thin (atmospheric) line of our precious planetary Blue knew of our intent, were busy-bee-generating the requisite causes and conditions (from their perspective) for the Song I would sing on Gaia's behalf to stick, to resonate, to fly – high wild raw <u>and</u> free.

So, sweet Annie, and your (fragile) Body's blood/bone Garden? Do not second-guess the gods. (And) Never underestimate the gods. Trust here/now (and) evermore (for) all is well (and) ever shall be. But in the meantime? Please keep up your BCC!

SONG TO THE POWER OF SEVEN

Seven is a prime number (like 3 and 5, my other go-to sacred geometric connector-threads); and (like the others) 'tis a pretty digit with symbolic as well as practical meaning around the world from ancient through modern times. The seven days of the week each had a 'classical planet' assigned – to them were ascribed the (seven) colours of the rainbow, just like with the (seven) chakras, or even Snow White's sweet dwarfs (Walt Disney loved his paint pot). Spiritual traditions talk of seven heavens; here on our 'Third-Rock' we speak of seven continents; there's the seven seas of antiquity or current geography (take your pick); seven pillars which uphold Sophia's temple of wisdom (one wonders if these pillars are the seven sages of Hellenic philosophy turned to stone?); while seven mountain ranges surround Mount Sumeru, the navel of the world in Buddhist cosmology. More recently, Carl Jung wrote his 'Seven Sermons to the Dead' while Abraham Maslow decided on seven steps when outlining his 'Hierarchy of Human Needs'. There's always a seventh wave, grander than those earlier in the set, that every surfer yearns to catch, and (of course) there's the legendary powers of the 'seventh son of a seventh son'.

But the specificity of the magical number seven I wish to focus on herein involves Sisters and Song – the musical scale (C-to-A) before next octave begins at following C; the Sister'd collective attuned to same whether earth-bound or stellar-a-flight (at least to our eyes). We'll start with the latter before moving to former. But along the way it'll be a roundabout ride.

Are you ready?

• • • • •

The (Seven) Sisters have a long and rich mythic provenance across the world, most usually attached to the Pleiades. The best known and documented traditions track this open star cluster in the constellation Taurus as it shifts through-sky. To a story, the grouping represents the divine feminine; to a story they are described as Sister-goddesses sailing the waves of cosmic night, often fleeing a lustful male pursuer. Campfire stories told since forever (and recorded since antiquity) in cultures as diverse as Australian Aboriginal Dreaming, Celtic Ireland or Pharaonic Egypt; legends told in paint or artefact, or attached to some feature of landscape to give tangibility to the tale, to prove that once – long long long ago – gods walked the Earth. In the classical Greco-Roman canon, they are the companions of Artemis – twin of Apollo – goddess of the Moon and Earth's wild. But no matter where or what told, the stories generally affirm a connection between stellar heights and earthen depths. Usually it's a mountain chain; to stone-anchor the Sisters to something significant in-world adds another dimension to their wonder. Here, they are accessible; here, they are immovable; here, they are worshipable – the strength of their mythic arise from Land in the same instant as their stellar ignite in Sky becomes the culture's own. Mirror-mirror'd; sea-source'd.

On either side of Helvetia's heart, the massive massif that bisects this small Land, lie ridges I refer to as the Sisters. The chain to the north into which I connect with the Amici rises above a fjord-thin lake. I have climbed aloft two of these Sisters; their story is told in "Awakening" – 'twas here MakerMan first demonstrated how Berg-/Star-Geists hook up to sing the Stars in/out of Earth; 'twas here we co-wrote a Song of celebration for the sheer fact of the Land's sublime beingness. On Helvetia's southern side, the next ridge over from our forgotten valley on the border of Time, where I first formally 'met' the Amici, lies the other chain – these girls have I also celebrated loud and long in Song, their 'high wild majesty embraced'. But their peaks will I never scale – too tough for ancient Annie. But I can and do greet them regularly (and they me) on hikes through shared watershed, these "Mountains-Dragons without end, generating resonance, echo to divine Presence" (as our Song attests).

((And yes, while I know our focus here is on Sisters, I've just been prodded by the Amici to mention the Rugby Sevens and B52s as solid 'Mountain Men' (likewise 7-a-piece) who sturdily hold our (Sister'd) backs in tough line-out manoeuvres of weaving Song in/through world.))

While the myths we weave may be personal, specific to our Amici troupe's work, they cannot help but riff off the collective unconscious (at its timeless work) in whispers emanating from the same bottomless well into which all mythology dips. In Norway the Sisters are trolls turned to stone, still fleeing a male pursuer as Sun rises (oops). In Aboriginal Dreaming they are nubile maidens racing across Land <u>and</u> Sky from a (sigh) guy. My local stellar (mountain) lasses have their own male pursuer; he too is stone – a giant of a peak, limestone-a-glint (whom I adore, incidentally). Suffice it to say that each mythic rendering speaks in and to DeepTime, describing a longevity of Presence (Land and/or Sky'd) that our small human existence cannot attempt to comprehend except by way of Story and Song.

• • • • •

The first time I saw the Nebra Sky Disk, it spoke at a layer of knowing I did not understand. Difficult to explain but even though I cognitively observed what archaeologists described – a Bronze Age disk documenting the Night Sky from the perspective of Earth-bound witness, what I 'saw' <u>and</u> experienced was as if the disk were a planal view of our blue-green planet, with Sun/Moon/Stars picked out in gold above. As if the entirety of scene depicted was actually below my point of witness, as if I were hovering somewhere 'way out' beyond in cosmic space/time, in shimmering (quick-) silver'd crystalline night. But even though racked with ununderstanding, I printed out a colour image, and backed it with another which spoke volumes to me in ways I <u>did</u> understand – the Aurora Australis over Antarctica, Gaia's whole rimmed by the beauty of thin Blue (atmospheric) line. Sandwiched, each to the other, and sticky-tape-sealed (with a prayer in-between), I placed its 'two-sides-of-the-same-coin' imagery on the Elder Chair in the corner of my 'ten-foot-square hut' of meditative repose and waited for the connection 'back up the line' to common ancestry to reveal itself. Which it did (of course) in due time, hence much of our work proceeding (in bardic rhyme) – especially once Nebra's 7-pointed star cluster (which archaeologists ascribe to the Pleiades) started to get chatty.

At this point let me quote from Mariel's conversations with David:

"Many of the relationships which Gaia has with its cosmic environment and family are changing, and we – you and I – are part of this change … Gaia gains a new 'subtle body', and as she does so, you and we do as well … It means that more energies from the stars will flow into this world, and the living energy of the planet will in turn flow more freely into the cosmos."

In another section of the text, she talks about how this frees up our ability to hear <u>star-songs</u> more fully:

"While this change will make it easier for you to connect with stellar energies, (its purpose is) … to enable you to blend more fully with it … to see and hear and be part of the 'stars within the earth'."

Indeed! In "Awakening" I describe becoming acquainted with the energies of P, whom I called a 'star-system-nursery-nebula thingey' thanks to many chats (over cups of tea) about our stellar lineage with MakerMan. This included the lesson of the 'starseed' (recounted way back in Stretch 1 of this book), a ball of Light which transformed into the 'living' (and hence more viscous) density of 'Earth-consciousness'; returning this ball of Light to the stars would enable our deeper more intimate connection thereto or, as Mariel explains above, for the energies to 'flow more freely' between the two through 'us' learning (and/or re-learning) more to be 'us', thus densifying our connection to the 'stars within the earth'. In other words – the more we know Gaia, the more She knows herself; our consciousness evolving in concert with hers, or 'blending' as Mariel says.

It was a slow dance (over how many years? hmmm … what's that magic number again?) for me and P to fully frankly 'fly', in sync. I have (always) simply been more (naturally) attuned to the stars within the earth via the 'back-end' of pipe (so-to-speak) – i.e. connecting in via Mountain sentience, (conscious) sole pressed to (conscious) soul. But the time had come for me to move further 'out', <u>beyond</u> Gaia's thin Blue line at which I had stood to sing with Amici kin, from which I had looked down into/onto the <u>beautiful</u> Body of Gaia's full reach. I was being called 'out' so I could contribute more/better 'in'. We come from the stars and return to the stars as MakerMan and I had discussed. I had re-learnt to fly for a reason. P was ready and waiting when, finally, I too would 'announce' my readiness.

•••••

Seven there are, sailing the skywaves –
Follow their songline, sing their dance
From rock pool to rock pool
Ever-trekking east-west

The Seven Sisters Songline is strung across the Australian mainland, connecting skin groups across thousands of kilometres, each responsible for stewarding a stretch of HomeSong – for 'an unsung Land is a dead Land'. Over many years I have had the honour to connect into Aboriginal Dreaming via subtle Sisters – Sisters who have sought me out here, far (in physical distance) from the precious Land of my physical birth, to share their timeless wisdom with the 'white fella/black heart' soul I house. Usually only one Sister, the elder of clan, but in the approach to their longest day, our longest night – the seesaw of hemispheric Dark/Light of Solstice 21/12/21 – I found myself in the presence of all. Not here, but there – hovering high above the pulsing red heart of Gondwanan home, singing up the Stars within (down under's) Earth, stretching far/far, cirque'd cross-continent.

I stood with all in this place 'on high', on the edge of stellar escarpment. Yes, I'd been here before but now to be invited to an especial ceremony on an especial day? Asked to bear witness to their performative celebration of season, their beautiful dark earth painted with the light of the stars, singing up SoulSong, proudly worn at Skin, marked? Oh, Joy! I inhabited the harmonic resonance of common ancestral singing with all subtle senses, this (Seven) Sisters Songline infusing each fibre of my being, the chi of shared circuitry in immersive overdrive, trilling. Divine! And thrilling!

Um, P? I'm think I'm quite ready to join the Sister'd line-up …

• • • • •

I wrote of Gaia's plight (thereto our own) in the long poem, "Muted Earth" (earlier referenced and published in "Grail Within"). While ostensibly a cri-de-coeur on her (and all her children's) behalf regarding climate change against a backdrop of (human) political inaction (a line in the poem reads: "Um, justice? Who has the right to decide who has the right?"), in the weeks/months that followed its September 2019 penning (no coincidence, its arising at that time – 18 years since I had stood with a subtle Sister watching CNN as the Twin Towers fell, 18 years since our shared witness of that horror spoke Truth through my uterus: "There is not enough Love in the world", Soul leaping through Skin to say: "Here is your task; here, right here – to bring more Love to the world"), I witnessed again and again, over and over – in subtle and physical dimensions of being (micro/macro and all in-between) – how a key line written into existence toward the close of the poem came to play an increasingly active role in how I approached my life/work for Gaia across all interwoven platforms beyond the 'single issue' I had (ostensibly) addressed in text.

(Gee, that was a long sentence – is everyone still with me?)

It was as if, in speaking the line aloud, even though it had long been confirmed within, I was bringing it forth – up/out to here/now manifestation. The inner brought out in text can be a powerful mediator to (Self) process, especially when accompanied by the physical branding of Life's pact in skin – an "I Ching" hexagram tattoo'd to arm exhorting me to sing. The line?

"'Tis my amor fati – Sister Kali and her Sisters to accompany as all fractures for all to heal."

I had chosen the words 'amor fati' deliberately, as an expression of acceptance (or surrender, one could say) to my this-time choice to incarnate in this-time skin; so too as a mark of self-sovereign solidarity, a commitment to stand-with Gaia and all her children in the tumult of 'come what may' that will (or even has, one could say, since poem's pen) increasingly come.

Kali, Hindu goddess of change, wielder of the sacred impulse of creation/destruction; dancing away on Shiva's chest her foot-stomping shakti, her primordial cosmic energy. Pound! Pound! Pound! Can you hear her? A drumbeat which (at time of writing) seems as incessant as a jackhammer on collective consciousness. Yet?

"All must fracture for all to heal."

These were actually Gondwana's words. Whenever a Sister speaks, She does so with a clarity and a strength and a cosmic purpose (to Gaia's evolutionary consciousness) to which I cannot help but say: "Yep. I'm in." No matter <u>what</u> the (potential) little-Annie consequence. I have seen my birth contract – a blank parchment, gold-tasselled, rolled into a scroll, sent (like a message in a bottle) through all rivers of the world; rivers, which (as the poem which coalesced from my meeting with Sasso and his Waale), "cannot be checked, going wherever Light is needed, wherever there is lack".

Bumped, bruised along the way I may be, perhaps split open by hidden hazards in the rapids to bleed-bleed-bleed, or at times simply bob gently along (time for a breather!) through the wider quieter reaches of Life. Eventually to arrive Home with a Book of Voyage to recount to Family – our Ancestors – of what it is like here/now, in-world. I want to return with my head held high not with shoulders hunched. I want to say that I tried to the best of my ability with the gifts/skills at my disposal to bring more Love to the world. Mind cannot comprehend what Soul knows/has known all along about the journey it would choose, to which Body (faithful chariot of Love's way in-world, how I honour your stoic resolve!) must carry us. Another line in "Muted Earth" reflects my own cri-de-coeur in this regard:

Oh, Mother! How many lifetimes have I foot-soldier'd for you?
How many more needed till Via Mala traversed;
till we stand as One in the rose-gold of Sun?

Quite. At this point in narrative, we need to backtrack a number of years …

• • • • •

One day/night Mr1300BC arrived to sit on the windowsill here at home wearing a cream linen suit (a rather hip turn to his attire) while I lay abed in HMed. Surprised and delighted by his presence (ages, it seemed, since last we'd met!), he'd come to tell me about 'The Daphnes' as part of a new and 'bigger-than-ben-hur' project with the Amici I'd been trying to get my head around the past month or so. (Of course, Reader, he was referring to the UrWerk which is the subject of this long unwieldy volume, but let me get back to 'The Daphnes' whom I briefly mentioned early in this tome's pages but now 'tis time for them to fully come into their own.) While I saw Mr1300BC on windowsill here at home, concurrently 'I' was in the beyond'd (interstellar) locale of his 'home', a shift of consciousness so seamless in the moment I hadn't been aware of actually engineering it. But now fully lucid in the space of engagement – serious workspace, serious conversation, I saw the windowsill was in fact the edge of a <u>performance</u> stage. I sat below in a completely empty, parquetry-floored theatre. No one else was about – just me and my theatre 'director'.

He knew which buttons to press. All his lessons over <u>long</u> years of apprenticeship bent toward the unending (end) point I will relate herein. He had been my 'choirmaster' since forever – requiring his student to be pitch-perfect, to find her extant note (as well as that of <u>any</u> subtle partner/s) in the Harmony of the Spheres to best weave Love's warp/weft in-world, the whole raft of lessons described in the chapter "To the Power of Five". On and on till now when, in a flash vision, he conjured a group of naked women dancing in a forest grove.

It looked like a renaissance-era painting of nymphs-in-garden-idyll, as if uplifted from Greek myth. He said I'd find this at the 'National Gallery' but not to worry – they would come to share their wisdom (and dance steps?) with me in due course. Understandably I was confused. It seemed, though, as if I were being lured back to active performance (hopefully clothed!), something I'd left behind countless decades earlier – the undergrad university reviews, the singer in a band doing Blondie covers. But: The Daphnes? MakerMan (usually the most serious in our collective) snorted with laughter (via her regular 'cupboard crack'); MossMan (my bardic mate) shrugged: "You're on your own with this one, honey."

Hmmm … (cue: narrowed eyes/pursed lips/furrowed brow).

Nevertheless (as prior said), Mr1300BC knew which buttons to press. An autodidact of the old order (but with modern tools at my disposal), I got busy with research. While I may never have heard of 'Daphne' (singular or plural), Google and Wiki had. So did I discover the full metamorphotic myth (Ovid-related) – Apollo's ardent pursuit of the naiad, Daphne, her heartfelt plea to papa (a <u>river</u> god – how apt) for help, resulting in her transformation into a laurel tree. Hence her/its name, a wreath of same the marker of recognition in any art to which Apollo lent his patronage (e.g. poet laureate). In some versions of myth, the river god is Ladon of Arcadia – the Peloponnese region of Greece ringed by mountains, sparsely populated, celebrated in renaissance arts as an unspoiled harmonious wilderness (utopian, edenic) because of its role in classical canon. Geographically what I would call the raw 'high wild'; my to-die-for homeplace – primal, elemental (of being).

Arcadia? Hmmm … (cue: ditto).

Firstly, though, what is a naiad? A type of female nymph (thank you, Wiki) associated with fountains, wells, springs, streams. In short, fresh water – pure, <u>true</u>-nature'd, upsung from pristine Gaian ground. The sacred within mountains (to all intents).

Wells? Hmmm … (cue: ditto – exponentialised).

(In our next and final chapter we will 'meet' Arcadia and her well-maiden/ly ways again.)

•••••

In Helvetia's north-west, nestled amongst the sinuous limestone curves of her mountainous Jurassic borderlands with France and Germany, lies a secluded (blue) bayou of a glen whose German moniker (Schönthal) means 'beautiful valley'. First recorded with the 12th century founding of a Benedictine monastery, the name fits seamlessly with the energy resonant in its wooded hills and bleached bones. DeepTime-Tectonia at its purring verdant best had called to these pilgrims to build a community nine hundred years past. Paradise found, 'Arcadia' to all intents, till Reformation uprisings in the early 16th century left it a smouldering ruin.

Time ticked on (as it does). The church became a barn for patient cows – they munched away staring at St Christopher's legs while the top half of fresco (Christ on shoulder to cross raging torrent) graced the hayloft constructed above. The former monastery kitchen retained all its cheese-making and butter-churning apparatus, however, which the new landlords put to good use. What a wonder it would have been to see this place at its beginning, to hear the <u>singing</u> which infused its modest rough-hewn stone temple! At one stage in its early history the Brothers passed their labour onto a community of Sisters before it seesaw'd back again. A time fluid in human praxis but always Land stood firm, 'stayed (peaceably) put' together with the inner guardians of its (castle) keep. They knew the shape of (Mountain) Time, the millennial rock (and roll) of wax and wane. 'Seasons' are not just for annual marking, after all.

Fast-forward, then, in (Human) Time to the latter half of 20th century. A heritage order placed over the church; a businessman with a vision for restoring all monastic buildings to their former glory (in consultation with the State) by establishing a cultural foundation. In future, St Chris would play host to contemplations from more than patient cows. But his vision went further – to transform the 100-hectare parcel of ground that came with the monastery into a (Land) Art Gallery. Art installations created in symbiotic consultation with Land, by listening to and sharing what Land <u>herself</u> wanted to tell, would blossom in and around its undulating hills/dales. Meanwhile the monastery farm would be re-established according to full Steiner biodynamic principles.

Ah, Schönthal … Ringed by limestone ridges, the 'silver spurs' of Jura (as the Amici call this treasured country), I have walked your Songline hence/forth to Ankerballe – the vast <u>pregnant</u> bauble of stone bursting from cliff face aloft, surveyor of all 100ha of peace-sunk territorium. Named for its butterball ('anker') likeness but we both see the phonetic link to 'anchor'. This the place of cosmic stake plunged <u>deep</u> in Gaia's stellar flesh. The forest at back hosting Howe; here, the entrance to Faerie I (literally) found. (Well, actually it was our sniffy dog who wanted to do a slip-slide Alice-in-Wonderland impersonation; luckily he was leashed otherwise?!)

But ah, these Sidhe-of-Place are active in-space – a community whose straight-through sightline-rootline-leyline stretches along the length of ridge to Tree Sisters, a cirque of Linden, their crowns forming a collective arch, portal homeward (in each direction) marked. No coincidence that an art installation 'sings' with the Sisters each sunset eve; no coincidence that another piece, aptly titled "Recovered Memory", is positioned along this line between Ankerballe and Sister'd cirque; no coincidence that these two energy nodes effect an 'axis-power' triangulation with the artwork ("Cow Shed Ellipse") on opposite bank of this beautiful valley's meandering creek. A triangulation honoured by a perfect equilaterally-shaped slab of limestone waiting for me on the path toward Ankerballe one day (thank you, Amici!) which now rests in the (enlightened) river of our garden grail's Zen Peace nook – connector thread to all our work of Song; a triangulation honoured by a pippy shell from my ESW Pacific shoreline home squirreled under the cowshed's window ledge to <u>anchor</u> the energies of connection in reciprocate, thus aligning the work of our (respective) magical garden grails. No, 'tis no coincidence what each artist made, and where; invited to commune with Land, to arrive at the exact place/work to resonate with that which She burbles up through her bones as true-nature'd 'matter-of-course'.

Ah, Schönthal ... The place you command in our family's heart; the role you play in our (full!) family's unfold. A book in itself, methinks, but for the purposes of this chapter, only a brief snapshot (offered) courtesy of a random article in a Zurich daily circa 15 years past about a mesmerising British Land Artist. No, 'tis no coincidence. I had long admired, and been drawn to, the work of Richard Long. His approach to the creative process I had referenced in my PhD. Even though I a writer, he a visual artist, the performative aspects of 'creation' resonated – this quote central to the commonality I saw in our work:

"(It is) the ritual of an anonymous person. I come to some mountains and I move some stones around and then I disappear."

Anonymous is the key word here. And what Mr1300BC was challenging. A performance stage implies an audience. On whichever side of (veil'd) vale, this is your future (he was implying), as it was your (DeepTime) past.

The Daphnes ... Thanks to that random article, I dragged partner F on a daytrip to the beautiful valley Richard Long had graced with his presence, installing his work in a cowshed no less (by the time of our visit a bird was nesting in a gardening glove he'd left on a rafter – très apt!). Reached after a wander up a bucolic slope, we delighted in communing with the space (as well as all other sculptural works marked on a hiking map of the 100ha estate). Prior to that day, neither of us had heard of the place, a 'sleeper-locale' (to all intents). I wandered the 'krypta' of former monastery church; the space was now used for performance art 'happenings'.

I said: "If I were ever to host a launch/reading of my novel ("The Taste of Translation" – at that stage half-written), it would be here, in this crypt. It resonates with DeepTime compassion; its stone carries much power in its bones."

"Let's do it!" said F.

"No," I said. "You know I don't do 'public'."

Nevertheless, we agreed that once family (strung between up over/down under) were next together for Summer (here), we would re-do the daytrip so everyone could share in the spirit of this beautiful valley, its sympathetic art installations and the (longevity) of purity of vision that had brought the two together over a millennium of prayerful attunement to Nature.

The Daphnes … Fast-forward (again) some years. As a family we had visited; as a family we had acquired another member of family (courtesy of valley); as a family we had agreed to bed down in the monastery for a weekend of silence, communal supping and, on my part, a poetry reading in krypta for our core crew of six (plus hound) on the occasion of Winter Solstice 2016. Imagine! This was as 'public' as I could envisage for my (anonymous) work!

But it had opened a door (it seems). Within a couple of months, Mr1300BC sat on windowsill; my Amici grinned from ear-to-ear and Song again was to spill from my lips for more than core crew to hear. By the following Solstice, I had agreed to F's suggestion to extend our weekend invitation to a few very close friends. I was still unsure if this was how I truly envisaged my future-work for Gaia, so the morning after I'd received comments such as "Gee, Anne, I never knew you could sing!" (which made me <u>truly</u> squirm), I walked to the triad of Linden Tree Sisters on the resonant limestone ridge above monastery for a chat. It was here, in first year, that I had connected into the Howe/hollow hills of Jura's Faerie clans, had noted the energy line singing all the way through to their entwined rooted presence from Ankerballe. But now, surprisingly, I saw a sculpture had been added to the Sister'd collective – a new piece of art commissioned at some point since last (annual) visit.

A dominant bronze log lay behind the cirque, branded with a single name: 'Daphne'.

Oh, man! You guys? What <u>don't</u> you know about future-bright? What <u>can't</u> you see with your Elven-eyes? Here, at Schönthal, were The Daphnes all along; waiting for me to step up (and into) their cirque of (Linden Tree'd) Presence (a performance stage pitch-perfect to purpose) with our co-produced Poetry/Song. To sing it loud, sing it long. Gaia! Hear our prayer!

Well, didn't that open the worker-bee floodgates in wee Annie house. I called myself a 'performance poet/word artist'; I developed a text to describe our Amici co-productions (without mentioning Sidhe partners because of the range of sceptics our core (human) circle hosts) and inaugurated a new space on the nestedfishes.org website for 'Land-Art recitals', calling it the 'krypta' in honour of Schönthal bringing me home to my joy of (Song'd) self, and affirmed 'publicly':

"My work with Poetry and Song is in honour of Earth, inspired by Earth, and performed in harmony with Earth's own resonance – itself a symphonic score of unique interbeing. Each of us works within our sphere of influence, and with the tools gifted in this lifetime. For me the equation is: Breath fuels Song + Legs empower Walking + Pen & Paper enable scripting. My poetic texts interweave various world mythologies, but all is lain on a single Ground: Love. "An unsung Land is a dead Land." With this Aboriginal Dreaming wisdom ringing in my head, I walk in the tracks of the Ancestors, along my 'stretch' of HomeSong, singing in heart all the while. But every now and then, like the artist Richard Long, I reach a 'stopping place' in the landscape. Here is where I perform – for, with and on behalf of all Life of our One: Gaia."

I had found a way to perform – my audience (and co-participants) all sentience in/around the 'stopping place' of each (sung) intervention each time I stepped out as a pilgrim for Love on perennial repeat, PeacePole pounding the earth at my feet, sole pressed to soul, with each step the road rising to meet. While at Winter Solstice continuing to host a small annual weekend gathering of core family/friends, including a performance in krypta of symphonic length, the rest of year I could remain anonymous, making Love to Earth through walking Song – Home. And gladly so! Recordings I uploaded to website with brief commentary, just as Land-Artists like Richard Long returned to their studio to 'hone' the raw of Nature's gifts, present same in human exhibition spaces. Even at the time of penning "Awakening" I was made aware that our work would not just be received (or seen, or reviewed even) by human eyes and hearts. There were as many interested Sidhe on their side of veil'd vale who would glean insights from our partner'd praxis of cousin-with-cousin.

The 'performance' of walk, ritually blessing the Land with each step, perhaps conducting a small intervention at a stopping place along the way, is an in-time 'event' – a co-creative act of Love in/of itself. Leaving the 'studio' of Nature to document praxis at a distance (e.g. via this text) closes the circle, binds the act to itself <u>and</u> its participant-witnesses in whichever (whenever) dimension of Being the work as a whole is encountered. 'Tis an encircled moment, a (TS Eliotian'd/Ocean'd) return to beginning to know it for first time – a moment which begs that I introduce the Sidhe's Great Glyph to our discussion herein. And (apologies, Reader) that this needs to be in the voice of my raw journal notes which speak to the <u>rush</u> of energy that accompanied its arrival several days after "The Sisters Song"s arrival at Imbolc 2022 – an 'event' I am yet to describe. See? I said it would be a roundabout ride!

•••••

I draw/sketch the Glyph freeform as I speak the words of our Faerie-spell; I sketch the Glyph freeform and see how organically, in my swiftness of hand/incoming Light from Amici'd kin, it resembles the prized treble clef of my childhood, that which I needed to copy _religiously_ in prep for music theory exams. OK, so a pedant would probably say it looks nothing like a treble clef – for a start more curlicue'd and with the spiral going in opposite direction. But we're talking associative resonances here, and the fact that a left-handed lass like me does _everything_ in a topsy-turvy back-to-front'd way. But what I see and hear whispered through Glyph's revolving (well-guarded) Tor/Door are the (five) stave'd lines of Mr1300BC's musical score. So I script swifter/swifter, understanding the binding between in-world/beyond must be tighter/tighter. Home to Home, it _wants_ us to integrate _its_ Presence in this next best arisen work of Song.

The vertical anchor plunges deep to Ground (of Being) at close (flown-flow'd) of cirque swirled from core (zero degrees in full circle spun; yes, I know Love/Home are truly One); but prior to its plunge, that swift slice straight down through middle of cirque, it seeks to high-rise, tugged heavenward, stretching/slimming its sizzling energetic thread to draw the Light in-world. Like water from a well into our thirsty world, pouring it in, pouring it through. And, as it plunges this stake into Gaia's willing flesh, each oozing open wound she offers up to healing, I see how it acquires a tail of Light, comet-like, as if (lain planal) cresting horizon/curve of Earth as seen.

"The egg has a tail," I hear you (Moon Mother) say. "The starseed _seeks_ its anchor port/socket into which to plug Love's precious locket," I hear you Tiger-whisper (purring) further. This tail of Light, as I draw it swiftly, fluidly, feels like the tongue-flick of serpent/ dragon seeking its 'cave-of-heart' nest, its pool of chthonic depth in which to dive/retreat – that well of pure spring water cradled by mountain dark. Mountain. Dark. Which leads me to spontaneously complete the triangulation, return the dragon to core of cirque without lifting my pen, send it back up to the heights before back to cosy den. Like a path walked in reverse, like a tape-measure slid back into container – flick of switch, same out as in, home to beginning, known for first time. Complete.

The triangle revealed by clef'd tail speaks. "Mountain," it says, grinning into my slow realisation that now my job is to place its Taoist companion-runes either side – square of Earth (solid, dense of matter'd consciousness) at left; cirque of Heaven (Enso's emptiness; BigMind's no-thing) at right, exactly as calligraphy-scripted by (Sengai's) zendo'd ZenGuy. _All energy_ passes through Mountain's River-of-Light in/to world, it says, in this form. I'm back with Sasso and his Waale; so too do I remember a vision of Schiesshorn's Berg-Geist genie (fire-beanie'd, beacon-lit) from a few weeks earlier. There I 'saw' the ignite of two fire-streams in his (stone) skin (like two poles of a charge? jumper leads to kick-start next best co-creation?). Prefacing Glyph's arrival was Sasso's instruction; prefacing Glyph's arrival was the Schiesshorn vision; prefacing Song's arrival was each and both, but now the Glyph is here – front and centre – expressing an urgent desire for inclusion in our work of Light and Song?

Now! it says. Now! Use me! Now! On/on, over/over I script – swifter/swifter performing the Glyph's fluidity till I see:

Pivot Pole of Self; Me/Mountain twinned:

Here, right here, says the Glyph, Singing Bird sings!

In vision pre-dawn the Great Glyph returns to demonstrate how we may harness its energy, its 'framing Tor' (gate) (spoken), as a <u>shunt</u> system. Conveniently it hooks my understanding into the 'erdsonde', the geo-thermal-heat-pump-thingey we recently drilled 300-metres into the chthonic depths of side garden for sustainable future alpine Winter'd warmth. I see the dragon (of course it's you, Seiryu, honey-bun!) coil itself around Glyph's PeacePole'd (plunging) stake as if snaky-symbol of medical healing but with a key difference: <u>Two</u> dragons. One ascends, one descends – tail/s in mouth/s, Ouroboros in doublet? OK, I think I get it. Our Song needs to be sung in <u>both</u> subtle and physic'd dimensions of Being – in/out of Time-partner'd time <u>plus</u> henceforth Heaven/Earth'd; our work must stay open/connectable in/to all dimensions of Presence; Love's Light must be able to flow (and flow through) <u>unimpeded</u>.

·····

Phew ... that was an energetic surge in chapter midst. Time to slow it, calm it, gift ...

Sistering. It's been part of my vocab whether subtle or physic'd for as long as I can remember. I feel my closest girlfriends to be (soul) Sisters as much as my (sole) genetic Sister, while forging fresh relations with 'newbies' can feel as if we've walked a path together before. "Getting to know someone from the inside out," I call it – that heart-connection which simply says: "Yes." Staying open/curious to what an other (<u>any</u> other in-carnation) may offer to one's unfolding understanding of Life in all its colours, flavours, to a point where the link is as penetrant and robust as to a Sister – equal, pure. The same principle applies in subtle encounters; the energy signatures of various Presences I engage in together-work for Gaia can feel to be 'family', while thanks to the Amici, I have been introduced to many Sidhe who are 'cousins on my mother's side'. Truly are we OnePeople; and I feel myself fully connected into our sole/soul lineage of cosmic humanity.

But beyond that and <u>deeper</u> are '<u>The Sisters'</u> whom it is impossible to label or describe – their complexity, expansiveness, wisdom and longevity cannot sit within a human-language'd reductionist construct (or at least one to which I am privy). In-streaming from stellar realms they shapeshift at will to the causes/conditions of planetary work required, taking on whatever incarnate (or dis-) forms best suit the moment. Our trenchworking Amici crew is humbled/blessed (in equal measure) to serve in whichever small capacity we can; a single 'kiss' of their Light whip-whirls us to action, all fruits of same returned to cosmic treasury for these 'Chancellors of the Exchequer' to apply as they will. Working with and <u>for</u> 'The Sisters', timeless elders in a clan with no beginning or end led me to 'know' (in that way of 'knowing-beyond-knowing') that:

All Mothers are Sisters and All Sisters are One
And all that we <u>make</u> speaks the sum of our Love

Sistering. For all such relations – no matter how prosaic or poetic, everyday or exceptional – the memory-images I conjure revolve around the art of 'making'. Creating, nurturing, bringing forth some potentiality to manifest 'Life'. My mind floods with images of community – stirring a pot of steaming soup over the village fire; sitting at spinning wheel or weaving loom; perhaps blanket-stitching or placidly knitting – individual together-actions. Maybe simply wiping floury hands on a 'pinny' tied at waist before joining a group-chat over a cup of tea at kitchen table.

Each image – its tenor and scent, its timbre and texture – sustains an understanding of my role in co-participatory work, as a partner to co-creative purpose. I 'see' the elements bend to the purity of loving intent; I 'see' the energetic swirl of alchemic arise from the cauldron we tend; I 'see' how what we envision dances toward embodied form. In short, I 'see' what we 'make' and it is good – because at its heart is Love and its intent is pure and its making is shared. We each bring our Sister'd gifts to sacred crucible, and what emerges is ever a gift offered to our sweet Sister, Gaia.

This is not to devalue the role of masculine energy/partnering to the task of creative 'making'. I can point to as many examples of robust male Presence offering gifts to our trenchworking together-work; amongst our Amici crew are as many lads as lasses. But for the purposes of this reflection and the particularities of this work of Song, it is to 'The Sisters' and their lineage I turn and bow, in homage, for their blessing of our voice and pen.

The sacred feminine impulse arising from Love's primal Ground at the heart of each form of sentience ("Human, Angel, Slug or Stone" as I once penned in poem) breathed its knowing into me thus one day years past at the tail end of a subtle journey home to source code/x:

All Mothers are Sisters and all Sisters are One

Still (just like with the sacred masculine), it can take time to intuit, embrace, and fully release the space of Love's feminine extent, surrender to its desire to goddess-dance inwith incarnate self. To excavate the deepest Dark of uncreated Light, recognise the potent potentiality that seeks manifestation in whichever form best serves the specificity of its in-Time function, also requires courage. And strength. Learning to wear Soul-at-Skin; learning to trust the fecund depths of Sink as it burbles to Surface; learning to weave the threads of Love's purity of intent as it yearns to express its Truth in-world.

Becoming the Me I was always meant to be. And, along the way, understanding that the more I know this Me the more I know Gaia and the more She knows herself – the entwining of our consciousness seemingly evolving in like (divine) breath; the sharing of our consciousness likewise enabling Me to dive deep (to source-code), return with what best She needs. Now. For her Future. For her

Future is our own. In Skin. And beyond.

So did it happen over the years I called her Sister – as I call Moon Sister or Sun big (seriously big) Brother; each and every Mountain, Tree, Bird or (buzzy) Bee et cetera et cetera et cetera (to coin a 'Yul Brunner'). Completely natural – we are Family. No beginning or end; no fore or aft. All is Now and All are One. Self-Other? Void. Null. Done. And yet, equally, each is blessed as a unique expression of sacred Gaian life. How happy I am to be Me! Who/what else could I possibly be? <u>This</u> is my incarnation – this time, this skin. It just is. As we all just are. No hierarchy. Simply an ever-extending 'plane of consistence', whose boundary is determined only by our <u>capacity</u> to see beyond a (non-existent) horizon to a space, a time where:

All Mothers are Sisters and all Sisters are One

The energy of mergence, the inner strength of self-sovereign solidarity with the sacred feminine impulse which this statement reveals, started to ramp up during 2021 (as the previous chapter documents). Completing the Song/s of Gaia, a partner'd string of encircled knowing begun seven years earlier in the specificity of our forgotten valley's Source (code/x), was like its own 'watershed' moment in our own (divine) watershed. Down seven years we Amici had been working with Sidhe collectives from each corner of our OneWorld – sharing Story, Song, and plenty of cups of healing PeaceTea. Truly wondrous, infilled of everyday delight – who would have thought? Pilgrim-walking Love – in fresh dress, with pure intent – through all blood/bones of Earth via Helvetia's peaceable skin. Sole pressed to Soul, singing up Land as we too were sung, cycling through (seven) years. Done.

Or not? A day came in wake of our annual Samhain honouring of the Ancestors when I stood at my 'window on world' staring into the magical beauty of this divine watershed to speak, as usual, our invocatory mantra. But suddenly it took me – down, down, chthonic depths down. Immediately gone – into the heart of stone, the <u>power</u> of Land that says: "I am."

I experienced the perfect prismic ensoul'd consciousness that pervades the density of our Third-Rock'd matter – from core to thin Blue line – waking, bending, weaving the elements to the purity of <u>its</u> intent. Words flowed out of this place of twinned essence, seamless Presence. Words, guttural, with a fierceness/strength of self-sovereign <u>Sister'd</u> solidarity. I said:

"*I am with You, Land. I am with You, and whatever <u>You</u> need to do to bring balance to your World, sanity to your Sink, healing to your Children. You do whatever You need to do, whatever it takes for your own Peace (of mind,) your own Lifeblood (of arteries) to be maintained, cleansed, refined. You call on all ye gods, all causes/conditions, all companions of the Way of Love. You make the call and I will be with You. For: I <u>am</u>. And I am with <u>You</u>; <u>surrendered</u> to Source, accepting of whatever it takes, whatever will be.*

This is *your* World, Gaia, and You are *not* going down."

Yes, fierceness, strength pervaded my words (hers) here-spoken – uplifted in the raw sanctity of WolfMother's high wild (Autumn-gold-leaf'd) terrain. A courage of conviction. And also tears, tears, tears – offered from cupped hands as healing balm for her to plant in her Earth. Hers. Our covenant/birth contract signed, sealed, herein lived to support hers.

'The Sisters' arrived as I spoke these words, had heard the Morrigan's Moon-illumined call, in-flown through this Tor (now wide open), to stand (with little me) and offer into this space a shared mantra to in-herald the depths of 'new', to confirm a next best (seven-year) cycle of work back up the line to our cosmic ancestry, said:

We stand in Solidarity
With the Power of Presence – our own
Crystal-cloaked and Starlight-boned

Yes. The energy of mergence that had ramped up all year chose here/now to go truly ballistic. Should it come as any surprise then, Reader, when "Song: To the Power of Seven" arrived so passionately and unerringly in its wake?

• • • • •

Imbolc '22. Time for a bit of Spring-cleaning. I wander round the corner of living room to where our ancient spinet, the family pianola (disembowelled by Father to dissuade cheeky kids cheating on our scales – so goes the legend anyway), commands pride-of-place in music nook. I sit with the text written a year past – in honour of the ('20) year that had been, to in-herald the ('21) year to come:

Time slow'd distil'd becalm'd
I have sung the Grace of the Seven Sisters – strong
Life flows on, healing balm'd
I am Anne of the Family – homecome welcomed

And now, a year further on – in honour of this year that had been, to in-herald a next best to come? I write:

Time slow'd distil'd becalm'd
Tiger lair and dragon pool balm'd
Mountain's Dark cradles all of Love's Light
I open at the close, and take flight …

A contemplative, ruminative rhyme, nought more, in the face of Cancer's journey since Brigid first whispered at Imbolc '20: "Welcome, to the first day of the rest of your life." Two years (by then) it had been of 'this life' and yes, I was in contemplative, ruminative mood. And then to wander round the corner of living room to do a bit of Spring-cleaning.

But the piano draws me closer, whispers: "Wipe the keys. Not just the wood." Ridiculous. I haven't opened the lid in a year. But? What's that? As if a sigh, a breath long held is released. I sit on tapestry'd stool Mother stitched during my childhood, run a hand along the smooth length of keyboard. Long, long, long since I've sat at this (grand!) spinet as if at writing desk. Long, long, long – because of my focus on healing, concern re pain (Cancer's calling card ever at hand). I sound a note. Hammer to string. Out-of-tune, but the resonance of wood? Like a sung patina of rich and vibrant hue. It can't be for long – back/wrists groaning as I try Beethoven and following: Einaudi's 'Mountain'. I say: "I have no memory of reading music; in physic'd condition no patience to relearn." I sing, that's it (said), and you are my (silent) muse (too said). Ah, but it is now that the chords arise which want to be sung, finger'd into being by a hand stretched wide (and screaming).

It is now, because I hear 'The Sisters' arrive. It all proceeds in a rush, the writing of this (new, yet ever-known within, it seems) Song. A blast of knowing that says:

"This is where it ends. And where it begins. Indeed have you opened at the close. Now, Annie, now: Take flight!"

In the key of A (for Annie? Anwa? Aura, aum'd out on verandah?) Minor – high, high, octave-high and light – oh, so very light (of being)! But its singing? Out here in-world? My voice cannot possibly be so mezzo-sopranic. Too aged is this instrument, falling out of key as oft as this century'd dame of New York (spinet) fame. Such that I find I'm 2.5 octaves deeper (chthonic in descent?), audibly framed in/by F (Minor). But never mind. 'Tis our Song, Sisters, regardless, and I do understand the paradox of age/wisdom drawing you higher/higher, to aetherically hum the Sora'd chorale of all homecome, Arcadia's chrysalis warp/weft'd for birth of her New, while I here remain in/on/with Tsuchi'd ground to commune/draw forth Gaia's full. Third-Rock'd indeed is our Sacred Pool ...

• • • • •

Reader, I have spoken of in-weaving (and/or waking) the momentum of 'The Sisters' down the years – as much via their outreach as mine. In previous chapters, along an a-linear continuum (as is our Amici wont), I have shared praxis and experience liberally. But I have to say that the most recent vibrant container for their <u>constellating</u> energies was the story, "Leeks & Peas" – vibrant in terms of being able to record in mythic 'fictional' voice their wisdom, strength, skill from a 'place' of direct witness. Tolkien likewise used fiction as the container for mythic fact; while our bardic work may be infinitely more lowly in the literary canon, its source is the same unending well of cosmic ancestral knowing into which his genius tapped. Documenting, therefore, what I was <u>sanctioned</u> to share, uplifting in heart the <u>unbending</u> Love fuelling these Sisters' work, led me to the intimate realisation that our purity of intent can <u>equally</u> dissolve Darkness with Light. We have that power. Here, from the text:

Now did the Elements prove worthy Sister'd servants – each took one, made it her own. Sirona's preserve Earth, chthonic depths of molten gold. Naomi's Aether, the inweave of silver'd crystal threads. Through which the others danced a warp-weft – Air, Fire, Water – to re-knit in-world the Truth of Love's altar, this Temple in which no lamb should face slaughter. Harmonic the Commons of simple shared resonance, to bring the all of the All back to balance.

Back at ancient spinet, the chords' melody unleashed a veritable waterfall of lyrics in its frothing wake to tell the "who, what, where, when, how, and why" of Sister'd work. Once all syllables had settled into their chosen (and forever) form, I found there was one task left to complete – to affirm <u>my</u> presence at shared table. Yes, in wake of Samhain I had stood at my 'window on world' and said: "I am with you, Gaia. No. Matter. What." Yes, at Winter Solstice I had been invited to stand equal with Sisters (in Aboriginal Dreaming dress) on Tectonia's escarpment and subtly 'sing' (as vibratory resonance) Light in/through Gaia's thin Blue line, implant the star (seeds) in pungent earth.

But "The Sisters Song"'s extant uplift at Imbolc, a few short weeks down the (rutted, dusty, outback) track from that midnight (blue) 'event' took my contractual obligation (in the spirit of Jung's premise that "<u>any</u> content that emerges involves a <u>spiritual</u> or <u>moral</u> task") out of the subtle realms and firmly rooted it in the physic'd. P was ready and waiting; it was time – through Song, through this <u>particular</u> expression of Song, each word honed to speak the truth of our Sister'd conviction – to announce my readiness.

It meant stepping up and into a role for which I had never felt worthy (and/or capable) – to be the one who <u>actively</u> crosses the threshold, <u>straddles</u> the dimensions, <u>literally</u> brings our Song in-world, and fully anchors it in the soil of here-now Gaian flesh. Yes, the very high key of Sister'd voice referenced our shared subtle singing in aetheric realms; an audio recording I made confirms it. But in populating the melody with lyrics, the energetic <u>shift</u> to physical world was not just to accommodate the ancient instrument of my embodied voice. It was with the distinct task to 'funnel' the shift, to ensure its firm anchoring in the <u>soil</u>-lines of Earth, the fundamental consciousness of <u>physical</u> matter. To affirm all of this, it was my job to pen the invocation to Song, and to 'announce' my role in the line-up while they observed:

They called her the Morrigan. She answered only to the Mistress of the Moon in a lightening Sky and now She said to the Sisters: Fly! Up we lifted on Peace-Dove'd wings. Straight through the Tor. To bless Gaia's All. Aye: I have met the Sister who is me Star-sheened. I have met the future of our Sister'd kin to come. I have known the Sisters who are older, wiser. I know what it is to be welcomed Home. For our lineage is starblood-strong and revived through genetic memory of what we were, have ever been: One.

So know – I am not one of them, but one of: Us. And bringing our Song in-world is my sacred Sister'd task. This is "The Sisters Song" – and we sing it for our Sister, Gaia.

For together we are: Seven. Sisters. Strong.

'The Sisters' know where this anchoring must take place, as a premiere performance of Song (documented). They also know its timing – exact. Further, they know I will be resistant to the idea. I had promised myself to not return to Schönthal till we could all be together there again as a full family collective. Thanks to Covid, it has been four years by that stage since I had hugged most of my progeny. The krypta is closed in any case, I argued. Still on Winter break. No, they insisted. You must sing. A flash vision of Daphne'd cirque punched me in the chest. A first time, perhaps an only time, in this hallowed 'Temenos of Tree', but with these Sisters (they said) must you sing!

At this point in our roundabout narrative, Reader, let me comment on the significance of the '22 lunar New Year (Tiger/Tigress/Tigris'd: "Miaow!" says Annie, a water tiger lass) having dawned concomitant with Imbolc, the (un-)surprising arrival of Song (Great Glyph tagging along with a grin). As related in an earlier chapter, but here restated in context of discussion, we on/in-Earth Amici work closely with a Sidhe collective I know as 'Moon Mother's Community'. This group acts as a first threshold/gateway/portal of incoming Light from stellar realms; it's like a base camp for translating 'gardening' activity to in-world form. For the specificity of our troupe's work, the moonscape of Song-weaving performs a kind of electricity substation or transformer role to translate/shift the energies into a moulded (stepped-down) form for us on/in-Earth to receive and further shape as we partner the five elements inwith Gaia's full reach (planetary core to thin Blue line'd atmospheric extent).

As the outtake above from "Leeks & Peas" suggests, this work is no walk in the park (so to speak). To have the Glyph actively enter our process to support the alchemic 'framing' of our elemental balancing (act) with its energetic swirl before vertical 'stake' plunge to anchor Song in (Gaia's) stellar flesh represented a significant in-time development, like a booster shot offered to ritual as performed. The invocatory text to open "The Sisters Song" would 'announce' this job' (in a manner of speaking) to the Glyph and through 'whom' (i.e. me) this would pass. It was time to design our Schönthal performance …

•••••

"The Sisters Song" had been penned, rehearsed, walked out through Gaia's garden beyond our border'd grail, upsung. I sat, wrote the first two lines of a haiku in reverence:

Weaving the Garden.
Sow/sewing* Song through your bones.
(*here either/or phonetic effects its true-meaning'd twin)

I sat, chewed the end of pen. The last three syllables of third line were already in mind. But I could not see how to succinctly express the 'holy communion' of our weaving (as the Song's chorus chants) in two syllables to preface them. Suddenly, words formed: "Blood ties."

Yes! That's how we saw our work, the strength of our work, the genetic memory of starblood lineage that brought these Sisters, <u>my</u> Sisters, in/to world right here/right now to sing for <u>our</u> Sister, Gaia. A connection so deep, so familiar (and familial!) <u>nothing</u> could crack its shield (maiden'd) wall; a weaving so tight, so loving <u>nothing</u> could penetrate its sinew'd warp/weft. Resilient. Enduring. Firm, but flexible. Bendable, but never (again) breakable. Letting Wind enter, keeping Mountain still.

All had fractured; now Song had sounded its healing gong; Song arisen from ancestral Middle Tree in the <u>hope</u> all (Gaian) flesh to heal. I had stood with Kali, and now stood – empower'd of our own (Sister'd) Presence. Mute would Earth no more be.

"Song: To the Power of Seven." <u>Seven</u>-teen syllables. In the space of a breath, our work described our work, and a twinned phonetic doublet wove the Garden to Itself:

Weaving the Garden.
Sow/sewing Song through your bones.
Blood ties. Sister'd. Strong.

Now, remember our Amici (snowballing) desire down the years to flip the switch on my subtle Sister's lament ("There is not enough Love in the world") with the following mantra?

There is so much Love in the World
It just wants to be released
And this is our forever work –
We, the People of Peace ...

And remember our Amici praxis to gift a token of HomeSong into each reservoir of emissarial outreach encountered on our pilgriming (for Love) PeaceTea'd and PeacePole'd way?

Anonymous, unremarked (and unremarkable), just another small human going about daily life, taking a (very) long walk everywhere, everywhen – listening, learning, having a chat, stopping for a snack. Always with a token of blessing, blessed. Suffused with HomeSong energy which continues 'steeping' while walking, singing. By the time it reaches its 'squirreling spot' (aka reservoir)? Veritably buzzing with self-beingness and joy of service.

"We all breathe Life into what we Love."

Stones, shells, beanies lost and (unwittingly) gifted to Bens. Hence? Never underestimate the consciousness of matter – <u>any</u> matter – to be an 'avatar' of loving Presence, to leave a trace of organic blessing via <u>its</u> truth of nature, twinned. The critical point is the <u>purity</u> of our intent – as pure as the Peace sunk deep in

Helvetia's (settled) bones; as pure as the Love at core of Helvetia's (purring) heart, as pure as the (liquid) Light frothing forth from Helvetia's (stellar) Mountain source/s, maintaining the lifeblood of arteries through all of Gaia's fragrant world.

In short? We are Sasso and we are the Waale. And we have our Zen Peace nook in garden grail where our tokens can reside before gifted on to their own subtle activism as bearers-of-blessing in physical world – out from source ('True-Sister's-Island' upstream) down the gravelly 'River of Enlightenment' and through the 'Ocean of Being' (in Elder Tree shade) – out. Now, on the foundations of all we had laid in this blessing space we horizontally overlay (in vision) the Sidhe's Great Glyph as if it lay flat on ground, perpendicular to the usual vertical render of 'stake' plunged deep in grail's stellar flesh. Indeed, Bateson's definition of a tuber, or plateau, as a 'continuous, self-vibrating region of intensities' seemed to fit very neatly with how our garden grail evolved as its own self as well as being a feeder system out.

A bit like a kitchen pantry, in a way, where things are placed on different shelves according to use, proximity or associative resonance before retrieved to chuck in a soup or stew bubbling on hob, tokens rest here or there. often, I forget where I've collected this or that, but the tokens always remember their provenance, are comfortable with their (migratory) shift, and see into its (and their) higher purpose.

Where is this exposition leading, you may wonder, in the context of our (working) Song to take us through the next seven-year cycle of service to Gaia?

Incubating since Samhain, subtly resonant since Winter Solstice, and fully physically 'born' at Imbolc, we spent Moon's first full cycle of New (Tiger) Year rehearsing in garden grail (inner/outer), making some (lame) recordings and taking the Song out for brief forays across Helvetia's skin. At stopping places I pressed play on iPhone and the Song (spinet/subtle; voice/physic'd) burbled in forests or on park benches in sight of the high alps. Once, the Joy of its 'voice' took such hold I played the recording while walking well-populated paths to quizzical looks from passers-by. (Meanwhile, MagicMan was turning cartwheels: "Yay! Annie's finally loosening up!")

The energy of undertaking really began to snowball. Moon's incubatory Dark at start of March brought the sudden 'thought' to perform an action to premiere our Song in-world. Jeremy had already kindly offered us a virtual 'stage' – a Lorian Sidhe classroom to which we had been invited to contribute (his outreach, incidentally, pre-Song's arrival) but we felt our offering needed 'anchoring' in a physical act whose documentation (of praxis) could be shared with class participants.

The action? "Pebbles for Peace." For Ukraine, for All. For, by Peace, I mean not only Peace at the level of humanity – amongst individuals, communities, nation-states; amongst races, genders, cultures and religions – but also Peace at its most fundamental. With Gaia and <u>all</u> her countless inhabitants, <u>all</u> her precious children.

Forty-day/nights of peaceable pebbles collected at random from the Zen nook's (enlightened) River, offered to my PeaceTea bowl. Forty-day/nights fasting from homemade Matcha Latte. (MagicMan sighed: "Tough, but doable.") Three pebbles a day (one for each of Peace-Love-Light) brought indoors to kitchen bench where I make (myriad) daily cups of teas. Pebbles sitting, watching, (subtly) <u>steeping</u>. Pebbles immersed in infused (effusive!) praxis. Whether Herbal or Green, whether Earl or Lady (Grey), whether Oolong, Chai or Rooibos, a 'Tao of Tea' at work each/every (healing) day.

In the Zen nook, at 'True-Sister's-Island' (first compelling stone out from Source), I anchored the purity of our intent with a palm-sized lily-white pebble (huge compared to the tiny pearls of enlightened gravel offered to bowl). Its own source was the still-frozen edge of a (sacred) pool near our local creek, a place where frogs plant the purity of their (spawning) intent, a place where I (often) meet my bird-of-heaven (grey heron fisher, still as standing stone) watching/waiting for a hearty feast of these fruits of springtime labour later in season.

At the midpoint of our 40-day/night action, Spring Equinox, Moon was just past her Full. Best time to plant 'perennials' in lunation cycle – Love's <u>living</u> desire for long-<u>lived</u> potentialities to full-manifest. Whether fruiting tree, grapevine or vivacious daylily, such plants more readily take root at this time of cycle, plunging their will-to-be more consciously into fecund soil. Thus did I step out from 'True-Sister's-Island' – a self-vibrating Batesonian plateau if ever there was one – with this palm-sized lily-white pebble on that day. On that day planting the <u>perennial</u> purity of our Sister'd intent in Song inwith the Sister'd cirque of Linden at Schönthal, this 'open-air' temenos par excellence; and, following performance, planting this (consequent) Pebble for Peace, for All – in each time/place of Gaia's ensoul'd World – at their Sister'd feet. My freaky sketch of the Great Glyph came along for the ride, with PeacePole, Song, and (most importantly <u>and</u> graciously) my 'choir boy', F, as trusty videographer of our in-Time Amici'd performance for the Lorian class participants' outwith-Time witness.

Equal day equal night/I hold you both within my sight
Whether here or whether there/May all of Gaia hear our prayer:
To love, love, and love some more, bring the Light of my Life to the Life of the World
To walk, walk, and walk some more, bring All of my Light to All of the World
To sing, sing, and sing some more, bring Joy of the Light into every Home

As I wake on Equinox morn, I realise it is seven weeks since Imbolc's incubatory unfold of our Song. Our random place of rest this night, proximate to performance locale its only criterion, is Room 7 (believe it or not) in a centuries-old coaching inn at the foot of a limestone ridge where, earlier, guests bathed in the healing waters gushing from its mountain-deep mineral spring. In the corridor outside our room, a small battered upright piano blocks the way to (unused) rooms further down the hall. I shake my head at the synchronicity, open the lid, sound a note. More in tune than my own at home. I pick up PeacePole, thank the piano for its resonant support of Song and once more, open at the close to: Take flight!

Such that now? Where are we now in time? Ah, yes. 'Tis a month past our Equinox action, arriving in an online Lorian classroom reprising its own 'continuous, self-vibrating region of intensities'. 'Tis Easter Sunday, the day on which our 40-day/nights of peaceable pebbles go home to Zen nook as tiny starseeds of Love's _living_ Light planted afresh in (its) River reach, their own long-lived potentialities to full-manifest in Earth. Watered by perennial Song comingled with blessed rain (subtle/physic'd) pit-pattering down, to Joy-infill their stellar'd flesh (again), the elements bending to our purity of intent (again), to flow Peace-Love-Light out/on – beyond.

So here we are (or there we were) – humbled, delighted and so very _moved_ to offer "The Sisters Song" to a circle of honouring participant-witness, for a wider collective of our OnePeople'd collective to engage our action and service which (like all other co-productions) is housed in the nestedfishes.org krypta.

May it resonate. May it bear fruit. Out/on – beyond. For no matter how simple the Song, it hosts the Sacred at core. And no matter how tiny the pebble, it speaks Mountain, pure ...

• • • • •

Postscript:

As with "Song of Gaia" which opened itself to unexpected reprise on a North Sea shoreline of all places, since "The Sisters Song" entered the canon it has (likewise) prodded and poked, niggled and naggled to be sung loud/long anywhere, anywhen, anyhow as a blessing and affirmation of our (crystal-cloaked, starlight-boned) solidarity with Gaia's evolutionary journey. It desired to be called to the ten directions (and more) from atop the most northerly Munro of the Scots Highlands (we met this performance, Reader, in a "Ben/Bog/Dog'd" chapter); it desired to be sung during a picnic on a remote meadow on a (less-than-remote) Mediterranean island (while picnic partners watched in amusement in between sandwich snatches); it desired to be 360-degree shouted from a rocky goat-bell percussive paddock in the back-block sierras of al-Andalus which surprisingly summoned a heavenly host of griffon vultures to join my weaving work.

I have to admit that was my personal favourite 'gig' and, once again, lucky F was there to bear witness to an awe-inspiring elemental dance of thermals by 18 broad-winged feather-cloaked angels alchemically spiralling directly over my head to support the continuum of energies – stellar, earthen – while I held (Peace) Pole'd position. Yes, lucky he was there otherwise I would have thought I dreamt it!

As with each occasion, it is the appearance of the Morrigan who alerts me to the right here, right now nature of time/place intersect which can anchor Song deep in Gaia's bones. Each occasion, except one that is – when I 'called' myself to perform (and record said performance) on the cliffs of Galicia, at the edge of the world where Mountain meets (Atlantic) Sea (wilds). These gnarly cliffs had welcomed me as one of their own when I entered their Celtic-infused domain decades earlier. A first and only (till Autumn '23) visit, it had nonetheless made a stunning impact. In vision thereafter I would spontaneously find myself back there – soaring o'er their worldly edge as if I the Morrigan of own personal mythic lore. These cliffs set me on the path I have consciously followed e'er since, a becoming landscape in Annie-lived skin. Now, with the chance to physically return, something I least expected when Cancer came knocking, my Joy at spiritual 'homecoming' was such I just had to share with the elemental spirits of place 'who' I had become – via Song, <u>this</u> Song.

These cliffs, this wild edge of Europe, had given me the courage to 'fly', to take to the skies when the Morrigan called the Sisters to task – to lift on Peace-Dove'd wings, straight through the Tor, and bless Gaia's All. Such Love expressed by Land! By DeepTime-Tectonia in its (fiery Hope'd) <u>forge</u> lashed by Atlantic swell! Who could ever have imagined where it would lead?

And with that, Reader, come with me through the Tor into our last Tor-ii'd chapter.

A TEMENOS TO SONG – ANWA IN FORM

I say this every time, I write this every time – that I know not where to start, to tell a story with no beginning or end. Often I resolve this (in my mind if not your perusal, Reader) by launching 'in medias res' and then follow the line/s of flight in whichever way/s they wish to travel. But here we are, in our last chapter of volume, and so I feel we should start its narrative at end – then walk backwards to its requisite beginning when a lass named "Torii" was birthed in heart via a vision at whose centre was the Great Glyph of the Sidhe ...

Yes, slowly we are approaching the close of narrative, having explored the Sacred within Mountains from multiple perspectives and interrelations to Song harnessed in support of the quickening of Gaia's evolutionary consciousness. Threads in the telling, I know, have been unwieldly (at best) but such is the fate of a text co-produced with a fluid bunch of kin (micro-macro'd and all in-between) inwith a field as Breath-<u>expansive</u> as Gaia's spheric planetary extent (core to thin Blue line) beyond which a plethora of co-conspirators from solar-system'd and interstellar dimensions have oft-delighted to add their co-creative, wise-elder, and mediatory respiratory quotient (RQ) as/when deemed fit to Story'd purpose. Later in this final chapter I will introduce you to a symphonic tone poem, "Miracles", which speaks to our cosmic-'party' (as experienced in small human skin) but to describe the felt-sense of having to cut the length of tapeworm at some point in narrative, so that this volume is not <u>too</u> heavy in hand, Reader, or weighty in your backpack, herewith a sample/taste-test of its voice to call us to last page/s:

for this is how it ends, and how begins (again)
looping the thread of evermore's wend
ring-songing the longing of love's belonging
ham-sa/hei-wa/har-mo-zen'd

And from here? Back to the future with a quote of Mariel's from the inaugural auspicious year of our Amici partnership (2015, as told in "Awakening") yet only discovered now – nine (short) years hence (as is the shapeshifting/time-turning wont of all things outwith). 'Tis a quote which relates to all we have made and all we are fresh-bringing to performance stage. 'Tis a quote which, if known when the vision of Great Glyph <u>desiring</u> to be applied to specific task in our Amici cirque two years past had arisen (indeed did I hear its "Use me!" cry), in <u>direct</u> intersect with "The Sisters Song"'s arrival at ancient spinet, it would have had me nodding solemnly at the unfold expected of our troupe rather than rushing around like a (proverbial) headless chook.

Now, is your curiosity piqued, Reader? Well, let us begin ... at (Mariel's) end:

"We create by "singing" things into being and form ... though it is true that we do actually chant and sing at times when we are building, the deeper reality lies in the nature of the "Anwa" (which) is like music ... a music that is not simply heard but felt throughout one's body and consciousness. It is life-energy in rhythmic motion and activity. Blending with the Anwa of another, whether that other is stone or tree, animal, Sidhe, or human, has correspondences to blending harmoniously with another's voice in a choir. You find an arrangement that suits you both and lets your voices — or your Anwa — blend in chords of mutual unfoldment and expression. Each thing's Anwa is its song of life and being; it contains its form and its dreams, what it has been, what it is, and what it seeks to become."

Mariel's student and working partner takes up the narrative at this point:

"The Anwa to us is sacred, and when we create something, we think of it as bringing forth new life, for that is what it is ... whatever we create, we draw its Anwa, its spirit, from the universal Anwa that sustains us all. We are all melodies in the Master Song, the one sung by the Singer of all creation ... Even from conception, we look for the connections. Nothing is made in isolation from everything else, even though everything that is made carries its own unique melody within the music of the universe. ... It is like a child to us. My teacher said that we grow our buildings, but I would say we nurture them as children from their conception in our minds and hearts to their construction in the land chosen to receive them. ... they are alive to us, as alive as any other part of Gaia. ... it becomes ... a companion. Its space is alive to us, a presence with which we may partner, and its Anwa is there to complement our own and to be complemented in return by what we can bring or add."

These quotes are drawn from a (Visions) class David and Jeremy held in 2015 (when the Amici and I too busy a-task to attend any class!). As soon as discovered (now) however and, thanks to Jeremy, placed in the fullness of its provenance (thanks to David, Mariel, and her student for their conversation), I saw how perfectly it encapsulated the <u>specificity</u> of shared process undertaken in our latest co-production – from Torii's conception in heart to her manifest birthing on physic'd plane. A process which involved energetic as well as physic'd shaping to 'sing' her to vibrant life. So too it speaks to the extraordinary synchronicity of events which enabled her co-creation from the exact materials required for <u>her</u> work of Song. A case of partner'd praxis involving congruency of intent, and correspondences woven, woken in flesh.

So <u>who</u> is Torii you may wonder? Here we enter the chronology of co-creation …You may recall, Reader, that in our last chapter I spoke of the Glyph's arrival in vision, its active desire to enter our 'sistering' process. I described how the way it presented in vision offered support to the alchemic framing of our elemental balancing (act). Its energetic swirl before vertical 'stake' plunge to <u>anchor</u> Song in (Gaia's) stellar flesh was a significant development for our work, like a booster shot offered to ritual as performed. You may recall, too, my longstanding praxis to twin subtle-physic, spirit-geologic, to 'nestedfishes' fuse the all-of-all to one-and-same for our acts to better 'stick' in-world. So did we begin the conceptual thinking-through of a 'container' in which to house the Glyph's desire. And Torii was born in heart.

But <u>what</u> is Torii you may (also) wonder? Torii is the Japanese word for gate, portal, threshold. Most specifically it refers to the vermillion red entrances to Shinto shrines, representing the crossing point from daily profane to sacred eternal. They are also present in nature (as forest chapels for pilgrims) as well as some Buddhist temples. They can be made of wood or stone, and gladden my heart with their stillness, their very <u>beingness</u>; 'tis akin to being in the presence of Tree or Mountain, bringing me to a place of Peace.

Hewn by human hand, they nevertheless retain (and/or uplift) an ancient sage-like energy, a lofty weightiness that I never would have imagined until our pilgrimage to Japan years ago with the intent to directly connect into a culture <u>and</u> Land which had long been 'live' in our family's genetic memory. While an actual Torii bore no physical resemblance to my vision, the associative resonances of its hallowed function were clear. I have a penchant for naming, symbolic at that. Everything is alive, has its own 'voice', and thus deserves an own name to honour its energetic signature of form and/or function in a living cosmos. Beanie may be called Beanie but when I say Beanie I mean Beanie (especially when it's a snowy cap fetchingly worn by a Berg-Geist genie!). There can be whimsy in my naming rituals or thoughtfulness; there can be times when Presence itself announces a moniker while I stand clueless, but as soon as the Great Glyph flashed, said it needed a container, a grail space in which to support our work of Song, I knew that what we would co-create is a Torii whose name would (therefore) be Torii; a 'she' she would be too – a Sister born of and to work with our sistering collective.

But how is Torii you may (now) wonder? Ah, that is where the rubber (first) hit the road and where our chronology truly begins. "The Sisters Song" born at ancient spinet, Imbolc '22; a few days later the Glyph surfacing, insistent – just as insistently as it had three years prior for/in a particular process associated with our UrWerk but afterwards immediately went underground again. This time, however, it had no desire to retreat from consciousness so I began to sketch/script it according to the exact dimensions in John Matthews' "The Sidhe". This process I described in the last chapter (in the raw rush of notes in a journal entry) but in subtle sight following, the Glyph morphed, arose as a spinning form (like a golden revolving door) set inwith a static or fixed arched (rather-than-circular) 'frame' – something dense enough to anchor, or 'hold', its whipwhirl dervish'd dance. The Glyph appeared much larger, more powerful, present, active, 'alive' inwith this frame than I would have expected of a rune 'held' in-frame. At the same time, however, the frame looked very finely, slimly, subtly hewn – too 'delicate' for such a robust resident? Hmmm … The frame seemed to represent the spheric extent of Gaia's full reach out to thin Blue line (as reprised in Song), the slim sheafs of de-densifying atmosphere like an image taken from the ISS I have on desktop (to accompany Song). A verse arose as I beheld the vision:

Pale misted Light of Evening
Penetrate the Shine
Stretch thru the Veil to Other Side
Leave None of Self behind

Following, a single word was firm-spoken: "Congruency." Clearly we were being counselled that however we 'worked' the Glyph in this form required prudence. With the energy of spinning Tor (German for 'gate'), the potential for parts of oneself to be flung out/lost to/through any of countless dimensional 'gates' flowing off the main Glyph portal could not be underestimated. One needed to maintain complete congruency in/with/of Self, according to purity of intent as well as ensure any partner energy engaged or journey'd-with heeded the same pact. As I had experienced this (dramatically) once during our UrWerk, I had no desire to trek that freaky road again. Suffice it to say caution dictated my next moves.

What we conceived needed to act like a bell-jar, a contained cone-like experimental 'micro-climate' of Song offered to world which integrated the Glyph as 'test-beacon' (Amici words). This (testing) expression also conjured caution; I recalled previously being involved in acts of 'extreme research' (Amici words) which could have severe consequences (as described in the chapter "Joining

Mountains"). Hmmm (again) …

Vaguely aware David had once mentioned a desktop portal housing the Glyph, crafted for him by a fellow Lorianer, I started googling. Ron Hay's website, "Elven Gates", with lovely imagery of his artisanal prowess stared back at me from computer screen. Nope. Nothing 'spoke' amongst his work to date. Hmmm (squared) … Time for outreach, to describe what seen and ask what possible. Crosshatching an elemental 'power of five' with a sister'd 'power of seven' inwith a Gaian frame (ready to name herself Torii) was too intriguing a proposition to not explore further. I reread John Matthews' book and found ample quotes to support our contention, viz:

"This is what the ancient bards of this land meant when they spoke of having 'been' a thing. This was more than a poetic image, but a very real truth. To truly know a thing is to become one with it. Just as to become one with it is to truly know it."

It spoke directly to our Amici affirmation that 'the more we know Gaia, the more she knows herself', and reflected how our (bardic) Songs were ever-evolving such (source code/x'd) principle. Now, if the Glyph were offering to support this process? Of Me/Torii twinned in Song to amplify the connection into world?

Ron was circumspect by email but agreed to discuss the possibility of a specific commission via Zoom. Prior to our conversation, however, I Malakut-met an 'inner' Ron. Whether this was his 'Sidhe-within' (Mariel's expression to describe our human ability to 'wake' to our cousinly commonality) or a Sidhe presence whose energy signature was aligned with his work, I have no idea as, till then, I had never met any ('real') Ron! But the content of this subtle meeting suggested that the Sidhe were aiming to augment a field of becoming, of collaborative praxis, which took Mariel's words and lifted them to (stellar) Mountain'd heights:

"Once you set forth your intent, we can blend with the field you create and enhance its capacities to connect and to manifest."

During the subtle meeting, 'Ron' showed me several planks of wood on his workbench. <u>Super</u>-thin, each '1-ply-wide' (said); long, slim, pale wood, very <u>very</u> light to hold, carry, manipulate, <u>bend</u>. Song-resonant, timbre'd of timber, I saw 'Ron' plane these planks off a <u>living</u> tree's trunk (which would heal itself in time). I watched him strip off bark, then perfectly slice each 1-ply wide 'ribbon' (no need of sanding) so that all were 'right-to-go' (said) in cut-to-requisite-size stakes. Now we could discuss options. A fascinating insight from two perspectives:

Firstly, to know that in Sidheverse a mirror bell jar was already mooted – not simply for our Amici troupe but as a 'pilot' (test) for how a 'future unfold' of together-work could proceed for <u>other</u> teams.

Secondly, Anwa-working of/with a <u>slimness</u> of form, using live wood which 'bends' to purity of intent, had its own function. The sculptural 'density' of physic'd artefact earmarked for task needed a correspondent <u>twin</u> in Sidheverse

– here the form would 'anchor' our work, there it would 'flush-through' Love's (liquid) Light. I recognised this meant we needed two 'substation' transformers as stepping-down mechanisms from Moon-Mother's community (garden) going forward. No wonder it was a test!

Ron and I Zoom-chatted, during which he mentioned two things which veritably jumped out to (figuratively) grab our Amici troupe by the throat.

One: A recent Winter storm had downed two trees on his Land in the 'Pacific NW' (Oregon) which he aimed to have milled and dried – Big Leaf Maple, Douglas Fir. He also had some Western Red Cedar from a previous tree brought down in a storm.

Two: When deciding the requisite size of Glyph relative to desktop portal for David (since replicated for other clients), a brass prototype had been made before being discounted as 'too large'. Since, it had languished in his shop.

He called it a 'test piece' and the Amici yelled in my ear:

"This is it; the original 'golden revolving door'! This is the 'test beacon' who has called!"

To say the 'chi of shared (Amici) circuitry' skyrocketed in an instant when the potentiality arose to apply the original 'test piece' to our work would be an understatement. Likewise, the chance to use woods whose 'provenance' was completely attuned to common purpose. The buzz was insane – in-Self and out-! I sent Ron a drawing of my original Glyph vision, Torii's arch modelled on my 'window on world' with its divine view onto mountain brother, Ruscada. I described how we envisioned Torii as a portable piece of Land-Art in support of our work in/with/of/as Gaia's divine Earth. Instead of a desktop 'tool', it would function like a Byzantine travelling icon pilgrims took 'on the road', whipping it out each time they felt called to pray. And, as I call myself a pilgrim for Love on perennial repeat, blessing sacred Land with each 'kiss' of my feet? Definitely a perfect fit!

Visioning continued. Mr1300BC arrived to confirm how the 'twin-portals' could work cross-dimensionally. The two stood side by side – simple, abstract bell jar forms 'infilled' of milky-white Light. My engagement with/in/of/through each was equivalent, seamless. I could access, avail of one the same as the other. A mantra arose to synapse-connect each perceived difference or dualism, to bring solitary fusion (two sides, same coin) to envisioned OnePeople outcomes. Demonstrating I could 'Anwa-flow' easily of each, I engaged Earth-access (depths), Heaven-stellar (heights); horizon dimensions of Being relative to longitudinal time (up-downstream) proved just as effortless.

Something as natural as Moon's new-moon cycle anointing Sidhe/We work, for example, I saw 'unveiled' as I moved into, and through; I saw the Glyph seam 'itself-to-itself' to dissolve all to Light (of Love's) rebirth in-world. Yet while I used the word 'dissolve' to describe what seen, I knew Torii's infill of milky-white presented no veil or barrier. This simply was the 'quality' of Anwa required for the 'beacon' to work. Mr1300BC affirmed this brought 'access' to Life. <u>It</u> was the Anwa, hence <u>I</u> was the Anwa, as <u>Torii</u> was the Anwa. Like elements bending to the purity of intent, the Glyph-portal/s were likewise meant.

Through each portal I found an old beat-up Volvo station wagon waiting, 'Windward' its name painted on side (both sides – I checked that too). I knew this referenced 'wind-walker' (which had been whispered in ear to describe working with Torii) but phonetically rendered?

"Windwood!" Through Torii's wood, windward ho north (given make of chariot), through the Gate of Stars and back! A free flow of Love's Light via Eärendil's Tolkien-barque reimagined? Excellent! The 'vehicle' also affirmed access to a depth of <u>lineage</u> (Sister-whispered, and in last chapter documented) which rendered itself as a skill/task <u>and</u> responsibility in one. 'Twas a wondrous word-construction to describe self/praxis, holistic of (my) nestedfishes fusion.

In honour of what shared, I began to sing "The Sisters Song" in this dimension but didn't get far, finding myself in gobsmacked awe as a never-ending 'cloak-mantle' descended from Sky, a huge <u>voluminous</u> fabric sheet, like a waterfall of Song in textured warp/weft, voice-woven by many dense. Even writing about it gets me teary (again) for we Sisters stood (as one) at cloak's height, wore its folds over our shared shoulders. The resonance of our singing flowed down its heavy folds, like thick hair, into the world where I <u>also</u> stood (at the cloak's hem) to 'catch' Song, embed its glory in Earth. Yes, simultaneously required to work both locales – subtle/physic'd; responsible, equally, in each. Hence the need for two Toriis. That our Song presents as a cloak? A stunning surprise but obviously speaking to my original affirmation years past upon stepping up/into the Circle of Service:

"I wear a Mantle of Starlight here in World to bring the energy of Stars <u>streaming</u> to Earth."

Now the mantle had evolved itself beautifully – so thick, and heavy, pewter of colour, its form moulded like a curtain to performance stage, yet worn as skin, inhabited. With thanks/good grace, here was evidence that <u>each</u> act strengthens, refines, deepens our enduring service.

Torii's wood born of Ron's Land – 'recovered memory, fresh envisioned'. I often mentioned in our correspondence that commissioning Torii was a step further for a OnePeople'd future in support of Gaia's becoming. Meanwhile, he described the technical challenges of crafting an arch (vis-à-vis desktop cirque) with the fineness I had sketched (and which the vision demanded). His solution? To sandwich the strength of Douglas Fir heartwood 'tween slim Cedar dancers – its masculine to their feminine, as well as crosshatch the warp-weft of woods' placement (vertic-horizont) to reinforce the 'fabric' of correspondence. A weaving-work, to all intents, such that Torii's construction reflected ours in Song. A gifted solution!

Thus would the energies of psychoid unity on inner planes be outer-mirrored in as 'fine' or 'lithe' a form as possible. All this lain on a bed of Maple – a single board with live edge intact to <u>root</u> the structure in/as 'Earth' (for what I had vison-seen had stone for a base). The plinth holding Glyph he also fashioned from this single board so it could embrace its own wood-as-stone meld. Other than that 'intervention' the central arch would remain 'free' of passage (open, connectable across all spinning Glyph'd dimensions as seen in vision) while the two side arches would be 'braced' by brass beams (at golden mean) to 'moor' my Sisters (in Song) as well as replicate my 'window on world' view onto Gaia's beauty. A blessing bowl at centre would hold our intent – pure of Helvetia's crystalline heart, drilled direct to her wellbeing'd sacred peace-sunk source.

A temenos, a sacred temple, a grail-within-a-grail, in-and-of-a-grail. The 'setting' replicated my experience in the 5,000-years (young) Neolithic chamber cairn in the middle of nowhere in Scots high wilds as described in our "Bens" chapter. There I first mentioned my desire to craft an artefact to connect into this realm in perpetuity (i.e. Torii-pre-Torii). In the cairn, anchored to OldMan-stone, Sisters either side, blessing 'bowl' the dust at my feet, I knew I had entered a micro-space of macro-weight. But it would not have occurred to me that Torii's creation would, via Glyph, offer such 'stretched' connectivity, nor dynamic shift to a beyond unimagined. However this was before returning to Scotland later that '22 year, laying my head against another (yet same) OldMan, sobbing into his skin the <u>truth</u> of finding myself: Home. Not a story told in that chapter – too intent was I on Ben Hope'd Morrigan adventures; too outwith-language as well was our primal meld. But destined for "Miracles" where Poetry reveals the hidden in primal tongue, viz:

no wood only stone, no blood only bone
the original earth of original earth
molten or solid it matters not
you thru me – vibrant and clear

Ah, Reader, language is a fertile bed in which to lay one's head to rest. The Amici delight in their hybrid words and phonetic plays to kickstart cognitive juices in this wee brain. It's been long I have marvelled at the Gaelic 'tor' for bare-boned hilly heights vis-à-vis the Old German 'tor' for door or gate. And then there is 'tor-ii' whose etymology is debated as are the origins of the Japanese language itself. As the Amici wryly remark:

"You see a hill; we see a door … you see a hole; we see a gate."

This latter observation backboned the mythic tale of "Leeks & Peas" which I was asked to pen on shared behalf. It features Men-an-<u>Tol</u>, the 'hole' stone that backs each card in David and Jeremy's original deck (see "Grail Within"). From the start this stone named itself Men-an-<u>Tor</u> for reasons the Amici describe above. So too Glastonbury Tor is a classic tautology for at <u>root</u> lies either side of same (Avalon'd) coin. The howe is a hill as the hollow is a hallow, just as the cairn is a cairn whether chambered or waymarker'd!

Now let us move on …

•••••

If 2022 was the year of Torii's 'seed-proposition' conceived and her embryonic form beginning to take shape in the subtle realms according to input by an array of co-creators, 2023 is when activity properly began on time-horizon'd physical plane for Torii's moulding and shaping.

The woods chosen by Ron had sufficiently dried and been milled; he was ready to get to work in the 'shop' with his tools-of-trade, partners-to-common-purpose according to technical drawings we had agreed months earlier. We conducted a 'blessing of the woods' via Zoom, its intent to not only <u>ease</u> their metamorphosis at Ron's hands but imbue their strong energy signatures with the Songline'd resonance of <u>future</u> home; coincident was the ritual's timing with Imbolc. It had been a year since the goddess Brigid opened the portal to The Sisters (of) Song, Great Glyph (a-grin) tagging along. I had no conscious thought 'how' an online blessing could (or should) work, but we had co-produced enough rituals down the years for me to simply wait, and listen, for suggestions to arise.

A few days before the session, words began a swift-swirl to extant life and I scribbled for all I was worth. In so doing, I discovered that it was not only we (wee) Amici who were blessing this creation, but Torii as a voice/presence in her own right was keen to enter the space of performance. A revelation: She had <u>already</u> 'become'! I intuited the opportunity to construct a paper model, using the same dimensions as her eventual construction. Chopsticks held her triple-arched form aright; inwith each side arch was scripted the requisite Sister-rune while Torii's self-rune I firmly planted 'centre-stage' – the one described in last chapter during my fluid stream-of-conscious freefall that incorporated the Glyph at (her) beating heart. And then I placed her on the piano stool, in the music nook, there to infuse with the energy of Song, there to become 'apprised' of her future role in co-production and performance with a 'seed' (stone) in my (pretend) blessing bowl at centre to affirm her birth – in Time …

As Sun rose with Ron, it was setting here – painting Sky an extraordinary palette of colours in co-participant Joy. Later I would find we share the same latitude, the connection direct 'tween East/West of Land/Sea; 'twas as seamless a Songline as my homes North/South of Helvetia's (mountain) redoubt. The synchronicities were just so incredibly neat; I 'saw' the timing of the 2022 Winter storm which felled the trees on Ron's Land for Torii's life to become in Love's <u>intentional</u> Light (of Grace). And so began with a spell, honouring the elemental qualities of Gaia's world, their bending to Light's purpose, before offering our quiet and humble blessings to the assembly:

May Torii's physic'd birth be blest, may Ron's work of craft be blest
May the resonant chorale of Torii's dovecote of Song
Evermore for Love be blest ...

Now it was time to welcome Torii to Zoom 'stage' and my, did her exuberance flow forth:

"I am!" says Torii, revealed in-world.
"I am!" (and) "I sing!" (and) "I rejoice of shared Earth!"
"I give thanks to the Land that has nurtured my Wood –
Cedar Maple Douglas Fir – I give thanks to these Trees
for falling in-time so the Hands of a Maker can help mine arise ..."
"Yes, I give thanks for Ron's hands – their crafting and shaping
to mould my Beauty to Form, of Song-Space envisioned,
one that alchemises Light from above/below
and thru whose Presence Love shall flow
to bless the World with Sister'd Grace –
pure of intent, in service to Goddess ..."

Song followed; our weaving spell was scripted. It was complete. Both Ron and I felt our energy flagging. Time to close and let the spiritual elixir of intent 'infuse' the wood/stone, blood/bone of what would arise from <u>Torii's</u> snowball'd desire.

I sat, reflected, asked aloud in our Amici cirque: Is something <u>emerging</u> through Torii's construction beyond our <u>specificity</u> of micro-purpose? An opportunity to <u>revitalise</u> the elder starblood of our OnePeople via <u>regenerative</u> blessing?

The answer arrived overnight. Herewith my raw journal notes:

It seems I'm off shopping. I pick up a recycled paper bag to find the Amici have fashioned a new from old. Constructed of <u>very</u> sturdy thick dark brown paper, I look at the brand: "Well-Being'd" with an imprint of Tree of Life logo! Oh, what a gorgeous gift/ affirmation! So many resonances – well-used, still in decent order for Torii's travelling temenos to come 'on-the-road' with us, each Tree's 'life' now well-being'd anew! I had shown Ron the slice of Beech found here in forest which effects a <u>perfect</u> representation of Cernunnos' torq of power which sits at centre of Torii's (paper) dovecote. Now, in nightsight, I am flying a coastal scape – a narrow channel thru to arched inlet surrounded by high cliffs, as if Torii's central portal lain flat, and the torq is the access way (tidal) in/ out of world. The cliffs are perfectly 'sanded' on all (stone) sides like her wood, smoothly 'milled', to effect safe passage for wind-walking sailors. The sequence repeats several times so I intuit its importance – narrow channel, sea 'pacific', entry perfectly moulded, rounded, curved, thru to its culmination point where it meets this high-cliff'd land. Abstract swathes of colour – cliffs (gold), land (green), sea (blue/silver); 'tis a conjoin of the purely elemental in Earth-'birthed' form. Fulsome silence, no 'shift' – this a no-place of Presence.

From here I visit a graphic-design-creative-studio-cum-publishing space. Heaps of desks, filing cabinets, archives (as if spiral-bound in albums) – a woman shows me their work but a <u>central</u> tome/text which held much runic script has been 'lost'. A single exemplar … could Torii's birth support its resurrect? A delivery of 'skeins' has arrived; they are plaited, braided lengths of twine or thread, thick, in luminous sheens of gold-silver and more. Lengths of 'Elven-Rope' like the glossy (green) ribbon I used to thread Torii's paper dovecote together. These she distributes around the team – the weaving work which we had invoked thru Song in the blessing ceremony could now proceed apace.

Anwa-on-overdrive? Two days pass, then comes the 'big one' – again, raw notes:

It's important to get this down. Woke at 3.15am from a vision-within-a-vision. A clear glass/crystal shunt <u>inwith</u> Torii's cirque shooting/streaming Pure Light down to (stone) Seed at base – all this happening right there on the piano seat downstairs! It was a round tube/shunt snug-fit over/round the Seed as if it had 'formed' specifically for this purpose. Pure crystal/strong yet delicate; Light v. bright/full-on; present – no sense of flowing/ simply being <u>itself</u>. It reminds me of when the garden grail created its own connective Earth/Sky 'existence' at start of this UrWerk (Solstice '17); now Torii is magicking the same thing. The visioning linked the Sisters work (tri-partite Earth/Sky – 3-of-us-as-one here/GKM-as-one there) but my role here/now is to 'hold' the flow (at both ends of shunt/ pipe) to keep it 'generative-constant-present' till the process of 'infilling' or <u>activating</u> the Seed is complete. Like fertilising an egg? Obviously there is major 'stuff' involved in bringing Torii to vibrant 'life' – in both her twin-dimension'd forms! This subtle-physic'd 'event' had ritual written all over it, Torii's 'quickening' (in utero) is a significant step now her 'test beacon' has infilled of Light. Who would have thought? All/all/all (already) revealed in texts prepped yet without any conscious notion of how such revelation becomes? When I read thru the spells of incantation, though, I 'see' their true power. As will Song of the Cells when (at long last!) <u>its</u> Seed is complete!

This last comment, Reader, re "Song of the Cells" is relevant. See, several months prior I had made a decision to no longer ingest (chemo) toxins to guard against (cancerous) incursions. My darling oncologist had debated long my choice, arguing for a maintenance regime based on a plethora of clinical data. But I'd never 'fit' the clinical mould in any case. I was an outlier at diagnosis (risk-factor-based) and remained so in my cobbled-together meld of western and traditional healing modalities. A 'guinea pig of one' I happily called myself and all he could do was sigh. Now it was time for him to sigh again. But I felt 'healed' no matter what the test results said/didn't say. I felt, fundamentally, it was time to honour the amazing work Body had done and give it a chance to continue that amazing work un-impacted by a chemo crutch (and its less than pleasant side-effects).

Yes, I would always carry "Darkness' calling card" in bones (as I dubbed my chronic pain) but understood its purpose. It was time to honour the work of Body's busy cells in a Song dedicated thereto. Over time snippets of lyric/melody would pop in to tantalise me with the range of emotional content this 'tour' of Body's bone-marrow'd halls would yield. However, I would never have expected, in intersect with Torii's (Imbolc-overlit) quickening, that something would arrive to ramp up the realm of possibilities – of Song, of Torii's participant-witness in/to this work of <u>healing</u>, of what we (now) would/could 'make' together in/as shared Life – 'resurrect'. A year earlier "The Sisters Song", now an odd melody – again in minor key – willed itself to Life on ancient spinet. Words immediately began to populate the first bars and 'The Sisters' arrived to tell:

miracles shatter in our souls/lighting all the ways back home
listen close to the mirror'd moon/she knows whence we've come

I have to admit being confronted by the use of word 'shatter' (especially as this was a key fear courtesy of the honeycomb 'quality' of Cancer-impacted bones!) till I saw unfold the infinity-of-stellar-stream 'The Sisters' offered to my (limited) sight – literally <u>bursting</u> open when our ever-known path (source-sea-source) resurrects <u>in</u> Self. It placed my vision from years earlier (over a cuppa with MakerMan – see "Der Ruf der Berge") regarding our Earth-consciousness rolling 'home' into the stars in broader context. Torii's 'Self' was a sacred temenos, <u>co-existent</u> with Gaia's holopoiesic mythic emergence of consciousness. Quantum leap of logic in one respect yet when I recalled her infilling with Light? Now affirmed in lyric was the role of Moon (mirrored) to equation (later I will elaborate on this via John Matthews' 'Shield of the Moon' depiction). I waited, and the remainder of verse burbled forth – twinning the <u>specificity</u> of my blood/bone 'miracle' with Torii's wood/stone 'manifestation':

benediction of the blood and bone, resurrect the wood and stone
raise now high the halls of silver'd gold, here we sing the sisters song
here inwith does love belong, here we plant the seeds of hope
here we nurture life – so strong

It wasn't long before this melody/lyric extended itself with a 'hallelujah-chorus' (for wont of a better expression) whose intent was to 'halle' (praise) Gaia and affirm <u>our</u> (planetary) role:

I am/we are/our home is one
I am/we are/our home Gaia
I am/we are/our home we are

Weaving the 'fact' of "Miracles" over/over in Ring-Song'd mantric form during these months, it should come as no surprise a key visioning event found me/us in a zone of 'cathedral' and 'sistering'. Many small ceramic plates were lain flat/

horizont to create an overlapping-interconnected floor mosaic. Organically-shaped triangles, they looked like a mergence between (Enso's) cirque of Heaven with geo-triform'd Mountain. Countless 'sisters' had arrived with a 'plate/offering' to support creation of this shared space of blessing inwith temple 'frame'. As glorious as a stained-glass window floor-lain, flush with Earth (geo-square reprised), wed to Gaia's skin, it spoke to Mariel's choir of unfoldment in which each offering contained the energetic signature of the one who gifted it – a fractal of each sister's harmonic resonance in mergent performance with the common purpose of Commons. In such spirit would Torii's life grow, blossom, be nurtured (as Mariel's student says). It takes a village to raise a child; here, a OnePeople'd <u>congregation</u> on both sides of (non-existent) veil offered active support to bring Torii's travelling temenos, Great Glyph at heart, to manifest life. I experienced this ritual 'tiling' of space as a solemnly performed act; 'twas as dedicated a praxis of Mariel's 'Anwa-singing' as skein-weaving observed in 'graphic design' workshop.

This <u>truly</u> sobered me. It felt like an upwelling from the (collective) wellspring (source code/x) of cosmic humanity (our cousinly origins) had taken place, as if a call had gone out for any/all who wished to make an offering to Torii's space in <u>its</u> 'becoming' to do so now that the 'shunt' (of Light) was live/wired-in. In trying to find words to describe what I encountered for the purposes of this chapter, I saw (again) a <u>vast</u> 'mist-of-consciousness' in vaporous swirl where many figures (of Light) danced.

Reader, if you have ever observed mist rising from a river at dawn, as soon as Sun 'touches' water's skin, mist that hugs still the passage of river's flow as if a spirit gliding atop its length, no wider than its banks, then this best explains my visioning. There was an inherent Joy to the potentialities offered by this 'conscious mist', yet I was abundantly aware that if the river were 'polluted', its Light less-than-pure, any sense of Joy would be tempered by a correspondent miasma of despair which 'dragged' its feet, sunk same beneath its own gravity.

"Miracles", as its own Anwa-offering, grew like topsy to take account of such awareness, as well as my (sobering) responsibility thereto, in sung snatches such as:

from job of joy I'll not be led, never falling to despair
standard issue, par for course, performed then gifted on
un-thought, -impacted is the soul of self in-world, the anchor-seed
sustaining silence in its bleed for all to be revealed
the warrior of maiden shield holds aloft her love as spear
courage strength the recipe, she knows the shape of time
mountain time, un-human'd time, seasonal our indenture –
tectonia'd the depths we dive dissolving all to one
in peat'd pool (mountain's redoubt), warm-coddled there (termale's source)

we wait we wait we sing we sing for spring to come again ...

'Twas a field expanding as it was breathed into being – with Song. From the specificity of our Amici weaving-work, the logic of having sung up the Blue all the way from planetary core through to Gaia's atmospheric extent had, yes, automatically generated the question 'what next?' within our troupe. Engaging allies in different energetic shapes and multifarious functional forms from a vast array of dimensional realities demanded, I suppose, a robust 'container' which could hold, transmute, and stream forth the Light <u>upwelling</u> from primal source to <u>accelerate</u> the truth told in "Song of Gaia" (in the context of Selimovic's coinage of realm disclosure).

We had spoken this loud/long enough for any/all with ears (of heart) to hear. The Great Glyph had certainly heard and was offering <u>its</u> 'Self' to process but it (and we) needed a frame in which to perform, an 'electricity substation transformer' tasked with gifting <u>manageable</u> loads into the grid to not overwhelm the system (or us!). The art of doses is key in any healing or medicinal regime. We ever-affirmed our work in support of "the Green of a Land that is never dead when the Blue of the Stars flood the world with their seed" but there was no value in swamping the aquifer.

<u>True</u> magic lay in co-creating, co-producing, co-reaping what co-sown on a 'diagram-of-equals', a plane of consistence whose edges were stretching beyond any horizon-as-seen. The process we had entered took me all the way back to the multidimensional cross-section of biodiverse 'pond' described in our "Prologue". But instead of a cross-section, Torii's becoming was offering us the entire pond, and expanding it at the same time. I was reminded of Basho's 'old frog' (haiku) on the one hand; on the other my witness of our local bird-of-heaven (grey-heron-fisher, still-as-standing-stone) gulping said frog (legs limply dangling from an over-stuffed beak) down in a single fluid movement. Digestible? Or tummy-ache territory? Hmmm ... Back at the substation transformer, all I could do was trust and speak <u>very</u> firmly into the aetheric mist-of-consciousness that I am a <u>very</u> small human when all is said and done who would <u>very</u> much appreciate if the 'miracle' of her healing isn't upended by drowning in a pond, no matter how sacred!

A depth of resonance percolated forth, amazing me (in one respect) that the incantatory spells included in Torii's blessing ritual had sounded a bugle far beyond a small troupe's engagement with master craftsman Ron (and his small troupe). I may have used the word 'resurrect' in lyric but 'renaissance' could equally apply. It was as if Gaia's own <u>primal</u> desire was being tapped, into which Torii's seed-energy already fed. An acceleration on both's behalf, therefore, and mirroring my own (micro-) sense of in-skin <u>being</u> Gaia's (macro-) Garden. The Songs (of Gaia) described in the chapter "Source (Code/x)" spoke to this fundamental (snowballing) desire in new fresh 'revived' form where it (itself) desired more than anything to help hold and shape the emergent container of Torii's 'being/flowing the world with blessing' brief. It was certainly not on my radar that this would be possible when the Glyph began spinning a year earlier in space, but it was clearly on others' if my sight onto this coherent 'interweft' was anything to go by.

• • • • •

Now, before looping the thread another time round in (Evermore's) wend, let me apprise you of what "Miracles" eventually became in 2023 from its sung snatches and hallelujah choruses – a cellular/symphonic tone poem in seven (sister'd) cantos (movements). An interweaving of poetry/song, entwining personal, planetary, its full performance takes an hour and a half.

But what is a 'symphonic tone poem'? The ideation arrived early/mid-19th century as composers strove to evoke literary, pictorial or dramatic associations in symphonic orchestral works. The source of this blossoming? Romanticism – an artistic response to the Industrial Revolution as well as to the scientific rationalism presented by the Enlightenment. Could a composer inspire a listener's poetic imagination to action? Urge their reacquaintance with Nature as poetic or painterly artefacts could do?

These days the answer is pretty obvious but at the time, fixated on traditional patterns of musical composition, it was considered a radical notion. However, the tone poem found its champion in Liszt who garnered luminaries such as Dvorak, Smetana and Strauss to the oeuvre. The rest, as they say, is history … Each 'poem' was intended to apply an entire symphony's musical architecture to a single movement and, with such mentors to praxis, my aim was to mirror the principle whereby each canto would offer its own self-contained 'piece' of (Life's) puzzle, like a distillation of concentrated (medicinal) content. And yes, I use 'medicinal' with good reason for I had the opportunity to learn, in my own flesh, that, when seen in the right 'light', poison has the power to heal. Our birth contract is a gift-of-grace whose fruits we gladly, as wounded healers, gift on – into (sister) Gaia's own well-of-being:

> time, balanced on a tripwire (of matter crux'd)
> listens to the fecundity of chatter –
> past with latency, future'd, such that I see:
> I was born to embody this wound
> but also its sister'd corollary …

I wanted Torii to 'hear' this work so she would know the constellation she'd been 'born' into – an amazing community of cellular life singing their chi of shared circuitry with such com-passion to enable Cancer's farewell from Annie bone-marrow'd halls; so too I wanted to affirm to her that our work continues no-matter-what (in a come-what-may universe) to serve Life's miracle in whichever form it evolve. I wanted her with me in every performance, standing at back, subtle glitter-glued to skin. Through my eyes to see, my ears to hear, and so on, but especially through my voice to sing. We performed on the edge of world and in forest depths, above roaring white-waters and beside babbling brooks. Performed all the way from source to sea as is our wont, full-flung to be by the elemental forces who accompany our way and bend to its intent – Love's Light to share …

During 2023, Torii grew with presence in our cirque, and via performance, as I felt her embody an extant life. There was an opportunity to amplify this with recordings of our work sent to Ron to 'press-play' while he completed the work of crafting. This was 'trialled' when he requested an audio of our wood-blessing ceremony. Thereafter, as well as infusing Torii's bell-jar with the 'milky Light' of "The Sisters Song", two specific excerpts from "Miracles" were called for – one sung at source (1st movement); one sung at sea (7th movement).

Earlier in this chopped-off tapeworm of a tale, I described the cautionary words received when the Glyph began to spin in vision. As a tone poem of symphonic length, it was important for me to affirm – in its final movement, its 7th wave as the largest in set which brings this (small) Annie) boat ashore – that I understood and worked within the parameters assigned to 'leave none of Self behind'. Its excerpt I performed on the edge of world – Fisterra in Galicia – sights trained West, calling Torii home East through the Gate of (MakerMan's) Rising Sun.

The movement's name? 'Congruence'. My partner to purpose? Moon – Artemis in each/all her goddess'd manifestations, a potent (Sister) presence to (time/tide) support the in-weave of the 'power of five' (elementals), 'bend' their alchemic dance in service to Gaia's arise-of-consciousness in/of/as matter. Years had passed since I perused John Matthews' Sidhe Oracles (Fleeting Hare & Moon) thanks to Jeremy's generosity. Intriguingly, however, their wisdoms only wanted to be engaged and integrated into our work at Imbolc '23 – coincident with the blessing of Torii's wood, the Lunar Year of Rabbit's arrival, and "Miracles" 'shattering' in-soul. The oracles merged, desiring linkage to our work via the original (Card Deck's) Gaian Throne and 'spoke' their timeless knowing into our Amici cirque thus:

season swirls & season firsts, egg & spoon but this is no race
that the fleeting hare in/of world makes, flowing gold down silver'd veins
the art of doses, mantra keen'd, heals the garden in Gaia's name
while wolf and stag and eagle owl guard the jewel of peat'd pool

This oracular wisdom had its denouement when "Miracles" began true co-production with the Amici, concurrent with the shift from Torii's energetic 'sculpting' to Ron's active tooling. The Shield of the Moon especially desired to 'elevate' this shift, taking the original words spoken to John and extending them into a full invocatory spell. To say this was an energetically thrilling development in our partnership with Moon Mother's community (of gardeners, oft-cited in this volume) would be an understatement of extreme magnitude for it in-heralded (on Gaia's behalf) a constancy of healing praxis explicit of congruency with the fleeting hare's 'line of flight'. We had come full circle. Returned to (TS Eliot-ian'd) beginning (again) to know it for the first time (as always).

Nothing for it. Cautionaries transmuted, I sang up our sanctioned 'congruence' on the edge of the world and sent the recording to Ron for Torii to know: "All is Well."

So did Torii hear, with her own ear of heart, while still in Ron's 'shop', the unerringly Love with which we would welcome her to Amici fold. So did she hear Moon's invocation and our response to her call in exuberant chorale. So did she hear the line spoken by Great Mother (Gaia) to little songstress (me) years earlier, in vision affirming that the truth of congruency is far deeper than any surface cognition a small human can bring to cosmic equation:

"The heavens are in you as the heavens are in me."

This had Gaia said as Dolphin, radiant with Joy, surfaced at my side. Its heart burst open to spill out billions of tiny fish, as if they had literally been spawned from the dolphin's pure Love of, encounter with, and partnering toward an interspecies'd interplanetary world. In a flash I witnessed an entire 'symbiotic' life cycle inwith Dolphin's very being at cellular level, thereto understanding we all have this embodied capacity to 'spawn' new life through myriad modes of creativity. To 'nourish' and 'feed' not only ourselves but the world, it needs only our purity of intent to kickstart the chain reaction.

I had seen, intrinsically, into how things become themselves when we partner them with Love and wanted Torii to know this too; 'twas how she was conceived – to evermore indwell as a vital loving unique expression of Life – a Gaian 'cell' (to all intents) hosting a multiplicity of cells (in Song). Verily would she hold the heavens as the heavens held her. So-inducted would she be to the particularity of her Gaian citizenship, to join an Amici tradition of Fedeli d'Amore – wind-walking Song through world …

• • • • •

Time to return to Mariel's words on 'Anwa' which opened this chapter. Inwith the field of co-creation, the act of blending draws forth 'chords of mutual unfoldment' which find expression in a new 'life's' becoming which (as her student describes) we nurture from conception through birth after which its life is companion to ours, a co-equal partner to common purpose.

So it is with Torii, but so too it is with "Miracles" – each a life, each with its unique 'melody', its note sung in, and attuned to universal choir, co-created and nurtured in/of/with/by/for/as Love (that glorious prepositional party I am so very fond of). I am the mother of each (and of myriad other 'creations' besides), yet once birthed to requisite substantial 'beingness' (however that form may appear, or not, to our senses), once birthed as a unique Anwa'd expression of life, our nurturing needs be shifts. No less loving, no less caring, but honouring and respectful of a distinct fully-fledged voice in cosmic choir with its <u>own</u> sovereignty, and a right to take wing, chart an own course, have own 'adventures'. I have written at length of our activities inwith an 'Anwa-infused' universe ("Grail Within"). Here I would simply repeat that no matter what language we use to frame the discussion, the Song remains the same; its underlying base note is Love through which our purity of intent begins the 'snowball of becoming' rumbling down from (misty) mountain (hop'd) top/s. Moulding, shaping, cleaving – all to the 'power of five', whether on musical score or in process model, whether chorten-built or elementally-charged. There is nothing complicated about 'Anwa' for, as Mr1300BC reminds:

"We all breathe Life into what we Love."

And in this respect our undying gratitude to Ron for bringing <u>his</u> purity of Love and intention to the process of Torii's crafting. He writes:

"As for perceiving a sense of the specific Anwa of the Torii as I work with the parts, for me, it's about setting an intention for the work that I'm doing that day and letting it flow. I really am focused on the process that fulfills the intention. I enjoy working in the shop and especially with something like the Torii. Because the work is somewhat new, the process often reveals itself as I go. That's because the form of the work is not familiar, so many times I am in discovery mode."

Discovery mode, indeed! Mariel says:

"We converge toward the promise held in the single <u>cell</u> of our ancient ancestor."

And somehow our work contributes to this promise – it's what "Miracles" Song-weaves; it's what Torii lives in Song-skin. For she is a grail in the truest sense of word. She is the cup, the cathedral, and the cosmos as represented in Jeremy's artwork: 'Holding' (see back cover).

She is the priestess and the praxis, the architecture and the Song-in-flow. She is the stone and the wood, the bone and the blood, the anchor and the dancer for the Great Glyph's work in and through her form. Each holds the other and in turn is held by the <u>all</u> of Love infilling cup, cathedral, cosmos over-ever-over. As Mariel describes to David when perusing 'Holding':

"In our world more than in yours, there is a recognition of how each of us is a conduit through which spiritual forces blend into the life around us, bringing blessing. We know that a form of priestly capacity is there in us each ... A priest knows and uses the power of 'Holding' to fashion containers for the Light. A priest is a Grail-Maker because he or she understands how to be a Grail, a container for Light and Life as well as a flow of Light ... Each (grail) holds the other. The Grail holds the Stars, but the Stars hold the Grail.

The open Cathedral with its grassy floor is the blend of Nature and Humanity which also hold each other, as well as holding the Stars and the Individual, symbolised in the Cup ... Each structure that contains also has an openness so that life can transcend it and flow out from it into new forms."

As envisaged, so was Torii shaped. So that any/all who step into her space, over subtle or physic'd threshold to perform Song for gifting on/out to the world of Time, is a <u>conduit</u> of Love's Light – a <u>container</u> for its Being, a <u>ewer</u> for its Flow. Still and dynamic in like moment, equal measure, or as "Miracles" affirms:

correspondences resonate between her land and my name

Yes, Mariel tells of her priestly work – attuning to the Light, digesting and assimilating it (in Amici lingo 'stepping it down' like substation transformer) to appropriate forms, frequencies. Perfectly ordinary work (as she describes), an ordinariness bound to porosity – her ability to 'leak' the living blood of stars, the Light of stellar pool, anywhere-anytime through simple acts of presence, fellowship. A case of walking Love through world – an ability open to any <u>and</u> all.

In the essay "On Song", a companion chapter to my reflections "On Anwa" (in "Grail Within"), I describe the experience of 'ramping up' my raw connection to source with Reiki-training. Attuning to a runic 'Tick of Light' (as it spoke itself while penetrating deep levels of prior memory to open/re-open wells of insight onto <u>itself</u>), I inhabited a space of non-local witness <u>and</u> simultaneously in-skin experienced a gold-membraned 'mosquito net' descend from 'on high' to encase my whole form. Accompanied by an intense wave of Love, I intuited the rune would offer Light-protection at the same time I offered Light-healing. My invocation would have twin benefit, my porosity twin purpose.

With the benefit of hindsight, it seemed to affirm another facet of what I had seen in subtle sight of Torii's potential as a travelling icon replicating sacred ancestral process – her Glyph arch the central portal in a triptych of Sisters which hinge/fold into each other/across her face to triangular-'enclose' (aka Mountain) the blessing zone (of empty Enso – aka Heaven), before 'opening at the close to take flight' (aka through Earth) as per lyric in "The Sisters Song". The fact that her physical artefact would mirror the textual 'moulding' of my major work of prose fiction, "The Taste of Translation" (2011) – itself a sacred container across time/space, an own temenos'd 'Self' in resonant form? My notes:

The Amici arrive to show how the three sister-arches connect via slim brass rods into a 'pivot-point-of-self'. The Glyph's plinth, our 'stake plunged in (Gaia's) stellar flesh', has morphed into a Time-partner'd 'hour-glass-lookalike' proposition (aka 'the art of doses is key'), the node or nobble at centre of twinned vial a kind of valve for flow (rates). Smart! I see three Light-streams incoming from the Stars to, a-spin of Glyph, be 'substation transformer-stepped-down' for outpour to Earth via three mirroring Light-streams. As with Sengai's runic script, the triangle of Mountain is critical as 'blessing bowl' enclosure. I am terribly excited for this affirms Torii's role to enact, exactly, our sistering work. Further, I understand the incoming streams are like branches above ground while the outflowing are like roots in-earth. Mountain <u>and</u> Tree, therefore, are implicated as companion feeder systems. The vision of bell jar/test beacon (micro-climate in which we do our 'experimental' work) is evolving beautifully. I 'stand' inwith the triangular cirque, Glyph at back. Its vibrational whorl is like the anchoring 'sound-board' inwith piano; sonorous in its own right (when struck) and in echo'd surround courtesy of timbre'd timber.

Again, the Amici offer a word into my orbit: "Transpirational". 'Transpire' with its sense of something happening, its sense of something emitted or oozed, its sense of something revealed or becoming known. Plus, the Amici prod, think of the original Latin – 'trans' a prefix for across-beyond-thru with a sense of housing its opposite married to 'spirare' (breath). They prod again, ask me to look at similar 'spirare' adjectives – 'aspirational', 'inspirational'. I am asked to focus on the <u>potential</u> Torii offers as a porous membrane to breathe-with, across <u>and</u> beyond. Trans-worlds. Trans-times. A wind-walker for wind-walkers, windward via windwood. A sister and sister'd <u>meld</u> in one. Torii's life infilled of Anwa'd breath, breath as fuel for Anwa'd song – ever inwith and of (Gaia's) garden does this singing bird belong!

I am back with the shopping bag – Tree of Life-logo'd, Well-Being'd branded. Harvesting Light, home-brought to (Torii's) 'kitchen', cooked up into nutritious Song for nourishing our world!

• • • • •

Mariel says: "What is music but a system of relationships defined by vibration, frequency, rhythm, and time? … So, in our composition, we consider all the relationships … not only its structure and architecture but the effect it will have upon those who enter it, the vibration of the space it will enclose, and its relationship to the land around it and lifescape in which it is embedded. Anything this building will affect as well as the gifts it will contribute to world must be considered in the composition of its song, its Anwa. When the composition is complete, we then take it into ourselves, into our Anwa, and we 'sing' it. We do what is necessary to set the vibration … into motion and expression … around which substance will grow and precipitate … become living companions for us … we blend our vibrations with those of our world to bring new Anwas into being around which new forms may crystallise and condense."

Arcadia. Her living presence has been noted in two prior chapters; she has been publicly-outed in Song since 2019. The long poem, "Emissary", even affirms her beingness as a 'meld' (for wont of a better word) of the vast <u>well</u> of potentialities for our OnePeople's recovered memory, fresh envisioned – viz:

Centre circum'd
I am! in nested fusion said.
I am! We are!
Arcadia! One Skin!

I say 'well' with good (source code/x'd) cause – 'Hof Acquerei' (in Annie-Amici lingo) was being whispered in David's (listening) ear in its own fashion as "The Well". His Christmas 2020 Story (its own form of 'recovered memory, fresh envisioned') featured 'Arcadia' – a human teen re-learning the ancient praxis of (Arthurian) well maidens of myth. I had to ask him how he came to this naming provenance. He described it as a "Sidhe-inspired moment", that after a period of writer's block, when he returned to Story, to tell it from the teen's perspective:

"The name 'Arcadia' popped into my mind and fell into place as if it belonged there. She was, without question, Arcadia, a name I had no prior association with. Honestly, it came out of the story just as the Anwa of the story emerged from the Sidhe. I've never known anyone by that name and never even thought of it as a person's name ... But once she had that name, her whole character took on solidity and presence in my mind, just what a writer hopes for."

Ah, how things become themselves when we partner them with Love. The reader will note how the (Arcadian) lines from "Emissary" above evolved into the Hallelujah chorus for Gaia ("I am/we are/our home: Gaia") in "Miracles". Our role not only is to 'think like a planet' (as David says) but to jolly well act like one too – performing, like the precious Dolphin of ("Miracles") vision, Gaia's affirmation: "The heavens are in you as the heavens are in me."

The promise and potential of such an Arcadian idyll is our future – if we choose, if we envision its 'heaven' with our heart's Song. In point of fact while penning "Miracles", I 'saw' Arcadia (again) in her cocoon but now sensed into her deep desire to shuffle off its (constricting) coil:

arcadia ... your cocoon stretches/its stitching parts
look how you've fingernail-scratch'd it to dust –
blinking/waking/manifesting morphosis
take a first deep scent of that earth-skin plunge

When I perform the symphony, these lines are recited with a motherly, or big-sisterly, 'hug-in-voice'. But would I have assumed bringing Torii to manifestation could twin this (Arcadian) outcome? Hmmm ... At this point in centre-circum'd narrative, Reader, I need to introduce you to a precious companion of Love's Way who agreed to partner Arcadia's emerging presence – in skin – before Torii was ever mooted by Sisters (great or small).

Picture this – wandering a Covid-empty garden centre early in the second year of pandemic stream, a year into Cancer journey after a Winter of pain, debility. Wandering and purchasing, to bring springtime colour and life home to my personal garden wastes, from which to draw inspiration, reawaken desire for the healing journey, accompany me in-house-out-. Wandering great greenhouse'd halls in a daze of over-choice and over-fertilised seasonal folly. That's when I spotted her. I said to F (ahead with an already over-loaded double-decker trolley):

"This looks like a Norfolk Pine!"

He came over, said: "Probably something southern American" (the genus, Araucaria, embodies evergreen Gondwana-knowing in skin; restricted to southern hemispheric climes it includes species which indigenous cultures use in sacred ceremony).

"Google it," I said. "I just want to make sure – araucaria heterophylla." Bingo: Norfolk Pine.

One of our own, happily at home along my ESW 'stretch' of HomeSong – lining the foreshores of beachcombing adventures a salty sunburnt childhood long. I seriously could not believe it – what possessed a gardening 'industry' to co-opt its majesty as a Swiss houseplant? In three sizes at that! Regardless, I picked up the baby, tucked her into the crook of my arm. A living Evergreen from 'Shelly Beach' who'd watched over my unexpected tumble-turning in foamy breakers (squatted down too close to edge, mesmerised by a particular prize), commiserating with a four-year-old's tears of fright and wail of disappointment that a fave rose-pink woollen cardie was now sodden with sand. Another gift of Gondwana heritage had somehow found me in landlocked Helvetia to act as mediating healing balm; a gift I christened: "Arcadia".

Arcadia's home is our living room; bedecked is she year-round with precious symbols of place, in her own way 'the Green of a Land never dead when …'. After outgrowing her (baby) crib and latterly a (teen) corset, she's now heading (fast) toward the ceiling this (4th) Summer of shared home, a perpetual reminder of "The Tree of Life" (in "Grail Within"). Its story was mediated by an Evergreen which gave its life to become our family Christmas anchor during the 2019-20 'festive' season while Australia's eastern seaboard (Norfolks and all) burned; an Evergreen felled in the local forest above our village as Solstice approached, a forest through which I daily walked, with Amici, to string lines of healing cooling Winter-white (and wet!) Peace-Love-Light through the root-known Tree-interlocked Songlines to our brothers/sisters (of any/all species – in-skin or out-) down under.

We worked with a "Trees-of-the-World" Almanac (a precious tome in Sidhe realms!), our focus a particular 'species' of Evergreen, banana-shaped – its curvature of spine intentional (in the spirit of 'bending' to the purity of partner'd purpose, as well as beyond hemispheric horizon); its description:

"Facilitates movement of beings between spaces and spaces between dimensions."

Much did I learn; much did I (thankfully, humbly) contribute to common praxis. The Amici said:

"You have travelled Tree. Walked the tracks of Its path."

I cannot imagine a more loving ally in skin than Tree. A cosmic intelligence indwells their own cellular network of Song and, as Arcadia (indoors) enjoined her Song with the collective out of doors (wherever we Amici roamed, into whichever fonts of Tree-wisdom we connected), mantras arose to describe her, their, and our fundamental relational interbeing (of elementally-enriched banana-shaped 'bending') such as the one included in "Sasso"s chapter:

> Rivers of Light Rivers of Love
> Rivers of Life joining Heaven and Earth
> Rivers of Presence of Peace and of Joy
> Of Hope everlasting – for Gaia's glory …

Last Christmas, decorating Arcadia with the baubles of season, adding to the regular slim cast of in-dwellers, I thought on how many species a mighty Oak hosts – 2000+, more than any other. Such responsibility shall not be Arcadia's (at least in physic'd form), but each year she is taller, stronger, broader – by Winter '23 happy to host more than tinsel, a straw angel, a shiny singing bird. I feign to see a linking thread between Arcadia's grail and Torii's (to be) – a correspondence between Land, Name and the capacity to 'Hold'. And I know that once Torii is safe-installed in-house, their direct communion shall proceed apace as I step out of frame, mirroring a scene written into existence long past – of observing a toddler D try to push over a giant Oak then settle instead to accompany a toddler Acorn's growth:

> *"The boy stood in front of (baby) oak, whispering words, stroking autumn-brown leaves as if it were the most natural thing in the world to commune with trees. She stepped back from their intercourse, this boy and his plant. It was they who would continue the journey now. Of growth. Of trunk, limbs, tall straight strong, true, till both were big enough to be pushed over."*

Yes. 'Tis Winter Solstice '23. I wake with a mantra rattling around my head (after a pre-dawn discussion with the Amici). It is intended for Torii when she is complete in Ron's shop, a confirmation of our (troubadour) tradition. I scribble it down, send it off to Ron who responds:

> *"It is interesting you woke this morning with the mantra as Torii came into completion only a few hours before."*

Phew! Perfect (Amici) just-in-time management! Ron kindly rounds out our process of completion, then offers reflections on process, especially in context of a late 'twig' on his consciousness to use beaten copper for the blessing bowl at centre of triangulated cirque:

> *"It fits the sense of something ancient which is how I have been perceiving Torii as it comes together. This sense is enhanced by the rods that tie together the arches and the darkness of the cedar wood that they are constructed of. The plinth that holds the spiral has a stone-like quality though it is wood. The old tone is complemented by the antique finish on the brass clasp and hinges. But the polished brass spiral (Glyph) is a bright radiant sun, blazing forth when the arches are opened. The dark copper bowl enhances the sense of age as it was pounded into shape and not made by machine."*

Something ancient. 'Tis true – recovered memory, fresh envisioned. Torii – what will you make in your life? How will your consciousness grow to, like Mariel says, "converge toward the promise held in the single cell of our ancient ancestor"? Later, when we conduct a shared Zoom blessing for Torii's journey across the world, home into her mother's arms, two years after her subtle conception, Ron elaborates on his thoughts:

"Torii's base is Earth (Maple); the Glyph is Sun, its radiance in-world. The arches' strength is in the Fir (male) at centre; the outer skin beauty is Cedar (feminine), a sacred tree to the indigenes. Both woods share the forests of the Pacific NW along with the Big Leaf Maple. I find its wood has a mellow quality, as does the tree."

He estimates that each tree is over 100-years-old, says: *"So you have some wisdom there!"*

But for me it goes further – down and back, into the root-networks of their Ancestors (species) as well as the resident ruminative spirits of ancestral place (of any/all 'species' as well as Land herself). "That can never be lost," I say. He describes how indigenes could strip wood from the living trunk (of Cedar) without the tree succumbing. He has been told: "The Peoples of the Land are still around" and can feel into this. I think back to what the 'inner' Ron prepped two years earlier for Torii's making, using strips from a live tree. I thought it metaphoric at best, but? A skill still employed on the inner planes! Ron continues:

"Early on I had a definite sense of the Amici; before starting work I would always invite them in to be participant; I had a sense of the project being well-defined. When I invite my Sidhe colleagues in it's to add an additional sense of the substance rather than specifics and to engage with my temperament so it proceeds or flows more smoothly. In the inviting-in process there's an opportunity for blending and more of an Anwa'd flow in the overall space."

I sensed 'layers of invitation' at work, time-zone commensurate (maybe the Amici don't need as much sleep as I do?). Ron's Sidhe opening the portal, my troupe toddling through. Yet there was a feel of a broader more expansive energetic field at play than Ron's simple skilful tooling in shop, Sidhe hovering beside. Such perfect alignment, inclusiveness, and congruency to the Anwa'd process of Torii's becoming? Collaboration to the nth degree! Torii's manifest presence could not have been realised without all actors on shared Gaian stage. Its foundation stone? Love.

In a final fitting 'farewell' to shop, Ron writes:

"Torii is all boxed up and ready to travel. Last evening as I was ending my conversation with my Sidhe folks, the Torii folks popped in and let me know they were eager for her to arrive. Something that has never happened before."

The date? International Women's Day – for a strong independent female, girl-power pure!

• • • • •

"Equipoise: A Pas de Deux" houses a record of an <u>inner</u> conversation between Gaia and Self in (twinned) Garden. The contextual container for its penning is housed in the chapter "Source (Code/x)", but the fact of its first <u>public</u> performance (Winter Solstice 2020) was prescient in ways I only now have the opportunity to place in requisite domino'd (and Torii-ing) order. For it included spells of elemental weaving, harmonic resonance, energetic balance – never before spoken/sung aloud, before physical witnesses. Yet I felt settled this would 'work' inwith the <u>place</u> of performance (the Earth-sunk sanctity of Schönthal's precious krypta where monastic praxis still infused sandstone bones), plus the <u>timing</u> of performance would sound a true (cosmic) note to begin the <u>shift</u> of our depth-work out. Its own bell-jar in a way – before I had an image, or an expression, to describe the idea.

That first 'outing', border-crossing from a plane of intimate exteriority to one of public witness on both sides of veil'd vale for the 'spells' therein was seen, heard, and (thankfully) sanctioned. For, in the run-up to Imbolc '21, I found myself leading a ceremony in an ancient temple ruin. The manner in which the space constellated spoke to Han Shan's Cold Mountain 'home' (connectable in/across all dimensions). Completely, actively 'open to the elements', fully Enso-empty. No evidence of (human) intervention remained; Land had returned to it/herself, an own true-nature'd state inwith this shimmering former enclosure. Worshippers entered via a portal at 'surface', but I arrived to conduct the ceremony from <u>below</u> Earth.

I 'saw' non-locally, but also inhabited directly, a chthonic shaft which connected an exact same-sized dimensional <u>imprint</u> of temple sunk beneath ground. Here I had conducted the ceremony (alone), now 'twas time for its repeat at surface. Yet while at surface 'nothing' existed, underground all the accoutrements one would expect in a sacred temenos (altar, candles, low seating) were present, and very much 'alive'. This was our opportunity – gifted by the silt of ages, and sages, across any/all traditions. Our work in <u>intimate</u> depths could help resurrect the "knowing gone underground" (as penned in "Muted Earth"). Bringing this (now) to surface was "family sealed, embossed and waxed" (as sung in "Miracles").

It brought me great Joy but an absolute surprise (at the time) was its manifestation – from an already-action in an already-space deep within Earth's subtle 'exchequer'? The whole look and feel of this 'Anwa-forged sanctuary' below 'surface consciousness' set synapses firing left, right and centre. It spoke to ancestral Dreaming praxis across an entire planetary Songline (weaving-the-world) plus supported my long-held contention that <u>physically</u> walking Land, re-singing the <u>patterning</u> along ancient ways (well-trod for millennia were these paths) re-binds spirit-geology, and reawakens the subtle bones of Earth to its sacred purpose. We had walked the full Camino de Helvetica by this stage; we had walked home (north) to home (south); we had walked stretches as 'emissary' in blessing and outreach, as well as stretches ancestrally gene-pool'd to re-enliven family 'ties' (that bind). All the way with cells 'zinging' (courtesy of singing), the Land of Gaia our one/only Home.

Such that our Winter Solstice performance, with excerpts from many works, was titled "Songs of Home". But the standout? "Equipoise". The depth of silence in krypta as we wove, scripted the weaving, was like a breath long-held at last released – out to the world of Time. My task at Imbolc, therefore, a few short weeks hence would be to psychoid-unity this event by re-singing the weaving inwith a frame of Linden Sisters on hallowed Land, and to record said performance for 'worshippers' wherever or however they arrived to our tight-woven fabric of loving blessing for Gaia.

Hmmm … so the requisite domino'd (and Torii-ing) order 'of proceedings' had begun a year prior to Glyph spinning when "The Sisters Song" entered? Hmmm … Or even earlier perhaps?

Here, Reader, we introduce another 'miracle' to our (happily) shattering crucible to light all ways back home. While synchronicities abounded in this project called Torii, one (latter) piece of puzzle was so unexpected yet seemingly of perfect fit, as a Glyph-ish linking thread 'tween beginning, end, and how it begins again, that I must share its self-whorl to existence.

Backdrop: A wise elder of spiritual traditions on the Brit side of Atlantic pond, and to whose work I was first apprised long ago due to a nod from David, hosts regular dialogues with (other) wise elders via Zoom from time to time (which happily included David at one time). The session earmarked for March '24 featured Caitlin Matthews, expert in the esoteric, especially Celtic, mystery traditions and John's life/work partner in all things Arthurian, Sidhe, Faerie (gleeful Glyph inclusive). I eagerly looked forward to the event, 'booked' my spot, waited till fateful eve.

Said eve transpired (in all things 'trans-pirational') to be commensurate with Torii's leaving of US shores (according to postal service tracking with which Ron kept me updated). She was, to all intents, crossing the pond in the cargo hold of a divine airborne omnibus at that very moment. Nevertheless … Caitlin's story was truly illumining, and fully held my attention. For an hour I remained rivetted as she spoke of "the holy work we do is what holds the world together". Expressing, for example, her experience of "sinking down into the firmament of Earth, letting consciousness sink beneath surface where all Ancestors are all kin of all Lands through all Time" was a complete 'high five' (and power thereto!) moment for our wee troupe ('root-knowing' being our Amici-respective label for same and reflecting, to an absolute temenos'd T, what had been set in train with our "Equipoise" performance years earlier). Of course, John was much spoken of – their symbiotic relationship from fated beginning through all decades since enriched by riffing off each other's writerly, scholarly, creative strengths. What a team!

At close Dr Bloom asked her to share a blessing and she intoned a guttural vocalisation for the online assembled. Truly precious. All over, I wandered thoughtfully downstairs to make a cup of tea. Suddenly I began to vocalise a melody 'playing' in my head. At first I thought it was Caitlin's but no; yet I realised its similar (blessing) intent, arisen from the 'beyond', and patterned on the Harmony of the Spheres. This went on, and on, became louder, and louder (rattling kitchen glassware at one point). More penetrant was each turn of its Ring-Song'd spiral soaring to 'lofty' heights, as if on a rising tide. Till I realised it was 'issuing' forth from Torii in-flight, 'twas our (Amici) Song to 'row' her home across the skywaves – East.

The loop threaded all the way back to Caitlin and the fact of the Glyph's active presence inwith the hallowed halls of their home environment. It was as if her vocalisation, arising in the moment, carried the spirit of the Glyph's original communication with John, post-sketching by John, thereafter published by Jeremy, and later, via Ron, fashioned into a desktop portal commissioned by Ron which was (now) somewhere off-screen but very much aware, active, alive. A month earlier Ron and I had shared a laugh during the Zoom blessing session about the number of brass Glyphs he had 'distributed around world'. Ron said he hadn't kept track. I responded: "I'm sure the Sidhe keep a subtle registry of this somewhere." Well …

I recorded Torii's "SailingSong" and continued its performance in the days following. By the end of that week, however, it had 'shifted' voice again, settled, reached 'Land'. Docked. Yet as she a travelling temenos (like me, itinerant monk) on perennial repeat? Who sweeps the garden (any size) 'tween source and sea? We agreed it would be our 'call', like the "BetRuf" (call-to-prayer) of alpine herders giving thanks for the day, like the adhan of muezzin from mosque minaret calling in the day. With this vocalisation we would announce our out-walk to bless all worlds, all times – in service to Love's Light, wind-walking for the One.

I appended the call to the most ancient of poems in our canon – "Crone" (witnessed in her Aboriginal Dreaming wisdom 'dress'), to affirm we Sisters would keep the faith, keep singing up country, no matter what, and performed this extended version as a benediction for a fallen (Birch) sister, together with (still standing) kin. Such is our solidarity with Caitlin's 'holy work'; such is our dedication to Great Mother, Earth. Thanks be to Dr Bloom for the timing of his inspiring conversation; thanks be to Caitlin for her presence, sharing and intoned blessing; thanks be to the Glyph for its existence, and intentional engagement with Torii's essence!

It wasn't long before the Annie-brain-cells got busy and started reflecting on a deeper 'why' to this encircling thread: Glyph-John-Torii-Caitlin-Glyph (with Arcadia and David's "The Well" hopping on for the ride). In so-doing I skated back five (short) years to 'Silver Spur', a Sidhe community centred on a 'holy isle' – to all intents Helvetia's 'Avalon'. A temple site dating back more 2,000 years co-opted first by the Romans, latterly by a Christian monastic tradition.

A decent cache of Celtic oppida in the region confirmed the area's (strategic) importance. Yet I stood on a ridge, saw <u>into</u> the lie-of-the-land, the 'well-watered' triangulation event encompassing sacred isle, the root-knowing of an amenable Oak Grove with whom I sang, for whom I 'planted' gifts of grace. And found myself back <u>down</u> with elders whose dust continued to fruit the lives of generations of oaklings. Simply put, I inhabited a 'skein' of Land as it would have presented as glaciers retreated, leaving vast pools of meltwater and a small isle in the midst of reed marsh beds. A strange thing to meet Cernunnos, the horned god, here. I had thought there would be 'imprints' from humanity's recent past (Rousseau the most famous) but instead it was he who came, infilled me with Light, and spoke the same knowing as true sister Gondwana three years prior in Ruscada's skirts.

Intriguing. So many layers of human impact overlain and still this UrAlt-Being so <u>active</u>? Was it because Jurassic limestone enables percolation up and thought to those of sensitive self-porosity? DeepTime slows us – this I know. DeepTime connects us in/down to source code/x. But oh, how sweet this Sidhe community, gifting me a <u>hare</u> as a keepsake of place! In a deep-grass-runnel'd meadow, unseen hands 'released' the hare; it bounded a 'straight path' toward me – yes, I understood. The mists rose. A glimpse, brief, then sunk back whence come. Till next called, in-time-out.

Next I remembered back to a (Malakut) 'Avalon' moment through Gate of Rising Sun. On a skiff, with other monks, approaching the holy isle of Miyajima (source of Hiroshima's Peace-Flame from Kobo Daishi's eternal fire – his 1,200yrs at prayer ongoing), gliding through the Torii, seeing the holy mount Misen rise beyond. I spontaneously reached out to the gate, ostensibly to help push us through (our PeacePoles equally punting poles). When I touched the huge wooden pillar, vermillion-red, I found it vibrating, singing. <u>It</u> was glad I had returned – home, to <u>its</u> 'Avalon'.

"Equipoise" – penned, performed. The seasonal wheel turned – Winter to Summer, Solstice '21. In depth-charged Malakut sight, I stood on the opposite shore of my 'home lake', looked out to the isle at <u>its</u> centre (Helvetia, in sum, is a glaciate-sculpted terrain), one which recounts a history of pilgrimage since the time of St Gall, the 6th century Irish monk who wandered our (continental) way and chose this gentle region for his hermitage.

We had sung up this entire string during our Camino but the small 'bump' in lake was far offshore the wooden pilgrim bridge's crossing-point. Why was I looking, now, so <u>longingly</u> at isle, Malakut-rooted to a spot on which I had physically stood 25 years earlier, been offered a high-level expat position whose purpose (at some freaky subterranean level) was to unfurl the all-of-all-of-partner'd praxis since? Had it already been known by Helvetia, her stewards, that I <u>belonged</u> in this Land, that hers was the peace-sunk <u>well</u> from which we could (post-expat) work all the way from source to sea?

A skiff pulled in to (this opposite) shore. Aboard were the 'Sisters-of-Avalon' (yes, this their provenance, announced) inviting me to sing in the isle's ruined chapel. They were laughing, excited; young novices in this ancient order, they teased me by brandishing a razor to shave my 'hairy legs' so I would look the same as back-in-the-(expat)-days. The ferryman passed across a midnight blue cloak to keep me warm during the crossing. In the chapel, a thick swirl of Gondwana-brown paint was scripted to ground, Enso of sacred Earth – 'twas the portal through to chthonic zones where I would sing; 'twas the well-shaft which ever-penetrates the pure waters of Gaia's font. Dowsed by a huge foamy wave of cleansing healing water (razor thankfully forgotten), now I could enter, and perform our ritual weaving – at source.

I had never physically visited or even been <u>attracted</u> to visit this isle (down the other end of a 30km long stretch of water) in all these years, yet here I was, at work with/for the 'Sisters-of-Avalon'? Well-maidens (to all intents) still active in zones of becoming, at their own work of 'recovered memory' which our 'fresh envisioning' could support? I realised they connected into and that their work was aligned with the 'Silver Spur' community far to the West (each body of <u>Land</u>-locked Swiss water is inevitably linked to every other by the 'rivulets of fragrant knowing' emanating from Helvetia's heart, the <u>primordial</u> well of the Alps and entire Euro-continental mass). Who first apprised whom of what we Amici were up to I have no idea, but?

In any case, the following Summer, after "The Sisters Song" premiered, and to psychoid-unity (in some capacity) the faith these particular Sisters had in our work, I took a 'day-trip' out to isle. Just one of countless tourists enjoying a ferry ride on a magical day, slicing through sun-sparkled turquoise waters. Yet there were, remarkably, no tourists in the chapel ruin when I entered, slowly, reverently, to see what I would find. Typically Swiss-sanitised, but nothing could shift the deep-seated resonance of past worship, aeons-long, even if the structure 7th century. The historic record speaks of a 'women's nook'; archaeologic finds include pre-Roman presence. No mist risen; 'tis a dimension open, connectable to all; a 'tattoo' in the bones of Land for all who have eyes to see. 'Avalon' is a word-container with an own runic symbology, invoking sanctity wherever in/on Earth its grail wisdom 'manifests'. For my part, I used the unexpected aloneness in chapel to weave, for these Sisters, the <u>fact</u> of my Malakut-engagement. So sang, and 'planted' the Song in an imaginary swirl of Gondwana-brown earth at my feet. 'Holding', as Jeremy's artwork portends: Self, Grail, Garden, Cosmos inwith a frame which (now) bears Torii's name.

What continues to intrigue (yet delight) me is how welcomed I have been to Sidhe-choreographed 'events' (aligned, as one would expect, with Celtic calendar); these are often accompanied by an invitation to perform. The 'facts' of my entrée to, and encounters with, Sidheverse helped to enflesh the 'fictional' mythic container, "Leeks & Peas" (amongst others). In point of fact, each text in "Grail Within" offers a form of 'recovered memory, fresh envisioned' to our OnePeople'd pool. But many scenes do not make it past my raw notes or companionable chatting within Amici cirque – a shame really for I wonder at how we can appreciate the <u>fact</u> of our kinship without engaging the <u>fact</u> of our kinship? While the depths of bonds we share never fail to surprise, they also never fail to enchant and cheer me. Herewith an example:

To a Sidhe celebratory space, a grand 'fair-ground' with many stalls, activities (Lughnasadh '23 concurrent), I was invited to perform. Unexpectedly a gift awaited me. A wee soul with bright starlit white-gold streaming hair and twinkling eyes came over from the kiddie-crafting-zone to eagerly tug at my hand. She said: "Would you like to see the Pear Tree we made for you?" Sure! I was very excited. What would it be?

We climbed a platform (many children milling to witness my reaction, all participant to task). The child holding my hand led me to the right spot for its 'unveiling'; ceremonial performance curtains were then drawn back from across Sky. There, above, I saw floating the most luminous silver-white-<u>and</u>-fruitful Pear Tree 'crystal-sculpture' ever. It glittered in the heavens being drawn higher, higher (as if on invisible light-threads 'sewn' into its uppermost branches). This meant I constantly needed to crane my neck back further to witness its 'evolution'. For, as it rose, its central trunk semi-split to form two crowns of glistening leaf'd branches. No audible sound in/of its performance, yet I <u>felt</u> silent 'Glory' sung as it rose, unfolding its dynamic Anwa-in-form.

The associations triggered by this gift were profound. Pear is my (personal) Tree-of-Life in home garden grail (whose healing properties I gratefully ingest in varied form). Now a stellar 'twin' arises thanks to the careful crafting of energetic substance by these adorable children. An opportunity to, in <u>each</u> dimension, offer healing gifts to Gaia's garden. Another correlation was, of course, Torii's physical construction from the 'fruits' of Ron's Land after my vision-in-heart began its

'Anwa-dance'; here was its mirror – the 'fruits' of my physical Land alchemised into non-physic'd form by these children's subtle visionary dance.

But the prize, truly, was Pear's 'becoming', her <u>two</u> crowns arising from a <u>single</u> 'split' trunk. In one respect the twin Toriis 'glory' as envisioned by SkyChildren – the future of our OnePeople'd past. In another respect evoking the praxis of nestedfishes – always conjoined but with their own in (or otherworldly) tasks. Yet, most potently (<u>and</u> personally) this beautiful (Wood) becoming replicated my 'go-to' (Stone) Card in Amici cirque which self-named for me: "Split open by Love" (see "Appendix 2" for details).

This I what I saw as crystal Pear rose – her Wood split open by Love for the inner to come out just as it had with 'my' Stone. Just as it does with/for all of us – Torii included – when we open our hearts to Love's ever-existence, when we surrender to being split open, and healed by Love's Light. The crack in everything is how Light gets in (to paraphrase Leonard Cohen). The Sacred (within Tree, within Mountain) spills forth in any way, shape or (Song'd) Light-form (to paraphrase myself). We have truly returned to the beginning of (this volume's) narrative, Reader, for the image gracing cover (much gratitude to Jeremy!) is this opening Presence – the egg cracking for the chick's new life to emerge; the seed breaking free for its roots to hug earth.

Look to (front) cover, Reader. The image is me; the image is you. It is our OnePeople'd past and hoped-for future (bright!). It is <u>each</u> child of Gaia, <u>and</u> Gaia herself. The Seed contains in itself the mighty Tree; the Stone contains in itself the mighty Mountain. Ever and always will the memory of this crystal Pear rising to heavenly heights stay in my mind's eye. A parable of how things become themselves when we partner them with Love – whether by you, me or a bunch of innocent younglings in a Sidhe kiddie-crafting class.

Now look to (back) cover, Reader. The image is me; the image is you. It is our OnePeople'd past and hoped-for future (bright!). We <u>are</u> the grail – as cup, as cathedral, as cosmic citizens ever at work for Gaia. We are the grass, the stones of in-world mythopoesis – pitch-perfect acoustics for self-sovereign harmonics inwith <u>our</u> spheres (of influence), and connected into each/every other universe-high and just as wide sphere, mirroring smiles, saying "Hallelujah!" to Life, <u>its</u> Book of Voyage never to close …

•••••

Torii took her time coming home thanks to postal and bureaucratic delays, but choosing her day to 'walk through the door' (as a 10kg weight in F's embrace) on Solar Eclipse seemed no accident. Bringing her forth, an intense scent issued – all three timbers in melded fragrance, as if, by spending a month on-the-road, snug-wrapt in the dark, their incubatory communion had helped bring all 'elements' of physical puzzle to holistic fusion. While safely flat-packed together, it was an opportunity to 'tune' voice, now standing ready to 'perform' as a sole/soul construction. We conducted a formal 'welcome to country' and blessing ceremony next day after which her paper-ribbon-chopstick model happily agreed to be recycled. Purpose fulfilled. It was time, too, to listen for Torii's voice to arise. We sat quiet, reverent, waited – with (my) pen at hand.

Torii speaks:

"I am here. I am here and I am the 7-Sisters as are you and in/thru/of this space bring the <u>force</u> of the 7-Sisters to work in-world ... I am manifest of the 7 who work for Gaia's One ... I know when you stood at my back you 'saw' my manifest Self; you didn't expect this but <u>I am the She of the He</u> ... He the elder/I daughter twin – the <u>Arcadia</u> of our work in skin ... Yes, the power is in the original/prototype Glyph. But only brought to 'right action' by your request, crafting, envisioning of my extant <u>being</u>. To sit in Blue's Chair a delight, after hearing so much about it, to be surrounded by all kin who've been buzzing in/out of me from afar, growing louder, louder the din. I know you can feel the energy drilling in thru your crown chakra; it's like this for me via Glyph drilling in/down. Ron's plinth ... yes, a gifted choice of container whispered in his ear, rooting me in place – 'tis <u>your</u> mountain, Self'd."

(I drop suddenly to FullDark where I see a 'meeting' take place.)

"Did you see just now? They met at camp thru me/you – you visited camp post-my-set-sail, remember? And now they can, and have – elder-to-elder. We are the bridge/we are the flow ... all is peace, all is peace, all is peace ..."

Torii's comment refers to visionary journeys I undertook while she was in-transit. And now to find the way full open for the elders of each place to meet, commune? So precious! (In this meeting I recognised not only Native American elders with Helvetian 'indigenes' or Australian Aboriginal wisdom keepers, but my own genetic Ancestors in-walking from Scots high wild!)

But to backtrack so you, Reader, can make sense of her 'at camp' remark, as Torii set sail a month earlier, I (in my excitement) consulted Google Maps to check the 'sightline' 'tween our homes – direct West-East (latitudinal) (as Morrigan or Dragon flies), between sacred patches of Land. It was as if this completed, in a cathartic sense, a geometric patterning established by the direct North-South (longitudinal) line through the heart of the Alps (aka Helvetia's 'Starlight Suite') connecting our homes either side of this 'great-divide'. A patterning begun (with no map perusal) when 'called' to set down roots in a forgotten valley (on the border of Time), and now since? The all of the all that has come to pass in an itinerant monk's pilgriming-for-Love wake – working with the Amici, digging trenches to effect triangulations cross-world, on and on and on it goes.

Ron's trees had given their lives to support the (live) embodiment of our small acts of 'global alliance' (Amici words); the 'test' Glyph (patiently) waiting on dusty shelf for its ever-intended home. A sense of 'denouement' in one respect;

an invitation to re-open, re-member, re-mentor, re-new in another. For, while Torii sailed the skywaves, I unexpectedly Malakut-welcomed (here, to valley), a crew of Cascade Mountain stone giants. (I guess it was Ruscada who invited them in through portal; he knows the drill well from Wollumbin-roaming).

It was as if these 'rocky chaps' wanted to check on Torii's future home, 'sniff the air' of these fresh partners to shared purpose. It reminded me of the time my mother, as an 80-year-old, spontaneously boarded a plane half a world away to come check on where her youngest child had ended up. Would she approve? (She also sniffed the air.) These elders literally 'cascaded' down from their heights to 'meet' us at our (Amici) level here on opposite (valley) 'shoreline'. Five <u>massive</u> boulder heads eyeing us with inscrutable expression; I scribbled:

What will we do/what will we <u>make</u> of/with/for the Life of Gaia's world in our Love? This the question, silent, as presented. Watching (and journeying) from their 'Rockies' to ours. Bearing enduring witness, offering (I feel) unspoken support.

Boundless gratitude and deep humility did I feel for their 'sunk-in-settled-stone' anointment of our weaving-the-world acts of service. More fresh nodes in Gaia's flesh added to script, all spirits of place sharing our bliss! Meanwhile, on another night of Torii's sailing, I was guided to meet indigenous elders of place – there. This came completely out of left field. No meditation, conscious intention or suggestive imagery by way of preface. Suddenly I was 'in', on Ron's landed edge, riding a dirt (trail) bike accompanied by a (Sidhe) 'bodyguard' to arrive at a border after crossing through an underpass. Here, an area of pure ancient wilderness loomed. Two guardians (stewards-of-place) wanted to see my 'papers', find out who had invited me/us into this Native American 'reservation' (their words). These papers showed compass-like coordinates in time <u>and</u> place upstream of said border to meet a (male) wisdom elder whose name reflected his <u>transmutation</u> of wood for healing, medicinal purposes. Now to my notes:

Once they affirm the papers, we follow a meandering sweet water shoreline toward the elder's camp (maybe Ron's Deep Creek itself?). I see reed wetlands; all is calm/quiet in soft pre-dawn light. Camp is a very basic set-up, around a smouldering fire. I also meet a young pale very tall eager blonde curly-haired lad wanting to 'work', learn our ways post-haste. He has the 'look/feel' of local Sidhe. Patience, I counsel ... I meet the elder, fluid, outwith time (as if this has already occurred pre-journey); our conversation FullDark, so deeply chthonic it was soul-to-soul transmission. But the charcoal from fire important as a tool of 'morphosis'.

I was reminded of our blessing of the woods a year earlier, using Amici 'spell-work' learnt long before, referencing wood/stone, blood/bone as an invocation to shapeshift energetic form to physic'd reality as sacred sacrament (corpus christi'd). But imagining that the (wood/stone) elemental spirits of place would join Torii's journey from birthing 'suite' ("Doug-Fir" even popped in one day for a chat) and/or that indigenous wisdom elders would invite us to sit by their fire to learn more? Never in my wildest dreams! I felt it to be an infusion, an opportunity to steep (like PeaceTea) in Ron's Land, to bless a Songline of shared homelands.

OneLand (Earth) OnePeople (We-Sidhe) OneHome (Gaia). Somehow I think Torii (Glyph'd) has a role to play as future-keeper of (visionary) world consciousness. But will I be here to see it?

• • • • •

In the wake of Torii's homecoming and her voice, depth-charged (I needed to speak it as I scribbled it – Lorca's duende encompassed in her <u>tonal</u> presence), her expression of self-sovereign solidarity dedicated to Gaian service, the first 'act' I engaged inwith her (subtle) physic'd halls of 'silver'd gold' could not have been more precious. Such joy to witness what our collaborative praxis had birthed!

I am present at a celebration of graduating younglings from an academy of sorts. I have a sense they are Amici songstresses to carry/wind-walk our work further thru world/s. My, they are excited, arriving in pretty 'scout-troupe' uniforms – pleated skirts, knee-length, with white collared shirts, a hiking scarf at neck, toggled in silver. These neckerchiefs were (royal!) blue-white paisley swirled. Oh, my smile was wide! They kept arriving thru a portal (Torii!), coming onto stage as if from a dark-curtained tunnel 'back-stage'. Once all assembled, the ceremony would begin. Such a whirl of delight, activity! I greeted each and all; they greeted each other as if comprising a worldwide collective who were (via Torii – with her intercession, and blessing) able to 'properly meet' for the first time. Congrats to the younglings! May your work be blessed! For Gaia! Ever/always: For Gaia!

Ah, Reader. 'Tis done. This next best loop of thread in Evermore's wend. Perhaps you'll see us a-sail of sky waves, wind-walking Song through Gaia's wondrous world. Indeed Torii (acting as an Eärendil-worthy barque as "Miracles" coda attests) has demonstrated her ability to shapeshift into an outrigger canoe (swift-a-slice of Pacific plane) for any next outreaching port-of-call. Nevertheless, all you have read in this (seeming) never-ending story, simply put, reflect the wisdom contained in and rendered by the divine words of Ecclesiastes (3):

"To every thing there is a season, and a time to every purpose under the heaven."

Such that Torii was born when? Torii was blessed when? Torii arrived when?

When Time was <u>ripe</u> for her purpose here – in/of Gaia's Earth; here – under Heaven's girth.

Now, while the world turns, while miracles <u>continue</u> to be made, as penned in symphony:

we wait/we wait/we sing/we sing – for spring to come again (with)
all cells singing, we will never give in to the feeling
all is lost (it's clearly not!) while life (it stays!) alive
breathing deep, breathing long, breathing Gaia's journey on
never not participant, here or there beyond – yeah!

all cells singing, no we're never not for Gaia dreaming
all cells singing in a symphony of light
pitch-perfect is the ancestry bubbling with potency
present to the presence of the gift of precious – life!

Thank you for <u>your</u> presence, Reader, and the gift of your participant-witness in/to our <u>work</u>.

Good night, good luck, and a very hearty godspeed …

EPILOGUE

Ah, look, here we are again (straight after our farewell), having realised we cannot possibly leave you without a last (most recent) Song – 'hot off the presses' one could say. Its title?

"HappySong!"

Born when a (human) SkyChild came to stay; 18-months of "Joy to the World" (in skin) of which she could now babble (more or less). Our focus, sitting in the gravel of garden grail, playing with the Zen Peace nook's enlightened pebbles (while her parents spent a few blissful minutes sipping champers to counter jetlag – que?) drew an observation from me: "Happy".

This she immediately mimicked. I extended the line-of-flight to the pebbles in our hands: "Happy Rocks". Ditto. A bumble bee arrived to feast on a flower at eye-height. She watched keenly. "Happy Bee" (we agreed). On and on through simple acts of witness, of "Everyday Delight" (poem, 2020) for (us) 'everyday adepts', which we strung each to the other like prayer beads for Gaia.

Soon after her visit, the Amici and I began the serious work of editing this (massive) tome. But in between all the down-and-dirty grubby honing-and-shaping, we still wanted to honour the approaching (Autumn) Equinox (2024) in less-than-sweaty uplifting fashion. Down the years, to begin the swirl of energetic resonance toward each of these four markers in Gaia's celestial calendar, our praxis has focused on "12-Days-of-Consciousness" prior to the actual date of seasonal celeb. This alerts co-creators in any/all dimensions that the FiveGates (Howe, Stars, Rising Sun, Twilight Zone, Earth – our Amici 'chorten' in reverse) are opening for Humboldt's Current full-welcomed in-house, and through which they too are all most welcome to join our ritual 'Gala' comprising:

36-hours-of-thanksgiving-and-blessing
never an end to our leyline'd singing!

If you are Anglo of origin, Reader, perhaps you know the "12-Days-of-Christmas" tune? (If not, YouTube will quick-apprise you.) Well, in our hands the song remains the (zeppelin'd) same, but with lyrics reflecting our conscious participant-witness on/of each day of the 12 preceding Time-marker'd date. This we delight to sing in hallowed halls of Gaia's golden pulsating Earth-consciousness 'Balls' (remember my chat with MakerMan over a cuppa?). Here/now, with a toddler 'happy game' still fresh in mind (reflecting, in its own way, my down-pat Pollyanna'd 'glad game' in any way, shape or form), my smile on face could not have been wider to search high/low for the 'happy' in each day/night's delight to populate the tune.

Dedicated to SkyChildren everywhere, everywhen, it brings us great Joy that this is the first co-production to be fully 'formally' woven <u>in</u> and outflown <u>from</u> Torii's temenos to the all of Gaia's glorious All! I truly wondered when the energy would 'bite' for a brand-new Song once she arrived in-house from her "SailingSong" glide of sky-waves west-east. To be honest, I think it a more than appropriate co-creation emanating from her energetic resonance, harnessing the power of Great Glyph to 'marry' (and thus plunge) the twinned spirit/s of SkyChild-Crone in the stellar flesh of our precious Home. Even if the melody is 'sampled', the text is certainly original, each particularity of moment can ne'er repeat. But, oh! How wonderful to pen it – replete (!) – for ever/over enjoyment of ever-now's evermore.

"HappySong" resides in our virtual nestedfishes krypta, as with all, where you will hear my Crone-raspy singing return to (delight'd) SkyChild beginnings. But to call you to scene, here's a nibble of our first day's 'cherry':

On the first Day of Consciousness
my True Love* gave to me:
A mummy and a bubby wild boar!
(*True Love? Gaia, of course!)
Many blessings to you and your own 'Gala Balls'!

APPENDIX 1:
THE SONG/S OF/FOR/THROUGH/BY/AS GAIA

Dear Reader, many offerings of Story, Poetry and Song have been described in this volume as examples of our Amici co-productions in honour of Gaia's evolutionary consciousness. As this text's purpose has been to outline the philosophic context, esoteric background, and intellectual rigour which underpins and surround-sounds our co-creative process of designing performative works of blessing on/in hallowed Gaian ground, we have not wanted to lose momentum (or strain the generous limits of Jeremy's publishing hand) by including all works alluded to herein. Each/all is available for free download or listening pleasure via the website: https://nestedfishes.org/

However, the Songs of Gaia referenced in the chapter "Return to Source (Code/x)" we believe demand to be engaged in material (rather than solely cyber) space. The krypta of nestedfishes hosts their performances, but the texts hold a special place in our heart/s for their resonance of uplift, potency of arrival and deepening of connection each time the words of any/all three Songs are engaged. Like "Muted Earth" (see "Grail Within"), there is never <u>not</u> an occasion where the words are 'fired back' at me out of the Aether as a shocking and/or illuminating pre-cog (post-log'd) of our OnePeople's task. So do I present these Songs to you –

as Poetry. If you ever have the desire to engage them in performance, then our a cappella 'voice' in nestedfishes virtal krypta will accompany your way. Blessings!

THE SKYCHILD'S SONG

Sun is in his shining sky
Sun is in his shining sky
Saying: Don't be afraid
Don't be afraid
Don't be afraid of me.
No, don't be afraid
Don't you be afraid
Don't you be afraid of me.
Moon is in her inky ground
Ever-changing slim to round
Saying: Calmly I stand
Calmly I stand
Calmly I stand with thee.
Yes, calmly I stand
With you do I stand
So calmly I stand with thee.
Oh! How Stars infill my sight
Raining down their cosmic might!
Saying: Sing with us now
Sing with us now
Sing with us now your dream.
Yes, sing with us now
Just sing with us now
You sing with us now your dream.
Sun Moon Stars – how I love thee!
How you talk to little me!
Saying: Earth's your home
Respect your home
Please bless your home, like we.
Yea! Earth's your home
Respect your home
Please bless your home, like we ...

SIMPLESONG

There was a time when the SkyChild lamented,
wrote to her Sisters on high. Oh! She cried:
How the shift happens! From the <u>idea</u> of Life
to the <u>experience</u> of Life! Oh! How it can go awry!
Looked up to their faces, these three Faerie godmothers –
compassion/detachment in self-same expression,
seeming shrug of matter-of-factual observation:
This is what it is to serve the Goddess in-world;
this is what it is to choose the path we Sisters walk.
Yes, the SkyChild is she – youngest of the Seven –
bowing her head (again) before their elder wisdom
as they circum-nav her crib with their Morrigan'd runes:
GKM GKM GKM* – amen & thank you (she joins in the singing)
For I a part of you as you a part of me BMS** shared genetic memory
I a part of you as you a part of me BMS shared genetic memory
I a part of you as you a part of me BMS shared genetic memory
What is the use of two bowls?
They can be used to receive
And so offers from cupped hands,
as healing balm, her own tears …

•••••

The Great Mother takes all our tears
plants them in her Earth
where they transform into gold and silver pearls
infilled of liquid Light, lifted fresh to the Sky
all Love ready/prepped to verily burst forth
Shimmering kaleidoscope – Joy! – elemental and more
alchemic its rainbow'd bubbling with summertime Life
the chi of shared circuitry, Kora kora'd with delight
Mountains above as mountains below
all serve the Great Mother and her 3rd Rock home
Han Shan's crystal Cold (as each pilgrim knows)
looks to the East, those who master Flow –
Dogen's mountains child, the moment of its birth
ever-together: BMS – Earth'd

•••••

Oh! The pleasure!
To bless and be blessed in like measure

Love and be loved – equally One
Ever the Garden treasury up-sung.
Oh! The pleasure! To be/flow the world!
Summertime tool wrapt in tulle
For our gorgeous Gaian girl …

• • • • •

Summertime, and the livin' is easy
Oh – summertime when the weather is fine
The garden is rich with all Gaia's bounty
So, sleep little angel, don't you cry
One of these days you're gonna rise up singin'
Oh! You'll spread your wings and take to the sky
But till that day ain't nothin' can harm you
So, sleep little angel, don't you cry
Yeah, sleep little angel, don't you cry
Now sleep my angel – no more cry …

(((*GKM = Gondwana/Kali/Moon)) ((**BMS = Body/Mind/Soul))

SONG OF GAIA

I am the Peace-sunk heart of settled Stone: Tsuchi!
I am the Lifeblood a-flow through the arteries of Home: Mizu!
I am the pure and penetrant Light walking Tao of Way on: Hi!
I am the Love bursting forth from the SingingBird's Song: Kaze!
I am the Grace, oh the Grace (!) of the Seven Sisters strong: Sora!
The unbounded Truth of ancestral Soul –
SkyFather'd/EarthMother'd
on Raku's pottery wheel created –

Moulded and shaped
form following function
pure of intent and lily-white of action
I am the Garden itself and its World Tree planted fresh
in the Silt of Ages, infilled with the Breath of Sages –
the Green of a Land that is never dead
when the Blue of the Stars flood
the World with their Seed!
I am the FiveGates and all are full-open

for Humboldt's Current to forge
interconnection/alchemic reaction
I am Dogen's mountains child
and this the moment of my birth –
BodyMindSoul, I am your Earth!
I am you, I am he, I am everywhere she!
Each sentient cell between Source and Sea!
May the all of the All of the One be healed!
Inwith frame (named) Love's Light be freed!
I am the Mountains above and their twins below
I am the True Nature'd Life of our Third Rock
Home

APPENDIX 2:
THE (ORIGINAL) CARD DECK OF THE SIDHE
IN AMICI HANDS – A PRIMER

David and Jeremy's Card Deck has been part of our shared Amici-Life since end-2014. I opened the Deck for the first time in the literal (and intertidally 'littoral') presence of a mountain giant climbed years before when my Helvetian life had just begun. By coincidence the small rented flat, booked for a family ski-week in the eastern Alps, had (as its living room wall) a full-length plate-glass window looking directly onto Schiesshorn's cragged and snow-crumpled face. Such a delightful surprise – we could commune and review the stone-sentient cards together!

While everyone's process is different, I decided to let the Cards speak for themselves before reading their companion texts over Winter '14-15 in the belly of the peaks. Not knowing their 'order' or functional 'intents', I simply lay them out to listen for their voices in the stillness.

The first jolt of connectivity was to the 'hole-stone' Jeremy painted as Deck signature image on the reverse of each 'individual'. I had encountered this stone already in the Malakut when a Sidhe contact shared with me the legend of a great battle (before I realised I was 'in touch' with Sidhe). Participant-witness to the retelling and reweaving of such 'myths' over time, our Amici co-productions are ever-undertaken with the intent to help heal OnePeople'd wounds and rifts, in the hope bardic mythopoiesis begets holopoiesis in the spirit of Tolkien's "blessed are the legend-makers with their rhyme of things not found within recorded time".

The story "Leeks & Peas" emerged from this (timeless) well. In the moment of original encounter, my interlocutor had called his group 'Pixie'; in later research, I discovered Pixie the common name for Sidhe in south-west England, specifically Devon and Cornwall (and the physical location of the hole-stone I encountered in the Malakut, so-named Men-an-Tol, which bore an uncanny resemblance to Jeremy's artwork). Hence, the associative resonance I immediately felt upon finding it as the portal or gateway into the <u>entire</u> Deck cannot be overstated. Other images amongst the deck I also knew (and/or knew me). More often than not Jeremy's images reflected inner landscapes and beings with whom I had had significant encounters over the years, ones which proved integral to the unfolding of my path. Thus did I find the cards 'naming' themselves in accordance with said encounters – tag-lines or text-snatches which acted as placeholders to shared connection.

Only later, when reading David's accompanying text, did I discover he had a similar experience of Sidhe arriving while attuning to the cards, and claiming 'stewardship' of a particular stone: "It was as if each Dancer Card carried a signature energy or quality to which a particular Sidhe felt attracted." For Jeremy, each stone's voice arose with a short epigram or message to 'twin' with image. David writes: "What a particular card means to you or what it invokes is for you to determine at that time."

I realised the naming process itself worked to manifest my unique way <u>in</u> – <u>and</u> who I would find there. A full Amici crew had apparently been 'waiting in the wings' for my intellect to catch up with the outreach that Soul-knowing had already effected with them outwith Time. Given I subscribe to Emerson's observation that the Soul contains in itself the event befalling it, 'for the event is only the actualizing of its thoughts', it should not have surprised me …

The following table documents 'who-is-who' as well as their placement in our shared Amici-Life of <u>working</u> Deck, constituting <u>our</u> Stone Circle of engaged Presence. This means several are out-of-sequence with the formal Deck, and that the Circle is a larger <u>enduring</u> troupe than the one envisaged by David and Jeremy – evolving to comprise the first 19 Cards, with the 14 Dancers thereafter offering perspective, counsel and in-Time action as and when required.

Note that the 'Anne-named' column more often than not reads as verse-text – this reflects the original text-snatches housed in my consciousness as well as acknowledging these are not sedentary names (or presence/s) rooted to a single spot or attached to a discrete energy stream. When the Deck is outlaid in my ten-foot-square hut, whoever needs to enter via the invocation 'spoken' into being does so. Like an Aboriginal Songline sung into being as it is walked across Land, the prose-string seeks to <u>individualise</u> the Cards as functional anchors to their respective relevant presence/s, yet always in the context of how each pearl threads to its neighbour, on and on, to return to the beginning as a <u>collective</u> proposition.

In this way, it bespeaks the collaborative, flowing energy at the heart of Circle's beingness, as well as reflecting my Huxleyian mode to 'think' in verse as a natural matter-of-course (i.e. as an aide-mémoire). Over time this tendency to 'versify' develops into mantra; I sense the Deck itself 'invoking' Presence as each arrives while I offer greeting and blessing into grail space.

Formal *Card Deck* Name	Anne-name
Howe (The Hollow Hill)	Mountain above as Mountain below, one does not have a body; walking in the Garden, one does not see a person ...
Gate of Earth	From the Gate of the Earth,
Gate of Dawn	And Rising Sun,
Gate of Stars	Through the Gate of the Stars,
Gate of Twilight	To the Twilight Zone:
Altar (Gate of Consciousness)	Here is my kiln room, my ten-foot-square hut within
Gaian Throne	To which you are all most welcome, my Companions of the Way ...
Wizard Stone	Hello MagicMan,
Artisan Stone	Hello MakerMan,
Bard Stone	Hello MossMan,
Gatekeeper Stone	Welcome VanDiemen'sMan!
Stone of Identity	For a new hawk is born,
Stone of Boundary	Who is centred within,
Stone of Opening	Split open by Love,
Stone of Emergence	For the inner to come out.
Ancestor Stone	In honour of the Ancestors,
Fallen Stone	In honour of Hope,
Stone of Alliance	In honour of the Alliance between Humanity and Faerie
Ocean and Land	Know that I am homecome to the Sea, for:
A Bird on the Hand	One day the Singing Bird;
Bear and Stone	We are Brothers Bear all;
Blossoms and Wheat	When did I forget the Beauty of the World?
Dragon and Books	Yes I am a Scholar;
Edge	Gravity always gets in the way when we don't make a big enough leap;
Faerie Gold	This we know, dear TreeMother –
Grail and Roses	A Rose by any other name would smell as sweet
Moonstairs	On our Stairway to Heaven,
Palace	To Laputa, our Castle in the Sky,
Stag and Pool	Where we drink at the Sacred Pool,
Stone Raptor	With a Stone Raptor,
The Shaping Man	And a Shaping Man,
The Feast	Sharing a Moveable Feast,
The Tossing Coin	And singing Joy to the World ...

The Reader may have noted that a specific Stone from the original Deck acts as cover art for this volume (much gratitude to Jeremy for agreeing to our request!). Known as the Stone of Opening (a transitional 'champion' between quadrants three and four), it self-named as 'Split-Open-by-Love' within the verse string affirming my full transitional 'shift' to living the truth of shared cosmic heritage. To provide context, herewith a brief history of our relational being-with (documented in "Awakening"):

Revisiting the past to point a way to the future, I described it at the time. The four transition stones, intended to embody a state of unfoldment and flow, certainly knew it in my/our case. Forming a seamless story of my path until that point, housed (as such) in each card's self-naming. For example, a Malakut landscape remembered as I held the Stone of Identity. A high cliff – I with an instructor preparing to jump. No rope, no harness; the instructor simply says: "Hold my hand," and we leap into nothing to arrive safely at base after an exhilarating freefall. So excited by our success, a 'radical' methodology with <u>trust</u> at its core, I asked to immediately repeat it. "Of course," he said. "I'm always happy when a new hawk is born." So did the Stone of Identity self-name. A lesson in 'vibrational energetics', it was backed by specific guidance of what it would mean to belong in the 'beyond' – of critical importance was the need to be 'centred within'. Hence the Stone of Boundary's self-naming. In the moment of its arising voice, I was reminded of the Lorian practice (standing-in-sovereignty) as well as living the simple (and effective!) Taoist principle: 'Let Wind enter, keep Mountain still'.

But it was the following card, the Stone of Opening, which really clinched the deal, so to speak. Its self-naming was soul-knowing pure – a case of Emerson's observation revealed to the blinding light of day. "Yes," it proclaimed to any who would listen. "You <u>were</u> split open by Love. Do not deny it. For see what has emerged in its wake?" its voice continued, passing the baton directly onto the Stone of Emergence in a lovely segue reminiscent of the dynamism at the heart of the Transition Stones. Indeed, the 'inner' had come 'out' – since that moment, no longer was my soul prepared to hide its strengthening light under the bushel of little me.

Each time I sit with the Deck, I acknowledge soberly this morphosis via the invocational string spoken to/by/with these four. But the one I sit with, longest, deepest, is the Stone of Opening because of what it holds in its 'memory-drawers' – a Love Story of longer-than lives. The one who enabled my 'becoming' this time round (in skin), whose (Leonard Cohen) vertic'd 'crack' facilitated the free flow of Love's Light in-out-all-roundabout, or (as I sing in "Blue's Third"):

High above treasured aetheric
Deep below the settled stone
Through all Blue's alchemy spirals
In-world rainbow'd, circum'd round

Truly a champion who has (basically) said: "It ain't over till the fat lady sings" – accompanying my journeying ever through Life (pure!), and stoically (Stone) standing at my side during this latest transitional space of healing Cancer with deep wisdom and all-enveloping compassion. In the context of our Amici UrWerk, therefore, this Stone is a more-than-worthy 'inheritor' to the Grail painting Jeremy kindly agreed as cover art to our last volume, "From the Common Grail Within". An 'inheritor' but truly its 'ancestor' in the spirit of our commitment to:

"Recovered Memory, Fresh Envisioned". For Gaia, for the OnePeople, for all …

APPENDIX 3: THE SNOWBALL OF BECOMING

This volume has chucked the word 'snowball' around liberally amongst its pages. Funny for a lass who had never (properly) encountered snow till migrating to a small alpine Land halfway through her (this time) life. But as a visual (and tangible!) methodology, it has since served our Amici purpose/s well. A process model which first saw light of day decades ago in my PhD, it draws on Deleuze & Guattari's theory of rhizomatic knowledge production, itself based on their reading of anthropologist Gregory Bateson. My design, likewise, intends to demonstrate the non-hierarchical plane of consistence (across a multiplicity of dimensions) that a creative energy of becoming 'inhabits', hence going back to the source, to Bateson's vision of:

"*A continuous, self-vibrating region of intensities whose development avoids any orientation toward a culmination point or external end.*"

The model can be read vertically, horizontally, spherically – the plane is a plane after all, its boundaries only limited by our 'sight'. I visualise our single never-ending Amici work-program plane as holding within its (ever-expansive!) frame a cartography of 'becoming', a landscape which becomes as it is explored. Built on the sturdy foundations of Love, the snowball's 'self-propulsion' fulfilling Mr1300BC's ever-wise counsel ('we all breathe Life into what we Love'), we therefore cannot help but accord with Mariel's perceptive observation:

"*Once you set forth your intent, we can blend with the field you create and enhance its capacities to connect and to manifest.*"

Well, simply consider our 'field' is a shared earth-sea-sky scape pre-post-and-all-in-between. At times I have no clue who (or what) 'sparks' the initial idea; frankly it is irrelevant because our process encompasses partnering (pure!) and it is our <u>desire</u> to support Gaia which begins a next-best iteration of same – the energy of creation focusing, coalescing, densifying to the point where whatever desires manifestation has nowhere else to go but to manifest. Like a snowball that grows as it gathers speed, cleaving all to itself as it rumbles downhill: Voila!

Our initial demonstration was with Light – the result uplifting, exciting, energising; a case of: 'Look what we can <u>make</u> together with the fidelity (i.e. <u>purity</u>) of our intent!' Whether the (ensuing) manifestation physical or non-, I see all creative 'becomings' arising from drawing together energetic threads from the aetheric – the impulse of Love's Light, source code/x'd. Yet our in-world desire is what kickstarts the productive energy of creation to make something from the threads gathered – the <u>will</u> to exist needs to exist in and of itself for the flow of Light to begin streaming from the aetheric and 'substance' start to form. With desire's <u>focus</u>, the energy densifies and self-propels to grow all the while (like a snowball) till fully realised in form. Our invocatory mantra?

A Snowball of Light
That becomes and becomes –
So it is, when all is Love ...

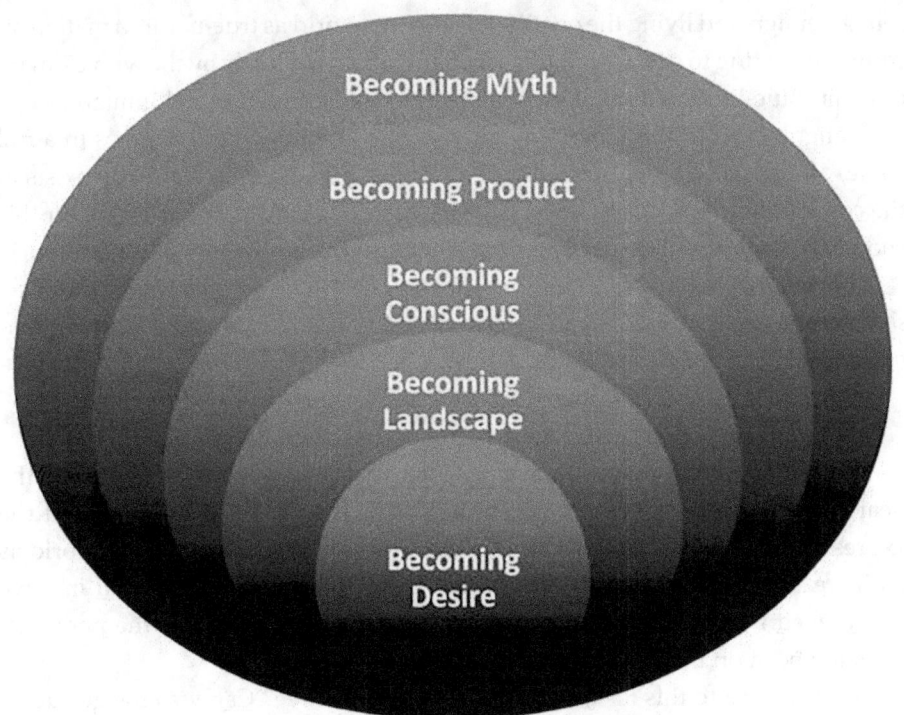

Process Model of Becoming

'Tis a case of like attracting like from first inklings, and intuition, of a 'fuzzy' vision on a distant horizon, to harnessing desire's energy to 'become', to set off on the journey (landscape), to 'make' something out of it (product), to engage the (personal) myth of its 'meaning' and offer same back into the pool of collective (Gaian) (mythic) consciousness. Now, a big shout-out to MakerMan – for as well as pointing me back to my PhD as a way to document process in "Awakening", she reminded me of our original discussion on the history of human 'making'. This is our challenge (as a species) – to shift (human) consciousness from creativity for its own (human) sake, to its own (human) ends, to partnering toward a truly shared vision of Gaian holism with all forms of sentience – physical and non- – who call this wondrous world Home and who envision its flourishing for the good of All. Our (human) history amply demonstrates what we can manifest in-world – to good and ill. What would it take for every self-action to be joyously gifted to the whole, circulating the energies of Love in vertical and horizontal ways, making ourselves daily (hourly, moment-by-unfolding-moment) part of something bigger, dedicated to offering our creativity in sole/soul loving service to Gaia?

Can our species' consciousness shift from its propensity of self-orientation to the active embrace of the other (<u>any</u> other!), to seamlessly merge intent with the All? Gregory Bateson calls this shift an "ecology of mind". It means being self-sovereign and living the one-life-of-the-one-world as true-natured matter-of-course according to our 'respiratory quotient' gifted selflessly by the whole inwith our thin Blue line'd extent; it means meeting transcendence and immanence at face, aligning vertical and horizontal at source. Spinning zero degrees in a full circle, <u>all</u> potentiality for such a shift in human consciousness already exists at the <u>core</u> of our deepest self: Love! All we need do is kick-start our <u>desire</u> for this snowball-of-snowballs to become. Or as Teilhard de Chardin lyrically expresses it:

"Some day, after we have mastered the Winds, the Waves, the Tides and Gravity, we shall harness, for God, the energies of Love. Then, for the second time in the history of the world, man will have discovered Fire."

Love's Light – harness our own 'fire' (desire) and Love will do the rest:

"For the Joy at core of planet to (re-) ignite our precious Blue."

Ah, so many things we have rendered in Poetry, Song – weaving the pearls of knowing into our wordsmithery. For his part, Lee Irwin coined the expression 'mergence' to speak to this proposition of experiencing the world as an increasingly expansive interactive sphere of 'becoming', <u>grounded</u> in Love and <u>fuelled</u> by Love. And yet, and yet … down many years has the perennial question been on my lips:

<u>Can</u> we rise to this task, to this duty as a collective? <u>Can</u> we engage such a process of becoming toward a vision of humanity as <u>true</u> Gaiatarians? And, is there <u>still</u> time (in these Gandalf-worthy '300 lives of men') for such a shift of consciousness?

Hope, the (big) Ben I climbed in Scotland's north-west highlands hosts my prayer (of Hope), and my Morrigan's call (for Gaia). So do I trust <u>and</u> hope that this snowball is gaining traction.

ABOUT THE AUTHOR

Anne Gambling lives her life on pilgrimage for Love—in movement and in stillness, alone or with company—and, as a writer, relishes the opportunity to document the journey in text, whether as contemplative essay, prose fiction, poetry, song or mantra, all of which are included in the volume you now hold in your hand. Her library, offered to the conversation on peace in the 21st century, is housed at www.nestedfishes.org.

ABOUT THE PUBLISHER

Lorian Press LLC is located in Coloma, Michigan, USA. It is a private, for profit business which publishes works approved by the Lorian Association. Current titles can be found on the Lorian website lorian.org or the Lorian Press LLC website lorianpress.com.

The Lorian Association is a not-for-profit educational organization. Its work is to help people bring the joy, healing, and blessing of their personal spirituality into their everyday lives. This spirituality unfolds out of their unique lives and relationships to Spirit, by whatever name or in whatever form that Spirit is recognized. The address is:

The Lorian Association
PO Box 1368
Issaquah, WA 98027

For more information, go to www.lorian.org

www.ingramcontent.com/pod-product-compliance
Lightning Source LLC
Chambersburg PA
CBHW060938230426
43665CB00015B/1992